THE
IRA
A HISTORY

THE IRA

A HISTORY

TIM PAT COOGAN

ROBERTS RINEHART PUBLISHERS

Dedicated to the memory of my Aunt Josephine Toal, and to my late friends John Taylor and Barbara Mullen, whose long marriage proved that an Anglo-Irish friendship can be strong and enduring.

Copyright © 1993 by Tim Pat Coogan

International Standard Book Number 1-879373-67-X
Library of Congress Catalog Card Number 93-85475

Published in the United States of America by
Roberts Rinehart Publishers, Post Office Box 666
Niwot, Colorado 80544

First U.S. Edition

Contents

Acknowledgments

I am under a heavy debt to a great many people for the assistance I have received in writing this book. Some, because of the nature of the subject matter, must remain anonymous; in the case of others it is inadvisable to be too explicit about who told me what. I shall, therefore, for the most part merely name them, with my sincerest gratitude for their help:

Anthony Heade, Frank Carty, Michael Traynor, Brian O'Neill, Frank Edwards, Seamus Byrne, Dan Breen, Laurence de Lacy, 'Pa' Murray, W. Roe, Pat Clare, Con Lehane, Sean MacBride, Mick Fitzpatrick, Seamus G. O'Kelly, Colonel Roger McCorley, Frank Driver, Pearse Kelly, Eoin MacNamee, the late Hugh McAteer, Paddy MacNeela, Tearlach O'Huid, Joseph Deighan, Sean O'Broin, Rory Brugha, General Sean MacEoin, Eamon MacThomas, Joseph Clarke, Charles Murphy, Eamon Boyce, Tom Mitchell, Donal Murphy, Pat O'Reegan, Myles Shevlin, Joseph Christle, Danny Donnelly, Terry O'Toole, Gerry Higganbotham, Lord and Lady Brookeborough, Noel Kavanagh, Harry Short, Stephen Hayes, Harry White, J. P. MacGuinness, Jimmy Steele, Jack Mulvenna, Roddy Connolly, J. F. Reegan, 'Micksey' Conway, Mrs Carmel O'Boyle, Lieutenant General M. J. Costello, General Michael Brennan, Jim Killeen, Jack Brady, Seamus Sorahan, Senator Gerald Boland, the late Peter Kearney, Detective Inspector James Fanning, Francis Stuart, Colonel Dan Breen, Ambrose Martin, Sean Dowling, Sammy McVicker, William McMullen, Miceal O'hAodh, Charles Gilmore, Anthony Butler, Pat Shanahan. (As Lord and Lady Brookeborough are included in this list it is probably superfluous to point out that not all the foregoing are connected with the I.R.A.)

I am particularly indebted to Commandant General Tom Barry for his lengthy, handwritten reminiscence of the Civil War; to An tAthair Columcille for much research on sources and, in particular, for a long dossier on the Civil War in Co. Tipperary; to Eamon Timmoney and Seamus Ramsey for their long assessment of the border campaign; and to the family of Fergal O'Hanlon for letting me examine his diaries. If I did not always quote from the material these (and others mentioned above) supplied me with, it was invaluable as background.

For American source material, I am indebted to Joseph McGarrity's daughter, Mrs Elizabeth de Feo of Philadelphia; to Sister Bernard Mary Tarpey, who has written a thesis on McGarrity; and again to Eoin MacNamee and Harry Short. For checking references and carrying out research, I must thank Professor Samuel Fanning and his colleagues at St John's University, New York, Professors Hogan and Griffith. Attorney Charles T. Rice of New York was helpful in checking information. My thanks are also due to Jim Ballance for much research and checking and to Sean Nunan for information on the role of the Clann na Gael in 1919–21. Professor Robert Stewart of the Fletcher School of Diplomacy, Tufts University, Boston, guided my hand through the State Department's volumes on American foreign relations that deal with wartime Ireland. To Dr Alan J. Ward my thanks for giving me his fine paper, 'America and the Irish Problem 1899–1921' (reprinted from *Irish Historical Studies*, March, 1968).

In London I must thank the British Museum for providing Photostats of material not available in Dublin and my friend Denis Lynch for being such a diligent and uncomplaining consulter of files and reference works.

In Belfast Jack Mulvenna and Andrew Boyd were unfailingly helpful in providing introductions or looking up information for me. The former editor of the *Belfast Telegraph*, the late Jack Sayers, his librarian Mr Gilbert and Mr Gilbert's successor also deserve my thanks for providing photos and cuttings.

In Dublin I must thank my many journalistic colleagues who covered I.R.A. trials or inquests for giving me their impressions and, for helping me with material and photographs, the staffs of the libraries of the *Irish Press* and the *Irish Times*. For providing me with other sources and reference books the staffs of the National Library and, in particular, of Dun Laoghaire Public Library are entitled to my gratitude.

And particular thanks are due to Ciaran Mac An Ali, Matt Russell and Maurice Manning for the time and care they devoted to checking the manuscript and proofs.

The opinions expressed in the book are, of course, entirely my own responsibility.

T.P.C.

Introduction

Had anyone told me, as I came to the end of the first U.K. edition of this book towards the end of 1969, that it was but the first of many editions, and that nearly a quarter of a century later, the book would be bigger than *War and Peace*, with the war more strongly in evidence than the peace, I would have replied to the effect that I had been shown the future and it did not work. Such a prospect was utterly inconceivable.

Yet, as the world knows, though the future did not work, it happened all the same. The reader will, I hope, have fathomed why by the time he or she has digested this relentlessly swelling tome of blood and violence, gallantry and squalor, cruelty and courage. To understand the I.R.A. is to understand Ireland and the Irish; their past, and regrettably, their present.

And by Irish I do not mean merely the Irish in Ireland. The Irish diaspora is so huge that at census time in America alone, some 43 million give their ethnic origins as Irish. Readers will see for themselves what the involvement of but a fraction of the Irish-American population has meant to the story of the I.R.A. I believe that if a larger percentage took a constructive, constitutional interest, the resultant political pressure could bring that story to a happy ending.

I do not believe that it is the karma of the Irish and the English to forever torture each other, acting out an ancient blood feud that should long ago have ended. However, my researches have driven me to the conclusion that until an outside force helps to fill the vacuum in constitutional progress which has existed for decades within six of Ireland's North-eastern counties, then that vacuum will continue to be filled by the I.R.A. and their mirror image Protestant paramilitary organisations.

A U.N. presence backed by the U.S., the E.E.C., and agreed to by Britain, is the best hope of peace. Others may come to different conclusions, but I can at least make this claim on behalf of my judgement: no other writer has devoted so much time and energy as I have to studying the I.R.A., and the reasons that young men and women join that organisation. It is a painful story, especially painful for an Irish author.

Embattled, controversial, countries like Ireland or Israel or Poland have developed a peculiar intensity of their own. They are not alone nation states, but states of mind.

Unless one has allowed oneself to develop a writer's necessary detachment to the point of becoming de-sensitised, interviewing people who have been through trauma of some sort is a harrowing experience. But it is as nothing to finding that 'contacts' cease to be merely one's normal sources of information, and become the names and faces of people you have recently talked with and who have suddenly been done to death.

In the world of the I.R.A., its membership and its victims, such incidents may become frequent, but never commonplace. Hatred, prejudice, and their all too frequent outcome, grief and bereavement, are not lightly encountered. Even the 'lesser' traumas of the Six Counties have a searing effect; finding someone, or some family you have known suddenly implicated in a shooting, a jailing, a knee-capping, a robbery or an arms smuggling. The pitch of intensity is far higher; the sense of personal involvement is incomparably greater.

Let me give an example of what I mean exactly as I experienced it. Early on in the troubles, shortly after the first, relatively slim volume edition of this book had appeared, I made contact with a Catholic West Belfast. I normally stay in Clonard Monastery, that strategically situated oasis of kindness and hospitality between the Protestant Sandy Row and the Catholic Falls Road, run by the Redemptorist Fathers. The monastery is one of the best listening posts in Ireland.

Things were getting bad on the ground and I could see trouble ahead. I asked if Father Superior could use the monastery's contacts to arrange for me to spend a weekend with a typical Republican-minded family so that I could judge for myself what sort of people supported the I.R.A. Father Superior, a grave and courteous monk, acceded to my request and arranged that I be guided to Andersonstown where I would meet my hostess for the weekend. 'She was,' he informed me, 'a good lady whose uncle was a member of the Monastery Community.'

Knowing the piety of Belfast Catholics at the time, this last detail made me uneasy. As I followed the monk in the car ahead of me, I calculated that, unlike the broad-minded atmosphere of the Monastery, the 'good lady's' household would certainly expect me to go to Mass. I could in fact, find myself in disfavour for not going to Holy Communion. I might even have to join in the family rosary that night, and a drink seemed out of the question. All of a sudden my research project did not seem such a good idea. But I resigned myself to seeing the thing through and as my guide rang the bell composed my features in what I hoped was a combination of courtesy and piety.

And then it happened: the door was opened by the 'good lady' with the uncle in the monastery. She turned out to be a beautiful blonde in her late twenties wearing a mini-skirt and halter top. While I was going through a spasm of mental readjustment that rendered me temporarily inarticulate, she bade goodnight to my guide, led me to a sofa, and inquired warmly: 'Would you like a wee go at my bush, or would you prefer something more exotic?'

Mood swing is, I understand, the correct term to describe the sensations induced by her use of the Belfast language. However it emerged that all she wanted to know was would I have a glass of the Bushmills 'Black Bush' Whiskey she was drinking, or would I prefer white rum, tequila or somesuch.

I poured a second tumbler full of 'Bush' over what remained of my shortlived hopes a little later when her husband arrived home with their three children. All girls, all favouring their mother; beautiful little blonde 'steps of stairs' aged four, three and two. They were still 'tryin' for the boy,' the parents informed me. I offered to assist in this laudable endeavour. The jest and the husband's bawdy riposte, embroidering the theme that he was 'up for Sinn Fein' which he translated as 'ourselves alone', set the tone for the night of ribaldry and hospitality that followed. They had arranged a party for me. There was so much laughter and singing that I could not accept that one tall, rather shy young man, their babysitter, was also the 'O.C. of the Third Battalion, a real good lad. You wouldn't believe some of the things he's done.' Nor could I accept that another innocous young chap who was pointed out as being 'dead on' had 'done in two of them.'

While I was discussing Spanish holidays with a couple who worked as spare-time marriage counsellors, a jolly, well-dressed woman was persuaded to sing. 'Her son's away,' said the marriage-counselling wife, nodding towards the singer. She meant not Spain, but Long Kesh prison. I had come to try to understand the mindset of such people, but the comfortable, semi-detached, house-proud normalcy of the surroundings militated against a grasp of the dark, brooding Belfast reality that existed outside the party—just outside it.

Next morning, as the 'good lady' prepared breakfast the, husband brought me into the garden to air our hangovers and to show me something. In the flower beds all round the house were large clear boot-prints. 'The B.A.,' exclaimed my host. He told me that the the British Army (B.A. in slang) often lay under windows, listening to gain information. 'The patrol would have seen the big Southern car outside the house, heard the party, wondered what's up.'

I subsequently found out that my host was telling the truth. Lying under windows was a primitive British Army intelligence tactic in those early days of conflict. As the I.R.A.'s terror campaign intensified, things changed. The army's techniques grew more sophisticated. Electronic surveillance gadgets, a network of spies, 'supergrasses', blackmail, 'shoot-to-kill' policies, torture; all the black, unacknowledged arts of counter-insurgency were deployed.

Things changed for my hosts also. For a time their lives moved out of synch with the troubles. As the overall situation got worse theirs got better. A new house, a new business. The boy they were 'tryin for' arrived. But for a family in West Belfast to remain unscathed by the troubles would be more remarkable than for one in the West Bank to remain untouched by the *Intifada* and what gave rise to it. Slowly, but inexorably, the situation began to engulf them. Did their Sinn Fein sympathies broaden to include some kind of I.R.A. supportive action? The police suspected that they did, and at different times both of them were locked up and interrogated for long periods.

I helped to secure their release. But the drinking increased as the business decreased. Eventually he had to leave the country, and I helped him to get a job in America. One of the lovely little 'steps of stairs' became a teenage mother. Her own mother, the once beautiful woman who had opened the door to me in Andersonstown twelve years earlier, grew less beautiful than the passage of years alone would have warranted. The pressures of Belfast, valium and vodka were taking their toll. Eventually the marriage broke down and the family home was sold.

The one bright spot on the family horizon was Sean, the boy. He had his mother's blond hair, was six feet, two inches tall and, though more gentle than either, possessing much of his parents' personalities as I remembered them when we first met: cheerful, fun-loving, hard-working, and with a good sense of humour. While he supported Sinn Fein, the political arm of the I.R.A., by a miracle, his temperament kept him clear of the troubles.

I was once visiting the family on a Sunday morning. The day was fine and we sat in the front garden drinking beer while lunch was being prepared. An army patrol came by, seven soldiers guarding one community policeman wearing a flak jacket. His mission was to win the minds and hearts of the people. But the Royal Ulster Constabulary are so hated in the area that he would have been killed within seconds were it not for the army escort. It reminded me of a similar doomed effort by the Americans which I had witnessed in Vietnam, the *Chieu Hoi* programme. The officer in charge of the patrol came into the garden, both ignoring us as individuals, and at the same time, sweeping the group with his rifle. After standing in the garden for five minutes, sighting his weapon at a non-existent target on the road, he left, still without saying anything. But the point was made: 'We have the guns. You can only sit out here, even if it is your own garden, because we let you.' And of course he had had a good look at the person driving the southern registered car. A commonplace, unremarkable Andersonstown incident.

It left me feeling rather angry, but Sean just smiled. Unlike most of the lads around the district, he had no knee-jerk reaction against the soldiers. Once, an uncle of his had been one of the two men in a car who blessed themselves passing a Catholic church. Two Loyalist paramilitaries who had been waiting for the Catholic passengers to identify themselves, immediately shot both men dead. Sean went to their funerals and mourned his uncle. The killings strengthened his support for Sinn Fein, but he did not join the I.R.A. to get even.

Then, nearly three years ago, approaching his twenty-first birthday, Sean came to see me in Dublin. By then he had acquired a pretty girlfriend and a steady job driving a van. There was talk of his taking up night classes. The family troubles had not brought him down at least. He said he had something to tell me. He thought I should be the first to know because, though I had not realised it, I meant a lot to the family. I smiled deprecatingly and prepared to congratulate him on his engagement. It was not that. His news was that he was 'joinin' the 'RA.'

His decision had been triggered by the fatal shooting of a teenager, with a rubber bullet, by a member of the security forces. To me, and to most people outside Northern Ireland, it was another statistic; just one of the 3,000 death roll created since the beginning of the troubles when I had first met Sean's family. But obviously events had been carrying him towards his decision for years, as I found out when I tried to remonstrate with him.

We were alone in my 'bunker' where I write and I had plenty of time to develop my arguments. But it was point, counter-point all the way. He had no faith whatever in any events which might bring about change. 'Sure what else can you do,' he kept saying. To him the rubber bullet shooting was not an aberation, merely a continuation of conduct on the part of the security forces. Even though charges had been brought against the man responsible, he was convinced by the evidence of similar cases in the past that the culprit would beat the rap and would be emulated by his colleagues when the heat died down.

So far as he was concerned, the British were responsible for shoring up a rotten situation and would have to be forcibly driven out so that a fresh start could be made. And if the driving process involved him in killing people?

'Sure what else can you do? It's a war isn't it? People get killed in war.'

Did he realise that he might very easily be killed himself or at best get a long jail sentence?

'Sure what else can you do?'

Did he realise what effect his decision might have on his family and girlfriend?

'Ah sure they understand—they'll get over it. They know in their hearts nothin' else'll do any good.'

He seemed to regard the I.R.A. as omnipotent. When I asked him had he thought about the career he was probably throwing away his answer was: 'Sure the 'RA'll get me a job, drivin' a black taxi or somethin'.' (Public transport did not run in the West Belfast area at that time because so many buses had been destroyed. Instead London taxis plied frequently and cheaply. The situation has changed lately with a few bus lines now running through the area.) I put it to him that he could conceivably face the worst case scenario of being captured, breaking under interrogation and then being shot by the I.R.A. as a result.

He replied: 'Ah sure what can them ones do to you? Sure the 'RA torture you before they let you in.' (He was referring to the I.R.A.'s counter-interrogation techniques.)

By this stage he had proved himself so steadfast that I almost felt I was in some way violating his integrity. But I tried one final objection. I pointed out that though up to then he had not been 'connected' he had attended several Republican funerals and demonstrations. As a result, particularly given his family background, he must have appeared on a myriad of Special Branch videos. I told him bluntly: 'You're all wrong for a guerilla. With your hair and your height you'll stick out like a spare prick.'

He replied: 'Ah sure the 'RA disguise you.'

And sure enough, when he called on me unexpectedly a year later, he did look different. His hair was much shorter, no longer curly, and appreciably darker. He had never been overweight, but now he seemed leaner, fitter. Instead of his normal denims he was wearing an olive-tinted khaki safari outfit and lightweight laced boots. His girlfriend was with him. If anything, she looked even prettier.

'I done that, Tim Pat,' he said.

'You don't have to tell me,' I replied, 'you're obviously an off-duty soldier. Some fucking guerilla you are!'

We talked for a while, joking, keeping it light. But he obviously knew that I was upset. As we said goodbye he held my hand for a moment and said: 'Cheer up, Tim Pat. One of these days we'll have a pint in Belfast in. . . .' He paused for a moment thinking of a suitable pub. And then this gentle young man, whom I had literally known since he was a twinkle in his mother's eye, said something that underlined the unconscious brutalisation of Belfast which had brought us to this parting.

He thought of a good place. 'We'll see each other in the Corporal's Rest.' He was referring to the Belfast club so cruelly nicknamed following the lynching of two British corporals outside it. (They had been set upon by a mob after accidentally driving into a crowd attending a Republican funeral.) As he drove off, with his girlfriend gazing adoringly at him, I consoled myself with the thought that at least he had been right about one thing. His girlfriend did get over his joining the I.R.A. But I had been correct in my forecast about the risks he was running. A few months later I received a 'comm'.

A 'comm' is a communication from a prisoner, inscribed in block letters on cigarette papers, stuck together, folded into a tiny square, sealed in cling-film and smuggled out at visiting time. As the 'comms' are not submitted to the censor, they have to be composed when the warder is not around; and hence, apart from the materials and methodology involved, even a small one takes quite a long time to prepare. This one was above average length, four cigarette papers. It was from Sean—he and a group of other young men had been arrested on explosives charges. It began like any other letter, 'Dear Tim', and continued:

Big Sean here, reporting here from the Crum (Crumlin Road, Belfast). Just thought I would drop you a line as things at my end are quiet at the moment...

He described his arrest and went on:

. . . Tim, Mary (his girlfriend) and I were only two days away from seeing you as we had planned to go to the Michael Jackson concert and call in on you. Well that's the way it goes, so if I can't talk to you face to face I will have a go at the writing....I was hoping to read Michael Collins, but they won't let it in in hardback. I should have read it on the outside, well I'll have plenty of time now, ha ha ha!

Things aren't too bad. I'm doubled up with a young lad from Ballymurphy. He's one of six lads that got lifted after an attack on the Brits. They are all between seventeen and twenty and all totally innocent, just like a lot of lads in here. He is eighteen and he's here a year now. His trial will come up in about ten months. When it does he'll probably walk. It's all just another form of internment.

Tim, things isn't great here. There's thirty six men on our landing. Twenty five republicans and the rest are prods, so you can picture the problems that brings. We are locked up twenty hours a day and some days we don't get out at all. Not even to empty our pots. So on those days you can get very down. We have a good structure (an I.R.A. command structure) when we get out, but things are still very hard in here. The cells are cold, the food is bad, but our spirits are high and that's what keeps us going.

Tim, I'm up for bail next week, my ma has her hopes up, but the way the courts work here I have no chance. The R.U.C. can get up and say whatever they want about you without any evidence, so I'm not expecting it. If the worst happens Mary and my ma will be wrecked. That's the hard thing, everybody gets effected [sic]. That's all that worries me. What a country we live in...

That was a year ago (1992) at the time of writing. Sean did not get bail and his case will not come to trial for at least another year. If he is found guilty, he can expect at least a minimum ten or fifteen year sentence. There is nothing very unusual about his case. There are thousands of young men like him in the jails of Northern Ireland. They see themselves as having been sent to a smaller prison from the larger one that formed them. Sent because they tried to change the rules by which the larger prison is run.

I do not condone the methods by which they seek to bring about change, but I understand why they try. If the Six Counties were not a sick society, Sean and his like would be sending people like me postcards from holiday resorts, or invitations to a christening—not 'comms'. My hope for the publication of this book in the U.S. is that it will help bring about change by peaceful means. I concluded the first U.K. edition of this book in 1969 by quoting a letter from a defiantly cheerful young prisoner, Conor Lynch. Almost a quarter of a century later I am commencing the first American edition by quoting from yet another young prisoner's jail correspondance. This is not progress. 'Comms' are definetely one form of Irish literary creativity that I want to see ended.

There is no possibilty of peace coming to Northern Ireland while the British link remains fixed and immovable. Britain has had to pass the greatest vote of no confidence in a vassal state recorded in Western Europe since World War II ended: the abolition of its parliament because it had proved itself to be unfit to govern. Stormont, the former Belfast seat of the Protestant and Unionist dominated regime, fell in 1972, not long after I first met Sean's family. Britain has since presided over a political vacuum. There is no more stark indication that a society has failed than the presence of combat troops on the streets.

The full history of how Stormont came to be set up in the first place and how and why it went, is told in this book. In brief, however, it may be said that the Unionist regime in Northern Ireland closely resembled that of the old Boer oligarchy in South Africa. There was the same fundamentalist form of Protestantism, the same apartheid culture in which Catholics got the sanctions of the law, but not its protections. It was this denial of civil rights that finally drove young Catholics into the arms of the I.R.A., as it drove many young blacks into the military wing of the A.N.C. Unlike South Africa, however, the recognition of the need for change in Northern Ireland has not been followed by a sustained move towards sharing power and guaranteeing the position of the former Unionists within the majority culture of Catholic Ireland.

The British, after removing the Northern Ireland parliament and imposing direct rule from London, continued to assure the Unionists that they had a veto on change. So long as Protestants do not wish it, they are free to regard the rest of Ireland, in the words of one of their principal leaders, Ian Paisley, as a 'foreign country.' But a desire to remain united to Britain depends on the British people remaining united with Paisley and his like. The average Englishman wants nothing to do with 'Ulster', as they mistakenly call the Six Counties. It is inertia, combined with the political clout, and prejudice, of old blood and old money, that keeps Britain in Ireland. A combination of the House of Lords element, many of them possessing Irish titles, and the 'Shire Tories' or 'Euro Sceptics', who not alone mistrust Dublin, but Europe into the bargain.

The tragedy is that while there is no widespread enthusiasm for staying in Ireland, lack of affection takes a long time to build into a positive policy. Meanwhile, the British Government is distracted by internal economic problems and, externally, the country's continual decline in world standing. A Ministry of Defence so strapped for cash that it has had to disband that treasured centrepiece of British military pageantry, the Coldstream Guards, cannot afford either to keep half its dwindling army in Northern Ireland, or to endure the heart being blown out of its financial district in the City of London.

Nevertheless, bereft of any leap of the political imagination, the British continue to make sporadic attempts to cobble together a short term political solution within the confines of the Six Counties. This is like trying to mend a broken leg with bandaids. Firstly, the Unionists resent being told by London that they will remain in the United Kingdom for as long as they wish while at the same time being pushed towards Dublin. Secondly, they can resist that push simply by invoking the veto which London has given them. Then, as if this Catch-22 situation were not bad enough, the motor force of the entire process (albeit a destructive one), the Republicans, the I.R.A. and Sinn Fein, are excluded from the peace process.

The British and the Unionists won't talk to them until the violence ceases. The I.R.A. won't desist from the violence until they can see some sort of return for all the infliction and endurance of the past quarter century. As readers will see within, when the I.R.A. have had truces with the British before now, the interludes were not used for meaningful political dialogue (in their terms), but as an opportunity for intelligence gathering by the British, another Catch-22 situation. It is like the Americans attempting a Vietnam solution without talking to the Vietcong. Sinn Fein want an end to the Unionist veto, and progress towards a post-British withdrawal Ireland. In other words, self-determination. The President of Sinn Fein, Gerry Adams, spells out how he sees this being achieved in the concluding chapter of this book. But his goals are, publicly at least, anathema to the British and not on the agenda.

This is the position at the time of writing. It is unlikely to be altered for the better in the short term, at least by the present weak and faltering British Government. Yet, Irish diplomats articulate a view which is widely met in Northern Ireland: 'the Brits are letting the air out of the tires gently.' This would appear to be the long term scenario, but it is not as optimistic a prospect as might at first appear.

Firstly, it naturally puts up Protestant paramilitay blood pressures. Secondly, the Protestants' hates and fears are also being added to by the demographic shifts within the Six Counties. Last year's census figures show that the traditonal population balance has altered sharply. The seemingly permanent two thirds Protestant to one third Catholic ratio has given way to 53 per cent Protestant, 41.5 per cent Catholic, with the remainder prudently styling themselves 'others'.

These changes have encouraged the Protestant paramilitaries to go in for some pre-pre-emptive 'ethnic cleansing' before the tires go flat. For the last two years, Protestant paramilitary groups have killed more people than the I.R.A. There are suspicions, which for the first time, as readers will see later. I have been able to give a disquietingly authentic colouration to, that the security forces have been grooming Protestant undercover squads. The process is part of the 'Ulsterisation' policy, the British equivalent of the American 'Vietnamisation' policy towards the end of the war. In plain language: get the natives to do the fighting and the dirty work while the tires slowly subside.

Too slowly, that way leads to too many deaths, too many Seans. The I.R.A.

has a practically inexhaustible source of recruitment in the high birth rate of the unemployment ravaged ghetto Catholics. And their recruitment is far from being confined to ghettos. As I write, after the longest continous period of warfare in the Western World, the I.R.A. is better armed, better organised and stronger than ever before. It is for all the foregoing reasons, therefore, that I pray that the publication of this book in the United States will help to move American public opinion, particularly Irish-American public opinion, towards helping to find a solution to the Northern Irish problem. Britain is not part of the solution, it is part of the problem. Nor, as Britain claims, is the matter 'solely domestic to the U.K.' thus frustrating any U.S. backed or E.E.C. backed intervention. If it is solely domestic to the U.K., why do so many British politicians spend so much time trying to influence American decision takers? Why, for example, are British decision makers so hostile to President Clinton's admirable proposal to send a peace envoy to Northern Ireland? What are they afraid he or she will find there? The envoy suggestion is a good one. It would help to prioritise the Irish issue and help to accelerate a solution.

The Anglo-Irish problem was already old when Columbus discovered America. In so doing, he blazed a trail that millions of Irish have long since followed. It is time that we in Ireland and you in America co-operated to end this quarrel, this relic of a retreating colonial glacier. Ireland is not Bosnia or Croatia. Neither the problem nor the terrain raise the same spectre of huge committments of manpower and long term involvements. Given American support, Ireland, and England, could be at peace. Ireland and England are both mother countries. There is a time in life when parents look to their children for support. That time is now.

Tim Pat Coogan, Dublin, September, 1993

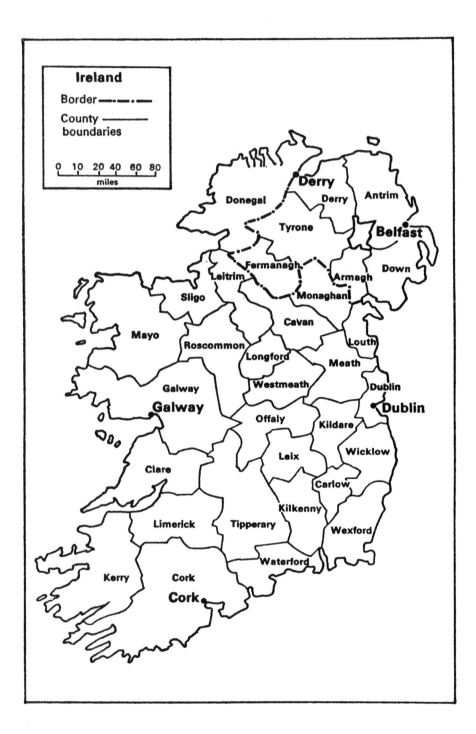

Ireland

Border —··—··—
County ———
boundaries

0 10 20 40 60 80
         miles

Part I
Beginnings to 1969

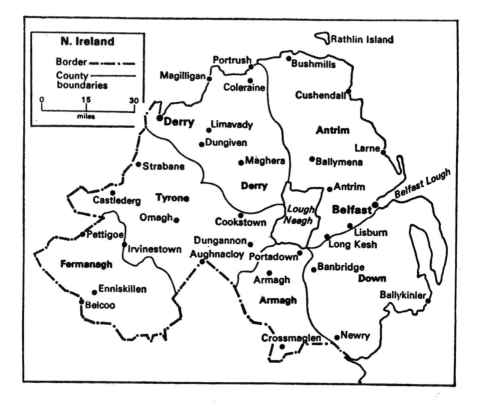

N. Ireland

Border — · — · —
County boundaries ————

0   15   30
miles

Rathlin Island

Portrush
Magilligan
Coleraine
Bushmills
Cushendall

Derry
Limavady
Dungiven
Antrim
Larne

Strabane
Maghera
Ballymena

Castlederg
Tyrone
Derry
Antrim

Omagh
Cookstown
Lough Neagh
Belfast
Belfast Lough

Pettigoe
Dungannon
Lisburn
Irvinestown
Aughnacloy
Portadown
Long Kesh

Fermanagh
Armagh
Banbridge
Down

Enniskillen
Armagh
Ballykinler

Belcoo

Crossmaglen
Newry

1

The Origins of the I.R.A.

What is Ireland? To many people it is a green and misty isle far out in the western Atlantic. A nation of saints and scholars, of drunkards and blasphemers, of priests and publicans, of piety and machine-minded politicians. A land where Christ and Caesar are hand in glove so that churches are full, and homes empty into the migrant ships, leaving behind saddened mothers consoling themselves on the diaspora of their vast families with the three great reassurances of a peasant people—mystery, miracle and religious authority.

All of these stereotypes reflect an Ireland that can still be seen behind the facade of Cathleen Ní Houlihan's latest expression—the neon Ireland of office blocks and traffic jams, the fashionable eating places and the tourist trade. You can still find the Ireland of your choice in the pinking masses of cumuli that shift and melt into purples and greys under a blue sky over the Sugar Loaf, in the shy smile of the mantillaed girl who, unhappy in a love affair, joins the thronged congregation in Whitefriars Street Carmelite Church in Dublin to hear the priest read her petition 'that a friendship may be restored', along with other petitions seeking God's mercy on a mother suffering from an incurable illness, His help for a wife who is a dipsomaniac, or a pregnant wife's prayer that her first child be a red-haired boy. All these form a pattern forged many years ago from great issues involving conquest, land, religion and politics.

In the North Christ and Caesar are commonly—though not inevitably—honoured in roars of bigotry and defiance to the rattle of the Lambeg Drum as preachers such as the Rev. Ian Paisley call down contumely on the head of Pope and Papist whom they see as working to overthrow the constitution of Ulster and the Protestant religion, aided by a constantly cited organisation known as the I.R.A. It is an organisation which more than any other shows us what the real Ireland is like.

Why should God elicit such a different response from a congregation in Whitefriars Street Church in Dublin, the capital of Southern Ireland, and from a congregation in the Rev. Ian Paisley's church on the Ravenhill Road in Belfast, the capital of Northern Ireland?

To understand it is necessary to turn to Irish history and to look particularly at the Irish Home Rule movement, the formation of the Ulster Volunteers and the 1916 Rebellion. As taught in the South, Irish history has tended to portray Irish revolutionary movements as occurring in cycles which always ended in disaster until the triumphant self-immolation of the 1916 leaders, whose sacrifice and courageous example put new heart into the Irish people, and gave rise to an independence movement from which came liberation and prosperity. This oversimplified view is true to a certain extent in so far as liberation goes, but it overlooks the central fact that the 1916 Rebellion by the Irish Volunteers was in fact an armed gesture by a body which came into being only *in reply* to an earlier gesture by the Protestants of Northern Ireland—the formation of the Ulster Volunteer Force to frustrate the British Liberal government's plans to introduce Home Rule to all Ireland. Had the Protestants of the North not acted thus Home Rule would have been passed, and it is difficult to see what force would have existed to stage the 1916 Rebellion. It seems certain however that there would have been no Irish Republican Army; no I.R.A.

The partition issue that helped to keep the I.R.A. alive for fifty years after 1916 dates back to the 'Plantations' begun under James I, in which six Ulster counties in north-eastern Ireland were handed over to 'Undertakers' to be colonised by Protestants, mainly Scots Presbyterians. In other parts of Ireland land was also given over to 'Planters' but in the North tenants as well as landlords were dispossessed and the plantation was therefore most complete.

The ensuing centuries of rebellion and massacre, when Protestant fought Catholic, were as much an effort by the native Catholic landowners to win back their land from the usurping English and Scots as they were religious wars, but they imparted to Irish affairs an all-pervasive tint of religion. The most notable Protestant victory was that of the Battle of the Boyne, July 12,1690 (July 1 in the Julian calendar of the day), which is commemorated annually and vigorously in Ireland today. 'Good King Billy', William of Orange, routed James of England and enthroned in power in Ireland a Protestant ascendancy. For long this was Anglican in character regarding Presbyterianism with only a little less disfavour than Roman Catholicism.

By the last generation of the eighteenth century a situation similar to that with which we are now familiar in Rhodesia prevailed in Ireland. There was a parliament of planters largely independent of England and equally largely indifferent to the sufferings of the Catholic peasantry whom they ruled and exploited. (This is not to say, however, that had an independent parliament ruled it might have evolved into a more democratic and equitable form of government.) Then in September, 1791 a young Trinity graduate from Kildare named Theobald Wolfe Tone attempted to change the existing situation by issuing a pamphlet, *An Argument on Behalf of the Catholics in Ireland*. Tone was himself a Protestant and the pamphlet met with an immediate success. Within a month of its appearance societies of 'United Irishmen' were formed in Dublin and Belfast.

In 1795 Wolfe Tone and his fellow United Irishmen—Russell, Neilson, Simms and McCracken—stood on Cave Hill overlooking the present Stormont parliament and swore 'never to desist in our efforts until we have subverted the authority of England over our country and asserted our independence'. The United Irishmen hoped to form a 'brotherhood of affection, a communion of rites and union of power among Irishmen of every religious persuasion, and thereby to obtain a complete reform of the legislature founded on principles of political and religious liberty'.

Wolfe Tone was a gay, ardent, outgoing spirit, clearheaded and far-seeing in his political thinking. The failure of his movement was to be a tragedy for Ireland. His effort at revolt in 1798 cost him his life and set in train many consequences which have their effect on Ireland yet. First there was the Act of Union in 1800 whereby Pitt and Castlereagh linked Ireland with England, greatly to Ireland's detriment. Ireland could no longer legislate for herself under the British crown, and the hundred or so members that she sent to Westminster were able to make very little impression on an assembly of 670 when it came to matters affecting Irish interests. Irish trade and industry were discriminated against in favour of British interests throughout the nineteenth century and several evils flowed from this. The Irish system of land tenure resulted in the parcelling out of land into minute, badly worked holdings and to rack-renting by landlords, many of them absentees who did nothing to improve their lands. Then, in the 1840s an ignorant population, grossly inflated beyond what the economy could support by the Catholic birthrate, was struck by famine and a new chapter of horror in Irish history was written.

Between 1841 and 1951 the population fell by two million people; approximately one million died, and another million emigrated. Many of these died on the way to England, Scotland or America, but enough survived to live rise to a tradition of emigration which continues to this day, and created in America the political force of the Irish Americans which subsequently provided much of the impertus and finance for Irish revolutions against England.

The Act of Union was to have three major effects. One was that by its very presence it generated a current in Irish affairs dedicated to the destruction of the act by armed force. It was this current which gave rise to Robert Emmet's rebellion in 1803, that of the Young Irelanders in 1848, and of the Fenians in 1867 whose lineal descendants, the Irish Republican Brotherhood, blossomed forth again in 1916.

The second great development was the growth of a constitutional movement for the repeal of the Union and for Home Rule. First Daniel O'Connell, then Isaac Butt, and finally Charles Stewart Parnell made repeal of the Union and Home Rule for Ireland their political platform. It was under Parnell that the constitutional and revolutionary movements began to coalesce. In 1879 he launched, through the initiative of John Devoy and Michael Davitt, a new departure whereby the revolutionary and constitutional movements met and mingled with the third force in nationalist Catholic Irish affairs, the Land League. This was begun under the ex-Fenian Michael Davitt at Irishtown, Co. Mayo, on April 20, 1879, and although it immediately fell foul of the Church—its first success was to get a parish priest, Canon Burke, to reduce his rents—the League prospered, and was a principal force in introducing the Land Acts through which by the opening of the twentieth century Irish farmers had won the 'three Fs': Fixity of Tenure, Fair Rents, and the rights of Free Sale.

This largely settled the land issue in Southern Ireland and as there were fewer Protestants than in the North conflict between Catholic and Protestant was also rare. Thus despite the fact that Parnell's fall after the O'Shea divorce scandal left the Home Rule issue in the doldrums, the South became relatively peaceful. The North, however, was less peaceful. O'Connell's Catholic agitation in the South and his conjuring up and utilisation of Catholic power accelerated the drift of Protestant wealth and interest from the South to the North—the third effect of the Act of Union. Industrialists moved North, although land owners retained their holdings in the South. As the industrialists moved North, bringing with them knowledge, drive and initiative, they created jobs in the linen, shipbuilding, and rope-spinning industries which they founded. Catholics flocked to Belfast in pursuit of these jobs and sectarian feeling was aroused by their arrival.

Beginning principally with the activities of the Rev. Henry Cooke, who died in 1868 and whose statue stands in Belfast today, there arose a line of Protestant clergymen agitators which stretches from Cooke to the Rev. Ian Paisley in a line of unbroken turbulence. From Cooke's day on, one can date no less than seven occasions between 1857 and 1912 when Belfast was the scene of fullscale sectarian rioting resulting in tragedy, loss of innocent lives, evictions, destruction of property and an embittering of relationships between the Catholic and Protestant sects. As Emrys Jones says, in his *Social Geography of Belfast*: 'the support which was given to the extreme anti-Papist attitude of Henry Cooke was probably an expression of Protestant dismay at the great increase in the numbers of the other sect. Tensions certainly rose as their numbers increased.'

These tensions focused upon an Orange Order founded by the Protestant privileged classes 'to maintain the laws and peace of the country and the Protestant constitution' as a reply to Wolfe Tone's United Irishmen.

The Order became such a force in Northern life that its influence in jobs, politics and religion is commonly held to be all-pervasive, and at all times its intent is to divide Catholic from Protestant so that the working classes of either sect will never unite to overthrow the Protestant ascendancy. In times of peace, the Order may only be used to ensure that Catholics do not get houses or to see that the Orange Brethren circulate through the lodges such choice items of anti-Catholic propaganda as the more incautious utterances of some Southern Irish Catholic bishops.

In peacetime one only becomes publicly aware of the Orangemen when they stage their annual picturesque march on July 12, the anniversary of the Battle of the Boyne, to commemorate 'Good King Billy' and Orange triumphs such as the routing of Catholics at the 'Battle of the Diamond' in Co. Armagh in 1795, after which the Orangemen were encouraged to take over Catholic land. But at times of civil disturbance the Order becomes an instrument of savagery, and burnings, lootings and shootings bestrew its unlovely history.

It was to this history and this Order that the English Conservatives under Lord Randolph Churchill turned in 1886 when they seized on the issue of Home Rule for Ireland to smash Gladstone's Liberal government. Lord Randolph summed up the Conservative policy in the historic letter he wrote to his friend James Fitzgibbon: 'I have decided some time ago that if G.O.M. [i.e. Gladstone] went for Home Rule, the Orange card would be the one to play.'

He played it in Belfast, giving to the Orangemen their still emotive slogan: 'Ulster will fight; Ulster will be right.' Gladstone, under pressure from Parnell, took up the issue and foundered under the weight of Tory opportunism and Ulster bigotry in the 1886 elections. The fall of Parnell in 1890 wrecked his Irish Parliamentary Party and years of painstaking reconciliation and manoeuvring lay ahead before the party, under John Redmond, again brought Home Rule to the edge of realisation.

Herbert Asquith, the British Liberal prime minister, became dependent on the

Irish Party for support against the Conservatives and attempted to implement his Home Rule pledge with such determination that the House of Lords' veto, an habitual stumbling block for Home Rule proposals emanating from the House of Commons, was removed in 1911. Once again, however, the Orange card was played.

As a result of religio-economic clashes, and the rantings of political priests the average Protestants of Ulster were conditioned to believe that Home Rule was Rome Rule, which would deliver them into the power of the Papacy, the bishops, the priests.* (To further incite these fears *circa* 1910–12 there was a controversy involving the *Ne Temere* decree promulgated in 1908, which declared that marriages between Catholics and Protestants were null and void if the children were not brought up in the Catholic religion.)

George Bernard Shaw correctly summed up the feelings of the Protestant rank and file in Ulster when he wrote:

. . . political opinion in Ulster is not a matter of tact and bluff as it is in England. No English Home Ruler has the faintest intention, in any event, of throwing actual paving stones at any English Unionist . . . the Ulsterman is not like that. He is inured to violence. He has thrown stones and been hit by them. He has battered his political Opponent with fist and stick, and been battered himself in the same manner . . . he has to avenge not only the massacre of St Bartholomew and the wrongs of Maria Monk, but personal insults, injuries and blood lettings of quite recent date and considerable frequency. Consequently, when he sings 'Oh God Our Help in Ages Past', he means business. And there is a strength in his rancour which lifts it above rancour.

Bonar Law, the Conservative leader, was unquestionably largely motivated by political expediency in his espousal of the Unionist cause, but he was also the son of an Ulster Presbyterian clergyman, the Rev. James Law, born in Coleraine in 1822, and he was a frequent visitor to Ulster. He was not altogether indulging in mere rhetoric, when at a Unionist rally at Blenheim Palace in July, 1912 he said 'I can imagine no length of resistance to which Ulster can go in which I would not be prepared to support them, and in which, in my belief, they would not be supported by the overwhelming majority of the British people.' And though the leader of the Unionists may have been a Dublin man, Edward Carson, one of the two members returned to the House of Commons for Trinity College, Dublin, he was also totally convinced that Ireland's future lay in union with England, and he advocated this view with all the forensic skill which had destroyed Oscar Wilde, and remade Archer-Shee.

It was Carson who, in 1912 standing on the steps of Craigavon, read the Ulster Covenant:

Being convinced in our consciences that Home Rule would be disastrous to the mental well-being of Ulster as well as the whole of Ireland, subversive of our civil and religious

---

* The actual measure of Home Rule to be granted was quite minute. Ireland was really only to have been granted local government powers under the Crown with severe limitations to her autonomy in the spheres of law, education and finance. The king was still to rule and Westminster to control the British troops who would defend the country in time of war and the Royal Irish Constabulary would police it in time of peace, although after six years this control was to be ceded to Dublin and in peace time the Irish parliament was to make its own laws relating to law and order.

freedom, destructive of our citizenship, and perilous to the unity of the Empire, we, whose names are under written, men of Ulster, loyal subjects of His Gracious Majesty King George V, humbly relying on the God whom our fathers in days of stress and trial confidently trusted, do hereby pledge ourselves in solemn covenant throughout this our time threatened by calamity to stand by one another in defending for ourselves and our children our cherished position of equal citizenship in the United Kingdom, and in using all means which may be found necessary to defeat the present conspiracy to set up a Home Rule Parliament in Ireland. And in the event of such a Parliament being forced upon us we further solemnly and mutually pledge ourselves to refuse to recognise its authority. In sure confidence that God will defend the right we hereto subscribe our names. And further, we individually declare that we have not already signed this Covenant. God Save the King.

This document owed as much to memories of the Reformation and the Scottish Covenanters as it did to any loyalty to the King. Imbued with this spirit during 1912 some 471,414 people are said to have signed this Covenant, some of them with their own blood. This was the origin of the Ulster Volunteer Force.

The Unionist lawyers were not long in discovering that an anomaly in the law allowed two justices of the peace to authorise drilling and other military operations within the area of their jurisdiction, provided that the object was 'to render citizens efficient in military arts for the defence of the United Kingdom Constitution and protecting their rights and liberties under this Constitution'. Ulster justices granted licences so enthusiastically that it was possible for the Unionists to recruit, arm and drill upwards of 100,000 men. Behind them was a network of sympathisers who provided contingency plans, transportation, an army of nurses in case of war, and sufficient manpower to immobilise every bridge, road and canal in the Province. A fund of over one million pounds was set up—Rudyard Kipling sent £30,000 and the Unionists were able to call on powerful support in high places in England also, men such as F. E. Smith, Lord Charles Beresford, Lord Salisbury, James Campbell, Lord Hugh Cecil and Lord Willoughby de Broke.

Moreover the army signified its sympathy with the Ulstermen during the celebrated 'Curragh Mutiny' affair of March, 1914, when a group of cavalry officers stationed at the Curragh, Co. Kildare, the largest British garrison in the south of Ireland, decided they would not engage in hostilities against the Ulster Volunteers. In fact, the Unionists had a staunch if devious champion in the very highest echelons of the army command in Sir Henry Wilson, the Director of Military Operations. Wilson was the archetype of those many senior British officers who felt that it was shocking to throw the loyalist Ulstermen to the Southern Papist wolves with their history of disrespect for the Crown and perhaps more important to the military mind, disrespect for British uniforms. Wilson openly connived with Bonar Law and supplied him with military intelligence and guidance.

Behind the Ulster Volunteer Force there was an Ulster provisional government set up by the Ulster Union Council, and this government gained some teeth by the Larne gun-running of April, 1914, in which the Unionist Volunteers landed 35,000 rifles at Larne, Co. Antrim, unloaded them, distributed them and secreted them without the loss of a rifle or a single arrest. The Home Rule movement was visibly grinding to a halt.

In so far as the Liberal vacillation was concerned, Asquith was afraid that an attempt to put down the Ulster Volunteers by force might provoke a civil war in England as much as a war between the Crown and its Ulster subjects. Also he doubted, possibly with good reason, whether he had sufficient backing in English public opinion to invoke the Crown against a minority of the King's subjects whose crime was that they wished to remain under the Crown. A poem by Rudyard Kipling in the *Morning Post* articulated the sentiments of those who felt that to drive Ulster out would be wrong:

> The blood our fathers spilt
> Our love our toils our pains,
> Are counted us for guilt,
> And only bind our chains.
> Before an Empire's eyes,
> The traitor claims his price.
> What need of further lies?
> We are the sacrifice.
>
> We know the war prepared
> On every peaceful home,
> We know the hells declared
> For such as serve not Rome—
> The terror, threats, and dread
> In market, hearth, and field—
> We know, when all is said,
> We perish if we yield.
>
> Believe, we dare not boast,
> Believe, we do not fear—
> We stand to pay the cost
> In all that men hold dear.
> What answer from the North?
> One law, one land, one throne.
> If England drive us forth
> We shall not fall alone.

However it was not England that drove the Home Rule issue forth, but Germany and the onset of the First World War. John Redmond, leader of the Nationalist Party, agreed to postpone the implementation of the Home Rule Bill until after the war and there the matter rested until 1916. By then a number of things were established concerning the Irish question. One was the form Home Rule was intended to take. Another was the extent of Northern Irish resistance to it, which prior to 1916 had the important effect of raising though not defining the question of partition.

On June 11, 1912 when the Home Rule Bill discussions had reached the committee stage a Liberal M.P., Agar-Robartes, had moved an amendment to exclude Antrim, Armagh, Down and Londonderry from the Bill because he said he didn't think that 'Orange bitters will mix with Irish whiskey'. The Unionists supported the amendment which was ultimately defeated, but it brought home to the Unionists the fact that effective resistance to Home Rule could only be carried on in certain Ulster counties: in fact in the six ultimately decided on, the four mentioned above, with the addition of Fermanagh and Tyrone although they have large Catholic populations.

Most importantly it also convinced a group of young men in Southern Ireland that if they wanted independence they would be better off fighting for it rather than waiting for the constitutionalists at Westminster to decide how little and how late would be the amount of Home Rule which they could enforce upon the alliance of the Orangemen and Conservatives.

These young men, and one Thomas Clarke who was not so young, were our Fenians or members of the Irish Republican Brotherhood. Padraig Pearse, Sean MacDiarmada, Joseph Plunkett and many others were to give their lives in a tradition of revolutionary activity which had flickered sporadically and unsuccessfully since Wolfe Tone's rebellion in 1798; during Robert Emmet's insurrection of 1803; the Young Irelanders' outbreak of 1848; and the abortive Fenian uprising of 1867. The latter degenerated into a debauch of floggings and firing squads as the British scotched plans for what was intended to be a year of destiny for Ireland with an efficiency made easy by equal parts of Irish bungling and British spies.

The Fenian tradition still persists in Ireland in the form of the I.R.A. and it merits examination. The movement was originally founded in Ireland on St Patrick's Day, 1858, by James Stephens and Thomas Clarke Luby, following the suppression of an earlier revolutionary group, the Phoenix National and Literary Society. The Phoenix Society had been set up by Jeremiah O'Donovan, better known in Irish history as O'Donovan Rossa after his birthplace at Rosscarbery, Co. Cork. Stephens and Luby called their organisation the Irish Republican Brotherhood, or I.R.B. The American wing became known as the Clann na Gael. (In Ireland it was sometimes called 'the Organisation' and sometimes the I.R.B.) Both wings came under the blanket description of 'Fenians' because John O'Mahony, the Clann's principal leader in America, was a man of literary tastes, who saw in the Fianna of Irish legend (who were something of a cross between the knights of the Round Table and Japanese Samurai) an appropriate title for an Irish republican organisation. Stephens saw the Fenians as being part of the same revolutionary movement which had shaken the Continent but in Ireland the Fenians depended for their support on the Catholics. In America and in England, their propagandists and financial supporters were also Catholic emigrants.

The I.R.B.'s organisational plan was as follows. In each parish there was a circle of nine men, one known as the centre or leader. The county centres were elected from the parish centres and the idea was that only the centres knew each other or knew who the members of each circle were—how far in fact this was true could only be judged by having recourse to the files of the British Intelligence Corps of the time! Membership of the I.R.B. was confined to Irishmen who were sworn to accept the organisation's constitution and who were prohibited from joining any other oathbound society without its permission.

The following are key extracts from its constitution:

1. The Supreme Council of the I.R.B. is declared to be the sole Government of the Irish Republic.

2. The President of the I.R.B. shall be in law and in fact the President of the Irish Republic.

3. The Supreme Council being the sole Government of the Irish Republic retains the right to make treaties and declare war, and negotiate terms of peace.

Penalties for breaches of these stipulations were to be 'in accordance with the nature of offence'. These penalties were framed to include death, banishment, or lesser punishments. Sentence of death could only be carried out for treason, and then only with the permission of the Supreme Council. (Treason was defined as being disloyal to the objectives of the I.R.B.—not to the Republic.)

In so far as the social philosophy of the Fenians' founders was concerned, it was arguably international and beyond mere separatism. Writing in his recollections of Fenians and Fenianism John O'Leary, himself a Fenian, said of O'Mahony that he was 'an advanced democrat of socialist opinions'. *The Flag of Ireland*, published in London following the suppression of the Fenians' own organ the *Irish People* in Dublin, 1865, said of the Fenians: 'It took its rise in the Latin quarter of this city when John O'Mahony, Michael Doheny and James Stephens were here in exile after 1848.' (The paper was quoting from a Paris correspondent.)

The ranks of the Catholic laity were keenly defended against Fenian recruitment by the upper echelons of the Irish Church. Some clerics went to extreme lengths in their condemnations. Bishop Moriarty of Kerry said that 'Hell was not hot enough nor Eternity long enough to punish such miscreants'. Others such as the ultra-montane Cardinal Cullen, archbishop of Dublin, saw Fenianism as a kind of Irish manifestation of Mazzini's views and opposed it by more subtle, but no less effective, methods, a pattern which continues to this day. However, in another pattern which also still exists, the Fenians found many supporters among the younger clergy, who returning for their holidays to their home towns from seminaries in which they were acquiring a Jansenistic brand of theology, found that these horned Fenians were, in fact, no more startling personages than their younger brothers, cousins and friends.

The Fenian Brotherhood displayed all the characteristics of Irishmen throughout the ages. The Fenians had colossal energy, daring, flair, suspicion, illogicallity, a tendency to disunity and splits, lack of organisation, courage, naivety and sometimes a high degree of shrewd commonsense coupled with an extraordinary tenacity that did occasionally bring spectacular consequences. Despite the damp squib at home Fenians were active abroad. The Fenian invasion of Canada in 1867 was a full-scale affair involving some thousands of men (predictably estimates of the numbers differ). The sailing ship *Catalpa* was chartered to sail around the world to western Australia in 1876 to rescue a group of Fenian prisoners. And it was the Fenians who commissioned the first American submarine, the *Fenian Ram*, designed by John P. Holland and launched in 1881.

The Fenian movement or off-shoots of it, such as the 'Invincibles', or members of the Clann na Gael, known as the 'Triangle', were also associated with some darker activities. To the Invincibles may be ascribed the murder of T. H. Burke and

Lord Frederick Cavendish the newly appointed chief secretary for Ireland, on May 6, 1882. It was a terrible deed and a great setback for the Irish Home Rule movement because of its effect on British public attitude. In America members of the Triangle were eventually sentenced for the murder of Dr Henry Cronin, a fellow-member of Clann na Gael who had been asking awkward questions about the misappropriation of Clann funds.

But there were other incidents which served to give both heroes and a folk memory to the movement, such as the execution of the 'Manchester Martyrs', Allen, Larkin and O'Brien, hanged in Manchester Jail for the death of a constable who was accidentally shot as a group of Fenians attempted to rescue a prisoner from a police van. (It was their deaths which inspired the ballad 'The Smashing of The Van', which I first heard sung by Brendan Behan, who had himself walked in the footsteps of the Fenians.)

On the heroic side also the Fenian movement gave tradition such figures as that of O'Donovan Rossa. Arrested in 1865 on the suppression of the *Irish People*, of which he was business manager, he was sentenced to life imprisonment on December 13, 1865. He was released on January 5, 1871 after experiences in various British prisons that were authenticated by the Devon Commission. These included having had his hands handcuffed behind his back for thirty-five days in Chatham Jail, and being kept naked day and night on a punishment diet of bread and water, in solitary confinement in a darkened cell, because of his intransigent attitude towards his jailers—an attitude which many Republican prisoners afterwards attempted to emulate.

After his release Rossa went to America and became a prominent member of the Clann na Gael, and one of the prime movers behind the 'dynamite campaign', a series of dynamitings carded out by young Irishmen throughout England for approximately two years beginning in 1883. Like its later offshoot, the I.R.A. bombing campaign in England of 1939, the dynamiting campaign seemed to end with small loss of life, the alienation of English public opinion, and the imprisonment of a number of patriotic young Irishmen, with no other effect than to embitter them and deprive their friends and families of their company and support.

But when an amnesty was granted to the Fenian prisoners in 1898 one such young man emerged from jail determined that this would not be the full story. Following the amnesty Thomas Clarke went to New York, but he returned to Ireland in 1907 because foreseeing a European war he decided that a time was coming when John Mitchel's doctrine 'that Ireland's opportunity would come when England was in difficulty' might have a chance to prove itself.★

In the colonial Ireland to which Clarke returned opportunities for revolution were few. Free primary school education was widespread throughout the country, County Councils and Urban District Councils were controlled by members elected by the Irish themselves by democratic franchise and generally

---

★ John Mitchel, the leading polemicist of the 1848 militants, had outlined his theory in his paper the *United Irishman*. The idea of striking at England while she was preoccupied with war was used again in 1939 when Sean Russell master-minded the I.R.A.'s bombing campaign against England.

supported the Irish Party. Tenant farmers were buying back their holdings from the landlords by a system of annuities payable to the British government which had compensated the landlords in the first place. Granted, slum conditions in Dublin were appalling—twenty thousand families were living in one room each according to a survey in 1910, and the infant mortality was 142 per thousand as compared with 103 in London—the bulk of the country was peaceful. Men of Clarke's generation in the I.R.B. did little for the movement beyond talk of the old days which grew more heroic with each telling.

However a group of young men—Denis MacCullagh, P. S. O'Hegarty and Bulmer Hobson—had been active in the north in setting up Dungannon Clubs, called after the town in Co. Tyrone where the Irish Volunteers were founded in 1782. These literary and debating clubs were a cloak for I.R.B. activities which consisted of little more than preaching separatism and republicanism and introducing new recruits to the writing of other authors of either a revolutionary or nationalistic nature—the Republican and separatist Wolfe Tone, John Mitchel, nationalists Charles Kickham, who had edited the Fenian newspaper the *Irish People* and Thomas Davis the leader of the Young Irelanders of the 1840s. The poetry of Eithne Carbery and Alice Milligan and James Fintan Lalor's writings on the land issue all helped towards creating a body of opinion, however small, in favour of staging a rising against the British.

This opinion was shared by very few people outside I.R.B. circles, and though they had a newspaper, *Irish Freedom*, Clarke and the young I.R.B. men cannot have had more than a handful of active members spread throughout the country at the onset of the Ulster crisis. None the less using the Communist tactic of infiltration they had manipulated themselves into positions of influence in a number of what might be termed 'Irish Ireland Societies'—notably the Gaelic League and the Gaelic Athletic Association, both of which had a nation-wide following by 1912. They were non-sectarian (the Gaelic League in fact was founded by a Protestant, Douglas Hyde) and in the period of relative peace and prosperity that followed Parnell's death these associations combined with the influence of the Abbey Theatre and W. B. Yeats to arouse a very definite awareness among young people of a distinctively Irish culture and identity.

The I.R.B. seized its chance to capitalise on this sense of identity when Eoin MacNeill, vice-president of the Gaelic League, wrote an article in the organ of the Gaelic League, *An Claidheamh Soluis* in October, 1913, proposing that a body of Southern Volunteers be formed on the same line as the Ulster Volunteers. Using the respected name of MacNeill as a front, the I.R.B. organised a meeting to which all parties were invited, at the Rotunda Hall, Dublin, on November 25. At the meeting MacNeill said: '. . . the more genuine and successful the local Volunteer Movement in Ulster becomes, the more completely does it establish the principle that Irishmen have the right to decide and govern their own national affairs. We have nothing to fear from the existing Volunteers in Ulster nor they from us. We gladly acknowledge the evident truth that they have opened the way for a National Volunteer Movement . . .'

It was put to the meeting that the formation of the Southern Volunteers was a reply to the course of action 'deliberately adopted by one of the great English Parties

. . . to make a display of military force, and a menace of armed violence the determining factor in the future relations between this country and Great Britain'.

Unlike the Ulster Force which was unified in a single aim under the discipline of regular British army officers the Volunteers suffered from conflicting motives behind their creation and different views as to who should control them.

MacNeill and the vast bulk of those who joined believed, until the 1916 Rising, that the Volunteers would only be used to fight if by some chance the Conservatives and Orangemen were to use the U.V.F. to attempt to frustrate the introduction of Home Rule. Redmond insisted that the Volunteers should be controlled, at least in part, by himself, not wishing an armed force to spring up in Ireland, and thus jeopardise the prospect of Home Rule. The Volunteers split after he made a recruiting speech in favour of the British army at Woodenbridge in September, 1914 leaving the Republican element in control of approximately 10,000 men against Redmond's estimated 170,000. Next, on the very eve of the 1916 Rising itself there were splits, postponements and the capture of arms being sent from Germany at the instigation of Clann na Gael and Sir Roger Casement, who paid with his life on the scaffold for his enterprise. These setbacks dearly doomed the movement to failure and Eoin MacNeill, learning at the last moment of the I.R.B.'s plans for rebellion, countermanded their orders for a mobilisation of Volunteers on Easter Sunday. Consequently when the Volunteers marched out to challenge the might of the British Empire on Easter Monday, April 24 1916, under the leadership of Padraig H. Pearse, poet, schoolteacher and principal source of inspiration of Republicans thereafter, the total force comprised roughly 1,200 Volunteers and members of James Connolly's Citizen Army.

This army had been founded by Captain Jack White, a son of White of Ladysmith fame, to defend the workers in the great 1913 lockout in which the strikers were finally defeated, forcing their leader James Larkin to emigrate to America. However, Connolly stayed, having succeeded Larkin as head of the Irish Transport and General Workers Union, and having himself founded in 1896 the Irish Socialist Republican Party. (In 1903, while living in America he was to become a co-founder of the International Workers League.)

However Connolly himself would never have got much widespread support had the revolution of 1916 been confined to his followers only. In a small-farmer economy, strongly influenced by the Church, the emasculated Labour Party which succeeded him had to expend so much of its time assuming the hierarchy that it wasn't Communist that it never even gave the appearance of being likely to form a government until, after Pope John, its leaders felt it safe to declare that the Labour Party was in favour of socialism and a workers' republic and as a result was beaten badly in the elections of June 1969. Nevertheless by 1916 Connolly's continual incitements to riot and rebellion were such an embarrassment to the I.R.B.'s plans that it co-opted him onto the Supreme Council, and he, with Joseph Plunkett, worked out the plans for the Rising of April 24.

There is no need to go into the oft-told story of the events of that week. The insurgents fought with a typical Irish gallantry, attacked by soldiers using artillery and outnumbering them twenty to one. Cut off from all possible support from the country, or from reinforcement of any kind, they held out for almost a week, during which Dublin was badly damaged and over three thousand people died. The leaders knew their rising was bound to fail, but they were prepared to batter their lives against the possibilities of their various dreams coming true after their deaths.

Some, such as Pearse, Plunkett and MacDiarmada wanted to set up an Ireland that would be 'not merely free but Gaelic as well, not merely Gaelic but free as well'. In so far as his anti-British separatist feelings went Clarke was still the same young man who had gone to jail nearly thirty years earlier. Connolly, a long-time exponent of force, also hoped for the dawning of a socialist republic that would guarantee equality of opportunity to every citizen. Other activists, such as sixteen-year-old Sean Lemass, a strange mixture of idealist and ruthless political opportunist, who later became a successful Irish prime minister and principal architect of Southern Ireland's industrial drive, merely wanted to carry on the tradition of a rising in every generation, a tradition which had lapsed in their parents' generation because of the Conservative policy of 'killing Home Rule by kindness', a carrot and stick policy of ameliorative and coercive legislation.

All found their aspirations expressed in large measure in the 'Declaration of the Republic' drawn up by Pearse and Connolly and read outside the General Post Office on the morning that the Rising began.

Poblacht na h-Eireann

The Provincial Government
of the

IRISH REPUBLIC

To the people of Ireland

Irishmen and Irishwomen: In the name of God and of the dead generations from which she receives her old tradition of nationhood, Ireland, through us, summons her children to her flag and strikes for her freedom.

Having organised and trained her manhood through her secret revolutionary organisation, the Irish Republican Brotherhood, and through her open military organisations, the Irish Volunteers and the Irish Citizen Army, having patiently perfected her discipline, having resolutely waited for the right moment to reveal itself, she now seizes that moment and, supported by her exiled children in America and by gallant allies in Europe, but relying in the first on her own strength, she strikes in full confidence of victory.

We declare the right of the people of Ireland to the ownership of Ireland and to the unfettered control of Irish destinies, to be sovereign and indefeasible. The long usurpation of that right by a foreign people and government has not extinguished the right, nor can it ever be extinguished except by the destruction of the Irish people. In every generation the Irish people have asserted their right to national freedom and sovereignty: six times during the past three hundred years they have asserted it in arms. Standing on that fundamental right and again asserting it in arms in the face of the world, we hereby proclaim the Irish Republic as a Sovereign Independent State, and we pledge our lives and the lives of our comrades-in-arms to the cause of its freedom, of its welfare and of its exaltation among the nations.

The Irish Republic is entitled to, and hereby claims, the allegiance of every Irishman and Irishwoman. The Republic guarantees religious and civil liberty, equal rights and equal opportunities to all its citizens, and declares its resolve to pursue the happiness and prosperity of the whole nation and of all its parts, cherishing all the children of the nation equally, and oblivious of the differences, carefully fostered by an alien government, which have divided a minority from the majority in the past.

Until our arms have brought the opportune moment for the establishing of a permanent national Government, representative of the whole people of Ireland, and elected by the suffrages of all her men and women, the Provisional Government, hereby constituted, will administer the civil and military affairs of the Republic in trust for the people. We place the cause of the Irish Republic under the protection of the Most High God, Whose blessing we invoke upon our arms, and we pray that no one who serves that cause will dishonour it by cowardice, inhumanity or rapine. In this supreme hour the Irish nation must, by its valour and discipline, and by the readiness of its children to sacrifice themselves for the common good, prove itself worthy of the august destiny to which it is called.

Signed on Behalf of the Provisional Government,

Thomas J. Clarke

Sean MacDiarmada	Thomas MacDonagh
P. H. Pearse	Eamonn Ceannt
James Connolly	Joseph Plunkett

It will be seen that this document, which has subsequently become the Magna Carta of all Irish Republicans, North or South, whether constitutionalists or not, was irreconcilably opposed to the claims of the signatories of the Ulster Covenant. The proclamation of 1916 expressed a distillation of the traditions and hopes of Catholic Ireland, leavened by Connolly's socialism, and asserted independence from England, equality of opportunity, and sovereignty over the whole country. The Ulster Covenant of 1912 spoke for Protestant Ireland, descendants of English and Scottish settlers. Its signatories wished to maintain their link with the Crown with all its consequent liberties and safeguards. To the Northerners 'equality of opportunity' in the Southern document meant putting the Catholics in a position from which they could overthrow Protestant hegemony. And in fact, revolution, time and the Catholic birth rate did do just this. In the North the Protestants circumvented the Catholic birth rate by gerrymandering the electoral system, and a policy of discrimination in employment whereby the Catholic and Protestant ratios remained almost static from the time the northern state was set up in 1920 to the time of writing. To the Northerner the proposed Irish Republic was a cloak for 'Catholic authoritarianism'. To the Catholic 'Protestant liberties' meant Catholic enslavement. It is an interpretation of terminology on which the Irish are still far from agreement.

After the 1916 Rising events took their predictable course. Great roaring fires of patriotism banked up as the British executed the principal leaders of the revolt, imprisoned others, imposed martial law, and hanged Sir Roger Casement in August, long after any danger of another Easter Rising had passed.

British efforts to arrest the development of events were swept aside. An attempt, shortly after the Rising, to forge an agreement between Carson and Redmond on the introduction of Home Rule, with the exclusion of the northern counties until after the war, broke down.

In this new atmosphere public opinion began to focus on the prisoners in English jails. The uncommon-sounding name de Valera, elected leader of the prisoners in Dartmoor, and the last commandant to surrender in Easter Week, became familiar. In Ireland people began to turn their eyes away from Westminster and to examine the doctrines of Sinn Fein, founded in 1905 by Arthur Griffith, who was neither Republican nor a revolutionary. In social and economic matters he was inclined to capitalism, believing in protection and condemning strikes. He was influenced by the writings of Deak, a Hungarian patriot, and saw a link between Hungary and Austria and Ireland and Britain. Griffith proposed that the Irish members withdraw from Westminster, rejecting that parliament's claim to legislate for internal Irish affairs. He advocated a dual monarchy similar to that of Austro-Hungary, in which the British monarch would act as king of Ireland and England, with separate parliaments in both countries—in effect restoring the pre-Act of Union position in Ireland.

In February, 1917 a by-election fell due in Co. Roscommon and Count Plunkett, father of the executed Rising leader Joseph Plunkett, was elected on a platform of non-recognition of the British parliament. Using the banner of a monarchist he inspired the party to press a demand for the implementation of the 1916 declaration of an all Ireland republic. In May Sinn Fein won another seat when a prisoner in Lewes Jail, Joseph McGuinness, was elected in a campaign during which the Sinn Fein supporters largely based their appeal on 'putting him in to get him out', and overruled the appeals of the Irish Parliamentary Party veteran Joseph Devlin, a Belfast man who could see the difficulties of implementing the Sinn Fein policy and warned the electorate that Sinn Fein stood for 'a hopeless fight for an Irish Republic'. In June and August the two men who were to lead the political struggle on opposite sides of the fence in post-Civil War Ireland, William T. Cosgrave and Eamon de Valera, were elected for Kilkenny and Clare.

Behind the scenes I.R.B. organisers, principally Michael Collins and Thomas Ashe, both of whom had taken part in the 1916 Rising, were directing this activity as they went about the country reorganising the I.R.B. and enlisting more and more young Irishmen in a volunteer army sworn to fight for an Irish republic. Ashe was arrested and died of forcible feeding while on hunger strike. Collins, a guerrilla chieftain of Mao-like stature escaped the net, and day by day the Volunteers grew stronger, drilling more openly and waving tricolours. The clang of prison doors on the ever increasing numbers of young rebels picked up under the Defence of the Realm Act (D.O.R.A.) failed to drown the defiantly swelling chorus of 'Up the Republic'.

A Lloyd George-inspired Irish convention set up to frame proposals for Irish self-government within the British Empire on July 25, 1917, was boycotted by both Sinn Fein and Labour on the grounds that its membership was representative neither of Sinn Fein nor of post-revolutionary Irish sentiment. Sinn Fein held its own convention (known in Irish as an 'Ard-Fheis') at the Mansion House in Dublin on October 25, and de Valera was elected president of Sinn Fein. Then on April 16, 1918, the British delivered the initiative to the Sinn Feiners by passing the Conscription Act. The Irish Party immediately withdrew in protest. The party then joined Sinn Fein and Labour in drawing up a joint anti-conscription pledge which was signed, with a solidarity like that accorded to the Ulster Covenant, at church doors following Sunday Masses. Even the Catholic hierarchy denounced conscription, a major shift in authoritative opinion as prior to the 1916 Rising Cardinal Logue's name had appeared on recruiting posters urging young Southern Irishmen to join the British army. To compound this error of judgement on May 19 the British authorities cooked up 'a German plot' and used it as an excuse to arrest Griffith, de Valera and many other prominent Sinn Fein leaders.

The election of December 14, 1918 completely discredited parliamentarianism on the old British model. Redmond's party won only six seats, and over a hundred years of Irish political development disappeared, taking with it Redmond's health, happiness, and, most unfairly, his reputation, which deserves to stand high with Irishmen. The newly elected Sinn Fein deputies held their first Dail (parliament) on January 21, 1919 in Dublin. This revolutionary parliament was not, of course, recognised by the British. Thirty-six of its seventy-three members were in jail, including de Valera, but it appointed delegates to the peace conference in Versailles and it adopted a 'Democratic Programme' based on the proclamation of Easter Week, watering down James Connolly's socialistic principles, but retaining the 1916 proclamation's demand for an all-Ireland republic. (To some members of the I.R.B. its constitution meant that the Irish republic was in fact established before 1916 and had existed *de jure* if not *de facto* since James Stephens had set up a provisional government in February, 1867 to take command of the revolution which failed to take place the following March.)

The I.R.B. had joined Sinn Fein seeing it only as another nationalist society that might help its aims. But at the Sinn Fein convention of October, 1917, working towards an Irish republic within a political party which advocated setting up a king in Ireland, the I.R.B. agreed to frame an article in the Sinn Fein convention declaring the movement's aim to be the securing of international recognition of Ireland as an independent Irish republic. The Irish people would then 'by Referendum freely choose their own form of Government'.

Constitutionally therefore the party kept its options open on the form of settlement it was prepared to make with England. In character however it was becoming a markedly republican organisation. Parallel to the rebirth of Sinn Fein after 1916 there occurred the reorganisation of the Volunteers, formed to defend Home Rule but now directed by I.R.B. men such as Collins and Richard Mulcahy. By 1918 the August issue of *An tOglach*, the Volunteer organ, could declare that 'The Irish Volunteers are the Army of the Irish Republic'.

The Volunteers however had their own executive and constitution, and though there was some overlapping of membership between individual volunteers and other national organisations they had a largely autonomous existence from Sinn Fein and the Dail. The first shooting of policemen, for instance, was not sanctioned by the Dail. It took place at Soloheadbeag, Co. Tipperary, on the day the first Dail met. A number of volunteers, led by Sean Treacy and Dan Breen, decided to strike a blow for Ireland and shot two policemen dead in a hold-up for gelignite.

The attitude of many rural volunteers, who subsequently took action like that of Breen and Treacy, was summarised in a remark made to me by one of the most famous guerrilla leaders—Tom Barry—who said of the Volunteers' relationship with headquarters, 'if we pulled off some action that worked they sanctioned it'.

However, this fairly typical reaction of the man in the field to a G.H.Q. anywhere does not minimise the fact that G.H.Q. did co-ordinate policies which emerged from leaders in the field, such as Liam Lynch who advocated the mass destruction of R.I.C. barracks, or Dick McKee who thought up the flying columns, small highly mobile groups of guerrillas, or Collins himself who originated the most effective weapon of all, the destruction of the network of spies which the British used as their eyes and ears in keeping control of the country.

Throughout the course of the Anglo-Irish War the Volunteers and the Sinn Fein party pursued separate though complementary courses of action. Sinn Fein gradually took juridical control of the many county councils, setting up courts and settling land disputes, and the Volunteers sought to achieve military supremacy where they could.

During all this period the question of the Dail's control of the Volunteers remained one of some doubt and even controversy, partially through the antipathy which some members of the cabinet, notably Cathal Brugha and Austin Stack, felt towards Collins in particular, and the idea of secret societies generally. Brugha had left the I.R.B. after the 1916 Rising, as had the 'Priomh Aire' or First Minister of Dail Eireann, Eamon de Valera, and after his election as minister for defence in the First Dail Brugha sought to bring the Volunteers under Dail control. Collins rejected the idea of trying to run an army under a civilian council. (Michael Collins was president of the I.R.B., the Dail's minister for finance, the Volunteers' director of intelligence and adjutant-general.) The clearest statement of the position, which de Valera felt free to make a few months after the setting up of the Dail, was a statement to the Dail on April 10 that the 'Minister for Defence is of course in close association with the Voluntary military forces which are the foundation of the National Army'—'in close association with' only, not 'in control of'.

Brugha, who disliked and mistrusted Collins, tried again on August 20 when he proposed to the Dail that Volunteers and Dail deputies alike should take an oath 'to support and defend the Irish Republic and the Government of the Irish Republic, which is Dail Eireann against all enemies, foreign and domestic, and I will bear true faith and allegiance to the same'. Arthur Griffith, acting in place of de Valera, who had gone to America on a publicity tour, backed the proposal and the Dail approved the oath. However under pressure of the military situation the Volunteers never made a similar formal acceptance of the oath. The individual commanders were left to discuss it with their troops, most of whom, in the light of their subsequent alignments during the Civil War, seem to have decided in favour of the oath.

The I.R.B. in secret session amended its constitution to delete its claim that the president of the I.R.B. was also president of the Irish Republic, and to recognise that the Dail set up as a result of I.R.B. policy was a 'duly elected public authority competent to declare the will of the Irish people'.

But still the issue of autonomy of the Volunteers persisted. It was not until March, 1921, only a few months before the truce which ended the Anglo-Irish hostilities, that the Dail agreed with de Valera that the Dail should take public responsibility for the Volunteers' military actions, and formally accept the fact that a state of war existed. It was left to him to issue a statement to this effect saying that the Volunteers were 'under the Civil Control of elected representatives, and that their officers held their commissions from these representatives. The Government therefore is responsible for the actions of this army.'

During the course of the war, backed by a sympathetic population, the I.R.A., as the Volunteers became known after the first Dail, carried out a campaign of ambushing, raiding police barracks, and inflicting casualties which were estimated, between the time of the sitting of the first Dail and the truce, at 600 killed, and 1,200 wounded on the British side, and 752 I.R.A. men killed and 866 wounded. In the South these incidents were coupled with midnight police searches, martial law and a fear and tension which were grim enough, but as nothing compared to the situation in the North. There the I.R.A., being fewer in number and relying almost exclusively on Catholics for recruits, was unable to make much progress. The sectarian question continually threw itself across the path of the conflict in the north-east. Derry was the scene of a fierce Protestant onslaught on the Catholic quarter on July 19, 1920 after Carson made a speech at an Orange celebration on the 12th, during which he said, 'I am sick of words without action'. The rioters carried the Union Jack and were not halted by the military over the five-day period during which looting and street fighting went on unabated. When the military did intervene, it was to fire on I.R.A. men who were standing guard on Catholic property.

Other Ulster towns had a similar story. In Belfast, after prominent Unionists had addressed Protestant workers in the Belfast shipyards on July 12, calling for a 'show of revolvers' to drive the 'Fenians' out, an orgy of looting, shooting and petrol bombing broke out. Catholic workers were driven out of the shipyards, homes were burned and, again, the military did not offer protection to the beleaguered Catholics. Commenting on these incidents in a report to the *Westminster Gazette* in London on July 24, 1920, a correspondent wrote: 'It is common knowledge in Belfast and had frequently been admitted by individual Unionists, that plans were matured at least two months ago to drive all the Home Rule workers in the shipyards out of their employment.'

The steps towards the truce were initiated in a conciliatory speech which King George V made at the Stormont parliament which he opened on the coming into force of the Government of Ireland Act on May 3, 1920. What this act did in real terms was to recognise that there was in Ireland a large Protestant element in the North who did not want to be governed by the South and, in fact, it effectively partitioned the country from that time on. Under the act, by which Northern Ireland is still governed, the South was to send thirty-three members to Westminster and to have 128 members in a Dublin parliament. The North was to send representatives to Westminster and to have its own parliament. Both Irish parliaments were to have senates. However, the Dail refused to recognise the elections for the Southern senate because the act entitled the Crown to nominate some of the members. It regarded the elections for the lower house as being held for the second Dail, not for the Dublin parliament. In the South, the 124 Sinn Fein candidates were returned unopposed, the only non-nationalist candidates being the four senate members for Trinity who were unopposed. When the Dublin parliament opened, on June 28, only the Trinity representatives and the Crown-nominated senators turned up. This 'parliament' sat for fifteen minutes and was adjourned *sine die*.

This act was both a tragedy and a triumph for the Unionists, a triumph because it prevented them from being placed under any Dublin government in the future, a tragedy because the North, no more than the South, wanted Ireland partitioned. However, partitioned it was and the treaty which the Irish negotiators signed with the British on December 6, 1921 accepted this fact.

How strongly extremist Republican feeling ran against the treaty may be gauged from Brugha's speech against it on the day he left the Dail, never to return:

If instead of being so strong, our last cartridge had been spent and our last man was lying on the ground and his enemies howling round him and their bayonets raised, ready to plunge them into his body, that man should say—true to the traditions handed down—if they said to him: 'Now will you come into the Empire?'—he should say, and he would say: 'No, I will not.' That is the spirit which has lasted all through the centuries and you people in favour of the Treaty know that the British Government and the British Empire will have gone down before that spirit dies out in Ireland.

The treaty set up an Irish Free State, as a self-governing dominion of the British Empire, with the same constitutional status as Canada, Australia, New Zealand and South Africa.

A representative of the Crown was to be appointed in the same way as a dominion governor-general and the members of the Irish parliament were to take an oath of allegiance to the constitution of the Irish Free State which pledged them to 'be faithful to His Majesty King George V, his heirs and successors'. The Free State was to assume responsibility for part of the United Kingdom's public debt, yield certain defence facilities to the British forces and in time of war give whatever assurance might be required by the British.

Furthermore, the treaty granted to Northern Ireland the right to withdraw from the jurisdiction of the Dublin parliament. Of these provisions, the oath, partition and the office of the governor-general were clearly incompatible with the republican aspiration of the nationalist movement and the affection with which Collins regarded it may be seen from his prophetic statement that he was signing his own death warrant. He felt, however, that it was the best 'stepping stone' as he put it, that could be got for the time being towards a full republic.

Moreover while to the public mind the I.R.A. seemed all-powerful the guerrillas were in fact almost at the end of their tether. Losses had been heavy and arms were running dangerously short. Unlike the Viet Cong who had a friendly landmass at their backs from which arms and medical supplies can readily be secured, the nearest landmass to the Irish was that of their enemy, England, and all military and other supplies had to run the gauntlet of British ships. Once the truce was signed and the I.R.A. lost the momentum and anonymity which had been among its greatest assets in the struggle, any attempt to restart the war would have been disastrous—precisely the consideration which has made Hanoi turn down so many American offers of a cease-fire pending negotiations on the Vietnam war.

The treaty was ratified by the Dail on January 7, 1922, by sixty-four votes to fifty-seven, and an administration was formed three days later led by Arthur Griffith The constitutional opponents of the treaty, including de Valera, Austin Stack, Cathal Brugha, Robert Barton and Erskine Childers, left the Dail in protest. Outside the Dail the Church, big business, labour and a large proportion of the general public supported the treaty and peace. Opposed to it were the deputies who had left the Dail under de Valera, a high proportion of the I.R.A. and the women's organisation Cumann na mBan, an auxiliary of the I.R.A.

The great polemicist on the Republican side was Erskine Childers, and his influence coupled with that of the women deputies led to those who supported de Valera becoming derisively tagged as 'The Women and Childers Party'. He was not as influential on the Republican side as the pro-treaties supposed as they winced under his barbs,* but in addition to his polemics they blamed him for using his influence with his cousin Barton who had signed the treaty later to reject it, and for having much to do with influencing de Valera's attitude also. Consequently when he was captured during the Civil War he was executed on a trumped-up charge of being in possession of arms a revolver given to him by Michael Collins.

But it was not the de Valera faction or the constitutional group which now proceeded to make the running against the wealthy. This opposition came mostly from the advocates of physical force—young men who had sworn an oath to an Irish Republic. Their leaders were men such as Liam Lynch (the only member of the Supreme Council of the I.R.B. to vote against the treaty), Tom Barry, Rory O'Connor, Liam Mellows, Sean Deasy, Joseph McKelvey, Eaman O'Malley, Sean Moylan, Sean Dowling, Peadar O'Donnell, George Gilmore, Maurice Twomey, Sean Russell, Sean MacBride and many others.

Though the Irish Civil War like any civil war was a terrible business it was not an unmitigated evil. At first sight it might appear difficult to see how this might be. Reports of deaths and damage so fill the columns of contemporary newspapers that little space remains for other news. The bill in money for the cost of the war was probably £20 million, in deaths approximately 700 and in long-term effect the embittering of Southern political life has still not entirely run its course. But at the same time a democratic two-party system did emerge from the Civil War as first the victorious and then the vanquished formed political parties, and above all the Civil War, centring as it did on the refusal of young men who had taken an oath to an Irish Republic to accept anything else, diverted Southern energies from the possibility of a North-South, Orange against Catholic conflict which would have been much greater in scale and horror, and which would also have inevitably brought in the British again on the side of the North. (As matters turned out the Conservative-Unionist section of the British cabinet so disliked the treaty that everyone who signed it was out of office in four years.)

Inevitably, also, given the Northern background, sectarian strife did break out in places and neither police nor army did very much to help the Catholics. Sir Henry Wilson was so active in his unofficial post as military adviser to the Northern Irish government that Collins had him shot dead in June, 1922, on the steps of his London home by two former British service men named Dunne and Sullivan. This shooting was held by Republicans to be the precipitating factor of the Civil War, but in fact a state of virtual civil war had existed for some time earlier. From February and March of 1922 groups of Republicans, most notably those in the South who gave, nominally at any rate, allegiance to Liam Lynch, and those in Dublin who followed Rory O'Connor, were conducting operations of a paramilitary nature to obtain funds either to maintain the troops or the republic—the staffs of the various post offices and banks which involuntarily provided the money were never quite clear which.

---

* Childers' high-pitched polemical style continued to be emulated by Republican controversialists down the years and even today the style of the *United Irishman* is evocative of that employed by Childers in the broadsheets which he turned out against the treaty and its upholders.

Attempts to bring the I.R.A. into line with the Dail failed when the cabinet refused to sanction an army convention timed for March 15 lest it lead to the setting up of an army dictatorship. General Mulcahy suggested on March 20 that a joint council be set up 'to frame definite proposals for associating the I.R.A. with the government elected by the Irish people'. The militants' acceptance of this proposal was conditional on a provision which the cabinet found totally unacceptable: that recruiting for the new Irish police force, an unarmed body known as the Civic Guard, be suspended.

Following this the militants made a clean break with the.cabinet section. And on March 23 a manifesto signed by leading anti-treaty I.R.A. men appeared in the public press summoning the convention for March 26 in defiance of the cabinet's order. At a press conference on March 23, Rory O'Connor said 'that the Army would not obey President Griffith' because 'he had violated his oath'. He said that there was no government in Ireland to which the army gave allegiance, that the holding of the convention meant that 'we repudiate the Dail' and he announced the setting-up of an executive which would issue orders to the I.R.A. all over the country. In response to a question as to whether this betokened a military dictatorship he said, 'You can take it that way if you like.'

The convention was duly held at the Mansion House in Dublin on March 26. Only anti-treaty men attended, and the meeting unanimously reaffirmed allegiance to the republic, and placed its forces under the supreme control of an executive to be appointed by the convention. It adjourned when a new constitution was drawn up stipulating that:

The Army shall be known as the Irish Republican Army. It shall be on a purely volunteer Army basis. It objects shall be:
1. To safeguard the honour and maintain the independence of the Irish Republic.
2. To protect the rights and liberties common to the people of Ireland.
3. To place its services at the disposal of an established Republican Government which faithfully upholds the above objects.

A sixteen-man executive was chosen and it was to this body that the anti-treaty Volunteers were to subsequently hold themselves responsible. The executive established an Army Council, composed of Liam Lynch, chief of staff of the Irish Republican Army; Joseph McKelvey, deputy chief of staff; F. O'Donoghue, adjutant general; Eaman O'Malley, director of organisation; Joseph Griffin, director of intelligence; Liam Mellows, quartermaster-general; Rory O'Connor, Seamus O'Donovan and Sean Russell, directors of engineering, chemicals and ammunitions.

On April 13 this council decided to occupy a number of strong points in Dublin, the principal one of which was the Four Courts, the seat of juridical control in Ireland. There ensued a confused dangerous period with barracks being seized around the country, banks being raided, people being shot, and in the South an effort by the Four Courts garrison to countermand the authority of the constitutional authorities. These derived their authority as follows: as required by the treaty the Southern parliament met on January 14, 1922. This parliament was composed of the sixty-four pro-treaty members of the second Dail who were elected in May, 1921 in the elections called for by the Government of Ireland Act. There were also the four representatives of Trinity College. This parliament elected a provisional government for the twenty-six counties and declared itself in favour of the provision in the treaty whereby the provisional government was to evolve into the government of the Irish Free State the year after the signing of the treaty. That much was settled although not of course in the minds of the dissident Republicans. The second Dail never met as the Republican deputies never returned to it, but it was to this 'second Dail' that a number of Republicans subsequently looked for legality—not the meetings which stemmed from the provisional government.

The shades gathered around their aspirations during what was to prove to be all too literally a flaming month of June. Collins had kept in touch with a section of the dissidents, those led by Liam Lynch who was nominally the commander-in-chief of all the Republican forces, to the extent that with Lynch he arranged the planning and armament for a campaign in the North in support of the beleaguered Catholics. This was in March. In May he concluded a pact with de Valera, both sides agreeing to go into the elections of June 10 under a shared Sinn Fein banner calling on the electorate to vote only for pro- or anti-treaty candidates and to forget about such light considerations as the interests of farmers, labour, Unionists, etc. The pact also provided for the enactment of a republican constitution after the election, although the day before the Four Courts was seized Winston Churchill had declared in the House of Commons that: 'If a Republic was set up, that is a form of Government in Ireland which the British Empire in no circumstances whatever can tolerate or agree to.'

Understandably therefore the pact displeased the British who exerted pressure to have it abrogated—which Collins did on the eve of the election, in a speech in which he urged the electorate to vote for anyone it fancied, thus ending the prospect of a coalition government about which his colleagues had been unenthusiastic anyway.

Three days before the elections were held Sir Henry Wilson was shot and on the same day the Four Courts prison arranged for the kidnapping of General O'Connell, the Free State army chief of staff. Either happening would have provided a catalyst for momentous events. Together they were irresistible and, on June 28, field pieces borrowed from the British loomed across the Liffey and blasted the Four Courts garrison from their fortress. The bombardment brought the issue of the treaty from the debating table to the sterner tests of ambush, reprisal, military action and execution.

It was a war of young men. Kevin O'Higgins, the strong man of the Free state government, said that: 'The Provisional Government was simply eight young men in the City Hall standing amidst the ruins of one administration, with the foundations of another not yet laid and with wild men screaming through the key hole.' The Republican leaders were young men also, in their late teens or early twenties. They hadn't the cohesion and resources of their opponents, nor did they have the backing of a sympathetic population. Houses that were friendly to the I.R.A. during the Anglo-Irish war were closed to them during the war of brothers. The worst of them contributed to the statistics of death and crime of the period and all the best of them had to fight a war were the qualities exhibited in these extracts from his last letter to his mother, written by Liam Mellows:

Mountjoy Prison, Dublin.
Dec. 8th 1922.
5 a.m.

My dear Mother,

The time is short and much I would like to say must go unsaid but you will understand in such moments heart speaks to heart. At 3.30 a.m. this morning, we (Dick Barrett, Rory O'Connor, Joe McKelvey and I) were informed that we were to be executed as a reprisal. Welcome be the will of God, for Ireland is in His keeping despite foreign monarchs and treaties. Though unworthy of the greatest human honour that can be paid an Irishman or woman, I go to join Tone and Emmet, the Fenians, Tom Clarke, Connolly, Pearse, Kevin Barry and Childers. My last thoughts will be on God, and Ireland and on you.

You must not grieve Mother Darling. Once before you thought you had given me to Ireland. The reality has now come. You will bear this as you have borne all the afflictions the cause of Ireland brought you—nobly and bravely. It is a sore trial for you, but that great courageous soul of yours will rejoice for I die for the truth—life is only for a little while, and we shall be returned hereafter.

Through you I also send another message: it is this, let no thought of reprisal or revenge dominate Republicans because of our deaths. We die for the truth, vindication will come, the mist will be cleared away, and brothers in blood will before long be brothers in arms, against the oppression of our country and imperialist England . . . in this belief I die happy forgiving all, as I hope myself to be forgiven. The path the people of Ireland must tread is straight and hard and true, though narrow; only by following it can they be men. It is a hard road, but it's the road our Saviour followed—the road of Sacrifice. The Republic lives, our deaths make that a certainty.

I have had the Chaplain to see me. It is sad but I cannot agree to accept the Bishops' Pastoral, my conscience is quite clear, Thank God, with the old Gaels. I believe that those who die for Ireland have no need for prayer.

God Bless and Protect you,
Your Loving Son Willie.

Mellows' reference to the bishops' pastoral concerned the issuing by the hierarchy on October 10 of a joint pastoral letter condemning the Republicans' war effort as 'morally only a system of murder and assassination of the National forces'. The bishops wrote of the Republicans' oath that 'No oath can bind any man to carry on a warfare against his own Country in circumstances forbidden by the law of God.' Following the publication of this pastoral many priests began to refuse confession to Republicans who would not repent of their ways. As a result men under sentence of death sometimes could not receive communion and died without the Viaticum, although as in Fenian times there were always some priests who defied the ban and heard Republican confessions.*

---

* It is still not clear whether or not he did receive the sacraments but a letter to the press in Dublin on April 24, 1968, from Captain Ignatius O'Rourke who was present at the execution, seems to indicate that he may have. According to the letter, a few minutes before Mellows was executed he sent for the prison chaplain, Father McMahon, and O'Rourke describes how, 'A few minutes later' he saw Father McMahon leaving the room 'accompained by Liam Mellows with his right arm around Liam's shoulders and they walked along together leading the group as we all walked to the sandbags. Liam and Father McMahon appeared to be in deep, friendly conversation, with no sign of discord, disagreement or argument, just like two men discussing some point in a friendly fashion. They continued to talk until Father McMahon left Liam in the number one position at the sandbags . . .'

This was and is a continuing trait of sane Irish priests, best exemplified by an anecdote from the period of preparation (1938) for Sean Russell's bombing campaign against England.

At the time a reservoir was being built at Poulaphoucca, Co. Wicklow, and upwards of thirty young I.R.A. men were in the habit of stealing gelignite and angle irons (for testing the strength of the charges) from the site. One of the lads went to confession:

'I stole Father.' 'What did you steal my son?' 'Explosives Father.' 'For use in Ireland?' 'No Father—in England.' 'That's all right my son,' said the priest, who gave the young bomber absolution, told him to send along his colleagues to be absolved also and wound up by getting the O.C. of the group to carry the Eucharistic flag at the head of a procession held to mark the closing of a mission.

However, the Civil War period was a rougher era and the bishops' pastoral took note of another grim factor then entering the war and urged the Republicans to take advantage of an amnesty which the government offered on October 3— because military courts were due to come into operation on October 15.

When the courts did begin functioning on November 17, they condemned seventy-seven men, including Childers and four leading members of the Courts' garrison who were executed as a reprisal after two pro-treaty deputies who had voted for the military courts were shot, one fatally. The executed men were Rory O'Connor, Liam Mellows, Richard Barrett and Joseph McKelvey. The executions of those leaders on December 8, two days after the Free State by the terms of the treaty officially came into existence, initiated a policy of reprisals whereby men who were already imprisoned were liable to execution if an I.R.A. operation took place in the district in which they were held.

It was against this background of religious and military pressures that an executive meeting was held in the remote Nier Valley in Co. Waterford on March 10, which de Valera attended as the political leader of the Republican side. He voted for peace, but Liam Lynch stood out for a continuation of the struggle. Further meetings were held in April on the run near Mullinahone, Co. Tipperary, and in Dublin between which Liam Lynch was killed and Austin Stack captured.

At the Dublin meeting a special Army Council formed from the depleted executive and consisting of Barry, Liam Pilkington, Sean Hyde and Frank Aiken agreed with de Valera and the three members of the Republican cabinet who were not in prison (P. J. Ruthledge, M. P. Colivet and Donal O'Callaghan) to issue a proclamation calling a halt to hostilities. Frank Aiken succeeded Lynch and on April 30 issued an order calling on the I.R.A. to suspend 'all offensive operations' and on May 24 the Civil War came finally to an end with a 'cease fire and dump arms' order also signed by Aiken.

As far as the ending of partition was, or is, concerned, the Civil War was a total irrelevance—as even the briefest of chats with any Northern Unionist would show. The point is vividly demonstrated by my talk with Viscount Brookeborough, from 1943 until his retirement in 1963 the prime minister of that strange political entity that the Government of Ireland Act created in the north-east, like a political left-over from the Reformation.

Coincidentally, the day before I went north to see Brookeborough I was in Dublin for the funeral of Dunne and Sullivan, the killers of Sir Henry Wilson, whose remains were brought back to Ireland on July 6, 1967. A guard of honour of the contemporary I.R.A. marched openly on either side of the two coffins through the streets of Dublin. The guards were set-face, stern young men, moving to military commands and dressed in a strange 'uniform' of ordinary peaked caps and gloves. Police kept the crowds back as men who had been under sentence of death by the state which those police were guarding honoured their dead, some praying openly.

The Brookeboroughs lived on a huge estate, Colebrook, near Brookeborough, in Co. Fermanagh. Outside the door stood two howitzers in memory of two relations of Brookeborough who were awarded posthumous Victoria Crosses in the First World War for gallantry at Ypres and at Givrenchy.

The relations and admirers of Dunne and Sullivan also remember Ypres. It was there that Sullivan lost a leg so that he could not flee after the shooting of Wilson, and Dunne stayed with him to save him from the enraged London mob, thereby ensuring his own execution also. At his trial, which was of course only a legal halt on the way to an inevitable execution, Dunne prepared a statement which said that they had 'fought for small nationalities . . . The same principles which led us to shed our blood on the battlefield of Europe led us to commit the act we are charged with.'

Lord Brookeborough and his wife said frankly that they considered Dunne and Sullivan to be murderers. Brookeborough had lost several relations in war for England, including two sons in the Second World War. 'I'm a Britisher,' he said, but he reminded me of the French General Massu of the O.A.S., both facially and physically and indeed in other ways too. He lived in almost feudal style at Brookeborough, pottering around in corduroys with a large clasp-knife dangling from his belt. In the wooded grounds around his mansion deer stalked through the trees, fat cattle grazed, and yards, barns and clusters of agricultural equipment, tended with nonchalant competence by innumerable workmen, combined to give a picture of a typical English demesne set down in an Irish countryside.

Lady Brookeborough, a woman of character rather than beauty, made me welcome, offered me coffee and then gave up a chance to watch Wimbledon on television to sit down and attempt to put me right about loyal Ulster. The contrast between the Brookeboroughs and the I.R.A. men whom I had seen in Dublin the previous night could not have been more striking.

Lord Brookeborough told me that he first heard of the 1916 Rising in his family pew at the local church. Just back on leave from the war, his first reaction was shame. He felt embarrassed for the country, for his regiment and for those who had died in the war. At the time of the Rising his wife was having a baby in the Rotunda Hospital in Dublin and both were impressed at the manner in which the rebels paralysed the city. This made them determined to withstand any such rising in the North.

When Brookeborough returned in 1918 he decided that nothing serious was being done to put down the menace of Sinn Fein. The I.R.A. was becoming active locally and by the end of 1919 he had lost his faith in the efficacy of the R.I.C. as a police force. Demoralised R.I.C. men were being sent north as Sinn Fein and the I.R.A. took control of the South. Brookeborough felt that something had to be done. At Dublin Castle he saw Sir John Anderson and General McCreedy who told him that a force was to be established in the North, issued with whistles. Brookeborough believed that even more should be done and decided to form his own force and issue them with something more lethal than whistles.

Thus began the celebrated B-Special Corps. He organised it first in Brookeborough, from men who had been Ulster Volunteers and from former members of the British army, then moved throughout the six north-eastern counties building the force to the strength of the pre-First World War Ulster Volunteer Force. He and his men regarded Catholics as potential traitors and Sinn Feiners. The B-Specials were the rock on which any mass movement by the I.R.A. in the North inevitably foundered.

2

Dilemmas of Violence and Politics

From the end of the Civil War until the present day a debate on the use of force has continued within the I.R.A. and the Republican movement generally. At some stages in the I.R.A.'s development the debate takes the form of Force *v.* Six Cos., or Force *v.* Free State; at other times it is Force *v.* England or Force *v.* Six Cos.; and sometimes it is Force *v.* a concentration on economic and social issues.

The use of force is a dilemma which the movement can never solve. The guns, the excitement and the secrecy attract new members thirsting for adventure. The guns go off and the authorities act. Take away the guns and the excitement and how do you offer a credible possibility of achieving the I.R.A.'s objectives and so attract new members? Even in 1970 when the movement had, for some years, rejected the ending of partition as its main objective (speech by Cathal Goulding, reported in *United Irishman*, July, 1967) and committed itself instead to a radical social and economic policy somewhat to the left of Albania, it still found it necessary, for recruiting purposes, to hold out the lure of the use of force to 'disrupt the existing state'. The ploy cut it away from the significantly large Republican socialist element in the country who would have supported a constitutional movement, no matter how radical its policies. Thus it was in 1970, and thus it was in 1924 when Eamon de Valera emerged from the jail where he had spent the year following the end of the Civil War.

The best illustration of de Valera's attitude towards the treaty is contained in a letter of September 10, 1922 to Joseph McGarrity in which he said, 'If the Republicans stand aside and let the Treaty come into force acquiescence in it means the abandonment of National sovereignty [for which of course he had fought in 1916] . . . if the Republicans do not stand aside . . . resistance means armed opposition to what is undoubtedly the decision of the majority of the people . . .'

It was a circle that could not be squared. On the one hand his speeches and actions were, to the pro-treaty side, at the worst outright incitements to bloodshed and violence and at the best were designed to wreck their efforts to make the treaty work. On the other hand to the militant Republicans these speeches and attitudes, while they showed that his heart lay in the right place, gave no indication of where his head lay. Politically his concept of 'external association'—an Irish Republic externally associated with England in the same way as later led to Indian independence—was ahead of his time and found little acceptance. The treaty was signed and he was forced to live with a *fait accompli*.

De Valera, coming out to freedom under the tattered banner of Sinn Fein, saw in the confused landscape confronting him, little hope of implementing his own kind of policies. On the other hand, having spent the Civil War somewhat outside the military councils which had made the running throughout the conflict (he had stipulated that while he honoured his responsibility to stand by his comrades he was not to be regarded as a leader of the armed wing) he was the most popular political leader on the Republican side if not in the country. The war had claimed the lives of Collins, Liam Lynch, Childers, Rory O'Connor, Liam Mellows, Arthur Griffith and many others and despite their military defeat Republicans had done remarkably well in the general elections of August, 1923.

Roughly 15,000 Sinn Fein and I.R.A. prisoners had been released from internment camps all over the country by July 16, 1924, when the three most important Republican prisoners, de Valera, Austin Stack and Liam Deasy were set free. In the six north-eastern counties, now beginning to settle down to the idea of partition, the I.R.A. were smashed. The remnants that had survived the brutalities of the preceding years had to contend with the B-Specials, a large and well armed Royal Ulster Constabulary, the British army and the full force of the Protestant ascendancy controlling business and industry.

At Stormont, the Nationalist M.P.s were still boycotting that institution. In the South, the Republicans emerging from jail and internment camps had to face a largely hostile population also. Many people agreed with the bishops' pastorals condemning the Republicans, or at least Republican militants, which stated:

They have wrecked Ireland from end to end, burning and destroying national property of enormous value, breaking roads, bridges and railways, seeking by an incessant blockade to starve the people or bury them in social stagnation. They have caused more damage to Ireland in three months than could be laid to the charge of British rule in so many decades . . .

Formerly friendly houses shut their doors on I.R.A. men seeking shelter. Such jobs as were available were being swallowed up by demobilised Free State soldiers, and throughout the ranks of the I.R.A. there was much confusion and bitterness at their leaders, and particularly at their political leaders in Sinn Fein whom they felt had let them down, by opposing the treaty but offering no viable alternative. They could not understand how the pro-treatyites were able to defeat an I.R.A. which, prior to the truce, had been in control of the greater part of the country. Increasingly in the I.R.A. also there was a feeling that the political leaders had not been as intent on directing the struggle as they had been in making political capital out of their opponents. Many of the young men were simply waiting for the call, believing that the 'dump arms' order by Frank Aiken was a bluff, that the war was going to start again any moment and that this time they would win.

Part of their determination was based on the bitter experiences of the Civil War. In Kerry, in particular, terrible things were done. Men were chained to mined barricades and blown to pieces, interrogations were conducted with the aid of a hammer and men went mad or were found to be castrated. Bitter Civil War memories are one reason why to this day Kerry is a fertile breeding ground for the I.R.A.

To the Free State side any Republican killing was an atrocity, no matter how justified such action may have seemed to the Republicans. The pro-treaty side regarded the anti-treaty forces as irregulars who had murderously turned on their fellow Irishmen in defiance of the lawfully constituted state for which they had successfully and with great sacrifice fought. Some Free State soldiers reacted against the Republicans with a rigour born of this attitude.

The Free State army intelligence department was believed to have been implicated in many of the killings. On August 26, 1922, shortly after Collins was killed in an ambush, three teenage youths were taken out of a lorry and shot dead near Clondalkin; a week later a prominent I.R.A. man called Banfield was killed in the same area, and there were sufficient other such deaths as to embitter the young I.R.A. men and make them wish for revenge. Michael Fitzpatrick, who in the 1930s was to be one of the most prominent members of the I.R.A., told me that while being interrogated after capture in the Civil War at Oriel House in Westland Row, the headquarters of the Criminal Investigation Department, he was forced to walk up and down a downstairs cell while shots were fired from a .45 pistol at either side of his head. He had become so desperate that he had decided to turn his head into the path of a bullet, when the interrogation ceased. Another life-long Republican, Joseph Clarke, a vice-president of Sinn Fein, told me how his moustache was ripped off during an interrogation, and that while he was waiting to enter the room where this happened he saw another prisoner being taken out with his entrails hanging out through his anus after a kicking.

Whether all these stories are true or not one can hardly vouch but the important thing is that they were believed, and used extensively for propaganda.

However, it is worth noting that unlike either the Russian or Spanish Civil Wars, the Irish affair differed in the degree of magnanimity shown by the victors towards the losers. There was no seizure of land or possessions for instance, and the losing side was left free to form political parties and to pursue professional or business interests uninterruptedly. On the I.R.A. side those who preferred to struggle on towards the Republic on leaving the jails or internment camps had first to answer the question—why had they left the jails or internment camps! All intending recruits were presented with a document in the name of Oglaigh na hEireann in which they were asked to state as follows:

1. Did you sign on any undertaking in order to obtain your release from Free State custody?
2. If so, give reasons why.

Those who signed out were either not allowed into the army, or if let in court-martialled and then rejected once they were found out. Selectivity was also enjoined in general order No. 21 issued by the chief of staff, Frank Aiken, on July 14, 1923, on the matter of recruits. This made three points:

1. No man would be permitted to join the ranks who was over 19 years of age on 12 July, 1923.
2. No recruit would be accepted without the express sanction of the battalion O.C. to whom full particulars must be forwarded.
3. Recruits when sanctioned by the battalion O.C. would be sworn in by the company O.C.

The I.R.A. was trying to exclude both faint hearts who might have been old enough to take part in the Civil War or War of Independence and had not, would-be spies and of course those who had committed the heinous crime of 'signing-out'. And despite the setbacks of the Civil War, jailings, internments and loss of life, the I.R.A. had sufficient strength by July, 1923 to hold a two-day meeting in the Elliot Hotel in Harcourt Street, Dublin. Here organisational plans were drawn up, and a draft constitution and rules agreed upon. At this meeting also it was decided to have nothing more to do with the I.R.B.

At this time the principal I.R.A. leaders were Frank Aiken, Andy Cooney, Maurice Twomey, Micky Carolan, Sean Russell, Jim Donovan, Sean Moylan, Sean Lemass, Tom Daly, Sean MacBride, Michael Price and Jim Killeen, who constituted the headquarters staff. Next in importance were prominent figures such as Peadar O'Donnell, George Gilmore, David Fitzgerald, Tom Maguire in Mayo, Ben Maguire (no relation) in Leitrim and Michael Fitzpatrick, all of whom were Civil War veterans. And there were other districts in the country that also provided recruiting grounds and sources of strength for the I.R.A.

I found in my interviewing that it was always safer to ascribe I.R.A. strength or influence to a particular leader, or to a local tradition, than to the formal organisational title held by a member of the organisation. The organisational blueprint that emanated from the July 12 executive meeting contained twenty-five closely typed pages, but in my experience the elaborate provisions it made for scouting, signalling, captains of right-half companies, captains of the left-half companies etc., existed only on paper, partially to impress young men. Whatever work was done in any given district depended on one good man.

As far as a social or economic policy was concerned the I.R.A. organisation at this stage was blank and provided only for a military organisation. The following. extracts from the constitution are the most important ones:

(3) Its object shall be:
    (a) To guard the honour, and maintain the independence of the Irish Republic.
    (b) To protect the rights and liberties common to the people of IRELAND.
    (c) To place its service at the disposal of an established Republican Government which faithfully upholds the above objects.

(4) CONTROL OF THE ARMY
The army shall be controlled by an Executive of 16, which shall be appointed by a Committee of twenty-five elected as follows:—

Each Province elects five delegates.
Each Province nominates five further delegates, from whom the whole Convention will elect the remaining five. Any serving Volunteer to be eligible to act on the Executive.

This Executive shall have supreme control of the Army, and the Executive shall not itself, directly or indirectly, be subordinate to, or be controlled by any other body; subject to any alterations necessary to put into operation Section 3, subsection (c) above.

Such proposed alterations to be sanctioned by a General Convention.

(5) DUTIES AND POWERS OF EXECUTIVE
The duties of the Executive shall be to define policy for the Army. It shall have supreme control over the Army Council, and General Headquarters Staff. It shall not, however, have power to interfere with General Headquarters Staff in respect of purely Army matters such as

Organisation, Training, method of conducting operations etc.

Ten shall form a quorum at meetings of the Executive.

(6) FINANCIAL POWERS

The Executive shall be responsible for the raising and safeguarding of funds for Army purposes.

(8) ARMY COUNCIL

The Executive shall appoint an Army Council of seven, of which four shall be chosen from members of the Executive, and the remaining three may be appointed from outside the Executive. Four shall form a quorum at meetings of the Army Council. In the event of a vacancy occurring on the council, it shall be filled by co-option, to be approved by the Executive.

(9) GENERAL HEADQUARTERS STAFF

The Executive shall appoint a Chief of Staff, who will appoint his Staff.

(10) GENERAL CONVENTION

A General Convention, representative of the whole Army, shall meet at least once in each twelve months, and shall elect a Committee to appoint an Executive as in Section 4, who shall hold office until the next General Convention. It shall also receive a report from the Chief of Staff, and a Financial statement from the Executive.

(14) GENERAL CONVENTION

The constitution of the General Convention shall be as follows:

- (a) All members of the Executive.
- (b) All members of the Army Council.
- (c) An member of the General Headquarters Staff.
- (d) All Divisional Commandants, and two other members of the Divisional Staff as elected by that Staff.
- (e) The delegates elected at the Brigade Convention.

(20) OATH

The oath of Allegiance to be taken by every member of the Army shall be as follows:

I .... do solemnly swear that to the best of my knowledge and ability I will support and defend the Irish Republic against all enemies, foreign and domestic, that I will bear true faith and allegiance to the same. I do further swear that I do not and shall not yield a voluntary support to any pretended Government, Authority, or Power within Ireland hostile or inimical to that Republic.

I take this obligation freely without any mental reservation or purpose of evasion—so help me God.★

The principal organisers of the I.R.A. chosen at the July meeting were Patrick McLogan, David Fitzgerald and James Killeen.

By April, 1924 the I.R.A. felt strong enough to express itself politically at least, and it was decided to support the Sinn Fein party. On April 28, a memo to this effect was issued to all volunteers urging 'every officer' to see 'that the men of his Unit not only join Sinn Fein Clubs, but that they work the clubs with the proper spirit of enthusiasm and along the straight lines of Republicanism. It is necessary to

---

★ Over the years the Church's opposition to the I.R.A.'s being an oath-bound society led to the recruit being asked not to 'solemnly swear' but to make only a 'declaration' of loyalty to I.R.A. This is the position at the time of writing.

have a sympathetic civilian population. We must begin to develop it immediately and our starting off point is the Sinn Fein Clubs. We must join Sinn Fein Clubs.'

The sort of activity which the I.R.A. reorganisation and planning led to in the subsequent decade was not calculated to win 'sympathetic civilian population'. Here it is important to recognise the two ways in which I.R.A. activity has to be assessed: how the I.R.A. judged itself and how the public judged it. The I.R.A. did contain many a laughing cavalier, such as Frank Ryan, who saw nothing wrong in either a drink or a pretty face. But officially the organisation took itself with deadly seriousness, laying great emphasis on conventions, the holding of meetings, the keeping of records and on styles and titles. Was a man properly appointed or not? Was this the adjutant general's job or should the instruction come from the chief of staff? These questions mattered and I.R.A. policy was viewed as something sacrosanct.

Individual deviations from policy, or interpretations of it, were regarded by the many and implacable purists with the same severity shown by the Roman Curia to errant theologians. And what I.R.A. policy came down to is evident in an agreement between the I.R.A. and the American Clann na Gael of September 15, 1926. Luke Dillon, secretary of the Clann, pledged to Dr Andrew Cooney, chief of staff of the I.R.A., that the Clann would give 'its undivided support, physically, morally and financially to Oglaigh na hEireann [Irish Volunteers] to secure by force of arms the absolute independence of Ireland'. This policy was, of course, easier to state than to implement. And even though the whole I.R.A. ethos was antipathetic to politicians, circumstances continually forced political debates upon the organisation and even sometimes forced it into positive attempt at political action.

The public was not aware of the time and energy which the I.R.A. devoted to planning and manoeuvring. But it was very much aware of the army's overt activities which followed from its policy of using physical force.

Some of these activities were directed by I.R.A. headquarters; others were not. One of these latter was the shooting of a British private, who with a party of other soldiers, women and children, was coming ashore on a tender from Spike Island, at Cobh, Co. Cork. This was motivated simply by anti-British feeling and was carried out by four I.R.A. men who had been on the I.R.A. side during the Civil War. Like many another incident it was their association with the old I.R.A. and access to guns rather than a deliberate policy decision which led to the killing.

There were other shootings too in 1924 such as that on May 6, when two guards were fired on by an I.R.A. man at Creag, Co. Tipperary, as he was about to be arrested. One of the guards died five months later, but the I.R.A. man escaped unscathed to America. The following year there were incidents such as the shooting of a man, Stephen Joyce, in Claremorris (as he was coming home from a dance) by armed men, presumably members of the I.R.A. Other incidents can be attributed to the I.R.A. with more certainty. On November 6 the Hill of Down railway station, Co. Westmeath, was taken over by a party of I.R.A. men under George Plunkett (a brother of the executed 1916 leader) to rescue Jim Killeen when the train arrived at the station. But the train had left five minutes earlier and Killeen went to court and to jail (he had been arrested for organising the I.R.A.). With eighteen other prisoners, he was rescued by an I.R.A. party under the leadership of George Gilmore on November 27.

An I.R.A. policy directive of 1925 concerned the showing of 'British Propaganda Films'. In Dublin, the Masterpiece Cinema was blown up after the film *Ypres* was shown, and in Galway the film *Zeebrugge* was seized and burned. Cinema managers were warned by the I.R.A. that if such films were shown they would be 'drastically dealt with'. And the year closed with a garda, Thomas Dowling, being 'drastically dealt with', by armed men who shot him dead at a graveyard in Fanore, Co. Clare, as he was coming home after patrol duty. As far as can be determined the shooting was in line with the general I.R.A. policy not to interfere with guards who did not take any particular interest in the I.R.A., but to discourage, and if necessary to shoot, those who did. (Surveillance of the I.R.A. was normally carried out by the armed Criminal Investigation Department.)

The I.R.A. paid dearly for issuing voluminous reports and directives. On July 30, 1925, police raided 68, Adelaide Road, Dublin, and in a secret room captured Michael Carolan and his secretary Margaret Clancy, and seized a vast pile of documents, publication of which as the trial proceeded (it opened on November 22) gave the public an embarrassing insight into the workings of the I.R.A. This fondness for paper work often amazed me as I attempted to research the subject. On the one hand I frequently met with evasions or refusals to live any information on the grounds that the I.R.A. was an oathbound, secret organisation, or that somebody might be incriminated yet this same organisation churned out mimeographed documents in vast and incriminating quantities, inevitably to be found or seized by the authorities.

This urge to conceal and at the same time express oneself is a very Irish characteristic, and on June 20, 1925, it found a noble expression in the launching of an I.R.A newspaper *An Phoblacht* under the editorship of Maurice Twomey. An article on its front page entitled 'Wolfe Tone and Ireland Today' was written by Frank Gallagher (who was later to become the first editor of the *Irish Press*). One would imagine that no secret society would dare sponsor a newspaper, which, when analysed by trained scrutineers in the secret service, would certainly yield important information as to changes in policy or personnel, but the I.R.A.. apparently found this disadvantage outweighed by the tremendous influence, not alone on Republicans, but on left-wing young people, which the paper very shortly began to enjoy.

In 1926 the following, among other incidents, occurred:

June 2—Raid on sheriffs office, Dublin, by armed men. The jury list was seized, intimidation of jurors being a favourite I.R.A. tactic.

August 20—John Doyle, Seatown Place, Dundalk, was shot dead by a party of armed men.

November 14—A number of Garda stations were raided by I.R.A. men. A Sergeant Fitzsimons was killed in the course of a raid in Cork, and a guard was killed as a result of a raid on Hollyfort Station, Co. Tipperary. These raids resulted in considerable controversy when, following a number of arrests, allegations were made that the police had maltreated some of the prisoners. A sworn inquiry resulted in a number of police being severely reprimanded.

November 20—Crumlin Barracks in Dublin was attacked. A guard was wounded and the attackers driven off.

November 24—Knockanore Garda Barracks, Co. Waterford, was raided by armed men, who, after locking the guards in a cell, took away station records.

The same night Guard Hanly, Ballinakill, Leix, was badly wounded by two cyclists whom he stopped because they had no lights.

A touch of anti-Semitism also showed in a series of armed raids on money lenders in Dublin, Limerick and other centres from July to October. The parties concerned, who were mainly Jewish, were threatened and all their books and records seized, the raiders in each case producing official authority from the I.R.A. Cars were stolen to carry out operations which were, to be fair, at least as much motivated by a desire to stamp out the practice of money-lending as to strike at Jews.

In 1927 there were the following incidents:

July 10—Murder of Kevin O'Higgins.

August 27—Detective Officer O'Donnell of Mallow was fired on by a wanted member of the I.R.A., named Con Healy (known as the 'One Eyed Gunner'). Healy was subsequently sentenced to five years' penal servitude for this offence.

There were innumerable arrests for I.R.A. activities during the year, illegal drilling being the most common offence.

In 1928 there were the following activities:

January 23—Three I.R.A. men fired on Robert Grace, the principal warder, Mountjoy Prison, North Circular Road, Dublin, after complaints had circulated in I.R.A. circles about ill-treatment of prisoners.

January 28—When Mr Sean Harling was entering his home, Woodpark Lodge, Dartry, Dublin, he was fired on by two men. He returned the fire and after an exchange of shots one of the attackers, a man named Coughlan, was wounded and died later. On February 15 the government appointed a tribunal which was satisfied that Harling did not fire until he had been fired at by Coughlan.

April 10—During a police search of a Sinn Fein office in Dawson Street, documents were found which led to a search of the home of Miss Florence McCarthy. Further documents were found which included a jury panel for the February sitting of the Central Criminal Court, and a circular addressed to each member of the jury panel signed 'Ghosts'. She was subsequently sentenced to six months imprisonment.

The rest of this year was characterised by an increase in the number of attempts to intimidate jurors, and by incidents of a markedly anti-British character. The Grafton Street, Dawson Street, Dame Street part of Dublin, a predominantly Protestant area of fashionable business premises, customarily displayed Union Jacks in shop windows around Armistice Day or on occasions such as royal birthdays. Throughout the year these were torn down and destroyed by young I.R.A. men. The subsequent prosecutions frequently failed when an intimidated jury feared to convict. British Legion and scouting halls were also burned down throughout the year.

The pace of violence really stepped up in 1929 when intimidation of jurors took the form of shooting them.

January 23—John White was shot in the stomach as he stood at the doorway of his home at Terenure in Dublin. He had served on the jury that tried Con Healy.

February 2—Albert Armstrong, an insurance inspector, was shot dead while he was putting his car in his garage. He had given evidence against I.R.A. men accused of removing a Union Jack from his insurance company.

June 11—Detective Officer T. O'Sullivan was killed by a trap mine at Tullycrine, Co. Clare. Detective O'Driscoll of Knock Station had received an anonymous letter: 'I found a box of ammunition and papers in a butt of hay in the haggard. The times are so dangerous I was afraid to keep it near the place. I threw it inside the ditch at Lahiff Cross in Ardil's Meadow yesterday. I want you to take it away. I do not want to get into trouble with people around here. [Signed] Farmer.'

O'Driscoll found the box and carried it to Tullycrine. There he met O'Sullivan and another guard. While O'Sullivan was attempting to open the box it blew up killing him outright and badly wounding O'Driscoll.

November 8—The roof of the British ex-Servicemen's Hall, Inchicore, was blown off by an explosion which shattered glass in several adjoining houses. This hall had previously been blown up on November 10, 1927.

December 11—Arms and an ammunition dump were found at the home of Sean Russell at Spring Garden Street, North Strand, Dublin. Russell was arrested and sentenced to three months' imprisonment.

Attacks on the police continued the following year though not on the same scale. The three following incidents in 1930 are worth mentioning:

July 27—A warder of Mountjoy Prison was chained to the railings of the 'Black Church', off Mountjoy Street, with a placard alleging ill-treatment of prisoners in Mountjoy pinned to him.

September 20—A member of the Garda Siochana was chained to railings in Drumcondra with an inscription: 'Informer Farrell arrests Republicans.'

November 23—Sergeant O'Regan, while on protection duty at the residence of the Ceann Comhairle (chairman of the Dail), Rathgar, Co. Dublin, was shot in the leg.

The year 1931 was notable for a tremendous upsurge in I.R.A. activity, for killings, shootings and for continual seizures of arms and explosives by the police, and by October it was obvious that the normal process of the law could no longer deal with the I.R.A. and a military tribunal was instituted. The shootings of jurymen and police witnesses made it almost impossible to get a verdict in an ordinary court, and the I.R.A. paper, An Phoblacht, was continually stoking the fires of revolt with statements such as the following for June 20: 'An Phoblacht states that members of the C.I.D. should be treated as "social Pariahs" . . . that treatment must be extended to . . . Judges and District Justices, to uniformed police—to every individual who is a willing part of the machine by which our Irish patriots are being tortured.'

After a month in which several ammunition dumps were discovered by the police, Patrick Carroll of Inchicore, Dublin, was shot in Dublin by the I.R.A. as a police spy and the coup de grâce administered by a hand grenade which blew part of his head off. This occurred on January 30. A police superintendent named Curtin was shot dead in Tipperary, March 21, as he entered his house late at night.

April 5—a hundred members of I.R.A. were found drilling openly at Daingean, Offaly, under Sean McGuinness.

April 15—A campaign to boycott British goods began in Dublin and shop-keepers were intimidated.

April 23—While an I.R.A. party was drilling at Killakee, Co. Dublin, two students chanced by and were fired on by an I.R.A. man who thought they were policemen. Fortunately his cartridge was defective and the bullet merely wounded one student.

June 10—A large I.R.A. dump at Killakee, constructed by the Gilmores was discovered. It contained twenty-nine rifles, thirteen revolvers, four automatic pistols, one Lewis machine gun, three shotguns, three Very light pistols, bombs, explosives, 3,137 rounds of assorted ammunition, spare parts for firearms, documents, the head of King William of Orange whose statue had been blown up sometime earlier, and ironically in such surroundings the original of the Sinn Fein document addressed to the Versailles peace conference in 1919.

July 20—Killing of John Ryan at Oyle, Co. Tipperary. His body was found with a placard around his neck reading: 'Spies and Informers Beware. I.R.A.' Ryan had given evidence in a prosecution for illegal drilling. He received a threatening letter on April 29 purporting to come from the adjutant, South Tipperary brigade, I.R.A., stating that he had been found guilty of treachery and warning him that if he were found in the country after May 17 his life would be forfeited.

September 12—New and unoccupied Garda barracks at Kilreekle, Co. Galway, blown up.

September 13—Attempted murder of William McInerney, Kilrush. He was seriously wounded by revolver fire while examining a notice, 'Spies Beware', that had been posted on his hall door. McInerney had been very outspoken in his denunciation of the I.R.A. and of Republican activity generally.

Very early on in this appalling sequence of events it became clear to de Valera and other pragmatists such as Sean Lemass that militarily the Republican movement had neither arms nor the organisation to attempt a rising. They also saw that Sinn Fein, to which the I.R.A. gave allegiance, by its policy of refusing to recognise this Dublin parliament, was clearly isolating itself from the main stream of Irish political life despite the grandiloquent directives in the name of the Republican government from the Sinn Fein headquarters in Suffolk Street, Dublin.

Nevertheless, to the hard-core I.R.A. militants any other course was a betrayal of the Republic. When it became publicly known at an I.R.A. convention on November 17, 1925, that discussions had taken place among leading Republican figures to find a more fruitful political and constitutional role, uproar broke out. Peadar O'Donnell secured an overwhelming majority for a resolution cutting away 'the army' from Sinn Fein, which more or less disappeared into a world of political make-believe. Subsequently the I.R.A. was to be a purely military organisation, thus frustrating the basic intention O'Donnell had had in proposing his resolution—an attempt not merely to cut away from Sinn Fein but to shake off the organisation's preoccupation with partition, the oath, and the second Dail, and to direct its energies into a leftward path of socialist Republicanism inspired equally by O'Donnell and Karl Marx. This was to aid in the formation of three other political organisations from within the womb of Republicanism: Saor Eire which lapsed without greatly influencing the movement one way or another; the Republican Congress which split the 'army' in half; and Fianna Fail which became the dominating political movement of Southern Ireland.

Three days after the I.R.A. convention passed O'Donnell's resolution the Ard Fheis of Sinn Fein itself was held. In private session a resolution opposing the discussions that were taking place within Sinn Féin, along the lines advocated by Lemass and others, was discussed. The resolution was:

Owing to the insidious rumours that Republicans will enter the Free State Parliament if the oath be removed, we call on Sinn Fein to get a definite statement from the Government [The 'Government' of the non-existent second Dail] that they will adhere to the policy of Cathal Brugha, Erskine Childers, and their fellow martyrs and enter only an Irish Republican Parliament, for all Ireland.

De Valera, as president of Sinn Fein, held that no declaration should be made which would appear to prevent the consideration of 'any honourable line of policy, or to hamper any tendency towards the unification of the Irish people'.

Finally the following resolution in the names of Countess Markievicz and Sean Lemass was passed by a majority:

That no change be made in the policy of Sinn Fein at this Ard Fheis, but it is agreed that no subject of discussion is barred from the whole organisation, or any part of it, with the exception of the questions of the accepting of allegiance to a foreign king and the partition of Ireland, and if at any stage a change of policy is proposed an Ard Fheis must be summoned to deal with the proposal.

But it was soon clear that major political developments could not be influenced from outside the Dail. On November 25 the *Morning Post* published the findings of the Boundary Commission showing that the border was to remain as it had been since the treaty was signed.

This report, which caused a sensation in Ireland, requires some explanation. Following the royal signature of the constitution of the Irish Free State Act on December 5, 1922, the North, by provisions in the treaty, availed itself of its powers to opt out from under the rule of the Irish Free State by presenting an address to the king from both houses of the Northern parliament. The treaty provisions however had called for the setting up of a boundary commission, with a representative from each of the Irish governments under a British–nominated chairman. But the North refused to nominate a representative and the British nominated J. R. Fisher under the chairmanship of Judge Feetham of South Africa to negotiate with Dr Eoin McNeill, the South's minister of education, who immediately resigned his portfolio on publication of the *Morning Post*'s report. The South seethed with rage at the loss of expected portions of the Catholic areas of Tyrone and Fermanagh. Even those who were hostile to the Republicans in the Civil War for a moment contemplated renewing the struggle to get back the six north-eastern counties and Sir James Craig, the Northern prime minister, sternly warned that Ulster was prepared to fight against anyone who would take away 'the loved soil of Ulster from any of the loyalists who want to remain there'.

It had been wishful thinking on the part of supporters of the treaty to imagine that any such commission could have, or would have, altered the border in favour of the South and in the circumstances the Free State government had no option but to sign an agreement, on December 3, whereby the border stayed as it was. The Free State was freed from making various contributions to the United Kingdom's public debt and the payment of pensions to former members of the Royal Irish Constabulary. However it was not a popular settlement and told against Cumann na nGaedheal (the government) long afterwards.

The Ard Comhairle of the Sinn Fein executive agreed to call the extraordinary Ard Fheis provided for in the Markievicz-Lemass resolution on March 9. At this meeting de Valera asked Sinn Fein to accept the proposition that 'Once the admission oaths of the twenty-six and six county assemblies are removed, it becomes a question not of principle but of policy whether or not republican representatives should attend these assemblies'. It was also suggested that in the next general election candidates should be put forward who would 'assert their right to enter any assembly where the other electorate representatives meet for public business'. These proposals were rejected and de Valera resigned as president of Sinn Fein.

On May 16 in the La Scala Theatre, Dublin, he founded his own party Fianna Fail (the 'Warriors of Destiny'). The Fianna Fail attitude was that while the Free State Dail was not the legitimate parliament of the Republic, it would use it to achieve such a parliament. Members would assert their right to represent their constituents without being forced to take the oath. If the oath were to continue in being they would attempt to create a majority of representatives in the Republican interest, to meet outside the Dail and take over the administration of the country.

The I.R.A. met the new situation with a meeting at Peadar O'Donnell's house, in 39, Marlborough Road, Donnybrook, and decided on a programme for uniting Sinn Fein, I.R.A. and Fianna Fail. There was to be a three-party delegate conference with a panel of candidates to go forward at the forthcoming election with I.R.A. support. These candidates were to 'win a majority'. With this majority secured, they would meet outside the Free State parliament, agree on a government and 'restore the Republic peacefully'. The Republicans were to enter the Free State parliament and take over all the instruments of state. Restoring the Republic peacefully would entail repudiation of the treaty, of the boundary settlement, and all agreements with Great Britain. The I.R.A. was to get control of all arms in the Free State, and all enemy forces (that is the Free State Army) were to be withdrawn from Dublin, disarmed and demobilised 'to prevent clashing and overlapping'.

Sinn Fein agreed to this conference but stipulated that Fianna Fail must not 'enter any foreign controlled Parliament as a minority or majority, with or without an oath, or other formal declaration'. The national executive of Fianna Fail turned down these proposals unanimously.

Elections were held on June 23, 1927 and Fianna Fail won forty-four seats, but when the deputies presented themselves at the Dail they were met by the clerk of the Dail who told them that first they must comply with what he called a 'little formality'—the taking of the oath prescribed by Article 17 of the constitution. That blocked the line of approach to Dail Eireann, but de Valera announced that he was going to try another, also provided for by the constitution, which stipulated that a national referendum could be held on the oath question provided that 75,000 signatures were collected. Legal proceedings to test the constitutionality of Fianna Fail's being debared from the Dail were also instituted but before either of these manoeuvres had a chance of succeeding a political murder occurred which changed the whole tenor of Irish politics.

Kevin O'Higgins, vice-president of the Executive Council, the cabinet formed by Cumann na nGaedheal, was murdered on his way to Mass on July 10. O'Higgins was the most able man in Irish parliamentary politics at the time. Apart from the reconstruction work which the Dail undertook after the Civil War, he had sustained the government throughout the war itself, and through many crises afterwards. He was a principal architect of the Statute of Westminster which came into being two years after his death and which de Valera was able to use to get rid of the oath. As often happens when a man of that calibre is killed, the shooting was not the result of a deep-laid plot, but the impetuous act of two young I.R.A. men acting unofficially and without authority from the movement. One of them had been chosen to play in a football match in the south-east of the country, and they escaped the police dragnet by driving to the game as though nothing had happened. They were never brought to justice although one of them was killed in cross-fire years afterwards when the I.R.A. unsuccessfully tried to execute one of its opponents.

The government replied to O'Higgins's murder by introducing three bills designed to bring stability to the country and Fianna Fail into the Dail. The public safety bill gave the authorities the most drastic powers; another required candidates at all future elections to make an oath-bound declaration, that if elected they would sit in the Dail and take the oath of allegiance. The third bill would have disqualified the election and vacated the seats of the Fianna Fail deputies who failed to take the oath. The bills did not have to become law. The day after they were introduced on August 11 de Valera and the Fianna Fail deputies took their seats.

De Valera addressed the clerk of the chamber in Irish as follows: 'I am not prepared to take the oath, I am not going to take an oath, I am prepared to put my name down on this book in order to get permission to go into the Dail, but it has no other significance.' Putting aside a Bible which lay on the table he said, 'You must remember I am taking no oath.'

Fianna Fail had lost for both political and emotional reasons for sounding militantly Republican. Speaking in the Dail on March 12, 1928 Sean Lemass, who had been 'minister for defence' in the underground Republican government in his Sinn Fein days, said: 'Fianna Fail is a *slightly* constitutional party. We are open to the definition of a constitutional party, but before anything we are a Republican party. We have adopted the method of political agitation to achieve our end because we believe, in the present circumstances, that method is best in the interests of the nation and of the Republican movement, and for no other reason. Five years ago the methods we adopted were not the methods we have adopted now. Five years ago we were on the defensive, and perhaps in time we may recoup our strength sufficiently to go on the offensive. Our object is to establish a Republican government in Ireland. If that can be done by the present methods we have, we will be very pleased, but, if not, we would not confine ourselves to them.'

The following year on February 27, Sean T. O'Kelly referred to the Cumann na nGaedheal minister for defence as the 'so-called minister for defence', when speaking in the Dail, and on March 14 de Valera made one of the most important statements of all on the legitimacy of the state: He said:

I still hold that our right to be regarded as the legitimate Government of this country is faulty, that this House itself is faulty. You have secured a *de facto* position. Very well. There must be some body in charge to keep order in the community, and by virtue of your *de facto* position you are the only people who are in a position to do it. But as to whether you have come by that position legitimately or not, I say you have not come by that position legitimately. You brought off a *coup d'etat* in the summer of 1922 . . .

If you are not getting the support from all sections of the community that is necessary for any executive if it is going to dispense with a large police force, it is because there is a moral handicap in your case. We are all morally handicapped because of the circumstances in which the whole thing came about. The setting up of this State put a moral handicap on everyone of us here. We came in here because we thought that a practical rule could be evolved in which order could be maintained; and we said that it was necessary to have some assembly in which the representatives of the people by a majority vote should be able to decide national policy. As we were not able to get a majority to meet outside this House, we have to come here if there was to be a majority at all of the people's representatives in any one assembly . . .

As a practical rule, and not because there is anything sacred in it, I am prepared to accept majority rule as settling matters of national policy, and therefore as deciding who it is that shall be in charge of order . . .

I for one, when the flag of the Republic was run up against an Executive that was bringing off a *coup d'etat*, stood by the flag of the Republic, and I will do it again. As long as there was a hope of maintaining that Republic, either by force against those who were bringing off that *coup d'etat* or afterwards, as long as there was an opportunity of getting the people of this country to vote again for the Republic, I stood for it.

My proposition that the representatives of the people should come in here and unify control so that we would have one Government and one Army was defeated, and for that reason I resigned. Those who continued on in that organisation which we have left can claim exactly the same continuity that we claimed up to 1925. They can do it . . .

You have achieved a certain *de facto* position, and the proper thing for you to do with those who do not agree that this State was established legitimately, and who believe that as a matter of fact there was a definite betrayal of everything that was aimed at from 1916 to 1922, is to give those people the opportunity of working, and without in any way forswearing their views, to get the Irish people as a whole again behind them. They have the right to do it. You have no right to debar them from going to the Irish people and asking them to support the re-establishment, or if they so wish to put it, to support the continuance of the Republic . .

The Executive have been trying to use force, and have been using it all the time. If they are going to meet force by force, then they cannot expect the co-operation of citizens who wish that there should not be force.

Of all this, the most important point is de Valera's proposal that those who continued in the I.R.A. could claim the same continuity that Fianna Fail had been claiming up to 1925. New I.R A. men I spoke to from this period said that this statement gave it, the I.R.A., a particular standing of responsibility in their eyes. Thus when President Cosgrave finally introduced the constitutional amendments setting up the Military Tribunal on October 14, 1931, de Valera replied to him the following day saying: 'These men are misguided, if you will, but they were brave men, anyhow, let us at least have for them the decent respect that we have for the brave.'

This sort of Fianna Fail utterance, of course, was given much wider circulation within the I.R.A. than were appeals to moderation like that of de

Valera at the Fianna Fail convention on November 9, 1933, when he expressed disappointment at the Republican continuation in militancy despite the fact that he had abolished the oath.

However though the broad mass of I.R.A. supporters remained sympathetic to Fianna Fail while infuriating Cumann na nGaedheal constitutionalists they buttered no parsnips for the socialist-minded members of the I.R.A. Some, in particular, Peadar O'Donnell, David Fitzgerald and Michael Price, tried to harness the mutually antipathetic currents of force and constitutional socialism within the organisation after a great deal of debate with those who wanted to concentrate mainly on building the movement as a purely military organisation. And this of course says in a sense all that needs to be known of the strength and weakness of the movement, for although the organisation grew to the point of being a dangerous nuisance to law and order and of contributing significantly to the overthrow of the Cumann na nGaedheal government, it remained an organisation whose hour had passed and which refused to recognise this. Its espousal of physical force wrecked its political chances and it was so weak that when the crunch came and the constitutional government really exerted strength against the movement it did not have the broad-based national support to withstand the setback, even though the government itself was shortly to be defeated by Fianna Fail.

The I.R.A.'s 'politicals' however scored a temporary victory when an organisation of workers and working farmers was set up in May, 1931, following a decision of the I.R.A. convention of February, 1931. The chief organisers were David Fitzgerald, Peadar O'Donnell, Michael Price, Sean Russell and Michael Fitzpatrick. At a parade of the Dublin brigade, I.R.A., on June 7, Peadar O'Donnell said that the days of active service were over for the present and that the need for a Republican Workers' Party, working for a 'Peasants' Republic' and controlled jointly by peasants and workers, was very pressing.

The first congress was held in Dublin on September 26 and 27, 1931, with about 150 delegates present. The draft constitution contained the following proposals:

To abolish, without compensation, landlordism in lands, fisheries and minerals.

To establish a State monopoly in banking and credits.

To create a State monopoly in export and import services and to promote co-operative distribution.

To make the national wealth and credit available for the creation and fullest development of essential industries and mineral resources, through Industrial Workers' Co-operatives, under State direction and management, workers to regulate internal working conditions.

The names of the national executive of Saor Eire, as the party was called, were as follows: Sean McGuinness† (Mountjoy), (substitute, Fionan Walsh, Kerry), Sean Hayes (Clare), May Laverty† (Belfast), Helena Moloney, Sheila Dowling, Sheila Humphries†, D. McGinley, M. Fitzpatrick, Sean MacBride, M. Price†, Peadar O'Donnell†, David Fitzgerald (Dublin), M. Hallissey (Kerry), M. O'Donnell (Offaly), Patrick McCormack (Antrim), Tom Kenny (Galway), L. Brady (Leix), Nicholas Boran (Kilkenny), John Mulgrew† (Mayo), and Tom Maguire† (Westmeath). (The daggers denote those who also signed the manifesto of the Republican Congress.)

But there was a strong body of opinion which was unenthusiastic about the new movement. Maurice Twomey in particular was cautious, not alone about entering constitutional politics but also about the possibly damaging effects of any taint of Communism attaching to the movement. Twomey, a Corkman who became the outstanding influence on the I.R.A. after the resignation of Frank Aiken (whom he eventually succeeded as chief of staff)* remained a formative influence on the I.R.A. until the outbreak of the Second World War. A dedicated, right-wing Fenian, scrupulous in his religious observance, it is generally agreed in political circles that had he abandoned his republicanism to join Fianna Fail a cabinet post would have automatically been bestowed upon him. (Although often condemned by bishops and clergy, most I.R.A. men shared Twomey's strong Catholicism. Jack Brady who became an organiser with Jim Killeen told me that one of the hazards that he and others like him regularly encountered was identification by local police, who would immediately notice their strange faces when they attended Mass in some small country village. Yet Brady would never think of not going to Mass because of this.)

The 1932 army convention's support for Saor Eire was restricted to a not very enthusiastic resolution: 'That we approve of Saor Eire. That the activities of Saor Eire be confined to an effort to educate the people in the principles of Saor Eire without publicly organising it as Saor Eire.'

The caution of this wording also was vindicated in at incident which may be seen as a microcosm for the failure of Saor Eire. David Fitzgerald addressed a meeting in Co. Louth to explain Saor Eire policy to a farming audience—all of them sympathetic towards Republicanism. He was describing how Saor Eire would break up the landlords' holdings and distribute them to the landless when he was interrupted:

'Be Jasus then,' said the proud owner of 200 acres sitting in the front row, 'an you'll not take my land.'

Saor Eire received its national quietus when it was declared an unlawful association on October 20, 1931, along with the I.R.A. itself, Fianna Eireann, Cumann na mBan, Friends of Soviet Russia and a group of other Communist-sounding organisations. On the same day the Special Powers Tribunal was set up consisting of five military officers. Introducing the bill which made this possible (Constitution Amendment No. 17) President Cosgrave said: 'The powers and machinery provided by this Bill are necessary not merely for this Government, but for any Government that may be in power if the will of the majority is to prevail.' (The will of the majority was shortly to prevail against Cosgrave, at least partially through the influence of the I.R.A. at whom his statement was aimed.)

The I.R.A.'s involvement in Fianna Fail's defeat of Cumann na nGaelheal took place in three ways: by working enthusiastically for Fianna Fail candidates at grass-root level, in the land annuities affair, and in the 'Release the Prisoners' campaign. Fianna Fail party campaigning was carried out by rank and file I.R.A. men. For the most part these men were united in outlook and social background with Fianna Fail supporters: small farmers, labouring men, tradesmen, people who in another country

---

* Aiken was succeeded for a period by Dr Andy Cooney.

would be associated with a Labour Party. Though the scale and membership of the I.R.A. support (the best estimates place its membership on paper at this time as around 30,000) was considerably less than that of Fianna Fail it was an extremely valuable asset in an election campaign, being both energetic and vocal.

The I.R.A. seems to have extracted almost no concessions from Fianna Fail in return. Some prominent members grumbled at the policy of support. One, Michael Conway, told me how he had warned his colleagues against de Valera, saying: 'I'm telling ye that fella will be as bad as Cosgrave, he'll hang ye when he gets in, mark my words he'll hang ye.' Conway was close to being a true prophet: de Valera very nearly did have him hanged.

The second great I.R.A.-based issue from which Fianna Fail benefited was the 'Release the Prisoners Campaign', a loose-knit movement centring upon a number of Republican women: Madame Maude Gonne MacBride, Helena Moloney, Mrs Sheehey Skeffington and Madame Despard.

Madame MacBride was the widow of Major John MacBride, the executed 1916 leader; Helena Moloney was a life-long socialist and trade unionist, sympathetic always to underdogs. Mrs Skeffington's husband had been murdered by a British officer in 1916, and Mrs Despard, a friend of Stafford Cripps and other British socialist leaders, donated a house in Eccles Street, Dublin to be used as a workers' college, only to have it set fire by a right-wing mob.

These ladies organised a 'Republican Prisoners' Dependents Fund' to alleviate hardships caused by the jailing of I.R.A. men. 'Release the Prisoners' is always an emotive cry in Ireland and public opinion was easily stirred by rules of prison hardships endured by idealistic Republicans. Some were genuine, the traditional Fenian defiance of prison regulations often bringing warders and Republicans into abrasive contact; some were self-inflicted, such as those of George Gilmore who refused to wear prison clothes, because of his political status and spent from October, 1931 to February, 1932 naked in a windowless cell. (By contrast his brother Charlie, who wanted to see for himself how poor George was getting along, told me that he spent the best part of an afternoon walking up and down outside Rathfarnham police station with blankets under his arm. Supposedly badly wanted by the police, he was trying to get himself arrested. He was, finally, after threatening to put a brick through the station window.) The issue of the prisoners played a considerable part in Fianna Fail's win. Actually it should have rebounded to the I.R.A.'s advantage but the movement failed to realise how sorely it was trying Cumann na nGaedheal. The setting up of the Military Tribunal had been a last desperate throw on the part of the administration, at its wits end to know how to combat the I.R.A.

Generally speaking the I.R.A., not recognising the state which set them up, did not recognise the courts. Any I.R.A. man, or woman, charged before a normal court generally refused to plead and announced that he 'refused to recognise the court'. However, the police, in order to place some curb on known I.R.A. men's activities, resorted to a tactic, known as the 'cat and mouse', of picking up suspects, holding them for a few days, releasing them and picking them up again shortly afterwards. But apart from the damaging publicity which this practice engendered, some members of the I.R.A. shook Cumann na nGaedheal badly by retaliating in March, 1930, by claiming damages for wrongful arrest and false imprisonment.

The four men concerned, Patrick McKee, Charles O'Neill, John Sugrue and Donal O'Donoghue succeeded in the circuit court in winning damages of £100, £80, £40 and £100, respectively. We need not discuss the merits of the cases of the first three plaintiffs, but O'Donoghue was at the time on the I.R.A. Army Council, so his legal victory had considerable implications for the police and the Department of Justice. The success of these four was followed up in the courts by eight other I.R.A. suspects who if they did not recover anything worth having in the way of damages (£5 to £10 each) further underlined the government's almost complete inability to deal with the I.R.A. But curiously enough the I.R.A. did not appear to be aware of this near immunity and did not push its activities to the extent it might have.

Some members of the executive, however, either through natural bellicosity or an appreciation of the true situation, did push their luck pretty far. Frank Ryan, for instance, gave an interview to the *Daily Express* (published August 24, 1931) in which he not only justified the killings of Ryan, Carroll and Curtin, but claimed that the I.R.A. could act on an even wider scale. It was this speech, I understand, which led the Department of Justice to advise President Cosgrave to reinstate the Tribunal. Peadar O'Donnell addressed a parade of I.R.A. men (which the police had tried and failed to prevent) from nineteen counties on June 20 in which he said of the government: 'All the powers in their hands we must take into ours, and in the final phase we must meet force with force.'

In the event whatever 'powers' lay in the hands of the I.R.A. were allowed to slip into the grasp of Fianna Fail. There was friendly personal contact between some I.R.A. men and Fianna Fail ministers such as Sean Moylan and Oscar Traynor, but no formal alliance. The I.R.A. let the political initiative drift away from it, apparently because, in Peadar O'Donnell's phrase, the I.R.A. felt that its cause would be best advanced by 'nipping at the heels of Fianna Fail' to push the party along paths favoured by the I.R.A. However the heels of one Eamon de Valera were not for nipping at and he gratefully accepted the present of the final weapon presented to him by the I.R.A. —the land annuities campaign.

The land annuities dispute had its origin in a campaign sponsored by Peadar O'Donnell, in his native Donegal. He describes in his book, *There Will Be Another Day*, how 'in late 1925 or early 1926' on the run from the police he discovered that neighbours of his were being served with summonses for non-payment of land annuities which had accrued in the trouble times (roughly from 1916 onwards) and decided to help them. With the aid of Colonel Maurice Moore, brother of George Moore the novelist, O'Donnell organised a campaign to help people hide their cattle so that they couldn't be seized by bailiffs, and urging more people not to pay either arrears or any annuities at all. The annuities were the sums which the farmers paid to the Irish Land Commission, which in turn passed the money over to the government for payment to the British national debt commissioners to meet the loans raised for the purpose of buying out the landlords in the 1891–1909 period. After the treaty these payments were made pursuant to the financial agreement of February 12, 1923, which was signed by W. T. Cosgrave and Major John W. Hills, the financial secretary to the British Treasury, and to the Ultimate Financial Settlement, as it was called, of March 19, 1926, which was signed by Ernest Blythe for Ireland and Winston Churchill for England. Between these payments and others covered by the two agreements specified for payments of pensions to former members of the Royal Irish Constabulary the total amount involved per year came to £5 million.

O'Donnell's Donegal agitation, which later spread to adjoining counties west of the Shannon, eventually petered out, but it generated sufficient support for Fianna Fail to take it up and make the retention of the land annuities by the Irish government seem a very attractive idea to small farmers in the 1932 election campaign.

All these factors and the fact that Cumann na nGaedheal had been in power for ten years ending in a period of economic slump helped to win the February election for Fianna Fail, and a sense of relief went through the I.R.A. when Cumann na nGaelheal was defeated. One man, a prominent Dublin lawyer, said to me, 'I felt a tremendous release. It was a marvellous thing, we really hated those buggers, it was great to see them out.'

3

The Triumph of Fianna Fail

The defeat of Cumann na nGaedheal was not, however, to herald a new dawn for the I.R.A. In power de Valera immediately began taking steps to abolish the oath, and he released the prisoners from Arbour Hill Barracks on March 10, after he had formed his cabinet, amid scenes of great rejoicing in the streets of Dublin. Two days later *An Phoblacht,* which had been banned for the previous three months, appeared with an article by Maurice Twomey which said: 'Fianna Fail declares its intention to chop off some of the imperial tentacles; every such achievement is of value and will be welcomed. Notwithstanding such concessions, the Irish Republican Army must continue its work, and cannot escape its role as the vanguard of the freedom movement.'

Six days later on March 18 the Military Tribunal was suspended, and the orders which had declared the I.R.A. and Saor Eire to be unlawful were revoked. On June 19 the I.R.A. marched in strength to Wolfe Tone's grave at Bodenstown where an oration was delivered by Sean Russell to a gathering estimated at over 15,000 members of the I.R.A. At a big demonstration to welcome the prisoners, held in College Green, Dublin, a few days after their release, one of the freed prisoners, Sean McGuinness, was reported as believing that 'The members of the defunct Executive Council were . . . a menace to society and the independence of Ireland, and it behoved all Republicans to unite and wipe out that menace at all costs.' (*Irish Times,* March 14.)

On October 15 and 22 *An Phoblacht* announced in successive issues that 'Free speech and the freedom of the press must be denied to traitors and treason mongers.' Speaking in Dublin at a public meeting two of the most prominent members of the I.R.A., Frank Ryan and Peadar O'Donnell, both spoke against allowing Cumann na nGaedheal speakers to be heard. Ryan said, 'No matter what anyone says to the contrary, while we have fists, hands and boots to use, and guns if necessary, we will not allow free speech to traitors.' O'Donnell said, 'The policeman who puts his head between Mr Cosgrave's head, and the hands of angry Irishmen, might as well keep his head at home.'

These were not cheering words for Cosgrave's supporters. Three days after McGuinness made his statement a convention of the Army Comrades Association was held to appoint a national executive. This body drew its membership from members of the army who had fought on the Free State side in the Civil War. Its aims were claimed to be benevolent, such as securing jobs in County Councils for out-of-work former Free State soldiers and its committee contained figures such as General Richard Mulcahy, and Dr Tom O'Higgins, a brother of the murdered Kevin O'Higgins.

Prior to Fianna Fail's taking office, rumours were rife that sections of the army and of the police would not allow this to happen. The rumours made the pre-election formation of the Army Comrades Association a highly suspect move to some Fianna Fail and I.R.A. supporters. This suspicion deepened after some Fianna Fail followers began to apply the I.R.A. policy of denying Cumann na nGaedheal speakers, in particular W. T. Cosgrave and Richard Mulcahy, a hearing at public meetings. The Army Comrades Association started to provide bodyguards to put down the bully-boys.

The I.R.A. and the Army Comrades Association also came into conflict when the idea of boycotting British goods, which was always flickering at the edges of I.R.A. planning, arose. A senior executive of Bass, the English brewing firm, made disparaging remarks about Ireland and a lorry load of Bass was destroyed in Dublin on December 14, 1932. Following this, the Dublin vintners appealed to the A.C.A. for protection and shipments of Bass were guarded by bodyguards of A.C.A. without further incident.

But the I.R.A. became involved with the A.C.A. most damagingly over the backlash of the land annuities campaign. On July 1, 1932, following its election pledges, the Fianna Fail government defaulted on the annuities due that day, and the British retaliated with a bill of July 11 allowing the government of the United Kingdom to recoup itself by imposing extra duties on imports from Ireland. The Irish struck again on July 23 with a similar bill, and what was known as the 'economic war' began. As Fianna Fail both reduced the amount of land annuities payable by the tenants, and at the same time funded arrears for three years, and sometimes longer, this was a highly popular policy with the small farmers.

The larger farmers, however, whose products were excluded from England by the tariff wall raised by the economic war, were incensed. A custom sprang up among the larger farmers of refusing to pay their land annuities, so that the Land Commission had to take legal proceedings in separate cases, involving thousands of defaulters, thereby clogging the courts. The government countered this move by passing the Land Act 1933 under which a warrant issued by the Land Commission took the place of legal proceedings, and over 400,000 of these warrants were lodged in twelve half-yearly periods, beginning in November/December, 1933 and ending in May/June, 1939, as a result of which a sum of over £2.5 million was levied or collected by the end of 1939.*

In the midst of this uproar a new complication arose on February 22 1933. General O'Duffy had been dismissed from his post as commissioner of police by Fianna Fail. As Cumann na nGaedheal had been unable to hold meetings unscathed under a friendly police chief his going led many people on the Cumann na nGaedheal side to believe that they were in for an I.R.A.-Fianna Fail onslaught.

But although the Cumann na nGaedheal was not to allow this the leadership of the I.R.A. and of Fianna Fail had already come to a parting of the way. Only

---

* It would be impossible to chronicle all the deeds of violence and acts of sabotage, which the 'no annuities' campaign inspired —in east Cork alone there were hundreds of such incidents.

four days before O'Duffy was dismissed the following directive was issued by the Army Council to the 'Commander of Each Independent Unit':

OGLAIGH NA hEIREANN
(Irish Republican Army)

ROINN; A/G
UIMHIR: BB 74

ARD OIFIG,
ATH CLIATH
18adh Febhra, 1933

To:
The Commander of
Each Independent Unit

GENERAL ARMY CONVENTION, 1993

A chara,

The following statement from the Army Council will be read at each parade and Battalion Staff meeting called for the purpose of electing delegates to the Battalion Convention. Copies of the Army constitution are here with enclosed.

1. In accordance with the constitution the Army Council had decided to convene the annual General Army Convention.

Briefly, the aim of the volunteer organisation is to assert the sovereignty and unity of the Republic of Ireland in which the ownership of the means of production, distribution and exchange will be vested in the Irish people. It will be the function of the forthcoming General Army Convention to consider how the task of achieving this object can be faced and to decide upon the policy of the Army.

2. The position of the Irish Republican Army from a military standpoint is dealt with in the Adjutant General's report which will be submitted to the General Army Convention. From this report it will be seen that the strength, training and discipline of the organisation have improved since the last convention. Whilst the strength of the organisation has shown a marked increase every year since 1925, the Army Council is of the opinion that the wide field for recruiting at the disposal of our forces has not been availed of.

In considering the policy of the Army, the General Army Convention will have to decide how the changes in the political situation, North and South, can best be utilised.

3. THE TWENTY-SIX COUNTIES: At the last Convention it was decided not to take any action which would actively impede the newly established Fianna Fail 'Government'. This decision governed to a great extent the policy of the Army Council, and every effort was made by the Council to avoid clashes. On the other hand, to put it mildly, not much assistance was given by the Fianna Fail 'Government' in carrying out this policy; the police and C.I.D. tried in many instances to provoke conflict. The Coercion legislation passed under the Cosgrave regime was not repealed—on the contrary in many cases it was actually used against Republicans, and thus we have witnessed the jailing of many of our comrades.

In dealing with England, the Fianna Fail 'Government' agreed to submit the question of the payment of tribute to arbitration. The payment of any tribute to England is an encroachment on the sovereignty of Ireland, which sovereignty is, and must remain, non-judicial. The oath of allegiance has been abolished, but the over-lordship of Britain was recognised by the appointment of a Governor General.

In its economic policy the Fianna Fail 'Government' has upheld and bolstered the capitalist system so that the economic war with England is being used for the advancement of both British and Irish capitalism within our shores.

Thus, these facts bring us to the realisation that the policy of the Fianna Fail Government is not directed towards the achievement of our aims.

4. It is the opinion of the Army Council that the policy of the Fianna Fail 'Government' is bound to lead to widespread dis-illusionment amongst a great proportion of its Republican supporters, and of the workers and working farmers. One of the principal tasks of the convention will be to decide whether such dis-illusionment can be availed of to assist in the achievement of the aims of the Irish Republican Army.

If it is considered that the title of Republicanism arising from the dis-illusionment in the Fianna Fail policy can, and should be harnessed, the next consideration will be the means by which this should be done. Four means present themselves:

1. Through the medium of the Irish Republican Army alone.
2. By the re-organisation of Saor.
3. Through the medium of existing political organisations.
4. By the creation of a new organisation.

5. The next problem for consideration will be the policy of the Volunteer Organisation towards the Free State 'Government'. Since the last General Army Convention there has been no change in the attitude of the 'Government'. It claims that it is the legitimate government of the Twenty-six Counties, and that the Irish Republican Army is usurping its powers. In brief, it makes the same claims as regards the control of arms, and as regards its legitimacy as the previous 'Government'.

6. The proposed creation of a Volunteer Reserve Force★ as an auxiliary to the Free State Army will also require the attention of the convention. It is the opinion of the Army Council that the creation of this new appendage to the Free State Army is aimed at diverting the activities of the manhood of Ireland from the Revolutionary Movement, and that is ultimate purpose will be to uphold the Treaty and Constitution of the Free State. The Convention will have to consider how best the threat of the creation of this force can be met.

7. Since the last convention the Army Council has approved of the initiation of the Boycott British Campaign. It is to be regretted that this campaign has not received the support that might have been expected from the volunteer organisation. It will be for the Convention to advise whether this campaign shall be intensified or discontinued . . .

10. The Army Council must again draw the attention of all ranks to the absolute importance of training, both in a military and economic sense. It is vital that every member of the Organisation has an intelligent conception of the task to which the Army has pledged itself.

The influx of recruits to the Army further intensifies the necessity for renewed efforts by unit commanders to raise the standard of training and discipline to the highest possible point.

The last General Army Convention decided:

THAT THE ARMY COUNCIL BE INSTRUCTED TO ESTABLISH AN OFFICERS' TRAINING CAMP FOR THREE MONTHS, JUNE, JULY AND AUGUST: THAT EACH UNIT BE COMPELLED TO SEND AT LEAST TWO OFFICERS TO THE CAMP FOR ONE WEEK

The Adjutant General's report shows how it was found almost impossible by General Headquarters to get units to provide suitable venues for these camps. The Army Council must express its regret at the lack of co-operation given by unit commanders to the General Headquarters Staff on this important matter.

11. The absolute necessity for the provision by units of financial support for the maintenance and equipment of the Army must again be emphasised. It is for that which some units are worthy of every commendation, many others have made no efforts to fulfil the obligations undertaken by them in this respect.

★ This was a kind of territorial army which Fianna Fail was setting up at this time. Recruiting opened on February 20, 1934, and the volunteers were a frequent target for assaults by the I.R.A. afterwards, particularly in Kerry. No loss of life was ever involved, although volunteers were sometimes raided in their homes, and their uniforms stolen. The uniforms were modelled on those designed by Sir Roger Casement for the brigade which he unsuccessfully attempted to raise among Irish prisoners of war captured while fighting for England during the First World War.

Do chara,

D

Adjutant General

The conditions of the time prevented Cumman na nGaedheal from trusting to Shakespeare's dictum that 'Two stars keep not their motion in the one orb', which in fact had begun to assert itself and continued to do so to the detriment of the stars of the I.R.A. Out of these conditions there arose a movement for whose creation the I.R.A. was largely responsible—the Blueshirts.

On July 20, 1933 an organisation known as the National Guard was formed from the Army Comrades Association to safeguard 'National interests and National culture'. Its director-general was General Eoin O'Duffy. At the suggestion of the secretary of the Army Comrades Association, Commandant Ned Cronin, it had adopted a blue shirt as uniform in April.

Its philosophy was militant from the start. The *United Irishman* of July 12, 1933, said, 'If a comrade is subjected because of his membership of the Association, to gross abuse his reply should be a swift blow or series of blows.' (The *United Irishman* was, at this time, the organ of Cumann na nGaedheal, edited by Ernest Blythe a former minister. The present day I.R.A. paper is also called the *United Irishman*.) By this time, *An Phoblacht* was coming out in successive issues with demands for the nationalisation of the banks and the breaking up of the larger farms but Professor M. Tierney, one of the secretaries of the A.C.A., wrote in the *United Ireland* on December 13, 1933: 'The corporate state must come in the end to Ireland as elsewhere', and the other secretary, Professor James Hogan, wrote a powerful series of articles attacking the I.R.A. which were later reprinted in a widely sold pamphlet, 'Could Ireland Go Communist?'

Another correspondent in *United Ireland*, 'Oghnach', suggested that the blue-shirt audiences should imitate the Nazis when greeting their leaders and 'give three sudden staccato bursts of mass cheering, each burst consisting of one sharply ejected syllable . . . the word may be Heil (Hail) pronounced sharply or it may be Hoch (Up)'. This sort of thinking was like a red rag to a bull to the leftists of the I.R.A. The spectacle of the bigger farmers, who had not helped very greatly in the struggle for independence and were tainted with the brush of 'landlordism', particularly in the Cork area, joining the rates campaign was also highly distasteful. These conflicting ideologies coupled with Civil War memories were enough to set the I.R.A. against the Blueshirts in a weakening and disastrous interlude for the I.R.A.

O'Duffy's first major effort as director-general of the National Guard was timed for Sunday August 13, 1933—a march of the National Guard to government buildings to revive a ceremony of laying wreaths on the graves of O'Higgins and Collins. Inside the Dail the idea of thousands of blue-shirted O'Duffy supporters bearing down even on Sunday aroused Fianna Fail reactions. The government hastily set up what was known as the S-Branch, or 'Broy Harriers', called after Colonel Broy, the commissioner of police who had replaced O'Duffy. The S-

Branch was drawn from members of the Republican armed forces during the Civil War and must have been the most hastily organised police force in the world's history. One man, Sergeant Willie Rowe, told me that he was asleep at midnight one Saturday evening and a knock came to his door. Somewhat fearfully he looked out the window—in those days midnight knocks could mean anything—to find not a hostile figure but a man who wanted him to come down immediately to Dublin Castle to be enrolled in a 'new police force they were founding'. One senior officer of the ordinary police force told me that he was on duty at a meeting of Cosgrave's in Dublin which was attacked by a number of Fianna Fail supporters and four I.R.A. companies who marched to the meeting in open formation. Many a head was broken and many a backside kicked at that meeting before Cosgrave was given a hearing through the efforts of the police and his own supporters. But to the officer's consternation a number of the I.R.A. attacking party were among the recruits who were admitted to the new force.

The Army Council of the I.R.A. decided to attack O'Duffy's marchers when they got as far as the Ballast Office at O'Connell Bridge, Dublin, a point where high buildings on either side make an ideal ambush site, and a headquarters to mastermind this operation was set up in Kevin Barry's old house in Fleet Street.★ The I.R.A. also arranged to have armed men near every railway station and government building in Dublin. In addition, individual members of Fianna Fail armed themselves with a view to fighting off what seemed to all concerned like an attempt at a Mussolini-type coup. However on the very eve of the march the government revived the stringent public safety measures of the Cosgrave regime, which it had repealed on taking office, banned the parade and revived the Military Tribunal. O'Duffy called off the parade and changed the name of his now proscribed organisation to that of the Young Ireland Association.

For the moment O'Duffy's personality added a new and significant dimension to Irish politics. On September 8, 1933 Cumann na nGaedheal and a farming party known as the Centre Party united to form a new party, Fine Gael (Tribe of Gaels), under the leadership of William T. Cosgrave, and of James Dillon and Frank MacDermot of the Centre Party. These men were to be its parliamentary leaders, but in national organiser and leader was O'Duffy. Cosgrave, to the architects of the new merger, though a man of supreme integrity, did not appear to have the flamboyance and panache necessary to combat that of de Valera.

The Young Ireland Association was banned on December 8 following clashes between it and the I.R.A. The bulk of the I.R.A. leadership, Maurice Twomey and Sean MacBride in particular, deplored these futile fights. On January 17, 1934, a document was issued as a directive to I.R.A. company commanders stating that 'The present policy of the Army Council is that clashes between Volunteers and Imperialists are forbidden, and that conflicts are to be avoided.' This was largely ignored. Nor indeed did the government's actions during this time do a great deal to assuage opposition fears that Fianna Fail and the I.R.A. were closer than the public knew and that therefore Blueshirt militancy was necessary and justified.

★ Barry, one of the youthful heroes hanged by the British during the Anglo-Irish struggle, gave his name to the ballad 'Kevin Barry' which is a favourite with nationalist Irish men and women of all shades of public opinion today.

The historic incident in particular caused a great deal of uneasiness. Mrs McGrory was fatally injured on the night of February 11, 1934, when the house of Joseph McGrory, Chapel Street, Dundalk, was blown up by a mine thrown through the front window. Two children also received serious injuries. Very little satisfaction was granted to either the public or the McGrory family over this outrage, which was in fact carried out by members of the local I.R.A. as an act of revenge. Joseph McGrory had given evidence against two members of the I.R.A. who were released by the Military Tribunal after the armed hold-up of a Blueshirt collector in Dundalk on January 9.

Thomas Lynch of Dunleer, Thomas Greene of Dundalk, and four other members of the I.R.A. in the Dundalk area were brought before the Military Tribunal on March 19 on charges of refusing to account for their movements. Lynch was convicted of this and an additional charge of unlawful possession of ammunition, and was sentenced to six months, three months not to be enforced if he entered into recognisances (he was granted a 'free pardon' on September 27, 1935). On March 23, Richard Goss, James Finnigan and Matt McCrystal were sentenced to three months' imprisonment in default of entry into recognisances, and on May 3, Thomas Greene and Bernard Murphy were sentenced to six months' imprisonment, three months not to be enforced if they entered into recognisances. After release Finnigan left the I.R.A. and joined the Republican Congress group. Later he abandoned this organisation and operated on his own—as a battalion quartermaster in the I.R.A. he had had control of arms and ammunition and after leaving he refused to give them up to the I.R.A. On October 14, the I.R.A. kidnapped him and held him prisoner for a week before he escaped. Arms were discovered in Finnigan's possession on November 10 and he was arrested and brought before the Military Tribunal. On November 26 he was sent to prison for fifteen months. In July, 1935, while still serving this sentence, he was charged jointly with Richard Goss, Eamon Coffey, Thomas Walsh and Bernard Murphy, all of Dundalk, with the murder of Mrs McGrory. McCrystal was a state witness. This was the first murder trial before the Military Tribunal. On July 20, after a five-day hearing, all the accused were acquitted. (Goss was later executed in connection with a shooting incident in 1940.)

Before this, however, the country was swept with rumours concerning I.R.A. and Fianna Fail links when on February 16, speaking in the Dail, W. T. Cosgrave stated that a meeting of the I.R.A. had been held in 44, Parnell Square on February 11. On the same date he said police officers entered 5, Parnell Square, which was closed by order of the Military Tribunal. From here, he said, police officers kept number 44 under observation with field glasses. The meeting, he alleged, was to give instruction in the use and construction of a land mine to be exploded the following day. But the only explosion which took place the following day was in Dundalk, resulting in the death of Mrs McGrory. On February 21 the Minister for Justice, replying, said that all he was prepared to state to the house or to the people outside at that stage was that the police were satisfied that there was no relation between what happened in Dundalk and anything that took place in Dublin on the previous day.

Following the banning of the Young Ireland Association O'Duffy retaliated by founding the League of Youth six days later. Immediately an application was lodged in the high court seeking a declaration that the League was a lawful association, the object being to prevent the government's banning it. The hearing of this case dragged on for a number of years during which the Blueshirt movement wore itself out in a series of unconstitutional activities.

Whether the Blueshirts' shirt was a gesture of solidarity with shirted Fascist movements on the Continent, as the I.R.A. and Fianna Fail claimed, or whether it was adopted merely, as its originator claimed, to keep members from hitting each other in mistake for I.R.A. men at meetings, is a moot point. Certainly the movement was associated with the idea of the corporate state, then so fashionable with right-wing commentators. Certainly also its membership and support tended to be drawn from among the larger farmers and bigger businessmen, whereas that of the I.R.A. and Fianna Fail tended to come from the smaller farmers and the working classes.

Equally certainly however there had been a civil war and the I.R.A. and Fianna Fail members were breaking up Cumann na nGaedheal meetings. Both circumstances contributed to the speedy rise and fall of Blueshirtism. O'Duffy's personality was not suited to politics. His tactics included paying young lads to turn up in their blue shirts to rallies. As they also got their meals and free transport he both ensured large meetings and a correspondingly large strain on the organisation's resources. (The fee varied but some ex-Blueshirts told me they got ten shillings a meeting, a lot of money in those days.) He also boasted that the local government elections of July, 1934 would give Fine Gael a sweeping victory—Fianna Fail swept the boards. In August, he backed a motion at the Blueshirt congress which called on farmers to refuse to pay their rates under the economic war ended. He followed this up by declaring that Britain was fortifying her outposts in the six counties and the Free State, and if this meant war he, O'Duffy, would be in along with 'ninety-five per cent' of the Blueshirts. 'The other five per cent should give up their shirts.'

That was the end for the constitutionalists of the movement. Professor Hogan resigned from the Fine Gael on August 31 as a protest against 'the generally destructive leadership of its president'. On September 21 O'Duffy was pushed out of Fine Gael under pressure from its central council. He set up another League of Youth and subsequently a National Corporate Party, both unsuccessful. W. T. Cosgrave was elected president of Fine Gael and by the following September the League of Youth was amending its constitution 'to alter the dictatorial status which had been given to the office of Director-General'. By the following September the general was in Spain leading a group of ex-Blueshirts in Franco's army.

Tactically, it would have been far better for the I.R.A. either to have stayed aloof from the Blueshirts versus Fianna Fail struggle or else to join in on the side of the Blueshirts and Cumann na nGaedheal and attempt to disrupt the government, but the rank and file of the I.R.A., particularly in Cork under the leadership of Tom Barry, threw itself enthusiastically into the struggle. The following table gives an idea of the volume of incidents which the police were able to bring before the Tribunal:

Year	No. of days on which the Military Tribunal sat	No. of persons convicted by the Military Tribunal I.R.A.	Blueshirts	Others	Total
1931	23	28	Nil	3	31
1932	23	17	Nil	2	19
1933	28	34	11	—	45
1934	110	102	349	—	451
1935	107	112	74	—	186
1936	43	129	Nil	—	129
1937	5	12	Nil	—	12
Total	339	434	434	5	873

Of the I.R.A. men and Blueshirts it is the Blueshirts who were sentenced to any lengthy period who are more to be pitied—the I.R.A. members at least emerged to find some sort of an organisation still in existence as a reminder of their sacrifice, but the speedy end of the Blueshirt movement meant that politically its members became nobody's children.

The elimination of the rightist Blueshirt movement should have led to a strengthening of the left. In fact the I.R.A.'s continuing and bedevilling debate on the use of force against some or all of three enemies—the Free State authorities, the Stormont government and the British—erupted again in such a way as to split the movement and leave Fianna Fail indisputedly the strongest force in Irish politics.

In a sense the Blueshirt upheaval and the I.R.A.'s preoccupation with economic issues brought about the rupture, because in allying itself against the right the I.R.A. allowed itself to be driven further to the left than many of its members, Maurice Twomey in particular, thought either appropriate or prudent. Two incidents in particular alarmed the conservative element and brought matters to a head. These were the Gralton case and the Connolly House burning.

James Gralton of Effernagh, Co. Leitrim, a naturalised American citizen, had emigrated from Ireland to America in 1909. He returned in 1932 an avowed atheist and Communist, and became very active in propagating Communist doctrines. He was the owner of a dance hall in which he ran free dances to entice workers and young people to listen to his views. As the local clergy frowned on dances of any sort he drew large crowds and provoked corresponding resentment in clerical rightist circles. His dance hall was attacked and shots were fired into it. On February 9, 1933, he was served with a deportation order. He gave a personal undertaking to leave the country before March 4, but in the meantime he went on the run. As soon as he was caught he was arrested and deported.

The matter was taken up by the Revolutionary Workers Groups, as the Communist Party then styled itself, and by left-wing notabilities such as Mrs Sheehey Skeffington and Captain Jack White who had founded Connolly's Citizen Army, and a public campaign to 'Keep Gralton here' was launched.

In so far as the I.R.A. was concerned if Gralton had not existed Peadar O'Donnell and Frank Ryan would have been delighted to invent him, and *An Phoblacht* almost drowned out the *Workers Voice*, the Communist organ, in demanding the retention of Gralton. At a mass meeting in the Mansion House, Dublin, on February 27 to protest his expulsion a statement from the I.R.A. adjutant general was read saying that the army had already 'taken up the matter with the Army Unit in Leitrim and urged that everything possible be done to organise protests against the expulsion of James Gralton from his native land . . .'

What the statement did not say was that the Leitrim I.R.A. commandant, Sean O'Farrell, had advised against becoming involved with Gralton and allowed his men to stand neutral in the affair. Moreover Peadar O'Donnell had been pelted with mud and stones when he attempted to address a meeting in Drumsna, Co. Leitrim, and in fact while prominent left-wing I.R.A. men did attend the meeting the Army Council did not permit the adjutant general to deliver his statement in person and Michael Price and Frank Ryan were ordered not to speak either.

Gralton was caught and deported a few days later, but before the I.R.A. had had time to expunge the red hue he had imparted to their colours the Connolly House fracas blew up. As mentioned above Mrs Despard's house in Eccles Street was used as a workers' college by the left-wing I.R.A. It was also the headquarters of the Irish section of the Friends of Soviet Russia. Connolly House in Great Strand Street was the headquarters of the Irish Revolutionary Workers' Party. Both premises came under public scrutiny during February and March of 1933, largely because the Lenten lectures took note of the Gralton affair and the dangers of Communism generally. The preacher in the Jesuit church in Gardiner Street, not far from Eccles Street, was particularly strong on the issue.

Then a group of socialists formed an organisation known as the St Patrick's Young Men's League which at first merely marched in the streets, occasionally stopping pedestrians in O'Connell Street to ask if they were wearing their scapulars! However on March 27 either this organisation, or a like-minded group attacked the houses in Eccles Street and Strand Street, causing some damage to fittings. Two nights later the mob looted and wrecked Connolly House before setting it on fire.

Charlie Gilmore, who had attempted to defend the place with a revolver, was arrested, charged with illegal possession of firearms and the attempted murder of a police officer. He conducted his own defence and was acquitted but the I.R.A. was deeply driven by the incident. He stated in court that he had had authority from the I.R.A. to bear arms in the defence of the Communist building. This was denied in an I.R.A. communique to the *Independent* on March 30. On April 1 however, the man who had given him permission to carry a weapon, his brother Harry, wrote contradicting this statement.

Harry was court-martialled on Sunday April 9, but was acquitted on all counts even though he refused to sign a prepared letter to the press exonerating the I.R.A. of having dealings with Communists.

These two incidents imposed a severe strain on the I.R.A. To the right the movement was in danger of being ground between Communism and Fianna Fail. To the left the army soldiered to no purpose. In March, 1932 a 'Constitution and

Government Programme for the Republic of Ireland' had been issued and the Army Council's manifesto for Easter 1933 said the I.R.A. believed that 'the reorganisation of Irish life demands the public ownership of the means of production, distribution and control' but neither 'constitution' nor 'programme' nor 'reorganisation' seemed to make any progress amid the welter of Blueshirtism, drilling and fisticuffs. What was needed, said the left, was a new political party. On March 17 and 18, 1934, a convention was held in Dublin to resolve the issue. It voted against the creation of a new political party. The margin was only one vote, that of Maurice Twomey, but Ryan, Price, Gilmore, O'Donnell, Fitzgerald and some of their supporters walked out of the convention and immediately set about trying to form a new movement without trying to win over their opponents. Offices were taken at 202, Pearse Street, later at 112, Marlborough Street, and on April 8 a conference was held at Athlone at which the new Republican Congress Party was launched, proclaiming itself 'So revolutionary that its achievement means the overthrow of all the existing political and economic machinery which at present holds this country and our people in subjection. Therefore our call is: Workers and working farmers unite on to the Workers Republic.'

The manifesto from which this extract is taken was printed in the national press and drew an immediate rejoinder from the Army Council, published in part in the national press, and in full in *An Phoblacht* on April 4. This said that 'in so far as the statement referred to is an attack on the present social and economic system, and an indictment of the policies of the Governments of the Six and Twenty-Six Counties, the Army Council is in complete agreement with it . . . this statement is merely repeating what has been stated over and over by the Army Council in its public pronouncements and through the columns of *An Phoblacht*.' But the Army Council went on to disown O'Donnell and Gilmore and said that 'This attack by Republicans can only assist the campaign of the Capitalist and Imperialist elements.'

The Army Council statement contained a passage which illustrates the very core of the hard-line, Fenian-cum-I.R.A. attitude towards constitutionalism: 'This Party will, in course of time, contest elections and enter the Free State Parliament. Inevitably it will follow the road which has been travelled by other constitutional Parties which, though setting out with good intentions, ended in failure. It is not very long ago since Fianna Fail leaders told us that they wanted to go into the Free State Parliament only for the purpose of smashing it up, but they now hold this institution and the whole Free State machine as sacred.'

The Army Council did not content itself with issuing this document, but continued to exert less public pressure on the Congress movement. Price, O'Donnell, Gilmore and Ryan were court-martialled *in absentia*, and expelled with ignominy—O'Donnell sending back word on hearing of the verdict that 'as he had been court-martialled in his absence, the sentence could be carried out in his absence also'.

However, Sheila Humphries, a prominent member of Cumann na mBan, and Eithne Coyle, another signatory, withdrew from the new movement on July 18, 1934, because of the feuding which the new departure generated between the two organisations. Three well-known members, Charles Reynolds, Seamus de Burca

and George Leonard, publicly recanted and reaffirmed their allegiance to G.H.Q.
in a letter which appeared in *An Phoblacht* on April 21, 1934. 'We are satisfied,' they
said, 'with the Army Council's expression of agreement with the [Athlone]
statement in reference to the attack on the present social and economic system.'
The Army Council forbade I.R.A. men to have anything to do with the new
movement under threat of dismissal and a few who disobeyed were in fact
dismissed, but a much greater number—mostly in Dublin*—voluntarily resigned
and went over to the Congress. Liam Kelly and Joseph Doyle were recruited in this
way. Other active recruits were Norah Connolly O'Brien, a signatory of the
Athlone manifesto; her brother, Roddy Connolly—both children of the executed
1916 leader James Connolly; Cora Hughes; and Frank Edwards, a Waterford school
teacher who was later involved in a public controversy with his bishop following
his dismissal, at the Bishop's instigation, for joining the Congress. All in all the
effect of the Congress was to split the I.R.A. down the middle.

The Congress inaugurated its public campaign at a meeting in Rathfarnham
on April 23, presided over by Liam Kelly, and on May 5, a newspaper, the
Republican Congress, 'Organ of the Committees of Workers and Small Farmers
working for the United Front against Fascism and for the Workers' Republic'
made its first appearance.

Differences, however, built up within the Congress and came to light at a
convention in Rathmines Town Hall on September 29 and 30. Michael Price
differed from the majority of delegates on methodology and consequently was
not elected to the executive. Price wanted the organisation to concentrate on
strikes, resisting evictions, and the creation of a political organisation to contest
municipal and Dail elections. O'Donnell, Ryan, Gilmore and others did not
consider the time opportune for such a programme. They wished first to establish
'cells' in trade unions and to place their men in key positions in political
organisations. Subsequently Price broke away from the Republican Congress and
joined the 'Citizen Army'. (A sort of hangover from Connolly's 1916 army, which
still kept itself within the Republican ethos, dimly hoping someday to achieve
Connolly's goals.) Here again he opposed the majority, and in a short time he left
that body. By 1936 his views had carried him on the platforms of the Irish Labour
Party advocating the cause of the constitutional Labour Party.

At the end of 1934 the Republican Congress movement was in debt. George
Gilmore had been sent to America to look for funds and meantime the Congress
weekly was forced to suspend publication, flickering into life for an occasional issue
as did the movement itself at times such as strikes when members came into conflict
with police. There were activities such as those of January, 1935, when the Dublin
chain, Bacon Shops Ltd, was strike-hit by Michael Fitzpatrick, a trade unionist who
was also on the I.R.A. Army Council. The strike of the Dublin tram and bus workers in March, 1935, provided another basis for a united from with the I.R.A., as did

---

* I was persistently given a figure of 4,000 for this defection, but I cannot estimate
exactly either this or most other numerical claims for the I.R.A. Numbers of names on
roll books did not in themselves give an exact picture of the numbers available to fight.
However it can be safely assumed that the I.R.A., in the South alone, had upwards of
30,000 in its ranks at this time.

agitations for the release of political prisoners, or events such as the I.R.A. Easter
Week commemoration during which there were special contingents from the tram-
way strikers, the Workers' Union of Ireland, the Republican Congress, the Communist Party and the Unemployed Workers' Movement. At a May Day demonstration
in College Green, the Republican Congress, the Communist Party of Ireland and
the Unemployed Workers' Movement were represented. But relationships with the
I.R.A. ruptured again at Bodenstown in June. The attitude of the I.R.A. was
criticised in a leader in the June 29 issue of the *Republican Congress* which said:

> From 1932 on it was clear the I.R.A. should rouse the Republican population of
> Ireland into the new national advance.
>
> Instead, Volunteers were sent out on silly attacks on neighbour lads of the same home
> circumstances who, in the absence of any lead from the I.R.A. were joining the Fianna Fail
> Reserve in the belief that it was to be used against the Fascists.
>
> Instead of raising the economic war into an assertion of the nation's sovereignty,
> I.R.A. Leaders tried to develop it into a squabble over Bass bottles in public-houses.
>
> Instead of opening the road for afterwards movement. the I.R.A. leaders, to the cheers of
> such men as Professor Hogan, opened an attack on their own left-wing elements.
>
> They took the same attitude as the Irish Hierarchy and the *Independent*★ towards the
> revolutionary workers within their ranks.
>
> I.R.A. leaders refused to permit Northern workers to carry banners in 1934, and
> actually tore the banner—'United Irishmen of 1934'—carried by the Shankhill contingent.
>
> And in 1935 I.R.A. leaders ordered country units to attempt to smash up Republican
> Congress marchers.

But the shades were drawing in on the Republican Congress Movement.

Peadar O'Donnell announced the formation of an 'Active Service Unit' one
hundred strong, on January 3, 1936. His proposals were:

> The active service unit will meet once a week; full strength. It will be in four sections:
> First Section will take on the task of penetrating the Fianna Fail Cumainn, I.R.A. units and
> Trade Union branches with a view to developing demonstrations to reveal the strength of
> Republican feeling and to accelerate the independence ferment.
>
> Second Section will organise the housing struggles and extend Tenant Leagues
> throughout the City.
>
> Third Section will co-operate with the unemployed workers' movements, and also
> bring to general notice and support those small strikes that have become a feature of
> Dublin in these days when an injury to one is no longer the concern of all, and it will co-
> operate generally with strike committees.
>
> Fourth Section will cater for the social, financial and educational side of the
> movement; will organise outings, collections and classes.

The 'Independence ferment' was far less than O'Donnell hoped. Early in 1936
the *Republican Congress* weekly was forced to suspend publication, and by the end
of the year the Congress offices at 57, Middle Abbey Street had to be vacated, as
there was no money to pay the rent. An attempt was made to revive the paper
under the name of the *Irish People* (the name of the first Fenian paper edited by
Charles Kickham in the 1860s). Like its predecessor, it was printed by Frank
Ryan, at the Co-operative Press, St Anthony's Place, but only one number seems
to have appeared, on February 29, 1936.

★   Which after the 1916 Rising carried a leading article calling for the punishment of the
    leaders.

O'Donnell, Gilmore, Ryan, Roddy Connolly and Cora Hughes gamely continued their efforts, co-operating with the Communists, then under the leadership of Sean Murray, in connection with the visit to Dublin of the Scottish Communist, William Gallacher, M.P. in April, 1936. Gallacher attended the I.R.A. Easter Commemoration on April 12 as one of the Communist and Republican Congress contingent. The presence of this group—whose members displayed a red button in their coats—provoked a good deal of public hostility and the marchers were stoned by one section of the crowd. The next day a large crowd assembled in College Green and prevented the holding of a public meeting at which Gallacher had been announced as a speaker. Peadar O'Donnell had to be rescued from the mob by the police. The crowd, on breaking up, marched through the streets and demonstrated outside the headquarters of the Communist Party. Subsequently the Congress group had to abandon a number of other proposed meetings through fear of attack

By November, 1936 the Republican Congress had pathetically ceased to exist, and the same may almost be said of the Communist Party of Ireland which was also in such financial difficulties that its organ, the *Workers' Voice*, ceased publication.

Meanwhile on the right the I.R.A. proper attempted to give itself a semi-constitutional role such as that of the Republican Congress. These efforts were not successful. In fact, its role in a bitter transport strike, which began in Dublin on March 3, 1935, led to widespread arrests. The government had placed army lorries on the streets to alleviate the distress caused by the strike, and on March 25 the Army Council issued the following manifesto:

> Oglaigh na hEireann,
> Ard Aifig, Atha Cliath,
> March 22nd, 1935.

Roinn: Army Council,
Uimhir: XD/61.

To the Joint Strike Committee,
Dublin Tram and Bus Workers.

A Chairde,
   The Army Council has had under consideration the dispute between the Dublin transport workers and the Dublin United Tramways Company.
   In the opinion of the Army Council, the situation is one in which more than the immediate causes of the dispute is involved. The action of the Free State Government in using the Free State Army for strike-breaking purposes, in the interest of a company to which the Government has given a monopoly, constitutes a definite challenge to all workers. That the complete transport system of Dublin should be at the mercy of a private monopoly is a matter affecting the welfare of all Dublin citizens.
   The Army Council takes the view that the matters at issue call for the intervention of all Republicans who stand by the proclamation of Easter Week, wherein equal rights and opportunities are guaranteed to all citizens.
   The Army Council, realising the importance of the principles involved, feels that the joint efforts of the Free State Government and of the combine must be defeated. To meet this attack, the organised support of all those who stand for decent working and social conditions is necessary. For these reasons, the Army Council hereby expresses its willingness to assist the workers in their struggle.

Further, the Army Council is interested, as the governmental programme of the Irish Republican Army on the question of transport provides:—

'Railways, canals, air and waterways, and all forms of public inland transport shall be operated by a body set up by the National Economic Council'

The Army Council offers the services of the Army to assist in mobilising the maximum support for the Dublin transport workers in their struggle, and is prepared to send representatives to meet the Strike Committee for this purpose.

le Sinne,

The Army Council,

Per.................Secretary.

This statement alerted the government and on the following day, the houses of prominent members of the I.R.A. and of the Republican Congress were raided by the police and forty-four men were taken into custody. Some of them, including Peadar O'Donnell, were released after interrogation, but on April 24–29 the Military Tribunal imposed the following sentences: Eighteen months' imprisonment on Con Lehane, solicitor (a member of the Army Council at the time) for sedition, membership of an unlawful association and refusing to give an account of his movements; six months' imprisonment on Claude O'Loughlin, Richard Batterbury, Leo Burdock, Thomas Farrington, Patrick McElroy, Thomas Merrigan, Donal O'Donoghue, James Hannigan, Andrew Walsh, John Farrington, Joseph Hendley, Sean Brunswick, James Cole, Michael Neary and Laurence Carwood, on charges of membership of unlawful associations, etc.; one month's imprisonment on John Nalty, William Scott and Michael Kelly for membership of an unlawful association, etc.

Sean MacBride, Maurice Twomey, Michael Fitzpatrick and Sean Russell went on the run, but Tom Barry, who had been arrested in Cork on March 26 on charges of seditious utterances at Tralee on January 6, was caught and got six months.

These setbacks promoted the growth of another burst of activity in favour of 'constitutional' advance, and at a convention held in Dublin on August 17 the agenda included proposals for contesting future elections and, in certain cases, recognising the courts. As usual those who believed in force objected strongly and there were threats of resignation. Nevertheless, another convention was held on September 21 and those present voted four to one to contest the next general election.

At a meeting at Barry's Hotel, Dublin on March 7, 1936, a new political party, Cumann Poblachta na hEireann, was formed. It was decided to try to have it both ways, by contesting parliamentary elections in the North and the South but stipulating that successful candidates would not take their seats. Maurice Twomey, who was lukewarm about the proposal, and Sean MacBride who was strongly for it, represented the I.R.A., and Republicans who abhorred Fianna Fail and Fine Gael and could see no sign of advancement in the nearly moribund Sinn Fein movement, also attended. Chief among these was the former chief of staff, Dr Andrew Cooney who had been particularly active in the I.R.A. in the 1920s; Dr James P. Brennan who was later to become active in Clann na Poblachta, a party Sean MacBride would lead; the Misses Fiona Plunkett, a sister of the executed 1916 leader; Florence McCarthy; Madge Daly of Limerick, sister of the widow of the executed 1916 leader Thomas Clarke, and Patrick MacLogan, the I.R.A. organiser who was at the time Nationalist M.P. for South Armagh. He was subsequently elected chairman of the new party.

However, the opposition, particularly in the Dublin brigade, to the proposal that the I.R.A. should have a political wing continued to be strong. A special convention was surrounded in Dublin on May 19 at which the two most prominent I.R.A. men were again Sean MacBride and Maurice Twomey. MacBride proposed that Cumann Poblachta na hEireann should receive the active support of the I.R.A. but Twomey objected and pointed out that there was no difference between this proposal and the first Fianna Fail proposal. The discussion was heated and finally Twomey walked out of the meeting followed by the more prominent Dublin Brigade officers: Claude O'Loughlin, James Coulton and Kevin Lawless.

The meeting revealed both the typical I.R.A. man's Fenian distrust of constitutional politics, and his native belief that once he entered politics power was his for the taking. This view was not shared by the public as is shown by a table giving the votes secured by Republican Congress and Clann na Poblachta. The Communists put forward no candidates in this election but worked for the Republican Congress candidates. (The elections were held on June 30.)

Republican Congress

Name	Area	Votes	Total Poll
Frank Ryan	No. 2	418	32,517
George Gilmore	No. 3	730	32,617
Cumann Poblachta na hEireann			
J. McGrath	No. 1	675	21,519
A. Lynn	No. 2	482	32,517
M. Fitzpatrick	No. 3	720	32,617
S. Malin	No. 4	630	21,556
Madame Maude Gonne MacBride	No. 5	689	29,733

For a personal assessment of how people generally felt about the movement I turned to my friend and colleague Anthony Butler, author, art critic, raconteur and television personality, who was both involved and at the same time sufficiently detached to be authoritative. He gave me the following characteristically humorous reminiscence:

'The first idea I had of the existence of the I.R.A. came in 1927 when police invaded my school to arrest one of the teachers in connection with the shooting of Kevin O'Higgins. I was in a low primary grade and since we all hated the teacher involved—a sadistic brute—we were all on the side of law and order. Rumour spread that the arrest was only a fake to get him for his use of the cane.

Mixed with this report was some mention of the I.R.A.s which we assumed was just a higher class than the ABCs. From that moment until the late 1940s the I.R.A. was a background to any thinking I might do on politics. It was the Mafia; it was truth; it was cruelty; it was justice —you didn't know what and this shifting assessment of their place in Irish life was one which most people shared.

'You couldn't escape the shadow of Republicanism and the I.R.A. in Dublin of the late 1930s. They weighed heavily on the nation; they were powerful and whatever the reality—menacing.

'The ebbing tide of revolution which was dying on the beaches of the new state had received some fresh impetus from the discontent generated by depressed economic conditions and the I.R.A. overlapped many other organisations in the labour field.

'In the great building strike of 1936 it played a large part even though the activities of its members were unofficial—this meant no more than an implied hand-washing by the Army: "Don't blame us if you're caught."

'While I was too cowardly—rather than too prudent— to involve myself with the I.R.A. I was like many others delighted to sniff the powder and vicariously enjoy the actions of others who were deeply involved, delighted to hang about the fringes of the movement and know people who were involved. One of my friends kept his private armoury in his cushions which didn't make for comfort or a peaceful mind, but he was an exciting person for a boy to know.

'The building strike went on for a long time and my father was involved in it so I, with little else to do at sixteen, took part as well. One feature of these days was the hunger march—the suffering artisans exposing their agonies to the people of Dublin. I marched with them but didn't last long.

'Plump, fresh-skinned and most definitely outside the classification of deprived citizen at least in appearance, I was poor propaganda material. But the whole thing introduced me to Paddy.

'Paddy was an I.R.A. hatchetman and executioner who, it was reputed, would shoot his own mother if the organisation demanded. Since she was faster on the draw than he was the reputation was purely theoretical. Through Paddy I was drawn into the Sunday morning discussion groups around the Nelson Pillar. Here a million plots were hatched although not one per cent ever reached fruition.

'Paddy would vanish now and then for a few days as the police made it a habit to pick him up no matter what happened through Republican activism. They always arrested him away from his home as it required siege tactics to take him in the bosom of his family and his mother was a deadly shot with a saucepan. Indeed until they learned to arrest him away from his home the political police tried as far as possible to take him on Fridays. It was much less dangerous to be hit by a fried kipper than to risk the scalding downpour of a stew outside the flesh-eating abstinence of that day.

'There was a vehicle builders strike on with the building strike and a number of "blackleg" workers were imported from England. Since this combined the national enemy with social justice Paddy offered himself and his "Peter the Painter" to the vehicle builders.

'Whether they accepted his offer or not I don't know but the decision was made to shoot the scabs. Knowing nothing of this I drifted into Paddy's small group one Sunday morning before the leader himself arrived. One of the faithful asked me if I was going to help Paddy the following morning and I said I was without being too sure what it was all about.

'When Paddy arrived I was an integrated if ignorant conspirator. The guarded language of the group, which stated nothing directly or concretely, contributed to keeping me in the dark.

'As arranged I turned up the next day outside the Northern Star Hotel in Amiens Street at 12.30. It was a hot steaming summer's day but Paddy and his two companions were ear-deep in trench coats that bulged in unexpected places as if they were carrying massive loads of scrap-iron. I wore an open-necked shirt, a sports coat and flannels and was the coolest man in every way amongst them. Paddy shook my hand and almost choked with emotion.

' "I didn't think you had the guts."

'Slightly puzzled I sat quietly on my bright new bicycle and discussed the weather, trying at the same time to work out what was involved. They didn't seem interested in chit-chat and kept looking up Amiens Street with fierce restlessness.

'An hour went by while I waited and talked and they displayed even greater apprehension and impatience. Finally we dispersed with Paddy thanking me profusely. I cycled away.

'It was a week or two before I found out Paddy's plans for that morning. A report in an evening newspaper told of the shooting in the leg of a British vehicle builder outside the Northern Star Hotel in Amiens Street. Paddy read it with a grin and nudged me.

' "Sorry, I couldn't ask you along for this one. Two of us was enough."

'He seemed a little ashamed of his neglect.

' "But don't worry, oul son. The next action is on I'll see you're in on it."

'The full horror of the event didn't strike me immediately but when it did I erupted in goose pimples. From that time on I kept clear of Paddy and put an end to my revolutionary career as an assassin.'

The year, 1936, that Butler abandoned his revolutionary career coincided with the government's coming to conclusions similar to his concerning the I.R.A. and for very similar reasons.

On April 29 and May 21 large-scale swoops on I.R.A. men in Cork and Dublin resulted in Twomey, most of the Dublin brigade and all the principal Cork I.R.A. men with the exception of Tom Barry (commanding officer Cork County), Tadgh Lynch (battalion adjutant), and Denis Griffin (County intelligence officer) being arrested. Sean Russell and Sean MacBride escaped the net but Donal O'Donoghue, who was then editing *An Phoblacht*, was arrested on July 8 in Co. Kerry. He went on hunger strike in Arbour Hill prison on July 11, remaining without food until August 7 when he was released.

The incidents that directed the government's attention to the I.R.A. varied from idiotic episodes like that which occurred on January 25 in the Masonic Hall at Tuckey Street, Cork, where a party of I.R.A. men struck a blow for Ireland by holding up the diners in the midst of a convivial occasion and smashing up plates and furniture, to incidents in which three lives were lost. The three deaths were those of Roderick More O'Farrell, who was fatally wounded on February 9, 1935; Vice-Admiral Henry Boyle Townsend Somerville, who was shot dead at 9.30 p.m. on March 24, 1936 as he stood at the door of his home at Castle-Townsend, Co. Cork; and John Egan, who on April 26, 1936 was shot dead in full view of everyone in Mitchell Street, Dungarvan, Co. Waterford.

The first two killings were not sanctioned by the Army Council but the death of Egan was as a result of an I.R.A. court-martial. It was probably never intended to kill More O'Farrell at all. This tragedy arose out of a rent agitation on the Sanderson estate in Co. Longford. Tenants were demanding a 50 per cent reduction in rent and the English agent, Captain Montague, was unable to collect any rents while the dispute continued. More O'Farrell, Senior, was appointed in his stead and the dispute simmered throughout 1934. On December 2, at a public meeting at Edgeworthstown, Co. Longford, official I.R.A. speakers, who had been formally invited by the Tenants Association to join in the agitation, made inflammatory speeches on the lines of: 'there must be plenty of pitchforks and boughs on the trees around Edgeworthstown but one strong bough should be left on a tree convenient to More O'Farrell's in case of need.' On February 9, 1935, a party of armed men raided the More O'Farrell house, outside Edgeworthstown, during a dinner pary. More O'Farrell and his son strongly resisted the raiders' attempts to take away More O'Farrell* and several shots were fired, one of them striking young More O'Farrell who later died. Seven members of the I.R.A. were arrested and charged with murder at the Central Criminal Court in Dublin, but on December 10, 1935, before the evidence for the defence was taken, the jury brought in a verdict of not guilty.

When Frank MacDermot, speaking in the Dail on June 16, 1936, asked Minister for Justice Gerald Boland why the case had not been heard before the Military Tribunal, the minister replied that a certificate was not issued empowering the Tribunal to hear the case as the minister 'could not conscientiously state that the crime was committed for the purpose of interfering with the machinery of government, or the administration of justice'.

MacDermot was reflecting an opposition view that the Fianna Fail government and the I.R.A. were still in some form of collusion. This unease spread to the public, so that when I.R.A. trigger-happiness claimed two more lives Fianna Fail was driven, both by the necessity of upholding governmental authority and the need to show people where the government stood, to act forcefully against its former friends.

Admiral Somerville was shot dead because the Cork I.R.A., strongly anti-British and anti-Protestant, took violent exception to his giving references to young local men who wished to join the British navy. The shooting of an elderly man who had come unsuspectingly to the door of his home to answer a knock

---

* I am informed that tarring and feathering, rather than shooting or hanging, was intended.

did more to alienate popular sympathy from the I.R.A. than any single act since the shooting of Kevin O'Higgins.

Then on April 26 came the Egan killing. Egan was an ordinary country lad, and his death horrified the countryside. He had been one of a party of five I.R.A. men arrested on July 12, 1935, for illegal drilling in Co. Waterford. On July 18 the commander of the West Waterford battalion of the I.R.A., William O'Donoghue, was arrested, and on July 30 received three months' imprisonment. He had been in charge of the drill session for which Egan and the others were arrested. At O'Donoghue's hearing Egan and two others were released, but the I.R.A. believed that Egan had earned their *nolle prosequi* by turning state's evidence, and that the other two men released with him were set free only as a sort of smoke screen. He was shot from a motor car (stolen earlier in the evening from the home of a district justice) and on May 14 four members of the I.R.A.— William O'Donoghue, John Tobin, Edmund Carraigan and Michael Conway— were arrested and charged with his murder.

Conway was sentenced to death but was released on May 4, 1938, his case having become in the meantime a *cause célèbre*. First, his counsel, Albert Wood and Art O'Connor, refused to appear before the Military Tribunal, saying that they would not act for him because they would not appear in any case before the Military Tribunal. Then his solicitors Messrs. Hogan & Lehane—Con Lehane being a former member of the Army Council, who had by then severed his connection with the army—sent the correspondence to the press. Only one paper, the *Mayo News*, printed it on July 18. After this, Conway's case proved a rallying point for I.R.A. publicists. 'Micksey', as he was called was one of the best-known I.R.A. men in Ireland at the time, and a classical example of a figure of menace to those outside the movement, and the epitome of decency, kindness, and sincerely to those within it. (He later became a monk.)

Twomey got three years from the Military Tribunal for membership of an unlawful organisation, on June 19, a day after the I.R.A. had been outlawed by an order from the executive council, after a two-day debate in the Dail. In the course of the debate the acting Minister for Justice, Gerald Boland, made the following significant statement concerning future government policy towards the I.R.A.: '. . . the fact that these murders have occurred . . . makes it clear that stern action must be taken against any organisation which claims to have the power of life and death over its members, or ex-members, or other citizens, or which claims that it is entitled to use force upon the community to compel obedience to its will. I now give definite notice to all concerned that the so-called Irish Republican Army, or any organisation which promotes or advocates the use of arms for the attainments of its object will not be tolerated . . .'

The next day he followed this up by saying, '. . . we smashed them [Blueshirts] and we are going to smash the others [the I.R.A.] . . . if there are people who know where arms are, and their sense of civic duty will not encourage them to tell where they are, then if any form of reward is necessary to induce them to do so, we will give it . . .'

The government also banned the Bodenstown meeting, fixed for June 21. Trains and buses heading for the meeting were stopped, an aeroplane hovered overhead, and on the ground armed cars and police were grouped. One band of young Limerick I.R.A. men seized a lorry and attempted to make their way to Bodenstown but were arrested and sentenced to nine months by the Military Tribunal. And a young man, Sean Glynn, committed suicide in Arbour Hill prison on September 13. A subsequent commission of inquiry investigating his death found that imprisonment had so worked on his mind that he became depressed and took his own life.

4

The I.R.A.'s Foreign Links

The I.R.A. did not make any great impact on the outside world after the end of the Anglo-Irish war, and the outside world has never impinged very greatly on the I.R.A. There were some peripheral contacts with European countries, and improbably enough with Russia, but the only country to which the I.R.A. looked for assistance in any sustained manner was America, where large-scale emigration from Ireland following the great famine of the 1840s had created a powerful source of strength. Embittered Irishmen in America were approached by Irish leaders as diverse in their policies and appeal as Parnell, Redmond, de Valera and Sean Russell.

The I.R.A.'s contact with Europe was, on the other hand, principally through its left-wing members, such as David Fitzgerald or Peadar O'Donnell. Fitzgerald was a frequent visitor to Russia during the 1920s and the I.R.A. was officially represented at the World Congress of the Anti-Imperialist League in Brussels in 1927 by Frank Ryan and O'Donnell, and by Sean MacBride and Donal O'Donoghue at Frankfurt on Main in 1929. As a result of I.R A. representations the Frankfurt congress (which met July 20–31) passed a resolution calling on 'the organised workers of Great Britain to withdraw the threat of war against Ireland and allow Ireland freely to organise her own life in accordance with working class ideals'.

The congress also pledged that the 'revolutionary organisations in Ireland' would receive the 'whole-hearted backing of the Congress' for their 'next attempt' to set up the desired state and elected an I.R.A. man called Magennis, who had been given two years hard labour for the possession of a revolver, as a member of the honourary praesidium of the congress. This was the most tangible result the I.R.A. deputation achieved.

Peadar O'Donnell and Sean Hayes introduced to Ireland an offshoot of the Third International with the formation of a branch of the European Peasants Committee which O'Donnell represented at the international congress of the movement in Berlin during March, 1930. However neither the I.R.A. nor the Communists thought much of each other. Police records of the 1930s show that two members of the British Communist Party who were deputed to visit Ireland during 1930 to study conditions on behalf of the Communist International reported that the Irish were 'too Mexican' to make good Communist revolutionaries. Presumably this means too volatile and unamenable to discipline. The Irish Catholic Republicans were certainly unmoved by appeals such as that of Peadar O'Donnell to 'think of the Army as the armed members of the toiling and working masses. The leadership must be that of a revolutionary working-class party whose membership may be all I.R.A., though the Army will be larger than the Party.'

First Saor Eire and then the Republican Congress failed to marry the class struggle to the I.R.A.'s efforts. In Irish circumstances such an outcome was inevitable as Stalin himself recognised when he had dealings with the I.R.A. not long after it had reorganised itself following the Civil War.

In the spring of 1925 I.R.A. headquarters considered seeking aid from Russia through 'Pa' Murray, a formidable figure during the war of independence and with extensive contacts in Russian circles in London. Through these he arranged for an I.R.A. delegation to be received in Moscow. The other militant Republican in the pay was Sean Russell, with Gerald Boland sent by de Valera to hold a watching brief on behalf of the more constitutionally minded section of the movement. The trio reached Germany and left Hamburg on June 27 with forged passports. (Ironically the outbreak of the Second World War would see Russell dying on a German submarine and Boland, as Minister of Justice in a government led by de Valera, distinguishing himself by the rigour with which he dealt with men who were still following Russell's leadership.)

At Leningrad the men were shown a variety of weapons—but 'Pa' was the only one who could use them! He has told me that his impression at the time was that the Russians simply did not have very much armament to give anyone, though this was not the reason which the Communists gave for refusing to help. After Leningrad they went to Moscow where Murray met Stalin. Stalin asked him what precautions he could guarantee against any weapons they might be given being seized by the Free Staters. He rocked Murray by producing a complete list of the amount of guns the government authorities had seized in Ireland to that date. In addition he wanted to know how many trained men the I.R.A. could guarantee to use the weapons. The interview lasted for about half an hour during which Stalin made it clear that he was worried that any weapons he might give to the I.R.A. would be discovered and used by Russia's enemies as a pretext for invasion. He thought that such a gift might particularly inflame the British.

All in all the interview and the visit were not successes. Stalin told Murray that, aboard the liner from Hamburg, the others had talked too much and that several people knew of their mission. Checking on this episode with Boland, he told me how they had met a friendly woman Communist 'who knew all about the Irish problem. She knew all about the Church and about our agricultural economy.' Whether or not the lady was a Cheka agent, the Russians do not seem to have been too impressed with the Irish revolutionaries. Boland told me that the first question he was asked on arrival was, 'How many bishops did you hang?' When he answered, 'None', his interrogator replied, 'Ah you people are not serious at all.'

This trip ended the I.R.A.'s chances, though not their hopes, of getting a large supply of armament from abroad. A trickle of Thompson guns with a significant history did continue to straggle in from New York. The guns were part of a consignment of 500 Thompson guns ordered from the Auto Ordnance Company, set up by Colonel Thompson in New York, on April 5, 1921. They were stored in a warehouse in the Bronx on La Fontaine Avenue, under the supervision of Lawrence DeLacy. DeLacy arranged to have them smuggled aboard the ship *East Side* for transhipment to Ireland on June 17. However on June 16 the consignment was discovered and seized as the *East Side* lay on her berth in Hoboken. The U.S. customs held on to the guns until September 14, 1925, when an order of discontinuance was issued allowing them to pass into the hands of Joseph McGarrity. This of course precluded their use in the Anglo-Irish war, but the I.R.A. did manage to smuggle some Thompson guns into Ireland during the war. On June 16, 1921, two of them were used to ambush a troop-train moving from Amiens Street to Kingsbridge—the first time Thompsons were used in warfare. (The ambush was carried out by a twelve-man party, led by Oscar Traynor, between Drumcondra Road and Botanic Road. The British admitted to three casualties, one of them serious.)

Eventually some of the American weapons found their way to Ireland, some in the personal luggage of a famous Kerry All-Ireland football team which visited America in 1927. Tom Barry told me that he had taken more ashore at Cork Harbour where he was an executive with the Port and Docks board. And Jim Killeen and Frank Driver recalled taking a lorry to Galway to pick up a consignment with Sean Russell. Killeen remembers the Galway episode vividly because two days after he and Russell had driven across Ireland with a lorry-load of illicit Thompsons he discovered that Russell had not taxed the lorry and that at any moment a vigilant policeman could have had them arrested.

The Russian episode convinced Murray, as it helped to convince other, more constitutional Republicans, that the I.R.A. had little future and he dropped out of the movement shortly after his return. By the end of 1925 the paths of the militants and of de Valera's followers had also diverged.

In America however the ground for Republican propaganda, though it shrank enormously after the end of the Anglo-Irish war, still continued fruitful as Murray could attest. Murray, who died at the end of 1968, was already an old man, interested in literature and history, when I first interviewed him in 1964. He told me of other incidents which he had taken part in during the War of Independence before going on to talk of America.

For instance at one stage during the war while the conscription crisis was raging Cathal Brugha took him along with a party of volunteers who, if conscription had been introduced, were going to machine-gun the British government benches from the visitors gallery of the House of Commons. As the debate wore on member after member of the group lost his nerve, but Murray, whose special task was the assassination of Balfour, stayed on in London, although the delay was telling on him too. One day he learned that Balfour was to preside at Oxford at a university function that afternoon and to test his nerve he went to Oxford and accosted Balfour on the street under the pretext of seeking directions. Balfour courteously walked with him for about a hundred yards, during which Murray satisfied himself that he could have carried out his mission if he had to.

When we spoke of America we were sitting in his house in Terenure waiting for a priest to call to hear his confession, because he had been unable to leave the house for some months following a car accident. He said to me that he had been in America and then said no more. I thought that his mind was dwelling on the priest's visit, and after a few moments silence ventured to prod him again.

'What were you doing there?'

There was a moment's silence and his kindly blue eyes flickered as though they had focused on something distasteful. Then he replied, 'Shootin' a poor divill'

The man had been condemned to death as a traitor by the I.R.A. after a party of Volunteers was betrayed to Crown forces at Clonmult, Co. Cork. After they had surrendered they were tortured and then shot out of hand. The man had gone to America and it was not until after the signing of the truce that Collins got word of his whereabouts in New York. Murray and two comrades were sent to carry out the sentence, but when they got to New York they found that their quarry had changed his address. However by extraordinary ill-luck the unfortunate man turned up to watch the St Patrick's Day parade down Fifth Avenue, across the street from where Murray and his confederates were standing. With the aid of an Irish-American policeman who was on duty at the parade they traced him to his new lodgings at 483 Columbus Avenue. Murray shot him with a revolver borrowed from a New York policeman on April 13th, 1922. Somehow the victim, Patrick Connor, a 29 year-old- Corkman, who worked as a book-keeper at Altman's Department store, survived the attack. Four bullets were removed from his body at the Reconstruction Hospital at Central Park West and 100th St.

Sitting in his red-bricked respectability in suburban Dublin nearly fifty years later Murray sighed and said, 'I was sorry after. We heard later that the poor devil had been tortured to make him talk. We didn't know that at the time.'

Even today it is conceivable that a modern I.R.A. party might receive similar assistance in New York, but it was not at all to be wondered at in the 1916–22 period. Current American statistics of the Irish population in America estimate that there are more than forty million people born in Ireland or of Irish descent, living there. The generation which lived around the time of the Anglo-Irish war had comparatively recent memories of crowding in ghettoes; persecutions by nativist groups such as the Know Nothings; of grinding poverty and hostility from the white Anglo-Saxon Protestants who denied them employment; of discrimination in boarding houses and sometimes in jobs with signs saying 'No Irish or colored need apply'; and of an anguished parting from the country they loved followed by a smelly, dangerous and often deadly voyage to the States in conditions which have branded the phrase 'coffin ships' into Irish folklore. Probably as many Irish died aboard these badly ventilated, over-crowded ships and were buried at sea as were claimed by every revolution from the time of Wolfe Tone to the signing of the treaty with England in 1921.

The Irish relied heavily on the consolation of relation, and took with them their own brand of ultramontane Jansenistic Roman Catholicism. To many a hungry immigrant Irishman or woman the Church was the only lifebuoy in a sea of hostility. Thus today in America while some Irish are organised in the service of the Democratic Party almost all Irish are organised in the service of the American Catholic Church. An annual display such as the St Patrick's Day Parade down Fifth Avenue is not organised by Irishmen to draw attention to Ireland, or to gain scholarships or industries for their native land, but as a predominantly Catholic festival which is organised under the direction of the archdiocese of New York by the Ancient Order of Hibernians.

Before 1922 the British were still in Ireland and it was relatively easy to canalise both religious fervour and patriotic anti-British nationalism into organisations of some power and significance. The combination of these emotions is caught exactly in an appeal which Joseph McGarrity issued in Philadelphia on June 4, 1914. Two days earlier the Clann na Gael executive had met in New York and set up a committee, headed by McGarrity, to attempt to organise and equip a volunteer force for Ireland. In his appeal McGarrity implored nationalist-minded Irishmen to attend a meeting at 726, Spruce Street, on June 7: 'In the name of God, in the name of Tone's bleeding throat, in the name of Emmet's severed head, in the name of Fr. Murphy of '98, and in the countless dead, who died for Ireland, we ask you to be there.'

These emotions may seem quaint today but they helped to create the 1916 Rising and change the course of Irish history. And earlier John Redmond with his constitutional United Irish League of America, founded in 1901, used these emotions to get contributions which paid for the Irish Parliamentary Party's expenses in the elections of 1906 and 1910 and, until salaries were introduced for M.P.s, a large part of the ordinary living expenses of the Irish M.P.s.

In America as in Ireland the constitutional movement for Irish independence had to contend with the influence of the revolutionary movement of the I.R.B.'s American offshoot, Clann na Gael. It was the army which in 1907 sent Thomas Clarke back from New York to help revivify the I.R.B. in Ireland. Through men like John Devoy and Joseph McGarrity Clann money and policies passed into Ireland, and in 1916 helped to destroy the influence of Redmond in America as in Ireland. McGarrity also played an influential part in saving de Valera's life after the 1916 Rising. After de Valera's baptismal certificate was procured from St Agnes Church, New York, thus demonstrating his American birth, McGarrity got a lawyer friend, Francis Doyle, a prominent Irish American to use it to bring pressure to bear on President Wilson (through Joseph Tumulty) who in turn contacted the American ambassador in London who successfully entreated with the British cabinet not to execute de Valera.

The Irish in America, like the Irish at home, were a fractious lot and there was an obvious conflict of interest between the United Ireland League—the constitutionalists —and the Clann na Gael, the revolutionaries. John Devoy founded a paper the *Gaelic American* in 1903 to combat the influence of Patrick Ford's *Irish World* which supported Redmond and parliamentarianism. The principal leaders of the Clann at this time were John Devoy, the old Fenian, Judge Daniel Cohalan, a Democratic politician of standing, and Joseph McGarrity. The Clann operated on a principle which was outlined by Cohalan that 'Ireland's true interest will be best served by a steady, resolute and progressive policy of organisation among our own people the world over and the cultivation of alliances with English enemies'.

The success of Clann propaganda may be gauged from the comment of the Irish-American *Chicago Citizen* of July, 1908—'There is not an Irishman in America today, in whose veins good red blood is flowing, who would not rejoice to hear that a German army was marching in triumph across England from Yarmouth to Milford Haven.' The 1916 Rising put the final seal on the decline of the United Ireland League which had been speedily going downhill since Redmond had pledged support to Britain in 1914.

The German ambassador to America, von Bernstorff, co-operated with the

Clann through John Devoy in assisting Sir Roger Casement in his attempt to organise an Irish brigade from captured prisoners of war. Through Devoy again, Germany supplied arms for use in the Rising, but due to muddling over dates they did not arrive in time, and were scuttled off Cobh.

Following the Rising the Clann rode high in Irish-American affairs and attempted to force President Wilson to include Irish independence in the post-war peace settlement, for Wilson had made the point that the war was being fought for the freedom of small nations. Wilson, however, though not antipathetic towards the Irish as such, was bitterly at odds with Cohalan and also hesitated to offend Britain, needing England's support in launching the League of Nations. He held out against the Irish claim despite strong Irish-American pressure but on March 4, 1919, the House of Representatives in response to this influence voted 216 to 45 that the peace conference should favourably consider Ireland's claim to self-determination, and on June 6 the Senate voted 60 to 1 in favour of de Valera, Griffith and Count Plunkett being allowed to appear before the conference.

The Clann na Gael leaders, through the 'Friends of Irish Freedom', founded in 1916, had set up an Irish victory fund which by the end of 1920 had collected almost $900,000. Only $115,000 found its way to Ireland, but $750,000 was spent in attacking the League of Nations—'Britain's League'. Cohalan and Devoy joined forces with prominent domestic opponents of the League such as Henry Cabot Lodge and William Borah and they organised huge protest meetings against Wilson during his speaking tour in September, 1919, taking full-page advertisements in the newspapers along his route.

This was the position when de Valera arrived in the States in June, 1919. He stayed first at McGarrity's home in Philadelphia, and formed a strong personal friendship with him. Indeed the *Irish Republic*, produced in New York by a group of McGarrity associates, in September, 1940 was correct in stating that it was McGarrity who persuaded de Valera to use the title 'President of the Irish Republic' instead of 'Priomh Aire', thus committing de Valera irrevocably to that title. Clann propagandists also allege that the tide was one of the reasons why he split with Cohalan and Devoy. They, as I.R.B. supporters, recognised Collins, the head of the I.R.B. as automatically 'President of the Republic'.

But there were more cogent reasons for this disagreement. Devoy, an old man, was very much under the influence of the dynamic Cohalan, who, while pas-sionately devoted to the cause of Irish freedom, felt that it was subordinate to the interests of America. Cohalan felt there inevitably could be a war between America and England, whose sponsorship of the League of Nations he saw as a part of a plot to overthrow America. De Valera felt he was entitled to control the Irish in America and set out to destory Cohalan's leadership. He was untimately successful, but the damaging split which ensued greatly weakened the 'clout' of the Irish Americans.

In January, 1920, an Irish bond drive was launched, with Irish bond certificates sold on a guarantee of exchange for Irish Republican bonds after the Irish Republic was recognised. It is estimated that $5.5 million were subscribed. De Valera prevented approximately half of this money from going to Ireland. It lay for years in American banks. Part of it was ultimately returned to the original subscribers, but de Valera also succeeded in getting control of sufficient funds from the bond drive to enable him to set up the Irish Press newspaper group in Dublin which became a de Valera family enterprise. By November, 1920, de Valera was able to set up his own Irish-American Association, popularly known as 'Growl' because of the sound of the acronym A.A.R.I.—for American Association for the Recognition of the Irish Republic. This organisation soon became dominant in Irish-American affairs. Out of it arose a self-appointed commission, the American Commission on Conditions in Ireland, which reported the sufferings imposed on the Irish by the British (for the purposes of the report these sufferings, though basically genuine enough, were somewhat overdrawn) and an American Committee for Relief in Ireland was formed. This collected an additional $5 million to alleviate conditions in Ireland.

De Valera, however, also aroused considerable controversy in Irish-American circles by attacking Cohalan and the *Gaelic American* and by appearing at the Republican Party's national convention against the wishes of Cohalan who also led a delegation there. The two groups made a bad impression with their quarrelling. Most of all he offended by an interview published in the *Westminster Gazette* on February 6, 1920 (after his return) in which he proposed a solution for the Irish question similar to the association between Cuba and America.

Yet by the time de Valera slipped back to Ireland for Christmas of 1920 he had so mobilised American public opinion on the side of the Irish struggle that it became clear to the British that American funds and public opinion could continue to support the Irish for an indefinite period. There was also a very considerable body of sympathy for the Irish cause in England itself and both facts weighed heavily with the British cabinet when it called for a truce and entered the negotiations which culminated in the signing of the treaty and the British departure from the South of Ireland.

In America the withdrawal of the British was hailed as a great Irish victory. The subtleties of Home Rule, self-determination, dominion status, partition, government by devolution and all the rest of it largely escaped the vast bulk of those who supported the Irish independence movement. From 1921 it is true to say that the Americans as a nation switched off the Irish problem. She had got her independence, the British were gone. What more remained to be done?

For the Irish-American politicians most involved in the struggle the issue was not immediately clear either. For instance, McGarrity who was to spend nearly twenty years trying to wreck the treaty in fact welcomed it with an editorial in his *Irish Press* on December 10, 1920. He said, under the heading 'Irish Republic Triumphs': 'Ireland's sovereign Independence is acknowledged by the British Cabinet and their action is approved by Britain's King. This much is certain . . .' After castigating sections of the American press for their 'despicable' attempts to 'make it appear that the citizens of the Republic of Ireland are to give allegiance to King George', he went on to show that the 'supposed Oath' was merely a 'very clever juggling with words' to give as little hurt to the British ministers and 'the King's pride as possible'.

The difficult hurdle of the new state's title he took without a blink:

Many people will say that the name Republic has been dropped. No such thing has happened. Ireland is to be a Gaelic not an English nation, and at the first sitting of Dail Erin the Gaelic name for the recreated nation was adopted. That name is Saor-stat, pronounced Seer Sthath. If England prefers the correct English translation of the Gaelic term, which is

Free State, instead of the Latin word Republic, Ireland should be quite happy that England has made such a choice.

He wound up by saying that 'putting aside all meaningless phrases if the Treaty made is approved and carried into effect, Ireland again becomes an independent sovereign nation among the nations'. The British, he said, would move out and the Irish take possession of their rightful heritage, boons for which he asked that 'every Irish heart be lifted up to his maker in gratitude'.

Michael Collins didn't go so far. He saw the treaty as not conferring full freedom, but 'freedom to achieve freedom', a 'stepping stone to the Republic'. Certainly de Valera didn't share McGarrity's view. He greeted the treaty's signing with a letter to the *Dublin Press*, co-signed by Brugha and Austin Stack, saying that the treaty was 'in violent conflict with the wishes of the Irish people'.

McGarrity soon swung back into line behind de Valera and a split paralleling the split in Ireland built up in the Clann. McGarrity sided completely with de Valera, Devoy with the upholders of the treaty (who gave him a state funeral through Dublin when he died in 1927). Clann na Gael split into two bodies: Clann na Gael, under Devoy, and the Clann na Gael Reorganised, or Clann na Gael and I.R.A. as it is better known, under McGarrity and Luke Dillon. This grouping remained imbued with the same sentiments as the I.R.A. in Ireland but McGarrity, though he became particularly bitter against Devoy, did not cool in his friendship with de Valera until the middle 1930s when de Valera began to jail I.R.A. men. (Once, however, de Valera entered the Dail in 1927 the Clann decided officially no longer to support Fianna Fail.)

After the Civil War Irish-American activities were mainly confined to the Clann. Broadly speaking New York City went to the Cohalan-Devoy section (as did a number of lesser centres throughout the country) but the principal Irish centres of Boston, Chicago, Cleveland, San Francisco, Philadelphia, Detroit and, in Canada, Ontario, all sided with McGarrity and his chief lieutenants, Luke Dillon, Connie Neenan, John Ryan and Major Enright.

McGarrity was born in 1874 near the village of Carrickmore in Co. Tyrone. He attended the local national school and worked on the family holding but at fourteen, during his parents' absence at Mass one Sunday morning, he ran away to Liverpool. About a year later a man in his lodgings who had bought a ticket to America had to return to Ireland on his mother's death. McGarrity, who had spent the previous nights praying to the Blessed Virgin for some way of getting to America himself, was able to buy the docket from him for £2. He travelled in a black jersey and corduroy pants without any luggage. After about a day at sea a ship's officer began questioning him about his lack of luggage, but an American overhearing him asked, 'Has that boy got a ticket?' The officer replied, 'Yes,' 'Well then,' said the American, 'why don't you mind your own business? What right have you got to question him?' He and a group of Indians befriended the young McGarrity for the rest of the passage. The incident never left McGarrity's mind and confirmed him in his belief that America was a wonderful country.

He must have had extraordinary personality because another passenger, who arrived with him in New York, discovering that McGarrity had no money, gave

1. Padraig Pearse, commander of the Easter Rising, addressing a meeting in Ireland in 1915. His writings and ideas formed the philosophical basis of modern Republicanism. He was executed by the British in 1916.

2. An early group of Volunteers in uniform.

3. Volunteers Jack Doyle and Tom McGrath inside the Dublin G.P.O. during the Easter Rising of 1916.

4. Republican prisoners being marched to the Dublin docks for transport to British prison camps after the 1916 Easter Rising.

5. The G.P.O. photographed from the top of Nelson's Column just after the Easter Rising.

6. The view of Nelson's Column (destroyed by an I.R.A. bomb in March, 1966) down Henry Street, showing the devastation in central Dublin after the Easter Rising.

7. Women picketing outside the U.S. Senate, and the British Embassy in Washington in 1919.

8. Eamon de Valera, accompanied by New York Governor Smith, arrives at a demonstration in support of Irish independence in New York, 1919.

9. De Valera in Syracuse, New York, during his 1919 tour of America to raise money for the Irish Republican war effort.

10. The huge crowd in Boston to hear de Valera speak in July, 1919.

11. Armoured car used by British forces against Irish Republican forces during Anglo-Irish War.

12. I.R.A. suspects at Bandon Barracks, County Cork, around 1920. These men were probably members of the Cork No. 3 Brigade, I.R.A., commanded by Tom Barry.

13. Michael Collins, Commander-in-Chief of Irish Republican forces, brought the British to the bargaining table and headed the team which negotiated the Treaty of Irish Independence.

14. Sir Hammer Greenwood inspecting a unit of the much feared group of British Army Auxilaries. (*Hulton Picture Library*)

15. On the brink of the Civil War, anti-Treaty I.R.A. gunmen patrol Grafton Street, Dublin, July, 1922. (*Hulton Picture Library*)

16. An I.R.A. patrol on the border between Donegal and Tyrone, May, 1922. (*Belfast Telegraph*)

him the fare to Philadelphia where McGarrity had a sister working in a hotel. Her first gesture of initiation into American society was to place a Derby hat on his head—which may have been why McGarrity always affected this type of headgear. He worked at the usual diversity of jobs which a young immigrant from Ireland at that period found himself lucky to get but being a teetotaller and enormously able and energetic, by the time he was twenty he owned a saloon in Philadelphia.

He brought his family to America and throughout his life continued the pattern of generosity he experienced on the boat. To give an example: at the time of the Irish independence controversy, McGarrity was driving a huge open touring car. Stopping one day at a street light he was surprised to find a passerby getting into the seat behind him without saying a word, and then after ten blocks tapping him on the shoulder and handing him a dime, thinking the car was a bus ! Years later, during the Wall Street crash, McGarrity happened to meet this same man weeping in the small hours of the morning in Philadelphia station. He had lost his money, his wife was very ill and suicide seemed to be the only outlet. McGarrity gave him some thousands of dollars on the spot. No one knew of this until after McGarrity's funeral when the man turned up with almost three thousand dollars and told the story as he handed the money over to the relatives.

No one can say how much time, energy and money McGarrity expended on the Irish cause. *The Irish Press*, which he founded in Philadelphia in March, 1918 because the American government was inhibiting the circulation of the *Gaelic American* and the *Irish World* (the two existing Irish-American organs) is estimated to have cost him about two hundred thousand dollars, and his subsequent support for other independence groups must have cost at least as much.

It is a measure of the calibre of the man and of his friends that people were prepared to act on an equally generous scale with him. During 1929 the Clann na Gael leader, Major Michael Enright, hearing that McGarrity was in difficulties gave him his entire savings and had to go to work as a clerk in city hall, Chicago, as a result. Connie Neenan, another prominent Clann figure, who had mentioned McGarrity's difficulties to Enright said, 'I'm awful sorry that I came and asked you to get money for Joe.' Enright's reply was, 'Joe McGarrity wanted it and if it was ten times as much and I knew I was going to lose it I would still give it to him.' When the Irish Hospitals Sweepstakes began to prosper in America about 1934 McGarrity was appointed an agent, and he became relatively well-off again.

He had a literary bent as well, publishing three books of poetry and contributing to Irish culture and literature whenever he could. His concept of what constituted art was, however, strongly influenced by his political beliefs. During the 1911–12 tour of America by the Abbey Players the Clann's Anglophobia caused it to regard Yeats and the players as 'fellow agents of England' because they considered the Abbey's work 'stage Irish' and so of benefit to English propaganda about Ireland. McGarrity was very active in the attempts to get the company prosecuted in Philadelphia and after causing a disturbance at *The Playboy of the Western World*, wrote to his friend Patrick McCartan in Ireland: 'There was nothing in the play that would cause anyone who would witness it to have love or admiration for the people and the country represented in it. If the *Playboy* is art, to hell with art and those who create it.'

Luke Dillon, son of Co. Sligo parents who had emigrated to America from Leeds when he was six, was an Old Testament figure, stern, scrupulously honest, and undying in his hatred of England. Men went mad or died in prison conditions which he endured, to emerge in good physical and mental health. In prison he had refused the entreaties of Clann leaders such as McGarrity that he acknowledge his guilt and petition for mercy, sending out a letter that such a course would mean that, 'The rest of my life would not be worth such a surrender of principle.' He had been jailed for an attempt to blow up the locks of the Welland canal to prevent the Canadians sending troops to aid the British in the Boer War.

Dan Breen told me that he visited Dillon on his death bed, and that the dying man said to him, 'Dan, I've bombed the bastards and I'd bomb them again, but you have tasted their blood.' He had been active in dynamite plots in England during the winter of 1883–84, being responsible for, among other explosions, those at the Carlton Club and the House of Commons. Cornelius Neenan, who had emigrated to America from Cork, and who succeeded him as secretary of Clann na Gael after his death in 1929 took part in these also. Breen told me that when a beggar set up a pitch outside the rebuilt Carlton Club with a placard on his chest saying 'blinded by the Fenian outrages' Dillon asked that all Clann sympathisers passing through London give the man a halfcrown. 'That's the way I'd like to see all the so-and-sos,' he said, according to Breen.

Other prominent Irish-Americans who continued in the Clann after the rifts and upheavals of 1921–23 were John Sullivan of Boston, Tom Pearse of Cincinnati, John Stanton of Cleveland, Jimmy McGee in New York and Harry McCarney in Philadelphia.

As with the I.R.A. in Ireland the same names recur over a period of decades. Those I have mentioned were men of above average ability, but they were deprived of strong public sympathy for getting the British out of Ireland and had many factors militating against the slightest chance of success. Moreover, the strong streak of sentimentality in Irish-American affairs tended to promote a situation in which Irish-Americans were swayed by what they would like to be true. They rarely applied themselves to finding out what the present situation was and how it differed from the land and problems of their youth. And if they were too young to remember Ireland or were born of Irish parents in America, they were subject both to parental memories and Irish-American education which, like that at home, had until very recently a strong anti-intellectual bias and an emphasis on inculcating devotion to the Roman Catholic Church.

The confusion, uncertainty and lack of initiative produced by this type of training predisposed most of those exposed to it towards accepting the *status quo* and the strong, simple certainties propounded on any issue from pulpit or platform. The day to day shifts in domestic Irish politics, the new allegiances, fresh groupings and new faces were a mystery to those in America who continued to send money and militant advice home to 'the boys'. They grew increasingly baffled and pained when the Irish refused their seemingly manifest duty of rising in wrath to drive the British out of 'Occupied Ireland'. McGarrity, for example, was so out of touch with the shifts in Irish politics that when Frank Aiken came to

America in 1926 after the formation of Fianna Fail he was unaware that Aiken was no longer chief of staff of the I.R.A. and was shaken when Neenan, who had been back to Ireland, informed him. McGarrity complained in a letter to Aiken that 'America has been asked to give its support for the past three or four years to the Republicans at home, but I have failed to learn up to the present time just what the platform or the policy of the party is.' Americans would always be in the position of never-knowing clearly what the 'platform or policy' was back in Ireland.

At the end of the Civil War on June 4, 1923 McGarrity had been receiving letters from de Valera, co-signed by Aiken as chief of staff, asking that McGarrity co-operate with 'Commandant General Moylan' whom Aiken and de Valera sent to America to build up support for the defeated Republicans. McGarrity does not seem to have appreciated the implications of another letter from de Valera, received a month later saying, '. . . the only hope for the future that I can now see is by *political* action. It would be a great mistake to imagine that the people were really in love with the Free State. With proper organisation we should be able to secure revision of the "Treaty" within four or five years. The main thing is not to let any time slip by in inactivity. If we could contest one seat in each constituency, we would have laid a solid foundation for the future. The trouble is the old one— money. Until we have made arrangements for the wounded and the army, we cannot use any of the money on hand for political purposes, even though the purpose is fundamental.' In the letter de Valera mentions that about $100,000 would be needed for the elections. This transfer of emphasis from physical force to political activity seems to have been lost on McGarrity who had rapturously accepted the now-to-be-revised treaty.

In a personal diary entitled 'Partial Records by Joseph McGarrity' (in the home of his daughter, Mrs Elizabeth Defoe of Philadelphia who kindly allowed me to see it) one can trace a growing disillusionment with Fianna Fail. He could not understand why de Valera should jail I.R.A. men and other prominent Irish-American figures were similarly bewildered. In June, 1935, the leaders of all the most prominent Irish-American organisations issued an appeal to coincide with the Bodenstown procession, asking Fianna Fail and the I.R.A. to unite. The pamphlet, called 'Republicans Must Unite', is addressed to 'Members of Fianna Fail and of The I.R.A.'.

Extracts from it show the lack of understanding among Irish-Americans about domestic Irish politics. Under the heading 'Who Wants More Civil War', the appeal says:

This year there are again rival pilgrimages to the grave of Tone—Tone who died for a United Irish Republic.

The rival processions occur because the Fianna Fail Government and the I.R.A. are practically at war. So serious is the danger of Civil War that LEADING SUPPORTERS OF FIANNA FAIL AND OF THE I.R.A. IN U.S.A. HAVE COME TOGETHER AND HAVE ISSUED AN APPEAL FOR UNITY AMONG ALL IRISH REPUBLICANS.

TO UNITE THE IRISH PEOPLE WAS THE AIM OF TONE. WHY CANNOT WE UNITE TO-DAY? OUR COMRADES IN THE U.S.A. HAVE SET US AN EXAMPLE; LET US FOLLOW IT!

Irish Republicans in America view with grave concern the present developments which, if allowed to continue, will lead to hostility between Republican sections in Ireland.

We believe that Ireland has reached the critical stage when the Republican enthusiasm of the people can be used to re-establish the Republic or may be dissipated in civil strife.

In this serious situation, we urge the Irish people to insist that representatives of all Republican thought in Ireland must meet in conference to find a means of reconciling their various differences, uniting on unswerving principle, presenting a solid front to the common enemy and re-establish the independence of the country as a Republic. Signed:

JOHN J. REILLY, National Chairman, American Association for the Recognition of the Irish Republic.
JOE MCGARRITY, representing Clann na Gael of America.
JAMES BRADY, Sec., Federation of Societies for Irish Independence.
SEAN HAYES, Chairman, Associated Irish Societies of New York.
JOHN STAUNTON, Chairman, Irish Societies of State of Ohio.
CON MOUNIHAN, Chairman, Irish Societies, Boston, Mass.
PAT HEGARTY, Chairman, United Irishmen of Springfield, Mass.
M. J. MULLANE, Chairman, Irishmen of Butte, Montana.
M. J. MCGING, Chairman, Associated Irish Societies of Chicago.
M. H. ENRIGHT, Colonel, Clann na Gael Guards of Chicago.
ROBERT MONTEITH, Captain, Casement Brigade.
GERALD O'REILLY, representing Congress Supporting Groups of U.S.

This appeal completely misjudges the tone and temper of the Irish electorate at the time. There was no danger of civil war. But the signatures on the appeal show how widespread was the feeling among Irish-Americans that the I.R.A. and Fianna Fail were somehow the same organisation having a family quarrel. In fact, they were two mutually antipathetic political organisations with different goals, or rather very different views about how to achieve the same goals of getting the British out and reuniting the country. In a way one can see in this sort of exchange a microcosm of the American bafflement in dealing with the shifts of Cypriot or South Vietnamese politics. If only they could have all got together and done the right thing! (Curiously, on another analogy between Vietnam and the Clann na Gael the Clann is known to its members by the code name of V.C.!)

The constitution of the V.C., adopted at a Clann convention in Philadelphia at which the nearly moribund body was revived in 1946, contains the following:

ARTICLE I.
Section 1

This organisation shall be known as the V.C., it shall be non-sectarian and shall not interfere in American Party politics.

Section 2.

Its objects are: *First*—To aid the people of Ireland in maintaining their complete national independence under a republican form of government with full civil and religious liberty guaranteed to all its inhabitants. *Second*—To foster and encourage a study of the language, literature, history, music, laws and traditions of Ireland at home and abroad. The Gaelic language shall be used at all public and private functions whenever feasible. *Third*—To foster a spirit of friendship between the Republicans of the U.S. and Ireland.

But the real favour of the organisation comes across in the initiation ceremonies, a mixture of cloak-and-dagger I.R.B.-I.R.A., Masons and Elks type ritual appealing both to the conspiratorial-minded and to those who like the mystery, miracle and authority of the Church.

The initiation ceremonies are laid down as follows:

Perfect silence should prevail during initiation. Nothing else should occupy the attention of the meeting.

The Warden will see that the Camp is not disturbed during the ceremony, and that every member shall avoid any needless movement or word. At such time a whisper may disturb a candidate or an officer, and mar the impressiveness of the ceremony. Each member shall endeavour to make the ceremony what it is designed to be—solemn and impressive.

S.G. [Senior Guard]—'Conductor, proceed to the anteroom and ascertain if there are any candidates in waiting.'

When the Conductor reports the names, addresses, etc., of the candidates, the S.G. asks:

S.G.—'Recording Secretary, have these candidates been duly elected?'

The Recording Secretary reports, giving data of election in each case.

S.G.—'Conductor, proceed to the ante-room and interrogate the candidates.'

The Conductor then retires and asks the candidates the following questions in their proper order:

Conductor—'State your name, age, birth-place and occupation.'

Conductor—'Do you believe in Ireland's right to be a separate and independent nation?'

Conductor—'As the Irish Republic is established, are you willing to sustain it by all means?'

Conductor—'Understanding, as you do, that the object of this Organisation is the freedom of Ireland and the elevation of the Irish race, are you willing to bind yourself by a solemn obligation to aid in carrying out that object and to obey the laws of this Order?'

Conductor—'Are you now, or have you ever been, a member of an organisation having for its object the freedom of Ireland?'

The Conductor having ascertained that the candidate has answered all questions satisfactorily to the Camp will return to the ante-room and collect the initiation fee. If any candidate admits being now, or having ever been a member of this or any similar organisation or if any of the answers should be unsatisfactory, or should call for special action, the Camp may act as may be required by the Constitution. If the answers are satisfactory, the S.G. will say:

S.G.—'Conductor, prepare the candidates and present them for initiation.'

The S.G. will detail a sufficient number of brothers to act as escort to the candidates. The Conductor will then take his sword and retire to the ante-room. The Conductor will then give three knocks at the door as a signal for his assistants to retire, one assistant conductor being selected for each candidate, who shall take a position on the right of the candidate. The Conductor will direct the march and place himself at the head of the escort. At the entrance door he will give three distinct knocks with his sword. The Sentinel will at once open the door and the escort will pass inside with the candidates, after which the Sentinel will close the door. When the escort has advanced three paces into the room the Sentinel will abruptly and in a clear voice say to the Conductor:

Sentinel—'Halt! Who comes there?'

(Escort halts.)

Conductor—'Friends who desire to unite with us in the cause of Ireland.'

Sentinel (to S.G)—'Shall I permit these friends to proceed?'

S.G.—'Advance.'

Conductor—'Forward, march'

The Conductor will lead the escort and candidates to within three paces of the S.G., making a circuit of the centre table and will command:

Conductor—'Halt'

The candidates will be aligned by the assistants facing the S.G.

Conductor (to S.G.)—'Sir, I present these candidates for final examination.'

S.G.—'Friends, you have come to us seeking the privilege of membership. That privilege is denied to unworthy men and granted only to those who can stand the test of a strict examination as to character and patriotism. We are engaged in a holy cause that can be served only by men of courage, devotion and loyalty. We are banded together to free the Land of our fathers from English rule and to sustain the Republic of Ireland as now established. We admit no man to our ranks who is not fully in sympathy with this object. Every man in our Order has taken a solemn oath binding himself to aid in accomplishing it. It is an oath which does not conflict with any duty you owe to God, to your country, your neighbour or yourself and which no true Irishman can condemn. It must be taken before you can be admitted to our Order. You have already signified your willingness to take our obligation, but we give you, even now, the privilege of withdrawing if you so desire. Answer honestly and freely, are you willing to take this oath?'

If the answer be satisfactory the S.G. will say:

S.G.—'Conduct the candidates to the proper office for obligation.'

The Conductor and his assistants will then march the candidates to the J.G. [Junior Guard and align them facing the J.G.'s chair.

Conductor—'Hold up your right hands.'

(S.G. gives two raps.)

The J.G. then administers the obligation, speaking clearly and distinctly, dividing the sentences into short clauses, so that the candidates may have no difficulty in repeating the words after him. He will not tell the candidates to kiss the book, the Ritual not being for that purpose, and the uplifted right hand being sufficient.

OBLIGATION

I (name), do solemnly swear that I will labour while life is left me to put an end to English rule in Ireland and to sustain the Republic now established on Irish soil and to elevate the position of the Irish race everywhere.

That I will obey and respect the Constitution and Laws of the V.C. and all orders coming from the proper authority.

That I will never reveal its secrets to anyone not entitled to know them, even if my connection with the Organisation should cease from any cause whatever.

That I will foster a spirit of Unity and Brotherly Love among Irish Nationalists.

That I do not now belong, and never will belong, to any organisation opposed to the principles or policy of the V.C

And finally I swear that I take this oath without any mental reservation whatever, and that I will keep it in letter and spirit until death. So Help Me, God.

All Present—'We are all witnesses to the obligation you have taken.'

Conductor—'Keep it as you love Ireland and value your honor as a man.'

J.G.—'Conduct the brothers to the S.G.'

(One rap.)

On arriving at the S.G.'s chair the Conductor will align the new brothers and say:

Conductor—'S.G., I present these brothers for final instructions.'

S.G. (Shaking hands with each of the new brothers)—'Brothers, I greet you and welcome you to our ranks in the name of Ireland.'

The name of the Organisation is the V.C. Its local subdivisions, or branches, are styled Camps, and each Camp is known by a number.

The Republican Congress break-away in Ireland was reflected in a similar split in America under Gerald O'Reilly who took most of the left-wing support with him. Then de Valera introduced a pension scheme for I.R.A. men who had taken part in the Civil War, and as many of these had emigrated to America after the war (where they supported the Clann) their acceptance of the pension cut them off from revolutionary activity against the government that was paying the money, and further weakened the Clann. And there were natural American disunities. For instance during 1930 the Clann split down the middle over the opening of a speak-easy to raise funds. One club, the James Connolly Club, led by James O'Mahoney, opposed the scheme and both the club and some individual members of other clubs broke away.

The greatest single weakening factor, however, was the spread of the Irish Sweepstakes movement to America. This took some of the ablest executive brains, as well as rank and file, out of the Clann organisation. Joe McGrath, principal founder of the sweep was astute enough to see the possibility of the old I.R.A. arms and letter smuggling network as a machine for smuggling illegal lottery tickets back to Dublin, and many Clann na Gaelite members devoted themselves more to ticket-pushing than to revolution. Other Irish Americans also supported the sweepstake enthusiastically, distributing tickets throughout the United States, sending counterfoils and money to the counterfeit addresses in Ireland or on the Continent, to be passed on to the sweep headquarters in Dublin. They behaved with that enterprising abandon that the Irish display when they can defy authority and make money at the same time.

Both the vigilance of the postal services and the enterprise of the Irish were well demonstrated on one occasion when a sweep agent, called Irwin, a steward on a Cunard liner, was arrested at Pier 16 and taken with his counterfoils and remittances to a neighbouring precinct station for the night before facing fines and confiscations in the morning. The fine was not serious, heavy though it was, because the sweep would remit this money to him, but the loss of the counterfoils meant that there could be a lack of trust on the part of subscribers. However, the following morning after being fined and losing his counterfoils and the money he had collected, Irwin walked out of the court whistling. All through the night while he was in custody the entire precinct staff, most of whom were Irish (and those who were not knew better than to protest) had laboured to fill in duplicate counterfoils made out on police stationery. These were duly sent to Dublin and accepted by the sweep authorities as being valid counterfoils under the circumstances.

All this meant of course that there was very little time left in Clann circles for fomenting revolution in Ireland.

Harry Short, who was present at the hall on 125th Street when Sean Russell announced, for the first time in America, his scheme for a bombing campaign in England, reckoned there were only forty people present.

5

The Bombing Campaign

Sean Russell's path to New York apparently began when he met Joseph McGarrity in Ireland in 1929. McGarrity's business had temporarily collapsed. He had been expelled from the New York Stock Exchange but a subsequent inquiry cleared his name, fixing the responsibility on his partner, a man named Kenny and restoring McGarrity to his seat. McGarrity had gone to Bolivia but returned to New York within months, full of plans for development in South America. When these met with no response from his associates he went to Ireland and there became friendly with Russell.

McGarrity's visit helped to create further dissension within the movement. On what might be called the 'physical force wing' there were two plans for action. One was Tom Barry's scheme for seizing a northern town, as the Dublin post office was seized in 1916, holding out for as long as possible and then falling back on the border at, say, Armagh, to rouse the people behind them. The scheme, known as the 'Barry Plan', was widely discussed but never became official army policy.

Unfortunately Russell's plan did. McGarrity had a friend approach a young German chemist in Cleveland who was an expert on explosives, and after talking to the chemist, became convinced that small, easily concealed and easily disposed of explosives with a high destructive content if let off in busy English cities would be the best method of freeing 'occupied Ireland'. Russell had seen too much of civil war in Ireland to want to embroil North against South on the lines of the Barry Plan and, moreover, he did not want to destroy Irish property or to take Irish lives if he could help it. To Russell, as Britain was, in his view, maintaining partition, Britain was the logical place to carry on the war.

The scheme was of course impracticable with the weakened I.R.A. and its position following the governmental crack-down, but it was the very weakness of the I.R.A. which enabled Russell to come to the top. The Blueshirt I.R.A. struggle took itself off to Spain at the end of 1936. Frank Ryan left from Dun Laoghaire (a borough of Dublin) on November 11 with a group of Republican Congress supporters, notably Frank Edwards and Christie Walsh, and O'Duffy's men began setting off two days later from Dublin. For the I.R.A. this meant a renewal of internal controversy as MacBride, Fitzpatrick and MacLogan tried to persuade their followers from going after Ryan, who was appealing to both socialist inclinations and the desire for 'action'. Russell was offering a possibility of 'action' nearer home and against a more familiar enemy than the forces in Spain. Moreover McGarrity continued to lend him moral and financial support. Probably as much as 80 per cent of the money required for the campaign was supplied by him and he grew more determined in his support as de Valera took an increasingly stiff line with the I.R.A.

In McGarrity's diary for August, 1936, are references to meetings with Russell, by then quartermaster-general of the I.R.A.; to Maurice Twomey's arrest by de Valera's 'Free State' police; to Micksey Conway's being charged with murder, and to reports of 'brutalities' against I.R.A. prisoners. He describes with sadness the sentences meted out to I.R.A. men who came from Republican families prominent in the time of the Anglo-Irish struggle. (Sean McSwiney, a brother of Terence McSwiney who died on hunger strike, and Sean Og MacCurtain, a son of the murdered mayor of Cork, were at that time before the Military Tribunal.) After noting that in the North the Craigavon government was also cracking down on the I.R.A. McGarrity writes, 'Craigavon and de Valera at least agree on one thing and that is that all those known to be Republicans must be jailed or hanged.' McGarrity was unimpressed with de Valera's constitutional attempts to give the Free State a more Republican appearance. These included removing the governor general, on December 11, 1936: enacting a new constitution by referendum on June 1, 1937, abolishing the senate's power of veto and altering its nature in an attempt to give it a 'vocational' character—which failed as the electoral colleges which put forward the senatorial nominees do so on party lines; and changing the name of the state from the Irish Free State to Ireland, or, in Irish, Eire. The changes were of course internal to the twenty-six county State and had no effect on partition.

In the midst of these changes de Valera set up a cabinet comimittee, on December 15, 1936, to make recommendations concerning the release of prisoners sentenced by the Military Tribunal. On the day this committee was announced an I.R.A. convention in Dublin, meeting not altogether in secret as police records of the time show, proposed that battalion commanders be given greater powers to deal with 'deserters' and those showing hostility to the I.R.A. This was the sort of thing which caused young Egan's death, for which Micksey Conway had been sentenced, but despite this Conway was one of those whom the Dail committee freed.

The case of the young Limerick man, Sean Glynn, who committed suicide in Arbour Hill prison after the proscribing of the Bodenstown procession affected McGarrity powerfully. He describes the I.R.A. prisoners being 'so unmercifully treated in prison that young Glynn was found hanging dead in a cell in Arbour Hill Prison, Dublin . . . This was the last straw for me. I had already spoken at a public meeting of the Clann in the Town Hall, New York, in protest at the jailings and prison tortures.' He went on to note that he had given an interview to the *Philadelphia Ledger* protesting the 'Free State Government policy and that of the Craig Government'.

Although he was still in touch with de Valera and growing increasingly friendly with Russell, McGarrity laboured under the old American difficulty of being out of touch. He was surprised to find that Sean Russell had had an interview with de Valera, in April, 1935, to talk over the possibilities of 'cooperation', as McGarrity termed it, between the I.R.A. and de Valera. De Valera's version of this 'cooperation' was that Russell and the I.R.A. would turn in their arms and disband. According to McGarrity's diary, Russell reminded de Valera of his statement after the Civil War about Republicans hiding arms and munitions—not to part with them 'until the country was independent'. This Russell said the I.R.A. was willing to do. According to the diary: 'Russell asked, or rather promised co-operation with the Fianna Fail party in every way for a period of five years from that date if Dev would promise to declare a Republic for all Ireland at the end of the final year period. Dev refused to agree to that saying "You want it both ways".'

McGarrity notes that he had been in Dublin during December, 1935 and on a visit to de Valera's house had a long talk about changes de Valera was proposing in the Free State constitution. But he had not been aware that de Valera had been in contact with the I.R.A. McGarrity wrote that 'Russell believes Dev has taken orders from Anthony Eden to suppress the I.R.A. in anticipation of some promised concession being fulfilled by England; there is no proof of this.'

An entry in the McGarrity diary for October 31, 1936 gives evidence of his naïvety in Irish affairs. He had arranged to send J. O'Hara Harte of the Society of Friends to Ireland to seek peace between the I.R.A. and the Free State Government, and the I.R.A. and the Craig regime in the six counties. McGarrity wrote: 'Have arranged a plan. $1,000 already provided for expense of the mission, balance of 1,000 will be ready by the time the mission is ready to sail—God grant it success.' McGarrity adds, 'de Valera has according to reports published his long looked for constitution for his Free State. Not a word about United and Independent Ireland, Six Counties forgotten—shame on Dev and his party.'

O'Hara Harte sailed from New York for Ireland on November 18, and a month later a baffled O'Hara Harte sent a cable from London recounting his interview with de Valera. He had told de Valera that the I.R.A. had signed a statement that they were willing to negotiate outstanding differences. Harte was amazed, McGarrity wrote, when the president said, 'he would not enter into any negotiations. Not only would he not meet the I.R.A. as a body or as individual persons but he would not accept my service as a mediator.'

So, mad though the British bombing campaign may seem to us, it must have appeared logical to men in Ireland in 1936 who thought it possible that de Valera, Craigavon and the I.R.A. (illegal on both sides of the border) should sit down together to arrange for the unification of the country under the chairmanship of an unknown Irish-American Quaker.

In America Russell first publicly announced his plan in early August, 1936, to a handful of Clann supporters. In an interview, with the *Daily Mirror* on August 14, Russell made a number of amazing claims:

You know, of course, that de Valera has betrayed the trust of the Irish nation by becoming the tool of Great Britain.

Instead of fighting, as he promised, for the Republic of Ireland, he has been content to allow her to be a nation subject to a foreign King.

Republican forces are awaiting an opportune moment to fight with all their might for the nation's freedom.

When the moment will come I do not know. It may come when the British become embroiled in a European conflict. But our plan of campaign is ready.

As de Valera knows only too well, we have splendid military forces in Ireland, with cleverly hidden arsenals.

Then, over in England, where we shall also take the offensive, we have another secret army of Irishmen, who meet quietly, for drill and target practice.

We have also quantities of ammunition and other war material in England.

Our Air Force may be small, but it is reasonably efficient.

When hostilities start we shall certainly send planes to bomb England.

It is a very definite plan in our scheme for an offensive.

Admiral Somerville was recruiting for the British Navy, and we won't tolerate a foreign Power recruiting for its navy or army.

I plainly warn the British people not to interfere with Ireland.

Russell's statement was pure propaganda. (There was a scheme in New York Clann na Gael circles at the time to fly an aeroplane across the Atlantic, bomb the British House of Commons, and then crash land on the coast of France, because there would not be enough petrol left to recross the Atlantic. There was not the slightest hope of laying hands on such an aeroplane, and the scheme never got beyond the level of discussion.) It is doubtful if Russell even had any title to make propaganda for the I.R.A. at home. Tom Barry wanted to have Russell court-martialled over the loss of two Thompson machine guns. He had no faith in Russell's plans nor had Sean MacBride who took particular exception to his involvement with the O'Hara Harte mission. But Russell directed his appeal at the younger men and with their help carried the day.

Some time during March, 1938, the die was cast at a meeting in Dublin. (Eoin MacNamee, a principal spokesman on Russell's behalf, Michael Fitzpatrick, then chief of staff and who presided at the meeting, and Sean O'Broin who stood guard at the door taking credentials were unable to tell me the exact date and place of the meeting.) Earlier on the morning of the meeting an unofficial convention was held in the home of Mairtin O'Cadain to plan strategy. MacNamee went to this meeting with the names of twelve Russell supporters from whom an Executive was to be picked.

These were, Jack McNeela, Tony D'Arcy (both of whom were to die on hunger strike), Victor Fagg, who, interestingly enough, was a Protestant from Westmeath, Charlie Dolan, John Tully, Jimmie Traynor, John James Kelly, George Plunkett, Ted Moore, Ned Kerrigan, Johnny O'Connor and Larry Grogan. Grogan was one of those who later signed the declaration of war on England, served on Lord Halifax. MacNamee also had a letter from Russell explaining his position. This was read by Maurice Twomey. The convention was a tense affair, run on military lines, each man giving his name and rank to Sean O'Broin who called it out from the entrance while the applicant stood to attention before being admitted.

The anti-Russell section was armed—one of the few times at which arms were carried at an army convention. Joseph McGarrity was present although he was a member of the Clann, not of the I.R.A. Russell himself was not present. In his opponents' view he was no longer in the I.R.A. through his refusal to take direction from the then executive. Barry proposed that as there were sufficient arms in Dublin to arm the Dublin brigade the I.R.A. should march on the North that very night, but the Russell scheme was carried at the end of an all-night sitting. Russell sensed the difficulties that had arisen and felt they should strike a blow at the earliest moment.

The fatal result was that the bombing party chosen to go to England was only half-trained in the use of explosives and hence some of the fatalities to the bombers and to innocent English bystanders. The destruction of property was all Russell aimed at, but badly made bombs in inexperienced hands went off at the wrong times with disastrous results. Russell possibly thought that more efficient explosives would be coming from America. MacNamee remembers passing Park Lane Hotel with him one afternoon and being asked by Russell, 'would he like to be able to blow that up with a pen?' MacNamee said, 'Certainly, but how?', pointing out that it was made of reinforced concrete. Russell smiled and went on to impress MacNamee with the sort of advanced methods of warfare to be placed at their disposal. (These were apparently pen bombs, mentioned to me by members of Clann na Gael as being talked about in America during the 1930s but they either proved impractical or could not be got out of the country for they never figured in the campaign.)

The campaign was appallingly ill-conceived. MacNamee told me that there was, as far as he was aware, only one Thompson gun and possibly six revolvers doing the rounds of the London units of the I.R.A. at the time. There was an Irish Republican Defence Committee, an open organisation which raised funds and carried out propaganda and Cumann na mBan, the women's auxiliary group which did somewhat similar work, but in terms of military power the I.R.A. scarcely functioned. In August, 1937, MacNamee, intelligence officer of the London battalion, returned to Ireland for a holiday and learned of the projected bombing campaign and of the differences concerning its merits. MacNamee, a Co. Tyrone man, supported the idea because he understood that it was to be accompanied by an attack on the North.

At the time, apart from its military weaknesses, the London I.R.A. was split into various factions. Jack Lynch, the officer commanding Britain, was arrested during MacNamee's visit to Ireland and Jimmy Joe Reynolds was appointed in his place. Reynolds, later to be blown up in a faulty mine explosion at Clady, Co. Donegal, made one of his first steps on being appointed O.C. the dismissal of all the battalion staff. The result was that officers from G.H.Q. in Dublin came over to set up the inevitable courts of inquiries. The row, a foolish affair involving Cumann na mBan women's gossip, was patched up and on MacNamee's recommendation London in 1938 was split into various companies with defined spheres of influence. During this period prominent Dublin I.R.A. officers such as Seamus Malin, Mairtin O'Cadain, Maurice Twomey and Thomas MacCurtain spoke in London.

From October on groups of handpicked I.R.A. men were brought back from England to be trained in Dublin and to return and spread their knowledge. The classes consisted largely of instruction in bomb-making and were held mainly in a hall known as The Green Lounge in St Stephen's Green. Other venues were also used around Dublin, one of the most important being Killiney Castle in Killiney. (Today in the summer amiable English tourists visit it unaware of the castle's history. Occasionally the words 'Up the I.R.A.' appear in large whitewash letters on the gates but these are speedily obliterated before they arouse any questions among the English visitors. In the 1938–49 period the castle was owned by a Dublin civil servant who was violently anti-British and, when the castle was commandeered on the outbreak of the Second World War by the military for use as a billet, he used to emerge from the basement which he retained for his own use, to run up the tricolour on the flag pole whenever a German victory was announced!)

The principal instructors in bomb-making were Patrick McGrath, who was later executed for the shooting of a policeman in Dublin, and Jim O'Donovan, Russell's former colleague in the war against the British. O'Donovan had come out of retirement at Russell's request to train a new generation of young Irishmen, a decision which was to cause him considerable loss. He was a member of a semi-state body, the Electricity Supply Board, in a comfortable position at the time and when the campaign misfired he lost his job and spent the war years interned in the Curragh. It was O'Donovan who drew up the 'S-plan', the official blue-print for the campaign, which called for the destruction of obvious military targets such as communications centres, B.B.C. transmitters, aerodromes, bridges and military installations.

Twelve handpicked volunteers crossed over to England during Christmas week 1938 and went to five centres: Walsh and O'Kennedy to Glasgow; Eoin MacNamee, Charlie Casey and S. McGuinness to London; Rory Campbell and Patrick Fleming to Manchester; Joe Deighan, G. Quigley, and M. Cleary to Liverpool; and Jackie Kearns and J. Fuller to Birmingham.

On December 8 Russell announced an event that he hoped would give respectability and authority to the campaign. This was the taking over by the I.R.A. of the authority of the 'Government of the Republic of Ireland' from the 'Executive Council of Dáil Eireann'. This meant that those who had recognised the second Dail as the *de jure* government of Ireland now recognised the Army Council (and Sean Russell as its head) as the legitimate rulers of Ireland. The announcement was printed on page one of the *Wolfe Tone Weekly*.

The people of Ireland were largely unaware of this transfer, but after it Russell could claim, as de Valera had said, that the authority of the Dail lay outside that assembly, that he now had this authority for his actions. Yet on the day the notice was published, an abortive effort was made, without his authority, to blow up the Nelson Pillar. Peadar O'Flaherty, believed to be Russell's right-hand man, planned the explosion for a Saturday evening, when the street would normally be full of people. To avoid fatalities, he planned to set the explosives, withdraw and notify the police, giving them time to cordon off the area. Joseph Deighan told me that he and the other members of the group actually walked down through O'Connell Street (from An Stad in Upper Frederick Street where most I.R.A. men stayed) with wads of gelignite on them, liable to be blown up at any moment by a jostling passer-by, but quite prepared to carry out the task. Arriving at the pillar they found that O'Flaherty had forgotten that it closed earlier on Saturdays in winter. When Russell heard of this harebrained scheme, he was furious and sacked O'Flaherty on the spot, but his control of the organisation was so loose that he could not prevent O'Flaherty signing the declaration of war on England which the I.R.A. issued a month later.

When the chosen twelve arrived in England they found organisation so lax that they had great difficulty in finding dumps for the explosives. Russell had excellent contacts in the customs service and in shipping circles and he managed to get the stuff into England. But once there it was no easy matter for young Irishmen living in 'digs' to find dumps for hundredweights of potassium chloride, sulphuric acid and iron oxide. Some willing friends who stored material knowing nothing about the campaign itself or what they were storing found their business gone, their families broken up and themselves behind prison bars after the campaign began and Scotland Yard began to round up suspects. One man who stored some stuff for Eoin MacNamee knew so little about him that he told the police that his name was McKenna. When the bombs started to go off he realised the position and in his desperation dug holes in the garden and covered them in. However, the police raided him before he had properly obliterated all traces and he got seven years hard labour.

A fact which cannot be too strongly stressed is the innocence, or if one wishes the ignorance, of the volunteers with whom the 'operations officers' in the various cities worked. Most were young men who, having left school around the age of twelve, emigrated to labouring jobs and had not the slightest resentment against England.

Paddy McNeela was a typical recruit. His brother Jack was to die on hunger strike and was at the time the principal I.R.A. officer in England. Paddy came from Ballycroy, Co. Mayo, where his memories were of the fiddler coming into the village, playing in one or two houses for a fortnight and taking up a collection at the end of the week, maybe getting thirty shillings in twopences for his work. Some overriding laws governed upbringing in Paddy's day. The Rosary was said every night; Mass was attended in all weathers though it meant a four-mile walk. At Christmas the average stipend to a priest was ten shillings, almost a week's wages. A wedding cost perhaps thirty or forty pounds but it was one great day out in everyone's lives and the money had to be found. The priest's authority was near absolute.* Paddy remembers a parish priest going to a house and burning what he called 'bad books'. In nearby Spiddal a cross was erected to poteen stills which were publicly burned by the famous Redemptorist priest, Father Conneally. Sermons were of the order 'two men will die in this parish' if mixed dancing or poteen drinking were not given up immediately. Growing up, Paddy and his companions firmly believed that the priest could, if he wished, 'put horns on you'.

Understandably, coming from this background, Paddy was far from mechanically minded. He remembers one drill session at which a hand grenade was thrown and failed to explode. Another young man picked it up, tested it with his teeth and said, 'Hm, it's alright, it should have gone off.' They tossed it around for some moments until their horrified instructor took it from them and threw it away, whereupon it duly exploded. When Paddy emigrated to England he was completely lost in London, but in a village in one of the Home Counties he found a life more like the one he had left and got on famously with the people. He remembers he found them very backward and simple.

'They'd listen to everything I'd tell them and take it in, jokes and all.'

When he was asked to take part in the bombing campaign, he no more associated those simple villagers with going to war for the Republic and the end of partition, than he claimed to have any knowledge of the rights or wrongs of the issues involved.

---

* A 'station' in Kerry was the following anecdote to the nation. A 'station' consists of Mass and communion followed by a large breakfast in a house, not a church. The custom, which dates from the penal days, is now dying out in Ireland except in the more remote areas, but at Paddy's time it flourished. A priest, who arrived at the house on a fine hunter, placed his umbrella in the kitchen, still open as he wished to dry it. Two of the menfolk of the place, not having seen him arrive were trying unsuccessfully to push it out the narrow doorway when the priest returned for it. They watched in amazement as he folded it with a flick of his thumb, and then Pat turned to Mick as the priest galloped off and said, 'Dey has de Power. Didn't I tell you dey has de Power?'

Paddy was lucky enough to escape detection but a more experienced colleague, J. F. Reegan from Cork, back from the Spanish Civil War and its hardship (the common diet was a few drops of olive oil in water, and a handful of grapes; with bread, meat, milk or coffee almost unknown) crossed to England and was captured, probably through an informer, and sentenced to twelve years' hard labour.

A leading contemporary Irish journalist, then just a homesick boy from Derry, was recruited when he went into Mooneys in the Strand in London where he hoped to pick up some Irish company. A man he knew slightly from his boyhood came up to him at the bar and spoke. Learning that the bombing campaign was being planned, he offered his services, was enrolled and began mixing 'Paxo', as the explosive was known, in his landlady's saucepans. The National Gallery in Trafalgar Square was to be his first target but his superior officer, a plumber, decided that there were too many tiles in it and that it wouldn't burn. Meanwhile his landlady, discovering the white substance, very sensibly flushed it down the lavatory.

MacNamee, who lived in Roseken Road, Fulham, used to test balloons in his fireplace, timing how long it would take for the acid to eat through the rubber and ignite the iron oxide. Once he went out while waiting for the acid to take affect, and came back to find that the landlady had cleared out the fireplace, balloons, iron oxide and all. She warned him that two yardsmen in a local scrapdealing business, whom he had prosecuted for stealing his bicycle, knew him to be an I.R.A. man and were going to get him locked up. MacNamee immediately quit the digs. The police called to pick him up that night.

Michael McInerney, former political correspondent of the *Irish Times,* disposed of some half ton of explosives down his landlady's lavatory after he learned what his Irish friends intended to do with the stuff that they had asked him to store.

Not all landladies were sympathetic although most of the young I.R.A. men of course stayed with established Republicans who had been in Britain for some years which, however, made it easy for the police to pick them up. Then the I.R.A. habit of keeping documents, writing out receipts, and leaving incriminating evidence lying around terminated many a promising arsonist's career. There was also the problem of accents. A group of young I.R.A. men from west Cork or Mayo going into a shop for an alarm clock, to be used as a timing device for a bomb, would give a cheery greeting to the assistant such as, 'Tell us, daughter, would ye be after havin' a few alarm clocks there?' They would be told, 'Certainly sir, do you mind waiting for a moment?' and would obligingly stay on the premises while the assistant went to telephone Scotland Yard.

Nevertheless some of the operation officers in the campaign did show considerable expertise in eluding the police. Joe Deighan told me that even though he was well-known in Liverpool as an I.R.A. suspect at least, if not something more active, and was continually shadowed, he was nevertheless able to set off a number of successful detonations—carrying his bombs in what looked like a lunch box on his knee in crowded public transport! (Public transport was frequently used by the I.R.A. Where a taxi driver might remember one fare, a bus conductor would not. It is a miracle that this did not lead to some really ghastly accidents. A jolting tram or bus is not the best conveyance for gelignite.)

It should also be pointed out that had the I.R.A. made more use of women it might have done better because women were less likely to be seized by the police. I met one lady who had emptied several cinemas on different occasions by letting off tear-gas bombs. She could have easily destroyed substantial installations.

The bombing campaign began formally on January 12, 1939, with an ultimatum to the British prime minister, the government in Northern Ireland, the British foreign secretary, Hitler, Musolini, and anyone else when the I.R.A. thought would be moved by such a document. It said:

I have the honour to inform you that the Government of the Irish Republic, having as its first duty towards the people the establishment and maintenance of peace and order, herewith demand the withdrawal of all British armed forces stationed in Ireland. These forces are an active incitement to turmoil and civil strife not only in being a symbol of hostile occupation but in their effect and potentialities as an invading army.

It is secondly the duty of the Government to establish relations of friendship between the Irish and all other people We must insist on the withdrawal of British troops from our country and a declaration from your Government renouncing all claims to interfere in our domestic policy.

The letter declared that neither the government of the Irish Republic nor the Irish people were actuated by any feelings of hostility towards England but warned:

We shall regret if this fundamental feeling is ignored and we are compelled to intervene activity in the military and commercial life of your country as your Government are now intervening in ours.

The Government of the Irish Republic believe that a period of four days is sufficient for your Government to signify its intention in the matter of the military evacuation and for the issue of your declaration of abdication in respect of our country. Our Government reserve the right of appropriate action without further notice if on the expiration of the period of grace these conditions remain unfulfilled.

(Signed) Patrick Fleming

Four days later on finding that neither the British nor the Orangemen seemed disposed to meet its wishes the I.R.A. issued another declaration. It was written by McGarrity* and said:

On the twenty-third day of April in the year 1916 in the city of Dublin, seven men, who were representative in spirit and outlook and purpose of the Irish nation that had never yielded to nor accepted the British conquest, set their humble and almost unknown names to the foregoing document that has passed into history, making the names of the seven signatories immortal.

Those signatures were sealed with the blood of the immortal seven, and of many others who followed them into one of the most gallant fights in the history of the world; and the Irish nation rose from shame to honour, from humiliation to pride, from slavery to freedom.

Three years later (on January 21, 1919), the Republic proclaimed in Easter week 1916 was ratified and formally established by the elected representatives of all Ireland and a solemn declaration of independence sent out to the nations of the world.

To combat that declaration and to prevent the proclamation of the Republic of Ireland from becoming effective, the Armed Forces of the English enemy made war upon the people of this country. They were met by the Irish Republican Army, and challenged and resisted so stubbornly that after five years of bloody warfare the English were forced to ask for a truce with a view to settlement by negotiation.

* McGarrity died in the 1940s but I.R.A. documents were still signed with his name as late as the 1970s, showing the continuation of his influence.

Unfortunately, because men were foolish enough to treat with an armed enemy within their gates, the English won the peace. Weakness and treachery caused a resumption of the war and the old English tactics of "Divide and Conquer' were exploited to the fullest extent. Partition was introduced, the country divided into two parts with two separate parliaments subject to and controlled by the British Government from London. The Armed Forces of England still occupy six of our counties in the North and reserve the right "in time of war or strained relations" to re-occupy the ports which they have just evacuated in the Southern part of Ireland. Ireland is still tied, as she has been for centuries past, to take part in England's wars. In the Six Counties, a large number of Republican soldiers are held prisoners by England. Further weakness on the part of some of our people, broken faith and make believe have postponed the enthronement of the living Republic, but the proclamation of Easter week and the Declaration of Independence stand and must stand forever. No man, no matter how far he has fallen away from his national faith, has dared to repudiate them. They constitute the rallying centre for the unsought manhood of Ireland in the fight that must be made to make them effective and to redeem the nation's self-respect that was abandoned by a section of our people in 1922.

The time has come to make that fight. There is no need to re-declare the Republic of Ireland, now or in the future. There is no need to re-redeclare the Declaration of Irish Independence. But the hour has come for the supreme effort to make both effective. So in the name of the unconquered dead and of the faithful living, we pledge ourselves to that task.

We call upon England to withdraw her armed forces, her civilian officials and institutions, and representatives of all kinds from every part of Ireland, as an essential preliminary to arrangements for peace and friendship between the two countries; and we call upon the people of all Ireland, at home and in exile, to assist us in the effort we are about to make in God's name, to compel that evacuation and to enthrone the Republic of Ireland.

> Signed on behalf of
> The Republican Government and the Army
> Council of Oglaigh na hEireann
> (Irish Republican Army)

Stephen Hayes	Patrick Fleming
Peadar O'Flaherty	George Plunkett
Laurence Grogan	Sean Russell

The ultimatum had been greeted with derision or disbelief, but the declaration of war was followed by explosions one of which immediately showed the futility of Russell's aim of conducting such a campaign without losing any life. A twenty-seven-year-old fish porter, Albert Ross, was killed on his way to work in Manchester when a bomb went off in a street main.

In London there were three explosions at electricity plants and throughout the north and the midlands other power units, gas and electricity mains, were damaged. On July 26 a young Scotsman, standing in the left-luggage office at King's Cross station, was killed in an explosion that severely injured his wife and fourteen other people.

On Friday August 25 the worst incident of all occurred. Five people were killed, including an old man of eighty-one, and a schoolboy of fifteen, twelve very badly injured and forty more less seriously hurt in an explosion at 2.30 p.m. in the thoroughfare Broadgate in Coventry. Two I.R.A. men were executed for this, one of them, Peter Barnes, being at least morally innocent. He had been involved in buying flour bags for the mixing and carrying of explosives (though he didn't know where these were to go off). The man who actually cycled into the street with a bomb in the carrier and parked the bicycle outside Astky's Shop, was a psycopath, who later received extensive treatment.

During the next fifteen months bombs went off in letter boxes, lavatories, telephone boxes, railway cloakrooms, cinemas, post offices and business premises of all sorts. Sometimes cinemas were emptied by tear gas.

Curiously enough it was the Irish government that first passed laws directed at the I.R.A. The British had of course been rounding up I.R.A. agents by the score but it was in Dublin that the Offences against the State Act was passed on June 14, setting up military tribunals (special criminal courts composed of army officers) and stating:

Every person who usurps or unlawfully exercises any function of Government whether by setting up, maintaining or taking part in any way in a body of persons purporting to be a Government or by any other action or conduct whatsoever shall be guilty of felony and shall be liable in a conviction thereof to suffer penal servitude for a term not exceeding ten years or to imprisonment for a term not exceeding two years.

The act also gave the government power to issue a suppression order against anybody who 'raises or maintains a military or armed force'. The following day the I.R.A. was declared an unlawful organisation and police and military clashed with the Republicans in a riot when the I.R.A. tried to make the annual pilgrimage to Bodenstown. Incredibly enough, in London after several explosions the previous day, some two hundred Irishmen marched through the centre of the city in honour of Wolfe Tone, carrying banners demanding the release of I.R.A. prisoners in the custody of Scotland Yard—their procession guarded by British police.

This tolerance wore thin. On July 24 when Home Secretary Sir Samuel Hoare introduced the Prevention of Violence (Temporary Provisions) Bill in the House of Commons, he told the House that sixty-six members of the I.R.A. had been convicted, and that 1,500 sticks of gelignite, 1,000 detenators, tons of potassium chlorate, a quantity of ferrous oxide, seven gallons of sulphuric acid, and four hundredweight of aluminium powder had been seized. By then there had been 127 terrorist attacks, fifty-seven in London.

Sir Samuel said the government had been informed that the I.R.A. campaign was 'being closely watched and actively stimulated by foreign organisations'. With the darkening face of Europe the House was not disposed to question whether the foreign organisations meant Clann na Gael or Nazis. Four days later the bill became law. It gave the Home Secretary powers to issue expulsion orders against suspected persons living in England and to issue prohibition orders against suspects wishing to enter the country. In emergencies, search warrants were to be issued by police officers not below the rank of superintendent and the police could arrest and detain suspects for five days without warrants. There might have been some opposition to these drastic provisions for Arthur Greenwood, the Labour M.P., said that while the opposition recognised the need for stronger powers, it regretted that the government should have quite so much authority. But on July 26 further explosions occurred at the left-luggage offices at King's Cross and Victoria stations. At King's Cross the Scottish doctor, Dr Campbell, lost both his legs in the explosion.

Speaking in the Seanad on the same day de Valera said, 'No one can have any doubt as to the result of the campaign in England, and no one can think that this government has any sympathy with it.' He appealed to those carrying on the campaign, asking them how they could hope to reach a decision by these means. He believed that a number of them were animated by high ideals, but that they were misreading Irish history and making no allowance for changed circumstances.

Although the horror of Coventry had not yet come there was by then no hope of the I.R.A.'s 'having a decision' from the campaign. Failure and disorganisation had done their work. Thus, after his near escape in London Eoin MacNamee had gone to the Leamington Spa and Stratford areas. With only a bicycle he could transport very little explosive and he asked for a car, but there was no money to spare. During mid-Lent in Coventry, MacNamee was told to report to G.H.Q. in Dublin. Here he found Sean Fuller, one of the Birmingham operations officers, who said that opinion within the movement was now swinging against Russell. Mairin O'Cadain, in whose house the plot to install Russell was given its final polish, was by now very anti-Russell. Nor was there any sign of the promised campaign against the North. This depressed MacNamee, now that most of his friends in London were captured.

He attended a meeting of G.H.Q. staff with Larry Grogan, Stephen Hayes, Micksey Conway, Sean Russell, Michael Traynor and Sean Fuller. Russell, depressed and waspish, asked MacNamee what he was doing there and wanted to know why he had not told the people in London where the dumps were. Confusion on the whereabouts of the explosives had led to MacNamee's recall to Dublin. He explained that he had told I.R.A. officers in authority where the dumps were, but that these men were now all behind bars, and that in any case he would always restrict the spread of such knowledge because he believed in secrecy. To which Russell replied, rather oddly for a conspirator, 'you're trying to create an air of mystery'.

· Russell next criticised Fuller's handling of operations, and Fuller, as chagrined as MacNamee, did not return to the campaign. He dropped out of the I.R.A. after his arrest later in a round-up by the Irish police. MacNamee went back to England with Michael Traynor via Rosslare. Keeping apart on the boat, they separated on docking to give MacNamee an opportunity of checking on the ammunition dumps.

When MacNamee met Leo Duigan, now officer commanding London, he found most of the 'stuff' had been disposed of. Checking a yard owned by a Jack Healy he learned that the explosive materials had been seized by Scotland Yard, and that Healy had been given ten years' penal servitude at the Central Criminal Court. Meeting his contact with Russell at Regent's Park he told him what had happened and advised against any intensification of the campaign because during that month (March) the cases of captured I.R.A. men were being heard at the Old Bailey and he felt it would prejudice them to have any further bombings for the time being. The contact disregarded this and said that continuation of the campaign would show the I.R.A. meant business. MacNamee knew how some of the prisoners were being treated and asked Russell to see that at least their dependents were cared for as cases of near starvation occurred when bread-winners were suddenly hurled into jail for storing a sack of white powder in a closet.

Ill-treatment of I.R.A. men in jail was by no means infrequent. Sometimes it occurred through the defiant attitude of the prisoner. Sometimes an episode such as the Coventry explosion prejudiced warders and police against the I.R A. One big row in Dartmoor broke out after the Coventry explosion and eleven I.R.A.

men were so badly beaten up that they had to be treated in hospital. After this, the I.R.A. prisoners in Dartmoor had to drill and work separately from the other prisoners. However, neither MacNamee's counselling, nor that of like-minded members of the movement had any effect.

When MacNamee returned to Dublin after checking on the dumps in London, he found that Russell, though depressed, had no intention of calling off the campaign. In fact he set out for America on April 8, shortly after receiving MacNamee's report, to publicise the campaign there and raise funds for it. But though he attracted enormous publicity in America, by the end of 1939 the campaign was dead. Only about a dozen incidents occurred in 1940, the last recorded one being in March when an unexploded bomb was found in a litter bin at Grosvenor Place. Another bomb that was not found went off at Westminster City Council refuse depot after the bin had been tipped into the heap. The most serious explosion of 1940, on February 22, was in a bus litter bin in Oxford Street, which seriously injured seven people. This can be seen as a kind of futile postscript to the hanging of Barnes and Frank Richards (alias McCormick) on February 7 for their part in the Coventry explosion.

This hanging aroused a wave of bitterness against England in Ireland. Emotional scenes recalled the height of the 'troubles' and every public body and the legislature itself pleaded for clemency for the condemned men. They have since passed into an only slightly lesser place in the martyrology of Ireland as have Dunne and Sullivan, the men who shot Sir Henry Wilson.

In English law, both Barnes and McCormick were guilty under the rule of 'Common Purpose' whereby if two or more persons agree to commit a dangerous felony, resulting in a death, all the persons in the combination or conspiracy are guilty of murder. Before being sentenced Richards said to the judge, 'My Lord, before you pass sentence of death, I wish to thank sincerely the gentlemen who have defended me during my trial and I wish to state that the part I took in these explosions since I came to England I have done for a just cause. As a soldier of the Irish Republican Army I am not afraid to die, as I am doing it for a just cause. I say in conclusion, God bless Ireland and God bless the men who have fought and died for it. Thank you, my lord.' Barnes said, 'I would like to say as I am going before my God, as I am condemned to death, I am innocent, and later I am sure it will all come out that I had neither hand, act, nor part in it. That is all I have to say.'

By English law Barnes's possession of a receipt for a flour bag and suitcases used in the incident, and a letter to a friend in the Republican movement in Dublin, made him an accessory. So far as intent to kill or complicity in the actual deed is concerned, Peter Barnes was innocent. Barnes was not in Coventry while the bomb was being prepared, and not there when it went off. The tragedy of Peter Barnes typifies the tragedy of all the confused, well-meaning, idealistic, uneducated young men who joined the I.R.A. without realising what they were letting themselves in for.

At thirty-two he gave up his job with Offaly County Council and went to an industrial England in 1939, while England was on the verge of a war with Germany, to free his country of 'British domination'. He probably never visited the North in his life, and had no inkling of the complexity of the Protestant-Catholic relationships. He paid for his idealism with his life on an English scaffold.

6

Years of Disaster

In Ireland the effect of the bombing campaign on the I.R.A. and on public opinion was to make a bad situation worse. The Offences Against the State Act, which allowed for imprisonment and detention without trial, became law on June 14, 1939. A few days later the I.R.A. was declared an unlawful organisation and the Bodenstown march was proscribed. The army was called out and the I.R.A. made no effort to defy the ban. Then on August 22 the special military court* for which the Offences Against the State Act allowed was proclaimed and from then until the end of the war the operation of the court was to cast a gloomy shadow over the I.R.A.

The international situation resulted in a declaration of emergency on September 2, whereby the government, both Dail and Seanad, resolved 'that arising out of the armed conflict now taking place in Europe, a national emergency exists affecting the vital interests of the State'. The Emergency Powers Bill was enacted the following day. From then on the government had control of supplies, tillage, transport, censorship, military matters and, of course, all measures to be taken against the I.R.A. To emphasise this hard line Gerald Boland became Minister for Justice on September 8.

The government also reorganised the Special Branch, although it was hardly the instrument upon which a government might depend for its internal security during wartime. The reorganised branch was headed by Chief-Superintendent Patrick Carroll, Chief-Superintendent Sean Gantly and Chief-Superintendent Michael Weymes. Its most colourful member, one Michael Gill a sergeant, at the outbreak of the war, was speedily promoted to chief-superintendent, through his talent for catching I.R.A. members. More than any other figure of the war, he was regarded as Nemesis by the I.R.A. and was feared and hated.

On the military side, the Director of Military Intelligence at the outbreak of the war was Colonel Liam Archer. He was succeeded by Colonel Dan Bryan with a formidable team, Lieutenant Colonel Joe Guilfoyle and Major Florrie O'Donoghue (who had both gained experience against the British under Collins) and Dr Richard Hayes, who later became director of the National Library. He was a cipher expert who trained himself to master every German code.

Junior officers who served under these men all later distinguished themselves in civilian life. Norman Hewitt became a top travel agent, Con McGovern an airline manager for an American company, and Douglas Gageby, one of Ireland's best journalists, founded the *Evening Press* and later became editor of the *Irish*

---

* The court's members were Colonel Bennett, Colonel McKenna, Major Joyce, Major Whelan, Major Tuite.

Times. This team, with more experience, education, energy and resources than the I.R.A. soon proved itself more than a match for both the I.R.A. and the spies whom the Nazis sent to Ireland. (They were sent, in part, to take advantage of the existence of the I.R.A.) The poor resources of the I.R.A. had been demonstrated the previous year when in November at Clady, Co. Tyrone, three I.R.A. men were killed when a faulty mine went off.

The three were James Joseph 'Jimmy Joe' Reynolds, one of the six men charged with the murder of Roderick More O'Farrell in Longford in 1935 (he was acquitted after the second trial) and also one of the prime movers in the British bombing campaign, John J. Kelly from Donegal, and Charlie McCaffrey from Tyrone. They had been making a mine to destroy some customs posts along the border. Blowing up customs huts had always been a favourite I.R.A. tactic and a number had gone up in 1937 in protest against a visit by King George VI and Queen Elizabeth. (This gave rise to the I.R.A. ballad 'A Bonfire on the Border'.) The 1938 explosions were intended to start Russell's northern campaign, to reproduce in Ireland the kind of onslaught made in England.

Tarlach O'hUid, who visited Charlie McCaffrey in hospital where he lingered for two days before dying of his injuries, remembers that McCaffrey, who never fully recovered consciousness, kept repeating over and over again, 'Stand back John Joe there's a wee thing wrong.' Clearly the bomb was inexpertly made. Children sleeping in the house where it was made had to be dug out from the debris, mercifully unhurt. Patrick Kelly, a brother of the dead man who was not in the I.R.A., had allowed his brother to use his cottage. He, his wife and daughter were flung across an adjoining room but escaped serious injury. A neighbour who had been saying the Rosary at the time of the blast said that it was her prayers that saved the family.

A number of customs huts that did go up were destroyed by bombs placed in attaché cases handed to bus conductors, carriage paid, with addresses to non-resistant people. The cases were then deposited in the customs hut awaiting 'callers'. It was intended that the cases should explode after the customs' officials had gone home. One time, a driver, Peter Lony of the Erne Bus Company, was given a case addressed to a Miss Eileen Douglas, Lisnascigh, c/o Clontivran Customs House. Like any rural bus driver in Ireland he made it his business to see that Miss Douglas got her case and took it on the bus from the customs hut where he found there was no Miss Eileen Douglas there for it. After inquiries for the non-existent lady he and his conductor took the case in the front of a crowded bus back to the Clontivran post and left it there to await Miss Douglas's arrival. Happily, the hut was still open. (When it was shut the normal procedure was for the driver to take the case home with him and deliver it again in the morning.) A few hours later the case exploded and parts of the hut were found a mile away.

Police activity in the North naturally increased after these explosions and deaths, and on December 22 the R.U.C. made a big swoop in Belfast, putting thirty-four I.R.A. men behind bars. Their arrest, which ruined any chance of a northern campaign getting off the ground, was accompanied by a statement from Sir Dawson Bates, the Northern Ireland Minister for Home Affairs saying, 'The fact having come to the knowledge of the police that plans have been prepared by the Irish Republican Army for attacks upon persons occupying prominent positions and upon Government and other property during that Christmas and New Year period, the Government decided . . . there was no alternative other than to arrest and intern well-known leaders and prominent members of this illegal organisation.'

In the South imprisonments after the English campaign had brought less established figures to the top of the I.R.A., in particular Stephen Hayes. Hayes, from Co. Wexford, an amiable ex-footballer, fond of a drink, and an official in the County Council, had been appointed adjutant-general by Russell in October, 1938. Before leaving for America in April, 1939 Russell had him promoted to chief of staff during his own absence. This appointment was never ratified in the normal fashion by an Army Council meeting. Hayes did not insist on regular meetings of the Army Council, and there were differences of opinion as to the proper course in the disasters which were occurring. Cork and Kerry I.R.A. split from the main body, and from each other, and the North began to look more to Belfast than Dublin for direction. In the South, Michael Traynor, Tony D'Arcy, Jack McNeela and Dom Adams, all new faces on the Army Council, were thinking of guerrilla raids on the North from southern bases. All were disillusioned with the routine of parades and confusion which existed in the South and realised that there was very little hope of overthrowing the southern state. Then sometime before Christmas 1939, Tom Doyle, a civil servant in the Department of Defence, presented an audacious scheme for raiding the Magazine Fort in Phoenix Park, Dublin, where the bulk of the Irish army's ammunition was stored. This idea appealed to Traynor and the others because, while they had a considerable number of guns stored around the country,* ammunition was in very short supply. Prior to Doyle's approach, Traynor had switched his emphasis from bomb making to guerrilla warfare, so the raid, although it involved fantastic risks, fell into their general scheme. An Army Council meeting, in the unlikely setting of the home of a Radio Eireann musician in Booterstown, Co. Dublin, decided to go ahead with the raid.

It began about half-past eight in the evening of December 23, 1939, and continued for two hours. The I.R.A. immobilised the entire garrison (an officer, two N.C.O.s and ten men armed with rifles and a Lewis gun) and got away with 1,084,000 rounds of ammunition in thirteen lorries. Entrance to the inner gate of the fort was gained when a military policeman left this open to answer a ring at the outer gate. There he met a man in civilian clothes who said he had a parcel for the officer in charge. The military policeman opened the gate for him and was promptly held up.

In a way, conditions in the Fort symbolised the attitude of the country as a whole to the threat of war. According to standing orders the inner gate should have been locked behind the military policeman, but in practice this was never done and Doyle knew of the laxity prevailing throughout the Fort. The policeman and the sentry on duty were captured with equal ease; the rest of the garrison was sitting around a fire in the guardroom when the I.R.A. burst in. Heads rolled in the upper echelons of the army for the unpreparedness that left the country virtually defenceless.

---

* Ballykinlar army camp in the North of Ireland was raided so often and so many Tommies stationed there were convicted of selling rifles to the I.R.A. that it became known in I.R.A. circles as 'the Stores'.

Stung by the I.R.A.'s audacity the government reacted with a ruthless speed and efficiency which showed results almost immediately. All army and police leave was cancelled, roads were blocked, cars and lorries had to pass checkpoints and money was liberally spent by intelligence agents. Beginning on St Stephen's Day, the ammunition was gradually recovered. Only about one lorry load got away to the Cooley mountain district of Co. Louth, where some incredible feats of endurance were performed by a farmer who made repeated journeys up the side of a precipitous mountain, carrying bucket loads of bullets.

'The arms were almost dragged out of me,' he told me years later.

On January 4 the Dail met in emergency session and by eighty-two votes to nine passed a measure allowing the government to set up detention camps at the Curragh headquarters of the regular army. Henceforward the I.R.A. men knew that, if captured, they might be thrown into the Curragh and left there until the government felt it was safe to let them out. This disturbed more people than those in the I.R.A.

Apart from the nose-twitching of the Magazine Fort raid, the government faced an ever growing number of unconstitutional activities by the I.R.A., legal challenges, and constitutional threats on its political front.

On October 22, 1939, a gelignite bomb had been exploded at the outer wall of Mountjoy Jail in an unsuccessful attempt to release four I.R.A. prisoners: Paddy McGrath, Willy McGuinness, Peadar O'Flaherty and Laurence Grogan. About the same time, the Killiney Castle bomb-making factory was discovered and machine guns, revolvers and large quantities of paxo were seized. On November 18, Amiens Street post office, in Dublin, was held up and £5,000 taken. Five days later the National Bank in Clonliffe Road was raided and £200 taken. In the wake of these doings the legal difficulty presented itself.

On December 1, Mr Justice Gavan Duffy, in the case of a *habeas corpus* application for Seamus Burke of Mayo, who was interned in Arbour Hill Jail, held that part six of the Offences Against the State Act 1939 was in conflict with the constitution and therefore invalid. He found that the minister's power, under the act, to order the detention of a person when he was 'satisfied' that it was necessary to do so was the assumption by a minister of the executive branch of powers reserved by the constitution to the judiciary. He consequently ordered Burke released. While an appeal to the Supreme Court was immediately entered this decision raised the question whether the other I.R.A prisoners in Arbour Hill should be set free. After a private debate to decide whether new legislation should be introduced, or whether the prisoners should be freed, the government released fifty-three I.R.A. men from Arbour Hill on December 2. On the same day a bread van was held up on the North Strand in Dublin, and nearly £500 was taken. The driver was badly beaten up.

December saw the sentencing of Barnes and McCormick, which had a power-ful effect on Republican sentiment in. Ireland, and the issuing of a circular from the Irish Republican Publicity Bureau to users of the Northern and Ulster Banks advising them to transfer their accounts to southern based banks, because 'those banks with headquarters in Belfast are considered to be operating against the best interests of national economic freedom'. Then came the Magazine Fort raid itself, the seizure on December 29 of an I.R.A. pirate radio station in a Dublin suburb and the fatal shooting of a policeman in Cork on January 3 as he attempted to arrest an I.R.A. man Thomas MacCurtain.

The government took parliamentary action following Mr Justice Duffy's decision. On January 5 the Emergency Powers (Amendment) Act, 1940 was passed, giving the government the right to intern Irish citizens without trial, in the same way as aliens could be interned without trial during the war which then existed. Because the emergency powers acts were passed pursuant to the resolution relating to the Second World War their constitutionally could not be challenged; the Offences Against the State Act, having been passed before the war began, was subject to judicial review. When part six of this act was declared repugnant to the constitution the government decided to carry out future internments under the Emergency Powers Act of 1939, as amended by the act of January 5 enabling it to intern Irish citizens. Such internments could not be challenged in the courts as the acts were not subject to judicial review.

All this legal manoeuvring aroused some showed misgivings on the part of responsible people. President Douglas Hyde, for the first time since the constitution came into force on December 29 1937, convened a meeting of the Council of State★ to advise him whether the act should be referred to the Supreme Court (under article 26 of the constitution) for a decision as to its constitutionality. After consultation he decided to do so. Even though both houses of parliament had passed the bill it could not become law until he signed it, and this he would not do until he heard the court's decision. On February 9 the court declared the bill to be valid in relation to the constitution and it was duly signed and became law.

The next day the I.R.A. again raided the Ballykinlar camp and got away with 100 rifles. This was an irrelevant episode as the I.R.A. did not have bullets of the calibre required for the stolen rifles. The raid was inspired by a false idea within the I.R.A. as to the strength of republican sympathy throughout the country. This false idea developed partially from reasons which have already been suggested and partially from what seemed to be tangible evidence that the public was swinging towards republicanism—albeit of a constitutional sort.

In Dublin at this time there was much take of a new political movement which was believed to be a challenge to the government and was popularly reported to be ready to take over the government on some form of corporative basis. This movement, which came to be known as Coras na Poblachta (System of Republicans), did in fact contain the nucleus of a party. Eight years later it formed the core of a coalition which introduced some new ideas into Irish politics and which took power from Fianna Fail. In the early months of 1940, however, its leaders were not capable of such a feat nor were the times right for a change.

The principal figures in Coras na Poblachta were Simon Donnelly, who had fought in Boland's Mill under de Valera in 1916, Sean Fitzpatrick, another War of Independence man, Con Lehane, who had lately left the I.R.A., Sean Gibbons,

---

★ It consisted of the prime minister, the deputy prime minister, the chief justice, the president of the High Court, the chairman of Dail Eireann, the chairman of the Seanad, the attorney general, Deputy William T. Cosgrave, Deputy James M. Dillon, Senator Robert P. Farnan, Senator John Keane, Deputy General Richard Mulcahy, Deputy William Norton, Senator Michael Tierney.

Tom O'Rourke, Sean Dowling, one of Rory O'Connor's principal lieutenants in the Civil War days, Colonel Roger McCorley, one of the principal I.R.A. leaders in Belfast who during the Anglo-Irish war had taken the Free State side in the Civil War, Frank Thornton, one of Michael Collins's top intelligence officers. Roger McHugh, a lecturer in English at University College, Dublin, Captain Martin Bell and Peter O'Connor.

Coras na Poblachta sought the formal declaration of a republic. Though it realised that its writ would run only in the twenty-six counties, it would claim that the jurisdiction extended over the six counties. Nobody bothered too much about how this writ could be enforced, either on a wartime England, or a wartime North of Ireland. In fact this declaration of a Republic was made eight years later by the coalition which ousted Fianna Fail. Its language policy required the use of the Irish learned at school, with Irish street signs, shop signs and government documents and bank notes. This policy was followed by successive governments. Coras na Poblachta also proposed to introduce national service, for educational purposes, to ensure that everyone understood his responsibilities.

The basic economic principle of the Coras na Poblachta founders was the statutory right to employment and a living wage. In other economic fields the party's thinking was strictly republican in the I.R.A. sense. It proposed breaking the link with British currency, the nationalisation of banks and the making of people employed in banks into civil servants.

Free education for all children over primary age was proposed as a right, as was a university education when feasible. This last proposal has become Irish governmental policy only since the mid-1960s, although another of the party's ideas, the introduction of children's allowances, was taken up by Fianna Fail three years after Coras na Poblachta was dissolved. Dissolution occurred because people tended to discuss the party rather than join it. Indeed some of the Coras leaders themselves, notably Frank Thornton, felt that duty lay in joining some of the forces then springing up to defend the country.

The I.R.A., meanwhile, elated with its upsurge, the psychological effects of the Magazine Fort raid and an undue reliance on the sympathy during the Barnes-McCormick hangings, persevered with plans for an attack on the North and a meeting was arranged in the Meath Hotel in Parnell Square, Dublin. The normal procedure for such a meeting was for delegates to visit a nearby hotel for directions, making their way unobtrusively in ones and twos to the chosen venue. But in this case each person was told to go direct to the hotel, and vigilant Special Branch men on duty at railway stations and bus depots realised that prominent I.R.A. men from Mayo, Donegal, Tyrone, Sligo, Galway, Belfast, Roscommon, Leitrim and other parts of the country were in Dublin, converging on the Meath. In a police raid everyone was captured. Knowing nothing of Traynor's, Dom Adams' and Paddy McNeela's plans the authorities thought the meeting was merely a gathering of I.R.A. men and sentences ranged only from three to six months.

Even so, these imprisonments began a grim chapter in the history of the I.R.A. In Mountjoy, prisoners were treated as ordinary criminals and there was continual agitation for political treatment. After the influx of new prisoners it was decided in February to back these demands by hunger striking. On March 1, Jack McNeela and

Jack Plunkett, both of whom had been seized with the ill-fated pirate transmitter in December, were due to appear before the Special Criminal Court in Collins Barrack, Dublin. It was decided to prevent their being taken to the court. The prisoners barricaded themselves in D-wing (which also contained the execution chamber), using their beds, tables and anything else they could get, and armed themselves with the legs of tables and chairs. Some very savage fighting broke out when the warders, augmented by members of the Special Branch, stormed the barricades.

Cornered, the prisoners fought fiercely and the police were not too particular how they subdued them. Traynor remembers seeing D'Arcy standing with his hands up after surrendering when a policeman brought down his baton across his head. On the other hand, Seamus Byrne, who had also been arrested in the transmitter swoop, recalls how a big sergeant approached him with a baton in one hand, and stuck out his hand to say, 'Musha is that yourself Mr Byrne?' He remembered him from his appearances as a solicitor in court. The two of them retired to an empty cell and smoked until things quietened down—after hoses had been turned on the prisoners. (Hosing is an effective form of riot control. It not only knocks down the protester but takes his breath away, leaving him chilled, shaken and unfit for further activity. With men who had been on hunger strike for four days this was a harrowing ordeal.)

Hunger-striking is a double-edged weapon. It damages the striker physically almost as much as it increases his moral stature among his sympathisers. Until February, 1940 I.R.A. hunger strikers had generally carried the day against the government, understandably in a country that had won its independence partly from deaths on hunger strikes during 1916–21 of men such as Terence McSwiney and Thomas Ashe. Fianna Fail had come under considerable pressure afterwards—both from those who wanted the prisoners let out, and from those who wished to have them kept in.

Within the six-month period before the Mountjoy strike, an I.R.A. internee in Arbour Hill Military Jail, Charles McCarthy of Cork (on hunger strike from September 16 to October 12) was released. On the same day Con Lehane* went on a hunger and thirst strike. His case was raised in the Dail on October 19 by the Labour leader Deputy William Norton. Lehane abandoned the strike two days later and was subsequently released.

The government had also been pressed into showing clemency towards a group of other Cork men, Jeremiah Daly, Richard McCarthy and John Lynch, who had gone on strike despite the government statement of October 31 '. . . that as arrest and detention in accordance with the powers conferred by Parliament are the only means available for the maintenance of public order and security they cannot permit the State authorities to be deprived of these means through the policy of hunger strike. The prisoners on hunger strike will, accordingly, not be released.'

Each of the strikers was told of this decision formally and individually. But on November 8 the Labour Party called on the government to release all prisoners on hunger strike. The next day de Valera defended the government's action but when Jeremiah Daly abandoned his hunger strike on the 11th he was released

---

* He had left the I.R.A. and was furious at being caught in one of the many I.R.A. sweeps of the time.

three days later, and Lynch and McCarthy, who had been removed to St Bricin's Military Hospital, were also released after treatment.

Above all there had been the case of Patrick McGrath the chief operations officer who had been severely wounded in the fight against the British, during which he had been an outstanding figure. His case was considered to be sufficiently important for the Government Information Bureau to issue a statement to the effect that a government order had been obtained for his removal on November 15 to Jervis Street Hospital from Mountjoy Prison, where he had been on hunger strike from October 23. He left hospital on December 4 and a *nolle prosequi* was entered in his case before the Special Criminal Court on December 7, his spell at liberty was not to be very long—he was executed the following year for shooting two policemen.

The sort of dilemma that these cases had presented to the government is well illustrated by the following passage from the debate in the Seanad on the Offences Against the State (Amendment) Bill, 1940.

Mr MacDermot: Might I ask the Minister one question? He said that he intended to intern these people. Does he intend to continue to hold them if they go on hunger-strike?

Mr Boland: I certainly hope so.

Mr Fitzgerald: Say 'Yes' or 'No'.

Mr Boland: The intention certainly is to hold them, hunger-strike or no hunger-strike because things have gone too far altogether.

Mr Fitzgerald: The last Senator who spoke here mentioned that the Taoiseach said: 'All Parties now know where they are', and he commends the action of the Government in releasing the hunger-strikers. How does the statement of the Taoiseach yesterday, that all Parties now know where they are, fit in? He went into the Dail and he stopped the operations of the Dail, departed from the whole procedure there, to give a public assurance that there would be no release for the hunger-strikers, and then he released them. Yesterday he gave us an assurance that the Government are going to take their responsibilities seriously and see that any means that may be necessary will be used to put down this criminal organisation. He may tomorrow change his mind, just as he did with regard to the hunger-strikers. How are we to know where we stand, and how are any Parties to know where they stand.

Mr Boland: As regards the question of vacillation and letting out the hunger-strikers, I do not want to run away from that either. I admit that, on the surface, it looks bad. It looks like weakness and it may be very hard to justify making a statement and going back on it. But there are all sorts of considerations. We have got to deal with a very delicate problem and members of a Government have to listen to cases made by responsible members of the Oireachtas who come to them and put up propositions. These propositions were not made in public, but I may mention a matter that was put to me. I am breaking no confidence because I shall mention no names.

A prominent member of the Opposition said to me in private—I mention no names and I hope I am breaking no confidence; this was a man who had taken very strong action against these people—that, in his view, we were not entitled to let these people die on hunger-strike because, due to our attitude and general policy towards these people in the past, they were entitled to believe that if they went on hunger-strike, we would let them out. He said:

'You did not make this announcement before they went on hunger-strike and I believe you are bound not to let them die.' Things like that had to be borne in mind, but I can assure this House that we are not going to let people take the law into their own hands and that we shall not be prevented from detaining them if we are satisfied they must be detained. Our patience has certainly been tried. Our policy of conciliation has got perhaps an over-trial; I think that is on the credit side, and I wish to pay a tribute to Senator Tierney for having said so much—that it was well worth while to have tried it. We tried that *ad nauseam*. We may have gone too far, but that has got to stop. There is no question of ruthlessness or rigour, but I am sure that there is going to be insistence that everybody in this country will obey the law.

A hunger strike begun shortly after Boland's declaration was obviously coming at a moment of peak determination on the government's part to resist such pressure and the seven men who rejected their food on February 25 realised this but were determined to die if necessary in order to achieve their aim.

The strikers were Thomas MacCurtain, Thomas Grogan, John Lyons, Michael Traynor, Tony D'Arcy, John McNeela and John Plunkett. Their principal demand was that they be allowed to walk around the jail freely without being confined to their cells at four o'clock each evening. They also sought to have John Dwyer and Nicholas Doherty, each serving five years' penal servitude in Mountjoy, transferred to military custody.

Doherty was convicted of being in possession of a rifle and ammunition taken from the Magazine Fort. He and Lyons went on hunger strike on February 25 but took food on March 6. Dwyer had been sentenced for having attempted to induce members of the defence forces to disclose information concerning Baldonnell Aerdrome. On March 1, John McNeela was sentenced to two years' imprisonment and John Plunkett to eighteen months' imprisonment on a charge of 'conspiracy to usurp a function of Government' (running a pirate radio). They were transferred to Arbour Hill and were removed to St Bricin's Hospital on March 7. Tony D'Arcy and Michael Traynor were sentenced to three months' imprisonment on March 5 for refusing to answer questions about the Meath Hotel case. They were transferred to Arbour Hill and were removed to St Bricin's Hospital on March 27. D'Arcy died on April 16 and McNeela on April 19.

Thomas MacCurtain, a son of a lord mayor of Cork who had been killed by the Black and Tans, had been in the I.R.A. since boyhood and was continually involved in its activities. He was awaiting trial for the murder of Detective Officer Roche and was removed from Mountjoy to St Bricin's on April 6. Thomas Grogan, awaiting trial in connection with the raid on Magazine Fort, was removed on April 1 from Mountjoy to St Bricin's suffering from pleurisy. On April 19, the day of McNeela's death, the hunger strike at St Bricin's was abandoned.

Michael Traynor recalled the strike for me without horror or bitterness.

'There were two nice doctors in the ward, one was Fianna Fáil and one was Fine Gael. The Fianna Fáil man was very embarrassed but the Fine Gael man was all in favour of us. Each evening we'd take it in turn to tell each other in great detail about the best meals we'd ever had or what the best meal we could ever hope to have would be like.

'The old bedboard had been done away with by Fianna Fáil and our beds were fibre mattresses with a spring upon an iron bed. After a while, we had to have all our joints bandaged because they were only skin and bone and bedsores or gangrene would have set in easily.

'After a bit, I remember, I couldn't even turn in the bed without help. We had to be rubbed down each day with olive oil to prevent the bedsores. I could smell death off myself, a sickly nauseating stench. We would have died except that we drank a great deal of water each day.

'But our other appetites went, and we concentrated on saving our energies and our lives to beat the strike. I'd been on two hunger strikes before in Crumlin

Road [Belfast's jail] but these were only canter strikes—this was a real galloping strike. Tony D'Arcy died first, he called out, "Jack, Jack, Jack McNeela, I'm dying." McNeela was in the bed opposite to D'Arcy and he insisted on getting out to go to his friend. I pleaded with him not to. There was no one in the ward at the time. The armed guard was outside a locked door. After the orderlies got the door open they lifted McNeela back to bed but he died two days later. Then we got word from Stephen Hayes telling us that all we had struck for was granted and that we were to call off the strike.'

Their first meal was two poached eggs on toast, tea, milk and sugar, followed by a dose of hydrochloric acid to replace their lost digestive juices. The acid treatment continued for a week and after every meal the prisoners could see the blankets rising round their distended stomachs

The prisoners' euphoria after the strike was short-lived because they did not get what they had struck for, and they were served either with internment orders or with notification of their prison sentences. This was stunning for Grogan who got fourteen years for his part in the Magazine Fort raid.

MacCurtain was one who survived to become a leader of the I.R.A. campaign of 1956–62. The Roche case, for which he was to be tried, began when in the course of a scuffle a shot was fired as Roche and detectives tried to take MacCurtain into custody in Cork on January 3, 1940. Roche was fatally wounded, dying the next morning.

This case aroused tremendous interest in Ireland because of MacCurtain's background. He was sentenced to death by the special Criminal Court on June 13, and the execution was fixed for July 5. But after an application for *habeas corpus* the execution was postponed for a week. The Supreme Court dismissed the appeal and the country seethed with controversy. MacCurtain's father had fought alongside many members of the present Fianna Fail for a thirty-two-county Republic and while everyone accepted that the I.R.A. and Fianna Fail travelled on parallel lines up to the point where the use of force was sanctioned, MacCurtain's case was seen as a test to whether Fianna Fail was prepared to kill to prevent force being used. It seemed certain that MacCurtain would die, but on July 10 a government statement declared: 'The President, acting on the advice of the government, has commuted the sentence of death on Thomas MacCurtain to penal servitude for life.' No one in Ireland outside the small circle from the government of that day knows the truth of what happened, but it is authoritatively supposed that a sister of Cathal Brugha's widow, the Reverend Mother of a convent in Armagh, interceded with Cardinal MacRory to have a last talk with de Valera, and that this final appeal decided him.

The hunger strikers' ordeal naturally excited much controversy throughout the country but government censorship restricted newspaper comment and coverage of the event. D'Arcy's death for instance was recorded in a short single column story on page eight of the *Irish Independent*. It was wartime and most people realised that episodes such as the Magazine Fort raid would jeopardise Ireland's claim to neutrality during the war. At the inquests on the dead men only relatives were allowed to attend. Sean MacBride appeared for the next of kin in both cases.

The verdict on D'Arcy was 'died of inanition, secondary to cardiac failure while on hunger strike'. This was the first time a coroner's jury had sat on a hunger-strike case since the death of Thomas Ashe, and the jury ordered a rider that, 'Immediate action should be taken with regard to the five men at present on hunger strike and in a serious condition. We desire to express our sincerest sympathy with the widow, relatives and friends of the late Anthony D'Arcy in their bereavement.' Most people in the country would have had sympathy with that rider but when McNeela died and the hunger strike was called off, the death of a bishop, Dr Hugh McSharry at the age of eighty-nine, was the main-page lead in the *Irish Independent* with a hundred and four lines of type. The end of the strike and the death of Jack McNeela rated only twenty-five. The *Irish Times* gave it a slightly bigger show but on a left-hand, inside page, and the *Irish Press* also played it down.

The inquest on McNeela on April 22 aroused some controversy because a Carmelite priest, the Rev. John J. O'Hare gave evidence that he had seen the prisoners on the day of McNeela's death, and that as a result of his conveying instructions to them from I.R.A. headquarters, the strike was called off. He said the strike could have been called off three weeks earlier and both lives saved, if de Valera and Boland had allowed him to visit the prisoners. He gave evidence of meeting with the prisoners to substantiate his claims. As he had already spoken at the D'Arcy inquest, making somewhat similar statements, Boland felt constrained to go into the box during the McNeela hearing and make a statement which in effect denied the allegations. This exposed him to a scorching cross-examination from Sean MacBride.

However, any sympathy the I.R.A. might have hoped to gain by the martyrdom of D'Arcy and McNeela was speedily dissipated by the tottering organisation's subsequent tactics. In retaliation for the deaths, a mine was exploded in the laneway off the Lower Castle Yard in Dublin Castle, headquarters of the Special Branch, injuring a number of guards and the castle's housekeeper (part of the castle and the Chapel Royal are open to the public) and two policemen were shot at in the streets of Dublin. Public sympathy for the I.R.A. dwindled.

The two detective officers who were taking mails from Pearse Street sorting depot to the Department of External Affairs were attacked in Holles Street by a group of I.R.A. men, armed with Thompson guns. The mails were thought to contain dispatches for Sir John Maffey, the British representative. Both policemen, Detective Officers McSweeney and Shanahan were immediately promoted to the rank of sergeant and the government offered rewards of up to £5,000 for information leading to the arrest and conviction of the persons who took part in the attack. (These were never claimed.)

The following day, after visiting the wounded men in hospital, de Valera, who had hitherto allowed Boland to make most of the stern public utterances concerning the I.R.A., went on the air from Radio Eireann to personally issue a statement:

'This moment, when small nations throughout Europe are devoting all their effort to strengthening national unity in order the better to defend their independence, is a moment that a group in this country has chosen to attempt to destroy our organised life.'

He referred to the 'dastardly attack made on two gallant policemen and the exploding of the time bomb in the headquarters of Dublin Castle'. He said, 'Were these deeds allowed to continue, Civil War would be the inevitable consequence and such a weakening of our strength as to make our country an easy prey to any invader.' He warned that no such situation would be permitted to develop and said to those 'now planning new crimes against the nation that they would not be allowed to continue their policy of sabotage. They have set the law at defiance, the law will be enforced against them. If the present law is not sufficient, it will be strengthened; and in the last resort, if no other law will suffice, then the Government will invoke the ultimate law—the safety of the people.'

He was backed up the next day by the leader of the Fine Gael party, W. T. Cosgrave, who speaking on a motion to issue a writ for a by-election in West Galway, announced that having heard the de Valera broadcast his party would not contest the Galway by-election. This election was for a seat formerly held by a government deputy, but Cosgrave went further and announced that neither would Fine Gael move a writ for a by-election in Co. Kilkenny where a seat formerly held by a Fine Gael deputy★ was now vacant. He said that Fine Gael had decided that a contest 'would not be in the interest of the country . . . if by any chance there was a marked reduction in the support accorded to the Government, it might be interpreted that that lack of support was due to the action which the Government, in recent months, had taken in connection with order in the State.' Fine Gael was 'particularly anxious that those engaged in unlawful activities . . . should realise that their activities should cease definitely once and for all and that there should be at least this much unanimity in the country that every citizen who respected his country would do his utmost to ensure that that sort of activity would cease.'

This inter-party co-operation was taken a step further and almost completely ruled out any prospects of I.R.A. recruitment of new members for the war years. An all-party defence conference was formed on May 28 and this body organised and propagandised to such effect that the prevailing spirit of patriotism was canalised within six months into the setting up of a Local Security Force of 133,000 men, drawn from towns, villages and baronies throughout the country.

Nevertheless between May and the following August upward of twenty incidents involving I.R.A. men with the police occurred. Arms dumps were seized; German spies hoping to make contact with the I.R.A. were captured; an I.R.A. man died after shots were fired at men digging a tunnel from Lapp's private asylum in College Road, Cork, in the direction of the Cork Jail which had recently been converted into a military detention centre.

Micksey Conway came into the news again. He had been on the run for some months and was captured at Harold's Cross Greyhound Track, after resisting arrest and being shot in the leg. Then on the morning of August 16 three detectives raiding No. 98a, Rathgar Road, Dublin, were fired on. Detective Officer Hyland was killed instantly, the other two detectives, McKeown and Brady being so severely wounded that McKeown died the following day in the Meath Hospital. On learning of the shootings the government immediately deleted from the

---

★ This seat was later won by my father.

Emergency Powers Act the right of appeal from findings of the Military Tribunal. That court was given a new brief under legislation which came into force on August 16. It was charged with the 'imposition and the carrying out of the sentence of death, and no appeal shall lie in respect of such conviction or sentence'.

Patrick McGrath and Thomas Harte, who were captured in the raid, were brought before the Military Court the following day. They were remanded until August 20 when they were found guilty of the murder of Hyland and sentenced to death by shooting. Sean MacBride defended them and appealed to the High Court and then to the Supreme Court, where after a three-day hearing (September 2, 3, 4) the appeal was again rejected. McGrath and Harte were duly executed by shooting in Mountjoy Prison at 6.45 p m. on September 6.

It might be noted here that the trigger happiness of both police and I.R.A. should be examined in the light of the prevailing circumstances. Nerves were strained to breaking point as a programme of searches and raids was carried out in the most intensive fashion at all hours of the day and night on the homes and haunts of suspected I.R.A. men. Members of the Special Branch and of the I.R.A. frequently came into verbal conflict and both sides began to develop personal grudges and fears as to what might happen if one should fall into the hands of the other. Public opinion had also swung away from the I.R.A. and behind the government that when on September 8 a communication similar to that circulated by the Cork I.R.A. on the execution of Barnes and McCormick was issued to cinema managers ordering them to close their cinemas as a mark of respect 'to the memory of Major-General Patrick McGrath and Thomas Harte, officers of the Irish Republican Army, who were murdered in Mountjoy on Friday', none of the cinemas closed—although all had shut for Barnes and McCormick. No incidents occurred, but to be on the safe side the police rounded up some forty-four I.R.A. suspects. Then on November 5 an event took place which stiffened the government's resolve to resist all pressures whether internal or external.

Speaking in the House of Commons on the U-boat sinkings in the Atlantic approaches to Britain, Churchill referred to Britain's being barred from using the south and west of Ireland to refuel her aircraft and flotillas. This, he said, was 'a heavy and invidious burden which Britain should never have to shoulder'. He suggested that if Britain could use Lough Swilly and Berehaven the whole situation could be changed.

De Valera replied two days later saying, 'There can be no question of handing over these ports so long as this State remains neutral.' He added that any attempt to bring pressure on the Irish government by any of the belligerents could only lead to bloodshed, and that so long as his government stayed in power it intended to defend its rights to the ports and to every other part of Irish territory. The following day two I.R.A. men were arrested in Dublin, after an exchange of shots, and given fourteen years each. On November 14, the police scotched a plan to raid a number of Dublin banks when they made a series of arrests which uncovered the plans of the banks.

As a result of the continuing decline of I.R.A. fortunes the belief became current in I.R.A. circles that the growing toll of arrests and set-backs was not so much a result of either bad I.R.A. planning or good police work, but of treachery within the movement. Where the I.R.A. was able to establish to its satisfaction that its code of honour had been infringed the punishment was drastic. For instance, on November 20 John Quinn, a lorry driver from Dundalk who had given evidence for the state after he had been arrested collecting ammunition for the I.R.A., was shot in the right thigh and in the left arm in reprisal.

To a group of I.R.A. men in Belfast, whom death and jailings had now brought to the top of the movement, it appeared that something more sinister lay behind the happenings in the South. Sean McCaughey, Liam Rice, Charles MacGlade, Liam Burke and later Pearse Kelly and Eoin MacNamee in particular, began to believe that there was a traitor at the very top of the organisation— Chief of Staff Stephen Hayes. The idea apparently originated with McCaughey who, like the other young men, was reared in the North and had very little contact with, or knowledge of, the South. Whatever reasons he had for becoming suspicious of Hayes in the first place died with him but investigations over a period of months led his colleagues to the conclusion that McCaughey was right. They decided that Hayes should be arrested, charged with high 'treason' and, if and when he admitted his treachery, executed.

Hayes knew nothing of their suspicions and arriving in Dublin for a routine meeting on June 30, 1941 he was immediately kidnapped. Then began a nightmare lasting almost two months during which, in Hayes's own words, he was both 'thunderstruck and gunstruck'. His captors took him and his brother-in-law, Lawrence De Lacy also of Enniscorthy, Co. Wexford (the man who had been instrumental in smuggling arms in conjunction with Joe McGarrity during the Troubles), to an isolated cottage in the Wicklow Mountains owned by Roger McHugh, a Coras na Poblachta founder and a Republican sympathiser though not a member of the I.R.A. or a party to the Hayes kidnapping. Prior to being taken to this cottage, Hayes was taken to the Cooley Mountains in Co. Louth, and then, after De Lacy had escaped from the Wicklow cottage, he was force marched to the Wicklow hills and down through Templeogue and Terenure to a house at Castlewood Avenue, owned by a friend of Pearse Kelly's aunt, a Mrs MacEoin, again a Republican sympathiser though not a member of the I.R.A.

There are two versions of what occurred during this period, that of Hayes and that of the I.R.A. It is not possible to say which is correct at this stage, without access to closely guarded Department of Justice files if, indeed, even these contain any information. It is possible to say, however, that the episode almost certainly caused two deaths and quite certainly wrecked the I.R.A. for the time being.

The I.R.A. version of the sequence of events is as follows. Immediately following Hayes's arrest a provisional Army Council was formed. Eoin MacNamee was brought down from Belfast to serve on it with McCaughey, MacGlade, Sean Harrington who later served for a month or two as chief of staff, Jack Lynch, Tom Mullally, Stephen Rynne, Andy Skelton and Joe Atkinson. It was an unusually large council because of the importance of the affair and the necessity of getting a broad measure of agreement within the organisation on a course of action. The I.R.A. says that Hayes was continually interrogated but not tortured or harmed in any way. Pearse Kelly told me that a light dog-chain was fixed to his legs but that he was not otherwise harmed and that it was arranged that after his court-martial

Hayes would be examined by a doctor, a member of a well-known Dublin family, who could then testify that Hayes had not been ill-treated.

Hayes was court-martialled on July 23. The court-martial consisted, according to his recollection, of McCaughey, Pearse Kelly and two I.R.A. men called McCarthy and Farrell, from Cork and Galway respectively. Also present were MacGlade, Liam Rice and Liam Burke. Pearse Kelly acted as official note-taker and procedural expert (because he had worked in a solicitor's office and as a reporter).

Sean McCaughey as prosecutor put the following two charges to Hayes:

1. That you, Stephen Hayes, conspired with 'The Irish Free State Government' to obstruct the policy and impede the progress of the Irish Republican Army.
2. That you, Stephen Hayes, are guilty of treachery for having deliberately forwarded information of a secret and confidential nature concerning the activities of the Irish Republican Army to a hostile body, to wit, the 'Irish Free State Government'.

The court-martial, which lasted from 9.00 pm. to 7.00 am., found Hayes guilty on both counts and sentenced him to death for being, as an official I.R.A. 'Special Communique' stated, 'a party to the most heinous conspiracy of crime in Irish history. The I.R.A. version adds that Hayes, after the verdict was announced, expressed a wish to write a confession.

The 'Special Communique' says that Hayes did this 'with the hope that it will undo some of the harm and injury I did to Oglaigh na hEireann [Irish Republican Army] through my co-operation with them [Free State government personnel].

'I decided on making this confession after I was made aware of the verdict of the court-martial. I further affirm that this confession of facts is the truth, the whole truth, and nothing but the truth, and has been made voluntarily by me.'

Pearse Kelly's recollection is that he and McCaughey were in a house rented by the I.R.A. in Gaeltacht Park, Whitehall and used as a temporary headquarters, when Liam Rice arrived and said, 'He's prepared to talk.' McCaughey and Kelly were surprised as they had been trying to collect additional evidence with which to confront Hayes, with a view to clearing up unexplained mysteries about some recent arrests.

McCaughey, Kelly, Rice and MacGlade then went to Castlewood Avenue and asked Hayes if he was prepared to talk. According to Kelly he replied, 'I might as well.' The next problem was, what form would his confession take, a question and answer or a straight handwritten account from Hayes himself? The latter course was agreed to and Kelly got rolls of the type of parchment used in solicitors' offices for Hayes to use. The writing took until September 8.

It had been decided to shoot Hayes on the morning of the all-Ireland football final later in the month. However, on the morning of September 8, Wright had gone to bed leaving Burke writing a letter in the same room as Hayes. Burke was called to the door by Mrs MacEoin and Hayes noticed that Burke had left his revolver and holster hanging on the mantelpiece. He grabbed the revolver, flung himself out of the window and shuffled down Castlewood Avenue, his legs still shackled, into the busy suburban shopping centre of Rathmines and through the bewildered shoppers to the Rathmines Garda station where he gave himself up.

Hayes's versions of what happened are quite different from that of the I.R.A. One is contained in a statement he wrote with the aid of a barrister, Eoin O'Mahony, on

March 18, 1949, in which he gives a point by point refutation of the statements in the confession and describes how he was tortured and starved. This written statement amplifies the evidence he gave during the trial of McCaughey before the Special Criminal Court.

Both statements say that he was captured at gun-point and taken to various places of detention where he was beaten, starved, continually urged to admit that he was a traitor and forced to write a confession admitting an the allegations put to him. In court he stated that he had partially met their demands by admitting some of the charges after beatings, threats of being shot or of being tied up and beaten to death. He said that he had finally decided to write a full confession when, after his court-martial, McCaughey threatened to hang him from a hook on a wall and to leave him there to die if he refused to meet their demands completely. He was prevented from sleeping for twenty-four hours and in this state of terror and fatigue, he finally gave in and began to write a confession of over 150 pages.

In the handwritten statement which he gave me, Hayes says that he purposely dragged out the confession to gain time. This statement says that the confession 'took over a month to write during which time I was being subjected to torture . . . Starvation diet, head beaten. All left side. Chained to bed at night. Tied to bed. Rope and chain fetters day and night. The substance of the confession was dictated by McCaughey.'

Hayes told me that he was beaten with a rifle butt all along the left arm so that it swelled up horribly. A broom handle was also used. His right side, he said, was spared so that he could write. He claimed that he never offered to write any confession and that the partial ones which he was forced to make before the trial were used in evidence against him. These, he said, were dictated by McCaughey and others. He denied completely that he was a traitor.

Hayes blamed the whole episode on the atmosphere of suspicion at the time. 'A man called Murphy by one group would be known as Smith to another, which could make his doing suspect if he were found out by the first group. That sort of thing.

'The Irish are rebels not revolutionaries,' he said. 'After the Magazine Fort raid, there was great debate about what we should do next. I favoured a coup, taking over the Dail, capturing the heads of the Government. There was no hope at all during the war of getting a man, let alone a bomb, across to England so the campaign there was finished. The atmosphere was very tense. George Plunkett had an idea that he would take four or five fellows down O'Connell Street, and if anyone stopped them they'd pull on them.

'The Army couldn't march anywhere. Our strength was overrated, we'd no arms. In my county of Wexford, for instance, there were about twenty rifles and two Thompson guns. The recruiting grounds of the ordinary young fellows grow-ing up in the country was closed to us because of the Local Defence Forces organised by the Government which took all the manpower. So the "Army" was back to the pre-bombing campaign stage of trying to build itself up to a point where we could "talk as equals" to Germany when they won the war. The main thing, as I saw it, was to try and keep the organisation intact and we were sending fellows round the country to try and organise things.

'We had a good bit of support at the time. Even though people would vote
Fianna Fail they would keep stuff in the house for us or do a run for us. But we
obviously hadn't a hope of doing very much. I only took over from Russell when
he went to America because there was no one else and Russell begged me to do
it. I remember, before he went away, he took me up to George Plunkett's house
to try to get him to persuade Peadar O'Flaherty not to sign the Declaration of
War on England because everyone was annoyed with him for trying to blow up
the pillar. But we had to let him sign it in the end.

'That shows you how things were even then, and you can imagine what they
were like when the Free Staters started to round us up and everybody got jittery.
Russell had been saying that the people would fall in behind the I.R.A. when the
campaign broke out and that the Government wouldn't take any action against us.
He put too much faith into an organisation that wasn't there. You can imagine how
everyone got more and more suspicious and nervy. McGrath had no authority to
carry a gun, for instance, but with the executions and deaths and hunger strike, no
one was too eager to check before they fired on someone. Everything was going
wrong and I suppose these fellows wanted a scape-goat. I don't think that
McCaughey was the full shilling anyway.'

Hayes's own written statement was drawn up to circulate among Republicans
to exonerate him but this plan fell through. The statement ends:

I am prepared to swear an oath that I never entered into any conspiracy with the Free State
Government, through Dr James Ryan, T.D., Minister for Agriculture, Thomas Deirg,
T.D., Minister for Education, Senator Chris. Byrne or Lawrence De Lacy, to wreck the
Irish Republican Army. Further, I would like to affirm an oath, that I made no confession
voluntarily.

Stephen Hayes

This comes at the end of a lengthy refutation of the I.R.A.'s 'Special Communique'.
In all, it deals with fifty-one points made in the communique. Checking Hayes's
statement against that of the I.R.A., any informed Irish person can see at a glance
that, if one must make a choice, Hayes's document is much more likely to be
accurate. Hayes, according to his confession, was supposed to have acted for the
government so that Russell would be confined in America and the British bombing
campaign go off half-cock. The Coventry bomb explosion was supposed to have
been done to discredit the I.R.A. Hayes is supposed to have carried out the Magazine
Fort raid at the suggestion of the government; to have deliberately timed useless
explosions in England at the time of the Barnes and McCormick appeals so that the
two men would be condemned in the outbreak of public indignation; to have
connived at the assassination of Sean Russell by British secret agents in Gibraltar; to
have arranged the murder of an innocent victim, Michael Devereaux of Wexford.
for which an I.R.A. man George Plant was subsequently executed; to have carried
out the Dublin Castle explosion at the express wishes of the government and to have
further attempted to discredit the I.R.A. by arranging a number of bank raids as a
result of which a young man called Richard Goss was arrested on July 18, 1941, and
executed in Portlaoise Prison on August 9.

These allegations do not merit a detailed serious consideration. On the Magazine
Fort raid charge, for instance, it is only necessary to remember the period when it

took place, and to ask what government in the world would allow an underground organisation deliberately to come and make off with all its ammunition. Such analysis shows that the statements in the I.R.A. communique are false and were obtained by force. It does not shed any light on whether Hayes was a traitor but if he was the government took a very strange method of rewarding him. On June 19, 1942, the Special Criminal Court gave him five years penal servitude for 'maintenance of an illegal force'. A similar sentence was handed out to a member of the Special Branch, James Crofton, who had been mentioned in the confession as being a link with Hayes through whom the government passed instructions.

Crofton was arrested for trying to get a Nazi spy, Herman Goertz, out of Kerry in a fishing boat from Fenit on the Dingle Peninsula

During the time Hayes was being held, McCaughey was approached to say that the life of Richard Goss, an I.R.A. man accused of shooting at military and police, might be saved if Hayes were set free. McCaughey refused this plea. Goss was executed at Portlaoise Prison.

Hayes's escape upset the I.R.A. It came at a time of great tribulation. McCaughey had been arrested a few days earlier as he sat on a train en route to the house where Hayes was writing his 'confession'. Immediately after the escape Burke left Castlewood Avenue to tell Kelly what had happened and Rice stayed behind to warn any I.R.A. men who might call to make themselves scarce. Rice was standing on the footpath watching for Kelly when a police car from Rathmines drew up. He fired on Detective Officer Dinny O'Brien. O'Brien and his colleagues fired back and Rice was badly wounded in the lung.

In this atmosphere, a meeting was held in Mountjoy Square to decide what to do next, and by whatever yardstick one judges the matter, an incredibly bad decision was taken. It was decided to publish Hayes's confession and Dr Lombard Murphy, chairman of the board of directors of the Irish Independent Newspapers Ltd, was contacted and asked if he would publish the Hayes confessions.

The idea was ludicrous. The policy of the *Independent* was right-wing, pro-clerical and anti-I.R.A. It was war-time and all papers were subject to censorship. Dr Murphy turned down the proposal at once and the I.R.A. decided to issue the document itself. Pearse Kelly and a number of helpers used a copy of *Thom's Directory*, which gave the addresses of Dail deputies, senators, bishops and other dignataries among whom they circulated the 'Special Communique' with disastrous results.

The vast majority of I.R.A. members had been quite unaware of Hayes's kidnapping, and this confession of deceit and treachery dismayed them. Tarlach O'hUid summed up the general reaction saying: 'As far as I was concerned the confession meant the end of the I.R.A. for me. There I was in Derry Jail, already fed up to the back teeth with my comrades, and with the circumstances which had led me there, and this thing came. To me it meant that though Hayes was a traitor, in which case the I.R.A. was a lousy organisation for having such a man at the top, or else he was innocent, in which case the I.R.A. was a doubly lousy organisation to extract such a document from him. Either way I was finished.' (Incidentally O'hUid, despite this, refused to sign out of Derry Jail, and stayed there for the remainder of the war, being in fact one of the very last prisoners to be released.)

Apart from all this, the publication of Hayes's 'confession' brought tragedy. It described how Michael Devereaux of Wexford, a battalion officer, was allegedly framed on government instructions. The I.R.A., believing he had given away dumps and information leading to the capture of some of his colleagues, had him court-martialled *in absentia*, found him guilty and ordered him to be shot. The I.R.A. communique said that the sentence was carried out by the divisional O.C. of the Wexford area. Within forty-eight hours of the communique being issued detectives were on their way to the area. Masquerading as I.R.A. emissaries from G.H.Q. they persuaded a local I.R.A. man, who could not read and accepted their credentials, to lead them to a cave on the Knockmealdown Mountains where Devereaux had been shot and his body buried. Whether Devereaux was framed and shot in error, or whether he was innocent but shot through misunderstandings, or whether he was, indeed, a traitor, the publication of his fate was more than indiscreet. It was clear that the man's former colleagues might be in jeopardy.

The finding of Devereaux's body opened one of the most distressing chapters in Irish legal history. After widespread police inquiries two I.R.A. men, Joseph O'Connor and George Plant, were charged with Devereaux's murder. Two former I.R.A. men, Patrick Davern and Michael Walshe, gave evidence against them. However, during the trial they withdrew their statements and the prosecution case collapsed. It was an open secret that I.R.A. pressure had been put on the two witnesses. Pearse Kelly told me that he met the two in jail and found them greatly disturbed. Being simple men, they had not realised their statements could incriminate former comrades. He advised them that they could retract their statements and destroy the prosecution's case. One may guess at what other pressures were brought to bear.

The government met this situation with a manipulation of the legal code, counteracting the I.R.A.'s tactics by issuing an Emergency Powers Order on December 30, 1941. This order dealt with the law relating to the admissibility of evidence before the Special Military Court. It provided that whether the offence was committed before the making of the order or not, 'It was proved that a statement relevant to the charge was made by any person including the accused and that such statement . . . was made voluntarily, lawfully . . . taken down in writing and was acknowledged by the person who made it, then at any stage of the trial the prosecution may read such a statement as evidence and may cross-examine the person who made it.'

The power of the court concerning such a statement were that it could act on the statement against the accused and that an application to read a statement could be made even though the person who made it was not present at the trial, or was dead, or was present at the trial even though he did not give evidence. The order further provided that if a military court considered it proper on any occasion during a trial that it should not be bound by any rule of evidence, whether of military or common law, then the court should not be bound by such rule.

Under this order Plant was put on trial again with the two I.R.A. men who had rescinded their confessions, Davern and Walshe. All three were sentenced to death. The last two sentences were commuted but Plant was executed in Portlaoise Prison on March 5, 1942.

Plant bore his sentence philosophically. He told one of the prison orderlies that 'those who live by the gun die by the gun.' Sean MacBride told me that of all the trials in which he took part during the war, he found that of Plant the most harrowing.

'He was a particularly nice fellow and seemed to have no fear. The night before his execution he sat up reading, completely composed all night, and went to his death wearing his best suit.'

After the Hayes affair, the I.R.A. in the South was smashed although it refused to admit it. Pearse Kelly became chief of staff after MacGlade was picked up within days of McCaughey being caught, and tried to resuscitate the movement. The Brugha family, Helena Molony, the businessman Lucas and Brian O'hUiginn worked with him to draw up a social and economic programme on which the I.R.A. could work.

In addition to all the setbacks the I.R.A. had little money. At the beginning of the war, police who were investigating the possible consequences of a visit to Ireland by Joseph McGarrity (he left on August 14) swooped on a house, 16, Rathmines Park, Dublin, on September 9, arrested the four I.R.A. men in the house and seized a quantity of ammunition, some I.R.A. documents and $8,265. Both Eoin MacNamee and Hugh McAteer told me that during the war bank raids were necessary to pay I.R.A. debts and to get enough money to continue operations. And certainly the treatment of the deportees who were sent from England as a result of the I.R.A. bombing campaign points to an acute lack of funds.

Clearing centres were set up to help the flood of deportees who arrived from England. But a letter from the deportees' committee shows how little money was available.

Deportees' Committee, 41 Parnell Square, Dublin

14/8/1940

A chara,

We enclose P.O. for ten shillings. We regret to state that this Fund is now completely exhausted, and except money is forthcoming from an unexpected source you cannot expect any remittance next week, or will you, we're afraid, any further remittance from this committee.

We extremely regret the necessity for sending this notice to you, but we have exhausted every source known to us. If, in the future, we see any prospect of getting further help for you, we shall communicate with you.

Yours sincerely,

L. Kearns MacWhinney   Agnes McCullough
Una de Staic   Helena Molony

No further help was forthcoming although Kelly pressed on and spoke to Eoin O'Duffy to see what help could be expected from the Italians or Germans. These activities succeeded only in placing him behind bars when he called on Herman Goertz, the German spy living in Dublin, to warn him that the police were looking for him. They were looking for Kelly too, and after arresting Goertz a few hours before Kelly's call, seized Kelly himself when he knocked on the door of Goertz's hide-out in Clontarf.

7

The I.R.A. in the North

Whether Hayes was a traitor or not, it is certain that the I.R.A. men who went to the South to assess his guilt or innocence were from backgrounds so different from his (and those of the average Southern I.R.A. man) as to make understanding between the two groups a very difficult business at the best of times, and almost an impossibility in the tension and suspicion of war. These differences in tone and background are basic not only to an understanding of the I.R.A. but to the whole partition issue. First, most prominent I.R.A. men in the North are Catholics and thus they are in an inferior social, political and economic position. Catholics drifted into the I.R.A. in great numbers. Protestants if they were militantly minded (and in the North in the 1920s and 1930s it was difficult not to be so), joined the B-Specials. So there was an armed 'them and us' situation. The Royal Ulster Constabulary was of course open to Catholics, but Catholics never showed much enthusiasm for it. Though one-third of the force was expected to be Catholic at its inception only about 12 per cent ever became so, and if one looks at the careers of some I.R.A. men one can understand why.

One of the most prominent I.R.A. men in Belfast after the end of the Civil War was Jimmy Steele, a baker's roundsman. Jimmy, who spent most of his life in prison, literally devoted his life to the I.R.A. He and his wife had only one week's holiday together before the end of the 1956–62 campaign in twenty-five years of marriage. Steele was reared in the famous Queen Street area of Belfast. Queen Street runs parallel to York Street, adjoining the dockland area. Queen Street is Catholic, York Street, Protestant, and between these two main arteries run a series of smaller intersections with names like Frederick Street, Lancaster Street, Great George's Street, Little George's Street, Henry Street, Cecil Street, Grove Street and Earl Street. At times of civil commotion, notably in 1932 and 1935, these were little more than shooting ranges. When disorder began anyone crossing those intersecting streets took the risk of being hit by a Catholic bullet coming down or a Protestant one coming up. So began the tunnelling through garden walls, and through the actual houses themselves, so that shoppers wanting to pass along one of these little death traps could walk the entire street without being fired on. But it meant little comfort or privacy in the lives of those who occupied these houses. In those circumstances, one did not have to ask, 'Why did you become an I.R.A. man?' of Steele. For a lad with his spirit and courage, there were few other courses open.

Much the same applied in the case of Michael Traynor, a man with a national reputation in the movement since the 1930s. He grew up in a mixed area of Protestants and Catholics and remembers regular bombings and shootings in the early 1920s. He recalled how as a small boy during the Anglo-Irish war in 1920 he and two friends went to see the naked bodies of three I.R.A. men found with crosses cut into their foreheads and insteps.

'There were small black holes in their heads,' he said. 'I remember they were found in Dan O'Neill's loanin [a Belfast term for a boreen or lane] in the Whiterock Road area. They had been shot as a reprisal for the deaths of three auxiliaries. I remember the MacMahon murder,* we didn't think that especially brutal for the time. I remember we thought that throwing hand grenades into the bedroom of two elderly sisters on St Patrick's night in Thompson Street was far worse because there was an awful job cleaning up afterwards with feathers and bits of bedding and pieces of flesh all splashed around the room. That was done by the B-Specials.'

The youthful Traynor and his family regarded the B-Specials as being outside the law. They seemed able to shoot anyone they wished and to get away with it. During the Anglo-Irish war there were sound reasons for Traynor's opinion of this group's immunity, and very sound reasons also for fearing another organisation known as the 'Murder Gang'. This flourished in Belfast during the period, carrying out assassinations and reprisal raids on Catholic strongholds. The gang was composed of former British soldiers, members of the U.V.F., and some sprinkling of R.I.C. men and B-Specials. Its members would set out from their cars and tenders in stockinged feet, with blacking on their faces to raid Catholic areas after dark. In the poor Belfast street lighting these marauders created terror among Catholics, as they loomed up out of the darkness to shoot a passer-by dead on the street or to hurl a hand grenade through a window, escaping like phantoms. Their tactics were eventually met by a simple strategy worked out between the civilian population and the I.R.A.

A custom known as the 'murder yell' sprang up. Anyone seeing a member of the gang gave a long, drawn-out, high-pitched keening yell of 'M - u - r - derr - eh' which was taken up by the entire district. Colonel Roger McCorley told me that this sound, with the banging of dustbin lids, pots and pails, was the most eerie he had ever heard. On hearing it, McCorley and his I.R.A. patrols would hasten to the spot, guiding each other with redtinted flashlights. When the shooting stopped and the invaders were driven off, the keening died away. The flashlights would be switched to green for 'all clear'. The custom of banging bin lids to warn either loyalist or British army incursions into nationalist areas was revived when the 'troubles' recommenced in 1968 and the the memory of those terrible days also survives today in a street ballad:

> Oh, she got up and rattled her bin,
> For the Specials were a-coming in,
> Tiddy-fal-la, Tiddy-fal-la.
> Oh, she got up and rattled her bin,

---

* This was committed by the 'Murder Gang' which, on March 23, 1922, broke into the home and shot male members of the MacMahon family and a man employed by them. The reprisal came on May 19. I.R.A. men went to a cooperage in Little Patrick Street, Belfast, and asked the coopers, 'Who are the Mickies here?' The Protestants pointed out the 'Mickies' (as the Catholics were known) whereupon the Protestants were lined up against a wall and five of them shot, three fatally.

For the Specials were a-coming in,
Tiddy-fa-la, Tiddy-fa-la.

Such a legacy of fear and hatred can still erupt. Two Protestant gunmen marched out one night in 1966, so moved by the songs and ceremonies with which the South was commemorating the 1916 Rebellion that they determined to kill I.R.A. men. They didn't find any, but they shot up some Catholic barmen, killing one of them. Such bigotry and tension lay behind the rioting and destruction which the world learned of during the fearful days of August 1969.

The principal I.R.A. Leader to emerge from Derry, the second city of the North, after the 'Troubles' was Hugh McAteer, who became chief of staff in 1941 for a time. His family had been nationalists for generations. One of his great-grandfathers was a 'reader'—a man who read *The Nation*, Thomas Davis's paper of the 1840s to neighbours at Ceili houses. *The Nation* cost sixpence, which in 1845–48 was a day's pay, and the fact that it should be so readily bought shows the strength of the nationalist tradition in the Derry area. Derry is, of course, a classical example of gerrymandering and discrimination. Today not even the most bigoted Unionist could deny that a Catholic majority in this city was unjustly denied its civil rights by a Protestant minority. That is why the civil rights movement had such a success in the area, making the world's headlines after an R.U.C. baton charge on October 5, 1968. Led by a Protestant, Ivan Cooper, and a Catholic, John Hume, it cut across sectarian barriers to the tune of 'We Shall Overcome' and demanded, not Catholic power, but civil rights and justice for all in the name of the city's noble traditions.

All the boys in McAteer's area joined the Fianna, the boy Republican's scout movement, as children in happier areas would join the Cubs, to become scouts later. McAteer remembers police surrounding them in a field as they drilled in 1928 and firing over their heads. Experiences like these, schooling by the Christian Brothers, attendance at Gaelic League classes (then controlled by the I.R.A.), readership of *An Phoblacht*, inevitably turned him to the I.R.A. Such social philosophy as he and his friends felt was expressed in trade unionism, or in discussions about the land war. To the young men of McAteer's youth it was a toss-up whether they joined the I.R.A. or became missionaries. Religious fervour and Republicanism were completely entwined.

'Independence was nearly as strong in our minds as religion,' said McAteer.

'We would go out unthinkingly after Mass at 11.00 am and we'd walk fourteen miles for our copy of *An Phoblacht*.'

He was a member of the St Vincent de Paul charitable organisation at this time, but it did not occur to him or his friends to apply St Vincent de Paul's social principle to his Republicanism. Independence, separatism, getting the British out, these were their goals. Success in these objectives would end the conditions they saw around them. The average house had concrete floors downstairs and there was little furniture or firing. But everywhere were numbers of children turning green with malnutrition. Were it not for the Christian Brothers, who dosed the children with cod liver oil daily, many of these children would not have survived the hungry 1930s. Some of them were known as 'half timers', being half-time at school and half-time at work, generally four-hour stints at each, and all under the age of twelve. McAteer formally joined the I.R.A. at Easter 1933. He remembers celebrating Fianna Fail's election victory that year by smashing windows. He and his friends had worked in Donegal as Fianna Fail election supporters.

In the countryside, for a young Catholic the differences were of degree rather than kind. Joe Deighan came from South Armagh outside Newry, a predominantly Catholic centre, not far from the border, and close to the Gap of the North through which (from the days of the Fianna legends) the men of Ulster sallied forth to attack the tribes of Leinster. It is a small farming area where memories of the 'Troubles' were much in mind. No Catholic in that area would join the British army although relationships between Catholic and Protestants were good. There was little hardship though in nearby Newry hunger was common among the Catholics, particularly in the 1920s and 1930s. Growing up, however, young Deighan realised there were more differences between him and the Protestants than the blue gates and blue cartwheels with which the Protestants adorned their property.

The sons of Protestant neighbours could get jobs in their own country but he couldn't. And in 1931, this fact, coupled with the songs about Emmet, Parnell and the stories of Fenians that he heard as a child, drove him to join the local I.R.A. at seventeen. They met in the mountains to drill in barrack-ground style unsuited to guerrilla warfare. There were a few revolvers, an occasional rifle, but anything larger, such as a Thompson gun, was as rare as plum cake in Oliver Twist's orphanage. Local people turned a blind eye to their activities and would hide them in times of trouble. At election times the young I.R.A. lads would back the Nationalist candidates in whatever way they could.

Deighan's first sentence was six months in Crumlin Road for 'promoting sedition'. In those years, constitutional politics in Northern Ireland for a nationalist-minded Catholic, like young Deighan, offered only frustration and disillusionment, or, if caught trying to lick the system by unconstitutional methods, jail. The Council for Civil Liberties issued a report on the Northern situation in 1936 which said:

Firstly, that through the operation of the Special Powers Act contempt has been begotten for the representative institutions of government.

Secondly, that through the use of Special Powers, individual liberty is no longer protected by law, but is at the disposition of the Executive. This abrogation of the rule of law has been so practised as to bring the freedom of the subject into contempt.

Thirdly, that the Northern Government has used Special Powers towards securing the domination of one particular political faction and, at the same time, towards curtailing the lawful activities of its opponents . . . The Government's policy is thus driving its opponents into the way of extremists.

Fourthly, that the Northern Irish Government, despite its assurances that Special Powers arc intended for use only against law-breakers, has frequently employed them against innocent and law-abiding people, often in humble circumstances, whose injuries, inflicted without cause or justification, have gone unrecompensed and disregarded.

This report was issued after the 1935 riots when there had been eleven murders, two attempted murders, 574 cases of criminal injuries, 133 cases of arson and 367 cases of malicious damage. Westminster had refused an official inquiry saying 'the matter was one which came solely within the jurisdiction of the Northern Ireland Government', when pressed by Catholic spokesmen such as T. J. Campbell, Cardinal MacRory and Bishop Mageean.

From the start, Stormont did not seem to be a seat of either justice or permanence to Catholic nationalists, who were split themselves between Sinn Fein and the Irish Parliamentary Party. In the early days of the Northern parliament the parliamentary faction, led by 'Wee Joe' Devlin, was paramount, but both sides boycotted the new institution, expecting the Boundary Commission to carve up Ulster and so make the new state unworkable.

After the commission's findings, 'Wee Joe' realised that the border was there to stay and took his seat. By 1927 he was the leader of a ten-man opposition, but unable to influence Northern affairs to any extent. One of the Unionists' first actions had been to abolish proportional representation in local government elections and to rearrange constituencies to give control to Unionists. In 1929 proportional representation was abolished in parliamentary elections also, wiping out independents and leaving a Protestant government finally entrenched by a majority of three to one over a Catholic opposition. Schooling was also firmly established on a denominational basis (by the Education Act of 1923 and subsequent amendments to it in 1925 and 1930) thus perpetuating the ghetto mentality on both sides.

The I.R.A. began to make inroads into the opposition support after the 1933 election, when de Valera was elected for South Down. He did not take his seat but his victor gave the Republicans an idea for an election strategy. They put up candidates for the 1935 Westminster elections, and to avoid splitting the vote the Nationalists stood down. The Sinn Fein philosophy overcame the traditions of the old Irish Parliamentary Party, but not that of the Unionists, and the ill conceived strategy cost the Nationalists seats in West Belfast, Armagh and Down. It also reintroduced abstentionism to the Northern political scene, and by the outbreak of war in 1939 only T. J. Campbell, who had succeeded Devlin as leader of the opposition, attended Stormont with any regularity. Catholic mistrust of Stormont was such that when Campbell accepted a judgeship from the government, this champion of the Catholic cause was dubbed 'Judas' Campbell by those he had striven to serve.

These were bad, bitter times. The rank-and-file of Protestant and Catholic followers heard declarations from Sir Basil Brooke that Catholics were disloyal and should not be employed, and from Cardinal MacRory that the Protestant Church was not part of the true Church of Christ.

It was their Northern Catholic birth which inevitably turned two of the most prominent I.R.A. men of the Hayes era towards Republicanism. Eoin MacNamee and Pearse Kelly were born in Co. Tyrone, Kelly in the town of Dungannon and MacNamee in the district of Broughdearg.

MacNamee's wild, mountainous, poverty stricken area had turned against the I.R.A. by the time he reached his teens, because around Tyrone and south Derry, the I.R.A. had lent themselves to a clerically-inspired anti-poteen campaign, smashing stills and pouring away the liquid which had been an impoverished people's only means of keeping out cold and reality. That the I.R.A. had survived at all was attributable to the traditions of the county, the home of the O'Neills and also the birthplace of Joseph McGarrity, and the fact that the Catholic majority was discriminated against by the Protestants through control of political power at Stormont and of local government bodies allocating houses and state jobs throughout the province.

MacNamee remembers being confused in his early days in the I.R.A. because the local I.R.A. were all Catholics, whereas in his early reading about the freedom movements of 1798 and 1805 there were copious references to Protestants. He could not grasp what had happened in the meantime. Nor could he reconcile the fact that local I.R.A. men saw no difficulty in shouting 'Up Dev' and 'Up the I.R.A.' in the same breath. Even as a boy of sixteen this slogan struck MacNamee as containing within it a certain paradox. However, the rebel streak was strong in him and he overcame these confusions and his distaste of the local I.R.A. who were rowdy and given to drink. He moved out of his own parish to the neigh-bouring Greencastle parish and joined a more orderly and responsible company. At that time in 1934–35, little was happening. After six or nine months he, like the young Deegan, emigrated to England and found his way to London where, at the age of seventeen, he became interested in socialism. He found his way into the Republican Congress, which was then active in London, principally under Michael Kelly, Charlie Donnelly (who was killed in Spain fighting for the Republicans), Sean Mulgrew and Tommy Paton. Eventually after the bombing campaign he returned to become ultimately head of the I.R.A. in the North.

Pearse Kelly joined the I.R.A. in Dungannon in late 1939 or early 1940. He was one of a group who had been to school together, attended Irish classes and shared a common Catholic nationalist 'Irish Ireland' outlook. War's outbreak saw troops billeted in the town, and the thoughts of fighting the British became more immediate. Kelly remembers, 'We thought the movement had reached very sad days when the people we saw in it locally were I.R.A. men.' They considered starting a movement of their own, but because of its tradition they decided to join the I.R.A. *en bloc*. They formed a company and absorbed those present. It was a good example of how the I.R.A. exists as a tradition rather than as a cohesive movement. Shortly before joining, Kelly, who was a junior reporter at the time, attended a court at which he saw Eoin MacNamee for the first time. He remembers him as being 'a solid indestructible man who seemed to have a rock-like tenacity'. MacNamee got six months after a hearing which apparently interested him as much as it did the flies on the wall.

It was after this case that Kelly joined the I.R.A. Kelly's area was apparently better armed than MacNamee's because he remembers Thompsons and rifles being used for training around Esker Lough and at his father's and grandfather's farms around the Dungannon area. His first active engagement was against the British when it was proposed that a hall in the Catholic part of the town be used as a billet. The local population regarded this as a slight because an Orange Hall in the Protestant part would have done just as well. Accordingly Kelly and his friends burned down the hall and ended the attempt to billet troops in the Catholic area.

Kelly, a very rigid and upright man, also established a Republican police in the Dungannon area, with a view to keeping the some fifty or so I.R.A. men under his command busy, and at the same time curbing a spate of petty hooliganism and larceny which had broken out in the area. Kelly's police rounded up those concerned in the hooliganism and took them to Edendork outside Dungannon and beat them up. The hooliganism stopped and the I.R.A. stock soared.

As a result of these activities Kelly was brought to Belfast where the principal leaders, Sean McCaughey, Liam Rice and Charlie MacGlade, were just beginning to get suspicious about events in the South and Stephen Hayes. They began to pay frequent visits to the South, thereby paving the way for MacNamee, McCaughey and Kelly to rise in the movement.

In Belfast Kelly was involved in a major I.R.A. coup. An I.R.A. sympathiser, Fergus Kelly, who worked for a chemist in Armagh, had been standing behind his counter when a group of, as he described them, 'British brass hats' came in, made some purchases and went off leaving a long, official-looking envelope on the counter. Opening it he found that it contained various documents which turned out to be the new code, complete with key, for British troops in Northern Ireland. It was due to come into operation in seven days.

Fergus Kelly immediately made an exact copy of everything in the envelope, and then called on Pearse Kelly with the result. They restored the envelope, and when the officers returned the next day they were met in the shop with courtesy, blandness and duplicity. 'Had they found anything?' the officers asked. 'Well what?' asked Fergus. 'An envelope?' 'Ah yes. There was an envelope somewhere.' Then after much searching, 'Would this be it?' and the envelope was taken down from a shelf where it had been shoved casually between two jars of medicine. Some very relieved British officers went off not knowing that the code had been cracked. It duly went into operation and was frequently broken by the I.R.A., although this did not add much to I.R.A. effectiveness. Shortly after Kelly's arrival in Belfast two I.R.A. men got drunk and raced up the Falls Road in a stolen car firing shots, one of which wounded a girl. Two innocent I.R.A. men were pulled in by the R.U.C. Kelly ordered an investigation of I.R.A. men and issued a statement. After describing the events this ended:

At a Courtmartial, James Murphy, ('Spotter') 7, Garnet St, was found guilty of (1) having taken part in the stealing of the car, (2) being in illegal possession of a Revolver the property of the Q.M G., Oglagh na hEireann, (3) endangering the life of Mary Teer by indiscriminate use of Revolver, while under the influence of drink. Accused was dismissed from the Army with ignominy and deported from Belfast.

Terence Donegan, 30, Milan St, was also ordered to leave Belfast, and the remaining three defendants [passengers in the car], were also punished by order of the Courtmartial. The sentences on all five have now been carried out.

Following the pronunciation of the Sentences by the Court-martial the Northern Command Staff made the appended announcement:—

'In view of the alarming frequency of incidents of this nature, and the fact that they are popularly attributed to Oglaigh na hEireann, we desire to issue a stern warning of our determination in future to take drastic measures to stamp out ruthlessly all such attempts to bring Oglaigh na hEireann into disrepute, and we are confident that we shall have the earnest support and co-operation of every loyal citizen of the Republic in our efforts to ensure the efficient administration of justice.'

Signed for and on behalf of the
Northern Command Staff.

Dated this 5th day of July, 1941.

This statement was accepted by the R.U.C. and the two I.R.A. men who had been arrested were released. Had a similar statement been issued by Protestant extremists in the Shankill Road area the R.U.C. would probably have accepted it also. In both areas it was the Protestants and the Catholics who reigned supreme, never the R.U.C or the government of Northern Ireland

This denominational solitary dated back to the days of the famine, when a census in Belfast showed that the population of the city was 35 per cent Catholic, the majority living along the line of today's Falls Road in western Belfast. Unfortunately, in the near vicinity, attracted by the same hopes of getting work that had brought in the Catholics, were the working-class Protestants who lived along the Shankill Road parallel to the Falls. The two sections were frequently in savage conflict because of economics, religion and political allegiances. Around July 12 each year the Shankill people come out in a blaze of bunting to honour King Billy, commemorate the Battle of the Boyne and swear fealty to the union with Britain. Lady's Day, August 15, was traditionally a time of Catholic fervour, though it was not so extreme.

While Catholic sympathy with the I.R.A. was heartening to its leaders, they knew that the influences that drove Catholics into the I.R.A. were also driving Protestant and Catholic apart to such an extent that the I.R.A. must inevitably be lost between them. To present themselves as armed Catholics on the Northern scene would gain no Protestant support, and without this a thirty-two county republic was impossible.

Accordingly the I.R.A. made two major efforts during the 1930s to bridge the religious divide. One attempt was defeated by the Protestants, the other by internal dissension in the I.R.A. itself. The opportunity for the first attempt came during the outdoor relief riots which disfigured Belfast in 1932. These arose over a governmental proposal to cut the rate of outdoor relief as an austerity measure, and it temporarily united both the Protestant and Catholic poor in common outrage.

The Army Council tried to take advantage of this feeling by issuing an 'address from the Army Council of the Irish Republican Army' to the 'men and women of the Orange Order' to coincide with the July celebrations:

Fellow Countrymen and Women,
    It is a long call from the ranks of the Irish Republican Army to the marching throngs that hold the 12th July Celebrations in North East Ulster. Across the space we have sometimes exchanged shots, or missiles or hard words, but never forgetting that on occasions our ancestors have stood shoulder to shoulder. Some day we will again exchange ideas and then the distance which now separates us will shorten. For we of the Irish Republican Army believe that inevitably the small farmers and wage-earners in the Six County area will make common cause with those of the rest of Ireland, for the common good of the mass of the people in a Free United Irish Republic. Such a conviction is forming itself in an ever increasing number of minds in north East Ulster.
    Working-farmers and wage-earners of North East Ulster! You surely must see that your future is bound up with the mass of the people in the remainder of Ireland. To preserve yourselves from extinction, you and they must combine and go forward to the attainment of A Free Irish Nation within which life and living will be organised and controlled by you to serve your needs and thus end the present economic and social injustices for ever. *The industrial capacity, and training of you industrial workers, of North East Ulster ensure for you a leading influence and place in the economy and life of a Free Irish Nation.*

EXPLOITATION OF RELIGIOUS PREJUDICES

To prejudice you it is emphasised that we of the Irish Republican Army and the mass of Republicans are mainly Catholic, and that your religious beliefs would not be respected in a free Ireland! It is quite true we are mainly Catholics, but in Southern Ireland the same political and economical interests and voices that tell you we are Catholics, tell the Catholic population of the South that we are Anti-God fanatics, and yearning for an opportunity to make war on the religion to which the majority of us belong!

The fact is we are quite unaware of religious distinctions within our Movement. *We guarantee you, you will guarantee us, and we will both guarantee all full freedom of conscience and religious worship in the Ireland we are to set free.* This is the simple truth, and just now when Imperial interests are attempting to conceal themselves behind the mad fury of religious strife, you and we should combine to make certain that no such escape should be provided them.

Do you not see yourselves queued shoulder to shoulder outside the Unemployed Exchanges waiting for the 'Dole', that crumb which the exploiters throw to the exploited of different religions? In these vital matters your religion or your membership of the Orange Order counts for little, nor does Catholicism to the unemployed and starving Catholics in Southern Ireland.

The fact is that the religious feelings of the masses of both Orangemen and Catholics are played on and exploited by the Imperialists and Capitalists the more surely to enslave them.

THE VICTORY OF THE BOYNE!

You celebrate the victory of the Boyne. This battle was a victory for the alliance of the then Pope and William of Orange; strange alliance for you to celebrate; strange victory for Catholics to resist. History has been muddled to hide the occasions when your forefathers and ours made common cause, and passions are stirred to manufacture antagonisms. If William of Orange and His Holiness could achieve an alliance, there is hope that 'No Surrender' may come from a throng which also roars 'Up the Republic'.

Your stock was the founders and inspiration, and North East Ulster the cradle, of the modern Revolutionary Movement for National Independence and Economic Freedom. Your illustrious ancestors and co-religionists, The United Irishmen, by their gallant struggle in 1798 set aflame the ideals of Republicanism which never since have been extinguished. We ask that you should join us to achieve their ideals—National Freedom and religious toleration.

The offer of friendship went further than that appeal according to rumours surviving from the period. One member of the Army Council told me flatly that these were not rumours—'We put guns into the hands of Orangemen for use against the B-Specials,' he averred. When I attempted to check the truth of this story with Lord Brookeborough he was thunderstruck. 'You shatter me,' he said and his wife and he shook their heads in disbelief.

But the old sectarianism of Belfast reasserted itself during rioting throughout October, 1932. Republicans said that this was deliberately fomented by some members of the R.U.C in baton charging and firing on Catholics. This is not impossible. In those bad times there was strong Protestant feeling on which the I.R.A. with its emotional appeals could never get a purchase.

The Ulster Protestant League, founded in 1931, adjured its members 'neither to talk nor walk with, neither to buy nor sell, borrow nor lend, take nor give, or have any dealings at all with them, nor for employers to employ them, nor employee to work with them'. The 'them' of course were Catholics and the League habitually paraded through Belfast with bands and banners flying, lambasting the government for being 'soft' on Roman Catholics, just as Paisley's followers did prior to the 1969 riot, calling for the resignation of the minister of home affairs. All this began to have an effect on Protestant support for the government and government spokesmen were driven to show their reliability to the Unionist cause by extremist replies. In his July address, Lord Craigavon made the first of his statements about Protestantism and government in the North—still quoted by long-memoried Nationalists. He said, 'Ours is a Protestant government and I am an Orangeman' and by July, 1934, he had escalated this to 'we are a Protestant parliament and a Protestant State . . . I am an Orangeman first and a member of parliament afterwards.'

Efforts to create unity still, however, continued. The *Republican Congress*, organ of the breakaway I.R.A. section led by Gilmore, Ryan and O'Donnell, had carried in its issue for June 2, 1934, a triumphant page-one headline proclaiming a 'United front between Orange and Green' following the formation of *one* James Connolly Cub for unemployed Protestant and Catholic workers.

Small though this beginning was, it was nevertheless a highly significant step forward, and it was arranged that a sizeable contingent from the Shankill Road would march later on June 17 to Bodenstown with banners bearing inscriptions such as 'Wolfe Tone Commemoration, 1934 Shankill Rd, Belfast Branch. Break the connection with capitalism', 'Connolly's message our ideal', 'James Connolly Club, Belfast, United Irishmen of 1934'. However, when the United Irishmen of the North reached the assembly field at Sallins en route to the graveyard of the founder of the United Irishmen of all Ireland they found the disunited Irishmen of the South waiting for them. A group of Tipperary I.R.A. men, led by a redoubtable figure called Matty Ryan, attacked the Congress group in an attempt to seize the Congress banners which had been proscribed by the Twomey-Fitzpatrick section of the I.R.A. The attempt failed as the two groups clashed to the accompaniment of 'Up Tipp' and 'Come on the Shankill Road'. Eventually the battered Belfast men marched on to Wolfe Tone's grave where further scuffles broke out in which the only lasting damage was to the United Orange-Green front.

Such were the efforts which the Catholic I.R.A. made to woo the Protestants. On the Protestant side another tradition existed which, properly cultivated, should have been more promising. This was the liberal Presbyterian strain of Wolfe Tone exemplified by Rev. W. Montgomery who, though worsted by Cooke, helped to give Northern Protestantism that more attractive vein which never quite dies out, even at moments of extreme religio-politico fervour. Thus during the Home Rule crisis of 1912 one of the sponsors of the plan which brought Winston Churchill to speak in favour of Home Rule in Belfast on February 8 of that year, was the Rev. James Armour of Ballymoney, a man whose memory is justifiably revered in the annals of Northern liberalism. There were Protestant subscribers to this tradition active on the Republican side during the Anglo-Irish war and it was still alive in 1939-40 both in constitutional and unconstitutional politics.

Constitutionally there was the Irish Union Movement, founded by Denis Ireland, a Presbyterian who later became a senator in the Dublin parliament through Sean MacBride's influence. This movement also attracted a considerable amount of liberal Protestant support in the North because of its programme of better relationship with the South, a programme which stemmed from Wolfe Tone's writings. However, on September 10, 1942, it was discovered during an R.U.C. raid on I.R.A. men that some of them, in particular one John S. Graham, had been active in the movement. As the Orangemen had always regarded Denis Ireland as a traitor and renegade because of his all-Ireland view, the I.R.A. men's arrest afforded an opportunity to detain and interrogate members of the Irish Union. This spread the suspicion that it was an I.R.A. hot-bed. Not surprisingly the movement collapsed.

(Graham and some of the other liberal Protestants, who constituted one of the best I.R A. companies in Belfast, had joined the Union, not for purposes of infiltration but through the same tradition that brought them into the I.R.A.: an interest in socialism, Wolfe Tone's writings, the Irish language and the Gaelic League. This group figured in a major crisis within the Belfast I.R.A.)

Despite all the speeches and slogans, the martyrs, commemorations and appeals to tradition the average young I.R.A. man's existence consisted largely of shooting around fields or back streets, holding drill sessions with obsolete weapons in disused halls and talking about 'action' that practically never came. The action that did occur was usually disastrous. In particular there were the two raids on the armoury at Campbell's College which resulted in the celebrated Crown Entry★ raid by the R.U.C. in the midst of an I.R.A. court-martial. The R.U.C. swoop settled some very big I.R.A. fish, including Jim Killeen, Michael Traynor and Tony MacLaverty, O.C. of the Belfast battalion, who was being court-martialled at the time. This was not for any misdemeanour but because he had issued instructions to some of the I.R.A. men who were caught in the armoury raids, allowing them to recognise the courts so that they had a chance of making a defence.

Increased wartime pressures on the I.R.A. made communication between Dublin and Belfast more difficult, and some Northerners began to think that a self-contained Northern unit was desirable. The principal architect of this idea was Charles MacGlade, a Belfast printer, and so 'Northern Command' came into being. The command in fact embraced seven counties, the six counties of Ulster proper and Co. Donegal. Eoin MacNamee, who later became its head, first heard of this unit in June, 1939, after his return from the bombing campaign in England. The formation of this command meant that the I.R.A. in the South was led from Dublin, in the North from Belfast, in England from God knows where and that each group carried on more or less independently of each other.†

Although it was widely discussed in I.R.A. circles, Northern Command's level of organisation may be judged from the fact that there were supposed to be two battalions in Co. Tyrone, Eoin MacNamee's native county, but when he began to organise there weren't twenty members in the whole county. But such was the spirit of the volunteers and MacNamee's expertise in training, that he remembers being able to set up fairly good battalions in both east and west Tyrone within six weeks. Their armaments, however, consisted only of a few weapons left over from 1922.

It is worth following MacNamee's career as it impinged on most aspects of I.R.A. activity. He was captured on June 11, 1939, charged with being a member of the I.R.A. and sentenced to six months in Crumlin Road Jail. After serving his time he told the authorities that he was going to Newry to give them the impression he was going to cross the border. He was issued with a Newry ticket, but on leaving the prison he was met by a girl, and placed in a 'pound loney' area of the Falls Road used

---

★   An 'entry' in Belfast is a narrow lane, or entry, for passers-by from one street to another.
†   This picture of a lack of communication is not exaggerated. Pearse Kelly, one of the first people I interviewed for this book, compared my lack of knowledge on starting my research to his incomprehension about Dublin's affairs when the Hayes investigation first took him to the South.

as an I.R.A. barracks. He remembers young men with guns and batons setting out on all sorts of military excursions. Everyone in the house was courteous to him but he soon discovered that he was under a form of house arrest! The Command had apparently decided to suspend him for illegal organising in Tyrone. When this news leaked out a mutiny took place in Tyrone. Then a communication arrived ordering MacNamee to return home. Part of this silly row lay in the fact that there is a traditional Tyrone versus Belfast animus somewhat akin to that existing between Cork and Dublin. However, since he was to be reinstated without trouble, the row blew over and Eoin returned to find himself a hero in Co. Tyrone.

He also found that there was little a hero could do apart from organising parades and training camps, but he was then appointed Adjutant General in West Tyrone and about April, 1940, he went on the run. He remembers that four or five other prominent Tyrone men had to do the same, so there were a number of full-time organisers working throughout Tyrone. (The adjoining Donegal, though partially in the Free State area, was much more difficult to organise because it did not have the abrasive reality of Union Jacks, British uniforms, gerrymandering and discrimination before it.) About this time he met Sean McCaughey for the first time. McCaughey was O.C. of the Northern Command, which had a headquarters in Carrickmore, near Joe McGarrity's old homestead. All seemed to be going well now, but the course of I.R.A. ways never run smooth. With the exception of MacNamee all the fulltime organisers in Tyrone were captured in a gun battle with the R.U.C. at Carrickmore.★

Eoin then moved up to become brigade O.C., reorganising the brigade staff to cover gaps left by the arrests, and despite these had the brigade whipped into a pretty effective unit by the autumn of 1940. It was at this stage that the issue of the Belfast battalion courts-martial blew up. For some time past volunteers had complained that battalion officers had been beating them up. There was at the time a strong Fascist influence in Belfast I.R.A. circles. An occasional I.R.A. man affected the Bersaglieri cap of Mussolini's crack troops and Fascist techniques, such as beatings with batons and doses of castor oil were frequently employed by what was known as the 'belt and boot brigade'.

Looking at newspapers of the time one will sometimes come across small paragraphs about young men being beaten up by unidentified passers-by. These incidents were the ones that came to the surface; others did not, and some were pretty savage. A favourite I.R.A. punishment of the time for serious dereliction of duty was wounding a man in the leg, or in both legs for more serious cases, with a revolver shot. Frank Morris of Convoy, Co. Donegal, one of the few reliable men whom Eoin had been able to recruit to the I.R.A. in the county, told me that his first noteworthy I.R.A. action was to attend a court-martial at which the sentence on a suspected informer was wounding in both legs. This was later reduced to wounding in one leg only, but the sentence was duly carried out.

★   They were Arthur Kearney, Jim Brogan, Pat McCallan and Jim Kirk. Another prominent I.R.A. man, Dan McMahon, was captured and left in his own home on the night of the raid under the guard of an R.U.C. man while the rest of the party went to surround the men at Carrickmore. However, when the R.U.C. man guarding McMahon heard the shooting at nearby Carrickmore he went to the door to see what was happening What he couldn't see happening was Dan McMahon making his escape through the back door!

Those who sanctioned these punishments felt that volunteers needed fear to keep them in line, whereas other prominent leaders, in particular Jimmy Steele, disagreed violently. To Steele, membership of the I.R.A. was an honour and privilege, and this fact alone enjoined a high standard of conduct. He first heard of these activities in Crumlin Road Jail, and began taking statements from incoming volunteers so that on his release he had a complete dossier. With this he had the entire battalion staff court-martialled in a little hall in a 'loney' off the Falls. It was a strange business and while it was being held Belfast was like an armed camp, with armoured cars, ordinary police cars and foot patrols four and five strong on every side of the street in the area. Evidently the R.U.C. had word of some impending I.R.A. activity, but didn't know what it was to be.

The outcome of the court-martial was that a number of officers were reduced to the ranks. This curbed the 'belt and boot' faction for some time, but the issue arose again when the command staff was arrested in the Hayes affair.

All that prevented serious trouble then was the fact that McCaughey's case was before the courts in Dublin. Everyone felt that any outbreak of shooting would prejudice a verdict. McCaughey was sentenced to death but was reprieved and sent to Portlaoise Jail. It is thought that his reprieve came through the intercession of Cardinal MacRory. The I.R.A. did make overtures to the Church on his behalf; MacNamee went to see the Bishop of Down and Connor, Dr Mageean, who was generally regarded in Nationalist circles as a Republican sympathiser, but he offered no encouragement. But perhaps the bishop took another line in private with the cardinal because McCaughey's reprieve was quite unexpected. On the other hand, although the government was incensed at the Hayes confession and the embarrass-ment it caused, McCaughey had not been captured bearing arms, or as a result of any affray that had cost life. So, even in wartime, his execution would have aroused violent reaction. (The I.R.A. had made preparations so that if he had been executed, a prominent intelligence officer from the Gardai who had been decoyed to Belfast, ostensibly to meet Eoin MacNamee, would have been ambushed and shot.)

After the reprieve, MacNamee and Hugh McAteer found that in the wake of the Hayes affair the activities of the 'belt and boot' brigade resumed and their own leadership was challenged. So, one night in November, 1941, MacNamee mobilised the Protestant company, led by John Graham. They drafted in a squad of men from county brigades and left a man on the Falls Road to tell Graham that, if they did not return very shortly, he and McAteer were to be followed into a house on the Falls Road where the battalion was meeting—with guns blazing if necessary.

MacNamee and McAteer were both armed and their appearance at the battalion meeting caused alarm. Eoin told the senior officer present that if the battalion failed to co-operate with the command, he would be shot. In a tense atmosphere, a member of the battalion staff, Patsy Hicks, one of its strongest figures, stammered out, 'I've seen these things before. I'm taking orders from the command O.C.' Hicks was known to have seen some stern affairs, so his reaction deflated the balloon of defiance at once. The atmosphere grew more cordial as allegiance was reaffirmed and every-body settled down to discuss future plans. Meantime, the Protestant squad, whom MacNamee had forgotten, rushed into the room prepared to shoot. Seeing MacNamee unharmed, they too calmed down and the incident ended peaceably.

After the Hayes affair it was clear that the I.R.A. had no immediate role in the South and a series of provincial conventions were set in train to decide future policy. MacNamee took over the one in Connacht; Sean McCool, who had succeeded Pearse Kelly as chief of staff, that of Munster; Hugh McAteer that of Ulster, and Frank Driver the Leinster gathering. Out of these conventions some degree of reorganisation took place with a view to transferring activities across the border and beginning a campaign exclusively in the North. About 20,000 rounds of the Magazine Fort ammunition, .303 calibre bullets for rifles, had found its way into MacNamee's custody in Tyrone, and between this and a quantity of arms still existing in various dumps throughout the South, it was felt that the I.R.A. was still relatively well-organised in the North. Against a backdrop of strong Catholic support, it could strike a reasonably effective blow against the administration.

But as with the English campaign the first blows were stuck by the Southern authorities against the I.R.A. MacNamee, who was attending Skerry's College in St Stephen's Green, Dublin, under the name of Diamond, ostensibly to learn Morse code, but in reality to provide a cover for his presence in Dublin, was picked up in Brandon Road as he walked towards a dump in the Drimnagh area of Dublin. Within a few weeks Sean McCool joined him in the Curragh.

However, the defiant and resilient Northerners pressed ahead with their plans for a campaign which was finally agreed to at a Northern Command convention held on March 25, 1942, in Belfast. The funds for the campaign were obtained by a raid on the Academy Street Civil Defence Headquarters, which netted about £4,200 of payroll for civil defence workers throughout the North. The I.R.A. was in debt at the time to landladies who had put up men on the run and part of the Academy Street money went to paying these bills. The rest went on buying information* from police sources, on the provision of medical attention for wounded men, for printing Tarlach O'hUid's newspaper, the *Republican News*, running radio trans- mitters and buying ammunition or guns from British soldiers. It would have been better if no guns had been obtained for the campaign. Three I.R.A. men died as a result, one by hanging, two by shooting on the streets of Belfast, and five members of the R.U.C. and of the special constabulary lost their lives.

Constable Thomas James Forbes, a married man with four children, was the first policeman to be shot in the North for ten years when he and a group of other police were fired on in Dungarmon on April 4, 1942. Constable William Mackey survived with fractured ribs because a bullet, aimed at his heart, struck a button in his coat. The following day Constable Patrick Murphy was shot dead in Cashmere Road, Belfast. A group of young I.R.A. men involved in this shooting, all of them under nineteen, retreated to Cawnpore Street, where they made their way into a house. Here they were arrested by four of Murphy's comrades, whom they could easily have killed as they came up the stairs, but did not. All six were sentenced to death for the murder of the policeman, and this sparked off the greatest agitation initiated by I.R.A. action during the whole of the war.

---

* Before being picked up MacNamee had established contacts with intelligence personnel in the Southern army who, he told me, showed him their reports before passing them on to their superiors.

In Dublin Sean MacBride set up a reprieve committee and acted as its secretary. No fewer than 207,000 signatures were collected, and huge meetings were addressed by such diverse speakers as Denis Ireland of the Irish Union, Jim Larkin, the trade unionist, and past and present Republicans of every shade and hue, including members of Fianna Fail. The agitation spread outside Ireland. Secretary of State Cordell Hall took up the matter after being pressed by the Irish minister to Washington, Robert Brennan. The execution of six I.R.A. men for the death of one would have jeopardised Fianna Fail's effort to keep order, to say nothing of the effect in the North.

Hull also saw Anthony Eden in Washington and put pressure on Lord Halifax, the British ambassador. In London the American ambassador, John Winant, made representations. In Dublin the American ambassador, David Gray, said that 'some measure of clemency is probably expedient. The British and Canadian representatives here hold the same opinion. Hanging six for one would shock public opinion.' However, Gray took a poor view of all the pressure for reprieves, and in a letter dated August 27, 1942, to de Valera wrote:

Those of us who like yourself have attempted and are attempting by diplomatic means to procure a measure of clemency for these young men, find ourselves embarrassed by the pressure exerted here upon the Northern Government. As you know, governments, especially in war time, do not like to be coerced and fear that clemency used under pressure will be interpreted as weakness.

I am afraid that if we fail, the originators of the pressure campaign will have a heavy responsibility. I appreciate your sincere desire to help this agitation within reasonable bounds and your considerable success in this direction, but repeat what I said in our recent talk—that, except for yourself and a few others, Ireland does not come to appreciate what the war means, the gravity of the situation and the danger of rocking the boat at such a time.

Yours sincerely
David Gray.

Irish sentiment in America was less sensitive than Gray's and influential congressmen such as the majority leader Senator McCormick, and many others urged the State Department to intervene.

The agitation was largely successful. Five of the six were reprieved, only Thomas Williams being hanged on September 2. It is believed in Belfast that the British cabinet favoured hanging all six, to deter the I.R.A. from activity for the rest of the war, but that Cardinal MacRory from Armagh approached Cardinal Hinsley, who was friendly with Brendan Bracken, Churchill's wartime minister for information. Bracken, an Irishman himself, could claim superior local knowledge and his word probably carried exceptional weight.

Williams's hanging was a frightful business that could have occurred only in Belfast. On the night before his death, Catholics kept vigil outside the jail saying the Rosary, while an Orange mob jeered them, shouting obscenities about Williams and singing Orange ballads.

Before his execution Williams wrote the following letter to McAteer:

Hugh, a Cara,

Just a note to let you know how my comrades and I are getting along. I do not expect an answer as your answer to Joe serves us all in that respect.

I am proud to know that you are our leader. My comrades and I are sure that you will use your utmost powers to free our dear, beloved country. And bring about the reestablishment of the Republic and its constitution.

It is beyond the powers of my humble intellect, to describe the pride of my comrades, in knowing that they are going to follow, in the footsteps of those who have given their lives to Ireland and the Republic. To describe the courage and coolness shown when sentenced to death. As Joe has previously stated to you. Our sorrow is not being able to attack the court and the 'Northern' Junta. But now you know the reason.

My God, can we tell you and our comrades who will carry on the fight, can we tell you of the gladness and joy that is in our hearts. To know that the Irish people are again united, aye, and well may England quake, Irelands awake, Irelands awake. After 20 years of slumber our nation will once again strike, Please God, at the despoilers who have infringed the nation's liberty, freedom and murdered her sons, her daughters, who have given us a foreign tongue; shall please God, strike and strike hard and make the tyrants go on their knees for mercy and forgiveness.

But shall we make the mistake of '21, no, no, tis men like you and your staff will see to it. That no farcical so-called Treaty shall in anyway be signed by a bunch of weak-kneed and willed Irishmen. Better that the waves of the mighty oceans sweep over Erin than take and divide our nation, murder her true sons again. Better would be that heavens would open and send fire to destroy Erin, than to accept another Treaty like it.

In writing this, dear Hugh, do not think that I am saying it to you or the gallant soldiers of Oglaigh na hEireann, it is from my heart that it comes to the weak-willed and ignorant Irish men who may put any trust in England. My only regret is now I will not be with you in the fight and last stand of Ireland's battle for freedom. But with the help of God and His Blessed Mother we may be in heaven looking down upon our dear, beloved, tortured, crucified Erin, and look with pride on the men and women who will carry on the battle until victory.

Well dear Hugh I'll close with the message to Oglaidh na hEireann, 'To carry on, no matter what odds are against you, to carry on no matter what torments are inflicted on you. The road to freedom is paved with suffering, hardships and torture, carry on my gallant and brave comrades until that certain day.'

Your comrade in Ireland's cause,
Lieut. Tom Williams,
'C' Coy. Belfast Brigade,
Oglaigh na hEireann.

For days before and after Williams's execution, tension hung over Belfast, particularly in Nationalist quarters. Two days before Williams was hanged, one of Hugh McAteer's principal lieutenants, Gerry O'Callaghan, was shot dead when the R.U.C. raided a dump at Harmanstown outside Belfast. O'Callaghan was moving arms to a safer place, for use in avenging Williams's death. Demonstrations took place in Dublin against business premises that refused to close and riots broke out throughout the city. In the North the reaction was grimmer—although the condemned man himself had sent a letter to his comrades asking that no reprisals be taken for his death. Within an hour of his execution police patrols were being fired on. At Clady, Co. Tyrone, Constable James Laird and Special Constable Samuel Hamilton were shot dead on September 5. In Belfast on the same day a shooting took place in Abercorn Street, when an R.U.C. man and a boy of sixteen were wounded. And of four I.R.A. men arrested under arms in Belfast on the same day, two were sixteen and one seventeen years old.

The wave of bombing and shootings finally led to a curfew in Nationalist areas of west Belfast. From October 10 no movement was permitted on the streets between 8.30 p.m. and 6.00 am. On the first day of the curfew a battle broke out outside Donegal Pass police barracks after a bomb was thrown there. Special Constable James Lyons was faulty wounded and a number of other police and passers-by received lesser injuries. All these incidents affected the nerves of Belfast people, but the campaign petered out with the enforcement of the curfew, although a shooting on October 1, 1943 claimed the life of Constable Patrick McCarthy, shot dead during a payroll raid on Clonard Mill at Odessa Street off the Falls Road.

The I.R.A. had intended to bring a number of other police officials and warders to their Maker but these plans misfired. One of the most celebrated policemen Northern Ireland has ever produced is District Inspector James Fanning, who was a particular scourge of the I.R.A. He was cycling to work one morning when a car passed him and a Chicago-style assassination was attempted. He was shot off his bicycle, and he described to me how he lay on the pavement with 'a feeling of cold and surprise. I felt the sting of the bullets, but no pain, just terrible cold.' The car carrying his would-be killers passed so close that he could see the men in it, handkerchiefs round their faces, as they fired through the windows at him. The bullets struck the pavement near his head and around his body. His wounds were so bad that when he was picked up blood ran out through the eyelets of his shoes, but he recovered after a lengthy stay in hospital and returned to duty.

He was not long back at work when one of those responsible for shooting at him (both I.R.A. and R.U.C. very often had a shrewd idea of what transpired in the enemy's camp without always being in a position to do anything about it) sought a permit to go to England. Fanning duly issued one, but could not resist asking the man if 'he was not ashamed of what he had done'. His assailant replied, 'Oh now Mr Fanning I don't want to talk about that at all.' In the circumstances, Fanning regarded his attitude as being entirely understandable, if reprehensible, and there the exchange closed.

All these incidents made the I.R.A. seem a formidable force to the public, but in fact, as in the South, the reality was quite otherwise. A week after the hanging of Williams, on September 10, the publicity headquarters of Northern Command was raided and the owner of the house, Sean Dynan, John Graham, the O.C. of the Belfast battalion, and David Fleming from Kerry were captured along with a complete issue of the I.R.A. paper the *Republican News*. This last loss was remedied by the efforts of McAteer, Gerry O'Reilly and others who sat up during the night producing a further 6,000 copies which duly were distributed.

Then on October 6 McAteer and O'Reilly were themselves captured. They had been decoyed to the home of a boyhood friend of McAteer's who was then a member of the R.U.C. and who had, by chance, bumped into McAteer earlier in the week and promised him some worthwhile information if McAteer would call to his home. The life of this young man hung by a very slender thread thereafter, but McAteer refused to have him executed as he could easily have done either later in the war or after it. (However, the man's father's undertaking business fell off and he went bankrupt as a result of an unofficial boycott against him.) After his capture McAteer received a fifteen-year sentence and was sent to Crumlin Road Jail, from which he immediately planned to escape.

The walls of the jail are more than three feet thick, the windows are barred and thick glass is set into steel frames. A twenty-foot wall surrounds the front garden overlooked by warders' quarters and the administrative offices and, during the war, this wall was patrolled by armed guards. If a prisoner did succeed in getting so far he then had to run past the windows of the warders' cottages outside the walls. Normally there was also a police patrol on Crumlin Road itself, a busy artery in the heart of Belfast. However, a trapdoor was discovered in the ceiling of the lavatory which led to an attic under the slates of the jail roof. McAteer, Paddy Donnelly, the prisoners' leader, Jimmy Steele and Edward Maguire decided to escape together. Ladders were made from sheets torn lengthwise in halves and the halves then sewn together end to end and bound with waxen cords. A hook was made from a brass bed end to catch the top of the wall and bandages were wrapped around it so that it would catch in the barbed wire with which the wall was protected.

On the morning of January 15, 1943, the four received permission to go to the lavatory and, standing on a table which was later removed by their friends, hauled themselves up into the attic, replacing the trapdoor underneath them. Once in the attic, they smashed their way out on to the roof. Incredibly, no one heard the noise of the breaking slates. They reached the wall without mishap, here to discover that the jointed stick which they had made to hoist the hook on to the wall was too short. Maguire stood on McAteer's shoulders in an attempt to hoist the hook on, but fell off. He and McAteer began squabbling as to whose fault this was when Donnelly intervened to say specifically, 'I think, lads, ye should finish this conversation on the other side of the wall!'

They eventually got over the wall safely, McAteer alone being injured with torn ligaments in his ankle and a badly reefed hand from the barbed wire. In the gloom of the January morning no one noticed them mingling with the crowds and, despite the fact that they were wearing prison clothes, Belfast's wartime shabbiness afforded them protection in this regard also. A £3,000 reward was immediately posted for the capture of any or all of the four, but Maguire and Donnelly stayed free to the end of the war, Steele lasted until May, and McAteer was not picked up until the following November.

The escape gave the I.R.A. a brief injection of life and McAteer and Steele figured in two spectacular exploits during their freedom. The first of these was the Derry Jail escape which was being prepared before McAteer's and Steele's exploit. The ground floor cells of Derry Jail were floored with wood, beneath which was nothing but clay. A group of prisoners—Liam Graham, Eddie Steele, John McGreevy and James O'Hagan—began to tunnel under the floor of Liam Graham's cell and, working for over five months, they and their prison comrades managed to sink a shaft extending twenty feet straight down and turning sharply to extend out under the roadway outside the jail and up into the coal hole of the Logue family in Harding Street. The clay was dumped into lavatories and twice the sewers clogged as a result, but although the sewers were laid bare and the clay discovered, the authorities apparently never connected its presence with an escape bid. The larger boulders which the diggers encountered were hidden under the floorboards of other ground floor cells. Once the escape nearly ended in tragedy when a tunnel collapse buried Graham, but he was dug out before he suffocated.

The escape was timed for March 21 and the day before this Steele hired a truck in Belfast and drove to Derry. En route the driver stopped at an R.U.C. barracks to deliver a message which gave Steele a nasty scare. While the driver was inside, for all Steele knew giving the game away, he had the unnerving experience of sitting on a level with a poster announcing a £3,000 reward for the capture of Hugh McAteer, James Steele, Paddy Donnelly or Edward Maguire who had feloniously broken out of Crumlin Road Jail. Nobody in the barracks connected the driver's helper with the photograph on the poster and the driver went on blithely to Derry where, to his horror, Steele produced a revolver and informed him of what lay ahead.

Twenty-one prisoners made their escape through Graham's tunnel, while outside the door one of the inmates played the bagpipes to cover the noise of their departure. The last prisoner to shoulder his way to escape was Brendan O'Boyle (who got clean away and remained at liberty throughout the war in Dublin only to die tragically later). Fifteen prisoners piled into the truck and made their way over the border where they were picked up by the Southern army and lodged in the Curragh for the duration of the war. Unknown to the army patrol which held up the truck, a woman with a camera was standing behind a hedge when this happened and took a photograph of the incident.

This escape created a fantastic impact on Nationalist sentiment, coming on top of the Crumlin Road breakout. The I.R.A. leaders began casting round for some similar exploit to impress public opinion and raise morale within the I.R.A. without, at the same time, endangering life. A young volunteer suggesting holding up either a picture house or a dance hall for the purpose of making a demonstration while volunteers guarded the doorways. Steele and McAteer were highly enthusiastic, but to avoid loose talk they told the volunteer that his idea was impractical. They themselves decided that the following Easter they would take over a place of public amusement. The Broadway Cinema not far from the Falls Road was selected as the target and on Holy Saturday afternoon, sixteen volunteers set off, two at a time, to converge on the cinema. The manager and projectionist were held up while armed volunteers guarded every exit and entrance. A slide was then flashed on the screen:

This cinema has been commandeered by the Irish Republican Army for the purpose of holding an Easter Commemoration for the dead who died for Ireland.

Jimmy Steele then read the 1916 Proclamation from the stage and Hugh McAteer read a statement of I.R.A. policy for the coming year. The proceedings closed with the observance of a one minute's silence for the dead and the raiders got away safely. Statements were issued to all the newspapers and Lord Haw-Haw included the incident in his broadcast from Berlin that evening.

While these exploits raised the stock of the I.R.A. enormously among its sympathisers they had the opposite effect on their enemies, particularly among prison warders. Up to the time when the war began to swing against the Germans, warders in Belfast generally treated the I.R.A. prisoners with some deference, but when it became apparent that the allies were likely to win, the I.R.A. came in for sterner treatment, and jail escapes marked a turning point in warder-I.R.A. relationships.

Hitherto, the hundred or so Republican prisoners in Belfast Jail had tried various methods to secure political treatment. These included not doing the prescribed prison work and going on hunger strike, and though they failed to gain their objective a kind of unofficial political status was accorded the prisoners. After the Crumlin Road escape, however, prison regulations were sternly enforced, and cell searches and bread-and-water diets became commonplace. One result of these antics was that the prisoners sent out word asking their comrades to shoot a particularly bullying warder, but the most popular warder in the prison was killed by mistake.

The prisoners then resorted to the 'strip strike'. John Graham and David Fleming had argued against a hunger strike, because it either weakened prisoners irretrievably or had to be carried through to the death. So a strip strike started in mid June, 1943. Twenty-two prisoners* in Belfast Jail took off their prison clothes and the authorities retaliated by taking every other article from their cells, including their handkerchiefs. Bedding and blankets were not restored until 8.30 each evening. Towels were taken after the morning wash and no reading material was permitted other than religious books. Cells were then left empty apart from the prisoner himself, the frame of his iron bed, his sanitary vessel and a carafe of water for the whole day.

An account of what the strip strike was like, was written by Seamus Steele in a journal he produced in 1954, *Resurgent Ulster.*

The prison bell goes at 7 o'clock. You awaken with a start. No nice slow leisurely wakening here but before the last clang you are wide awake. The cold bar walls stare back at you and you realise that you have another long day to spend naked. You ponder how long it is until you will see that bed again—13 hours—780 minutes—46,800 seconds and you have to live thru' every second. But you have a half hour yet for the warders do not come until 7.30. How you treasure that last half hour. The old lumpy fibre mattress, the army blankets, and the hard worsted sheets feel like down. For soon you hear the clang of the keys and the rush of feet. The warders have arrived. They are laughing and joking and full of the ordinary joys of life. You wonder if the fight is really worth while. But this passes very quickly and you get the courage to at least last another day. The slops are removed and the door is banged in your face again. You still have another minute or two and you get back into bed again. When the bed is moved you stand naked in your cold bare cell.

At eight o'clock the breakfast arrived. This consists of one pint of tea, eight ounces of bread, and half an ounce of margarine. Your table and chair have been removed so you take your treasure to the old bedstead. You try to eat it slowly as you know it will do you more good and it will last longer, but the hunger is so great that you eat it very quickly. Any stray crumbs are quickly retrieved. You drink the tea and all is finished and you are nearly as hungry as ever. It will be four and a half hours before you get any more.

Now the day has really begun. You hear the prisoners going out to work. How you envy them their warm clothes. They are happy people. Nevertheless the fight must go on. The day must be spent. You begin the parade again. Eight paces up, one at the turn, and eight paces back again. You begin this parade and people wonder what is the matter with you. Perhaps you make a football out of an old pair of socks and try to get the blood to circulate. You think on how cold it is even though it is the month of June. What will it be like in January? You put

---

* James Brogan, Tyrone; Frank Morris, Tyrone; David Fleming, Kerry; John McMahon, Portadown; Ned Tennyson, Portadown; Sean Gallagher, Derry; P. Heggarty, Derry; John Graham, Belfast; Joe Cahill, Belfast; Dan McAlister, Belfast; Gerry Adams, Belfast; James Hannon, Belfast; Joe Myles, Belfast; R. Dempsey, Belfast; H. O'Hara, Belfast; S. McParland, Belfast; P. Corrigan, Belfast; Charles McCotter, Belfast; T. Morley, Belfast; W. Doyle, Belfast; J. McCusker, and Seamus 'Jimmy' Steele, Belfast.

this out of your head at once. The sun is shining outside but this does not reach your cell. What is that? A knock on the wall and then a knock on the pipes. It is the signal that your next door neighbour wants to speak to you. You listen at the door and all is quiet. You get your enamel mug and use it as a kind of telephone on the pipes. Perhaps there is some news. But no! Your pal is finding it hard also and you try to encourage him. Stick it a little longer and there is no knowing what will happen. Suddenly the spy-hole is opened and an unfriendly eye looks in and gives a sharp order to get off the pipes. Even this small luxury is denied us. Well, on it must go. You begin the parade again or perhaps read a few pages of the Bible. You read but you do not take anything in. There is such a vast difference between what you read and the position you are in. Perhaps if you read the part on Job you get a little comfort. He has done his suffering for God, you are suffering for a principle. It helps a lot if you offer it to God too.

It is usual for them to search your cell. What do they expect to get in your empty tomb? Perhaps a small butt of a cigarette that you managed to get. At any rate everything is gone through, even at times your hair and beard. You will have a beard by this time for you are not allowed a razor. Perhaps if they did the death of Tone could be reenacted. You cannot see this beard for your mirror has also been removed.

The dinner arrives and you are just ravenous. This consists of one pint of soup, two ounces meat, one ounce vegetables and about three small potatoes. If one potato is bad it is a calamity. There is no use asking for another one for you will in all probability get another bad one and draw down the enmity of a warder on your defenceless shoulders. Well, you eat everything— potatoes, skins—every scrap, no matter how unpalatable it is it fills an empty space. It is now only twelve o'clock and you think it is only four and a half hours from the morning, that is another eight and a half hours to go until you get into that bed again. You lie on the cold bedstead and try to rest for you have been on the constant move since the morning trying to keep warmth in your body. You are so cold that you begin the whole parade again. Perhaps you have a visit from the prison chaplain. You are delighted to see him and at the same time feel embarrassed and ashamed. You do not like to detain him too long as he has to visit all the other fighters and perhaps some of the other prisoners as well. He has a very difficult job. You can see the light of sympathy in his eyes and at the same time he gives you to understand that he thinks you are striking your head against a stone wall. Perhaps you are too. You are in the grip of a mighty machine. What is the use? Others fought against it for years. Some went to an early grave, while others went mad. What was to be your fate? Nevertheless you must not let your comrades down. We are all in this to the end.

At two o'clock the noise starts again. The other prisoners go out to work and you have simply nothing to do. In these circumstances a man realises how incomplete he is on his own and how much a social creature he really is. How content you would be doing anything. Even the hateful monotonous task of sewing mail bags that you were doing before the strike began. Perhaps you climb on the back of your bed and look out of your window. There is very little to be seen. Perhaps some hapless creatures marching around a ring in the courtyard awaiting trial. Perhaps some of your own comrades who will get the same kind of a trial that you got and a savage sentence. If you are caught it will almost certainly mean a report followed by a sentence of 'bread and water'. They cannot confine you any closer but your diet will be reduced to a total of eight ounces of bread and one pound of potatoes per day. These morsels make you feel more hungry than if you get nothing at all.

At four o'clock the prisoners return from the shops and the tea arrives which consists of the same as the morning with one pint of porridge and half a pint of milk. This has to keep you going till eight o'clock the next morning. You could eat it at once and still be hungry but you must keep a little for later in the evening. Even though there is still four hours left you have the day's back broken. You have done nine hours and every hour you do leaves one more down and one less to do. If you get a chance now you try to get something from the prisoner next to you. This is done by using a string, which you had concealed, and a weight. Perhaps you have a few booklets to exchange that will while away the monotony of the evening. If you are caught it will mean punishment but it is worth the risk. Look at the satisfaction you get if you succeed. Even if it is only a small thing you have a feeling that you have beaten them.

Perhaps the prisoner below you who is in sympathy with your ideals sends you some of his food on the line. His own food is little enough and if he is caught it will mean punishment for him but he knows you are fighting his fight too. The time is passing but will 8.30 never come? At long last you hear the rattle of the keys. How welcome is that sound now. They start at the top. Will they never reach your length? The door opens and you get your bed. You are under the clothes in a few minutes. You are asleep in a few more. It does seem a pity to go to sleep as you don't find the time until that awful bell goes again.

Conditions seem to have been even colder than they would have been in winter for in prison the heating is switched off during the summer and the stone cells had no way of heating up. The strike was called off after about three months to allow John Graham to get treatment for a badly swollen knee.

McAteer was recaptured on November 21 as he was coming out of St Paul's Church, and with his capture the era of the I.R.A. as a significant fighting force in Belfast came to an end. In jail, prisoners still asserted their demands for political treatment by going on hunger strike, but outside, police pressure and the war itself combined to destroy the organisation. Protestants and Catholics who huddled together in air raid shelters during the Belfast bombings never had quite the same bitter animosity towards each other after the war. And the introduction by the British Labour government of the welfare state to the North (despite the votes of twelve Tory candidates from the North against these movitations) damped down rebellious feelings. Henceforward, Northern Catholics began to seek an end to gerrymandering and discrimination in housing and jobs, rather than a reunion of the country under a Dublin parliament. When the I.R.A. campaign broke out in 1956, it was obvious even to I.R.A. leaders in Dublin, who had grown up in the meantime, that Belfast was not a suitable theatre for operations. The city remained calm despite events along the border.

17. An early group of B-Specials. First organised by Lord Brookeborough in 1920, this Protestant Unionist volunteer militia rapidly spread to all parts of the Six Counties.

18. A group of I.R.A. men tunnelled out of a Derry jail in March, 1943, and fled across the border in a truck. They were picked up by Southern soldiers and interned. This photograph of their arrest was taken by a woman who stood unnoticed behind a hedge.

19. An R.U.C. man with a Sten gun outside his barracks in 1957. The poster offers a reward for information about the death of R.U.C. Sgt. Arthur Ovens.

20. Irish-American "Minute Men" picket the British consulate in New York in April, 1958. They were protesting against the trial and ill treatment of two men from County Tyrone for taking part in a booby-trap murder of R.U.C. Sgt. Arthur Ovens.

21. A British soldier describes his narrow escape from the I.R.A. to his compatriots, 1954. The photograph was taken through a hole in the wall surrounding the barracks, unbeknownst to those inside. (*Colman Doyle*)

22. A British Army patrol from the Royal Warwickshire Regiment on the streets of Belfast in the mid-1950s.

23. Rev. Ian Paisley's Ulster Constitution Defence Committee blocking Armagh city centre to civil rights marchers, November, 1968. Their cudgels had nails driven through them. (*Colman Doyle*)

24. Rev. Ian Paisley during his first campaign for election to Stormont. (*Colman Doyle*)

25. B-Specials in Derry, August, 1969. The handkerchiefs are for protection against gas. (*Colman Doyle*)

26. A young Nationalist citizen of Derry faces the R.U.C. during the Battle of the Bogside, August, 1969. (*Colman Doyle*)

27. A canister of tear gas lands on the Bogside barricades, August, 1969. (*Colman Doyle*)

28. At the height of the Battle of the Bogside, an R.U.C. armoured car burns in William Street. (*Colman Doyle*)

8

The Years of the Curragh

Ground between the Military Court and the Curragh, the I.R.A. men in the South shared similar experiences to those of the North with street shootings, individual acts of heroism, executions and defiance of prison regulations. While the provincial conferences were being held and the Northern campaign plans were being laid, it became obvious that the prime need to carry out such plans was the provision of some reliable men. Sean McCool sent word from the Curragh for a number of selected personnel to 'sign out'—that is, to give undertakings of good behaviour for the future.

Two of these were Seamus 'Rocky' Burns and Harry White. Burns was killed in a gun battle with the R.U.C. in Belfast on June 2, 1944. Even though he had 'signed out' under orders, such was the rigidity of the traditional Republican sentiment to 'signing out', or recognising courts, that several Belfast Republicans refused to attend his funeral because he had 'signed out'.

White, a plumber by trade, had been active in the bombing campaign in England before his internment. After his release he went on the run and escaped police surveillance until one evening in November, 1942, when he and a comrade, Maurice O'Neill from Kerry, were holed up in a house in Donnycarney, Dublin, and a party of Special Branch men made a lightning raid.

Shooting followed and Detective Officer Mordant was killed. White made a break and succeeded in getting out the back, across a number of adjoining gardens and walls until finally, hurling himself over a wall leading to a railway embankment, he fell sixteen feet into a dense thicket of briars. He lay there for two days with a gunshot wound in the leg while around him the police combed the area. Eventually, covered in mud and blood, he made his way to a bus-stop, boarded a bus, dismounted in crowded O'Connell Street in the heart of Dublin, and walked to a refuge in the Summerhill area of Dublin, where he learned that there was a price of £5,000 on the head of one Harry White, alias Anderson.

A few days later, Maurice O'Neill was executed in Mountjoy Prison for Mordant's murder. His execution provoked particularly widespread protests as he was a popular figure in his native Kerry, but the government, desperately trying to preserve its neutrality, was adamant. An iron-gloved approach to the I.R.A. was the order of the day with vigorous raids and interrogations. As a result relations between individual I.R.A. men and the Special Branch became understandably strained, and the I.R.A., in its shattered and disorganised condition, came to regard the Special Branch as a greater enemy than the British Crown.

On September 9, 1942, Detective Sergeant Denis O'Brien, one of the most prominent Special Branch detectives and a brother of Sean Lemass's secretary, was shot dead as he left his home in Ballyboden, Rathfarnham, Co. Dublin to go to work. The shooting greatly increased public feeling against the I.R.A., particularly as the murder was carried out almost in view of his wife. As she held her dying husband she watched his assailants cycling past.

A number of I.R.A. men were charged at various times in connection with this killing, but only one was executed for it—Charles Kerins, twenty-six, of Kerry, on December 1, 1944. At the end of his trial the president of the Military Court delayed sentence until later in the day to allow Kerins, if he wished, to make an application whereby he might have avoided the capital sentence. When the court resumed Kerins said:

'You could have adjourned it for six years as far as I'm concerned, as my attitude towards this Court will always be the same.'

He thus deprived himself of the right to give evidence, to face cross-examination or to call witnesses.

The Special Branch was equally tense when dealing with I.R.A. men, and in such an atmosphere guns blazed on both sides in cases where a prisoner would normally have gone quietly. The best one can say of a shooting on July 4, 1943, in Mount Street when a young I.R.A. man, Jacky Griffith, was machine-gunned off his bicycle by the Special Branch, is that it was the last fatal shooting in the South of Ireland between police and I.R.A. for over twenty years.

Through all this period, Harry White managed to stay free, remaining on the run for five years and surviving some remarkable adventures. Once he had the audacity to attend a public meeting in O'Connell Street, Dublin, to protest the hanging of Thomas Williams. Mrs Kathleen Clarke, widow of the 1916 leader Thomas Clarke, made a fiery speech threatening that if it took place, there would be a march on the border. As Mrs Clarke was a Fianna Fail senator and a former lord mayor of Dublin, White became enraged at what he considered hypocritical rabble-rousing and he called out, 'What about George Plant?' He was nearly lynched by Fianna Fail supporters but managed to get away. He later took a lorry-load of men in full daylight across the border, hoping to capture a British officer, any British officer, in reprisal for Williams's death.

Later that month he was attending a wedding in Ballyjamesduff, Co. Cavan, when police surrounded the house, shots were fired and the bride's brother, Patrick Dermody, was shot dead in a gun battle which also took the life of a guard. This affray provoked great bitterness, from police and public at the death of the policeman and, in I.R.A. circles, over Dermody's death. Dermody was so powerful in border areas that he held regular courts at which he settled land disputes and other squabbles. White managed to shoot his way out of this trap also and did not see the inside of a jail again until 1946 when he was picked up in Derry and handed over to the Gardai by the R.U.C.

I.R.A. apologists say that White was handed over because the R.U.C. hoped that the Southern 'death court' would condemn him to death. However Sean MacBride persuaded the court of the fact that while the bullet which killed Detective Officer Mordant was fired from White's gun he was entitled to defend himself as the raiding police had not identified themselves before opening fire. The court held that this was not murder, but excessive use of force by White when resisting unlawful arrest and it found him guilty of manslaughter. O'Neill had been tried and executed on the charge that he had murdered Mordant on the date in question. But it is clear from the evidence that White and O'Neill were separated at the time the fatal shot was fired and it is at least arguable that O'Neill knew nothing about it.

The years in the Curragh left their mark on those who remained in the camp after White and Burns. Most men, on leaving the internment camp, were so unable to deal with ordinary life that it took upwards of six months before any of them could screw up their courage to do normal things such as signing on at the Labour Exchange to draw unemployment benefit or applying for jobs. Even to cross the road was a terrible effort, the traffic, thin enough after the war, seemed fantastic after the years in the Curragh. The difference in women's fashion frightened them and added to the general air of unfamiliarity. After years in confinement with adult men, children seemed fragile and small-scale. Most remained Republican in sympathy but had no means of solving the border problem. Some were broken and turned to drink or developed nervous breakdowns.

Strangely enough, only one case of homosexuality in the Curragh has ever been mentioned to me. There was a great deal of horseplay. Sometimes the clothes were stripped off an internee by his friends, and he was left to run naked through the camp on a winter's day, but the over whelming majority of prisoners made a deliberate effort not to allow sex to unbalance them. Between almost frenzied bouts of football or other athletic activity and hours spent making medals, baskets, leatherwork and so on, sexual frustration was largely exercised. But dissension, the principal bugbear of Republicans, remained.

Pearse Kelly, who was camp O.C. during the greater part of his five years internment, described his first impressions of the Curragh in a prison record which he was kind enough to give me:

It was December with the usual dismal rain. The car stopped at a big, barricaded gate just above the camp and one of my escorts remarked 'well, you'll have plenty of time to hibernate down here. This isn't a health resort at any time, but it's at its worst now so you know what's in store for you.'

From my elevated position I had a panoramic view of the camp, a conglomeration of long low wooden huts erected in military lines, behind a quadruple fence of barbed wire and completely surrounded by a deep trench, evidently designed to prevent tunnelling. I was conscious of a slight shiver of apprehension as I took in the dead, drab look of the place

After being searched and stripped, I was given a dilapidated mattress and a pillow with four old army blankets. The compound gate was unlocked to allow me in and I entered to find no sign of life apart from a Military Policeman who directed me to Hut 314.

When I entered the hut, I stood aghast. For a moment I couldn't make out what was happening. The rise and fall of the babble of voices that filled the turbulent air, stilled momentarily as attention centred on the newcomer. Almost at once the din broke out again with men shouting at each other across the hut with voices raised to be heard above the general bedlam. A scene of apparent disorder met my eyes, all I could discern was a litter of beds with lines of discarded clothing hanging from the rafters and men, some squatting in silence on their beds, others huddled up in their blankets. Thirty men lived and slept in this hut and out of the forty in the compound there were sixteen similarly occupied, almost 500 internees.

Heating was supplied by small turf stoves and the walls and window-frames were of such inferior quality that, in bad weather, rain seeped through.

Before Kelly's arrival, the camp had been going through a particularly bad phase. On December 14, 1940, there had been an outbreak of rioting resulting in several bad injuries and one death. The cause was an ugly, brooding, hothouse atmosphere created by close surveillance, internment, frustration and a feeling among the internees that some stand had to be made.

The internees considered the food in the Curragh to be 'lousy bad', as Michael Traynor put it. It probably was, but it was the same food as army privates received, and when on December 14 the army's butter ration was reduced by a quarter this reduction was also extended to the internees' diet. It was the last straw. Peadar O'Flaherty, the prisoners' leader, lined them all up and gave a stirring address.

'Are we men or mice?' he asked, and gave the order to set fire to a prison hut.

Unfortunately, the fire spread to a number of other huts and six of them were destroyed with a great quantity of beds and bedding. And then, during investigations, it was discovered that the internees had been tunnelling for the whole summer and had almost reached the barbed wire.

Fierce fighting began when the military and military police went to put out the fires. Two internees and two members of the army were badly injured and taken to hospital. The internees were rounded up in the open, where they spent the day until being herded into two huts, one of them with a concrete floor. Being December this came to be known as the icebox. Throughout the night there was desultory shooting around the huts as trigger-happy military police fired at shadows. Inside the huts the internees were apprehensive that someone was going to be shot. For two days after the incident the men were kept in these two huts, only a cookhouse detail being allowed out to collect food and bring it back. Several of the internees had diarrhoea and dysentery, but the only sanitary facilities in the hut were buckets which provided an added dimension of unpleasantness.

The prisoners then refused to be counted and an armed guard had to be sent to the huts to check them. Only when it was certain that no escapes had occurred were the prisoners allowed to go to the dining hall. They lined up outside their huts facing a party of armed military police, nerves on both sides at breaking point. The military had been attacked during the fire with wooden trestle boards, iron trestle bars, broom handles and pieces of piping and fittings, and had replied with gun butts and rifle shots. In this instance the prisoners had no intention of rushing the armed party, but as their numbers swelled coming out of the huts, about fifty internees came to within ten yards of the armed party. Shooting broke out, one internee, Bernard Casey, of Co. Longford, being fatally wounded and another, Walter Mitchell, escaping with a bullet that lodged between the heel and the sole of his shoe.

Following this, a period of nearly two weeks of extreme tension ensued in the camp. The prisoners were penned into the icebox at night, hearing stray shots outside and fearing that something worse might occur. One night, a strong force of military police surrounded the camp and took selected leaders, among them Michael Traynor, to what was known as 'the glasshouse', a wing of the camp with a double row of cells under a high glass roof. Here, Traynor says, a fortnight of sheer horror followed. Jittery military policemen ran along iron stairs at night to quell suspected outbreaks. Beatings and kickings were more frequent than halfpence.

Readers who have seen Brendan Behan's play *Borstal Boy* will get an insight into the kind of fears that political prisoners engender in their captors. Traynor remembers his period here as a time of 'diabolical treatment'. Outside the camp, Sean MacBride tried to have the case of Bernard Casey brought into the open and debated publicly to focus attention on the appalling conditions in the camp, but this attempt failed. When those who were held to be the ringleaders of the disturbances were identified, they were brought before a military court and sentenced—to their great delight. Traynor, although he got five years, regarded being away from the military police 'as if I was in heaven'. They used the condemned cell in Mountjoy as a recreational centre and, with plenty of food parcels from outside, it was a relatively pleasant interlude for a man who had begun the year with a fifty-day hunger strike.

After Kelly's arrival things improved, *vis-à-vis* the authorities. But for a time, among the internees, they got worse. Basically the trouble stemmed from the unnatural atmosphere of the place and the divisions between the Dublin and Belfast wings of the I.R.A. But trouble also flared up over issues such as prisoners collecting their own coal, rather than having it delivered to the huts by the authorities; the reading of the Stephen Hayes's 'confession'; and varying political views, Fascism versus Communism, or the issue of whether, in the event of an invasion, the internees should offer to sign out and fight in the hitherto hated Free State army, in a common defence of their homeland.

When Kelly arrived, the camp O.C. was Liam Leddy from Cork and he continued as such for some months until Kelly, Eoin MacNamee and Tom Cullimore decided that the only way to establish morale was by electing a new camp council. This trio made the Hayes 'confession' widely known throughout the camp although some prisoners were already aware of it. Joe Deighan, for instance, told me he had seen the 'confession' before Kelly showed up, but the publicity given to it by the trio led to their ostracism by the Leddy wing and they were 'sent to Coventry'. However, about 150 prisoners eventually came over to their side and by the end of the war, all the internees were on the Kelly side. For a time, relationships between the two wings were extremely bad. Any man caught talking to a member of the opposite camp was disdained by his own side and considered not to be a true Republican at all. But the position gradually eased over the years as the Kelly wing began to win concessions from the authority such as an ending of the physical punishment by the P.A.s,* an increase in the fuel allowance and facilities for hobbies and camp concerts. The Gaelic Athletic Association secretary, Padraig O'Caoimh, himself an old I.R.A. man, sent in a set of footballs and medals that were keenly played for, and the prisoners got such control of their own affairs that one Christmas they acquired all the equipment and ingredients to manufacture a successful run of illicit alcohol.

'Gaelteachts', peopled entirely by Irish-speaking internees, were set up and Mairtin O'Cadain ran highly successful language classes. Other prisoners who had

---

* Military policemen, Poli Airim in Irish, P.A.s for short. Prisoners in the Curragh complained to me that in the early days of the Curragh it was not unusual for prisoners found guilty of some breach of camp regulations to be forced to run a gauntlet of P.A.s armed with batons which they used to strike at the victim's limbs, their heads being protected by the mattress and blankets which they were forced to carry on their way to the 'glasshouse' for a sojourn on bread and water.

more education than these fellows also gave tutorials in their own special subjects and many a young country lad, who had left school at twelve, emerged from the Curragh with a far better education than he could possibly have acquired any other way.

The even tenor of the prisoners' ways was threatened principally by the activities of Niall Verschoyle Gould, a devoted Communist who had been on the fringes of the Republican Congress movement and active in organising strikes in Dublin. Gould formed the centre of a coterie of other Republican Communists, in particular Michael O'Riordan, Johnny Power and Dermot Walshe. These three had fought in the Spanish Civil War, and they elected Gould as their tutor in Russian.

Gould did not confine his activities to teaching Russian. As the central premise of Irish Catholicism was traditionally, before the Vatican Council II, an unthinking acceptance of authority, his clever dialectical approach undermined several fervent young Catholic internees. They were unaware of the Church's association with Britain in the enactment of the Act of Union and the subsequent quashing through-out the nineteenth century of every manifestation of Irish nationalism. He also undermined their faith in their nationalist gods, pointing out how John Mitchel had fought in the American Civil War on the side of the South and slavery, and he was well on the way to distracting the camp's attention from British oppression and/or de Valera, to that of the class struggle, when Kelly decided to take some action.

A message was smuggled out to the Bishop of Kildare and Leitrim, in whose diocese the camp was located, telling him that the morals of the camp were being perverted by a notorious Communist who was undermining the teachings of the Church and making the Curragh a hotbed of sedition and Marxism. Within three days Gould was removed from the camp and deposited in Mountjoy Jail. (To be a Communist in Ireland requires unusual self-control and discipline. While the toler-ance of the people would rarely condone violence to a self-confessed Communist, such a declaration, even now, would inhibit his career in most fields, certainly in teaching.)*

In all some two thousand internees passed through the camp. The sort of men they were and the problems they faced are illustrated in this concluding passage from Kelly's camp memoirs describing the advice given to him by an old friend who had left the camp.

He urged me to get away out to the country where I would really appreciate freedom as he had done. The barbed wire had no terror for him then, he actually came to have a sort of regard for it when he found he could fondle it without being molested.

'Don't mind,' he added, 'if you find yourself talking to the animals in the fields. These were the first things I made friends with when I came home, for if the animal doesn't like you it walks away, and you know at once where you stand. One feels nearer to Heaven too, to stand on a hillside of a sunny evening in the harvest, and as far as the eye can carry

---

*   Gould apparently taught his beliefs to his son. In 1957, years after the Curragh and the war, family estates in Longford came before the courts for a decision as to what should become of them. Evidence was given that a lawyer acting for the court had gone to Moscow and found Gould Jr. working as a labourer digging a trench across a Moscow side street. The boy had refused to take any interest in his inheritance or to give any directions as to what should be done with it. The money was duly lodged in the court.

to watch the corn and crops and grasses with their glorious hues and they waving in the breeze and the sun dancing on them. As to the people, 'tis little I can say about them, for even yet I can't fit in no matter where I go, and I hate crowds. Back of it all, I am at times conscious of a deep yearning for my old friends of Tintown.'

The last sad act of the I.R.A. drama of the 1940s was a strip strike in Portlaoise Prison. In the Curragh, Arbour Hill or Mountjoy jails, the Republican prisoners were allowed to wear their own clothes. But on transfer to Portlaoise they had to wear convict uniform. When Sean McCaughey arrived there, in September, 1941, like the men who had gone before him he refused to wear these clothes.

From then until the middle of 1943, he and the others were kept in solitary confinement. They were not even allowed out to the lavatory and the confinement was made doubly rigorous by having an empty cell on either side of them. In 1943, their conditions were relaxed somewhat. They were allowed out of their cells into a larger cell together for an hour in the morning and the afternoon and they were also permitted a paper per week and a letter per month. By refusing to wear the convict clothes, the prisoners had set themselves in defiance of the prison authorities, so very little else was done to make their stay there enjoyable. McCaughey was allowed no visitors during the four and three-quarter years he was in Portlaoise Jail.

Like the others, he spent all this time naked except for his prison blanket. Finally on April 19, 1946, he went on hunger strike for release though it is alleged by his comrades that it was well understood by the prison authorities and by the government that he would have come off the strike if he had been removed to the Curragh. Whatever the truth of this, the early days of his hunger strike produced no result and five days later he went on thirst strike too. Seventeen days later Sean McCaughey died with his body in a condition better imagined than described. Patrick McLogan, who saw the body after death, said that McCaughey's tongue had shrunken 'to the size of a threepenny bit'.

The inquest was held in the prison and the deputy coroner refused to allow Sean MacBride, counsel for the next of kin, to cross-examine the governor. The following passage occurred during MacBride's cross-examination of the prison doctor:

Mr MacBride: Are you aware that during the four and a half years he was here he was never out in the fresh air or sunlight?
Dr Duane: As far as I am aware he was not.
Mr MacBride: Would I be right in saying that up to twelve or eighteen months ago he was kept in solitary confinement and not allowed to speak or associate with any other persons?
Dr Duane: That is right.
Mr MacBride: Would you treat a dog in that fashion?
Mr McLoughlin: That is not a proper question.
Mr MacBride: If you had a dog would you treat it in that fashion?
Dr Duane (after a pause): No.
Mr MacBride: Did you have to attend the prisoner for a nervous breakdown?
Dr Duane: He suffered from a nervous condition for a time.
Mr MacBride: By reason of solitary confinement?
Dr Duane: I don't know.

Replying to his own counsel, Major Barmys, the prison governor, said of McCaughey:

He refused to wear prison clothes, and a man could not go out in the air without clothes, from the health point of view. Decency forbade it, and apart from that, his health would not stand it. You cannot have a naked man walking about a prison.

The jury's verdict was:

That the conditions existing in the prison were not all that could be desired according to the evidence furnished; but there was no reflection on the Governor, Medical Officer or Staff intended.

So ended the Stephen Hayes affair. The only man who could really say what prompted his suspicions of the former chief of staff is dead. If the affair had not brought McCaughey southward he might have survived the war, though, given his temperament, he might have been killed in a police battle, been executed or died during one of the jail strikes.

The plight of the other prisoners in the jail, such as Thomas MacCurtain, Michael Traynor, Liam Rice and Harry White, led to support for the new party which grew up around Sean MacBride in those years and which put Fianna Fail out of office in 1948. Just as Fianna Fail had come to power in 1932 to the echoes of 'Release the Prisoners', the same call sounded against them in 1948. One of the first acts of the new minister for justice, General Sean MacEoin, who as a member of the I.R.A. had been sentenced to death by the British, was to 'release the prisoners'.

9

The I.R.A. and the Nazis

No facet of I.R.A. activities aroused so much distrust and alarm, at home and abroad, as did the organisation's links, real or imagined, with the Nazis. These must, however, be assessed against the background of Irish neutrality.

On September 5, 1939, Winston Churchill wrote to the First Sea Lord and other top figures in the Admiralty demanding a 'vigilant watch' on the I.R.A. in Ireland. He reasoned that 'if they throw bombs in London why should they not supply fuel to U-boats?' The I.R.A. of course did not have any U-boat fuel, nor did anyone else in Southern Ireland. But the mere existence of the I.R.A. made such a threat worth guarding against.

Churchill, moreover, was infuriated that in 1938 de Valera had negotiated both a satisfactory settlement of the economic war and an end to British rights, under the Anglo-Irish treaty of 1921, to what were known as the 'treaty ports'. Without control of these Irish neutrality would not have been possible. The ports were Berehaven and Cobh, both near the major southern port of Cork, and, to the north, Lough Swilly in Co. Donegal. From Lough Swilly the approaches to the Mersey and the Clyde could have been more easily guarded by British warships than from Derry, and from Cobh and Berehaven destroyers could have foraged westwards after the U-boats and linked up with incoming convoys far out to sea. Without them, such operations had to start from British bases such as Lamlash, Pembroke Dock or Falmouth, thereby reducing the British range of action by approximately four hundred miles.

Discussing a London *Times* comment on the 1938 agreement which said that 'The agreement releases the government of the United Kingdom from the . . . onerous and delicate task of defending the fortified harbours of Cork, Berehaven and Lough Swilly in the event of war', Churchill snarled in his memoirs: 'Further releases might have been attained by handing over Gibraltar to Spain and Malta to Italy. Neither touched the existence of our population more directly.' And during a victory broadcast on May 13, 1945, Churchill vented his irritation with de Valera in public, saying:

Owing to the action of the Dublin government . . . the approaches which the southern Irish ports and airfields could so easily have guarded were closed by the hostile aircraft and U-boats.

This was included a deadly moment in our life, and if it had not been for the loyalty and friendship of Northern Ireland, we should have been forced to come to close quarters with Mr de Valera, or perish forever from the earth. More, with a restraint and poise to which, I say, history will find few parallels, His Majesty's Government never laid a violent hand upon them, though at times it would have been quite easy and quite natural . . .

Throughout the war British opinion continued to be puzzled by the Irish position, much as if Wales had opted for neutrality after several hundred years of association with Britain. The British had reluctantly approved de Valera's constitution in 1937 and the abolishment of the voice of governor-general, but nevertheless did not concede Ireland's right to have an ambassador accredited to her. The governor-general was not replaced for three years, and then only in ambiguous fashion: Sir John Maffey, who was actually retired at the time, was appointed British representative in Eire in November, 1939. Britain still saw Ireland as belonging to the British Commonwealth, but Sir John could not be appointed as a high commissioner because the Irish did not recognise the Commonwealth, as Whitehall did not recognise the new Irish state. He was therefore designated a representative though with diplomatic status. In London, the Irish representative, John Dulanty, continued as he had since 1930 as high commissioner for Ireland.

Irish neutrality as regards Britain had been prepared for by de Valera as far back as May 29, 1935, when, in a debate in the Dail, he said: 'Our territory will never be permitted to be used as a base for attack upon Britain.' He reiterated this again on April 25, 1938, when signing the London agreements whereby he regained the treaty ports. He was equally far-sighted where Germany was concerned. Through Joseph Walsh, secretary to the Department of External Affairs, he had informed the German ambassador, Dr Edward Hempel, on August 26, 1937, that Ireland wished to stay neutral in any war, and would do so unless attacked first, perhaps by bombing. (Even at that early stage the Irish government learned to be more aware of the potential of the Luftwafe than did England.) Walsh also played the Irish-American card adroitly at a lunch with Hempel, pointing out that the Irish-Americans would set their faces against any Anglo-Irish tie-up, and would do what they could to make Britain pause before attempting to invade Ireland.

Hempel explained this position to Berlin and on August 29 the German Foreign Ministry telegraphed him:

In conformity with the previous friendly relations between the two countries the German government will refrain from all hostile activity towards Irish territory and will respect Ireland's integrity provided that for her part Ireland will observe strict neutrality towards Germany. In the event of war against England the German government will do its utmost to reduce to a minimum the resulting unavoidable disadvantage for Ireland and Irish trade. Germany is entirely clear as to the difficulties facing Ireland in consequence of her geographical position.

The Germans were not being altruistic about this. If the British *had* tried to take over Ireland, Germany would not have been in a position to prevent her. Also, as Paul Leverkuehn in *German Military Intelligence* shows, a central and crippling problem bedevilled Nazi-I.R.A. affairs. Apart from bad luck, spies being captured immediately on arrival and the I.R.A. being 'riven with enmity', German military intelligence found itself continually at loggerheads with diplomats who effectively stymied all its schemes because of the doctrine that 'military plans should play second fiddle to political decisions'.

The American position was simple. As Professor Bob Stewart, then of the Fletcher School of Diplomacy at Tufts University, Boston, and wartime member of the State Department section dealing with Irish affairs, put it to me, 'I sure wanted Ireland in that war.' To this end the ambassador to Ireland, David Gray, a relation of Roosevelt and a wealthy man but not a career diplomat, exercised a great deal of enthusiasm and energy, but little diplomacy, and as a result was virtually *persona non grata* with the Irish government towards the end of the war. This was a pity because he was a man who genuinely loved Ireland, but as he said, 'I had a job to do.'

The mind boggles at the way he sometimes went about his job. In one of his telegrams to the secretary of state (January 7, 1941) we find him saying that he had told de Valera that 'he had capitalised on hatred of Great Britain for political reasons and so must take some responsibility for the existing popular state of mind'. Later he describes another interview with de Valera, saying:

> He began to talk about his rights. I told him that . . . the only right that he and myself enjoyed was to believe in our religion, and be burned for it if need be. Every other right depended upon force to maintain it and that he was steering a very dangerous course if he thought otherwise. He called my views the greatest exponent of force he had ever met and made it clear that it was a case of facing reality. Curious, but almost friendly, I grow fond of Mr de Valera as we argue!

De Valera's determination to maintain neutrality seems to have checked this friendship and Gray, after an interview with de Valera in April, when, he says, 'de Valera flushed angrily and shouted that it was impertinent to question the statements of a head of state', reported:

> I think the effect of a stiff attitude will be sobering. It is the only way to impress him that there are realities closing in upon him. He always outmanoeuvred Chamberlain. I no longer hope to get anything from him by generosity and conciliation. He must be made to realise that it is possible that a situation is approaching in which if it be essential to survival his ports will be seized with the approval of the liberal sentiment of the world, that he will have only the choice of fighting on the side of Great Britain or Germany.

Gray later learned that de Valera told an opposition leader that Gray had misrepresented Ireland to the secretary of state and that if the situation were not so tense, and Gray not a friend of the president, de Valera would have asked for his recall.

Apart from all this, formal American policy frequently put the Irish national temperature up, particularly over the delays in supplying American ships to Ireland. Only two were made available. Then there was the unwillingness of the Americans to let Ireland have munitions and war supplies so long as she stayed neutral, the issue of conscription in Northern Ireland and the landing of American troops in the North. There was also the Americans' belief that the Japanese embassy in Dublin was filled with Japanese spies. In fact it contained four Japanese nationalists who behaved with diplomatic decorum. The German embassy was also supposed to be a centre for transmission of information to Berlin, though the only broadcasts from the embassy occurred at the beginning of the war and consisted of weather reports for the Luftwaffe. These had ceased by 1942, as Hempel's wartime dispatches make quite clear. Even so the British and the Americans refused to believe they had ceased.

The conscription issue and the American landing were the most important episodes, raising the possibility of loss of life if the British tried to enforce conscription on Catholics in the North or the Americans attempted to cross the border. The conscription problem made the last fortnight of May, 1941 a time of acute crisis. Southern Ireland and the Northern minority were inflamed at the proposal apparently motivated by the bombings in Belfast and the fact that very few volunteers were coming forward in the North. Even the pro-British Gray was aghast and on May 24 he cabled the secretary of state:

Opposition leaders yesterday informed me that conscription without a conscientious objector's escape clause for minority Catholic nationalists will constitute a major irretrievable and probably fatal political blunder at this time and play directly into de Valera's hands with grave possibilities for American interests. They predict draft riots, the escape of draft dodgers to Southern Ireland who will be acclaimed as hero martyrs by three-quarters of the population and the fomenting of trouble by Republicans and Fifth Columnists. The clearest headed leader predicts that de Valera will seize the opportunity to escape from economic and political realities by proclaiming himself the leader of the oppressed minority and with the blessings of the Cardinal will rouse anti-British feeling and call a Holy War. I think it a very likely prediction. All classes of opinion here unite in condemning the move as calamitous. It appears to be a repetition of the same fatal blunder made during the last war. The weak and failing Ulster Government is probably seeking to sustain itself by provoking a crisis. Unless Great Britain is prepared from a military point of view to seize the whole country it appears to be madness. So little can be gained and so much lost.

Eighty thousand Irish volunteers in the British army will be disaffected, there will be no material number of Nationalist conscripts, a government, a popular majority and an army inclined to be friendly to Great Britain rather than to the Axis will become definitely hostile, possibly giving active aid to Germany and most important of all the pro-British opposition will be helpless and the opportunity for dividing the country on the question of the ports will be lost for the duration. The effect on Irish-American opinion at this juncture is not for me to estimate. This is a grave situation.

In London American Ambassador Winant saw Churchill and Eden in lengthy sessions. A stern message from de Valera warned the British against imposing conscription on Irishmen. The London meetings ended with Churchill's agreeing that Winant send the following dispatch to Hull:

The Ulster Government has weakened considerably over the weekend and in consequence the Cabinet is inclined to the view it would be more trouble than it's worth to go through with conscription. No immediate decision will be taken and in the meantime the less made of the affair the better.

That ended the proposal. My information from Unionist circles is that Northern Prime Minister Andrews had drawn back leaving Churchill with no option but to call off the attempt. Andrews apparently took the R.U.C.'s estimate of the situation more seriously than did the hardliner in the cabinet, notably Sir Basil Brook, later Lord Brookeborough.

Relationships with the Americans were strained again when American combat troops armed with heavy artillery landed in the North on January 26. De Valera protested against the violation of the sovereignty which the twenty-six counties claimed over the six, and most of the civilian population feared that the landings were a prelude to an invasion of the South.

Time put an end to these apprehensions and the unofficial co-operation which the Irish extended to the allies helped considerably to improve relationships. British flyers who crashed in Ireland were speedily put on the mail boat back to England or, if their planes were still serviceable, these were refuelled and returned. Many an R.A.F. man got back to England this way with a cockpit load of butter, eggs and steak. His Luftwaffe counterpart ended up in the Curragh internment camp for the duration of the war. The Germans protested about this but de Valera had accepted the American argument that any allied plane forced to land in Ireland was clearly on a non-operational mission, whereas any German plane being so far from home was obviously operational. To return the flyer to Germany would be to infringe neutrality.

Sometimes it was necessary to intern British soldiers for the sake of appearances, but they managed to escape as a matter of routine. In contrast, the Germans were held behind bars until the end of the war. And when America's General Jacob L. Devers crash-landed in Ireland late in 1943 with a briefcase full of allied invasion plans concerning Operation Overlord (the D-Day code name) he was not subjected even to the pretence of internment. He was driven to the border in an official car and handed over to the Americans within a few hours of landing, his plans and his identity intact.

Also around the time of D-Day it became known in Dublin that the Irish officials were 'worried by the overcrowding in the Curragh, because of all the interned British airmen. There were so many of them that they were beginning to affect the health of the Germans.' A new camp was opened for these internees at Gormanstown in Co. Meath to the north of Dublin, and the internees were driven off by lorry. The lorries were stopped on the way and the internees, all badly needed flyers, were put into a fleet of waiting cars and driven to the border! The Irish government also allowed the Royal Observer Corps to set up plane spotting posts around the Irish coast. A British radio transmitter operating from a van went unremarked by the Irish authorities who took part in regular staff talks with the British army heads on the same basis of mutual trust and co-operation that the Irish Secret Service continually co-operated as a matter of routine with that of Britain.

But despite all these gestures of goodwill, Irish neutrality remained balanced against a precarious background of changing international conditions and every I.R.A. action threatened it. The Irish government's position would have been swept away overnight had the Nazi-I.R.A. links led to any serious trouble for the British. That they did not may be attributable to a number of factors: the efficiency of the Irish security forces, the ignorance of the Nazis about Irish affairs, German inter-departmental warfare and above all the disorganised nature of the I.R.A. itself.

Sean Russell's departure to America had been disastrous for his bombing campaign in England and for the I.R.A. at home. In Detroit on June 6, 1939, it became disastrous for him also in a manner which brought him into the arms of the Nazis, and to an extraordinary death. He was arrested by the Detroit police, apparently as a precautionary measure, because King George and Queen Elizabeth were at the time just across the border in Canada. The subject was raised in the House of Representatives by Congressmen Sweeney of Ohio and MacGranery of Pennsylvania, who called it 'a very stupid blunder on the part of our Government which demonstrated British influence in the U.S.'. Russell was released on bail after McGarrity had put up a $5,000 bond and some seventy members of congress had threatened to boycott the royal visit.

A temporary bonanza of publicity boomeranged on Russell when he was served with an expulsion order to quit America by September 10. He went on the run, but although he managed to stay hidden under the Clann na Gael cloak, reduced wartime shipping prevented him from getting a boat to Ireland. One chance remained. On January 24, 1940, the German Foreign Office in Berlin received a telegram from the German consul-general in Genoa asking 'whether the German Government would be prepared to provide transport to Ireland for Sean Russell, Chief of Staff of the I.R.A., who unknown to the American Government is still in New York. If this is possible, he will make his way here by a new direct line from New York under an alias.'

Russell's arrival in Berlin from Genoa is recorded in the War Diary of May 3. Ambassador Hempel's objections to becoming involved with Russell were over-ridden by the opinion of Wermann, the under-secretary of state, who in a memorandum dated February 10, 1940, pointed out that basically Fianna Fail and the I.R.A. wanted the same thing, the reunification of the country, and that their only difference lay in their choice of methods. Wermann thought that 'by reason of their militant attitude towards England, the I.R.A. is Germany's natural ally'.

An attempt to place Russell in contact with a German agent, Captain Herman Goertz, who was setting out for Ireland at that time, misfired because Goertz had taken off from Fritzlar airfield in the early hours of May 5, just a short time before Russell arrived at the airfield to brief him. Russell was then enrolled in a course at Legal Laboratory in, as the Abwehr Diary notes, 'the use of sabotage materials'. It was while attending his bomb-making class that he was reunited with an old friend—Frank Ryan, the Republican Congress leader who had been captured by Franco's forces during the Spanish Civil War.

Ryan, an acting brigadier in the Lincoln Washington Brigade, had been captured in the late summer of 1938 by a group of Italian troops. This fact saved his life as the Italians hoped that they would be able to exchange him for one of their own officers. Had the Spaniards captured him he would have been treated like every other captured member of the brigade and shot. The Italians failed to make an exchange but by the time they had turned Ryan over to Franco's troops some months had elapsed. In the meantime a group of American journalists, who had been allowed to speak to prisoners, discovered Ryan's presence and wrote about him. In Ireland people of all political persuasion signed petitions for his release. Somewhat pathet-ically I.R.A. slogans—'Release Frank Ryan or else'—appeared. Ireland had adopted a policy of non-intervention in the Spanish conflict and had an ambassador in Madrid but de Valera telegrammed Franco asking him to spare Ryan. No one in Ireland knew whether the telegram had any effect until after nine months Leslie Barry, Tom Barry's wife, and a sister of Michael Price, one of the principal figures in the Irish Red Cross, discovered his whereabouts through the agency of the Red Cross.

During this time Ryan lived in a cell with eighteen other condemned prisoners. Every morning nine of the eighteen were taken out and shot and their places filled by another nine. Ryan never knew which morning was to be his turn. All he could do was scratch his name on a comb which he hoped to be able to throw through the cell window of prisoners who had not been condemned and in this way leave behind some record of his fate. He had been wounded in the fighting and his slight deafness had become marked. In the terrifying isolation caused by deafness, imprisonment and language barriers, the arrival of Leslie Barry's first food parcel must have seemed like a message from heaven.

At the end of the Spanish war de Valera arranged through Leopold Kerney, the Irish ambassador in Madrid, for a Spanish lawyer for Ryan, and de Valera saw to it that the expenses of defending his former enemy were defrayed by the Irish state. Ryan's sentence was commuted to life imprisonment, and he was granted the further concession of a monthly visit from his lawyer, Señor Champourcin, and the right to receive food parcels. Meanwhile in Germany Dr Jupp Hoven and Helmut Clissmann,* who during their student days in Ireland had been friends of Ryan (a photograph of Ryan with Clissmann and Hoven appeared on the front page of *An Phoblacht* during Ryan's editorship), supported his case. Hoven officially notified the Abwehr that in his judgement the release of Ryan under German auspices would create a good impression in Ireland and would also place Ryan at Germany's disposal. His idea was eventually taken up. The Nazis approached the Spanish police authorities and Ryan's lawyer contacted the Irish ambassador, who in turn got in touch with his government. All parties agreed to Ryan's release, and he was handed over to German custody at Irun-Hendaye on July 15, 1940. He was emaciated and haggard and almost completely deaf. The Nazis drove him to Paris and took him to eat at the Tour d'Argent where Kurt Haller, section leader in Abwehr (II) Office I West in Berlin, remembers that he was 'completely flabbergasted by the whole thing and thought he was dreaming'.

When Russell and Ryan were introduced, according to Haller they 'embraced one another like brothers who had not seen each other for many years'. Russell immediately agreed to take Ryan with him back to Ireland on 'Operation Dove', a loosely defined mission which left Russell free to take any action he saw fit in Ireland. It was finally sanctioned at a meeting on August 5 of Foreign Minister Ribbentrop, Admiral Canaris, Lieutenant Colonel Lahousen, the Abwehr head and Dr Veesenmayer, in charge of Irish affairs at the Foreign Office, who introduced Russell to Ribbentrop.

Ribbentrop was offensive to Russell saying flatly that he doubted whether Russell was a genuine agent or indeed, if he were Russell at all. Apparently he disliked the Irish as a race. Despite this arrogance the Nazis thought enough of the Russell-Ryan mission to place a U-boat at their disposal, and it sailed from Wilhelmshaven on August 8, captained by Commander Von Stockhausen.

Neither Russell nor the U-boat ever reached Ireland. On August 14 Sean Russell died in Frank Ryan's arms, when they were some one hundred miles west of Galway. He had been taken ill with agonising pains in the stomach shortly after leaving and these got progressively worse. There was no doctor aboard, only a medical student as an orderly. Ryan persuaded this man to give Russell a purgative thinking that he was suffering from constipation. But it appears from the medical reports submitted to German doctors by Ryan, the orderly, the captain and the second in command of the U-boat, that Russell died from perforated ulcers.

He was buried at sea with full military honours, wrapped in a German flag. Not knowing what his mission was intended to be nor what conditions were like in Ireland, Ryan returned with the submarine to Germany. He never saw Ireland again. His last days were pathetic. On January 15 he suffered some sort of a stroke,

---

* Clissmann became a businessman in Ireland and married an Irish girl.

and his condition deteriorated progressively. It was wartime, the hospitals were full of wounded, there was very little food, and the aerial bombardment grew heavier and heavier. As he was so deaf that he could not be left alone at night because he couldn't hear the sirens, he had to sit at cafés with a cup of coffee so that people could warn him when the sirens sounded. His friends and contacts in the German establishment were gradually transferred from Berlin. An Irish friend, Francis Stuart, the writer, who was lecturing at Berlin University, comforted him as best he could, occasionally taking him out for a drive to one of the Havel lakes to spend a day on the beach, and Stuart also attempted to get the Irish chargé d'affaires to arrange a passage for Ryan back to Ireland. But Ryan's health had deteriorated so badly that he was unable to travel. In January, 1944 he was taken to a sanatorium at Dresden Loschwitz. He died on June 10, after a period of agony during which his breathing was so painful that he had to be placed sitting in an armchair with the back of another before him so that he could rest his head on his arms before speaking. He was buried in the Dresden Loschwitz cemetery. A wooden cross giving his name as Francis Richard appears above the grave with his date of birth and of death inscribed on it.

Apart from the Russell-Ryan affairs the Nazis made a number of attempts to win over the I.R.A.

Oscar C. Phaus, journalist and founder of the German Bund, returned from America to Germany on December 2, 1938, and was approached by the Abwehr and asked to establish links with the I.R.A. in Ireland. The Abwehr knew little about the I.R.A. beyond the fact that if it carried out bombing attacks in England it must be a potential German ally. Phaus landed in Ireland on February 3 and tried to contact the I.R.A. by approaching General Eoin O'Duffy, the former Blueshirt leader. If O'Duffy, on meeting a Nazi agent, did not actually put him in touch with the I.R.A. he at least made no attempt to have him arrested. Within a matter of days Phaus had established contact and was driven by Maurice Twomey to meet members of the Army Council.

Various stories circulate about this meeting, one of them being that Phaus thought that he was going to have to shoot his way out, so unfriendly did the atmosphere become and so disbelieving was the attitude of those whom he met. A telegram from Germany, in reply to one which had been sent immediately upon his arrival at the meeting, confirmed his identity. The story seems a bit unlikely but, at all events, from then onwards Seamus O'Donovan became the principal Nazi link with the I.R.A. and later in the month visited Phaus in Hamburg with a memorandum for the Abwehr setting out the I.R.A.'s policies and the strength of its equipment. Nothing was decided about sending equipment to the I.R.A. but discussions took place about Nazi policy in the event of war between Germany and England.

O'Donovan again visited Germany in April and in August, 1939, the third journey very nearly being the I.R.A.'s final contact with the Nazis. A row with the German customs infuriated O'Donovan. The Abwehr spent so much time trying to mollify him that it was only after he had left that the Abwehr realised it had arranged courier routes for messages and money, come to agreements on wireless transmissions and on possible arms and other supplies, but had forgotten to give O'Donovan the code word for the wireless exchange which would be needed to arrange these things. A few days after the outbreak of war a code phrase—'House of Parliament'—was devised and sent to London via a Breton, Paul Moise, working for the Breton underground movement Breiz Atao.

It was not until October 29 that the first message to Germany was received from O'Donovan's transmitter. It asked about arms, but the Abwehr could not help as the message had not indicated any likely supply routes. (This transmitter was the one which the police seized on December 29 in the raid on Ashgrove House which captured D'Arcy and MacNeela.) Very little of value passed over the transmitters either from Berlin or Dublin. The I.R.A. never did succeed in setting up a supply route, nor did it respond to the German requests to cease operations against de Valera and concentrate instead on military installations in Britain and the North. Indeed one of the messages which the Irish sent the Germans told of a direct rejection of advice—the report of the I.R.A. raid on the Magazine Fort.

One can be reasonably certain about the valueless nature of the I.R.A.'s messages to Germany. Major Florence O'Donaghue and Colonol Dan Bryan, the leading figures in the Irish Secret Service during the war, both told me I.R.A. transmissions were wordless. I also spoke to one of the chief broadcasters and script-writers connected with this transmitter—Seamus Byrne, a solicitor and playwright whom I had known since boyhood. (He was one of the four men arrested when the police raided the house.) I spoke too to the chief broadcaster from the transmitter which the I.R.A. operated from Northern Ireland, Tarlach O'hUid, now a journalist. From the statements of all it appears virtually certain that the transmitter's main use was for the dissemination of internal propaganda to give an impression of a strength on the part of the I.R.A., which it did not really possess. In fact the discussion which the Southern radio occasioned worried German Ambassador Hempel so much that he telegraphed a strong warning to his foreign office about rumours circulating in Dublin concerning the I.R.A.-German link-ups. Hempel felt that if the Germans were to be seen helping the I.R.A. this would prejudice them in the eyes of both Irish and English—the Irish because there was a widespread sympathy towards Germany on religious grounds and the British because it might give them an excuse to breach Irish neutrality. Hempel's advice was not taken but the Germans would have saved life and money if they had listened to him.

The most important German spy in Ireland was Captain Herman Goertz who parachuted from a Heinkel on May 5, 1940, landing in County Meath near Summerhill and then managing to remain free for nineteen months. Some irish army officers, who were not exactly pro-Nazi but were willing to make the war an opportunity for doing something about the partition issue, met Goertz. They decided against collaboration with him because of their contempt for I.R.A. security and their distrust of all military powers. There were also some nationalists, and others who had some influence with the government through language circles such as the Gaelic League, who were disposed to assist Goertz in his mission of creating difficulties for the British in the North. But here again his involvement with the I.R.A. stymied him.

He expressed a very low opinion of the movement in a series of articles, published posthumously in the *Irish Times* in August, 1947. (Goertz had poisoned himself the previous May rather than face deportation back to Germany.) He wrote:

The I.R.A. had become an underground movement in its own national sphere, heavily suppressed by men who knew all their methods. Inside the I.R.A. nobody knew what game was really played, not even their leader. Their internal means of communication were as primitive as boys playing police and brigands. They got no further than the open message in the sock of a girl. And what messages! There was no code—they did not want to learn the most simple code, they preferred to sacrifice their men and women. They had not a single wireless operator; they made no attempt to learn messages discipline; their military training was nil. I once said to one of them whom I admired for his personal qualities: you know how to die for Ireland, but of how to fight for it you have not the slightest idea.' In spite of the fine qualities of individual I.R.A. men, as a body I considered them worthless.

From the start the I.R.A. had meant trouble for Goertz who, upon landing, had marched seventy miles to Laragh, Co. Wicklow, and the home of Mrs Iseult Stuart, wife of a man who had befriended him in Berlin and a sister of Sean MacBride. Mrs Stuart gave him hospitality and brought him clothing, but a few days later, contact with the I.R.A. having been effected, he went, on I.R.A. advice, to the home in Templeogue of Stephen Carroll Held, a businessman whose father was a naturalised German. On May 23 Held's house was raided by police who missed Goertz, but seized his transmitter and some $20,000 in notes. This seizure alarmed the government more than any development since the Magazine Fort raid. Five days later the all-party National Defence Council was formed and on June 3 400 I.R.A. suspects were rounded up and interned in the Curragh.

The money which Goertz had suggests that the Germans thought highly of him. In his articles he describes sending money to a transmitting station in the North and makes other references to helping the I.R.A. financially. But it is very difficult to discover just what became of these sums. I.R.A. Leaders such as MacNamee, Kelly and McAteer impressed me as being among the most honest men I have ever met, and they all assured me that it was necessary to stage dangerous bank robberies in order to pay I.R.A. debts. Nor did the equipment of the rank and file ever indicate any degree of affluence. Goertz's money seems to have vanished into that murky limbo of espionage where nothing flourishes but crookedness, mediocrity and betrayal.

Reading his articles, and knowing that the man who wrote them committed suicide, one could not help feeling sorry for Goertz. He describes how all his efforts to get back to Germany failed, either because of police vigilance or treachery. A plan to get him away by boat from Fenit, Co. Kerry, in February, 1941 was scotched when the Irish authorities picked up his I.R.A. collaborators, and a British patrol boat waited just outside the three mile limit. He actually got away from Brittas Bay in Co. Wicklow but his engine broke down and he had to remain. He tried again in September while German planes circled overhead but, he wrote, 'again my boat failed. It was extremely hard on me to stand on a broad field near the sea and watch those friendly aircraft overhead.'

Assessing the I.R.A. and Goertz's role, Veesemayer, of the Irish Section in the Abwehr, in a lengthy report which he made on November 24, 1941, on a number of telegrams which Hempel had got from Dublin concerning the Hayes affair, said of Goertz: 'His communications are mostly one sided and therefore of a relatively valueless nature . . . both the Irish and the English police are informed as to his whereabouts . . . the value of his activity in Ireland has sunk to nil.'

The only spy other than Goertz to remain at liberty for any length of time was Ernest Weber-Drohl a former strong man in a circus. He was sixty-one when he appeared in the Dublin District Court on April 24, 1940, charged with entering Ireland illegally. He convinced the court that he was, as he described himself, 'Atlas the Strong', that he had come to Ireland to look up two missing children by a sweetheart whom he had loved and lived with in Ireland in 1907 and that he landed in Ireland in a small boat from a tramp steamer which had taken him from Antwerp. The boat, he claimed, had overturned and he had to swim for his life, losing in the process his passport, marriage certificate, pipes and letters. Weber-Drohl went on to say that a sailor who had come with him from the tramp steamer in the little boat had assisted him in righting it, and that the sailor had then made his way safely back to the steamer.

The strong-man story was a nicely blended mixture of fact and fiction: the sailor had made his way back in the little boat but not to a steamer. He had come from a German U-boat that approached the Irish coast. In a rough sea, the little boat had overturned and a wireless transmitter, which Weber-Drohl was supposed to hand over to the I.R.A. to replace the one seized in Rathmines, fell overboard. He had left Wilhelmshaven aboard U-boat U37, on January 28, 1940, so prior to his appearance in court he seems to have spent at least a month at liberty in Ireland. During this period he saw Jim O'Donovan and handed over money and code words to be used when another transmitter was found. This is about all Weber-Drohl achieved because three lapse after his acquittal the Secret Service picked him up.

The other German spies were caught almost on landing. One, Karl Anderson was arrested in Kingsbridge Station in Dublin on June 13, 1940 the day after landing in Kerry, and three others were picked up in July. These three agents were called Tributh, Gaertner and Obed, and they had landed in Baltimore Bay on July 18, with an incredible story of courageous seafaring behind them, having sailed from Brest in a yacht, the *Soizic*, rigged like a Breton fishing boat. The yacht had been commandeered for the voyage by a famous German yachtsman, Christian Nissen. They had passed close to British warships on a number of occasions on their thirty-six foot craft before landing and almost instant capture. Obed was an Indian, and three foreigners on a Cork road in wartime asking how to get to Dublin quite naturally attracted attention and they were arrested. None, of course, had made any contact with the I.R.A.

After 1941 the only German agent to make contact with Republican circles (and that only tangentially) was Gunther Schuetz, who made a spectacular escape from Mountjoy Jail in Dublin on February 28, 1942, after manufacturing a rope and grappling hook from some copper wire to scale the walls. He had earlier used some of the money given to him on departure from Amsterdam to buy women's clothes, allegedly for his fiancée, and dressed as a becoming young woman he made his way to the home of Kathleen Brugha (Cathal Brugha's widow) which was a centre of underground activity. Both Mrs Brugha and her daughter Noinin were active Republicans (Noinin afterwards married Sean O'Broin, one of the leaders of the raid on the Magazine Fort) and the police were actually coming to arrest her when they found Schuetz, who was using the name of Marschner. In the interval since his escape he had been put in contact with the I.R.A. and it had been arranged that a boat would be provided to take him from Dingle to Germany. However, on March 30, the day he was to go, the shipper of the boat, Charlie McGuinness, three men who were to act as crew, and the dining car attendant on the Belfast-Dublin train who was an I.R.A. courier were all arrested.

Churchill's fears about the possibility of an I.R.A.-Nazi tie-up proved groundless throughout the war. Eamon de Valera had wanted his country to be neutral and neutral it stayed, in one of the greatest diplomatic feats of the Second World War.

10

Republic and Republicans: I

The extraordinary doggedness of the Republican tradition persisting, despite many disasters, through the generations cannot be overlooked. Even with the disappearance of the border there would be some Republicans somewhere who would still claim to be the lawful inheritors of Ireland's revolutionary traditions, entitled to shed blood for what they believed a historically justified cause.

This sentiment was articulated on behalf of the Irish language by Diarmaid O Donnchadha* when he said:

It is charged that we pay more heed to the words of dead heroes than we do to living leaders. We accept that charge as a compliment . . . Comparison between the statements of aim of living leaders and the writings and speeches of dead heroes is the only way to be certain that the living pursue the aims of the dead. We want to make sure, to echo the words of Pearse, that they are preaching the same gospel rather than perhaps a saner and a wiser gospel.

This 'gospel of continuity' was in part responsible for the outburst of activity that took place after the Second World War. The campaign of border raids during 1956–62 was in some ways the most costly of all post-1921 I.R.A. activity. It occurred after the portcullis of years had been dropped on the events of the 1940s so that the bulk of those taking part knew of the leaders of other days only by hearsay—if at all.

And this is one of the extraordinary features of the I.R.A.: the manner in which the tradition of continuity exists side by side with a blank ignorance of earlier events and personalities. It goes far to explain the I.R.A. ethos, touching as it does on questions of Irish education generally, the I.R.A.'s own educative process or indoctrination, and the religio-politico nature of the division of the country, all of which combine so that the young I.R.A. man knows only as much about his country and Republicanism as the I.R.A. lets him know. Before turning to the 1956–62 phase of activity it is necessary to examine these forces.

It must first be understood that 'a Republican' or 'the Republic' in I.R.A. terms do not mean the same thing as they would, say, to a student of Plato, Rousseau or Jefferson.† A Republican is not merely a man who sees Ireland as

---

* Page 3, *The Case for the Defence; answers, based on facts and logic, to changes against the Irish Revival.*

† We may also discount the definition of an I.R.A. prisoner in Derry Jail who rose in disgust in the dining hall one Christmas Day, on being served with a herring, to proclaim as he held the offending object between finger and thumb, 'Any man who would eat these is no Republican.'

one nation, a geographical and cultural unit, and who objects to that nation being partitioned and to the spectacle of the flag and troops of another country giving daily evidence of that partition. There are such men, of course, but let us see how the question, 'What exactly is a Republican?', is answered in a pamphlet issued to commemorate the death of Austin Stack on April 27, 1929.

Stack was condemned to death for his part in the 1916 Rising, but his sentence was commuted to penal servitude. He underwent many subsequent terms of imprisonment, and some incredible hunger strikes and other adventures, such as the smashing up of Belfast Jail in November, 1918, when he was commandant of the prisoners there. He held various ministries in the underground Republican government, and during the Civil War itself was deputy chief of staff to Frank Aiken. He is venerated by his contemporaries as the very model of a perfect Republican.

The name Republican in Ireland, as used amongst Republicans, bears no political meaning. It stands for the devout lover of his country, tying with might and main for his country's freedom.

Such a man cannot be a slave. And if not a slave in heart or in act, he cannot be guilty of the slave vices. No coercion can breed the in the freeman.

Fittingly, the question, What is a Republican? fails to be answered in our memorial number for Austin Stack, a man who bore and dared and suffered, remaining through it all and at the worst, the captain of his own soul . . . What then was Austin Stack, Republican?

A great love of his country. A man without a crooked twist in him. One who thought straight, acted straight, walked the straight road unflinchingly and expected of others that they should walk it with him, as simply as he did himself. No man could say or write of him: 'He had to do it.' That plea of the slave was not his. His duty, as conscience and love dictated, he did. The force of England, of the English Slave State, might try coercion, as they tried it many times. It made no difference. He went his way, suffered their will, and stood his ground doggedly, smiling now and again. His determination out-stood theirs, because it had a deeper foundation and a higher aim. Compromise, submission, the slave marks, did not and could not exist for him as touching himself, or the Cause for which he worked and fought, lived and died.

Fifty years after 1916 another Republican, Joe Christle, who himself took up arms in the 1950s wrote an essay defining a Republic as he saw it. Christle split from the main body of the I.R.A. during his period of activity, but the sentiments contained in his essay would be acceptable to most members of the I.R.A. both past and present.

THE LIVING REPUBLIC!

The great purity of the Republic, the sublimity even of its object—the guarantee of equal rights and equal opportunities is precisely that which makes our force and our weakness. Our force, because it gives us the ascendancy of truth over imposture and the rights of public interest over private interest. Our weakness, because it rallies against us all the vicious; all those who in their hearts meditate the robbery of the people, all those who having robbed them seek impunity, all those who have rejected equality as a personal calamity and above all, those who embrace politics as a family trade and the nation as a prey.

It must not be forgotten that the desecrating voice of the establishment raged equally loud in denouncing Pearse in 1916 as it did in denouncing South in 1956. In Ireland the voice of the establishment has been and still is the voice of criminal and here crime massacres innocence to reign. If now no man is led out blindfold to be executed in an Irish prison yard, it is because no man rebels against the criminal in power.

In this situation the first maxim of policy for the Republic should be to conduct the people by reason and the enemies of the people by strength . . .

Let us commune with them who declared the right of the people of Ireland to the ownership of Ireland with equal rights and equal opportunities for all citizens The men who faced the firing squads of the establishment gave testimony to the truth of what had been declared and gave the lie to every Judas who would betray them.

The people can be relied upon to rally to take Republican ideals when Republicans themselves rally to the ideal . . . equal rights and equal opportunities. It was for this the Republic was proclaimed and for this alone is there any meaning to Republic.

But the establishment will be heard to shout 'Oh No! Republic means Democracy and this formula is guarded by the Ballot-Box.' That is a deceit and this deceit founded the Free State and was used by clever men to cloak the surrender of 1922 as a stepping stone to the Republic. These clever men were heard to say that 'the people fought for the right to vote.' In other words the people fought for the right to choose their masters. But this is blatantly deceitful, for the Founders of the Republic wrote—the people shall be master; the people who wept in Gethsemane and who died naked on the Cross.

The Republic is not a formula to be dispensed at Ballot boxes once in every five years. It is the way of life. It is not that some are chosen to be masters for this would be 'Beggars change horseback but the lash goes on'; it is, that all have admitted the reality of equality . . .

[The Republic] could not tolerate education based on privilege because in the Republic there can be no privilege . . . the Republic would encourage the fullest expression by writers, poets and artists [and] could not have troops of an alien enemy occupying part of the national territory . . .

We should with strength seek to destroy the establishment but not, after destroying it, seek wantonly to kill its agents for to do so would be to violate the honour of the Republic.

What made men join a movement dedicated to the establishment of such an ideal Republic? Family and environmental influences played a large part, as the careers of two of the I.R.A.'s outstanding figures show.

Sean O'Broin, one of the leaders of the Magazine Fort raid, comes from Kerry where the Civil War took a grisly turn. At Ballyseedy Republican prisoners were chained together and set to dismantle a mined barricade so that they were blown to pieces. Cathal Brugha's son Ruari, a successful businessman and Fianna Fail senator gave me this statement:

'I joined the I.R.A. at sixteen while I was still at school. It was the result of the environment in which I grew up. My father had been killed fighting in 1922 for the ideals of Easter Week, founded on a love of Ireland and its people, and an angry determination to save the nation from being completely smothered by English influences. In the struggle that followed 1916 against England, people had to endure many things. Hard decisions had to be made. Young men had been sent to their deaths in bitter fighting all over the country. Spies and informers had been executed but the leaders in this conflict were not fighting for military victory alone. The real struggle was for the mind and soul of a once proud nation, and now, at the end of it all, they were asked to swear allegiance to a foreign king and to acknowledge the right of the former enemy to keep troops in Ireland. These symbols of domination contrasted so violently with the inspiring vision of a free and independent Ireland that they were utterly unacceptable. This, I believe, is why my father made his sacrifice.

'Naturally, the atmosphere of my home was not only Republican and anti-treaty but also anti-Free State and generally derogatory of politics and politicians. I think my decision to join the I.R.A. was inevitable because, with my upbringing and background, it would have been shirking a duty not to do so. In any case, for the very young, there was an element of excitement in it. Raids, arrests, secret parades, arms classes and the occasional public parade, which were a challenge to authority, helped to make it attractive. You felt you were part of something and had a sense of identity with the high ideals of the past.

'I.R.A. policy, as I understood it, was confused. It was taken for granted that one joined the I.R.A. to get an all-Ireland Republic of which Ireland had been cheated by England with the aid of some Irish politicians. I learned that the Free State was a British dominion created by an English act of Parliament; that there was a governor-general appointed by the king of England; that we were British subjects; that Ireland was partitioned by Britain and kept that way by British troops against the will of the majority of the people. I was led to believe that the ideals of anyone who went into politics (i.e. Leinster House) would be under-mined or weakened; that he would become pro-British and that it was an act of treason to the Republic to acknowledge the state or the government. This was the type of doctrine one heard or read about in *An Phoblacht*.

'The things that stand out in my mind now as being significant did not seem so then. There was an instruction to the rank and file of the volunteers [I.R.A.] to refuse to recognise the courts if charged with political offences. The theory of the *de jure* authority of the second Dail was used to justify the existence of an armed force. This theory rested on the fact that the second Dail had not been properly dissolved and that those who had refused to enter the Free State Dail retained the *de jure* authority of the second Dail. That argument was supported by reference to a statement [by de Valera] made in Leinster House that "the real authority lies outside this House". I think that the idea of the continuing authority of the second Dail had considerable influence on some of us at that time. This theory was being upheld despite successive governments being elected under a free franchise. We became the victims of an illusion that could never become a reality. It prevented constructive thought about the country and how best to serve it. But for a young person to turn his back on this teaching would have been seen as an abandonment of principle.

'To some, in that atmosphere, to do so would have been as impossible as changing one's religion. As a result, normal judgement could not be exercised and such political steps as the removal of the governor-general and the oath of allegiance, the introduction of the Irish Nationality and Citizenship Act, the recovery of the occupied ports, the new constitution with a president elected by the people—all of which were milestones in our development towards political independence and which would have been welcomed in 1922, were regarded by extreme Republicans as political stunts.

'I had resolved from the beginning to avoid gunfighting involving Irishmen because I rejected the idea of civil war. Many of the things which happened during the 1930s caused me to have misgivings. There were indiscriminate actions and shootings which were not consistent with the aims of the movement. Those in charge seemed unable to cope. All this led me to think critically and therefore independently and prevented me from becoming too deeply involved.

'As I see it now, the dilemma facing the leaders arose from their complete acceptance of the theory that force was the only way to achieve their aims. They felt committed to this policy partly through loyalty to those who had already lost their lives and also because of a deep distrust and dislike of political methods. Any deviation from the accepted principle appeared to them to be an abandonment of the struggle for Irish freedom and unity. This prevented them from considering other means.

'It is easy to criticise that campaign [Russell's against England]. However unrealistic and ill-advised that policy may have been it is true that some brave young Irishmen, acting in good faith, took part in it for the sake of their country. They carried out extremely difficult tasks in the most dangerous conditions. They suffered ill-treatment and long terms in British jails. Some of them never fully recovered from their experiences. Their sacrifices must appear on the credit side somewhere.

'In the autumn of 1940, I was interned. In the Curragh I was struck by a curious situation. Irish soldiers were guarding alike I.R.A. and British and German internees in separate internment camps. I realised that Irish neutrality was a token of our sovereignty. I found it difficult to resent the government which had interned me because, in their view, I was not prepared to acknowledge their right to maintain order and defend the freedom of this part of Ireland. An unusual aspect of this situation was that many of us, certainly I myself, could have secured release simply by giving an undertaking. But this was what one could not do. It is one thing for a free man to declare his attitude of his own free will. It is quite a different thing for a detained political prisoner to do so in order to get out. And so many hundreds of men and some women (in Mountjoy Jail) remained in prison away from their families rather than "sign out" and lose their independence of mind and self-respect. As a result, many of them suffered torment—torn between responsibility for their dependents and loyalty to a cause.

'There is an interesting aspect of the later prison situation that is not generally known. During the invasion scare, sentenced I.R.A. prisoners in Arbour Hill detention barracks decided that, if there was a British invasion of the twenty-six counties, they would volunteer for service in the Irish army. This may not seem peculiar today, but for them it would have meant putting on the uniform of the former Free State army with its memories of deaths, executions and civil war.

'Circumstances had brought them into a cul-de-sac; they had been taught no way of serving their country except by arms and sacrifice. These were some of the best elements in the nation. The stream of idealism that runs in every generation was at that time partly diverted, as it were, into the desert. They could have helped to supply some of the patriotism together with the dynamism essential in national politics. They sought nothing for themselves; they only wished to serve their country.

'It was obvious to me that the twenty-six counties were politically free and that the sort of activity in which the I.R.A. had been engaged had not helped to end partition. The six counties is a largely planned area with all the ills that such areas possess wherever they exist in the world. There will be extremes of political differences and loyalties there for a long time. There is gerrymandering because of vested interests and because of inculcated mistrust and fear among the descendants of planter stock. We need to understand that the division in Ireland arises out of its tragic history and may not be quickly resolved.'

Another famous name in I.R.A. history was that of Micksey Conway who, when I interviewed him in 1969, was Brother Maolmuire in the Cistercian communique at Collon, Co. Meath. The formidable figure of the 1930s was no more. He was a low-sized, greying man with sincerity and decency radiating from blue, kindly eyes, from his weather-beaten, disciplined face and his warm, strong handshake. He was only a boy of twelve during the Civil War but he remembered incidents such as soldiers coming to Tipperary town and firing over the heads of looters who had taken butter from shop windows and were trampling it into the street.*

He told me he was first attracted to the I.R.A. by the dedication and religious fervour he saw in its leaders. It matched his own religious feelings and made him see the I.R.A. as something noble and pure. This dedication was to lead him into some pretty desperate situations. The Egan shooting, for instance, led to his death sentence, but when he was finally reprieved, he told me, he was disappointed. He had become resigned to the thought of death for imprisonment meant constant supervision by warders who sat beside him even while he slept, lest he attempt to strangle himself. This seemed a far worse fate than death in a cause he felt to be intrinsically good.†

Conway joined the Cistercians in 1951. When I met him seventeen years later he had been to Dublin only twice in the meantime. His normal daily routine was to get up at 4.15 and work all day, returning to bed at 8.30 pm.—which he found trying in summer. He was very hopeful of the reforms and the renewal of the Church set in train by Vatican II. Driving back to Dublin after interviewing him, my abiding impression was that it would be difficult to meet a more sincere man.

The sort of influences playing on the idealistic mind of young I.R.A. volunteers may be gauged from some typical Republican publications from the Civil War to the present day.

In an issue of a broadsheet, *The Fenian*, dated September 13 '7th year of the Republic', probably edited by Erskine Childers whose influence on Republican polemics has lasted until our day, one can trace the same threads of bitterness, high-mindedness, dedication and contempt for the institutions of the state other than those stemming from the mystical 'second Dail'. *The Fenian* always referred to the Free State as 'the Slave State' and defined its attitude thus:

In answer to some correspondents we wish to say that it is not our intention to devote space daily to the reports of the proceeding of the called 'Parliament' now sitting in the very appropriate premises of the Royal Dublin Society. The only parliament entitled to legislate and govern in this country is Dail Eireann, The Parliament of the Irish Republic. The Kildare Street debating club is not the Dail. It therefore is entitled to no respect or obedience from the Irish people. The only use of interest its proceedings have for us is to afford a certain amount of amusement, or of insight into the minds of the men who have endeavoured to sell their birthright for a mess of English pottage.

---

* Tipperary, a rebel county, the home of Charles Kickham the Fenian writer, had its share of bitter Civil War memories, executions and divided families. One court-martial of two men who had betrayed I.R.A. volunteers to Free State soldiers thereby causing their deaths, was guarded by a brother of one of the two accused, and subsequently executed, men.

† This is a common attitude towards loss of life in religious I.R.A. men. Oscar Traynor, who commanded the Dublin brigade in the Anglo-Irish war, and had to initiate and sanction some pretty stern actions, told how one morning in Wicklow Street he met a man on his way to Mass in Clarendon Street Church and it emerged that the man was also going to receive communion, 'But,' asked Traynor, 'weren't you the man who carried out——last night? I've just bought a paper and it says he was killed outright?' 'Yes,' replied the gunman, 'of course I am, what's that got to do with it? That execution was sanctioned by the legal government of Ireland. I was only doing my duty.' With that he went off to receive communion.

Another Republican apologist, Frank Gallagher, in a pamphlet 'By What Authority?' published in London during the Civil War, defined the Republican position in a manner which would stand today for many Republicans:

> Before the Treaty was signed, Civil War in Ireland was impossible. What made it possible? For five terrible years the nation had remained united on three great principles:
> 1. The existence of the Republic founded in Easter Week, and confirmed by national plebiscite in 1918;
> 2. The sanctity of our national independence declared by the Sovereign National Assembly in January, 1919; and
> 3. The territorial integrity of Ireland, which had outlasted history itself.
> The Treaty violated these three fundamental principles, destroying the Republic, surrendering our national independence, partitioning our ancient nation.

The significance of the Government of Ireland Act meant nothing.

The question of the oath was responsible for voluminous literature in its own right. One of the more notable pamphlets, 'The Oath of Allegiance and All that It Implies', by 'Skellig' (J. J. O'Kelly, a member of Sinn Fein's first Dail, and a noted propagandist on the Republican side) devoted most of its animadversions on the oath to 'The Lustful Henry the Eighth's' machinations, and traced those supporting (in 1925) the Free State back to the days of Henry. Throughout the pamphlet references to the debauchery of the royal line made it clear that anybody subscribing to the contemporary oath of allegiance was, if not quite incestuous, homosexual and degenerate, at least very lacking in patriotism.

Lest there be any religious scruples in the minds of I.R.A. men there was also a pamphlet entitled 'False Pastors' by Columban na Banban, who was very likely Father O'Flanagan, former vice-president of Sinn Fein, which said that the Irish bishops had the right and duty to lay down a code of behaviour for the faithful—except when they were in error. That the Irish bishops were very much in error we learn here:

> It is charged that through a long course of years they have been false to this nation; that they have time and again encouraged the enemy of our people; that they have blessed those amongst ourselves who stood for the compromise of our national principles and honour, and cursed the men who were ready to fight and die to win our liberty and independence. It is charged against them that when at last in 1921 victory seemed at hand, they sided with the men who betrayed the nation; and that then, encroaching on the purely temporal, prostituting their spiritual power and profaning the most sacred things, they conspired with a domestic enemy, the most terrible our people have ever known; and that they condoned by their criminal silence the perpetration of savage and inhuman deeds. It is charged against them that they are the principal cause of the blackest crimes which stain our history, not that they were the actual perpetrators, but because, by reason of their position and influence, the part they played makes them more responsible and guilty than the actual criminals.

The constitution of the I.R.A., published by the Republican Information Bureau in June, 1932, contains a passage explaining how it is that on one hand the I.R.A. might hold secret drill sessions, be bound by oaths and passwords, and on the other, drill openly, and publish newspapers and pamphlets:

> It is well to emphasise here that the Irish Republican Army is not, and never has been, what is termed a 'Secret Society'. Its existence, constitution and policy are openly declared. Secrecy as to its activiites is only maintained to safeguard it from attack. The policy of the Irish Republican Army is published and proclaimed in writing and speech as openly as circumstances permit.

The justification of having an army at all reads:

Until the Republic of Ireland is freed from foreign aggression and can function freely, the
necessity for the Irish Republican Army will continue. Only to a Government of the
Republic can the Army give allegiance. Should the time arrive when its services will be no
longer necessary to defend the nation's sovereignty, it will disband.

The flexibility of this last principle is demonstrated by the fact that in June, 1969,
when armed attacks on the North had clearly failed, the I.R.A. had turned itself to
defending 'the nation's sovereignty' by burning down the homes of Germans who
had bought land in Ireland.

Republican theology has always been subject to this kind of interpretation.
One of Peadar O'Donnell's pamphlets, 'For Or Against The Ranchers?' printed
by the *Mayo News* in Westport shortly after the outbreak of the economic war,
tells small farmers that:

This rancher-based cattle trade versus tillage fight now is primarily a fight on the national
issue. The ranchers are not fighting against exclusion from the British market; . . . It is in
their role as Imperialists that the ranchers and big farmers are warring now, and it is in their
role as Nationalists that the mass of the Irish people must overwhelm them. Any leadership
that does not take its stand on the full Separatist platform must, therefore, fall short of the
needs of the situation.

Young men reading *An Phoblacht* would find sentiments akin to those of O'Donnell.
Its editorial for March 26, 1932, contained the following:

The enemy of Irish Independence, British Imperialism, is still entrenched and active. Its
immediate aim will be to stir up conflict, seeking to drive a wedge into any movement that
aims at its undoing. British Imperialism stands for the maintenance of the present Social and
Economic system; it is for all National organisations accordingly to fight any influences that
tend to foster internal strife, mobilising en masse against the common enemy. The Treaty was
imposed by force; its alternative ruthless war: it is unnatural and immoral. Partition, its
changeling, is a degrading abomination, foisted upon us by the foreigner. To undo both is our
obvious duty.

The *Irish Workers' Voice*, official organ of the Irish Communist Party endorsed this
line in its publications. The Communist Party's inaugural meeting was held on
June 4 and 5, 1933, in Dublin, where Sean Murray, the great figure in the Irish
Communist Party in the 1930s, said that 'the manifesto was to be issued to the
working men of Ireland, to all fellow Fighters for national freedom. The delegates
here today from the four corners of Ireland are living proof that a society of
United Irishmen can be formed in this twentieth century.'

The *Wolfe Tone Weekly*, which began under the editorship of Brian O'Higgins in
September, 1937, though not as popular as *An Phoblacht*, was a journal of some
influence until its end in September, 1939. Brian O'hUiginn (the Irish version of his
name by which he was generally known) was a member of the first Dail. As a polemicist he lacked he grace and social content of Peadar O'Donnell, tending more towards
Gaelic revivalism than socialism. The *Wolfe Tone Weekly* was, however, well edited
and laid out, better than either *An Phoblacht* or the *Republican Congress*★.
O'hUiginn's first editorial set the tone for the two years of his papers existence:

★   O'hUiginn also produced tastefully designed Celtic art work. My father, who politically
    could hardly have differed more from him, would never allow any Christmas cards to
    be bought by our family other than those produced by O'hUiginn.

What we believe in our hearts . . . of the heritage we have revived from the unconquered and breathless dead. When we think of the many men who, in the full vigour and glory of their manhood, lay down their lives without a murmur of complaint or regret, we must ask ourselves this question—for what did they die? And if we are honest we must answer in their own words, spoken with their dying breath—they died for the full and complete and untrammelled freedom of an Ireland, of every sod of Ireland. They did not die for a prosperous so-called 'Free State', nor did they die for a cosmopolitan Republic. They died endeavouring, in the words of Wolfe Tone, 'to break the connection with England, the never-failing source of all our political evil.' They died endeavouring to make the Sovereign Republic of all Ireland, in the inspired words of Padraig Pearse, 'Not free merely, but Gaelic as well; not Gaelic merely, but free as well.'

Since 1916 the most important influence on all sections of Republican thought has been Padraig Pearse. Pearse's writings⋆ derive their strength from the manner in which they express the ideal of Irish separatism—'Ireland Free is Ireland Gaelic, Ireland Gaelic is Ireland Free'—and from the themes of self-sacrifice and communion with the dead, which are common both in the Irish missionary tradition and in the typical Republican attitude towards serving Ireland.

'Patriotism,' he wrote, 'is in large part a memory of heroic dead men and a striving to accomplish same task left unfinished by them.' (This later appeared on a memorial programme issued by the I.R.A. at Easter 1968.)

The way in which Pearse mixed revolution and religion was particularly powerful. His statement on 'freedom and the sword' embodies teachings learned by every Irish Catholic schoolchild of his time:

'One of the sins against Faith is presumption which is defined as: "A foolish expectation of salvation without making use of the necessary means to obtain it." Surely it is a sin against national faith to expect national freedom without accepting the necessary means to win and keep it. And I know of no other way than the way of the sword: History records no other, reason and experience suggest no other.'

This quotation appears on the late-page of a document on I.R.A. policy published in June, 1932 by the Republican Publicity Bureau. It is interesting to contrast it with an entry in the diary of Fergal O'Hanlon, nineteen, who was killed in the Brookeborough raid on New Year's Eve, 1957. Across two pages recording Easter Sunday and Monday 1956, Fergal wrote, 'I know of no way by which freedom can be obtained and when obtained maintained, except by armed men.'

The *Wolfe Tone Weekly* includes articles signed 'A Catholic Priest' on the 'Morality of Revolt', declaring that if one were revolting in the interests of the principles contained in the leading articles, one was not breaking the laws of God

---

⋆ Many of them, particularly a series entitled 'Tracts for the Times', showed a markedly socialist content, a preoccupation with death, a conviction, that all must end in sadness. This theme cropped up in short stories like 'Eoineen na nEan (Eoineen of the Birds), 'Bridget of the Sorrows', in 'Isogain', in his poem 'The Mother' with the statement, 'I do not grudge thee Lord my two strong sons' (both Pearse and his brother Willie died before firing squads) and in his celebrated statement on the outbreak of the First World War. This trend towards morbidity may have been heightened by the death of his sweetheart, Elaine Nicholls, who was drowned off Great Blasket Island, off the coast of Kerry, while giving another girl a swimming lesson in 1909.

or man. The late Sean Dunne, a Labour deputy who spent the war years interned in the Curragh for his youthful Republicanism, described this mentality to me as being that of a '—with a .45 wrapped in Rosary beads'. Earlier the *Weekly*, in a panel set in heavy black type that appeared in the issue of April 16, 1938, under the heading '1916' said, 'the men who took part in the Easter Week Rising were Irish in heart and soul, and their prayers were said on Irish Horn Rosary Beads. Do those who commemorate them follow their example?'

A poem in the *Wolfe Tone Weekly*, on September 11, 1937, from Jimmy Steel, at the time serving seven years, shows again how religion and Republican mingled.

A PRISON PRAYER

O, Sacred Heart of Jesus we pray to Thee today,
To aid our suffering Motherland
Upon her bloodstained way.
For loyalty to serve her,
For strength to set her free,
O, Sacred Heart of Jesus!
We send our prayer to Thee.

O, Sacred Heart of Jesus!
Look down on us today,
Make us strong and fearless soldiers,
Ever ready for the fray.
'Gainst Thine and Ireland's enemies,
Wherever they may be,
O, Sacred Heart of Jesus!
We put our trust in Thee

Another poem in the *Wolfe Tone Weekly*, in January, 1938 was reprinted in many other Republican journals in Ireland and America. Entitled 'Who is Ireland's Enemy?', it included these stanzas:

Who is Ireland's enemy?
Not Germany, nor Spain,
Not Russia, France nor Austria;
They forged for her no chain,
Nor quenched her hearths,
Nor razed her homes,
Nor laid her altars low,
Nor sent her sons to tramp the hill
Amid the winter snow!

Who spiked the heads of Irish Priests
On Dublin Castle gate?
Who butchered helpless Irish babes,
The lust for blood to sate?
Who outraged Irish maidenhood,
And tortured aged sires,
And spread from Clare to Donegal,
The glare of midnight fires?

Who scourged our land in '98
Spread torture far and wide,
Till Ireland shrieked in woe and pain,
And hell seemed fair beside?
Who plied the pitch-cap and the sword,
The gibbet and the rack?
O God! that we should ever fail
To pay those devils back.

Who slew the three in Manchester,
One drear November dawn,
While round them howled in fury
The devil's hungry spawn?
Who shattered many a Fenian mind
In dungeons o're the foam,
And broke the loyal Fenian hearts
That pined for them at home?
Who shot down Clarke and Connolly
And Pearse at dawn of day,
And Plunkett and MacDiarmada
And all who died as they?
Who robbed us of McSwiney brave?
Who murdered Mellows too,
Sent Barry to a felon's grave
And slaughtered Cathal Brugha?

Not Germany nor Austria,
Not Russia, France nor Spain
That robbed and reaved this land of ours,
That forged her rusty chain;
But England of the wily words—
A crafty, treacherous foe—
'Twas England scourged our motherland,
'Twas England laid her low!

Rise up, o dead of Ireland!
And rouse her living men;
The chance will come to us at last
To win our own again;
To sweep the English enemy
From hill and glen and bay,
And in your name, o holy dead!
Our sacred debt to pay!

While most of this writing was propagandist rather than literary, the *Wolfe Tone Weekly* also provided a fifteen-year-old Dubliner, Brendan Behan, with a vehicle for his poetic view of the deaths of Rory O'Connor, Liam Mellows, Richard Barrett and Joe McKelvey during the Civil War. The poem appeared on December 24, 1938, under the heading 'Four Great Names'.

The tragic events of the war also provided a deluge of pamphlets and broadsheets. One of the most interesting was showered on Dublin on St Patrick's Day, 1942, after George Plant's execution. The leaflet set out the facts from the I.R.A. point of view. But it is not the content so much as the manner of delivery that is memorable. With the aid of friends and relatives, including two Christian brothers, all of whom were subsequently arrested, Seamus G. O'Kelly, a victim of cerebral palsy but the father of four healthy children and a life-long I.R.A. and Republican publicist, arranged for 5,000 copies to be run off and then, while de Valera was attending High Mass in the nearby Pro Cathedral, had them all scattered down on Dublin from the top of Nelson's Pillar.

Brian O'Higgins's *Wolfe Tone Annual* also came out during the war years. This was a compendium of articles on separatist history, something on the lines of the *Wolfe Tone Weekly* though less detailed. In October, 1943 it was banned from appearing as a 1944 issue on the grounds that it contravened the Emergency Powers Order of 1939. It was subsequently published unaltered in 1945 and the banning reverberated through the Dail and the columns of letters to the editors for some years afterwards.

When a regular Republican newspaper, the *United Irishman*, began in July, 1947, the mixture was as before, with articles about I.R.A. leaders who had been executed, accounts of commemoration ceremonies, references to 1916 and a preoccupation with those who died for Ireland rather than with the living conditions of those who wished to live for her in the post-war years. As the younger spirits who master-minded the 1956–62 border campaign came to power, the paper developed a more militant tone and Eamonn Timmoney, O.C. of the I.R.A. group in Derry in that campaign, said, 'This little paper played an important part in developing sympathies with, and support for, the Republican movement.'

It gave articles of interest to Republicans, told the new generation about the indignities suffered by Irish patriots at the hands of the British and Irish authorities in the past and blended Feniansim, commentary on the contemporary political situation in the North and attacks on the Fianna Fail and Coalition regimes in the South. As the campaign developed the paper devoted itself to accounts of great victories won and battles fought. (Many were more apparent to the editorial staff of the *United Irishman* than to the public at large.) The 1960s' *United Irishman* was well written and laid out though the Fenian content had been steadily diminishing and, while occasional photographs of commemorations (in particular of Bodenstown) occurred, it tended to consist of articles reminiscent of the old Saor Eire and Republican Congress days. Articles on Dublin's housing conditions, on emigration and attacks on Ireland's plan to join the Common Market formed the bulk of its contents. These, like the slogans defacing the walls around Dublin—'E.E.C. No!'—hardly carried the same impact as the old 'Up the I.R.A.' which, leaping at you from dead walls, at least let you know where you stood.

But even in this more sophisticated era of Republicanism, the old dichotomy between armed force and cerebral political movement is still apparent in the movement's publications. Glossily produced, *The Separatist* sometimes appears on newstands showing a map of Ireland on page one with a Union-jacked hand lifting the six counties out of it, while in the foreground looms a figure of an I.R.A. man with a tommy-gun. In its introduction, the publication states that:

The I.R.A. cannot be dismissed as mere gunmen screaming for blood. There is over-whelming support in the Republican movement today for a more realistic approach to Ireland's ills. This school of thought is disgusted with the way Ireland (32 counties) has been ruled for the past forty years and advocates sweeping social reforms especially in education. They point out that Britain has changed its policy towards the 26 Counties and now rules by economic rather than by political means. They will fight this cheque-book invasion, changing tactics as it suits them. This does not mean that the I.R.A. will lay down the gun, for they still believe that the final changing of power will come only with the threat of, if not the actual use of, physical force.

As a result of all this pressure towards a sombre, brooding type of patriotism, in which death was used with something of the same spirit of the Japanese suicide flyers in the Second World War, it is not surprising that the I.R.A. should itself inflict death on some of its own members for real or imagined breaches of its code.

A man accused of a capital offence under I.R.A. law is normally given the opportunity to defend himself in a court-martial (though this did not happen in at least one case). I.R.A. court regulations stipulate that the accused be tried before three officers, that he be given the opportunity to nominate a defending counsel and that the prosecution be carried out in the same way as a lawyer for the state presents a case before a judge and jury in ordinary law cases. An accused man may summon witnesses and he is normally served with a copy of the convening order showing the personnel of the court, a copy of the charge sheet and a copy of any exhibits which may be produced, so that he and his 'counsel' may prepare a defence. The regulations provide for a number of oaths, modelled on those taken in legal courts. These are administered to all court members, the legal officer, witnesses and the shorthand clerk.

Much I.R.A. time and energy went, and still goes, into the holding of such courts-martial, courts of enquiry into misdemeanours real or imagined and attendance at commemoration ceremonies. (These are tragically increased by the malfunctioning of some bomb, weapon or ambush.) The more legalistic attach importance to courts-martial, but these can prove to be fairly arbitrary affairs so far as justice is concerned. During the 'Belt and Boot Brigade' era in Belfast one court-martial occurred at which Tarlach O'hUid was the note-taker when sentence of death was pronounced for a not very heinous misdemeanour. For some reason the principal officer of the court hesitated about sentencing the accused. A discussion began and the officer asked O'hUid, 'Well, should we execute him, or what will we do with him?' O'hUid replied, 'How about reducing him in the ranks?' This compromise was accepted but a compromise was not always forthcoming and a number of 'disappearances' that took place during bombing raids on Belfast were not from falling masonry, but from I.R.A. action. In one of these cases, the widow of the executed man was so well aware of the I.R.A.'s role that she asked a bishop to communicate with the I.R.A. for a certificate stating that her husband had been executed. The insurance company would thus have proof of death and would pay the insurance she badly needed.

The I.R.A. decided that such a comment would be too incriminating and refused her request so she never got her money.

No court-martial preceded the Admiral Somerville shooting but there was one for John Egan. I asked a member of the Army Council at the time (all such verdicts have to be sanctioned by the Army Council, in theory at least) how this action could be justified. He replied, 'These things are very necessary in an organisation like the I.R.A. They are very good for morale and they serve to release tension.'

Of all the I.R.A. courts-martial that of Dan Turley on April 5, 1933, in Dublin is probably the most contentious. Turley, who had been a gallant figure during the

Anglo-Irish struggle and was for a time O.C of the Belfast brigade, was at the time of his court-martial, intelligence officer to the brigade. The position of intelligence officer is a delicate one. To get information he has to make contacts with opposing forces, rendering him susceptible to their pressures and suspect to some of his colleagues. Turley fell under suspicion after a number of raids and arrests in Belfast pointed to an informer in the I.R.A. camp. Because of his position and record he was not informed of the feeling against him and he accompanied two other senior I.R.A. officers (one of whom supplied me with these details) from Belfast to Dublin where he learned that he was not being summoned to a convention but to a court-martial at which Michael Price was the prosecuting officer. He was found guilty of spying and sentenced to death, the sentence being commuted to banishment provided he never returned to the country again—on pain of being shot at sight.

Turley agreed to this and was taken to Glasgow by Sean Russell. However, Glasgow, for an insurance agent with his roots in Belfast and a young family to support, was not an attractive spot in the 1930s and after about six months he returned. Between then and December 7, 1937, when I.R.A. men shot him dead on the way to Mass, Turley must have lived a haunted life. He remained in a secret room in his house most of the time, only venturing out at night. Several friends visited him and warned him that the I.R.A. was going to kill him but he protested his innocence and refused to leave his native city. After his death his sons continued in the I.R.A., though refusing to believe their father guilty. With extraordinary loyalty to both their father's name and to the organisation that had killed him they continued membership while attempting to build up a dossier proving his innocence.

In addition to Turley I was given the names of three men in the North who, it was claimed, were executed, and four more reputed to have 'disappeared' during bombing raids on Belfast.

North or south of the border, I.R.A. training has always fallen into two categories—military and intelligence work. Recruits were trained in the use of rifles and small arms and in army drill. The guns used in these sessions were always carefully rushed away afterwards and only one or two weapons were ever available, even for a reasonably large company. This position did not greatly alter throughout the I.R.A.'s history between 1923 and 1963. Dumps have always been kept a closely guarded secret, but one that the police nevertheless penetrate. A Thompson gun at a drill session was a very rare event and the Derry unit of the I.R.A. put down a motion at the 1953 convention that asked that limpet mines and silencers for sten guns be provided. But they were not available. The chief explosive was the highly volatile 'paxo', made from potassium chlorate and paraffin wax.

I went, while researching this book (1969), on a drill session with a group of young I.R.A. men, and watched their military manoeuvres, mock attacks and advances over rough country under simulated war conditions, guns at the ready. This group seemed well armed, as a certain account of surplus American war equipment inevitably finds its way into the hands of those willing to pay for it. The 'soldiers' wore green battledress with peaked caps and looked a little like Roman soldiers. Armament was fairly good, with modern looking sub-machine guns, automatic rifles, walkietalkies, bomb-making equipment and useful looking revolvers. Physical fitness was excellent.

As this was a military operation, nobody was anxious to fraternise with me, though all were courteous enough.

The countryside in many parts of Ireland, even quite close to Dublin, is mountainous and well covered so there is little difficulty about concealment. I was told that local farmers were friendly and interruption by police seemed unlikely. As a precaution, I was called for at five in the morning before it was light and I did not reach home again until after dark, so that I could not divulge the route, if questioned.

Everyone in that group of twenty-five to thirty people was a small farmer, a clerk or a labourer. The disquieting thing was that, apart from the obvious dangers to themselves and others, they had no coherent political or ideological creed, nor even a sense of humour. Particularly with the spread of the ecumenical movement and the lessening of the horrors attending the word 'Communist', the I.R.A., I would say, of all revolutionary movements in Europe, would have been the most vulnerable to a Communist take-over.

The groundwork for the I.R.A.'s intelligence network was established in a memorandum of February 1, 1924. The document said that the intelligence information needed was:

(a) GOVERNMENT OFFICES: A list of Officials, Clerks, etc., employed in Government Offices annotated as to whether they are friendly (R), hostile (F.S.), doubtful (D), or neutral (N).

(b) NEWSPAPERS: A list of the Staffs on all Dublin daily and weekly newspapers (Marked as above.)

(c) RAILWAYS: A list of the permanent employees at all Dublin Termini. (Marked as in (a).)

(d) OFFICES OF PUBLIC WORKS: A list of the Staffs and permanent Officials of Dublin Corporation, Dublin County Council, Rathmines Council, Employment Officers, Labour Exchange, etc. (Marked as in (a).)

(e) TRADE UNIONS: a list of Officials, Clerks, etc. of all Trade Unions. (Marked as in (a).)

(f) CONTRACTS: Names and addresses of all employers, gaffers, foremen, etc., who have the giving of jobs with particulars as to their political sympathies, and as to how best they could be approached to employ released prisoners.

Modifications were introduced to this scheme over the years. One could today safely add a dossier of television personnel sympathetic or otherwise. In the 1950s photographs of Special Branch members, their home addresses, telephone numbers and registration numbers of their cars were also collected. But the principle remains that each volunteer is considered to be an intelligence officer who reports to his company commander anything he considers may be of assistance to the movement. The amount of reportage depends on the ability of the individual.★

Another continuing source of Republican influence is the annual Bodenstown march, usually held on the Sunday after Wolfe Tone's birth date, June 20. This occupies a position in the Republican calendar, analogous to that of Easter in the Christian religion. Bodenstown is three miles from Sallins in Co. Kildare, about

★ After the Second World War the paperback revolution inspired many young revolutionaries in the I.R.A. Eamonn Timmoney, O.C. of Derry, and Charlie Murphy, adjutant general of the movement in the early 1950s both remarked on the influence of books by foreign underground leaders.

thirty-five miles southwest of Dublin. Visiting Tone's grave on Bodenstown Sunday in the 1960s I learned a great deal about the I.R.A., and about Ireland itself.

Until the worsening situation in the North caused the Army-Fianna Fail commemorations to be held on spearate Sundays, it used to be the custom that the I.R.A. also marched to Bodenstown on the same day, though after Fianna Fail and the Army had departed. The first procession of the day was by the Irish army. A wreath was laid on the tomb, reveille was sounded and honour paid to the founder of Irish Republicanism. A little later came the Fianna Fail procession, when the prime minister or some other leading figure laid a wreath to the man from whom the Fianna Fail party derives its inspiration. All was quiet, decorous and generally sunlit.

After lunch came the I.R.A., the illegal organisation whose existence was not officially recognised, whose name could be mentioned publicly only while keeping a wary eye on the Offences Against the State act, and the grave of Wolfe Tone was again festooned with wreaths from various Republican organisations. Military commands were given, the flags of I.R.A. detachments were displayed and there was a fiery denunciation of everything symbolised by the previous two processions.

The annual Bodenstown oration is more than a mere denunciation. It sets the tone for the coming year's Republicanism, explains the policies of the movement, justifies them against criticism and urges those present on to greater efforts. One can judge the direction of I.R.A. policies by a study of the groups and personalities who attend Bodenstown in any given year. In 1931, for instance, though Cumann na Gael cancelled the special trains that normally run for the occasion, and police prevented some of the more openly militaristic from parading, the event was held with members of Fianna Fail marching together in a body. De Valera laid a wreath on Tone's grave after Peadar O'Donnell had called down the customary fire and brimstone on all those who stood in the path of I.R.A. policy. But the following year Fianna Fail were in power and the links between the two movements were becoming more tenuous. In his oration, Sean Russell said of the Dublin parliament, now led by de Valera, what Wolfe Tone had two centuries ago said of Henry Grattan's planters' parliament:

Of all parliaments beyond all comparison the most shameful and abandoned of all sense of virtue, principle or even common decency, was the Dublin government.

However, politics are politics and, this said, Mrs Tom Clarke, widow of the 1916 hero and representing the Fianna Fail, laid a wreath on Tone's grave on behalf of the Fianna Fail national executive. On this particular occasion the official army parade was held a week later, for the times were not propitious for the army and politics to mix safely.

In 1935 Tone's graveyard again rang to the sound of blows between the two sections of the movement, further weakening and embittering both sides. The next year, following the murder of Admiral Somerville the demonstration was banned altogether. It resumed in 1937 but was banned again in 1939. After the war it was the meeting place for those who initiated hostilities on the border in 1955, and was the venue for important public announcements, such as the speech by Christoir O'Neill in 1951 declaring that force would no longer be used against agents of the Southern Irish government but only against those maintaining the status quo in 'Occupied Ireland'.

But a casual observer is not normally aware of this significance. The Bodenstown marchers form up in assembly fields beside the shabby old limestone village of Sallins and then march out to the graveyard itself. All around the area there are encampments of various groups. Stalls do a roaring trade selling teas and ices and people go through the crowds selling booklets with the biographies of various patriots or distributing Republican literature. But the processional route is dotted at intervals by Special Branch cars with walkie-talkies and reputedly more lethal weapons. Special Branch photographers in plain clothes with miniature cameras normally mingle with the crowd taking pictures of those present.

Most of the marchers I have seen at Bodenstown were young men, generally from country districts, but there were also fathers and mothers wheeling prams, and elderly people. Behind the Republicans marched sympathetic groups. A contingent of Communists marched openly on at least one occasion. Here and there an American was to be seen, taking part in a pilgrimage. I once met one very fat old lady, barely able to walk, who had been coming for nearly fifty years. Although there were political overtones to her gesture she was making it in much the same spirit as any other woman of her generation would pay a visit to a noted shrine.

Even on my first visit men with wives and families chatted quite freely with me and, although the fact of my writing a book about the I.R.A. had aroused controversy within the movement (and throughout the day I was shadowed by two young men detailed to watch me by a senior member of the movement who objected to my writing), no one offered me anything other than friendly conversation and the hope that, whatever my views, I would put their case fairly. That was in 1967.

The oration that year was delivered by Cathal Goulding, a good speech which marked a radical turn in Republican policy. He said frankly that the movement's concentration on the removal of partition was a mistake and that social and economic goals must be pursued. Disquietingly and paradoxically, however, he added that to achieve these the option of the use of force must be retained. It was the old bugbear of Republicans manifesting itself again. How to get recruits and retain the support of the militants if force is eschewed? And if it is used how can the support of responsible public opinion be retained?

By a coincidence I listened to his speech in the company of Jack Mulvenna and Roddy Connolly, James Connolly's son. They were old Republican Congress stalwarts who had been involved in fights with the I.R.A. in 1934 and 1935 in that very graveyard for advocating the principles Goulding was putting forward then.

'It's fine but he's thirty years too late,' commented Mulvenna.

As we walked from the graveyard I was chatting with Charlie Murphy, one of the principal organisers of the 1956–62 border campaign. He paused to salute a neighbour, a friendly police superintendent in uniform.

'Force! My God, can you imagine anyone deliberately setting out to kill him?' commented Murphy.

Earlier I had noticed Murphy's wife Carmel standing rigidly to attention as the national anthem was played. She made an attractive picture against the sky, but she had tears in her eyes. As we drove home I asked her why.

'I was just thinking,' she said. 'Poor Wolfe Tone, the man who wanted to unite us all and there today we had three separate commemoration ceremonies and God knows how much bitterness as well.'

Violence and tragedy also fringe the edges of the major Orange parade—that on July 12 to commemorate the Battle of the Boyne. It finishes at Finaghy, about three miles from the centre of Belfast, and thereby takes the Orangemen through Catholic areas, with a consequent rise in tension. The Orange banners are gorgeously sumptuous. Brocaded and tasselled they show in bright colours 'King Billy' on a white horse leading his followers across the Boyne, Queen Victoria bestowing a Bible on a blackamoor or dour-faced men with names and styles such as 'James McFettridge, Founder of the Royal Orange Lodge, Temperance Loyal Lodge, No. 708, Shankill Rd.' Union Jacks flutter everywhere and, indeed, the Northern Irish march under symbols of divided allegiance. In the South the Republicans, divided from the Dublin government, nevertheless carry their country's flag.

The Northern speeches are frequently concerned with religion and, since Vatican II, increasingly denunciatory of the ecumenical movement. The Orange processions with their bands, banners and bowlers have a marked Kiplingesque air about them. When passions and Paisleyism subside in the North it is to be hoped that the Orange commemoration will be maintained as a colourful remnant from the past—attended by Irishmen from all parts of Ireland, including those who walk at Bodenstown.

In sport, too, the ugly effects of partition can be felt. Rugby chooses its international team from both sides of the border, but soccer is split between the two states. The Gaelic Athletic Association (G.A.A.), the largest sporting association in Ireland, confines itself to hurling, Gaelic football and handball, and its social occasions are devoted to the Irish language and céile dances. Until comparatively recently, anyone running foreign dances, or attempting to play 'foreign games' such as the former garrison games of rugby, soccer, cricket and hockey, is liable to be reported by the association's vigilante committee and expelled. There are very few Protestants in the G.A.A. and in the North membership of the G.A.A. carries political and religious overtones. Membership is denied to the British Army and the R.U.C. The authorities retaliate by sometimes harassing players on their way to training, or even, as in Crossmaglen, by damaging playing pitches and installations.

In athletics and cycling too, partition and the shadow of the I.R.A. are noticeable. The Irish Athletic Association, founded in 1885, was the first athletic body to bring working-class people within its scope, thus becoming a national organisation. In 1922, the G.A.A. by then more concerned with hurling and football, handed over control of athletic affairs to a new body, the National Athletics and Cycling Association. Most of the N.A.C.A. trophies were presented by the I.A.A. which joined the new N.A.C.A., offering fine, Republican-sounding awards with names like the Lord Ardilaun Trophy and the Wakefield Cup.

A new athletic association was founded in 1937 to provide an international outlet after the suspension of the N.A.C.A. in 1935 by the International Federation—because the N.A.C.A. maintained an 'anti-treaty' attitude and would not accept the border. The A.A.U. 'accepted' the treaty to gain an outlet for international competitors from the South. Those from the six counties were represented by the Unionist-minded North of Ireland Amateur Atlethic Association. In April, 1967, the N.A.C.A. and the A.A.U. combined to form Bord Luithchleas na hEireann (B.L.E.) (something similar, as far as N.A.C.A. was concerned, to Fianna Fail entering the Dail in 1932), which was hailed as a tremendous advance in healing old scars. However, elements in the N.A.C.A. refused to accept this settlement and led by ex-I.R.A. men such as Jim Killeen, Jack Brady and Joe Christle, they could be said to be the contemporary 'Sinn Fein of Irish sport'.

B.L.E. is recognised by the International Federation as controlling cycling and athletics in the Republic of Ireland, but the dissident wing of the N.A.C.A. which, under Christle in the 1950s was perennially engaged in clashes with the R.U.C. over carrying tricolours across the border during cycle races, is unworried by the lack of international outlet and this split will not readily heal.

The thirteen Irish language groups which would, on the face of it, appear to be I.R.A. breeding grounds, tend more to enhance existing tendencies than to sow the seeds of Republicanism. The oldest language group, the Gaelic League, was the avenue through which Tarlach O'hUid, then a young man living in London and rejoicing in the name of Hood, first became interested in an Irish Ireland, and ultimately joined the I.R.A. But he was an exception. Almost all I.R.A. men whom I questioned tended to regard the Gaelic movement as being 'parlour nationalist'. Interest in the language is a facet of their Republicanism rather than its motivating force

Before 1916 the founder of the Gaelic league, Douglas Hyde, had quit the league because he resented the I.R.B.'s infiltration of it for political purposes. Nevertheless, so many I.R.A. men join language classes, sometimes set up by the I.R.A. as front organisations, that after the 1956–62 campaign a former chief of the Special Branch told me that the branch had to regard the language movement as an I.R.A. stamping ground and to warn superiors of certain schools that individual Irish teachers were inciting classes towards militant Republicanism. Several times the police found that captured I.R.A. lads were from a school class that had been influenced by an Irish language enthusiast.

11

Republic and Republicans: II

To understand the post-war I.R.A. it is vital to understand also the intellectual and religious atmosphere in Ireland at the time and to look at the educational system under which young I.R.A. men had been raised.

Neutrality had screened Ireland from world affairs, leaving her with the literally insular political problems of partition and the I.R.A. Film and literary censorship had compounded the isolation, cutting off the flow of ideas and helping to stagnate the intellectual climate still further. Television had not come to Ireland except along the south-east coast where B.B.C. programmes could be picked up faintly. And there were the country's religious beliefs affecting the Republican movement through the educational system.

The attitude of Catholics towards Protestants in the South was one of uncertainty rather an of bigotry. An Irish schoolchild speaking of a man who did not go to Mass would not have said not say: 'He is an agnostic.' He would have said: 'He's a Protestant', because, to the average child, it was only Protestants who did not go to Mass. Only 5 per cent of the South's population is Protestant, so there is no overt Protestant-Catholic clash. Such visible strains as exist are generally confined to rival pressure organisations with a religious character. For instance, it was a matter of pride to the Roman Catholic Knights of Columbus in Dublin that the order had successfully broken the monopoly of the Protestant Masons on the executive board of the Royal Dublin Society.

Nevertheless the religious divisions ran deep and cannot be overlooked. One of de Valera's undoubted achievement was his allaying of the fears of the Protestant minority at his election in 1932. The Protestant *Irish Times* had urged its readers to vote for the Protestant-aiding Cosgrave regime because, 'If Fianna Fail takes office, the wealth and security of every citizen, including the ex-Unionist, will be impaired and perhaps gravely imperilled.' But in office de Valera nominated Douglas Hyde, the Protestant founder of the Gaelic League, as president under his new constitution in 1937. (When Hyde died, the then prime minister, John Costello, and his cabinet did not attend his funeral service because before Vatican II Irish Catholics were forbidden to attend Protestant church services.)

While the fears of Protestants were aroused by the prospect of de Valera in power or by any manifestation of clerical influence, the arms-length attitude which such fears engendered among Protestants was compounded by the fact that, as school children, Catholics learned nothing of phenomena in Church history such as bad popes, the Spanish Inquisition, what the word 'anathema' once signified or that the pope of the day had ordered a *Te Deum* sung in thanksgiving when he heard the outcome of the Battle of the Boyne. But they did learn in their catechisms that, 'There is only one True Church and no one can be saved out of it.' The statement was generally mitigated by a reference to Christ's statement that 'In my Father's house are many mansions' but Protestants were obviously defined as being in a very humble place in the queue for salvation.

Almost no member of my own generation, who left school in the mid-1950s, had the slightest notion of why Protestants should have wanted to remain under British rule in the North, or how religion and politics had become so interwoven that, even in the South, the flags of British regiments can be seen displayed in many Church of Ireland churches and that many Catholic Irishmen will not attend Landsdowne Rugby football ground because there are prominently displayed there the names of former Landsdowne and Wanderers' Rugby Club members who died in the First World War. In some circles, the main entrance to St Stephen's Green Park at the head of Grafton Street, which is similarly inscribed, is known as 'Traitors' Gate'.

The educational system, which furthered such prejudices, showed the marks of British influences and of the struggle between the claims of the Church and Irish nationalism which has been going on since the Act of Union in 1800.

The report of a council on education set up on May 5, 1950, to advise the government on the function of the primary school (for pupils under the age of thirteen) and its curriculum says:

'The school exists to assist and supplement the work of parents. Their first duty is to train the children in the fear and love of God. That duty becomes a first purpose of a Primary School . . . the child must *also* [my italics] take his place in human society as a citizen of the State . . . His training for this is essentially religious and moral.'

Primary schools were under the control of a clerical manager, the local parish priest or vicar, who was responsible for the appointment of teachers and the maintenance of the schools.

So much for the influence of the Church. The Nationalists too have their share. An important guide for parents, *Education in the Irish Republic*, prepared by Professor John O'Meara in 1965, describes the curriculum of a typical primary school of the period as being chiefly concerned with religious doctrine, reading and writing in Irish, and English and arithmetic. In addition there were history, geography, music and (for girls' schools) needlework. One can assess the time spent on these subjects if one remembers the primacy accorded to religious instruction in the council's report and considers the findings of Father John McNamara in his study, *Bilingualism and Primary Education in Ireland*, in which he claims that 42 per cent* of the time spent teaching in national schools was devoted to Irish. Father McNamara was a lecture in educational psychology in St Patrick's College, Dublin. In his book Father McNamara says that in an English test between two groups of twelve-year-olds, one Irish and the other English, the English children answered three times as many questions correctly as did the Irish. He says that the Irish children had all spent 42 per cent of their time at primary school learning Irish and only 22 per cent of their time learning English.

---

* In the Dail on July 22, 1969, the minister for education put the figure at 38 per cent in primary school classes and 20 per cent in the senior classes.

Arthur Griffith once complained that as a result of British influences, 'Irish education is a means of washing away the original sin of Irish birth'. But in the struggle between the claims of Irish nationalism and those of the Church, neither the Irish primary nor secondary schools' curriculum in the 1940s and 1950s would have given cause to retract his statement. And this was long after the British had left. The Irish language was not restored and if one examines the teaching of three subjects—history, English and Irish—one sees how the effect was to send young people out into the world generally unenlightened about the division of their country, with a strong anti-British bias but a paradoxically strong English bent towards literature, poetry and mode of expression. The courses for the three subjects during those years were laid down in the 'Rules and Programme for Secondary Schools', published annually by the Stationery Office.

History began with 'Early Christian Ireland, the Mission of St Patrick and the spread of Christianity' (which to Irish children, of course, meant the spread of Roman Catholicism) and ended with 'The Resurgence of 1916'. In between, the pupil learned of the invasions by Norsemen and Normans; the Elizabethan wars; the Plantation of Ulster; Cromwell; the Williamite wars; the penal laws; the famine, and the movements led by O'Connell, the Young Irelanders, the Fenians, Parnell and Arthur Griffith; and finally the 1916 Rising. European and world history were scarcely taught at all; only a smattering of European affairs was imparted, ending about the period of the French Revolution. Almost no Irish schoolchild, to my knowledge, learned anything about the pre-First World War era and from the Treaty of Versailles to Malta was a time unknown. Moreover the rules stipulated that, 'The Irish History Course will deal only with the period from 1014 to 1921'. This in practice meant that the teaching of history ended at 1916 and children never acquired a classroom knowledge of the Protestant drift away from Catholic power to the North and the emergence of a situation in which partition became possible, or the circumstances of the Anglo-Irish war and the Civil War. These were learned about later, either from the subjective viewpoint of relatives, or from polemic writings in republican journals.

The English literature course gave the student very little assistance in broadening his mind, and shuts off his access to the writings of his fellow countrymen. A typical leaving certificate English course (that for 1951–52) offered one Shakespearian play, Hamlet and one poem each by Shakespeare, Milton, Wordsworth, Shelley, Coleridge, Tennyson, and one by Yeats ('The Lake Isle of Innishfree'). Essays by Lamb, Leigh Hunt, Grey, Thackeray, Belloc, Addison, Ruskin, Newman and R.L. Stevenson were also included. Earlier in the intermediate course pupils would have done slightly better, with one essay by an Irish author, Thomas Davis. Their poetry course would have included one poem each by Aubrey de Vere, Emily Lawless, d'Arcy Magee and James Clarence Mangan.

In the Irish course students read works about the 1916 period such as 'Mo Dhá Rosin' (My Two Rosaleens), a tale of young lovers parted by death in the 1916 Rising and 'Mo Sceal Fein', by An tAthair Peadar O'Laoghaire, the story of an Irish parish priest at the turn of the century. This story, describing the priest's battles with the British authorities, gave me, at any rate, the false impression that the clergy were on the side of the language revival. They were, in fact, anti-Irish because a knowledge of English enabled the Irish Church to spread throughout the British Empire.

Irish stories in the secondary school courses recreated the struggle between Church and nationalist ideologies by imparting both a propagandist and religious favour. Themes such as the great famine were balanced by those about outwitting the power of the devil, as in the book *Seadna*, or supernatural manifestations such as that of the Christ Child in Padraig Pearse's *Isogain*.

Both Church and state were faced with a difficulty in teaching history. The system of education had given the Church a powerful source of strength through its ability to channel so much of the energy and talent of Irish boys and girls into its ranks, and to control the quantity of Irish intellectual life. In Europe, at this time, Ireland, with a population North and South of four million, ranked next to the Netherlands in the actual number of Catholic missionaries sent abroad, and above Germany and France. During 1968, a year of special emphasis by the Church on missionary endeavour, Church apologists pointed with pride to the fact that the proportion of Ireland's resources expended on missionary activities was equal in percentage terms to American military expenditure in the Vietnam war.

This position was achieved by skillful Church diplomacy in playing ball with the British. But the British were, by definition, Ireland's enemies. How could this diplomacy be explained to children? For the state, after the Civil War, the problem was to give children a knowledge of highly contentious issues involving not only living persons in the two major political parties, and hundreds of thousands outside, but also the memories of recent deaths, imprisonments, hunger strikes, burnings and the many brutalities associated with the Civil War, partition and the settling of old scores. The simple answer decided on by both parties was to teach no history after 1916, and to outline very sketchily events of the nineteenth century.

In the North a somewhat similar situation existed. The Catholic children received much the same historical instruction as do those of the South and some Irish was also taught. But the Protestant children learned almost nothing of Irish history and were instead instructed in the history of Britain. In both cases, North and South, Protestant and Catholic classrooms tended to impart the facts of the past with a gloss which took note of contemporary politics, though in both quality and volume the educational position had improved considerably since the 1950s. When I left school in Dublin in 1954 some six thousand secondary school pupils sat for their Leaving Certificate Examination. In 1969 this figure had increased to about seventy thousand.

A Telefis Eireann series of illustrated lectures on 'The Course of Irish History' during the 1916 celebrations, edited by Father F. X. Martin of University College, Dublin, and Professor Moody of Trinity College, Dublin, appeared in paperback and had an enormous sale. During this period I was shown in confidence a memorandum drawn up by a group of parents, educationalists and historians at the request of the government for use as a guide in creating more realistic history courses. It later became policy and helped to improve matters.* In the North a reappraisal of the history situation also got under way and the B.B.C. did valuable work in televising a series of programmes similar to those by Telefis Eireann and reprinting them in book form. In general, in the wake of enthusiasm for the study of Irish

---

★   Also appearing in 1966 was my own effort to provide the first attempt at an objective survey of the years 1916–66, *Ireland Since the Rising*. It proved popular and was made recommended reading for university students of history.

history (generated by the commemoration of the 1916 Rising in 1966) and the goodwill that sprang from meetings between Republican Prime Minister Sean Lemass and the North's Captain Terence O'Neill in January and February, 1965, contemporary interest tended to force on the civil rights movement rather than on how the border might be blown away—until the years after the 1969 upheavals.

It was the colourful Minister for Education, Donough O'Malley, who died in 1968, who led the move to improve the Southern Irish educational system—and it has improved out of all recognition. In the 1950s the kind of educational system I have outlined was the only one available to the vast majority of Irish schoolchildren. The governmental report, 'Investment in Education', prepared under the chairmanship of Professor Patrick Lynch, in 1966 revealed that over 50 per cent of Irish children left school at twelve.

Post-war politics had, of course, a great effect on the policies and organisation of the I.R.A. The general election of February, 1948 reaffirmed the high priority which partition and Republicanism were given in Irish affairs. Ireland had escaped the war but could not escape the post-war unemployment, high taxation, strikes and unrest. Fianna Fail had been in power for sixteen years and the country wanted a change. But while these issues were prominently discussed during the campaign, the political reaction which they generated was canalised by the Republican movement, or more accurately by a part of it, Clann na Poblachta, which came into prominence concerned not so much with the new problems as with the old problem of partition.

The formation of Clann na Poblachta was the most important break in the ranks of 'physical force' Republicanism since the creation of Fianna Fail in 1926. For Eamon de Valera there was now Sean MacBride, and in place of the land annuities' question the tuberculosis issue presented itself. Some old Republicans, most notably Patrick MacLogan and Maurice Twomey, said 'No' to joining. However, a number of old Republicans, including Con Lehane, Michael Fitzpatrick, Nod Hartnett, Jim Killeen, Donal O'Donoghue, Dr Richard Battenbury and Finian Brenacht came together under MacBride's leadership. At public meetings throughout the country and at private ones in the Teachers' club in Dublin, the new party mushroomed into vigorous life, even enlisting people who had been on opposite sides in the Civil War.

The scheme that most caught the public imagination was a proposal to concentrate on the eradication of tuberculosis, which was then both a social and medical evil. For some reason syphilis today carries less of a social stigma than did tuberculosis in 1948. The tuberculosis issue was the brainchild of Dr Noel Browne, not a Republican but a brilliant young socialist educated at Trinity. The Clann backed him in his programme for new sanatoria and immunisation which proved a success9 (deaths from tuberculosis had fallen to 431 by 1961 from 3,103 in 1948) but deserted him in 1951 when the Church hierarchy objected to a health act which would have provided sex instruction from state medical staffs and would have thus taken what the hierarchy regarded as *moral* instructions out of the hands of the Church. The hierarchy also objected to free care for anyone, regardless of income. The government fell in the ensuing uproar.

The Clann also introduced the novel idea of seating Northerners in parliament, but as far as ending partition was concerned, this was a flop. In Dublin the seating of the two Northerners in the senate was taken as a sign of crossborder unity but in Belfast the move was regarded with deep suspicion. One of the men was Denis Ireland, who in the Unionist view had shown a renegade's colours by the foundation of the Irish Union movement. The other, Liam Kelly, was known to advocate the use of physical force and did in fact lead armed attacks against the North.

In the South, however, for the moment all was excitement and optimism. Clann na Poblachta which got 173,166 votes won ten seats in the elections of February 4, 1948, and Sean MacBride and Dr Noel Browne, become ministers of external affairs and of health respectively on February 18 when the new Dail met.

The new prime minister was John A. Costello of Fine Gael. He led a heterogeneous coalition which ousted Fianna Fail, 75 votes to 68. The left-wing Clann na Poblachta formed a government with Labour, which was split into two factions: National Labour; and the right-wing Fine Gael. Costello said that 'the principal objective' on which these parties were agreed was the ending of partition.

In September, during a visit to Canada, Costello announced that the government intended to repeal the External Relations Act. The statement aroused considerable surprise in Ireland. MacBride and William Norton of Labour were on record as favouring such a course, but Fine Gael during the election campaign had reaffirmed its traditional support of the Commonwealth and had subsequently said nothing to indicate a change of heart. But despite much controversy and debate the Dail unanimously agreed to pass the Republic of Ireland Act which received the president's signature on December 21. The date when the bill would go into force was held over until the following year.

Then on January 20, 1949, the Northern premier, Sir Basil Brooke, announced that a general election would be held on February 10. On January 25, Costello invited the leaders of all political parties to confer on how their 'assistance can be given to the Anti-Partition candidates contesting seats at the General Election in The six N.E. Counties'. Two days later at an all-party meeting in the Mansion House, Dublin, it was decided that a public subscription should be opened to set up an anti-partition fund. This Mansion House committee and its offspring the Anti-Partition League provided a torrent of propaganda about partition and published a tide of pamphlets describing discrimination and gerrymandering.

The Mansion House committee collected more than fifty thousand pounds. Part was devoted to supporting anti-partition candidates in the North in the general election and the rest to purposes such as sending anti-partition speakers like Tom Barry and Denis Ireland on tour of America and Britain to inveigh against the border. (De Valera, too, went on a world tour to highlight the partition issue.) The all-party conference also chose the date of the Northern Ireland general election, February 10, to announce April 18—Easter Monday—as the date on which the Republic of Ireland Act would come into force.

All this of course played straight into the Unionists' hands. For years they had manipulated sectarian fears so that the average working-class Northern Protestant was conditioned to believe that if the border went, loyal Protestants would be trampled underfoot by hordes of I.R.A. gunmen egged on by Catholic clergy. For one instance there is an alleged version of the Sinn Fein oath which circulates through the Orange Lodges. It was published in the April, 1967 issue of the *Protestant Telegraph*, the organ of the Rev. Ian Paisley. The oath is supposed to read in part:

These Protestant robbers and brutes, these unbelievers of our faith, will be driven like the swine they are into the sea by fire, the knife or by poison cup until we of the Catholic Faith and avowed supporters of all Sinn Fein action and principles, clear these heretics from our land . . .

At any cost we must work and seek, using any method of deception to gain our ends towards the destruction of all Protestants and the advancement of the priesthood and the Catholic Faith until the Pope is complete ruler of the whole world . . .

We must strike at every opportunity, using all methods of causing ill-feeling within the Protestant ranks and in their business. The employment of any means will be held by our earthly Fathers, the priests, and thrice blessed by His Holiness the Pope.

So shall we of the Roman Catholic Church and Faith destroy with smiles of thanksgiving to our Holy Father the Pope all who shall not join us and accept our beliefs.

The Northern electorate rallied to the polls for the Unionists in such numbers as to blot out the Northern Ireland Labour party, even to the exclusion of the outstanding figure of Jack Beatty who had represented Mount Pottinger for twenty-four years, and to return the Unionists with the same majority as they held in 1921: 40 seats to 12.

In the South, however, the coalition government pressed ahead towards the Republic, which was born to the accompaniment of a twenty-one gun salute on Easter Monday. Fianna Fail boycotted the christening because de Valera said that the party stood for a thirty-two, not a twenty-six county Republic. The ceremony at the G.P.O. building was emotional and impressive, recalling memories of 1916. I was a child of twelve at the time and as I stood with my mother on the reviewing platform (my father, the general secretary of Fine Gael, had died shortly before), the flags, the *feu de joie*, the marching soldiers, all raised within me emotions which, had I been older, could well have drawn me towards the I.R.A. and its stand against the border.

Constitutionally as well as electorally the Unionists gained from the anti-partition campaign. In response to their alarm at the declaration of the Republic, British Prime Minister Clement Attlee introduced the Ireland Act in the House of Commons on May 3. This contained the following provision:

'It is hereby declared that Northern Ireland remains part of Her Majesty's Dominions of the United Kingdom and it is hereby affirmed that in no event will Northern Ireland or any part thereof cease to be part of Her Majesty's Dominions and the United Kingdom without the consent of the Parliament of Northern Ireland.'

The new Republic was outraged at this reaction to its birth. In the Dail on May 9 all parties agreed to Costello's resolution proclaiming 'indignant protest against the introduction by the British Parliament of legislation purporting to endorse and continue the existing Partition of Ireland', and calling on the British government to 'end the present occupation of our six North Eastern Counties'. Costello in his speech added, 'We can hit the British in their pride, pocket and prestige and every effort we can make we will make if they present us with that horrible alternative.'

The country responded with mass meetings, county council resolutions, thunder from the letters to the editor and editorials in all the leading newspapers. Slogans on walls all over the country announced that the 'Border Must Go'. But the Ireland Act became law the following June and for the I.R.A., trying to pick itself up off the ground after the war years, nothing could have been more welcome than all this concentration on partition.

These were the constitutional events that aided the rebirth of violence and death, a cycle that had for so long characterised Irish Protestant and Catholic failure to stop hating each other.

In the unconstitutional I.R.A., the principal figure in the reorganisation which took place when the detainees were released from the Curragh was the priest-like Anthony Magan, a bachelor and County Meath farmer who had given all his money, time and thought to the I.R.A., a deeply religious man of the old-guard school of Irish Catholicism. In the Curragh he and Michael Conway had been the main leaders of the pro-Irish and pro-Gaelic culture group In the camp. Conway actually went into the Church and several people I interviewed told me that they felt that Magan belonged there too: when he was again interned in the Curragh during the 1956–62 campaign he organised a flourishing branch of the Legion of Mary. He was taken into the I.R.A. by Jim Killeen but after Killeen helped to form Clann na Poblachta Magan ignored him. For a man who contributed most of his waking hours and all of his family inheritance to the Republican movement such deviation was treachery. He was continually in pain from rheumatism during the 1950s but he never allowed this to interfere with his lengthy drives, all-night meetings or day and night organisational activity. A stern, unbending figure whose intransigence drove many people out of the army, he nevertheless had a compassion for his men, especially noticeable after raids when his first question was never, 'How did it go?' but, 'Is everyone all right?'

When Magan, Conway, and to a lesser extent Sean McCool, began to reorganise the I.R.A. the situation was vague and confused, almost like that after the end of the Civil War. Organisation was practically non-existent and both the ex-internees and their sympathisers who had escaped the net were deeply divided. But Magan and Conway persevered. The first general meeting of Republicans came at Bodenstown in June, 1945. There, in the inner assembly field, Magan, Conway and McCool suggested a reorganisation. After Bodenstown the idea spread, very slowly, until an apparent reversal actually enhanced its chances and the post-war strength of the I.R.A. increased.

This was the Ardee Street raid on March 9, 1946, in which a number of prominent Republicans were arrested, including Peadar O'Flaherty, Patrick Fleming, Cathal Goulding and John Joe McGirl. Magan and Conway were also picked up the following morning. What changed this apparent set-back into a springboard for further activity was that a document found at Fleming's home was read out in court and reprinted by the *Irish Press*. Republicans throughout the country were thus informed that an I.R.A. reorganisation was taking place. The document container the following:

'That this meeting composed of representatives of the Cork and Dublin, Leitrim and Mayo units and of the surviving members of the 1938 Army Council resolves that the surviving members of the 1938–9 executive be summoned to a meeting for the purpose of bringing the executive up to full strength and electing an executive drawn from active volunteers.'

It was not realised at the time that publication would have an inspirational effect and Magan and Conway were convinced that disaster had befallen. They had arrived for the meeting in the Ardee Bar and found Special Branch men watching the premises as prominent Republicans walked past them, unknowingly, towards certain jail sentences. Their agitation was so great that they never thought of telephoning to warn those inside. Walking around the block, hoping to warn off late arrivals, they exchanged coats, but this ruse was noticed by the watching police who, however, allowed them to go free until the next morning. They were then both picked up at their digs, having spent a sleepless night trying to warn I.R.A. men who might have known of the meeting to prepare for visits from the police. They were given four months each and the eight other young men picked up in the raid received nine to twelve months each.

The I.R.A. also gained useful publicity that year from the death of McCaughey which occurred in the same month that the Stormont released a prominent I.R.A. man, David Fleming, because of ill-health, and from the trial of Harry White. I.R.A. drilling began again and, particularly in the North, 'the Army' began to infiltrate Irish language classes, debating classes, G.A.A. clubs and kindred bodies. The Sinn Fein party was reactivated and a newspaper, the *United Irishman*, was started in July, 1947. The state was set for a new outbreak of violence.

12

Prelude to the Border Campaign

Reflecting on the disasters of the war years Magan originated a new policy, stating publicly that it was to be used solely against the Northern administration. This policy was proclaimed at Bodenstown in 1949 by Christoir O'Neill when he said:

'The aim of the Army is simply to drive the invader from the soil of Ireland and to restore the sovereign independent Republic proclaimed in 1916. To that end, the policy is to prosecute a successful military campaign against the British forces of occupation in the Six Counties.'

This aim was unpopular with many of the rank and file, who wanted 'the Army' to turn what they conceived to be its limitless legions against the Special Branch, members of the government, and, above all, against Stephen Hayes. The subject of his elimination was discussed continuously until during a particularly stormy meeting Magan suddenly produced a revolver, handed it to one fire-eater and said, 'Here, you execute him yourself.' The subject was never mentioned again. However, splinter group activities, or some undisciplined I.R.A. man's firing of shots at a neighbour's house or letting off of gelignite bombs became magnified into nation-wide rumours of coups or assassination plots and the I.R.A. had, from time to time, to repeat its avowal concerning the use of force solely against the North lest the Southern government be prompted to take action.

The Army Council statement of Easter 1950 said that 'in order that no excuse may be provided for using coercion and to define quite clearly that the Irish Republican Army had only one enemy, England, no sanction will be given for any type of aggressive military action in the Twenty-Six County area'. The statement for the following Easter said 'all types of aggression in the Twenty-Six County area are ruled out'. But it was not until after the Omagh raid of October, 1954 that the Army Council formally told the various units that this was now official policy and incorporated it into the 'General Army Orders'. From that month, Standing Order Number Eight read as follows:

1. Volunteers are strictly forbidden to take any militant action against 26-Co. Forces *under any circumstances whatsoever*. The importance of this Order in present circumstances especially in the Border areas cannot be over-emphasised.
2. Minimum arms drill shall be used in training in the Twenty-Six County areas. In the event of a raid every effort shall be made to get the arms away safely. If this fails, the arms shall be rendered useless and abandoned.
3. Maximum security precautions must be taken when meaning. Scouts must always be posted to warn of emergency. Volunteers arrested during training or in possession of arms will point out that the arms were for use against the British Forces of Occupation only. This statement should be repeated at all subsequent Court proceedings.

4. *At all times* Volunteers must make it clear that the policy of the Army is to drive the British Forces of Occupation out of Ireland.

Despite an occasional lapse, such as that which caused the death of Garda Clerkin (see later), this policy still holds as of today.

I.R.A. influence over Sinn Fein grew between 1946 and 1949. Speaking at Bodenstown in 1949 Cristoir O'Neill, at the time vice-president of Sinn Fein, said:

'The Republican movement is divided into two main bodies—the Military and the Civil Arms, the Irish Republican Army and Sinn Fein. Each has an important task to do. In the final analysis the work of either is as important as that of the other.'

The drawbacks of a 'physical force' policy with the I.R.A.'s resources were very much apparent to the survivors of the violent era of the 1940s who now emerged as the principal Republican leaders—the 'three Macs', as they were popularly known, Anthony Magan, Thomas MacCurtain and Padraig MacLogan. For a period of almost ten years after the end of the second World War they discouraged an armed campaign against the North, and the decade gives evidence of political rather than military activity.

MacLogan, O.C. of South Armagh during the Anglo-Irish war, was the chief political thinker of Sinn Fein. He operated a public house in Portlaoise and his name became familiar during the agitation to release the prisoners in Portlaoise jail at the end of the Second World War. Like Magan, he was a man of deep religious conviction. Time-keeping in his pub was meticulous. No drunkenness or profanity was allowed. He met his wife on a pilgrimage to Lourdes and I think it symbolises his combination of religious and conspiratorial outlook that he should have kept his secret I.R.A.. papers hidden in an altar that he made himself. He also headed the co-ordinating committee between Sinn Fein and the I.R.A., and one can see how the degree of control which the I.R.A. exercised over the party had extended from the results of the Sinn Fein Ard Fheis of October 7, 1951.

Mrs Margaret Buckley, president of Sinn Fein throughout the war, was demoted to merely a member of the Ard Comhairle (the controlling body) which now included Anthony Magan. MacLogan became president and the vice-presidents were Michael Traynor and Tom Doyle, who had initiated the Magazine Fort raid. Charlie Murphy, who was shortly to become adjutant-general of the I.R.A., became joint secretary with Sean Kearney, who later left to become a priest. Patrick Doyle, who had been sentenced to life imprisonment in Belfast during the war, was also elected to the Ard Comhairle. (There were some differences in policy among them. Traynor, for instance, was not happy that the I.R.A.'s *de jure* position in the eyes of the movement should give the I.R.A. control over democratically elected Sinn Fein representatives and he felt very strongly that the I.R.A. should not control Sinn Fein.)

Traynor and the 'three Macs' shared, however, the view that Ireland's fortunes would improve if the link with England were broken. They all wanted an end to partition.

They also favoured the social teachings of the papal encyclical *Rerum Novarum*— generally in Ireland in the early 1950s opinion favoured vocationalism—and they opposed the welfare state, which (though they failed to grasp the fact) was steadily driving a wedge between North and South as the standard of living in the North rose because of the British ties they were trying to persuade Northern Catholic to break. The entire Ard Comhairle felt that the welfare state destroyed the concept of the individual, who to them was not a tool to be brought out on election day but a being who should have a continuing influence on his own economic set-up.

Their major political activity then was to draft a Sinn Fein programme to embody these beliefs within a movement that had traditionally rallied mass support not for social and economic policies but for the use of force, and which also held to two basic concept of Republicanism: Wolfe Tone's 'Breaking the link with England', and Terence MacSwiney's, 'When Ireland was wholly free Ireland was wholly Gaelic. When Ireland was wholly Gaelic, Ireland was wholly free.'

MacLogan, helped by Traynor and another prominent ex-internee, Frank MacGlynn, drew up a new constitution for Sinn Fein along with two other important plans: the 'National Unity and Independence Programme of Sinn Fein', and the 'Social and Economic Programme of Sinn Fein'. All were vetted by sympathetic clergy to ensure that they contained nothing contrary to Catholic teaching. The principles of the new constitution have a familiar look:

'That the allegiance of Irishmen and Irishwomen is due to the sovereign Irish Republic proclaimed in 1916.

'That the sovereignty and unity of the Republic are inalienable and non-judicable . . .'

Its objectives were:

The complete overthrow of English rule in Ireland.

To bring the Proclamation of the Republic, Easter 1916, into effective operation and to maintain and consolidate the Government of the Republic, representative of the people of all Ireland, based on that Proclamation.

To establish in the Republic a reign of social justice, based on Christian principles, by a just distribution and effective control of the Nation's wealth and resources, and to institute a system of government suited to the particular needs of the people.

To promote the restoration of the Irish Language and Irish Culture and the widest knowledge of Ireland's history; to make Irish citizens conscious and proud of their traditional and cultural heritage; and to educate the citizens of the Republic in their rights and responsibilities.

Other traditional I.R.A. policies which were retained included the non-recognition of the courts and Dail Eireann. No barrier, however, was placed on membership of local government bodies which levied a large proportion of the taxes without which parliament could not have functioned.

As the Republican movement gathered strength after the war the 'three Macs' planned, not border raids and the blowing up of bridges, but a policy of passive resistance. Michael Traynor told me that a scheme for withholding rates was worked out: the I.R.A. would protect the nationalist sympathisers who supported the idea. But the controversial question of the use of force caused a rupture within the movement as early as 1949 with the founding of the *United Irishman*. (Its first editor was Seamus G. O'Reilly, who worked from an office at 38, King St, Dublin, and produced the first issue in July, 1948.)

The paper was Republican in tone, but not controlled by the I.R.A., owing its origins to sixty pounds collected by members, principally Seamus Doyle and Tom Byrne, of a Republican club named after McCaughey. It was supported strongly by prominent Republicans no longer active in the I.R.A. But during 1948 the I.R.A. became interested in it and MacLogan demanded representation on the editorial board. A row developed over the suggestion that the paper advocate the I.R.A.'s blowing up customs huts along the border, to capitalise on anti-British feelings generated by recent political speeches. The row ended with Doyle, Byrne and Kelly severed from their connections with the paper.

Subsequent issues openly urged readers to 'Join the I.R.A.'. The paper was against the 'Free State' (the change to a Republic altered neither the I.R.A.'s attitude nor terminology), anti-Free Mason, anti-Communist, anti-British, and opposed to Irish newspapers carrying advertisements for jobs in England. The difference between the opposing parties was succinctly put in a letter of resignation from the paper which Michael Traynor wrote on January 4, 1949:

'The difference between us is tactical, we are fully agreed on basic principles. Yet, I have stated time after time, on the committee and before the committee was formed, that I would not be a party to organising the youth of Ireland to use force for the mere sake of using force.'

The difference between the activists and those who favoured passive resistance was more than 'tactical'. It was also the difference between one generation and another, between the men who had seen what 'action' could lead to and those who sought excitement without thinking of its consequences. As the movement gathered strength the activists gradually gained in influence and their urgings finally resulted in the campaign which began on December 12, 1956. But prior to this the exponents of force had incited the I.R.A. to carry out six raids, of which four were unsuccessful, and to plan a number of other operations, none of which came off. In this period the movement also suffered three splits: those caused by Brendan O'Boyle, Liam Kelly and Joseph Christle.

Within the I.R.A. proper the leading young activists were Charlie Murphy, Robert Russell, Eamonn Boyce, Tom Mitchell, Rory Brady and Joe Christle.

Charlie Murphy, a young Dubliner, was at the time a tall, striking-looking figure with prematurely grey hair. A clerk in the Guinness brewery, he had joined the I.R.A. in 1950, at nineteen, after anti-partition slogans such as 'Let's Finish the Job' had put a match to the powder trail laid by a nationalist family and his boyhood reading about the War of Independence. He answered an advertisement seeking help for Republican prisoners and met Tom Doyle of Sinn Fein. From the start he showed an unusual aptitude for intelligence work, one of his exploits being to obtain a camera in the shape of a fountain pen with which he photographed the entire Special Branch and compiled a card index system giving their names, addresses and numbers of their automobiles.

Robert Russell joined the movement because of family influences; he was a nephew of Sean Russell. (He later married May Smith who became chairman of Sinn Fein.)

Eamonn Boyce, who led the Omagh raid and was sentenced to ten years, later married and became a bus inspector. In 1953 he had not been aware of the I.R.A.'s existence until one day he passed a large hoarding advertising an English Sunday newspaper series about the I.R.A. and showing a trench coated figure carrying two guns. By chance, his companion at the time was Matty O'Neill, a former Curragh internee. He remarked on the garishness of the poster thinking that this portrayal had something to do with the War of Independence. He was surprised when Matty replied, 'Sure, them that's running it now don't mind.' Amazed that the I.R.A. was still in existence, Boyce made further enquiries which led to his becoming a member when he was twenty-two.

Tom Mitchell, who was also sentenced to ten years for the Omagh raid, became leader of the prisoners at the Crumlin Road jail in Belfast. Elected to Westminster as M.P. for mid-Ulster he was unseated as a convicted felon in 1955 and now works as an official with Dublin Corporation—appropriately enough inspecting dangerous buildings! A formative influence on him was a lay teacher at St Joseph's Christian Brothers school at Marino, North Co., Dublin. The teacher, later interned, was nationalistic in his interpretation of history and equated Republicanism with religion. Mitchell began to read about the wartime shootings and executions, attended Sinn Fein meetings in Abbey Street, enrolled in Sinn Fein and gravitated to the I.R.A.

Rory Brady is from Roscommon. His parents were dedicated Republicans and he himself took part in some of the most memorable events of the 1950s, including the Arborfield raid and an escape from the Curragh internment camp. He became chief of staff for a brief period in the later stages of the border campaign. (He was a vocational school teacher until 1969.)

These young men went on holidays together, chiefly to the Irish-speaking district in the west, the Gaelteacht, and, apart from their Republicanism, shared a common interest in the Irish language and culture. At the time none of them thought more deeply about the border issue than that the British should be driven out of the North and did not appreciate the part religion played in partition. The social or economic conditions which would follow if they succeeded in their objective did not trouble them greatly. They had only an undefined feeling that the new state ought to be somehow Gaelic.

In the 1940s and early 1950s the number of men coming and going seemed quite large but in fact the movement was neither strong nor widely spread. In Cork there was, of course, Thomas MacCurtain, and older Republicans such as Michael MacCarthy and Gerry MacCarthy (no relation), J. F. Reegan, who had fought with Frank Ryan in Spain, and a number of younger men of Murphy's and Mitchell's generation. In Limerick there was Willie Gleeson. In Portlaoise, MacLogan's base, there were some reliable men, in particular Terry O'Toole. In Lurgan there was Joe O'Hagan. In Leitrim, a county with a long tradition of rebellion, John Joe McGirl. In Drogheda Larry Grogan, who had signed the proclamation declaring the start of the bombing campaign against England. In Dundalk there was Liam Fagan. In Derry, Eamonn Timmoney and Seamus Ramsaigh were unusually good men.

In Belfast the movement was numerically strong— Charlie Murphy told me that he remembered inspecting parades, as adjutant-general, at which there must have been hundreds present. But the fire and passion which once animated the Republicans were missing. So was most of their motivation. There had been no sectarian rioting since 1935 and the comradeship of the years had taken some of the sting out of Protestant-Catholic relationship. Nevertheless, the I.R.A. group in Belfast was, willy-nilly, formed on a sectarian basis. No Protestants now attached themselves to the cause and the movement was almost entirely an armed Catholic one, although not representative of all Catholics. The welfare state having been introduced to the North many former Nationalists were secretly disposed to support the British link. Moreover security was weak. Incidents took place which made the Dublin I.R.A. think that the R.U.C had sources of information in Belfast which would prejudice any attempted rising there. Bearing these in mind and also the possibility of inciting reprisals against the Catholics, whom they would not be strong enough to protect, the I.R.A. Leaders decided to take no action in Belfast when the border campaign began.

The pendulum had swung from the time of the Hayes affair when Northerners went south to direct the I.R.A.—now it was to be Southerners who largely controlled the movement and directed its energies northward.

The major raids initiated before the outbreak of the border campaign were:
June 5, 1951, Ebrington Barracks, Derry.
July 25,1953 Felstead School Officers' Training Corps, Essex.
June 12, 1954, Gough Barracks, Armagh.
October 7, 1954, Omagh Military Barracks.
April 24, 1955, Eglington Naval Air Base, Derry.
August 13, 1955, Arborfield Depot, Berkshire.

Neither the Ebrington raid nor that on Felstead attracted much attention but they did alert the R.U.C. to the need for strengthening the Northern defence.

Before the Ebrington raid the Derry unit, like every other section of the I.R.A., had been subject to a high turnover of membership. The unit had been approximately one hundred and fifty strong in the years 1938–39 but wartime imprisonments cut down this strength and the unit was almost non-existent during 1943–45. However, following the release of internees in August, 1945, some reorganisation began, and by 1947 the unit was functioning again, at least to the extent of drilling. But this fact was so well concealed that no one was aware of the unit's existence until the I.R.A. issued a statement from Dublin saying that an arms haul had been made.

Even then a number of people in the North believed that the raid was a figment of some B-Special's imagination. Hugh McAteer's brother Eddie, the Nationalist leader, issued a statement to this effect but the raid was genuine. The I.R.A. seized twenty Lee Enfield rifles, twenty Sten machine-carbines, two Bren light machine-guns, six BESA 7.92 mm. belt-fed machine-guns and a quantity of .303 and .9 mm. ammunition.

After this raid the I.R.A. drills attracted more members and a spate of incidents occurred. R.U.C. intelligence improved and the R.U.C. began to build up defences against any large-scale campaign. R.U.C. commando units were formed, manned by personel who had seen active service during the Second World War; wireless communications were improved, and security and fortifications at all military installations were considerably tightened.

The raid on the armoury of the Felstead School Officers' Training Corps was more ambitious and was initially successful. The raiders got away with ninety-nine rifles, eight Bren guns, ten Sten guns, a Piat anti-tank gun, a 2-inch mortar and a Browning machine-gun. But the next morning, at Bishop's Stortford, the police, noticing a suspicious van with its rear windows obscured by strips of paper and smeared with whitening material, stopped it and found the weapons inside. Three men were arrested: Cathal Goulding, Sean Stephenson and Manus Canning. The next October they were sentenced to eight years after a jury in Hertfordshire had taken one minute to find a verdict of guilty.

After sentence Goulding, who accepted responsibility as leader of the raid, said, 'We believe that the only way to drive the British Army from our Country is by force of arms, for that purpose we think it no crime to capture arms from our enemies. We make no apology for our action.' However, this declaration by Goulding, a Dublin housepainter whose father had been active in the War of Independence, aroused little echo in Ireland as the raid had been a small one and had occurred in England. It was the Gough raid, in Armagh, which caught the Irish attention. It brought, furthermore, many young men into the movement as well as arousing considerable support in America.

Six months or so before the raid Leo McCormick, training officer for Dublin, noted on a visit to Armagh that the sentry outside the barracks had no magazine in his Sten gun. He felt that some use could be made of this discovery, but his plans were interrupted when he was picked up by the R.U.C. for having incriminating documents on him and sent to jail. Charlie Murphy and Eamonn Boyce then decided that the thing to do was to plant someone in the barracks.

They called on another young Dubliner (nameless as he is still in the I.R.A.) and told him they wanted him to join the British army. He agreed immediately and was posted to Armagh. To keep contact with him, Murphy, Boyce and various girls used to travel to Armagh on Saturday nights to attend the soldiers' dances. They would leave the hall, ostensibly to court the girls but really to contact their plant and reconnoitre the barracks. In this way they learned enough to plan a raid for June 12, 1954.

The operation was launched from a farm outside Dundalk about a mile south of the border. There they struck a snag when the expected lorry didn't turn up. They therefore sent word to a local haulier telling him that there was a load of cattle to be shifted, and when he arrived they hustled him into a tent and took his lorry. They also had a car, the occupants of which were to take over the guard-room. There were nineteen raiders, armed with Thompsons, short-arms, grenades and burglary implements. Everything worked perfectly. It was nearly three o'clock on a busy Saturday afternoon when the car drove through the barracks' gate. The gang held up the guardroom, hurried the sentry away from the gate and in his place put a man who, because of his training in Ireland's equivalent of the Territorial Army, was able to march up and down in front of the gate in con-vincing fashion. (The lorry coming behind the car overshot the gate and had to reverse and a British army lorry, also making for the gate, courteously pulled up to allow the I.R.A. in first and drove by without noticing anything amiss.)

Murphy raced up the stairs to the armoury ahead of the others. He had trouble getting his revolver out of his pocket and was further embarrassed when the two soldiers in the armoury refused to put up their hands. However another I.R.A. man arrived carrying a Thompson gun which overawed the pair. Positioning a Bren gun at the armoury window to command the barracks' square they started loading. As each I.R.A. man came into the armoury he held out his arms and

Murphy stacked him up with as many guns as he could carry. They got away with three hundred and forty rifles, fifty Sten guns, twelve Bren guns (most of which were non-operational), and a number of .22 mm. arms.

During the course of the raid a woman, noticing that something was wrong, had stopped an officer in the street and urged him to go into the barracks and do something. Once inside the gate the officer was taken under control and, protesting that he was an officer and a gentleman, refused to be tied until a gun was put to his head. An N.C.O. then noticed what was happening, got into a lorry and drove for the gate, intending to block the exit. But one of the raiders stood in the gate and brandishing a revolver said, 'Back', and forced the N.C.O. to back the lorry across the barracks' square. Then he too was placed under guard in the guardroom.

The lorry containing the arms was driven away first, Boyce and the group in the car following after locking every gate and door for which they could find keys. (The keys were subsequently auctioned in America to raise funds for the I.R.A.) Luck attended the men in the lorry all the way back across the border. At the Monaghan side of the border an obliging R.U.C. man gave them the right of way and they drove the remaining seven miles without incident. Boyce met them and handed over the small arms that he and the others had carted. Everyone got into the lorry and they drove on to a dump in Co. Meath where they met Magan. His first question was, 'Is everyone all right?'

The men were dismissed, some to find their way back to Dublin by bus, others, including Joe Christle and Eamonn Boyce to return to Dublin in the lorry. Boyce sat in the body of the lorry but Christle got into the driver's cabin and, instead of following the pre-arranged route, he ordered the driver to go by the main road. On the outskirts of Dublin, a squad car, alerted to the fact that the raid had taken place, attempted to bloke their path. Christle ordered the driver to ram the squad car, which pulled out of the way. Later, when the lorry was being returned to its owner, two men in it were captured and interrogated. They were subsequently released as the Southern government was embarrassed by the whole affair and wished to make as little of it as possible. It was given out that nothing incriminating was found in the truck, although in fact two revolvers were seized.

The raid was a tremendous source of morale for the I.R.A. but fears were aroused by an article in the *Irish Times* speculating that the arms were intended for use in the South. To prevent this idea gaining currency the speaker at Bodenstown the following Sunday, Gearoid O'Broin, repeated once again that I.R.A. policy was directed solely against British forces in the North and said categorically that the guns would not be used against the Southern government or police force.

The raids which the I.R.A. attempted between this time and 1956 were failures, yet the Omagh raid in October, 1954, and its aftermath, brought both recruits and money to the I.R.A.

The raid (which resulted in eight young men going to prison) was made in an attempt to seize ammunition and arms. The I.R.A. had not managed to obtain much information about the layout of the barracks until the same British army agent who had helped in the Armagh raid managed to spend a night in the barracks. With his briefing in hand the raid was fixed for the night of October 16. A week before this date Magan arrived at a house in Dublin with some twenty machine-guns and gave them to Murphy and Eamonn Boyce, who was to lead the raid. Murphy, it had been decided, was too valuable a man in Dublin to risk.

Boyce had thirty-five men in his party, three armed with knives to silence the sentry who patrolled the back wall of the barracks (a duty very few were eager to undertake). Gearoid O'Broin was in charge of transport, which was to consist of two cars and a lorry, and he took equipment with which to start the British army lorries which the raiders hoped to commandeer.

Omagh Barracks, Co. Tyrone, backs on to marshes, its main gate opening on to a narrow street leading to the town. Three sentries patrolled the barracks: two watched the wall facing the town and those at right angles to it, and the third guarded the approximate one hundred yards of the back wall. The raid had been planned for the changing of these sentries but O'Broin had trouble getting a lorry. Eventually he stole one but this had caused a three-hour delay. Boyce and fifteen men then scaled the wall at about 3.30 in the morning, the remaining twenty men staying outside the wall.

The men with the knives headed for an archway in which the sentry was expected to take shelter. When he did not the raiders attacked him, using not their knives but the butts of their revolvers with which they clubbed him. The sentry, however, was an exceptionally strong man and held off the attackers. His shouts both frightened other members of the raiding gang and alerted the British soldiers in the guardroom near the main entrance. In the event of something going wrong the I.R.A. men had planned to use this gate to escape but the soldiers in the guardroom began shooting and made this impossible. The raiders retreated to the back wall and climbed it with no trouble. They escaped into the marshes, leaving their twenty comrades impotently standing outside the main entrance.

The invading party split up and disaster befell Boyce. He was unworried about immediate pursuit and returned towards the I.R.A. lorry, watching for stragglers on his way. When he was fifty yards from the lorry it drove off. He ran for it but could not catch it and, still unworried, tried in vain to unlock an R.U.C car parked near by. He then began to walk towards the border twenty miles away but, exhausted, hungry and wet he was picked up as he attempted to take off his boiler suit in a ditch.

It is worth briefly examining here how I.R.A. prisoners were treated at this time, not least because stories of their hardships influenced I.R.A. policy and increased its recruitment. These stories also led to an I.R.A. reprisal which cost innocent lives.

Prisoners were certainly roughed up to some degree. Boyce for instance was cuffed about and forced to strip naked and then dress again in his wet clothes six times. But the worst feature of the prisoners' treatment seems to have been the method of their transportation during the time of the taking of depositions. Under English law these had to be taken in the courthouse nearest the scene of the alleged crime. As a result, the I.R.A. prisoners were taken from their cells at 5 a.m. each day, handcuffed to each other and to detectives and taken in a van across the province to Omagh.

Prisoners with weak stomachs got sick shortly after starting, and there was no sanitation available. The trips were never less than seventy miles, sometimes more. The vans often crossed into Donegal to avoid I.R.A. ambushes against the convoy which accompanied the vans. Once in Omagh the police escort was changed but the prisoners, often after a court appearance of only a minute or two, faced another five-hour journey back to jail.

Once, however, the prisoners had been sentenced they were not harshly treated beyond, of course, having to endure normal prison routine. Here the great enemy was 'the bonk', a term coined by Philip Clarke, who, with Tom Mitchell, was elected to Westminster but was later unseated as a convicted felon. 'The bonk' described the terrible depression which would descend on even the best adjusted. One of its effects was that the prisoner became unpredictable, likely to strike out at anyone—a serious matter in such an environment. Prisoners seldom dared become too friendly with each other lest they weaken the will and self-reliance, upon which they depended to get through their sentences.

The Arborfield raid led to the imprisonment of Donal Murphy, Charlie's brother. He had joined the I.R.A. in Dublin by taking much the same route as had Charlie. Interested in history he remembers being influenced in particular by the *Wolfe Tone Annual*, 'Scelig's' pamphlets and Tom Barry's book, *Guerrilla Days in Ireland*. Then came the familiar sequence of events: attending Sinn Fein meetings, quite casually at first, merely stopping for a few minutes after the pictures; meeting prominent Republican figures; driving speakers to Sinn Fun meetings at Charlie's request, and finally, in 1953, joining the Dublin unit of the I.R.A., aged twenty-one.

The following year a man who was to play an important role in I.R.A. affairs contacted Donal's brother Charlie through the *United Irishman* offices, and set in train events which led to the I.R.A.'s most ambitious coup of the postwar period—and to Donal's being sentenced to life imprisonment. The man was Frank Skuse, who in autumn 1954 was a serving member of the British forces, stationed in Monmouth. Skuse had a magnificent presence being over sis feet tall, red-haired and well proportioned. His father was a lieutenant commander in the British navy, and a brother is in the same organisation today. Born in rebel Cork, he had sufficient Irish blood to make him eager to place such information as he possessed concerning the British military at the disposal of the I.R.A.

The Monmouth Barracks would have been easy for the I.R.A. to attack because the surrounding walls were so low, but Skuse was transferred to Arborfield in Berkshire. There he familiarised himself with its layout and obtained maps for the I.R.A., which eventually decided to attack the Royal Electrical Mechanical Engineering Depot at Arborfield.

Donal Murphy only discovered what was planned by accident but he promptly volunteered for service. After a period of training, which laid special emphasis on things such as walking on tip-toes and small-arms drill, he and a group of eleven others, led by Rory Brady, were briefed in Dublin and shown a film of Arborfield, obtained by Charlie Murphy with Skuse's aid. On August 11, 1955, the party set off for England in the mail boat from Dun Laoghaire, pretending not to recognise each other. There were several other young Irishmen on board, either emigrating to England or returning after the holidays and one of them, in the bunk beneath Murphy, showed no surprise when Murphy's .45 slid out from underneath his pillow and bounced to the floor. Donal accepted the return of his revolver with the same courtesy with which he refused an offer of guidance from a policeman who came up to him at Euston station to ask could he be of assistance. This time Donal was carrying two revolvers, a .38 and a .45!

The entire group spent the night in the same London hotel and set off at midnight, August 12, for the raid. They had two hired vans and a car and had spent the day surveying the depot. About a quarter of a mile out Rory Brady lined them up at the roadside, in their dungarees and berets, and warned them not to fire first but if fired on to drop on one knee and aim low. Approaching the barracks they saw a red flare and feared something had gone wrong, but as this was followed by a green one they decided it was merely a routine drill and pressed on. They captured the sentry at the gate, took him into the depot, and left Skuse in his place.

Inside the guardroom the commander of the guard was cooking beans and sausages. He dropped the plate when they appeared and Donal grabbed a sausage—the last one he got for a long time. They tied up the eighteen-man guard without difficulty, but there were five men in the guardhouse serving punishment sentences and they had to use bootlaces and ties to secure them. Then they discovered that the keys to the armoury were not where Skuse had said they would be. He was summoned from the gate, after they had blindfolded the guardroom sergeant to prevent his recognising Skuse, but he couldn't find them either (the armourer had taken them home) and they had to jemmy open the doors. In all they took five *tons* of guns and ammunition.

There were 82,000 rounds of ammunition in the van in which Donal was captured. He should have gone in the car, but Joseph Doyle was unsure of the route back to London and they went together. They were passing Ascot when a patrol car flagged them down on a routine check. They did not use their weapons because they feared that if the police failed to report to their radio control a general alert would ensue and trap their companions who were still in the armoury.

While Doyle and Murphy were being interrogated in Wokingham police station they heard the other van go by. But the raid had been futile. James Andrew Mary Murphy, in charge of the dump at Pentonville, had hired the vans in his own name and the police traced him easily. He was captured in his digs, lying in bed. The police had little difficulty in recovering the ammunition, although the rest of the raiders got away safely. All of them except Rory Brady were back in Ireland within four hours of the raids. Brady decided to hide out in the Channel Islands for a fortnight before returning to Dublin.

Donal Murphy's imprisonment led to some far-reaching contacts between the I.R.A. and the wider world of revolution. Murphy had settled down to serve his sentence, determined that prison should not break him, when he became friendly with the Russian spy, Gordon Lonsdale, and a number of Greek Cypriots, including the guerrilla Nikos Samson. Lonsdale and he became particular friends and the Cypriots taught him Greek in return for lessons in Irish. Later these lessons developed into contacts between the I.R.A. in Dublin and the Cypriots with a view to having EOKA recruits sent to Ireland to be trained in guerrilla warfare. The I.R.A. also planned to rescue some of the Cypriots but the plans were rendered unnecessary by the signing of the London Agreements.

Murphy regarded Lonsdale as one of the most intelligent men he ever met. He had, Murphy said, an encyclopedic knowledge of world affairs and was able to talk informatively on all aspects of Irish foreign policy at the U.N., Irish domestic policies, the Church and the economy to a degree not then usually equalled by many Irish elected representatives. The warders and the prisoners apparently looked up to him, but apart from Murphy he seems to have made no effort to be friendly with any of them. With Murphy, however, Lonsdale made a point of being friendly, perhaps reasoning that with him he could fulfil the need for companionship which even the most disciplined prisoner must feel without running the risk of being undermined by a British intelligence agent. He would politely decline offers of company from other prisoners on exercise walks, until Donal joined him, and he never attempted to indoctrinate the younger man into Communism. He confided in Donal to a remarkable degree. For instance, the I.R.A. offered to help rescue him but he rejected the offer immediately, not because he thought that the plan could not succeed (at least that is what the I.R.A. says!) but because he was confident that there was no question of his serving his twenty-five-year sentence. 'If anyone thinks there is,' he said, 'they're crazy. My people are just waiting to grab a suitable British spy and they'll exchange him for me.' He was so explicit and forthcoming on the subject that the moment Greville Wynne was arrested neither the Murphys nor anyone in touch with the plan to rescue Lonsdale had the slightest doubt that here was the requisite spy.

Donal was eventually released through the intercession of Carmel Murphy, Charlie's wife, with Cardinal Heenan, a distant relative. The cardinal interested Lord Longford in the case and the earl secured a pardon for him.

In 1956 Magan decided that Cathal Goulding, in prison for the Felstead raid, should be rescued. Plans were laid and during October Sean Cronin's wife Terry chartered an Aer Lingus DC-3 in the name of a fictitious drama group, the 'Scelligs Players' (the title was derived from the name of Cronin's birthplace, Ballinascelig). The plane was filled with Cumann na mBan women and I.R.A. men, the women very curvaceous with sub-machine-gun parts, rope ladders and revolvers stashed in their underwear. Goulding was imprisoned in Wakefield and the plane was scheduled to touch down there. However it was diverted because of bad weather to Huddersfield R.A.F. base, and the party had to charter a bus to Wakefield. The group split up and made separate ways to the prison, intending to fling a rope ladder over the wall to Goulding, who was expecting the attempt. However when the rescuers got to the prison they found that there was a police patrol car circling the walls at regular intervals, and that alarm bells were sounding from within the prison. The raid was called off and the party regrouped at the bus and drove back over the mountains to the air base, unrecognised, and took off safely for Dublin.

The incident was in a way typical of the I.R.A. attitude: concern for a captured comrade, great daring and ingenuity, and a wasteful expenditure of money, energy and potentiality of personnel. The episode took £2,000 of the I.R.A.'s funds and had the police bring down the curtain on the 'Players'—practically all of the I.R.A. leadership, with the exception of Magan, of whom Scotland Yard was known to have a description anyway, and MacCurtain, who lived in Cork would have been arrested in England *two months* before the border campaign proper was scheduled to begin.

Another earlier scheme that never came to public knowledge took a tremendous amount of planning and cost life. This was the abortive second Armagh raid, intended as a reprisal for the severity of the sentences imposed on the men captured after the Omagh raid and their treatment. The raiders also wanted ammunition and to boost moral, after the Omagh failure.

Unlike the first Armagh raid this attempt was to have caused destruction and, if necessary, taken life. There were between fifty and seventy picked men involved in the attempt, some of them experienced from the earlier raids. It was made clear to all that this was not merely a raid for arms, but an armed attack on a barracks which was to be burned down if possible. The raid was set for March 6, 1955, but when two trucks containing the raiding party, under Charlie Murphy, approached Keady village en route to Armagh they found it swarming with police.

Murphy decided to try another approach and sent a patrol ahead into Crossmaglen village. The main party retraced its route back over the border so as to reach Crossmaglen from a different direction. They arrived safely outside Crossmaglen, picked up their foot patrol and found that this village too was buzzing with police and B-Specials, and that barricades had been set across the roads. Murphy decided that to attack these forces would tarnish the I.R.A.'s reputation for attacking only British installations and personnel, a reputation which had been gained as a result of the Omagh raid, and he called the attack off. The party got back to Dublin unscathed, where it was learned through Joe O'Hagan of Lurgan, who had a contact on the force, that the R.U.C. had expected a raid that weekend. (For reasons of their own Magan and Murphy decided that the leak in security had come from Belfast and this was a contributory factor in the decision not to begin hostilities in Belfast when the main campaign started the following year.)

The morning after the abortive Armagh raid it was discovered that a boy of eighteen, Arthur Leonard, had been killed when his van was fired on by a B-Special patrol at Ready. Two other young people, a sixteen-year-old girl who was with Leonard and a man whose car was fired on by another jumpy B-Special patrol while driving in Co. Fermanagh, were wounded.

Ironically these happenings played into the hands of the I.R.A. It was widely assumed that the shootings had taken place as a result of Northern trigger happiness engendered by unnecessary mobilisations. Throughout the South, county councils denounced the Stormont regime and demanded that the B-Specials be disbanded. The force was likened to the Mau Mau, protest meetings were addressed by Sinn Fein polemicists and were widely attended by students and young people. In Belfast a visiting Labour deputy from Dublin, Sean Dunne, was expelled from the Distinguished Visitors Gallery for uttering shouts of 'murder' during a Stormont debate on the affair. Even the *Irish Times* became temporarily aggrieved at Stormont, observing huffily on March 8 that it was about time the Northern government developed a sense of proportion in its methods of law enforcement because 'paramilitary forces are an anachronism in a democratic society'.

Another destructive proposal which occupied a good deal of energy in the early part of 1955 was 'Operation Thermite', intended to inundate Eglington Naval Air

Base, Derry, by blasting an embankment retaining the waters of the river Foyle. This scheme was eventually dropped, as was another plan to hijack an arms lorry from Omagh barracks. Throughout the period, and indeed as long as the I.R.A. has existed, plans such as these were, and are, continually being made and discarded.

Hoaxes also characterised the period: one at Rhyl, north Wales, involving four junior army officers doing National Service caused a major alert throughout England. Affecting Irish accents the officers tied up a sentry at a royal artillery training camp, and threw him into a truck, making off into the night when another sentry gave the alarm.

This occurred only two days after the Arborfield raid, at a time when English public opinion was outraged by the disclosure that sentries on duty at Arborfield were armed only with pick-axe handles. As a result the minister for war had to return to London from holiday to make a report to the cabinet which also received a special report on I.R.A. activities in Britain from the home secretary, Major Gwylym Lloyd George (later Lord Tenby). No sooner was this meeting over than the two ministers and the chief of the imperial general staff, Field Marshal Sir John Harding, were summoned to a further emergency conference with Prime Minister Sir Anthony Eden. The establishment was bracing itself for a repetition of the 1939 campaign when the four hoaxers confessed to their practical joke five days after the Eden conference, and the war office issued a communique apologising to the police for the trouble caused.

On September 13 more hoaxing came to light when it was announced that a sentry who had caused a widespread alarm by falsely reporting that three men had attacked him at St George's Barracks, Gosport, Hants, was to receive psychiatric treatment. On October 26 fifteen R.A.F. stations in the north of England were placed on alert by a false rumour of impending I.R.A. attack. Similar reports of bombs in planes and cinemas required checking and caused a not inconsiderable amount of inconvenience both in England and Ireland.

The public never learned, however, of the most extraordinary 'non-action' of the whole post-war period—the true story behind the attempts on the lives of the inspector general of the R.U.C., Sir Richard Pim, and his deputy, County Inspector A. H. Kennedy.

On September 26, 1957, as Kennedy and a friend, R. D. Ferris, were driving along University Road, Belfast, a bomb fastened underneath the car exploded. It was so slight a blast that the inspector garaged the car and continued his journey, believing merely that some mechanical failure had occurred. Investigation revealed what had happened and police realised that the attempt was similar to one the previous May. Then Sir Richard Pim and his wife were almost blown up by a bomb of the same type attached to their motor launch on Strangford Lough. Further investigation showed that the bombs had not been planted by the I.R.A. but by a disgruntled member of the Northern Security Forces who was, moreover, a relation of one of the leading figures in the Larne gun-running and in the creation of the Northern state. He had been disciplined after his drinking had led to repeated acts of bad conduct which, had they been committed by anyone else, would have resulted in instant dismissal. No influence could have saved him from charges of attempted murder after the bomb incidents, but, being tipped off by a friend, he entered a mental home as a voluntarily patient.

In between the raids and abortive raids I.R.A. training and reorganisation went on. A month after the Armagh raid a big camp was established in Ballinascorney above Bohernabreena in the Dublin Mountains. Here over seventy men at a time from different parts of the country were trained for a week, each then returning home and training volunteers in their areas.

Security at this camp was ludicrous. On the normal weekend training sessions volunteers were expected to observe strict precautions to prevent their being followed: not speaking to each other in buses, approaching the camp site in ones and twos and so on. But no sooner would the Rockbrook bus have pulled away from its starting point in Dublin than someone would start singing the old I.R.A. marching song, We're off to Dublin in the Green', and before long everyone in the bus would be joining in the chorus. The buses used to pass in front of my aunt's home in Kenilworth Square, in Rathgar, and I often encountered the young singers and thought they were campers. The police knew differently.

As Tom Mitchell put it to me, 'The Special Branch were at one end of a telescope and the I.R.A. were at the other.' He remembers cycling up the Navan Road, a large suburban estate on the northern outskirts of Dublin, with a Bren gun strapped to the crossbar, dismounting under the noses of Special Branch men, who greeted him cheerfully, and then entering a field beside the main road to conduct an arms class in broad daylight.

Relations between the Special Branch and I.R.A. (or at least parts of each group) had become so relaxed since the war that no one considered it unusual for a Special Branch man to greet an I.R.A. man with a friendly 'Hello'. Both Special Branch and I.R.A. members were younger now and had no personal knowledge of the Civil War. In fact some young recruits responded so effusively to the Special Branch that a rule was instructed forbidding volunteers to talk to Special Branch men. Even so, at Ballinascorney no one objected to Special Branch men watching as Charlie Murphy and Tom Mitchell shot a colour film of the training for use in America as propaganda. Bell tents were erected and the training sessions concluded with a shoot-off, using Bren guns, Lee Enfield rifles, a few Thompsons and revolvers.

The pattern of instruction at these training camps* was unrealistic for the conditions obtaining in the North. The theory of warfare used was taken from Tom Barry's book about events thirty years past. This overlooked the fact that in Barry's day reinforcements often took up to two days to arrive at a beleaguered barracks. These young men were going into action when it needed only ten minutes to bring troops, dogs and spotter planes to the scene of an attack. On top of this, of course, was the lack of modern heavy guns and armament.

Recruits were also taught ju jitsu and knife fighting. Some fainted at the thought of knifing (particularly at one especially realistic session in a hired room in Power's Hotel, Dublin, where a medical poster was attacked with carving knives

---

* At a camp at Kildare before the Omagh raid the I.R.A.'s armaments were almost lost. A short-sighted look-out dashed up to the officer in charge in inform him that there were 'tanks, red lights, white lights everythin' comin''. As previously arranged, the officer immediately got all the weapons placed in a heap, set explosives around them and prepared to blow up the lot, when someone else reported that the 'tanks' etc. were nothing but the traffic on the main road some distance away!

and had a terminal effect on the careers of some would-be freedom fighters) but after the success of the Armagh raid there was great euphoria at classes and in camps. It was assumed that the British would run away when the I.R.A. loomed up out of the night, the faces of the raiders smeared with blacking.

13

Splits in the Ranks

While raids and training continued so did another familiar I.R.A. activity—splits in the organisation. In the decade after the war the policies of Brendan O'Boyle, Joseph Christle and Liam Kelly, all of whom diverged from the main stream of 'physical force' Republicanism, occupied almost as much of the I.R.A.'s time as did preparations for the border campaign itself.

It is of interest here to turn briefly to America and the Irish-American societies in the post-war period.

The war and close surveillance by the F.B.I. put an end to the Clann na Gael's activities in 1939–46, but in March, 1946, it was reorganised following a convention of the various branches. Despite the war there was almost thirty thousand dollars in the kitty but a split occurred among the clubs and their members over whether this money should be used to build a monument in Dublin to Sean Russell or saved against the day when a new generation of I.R.A. would arise in Ireland and require funds for another uprising. The pro-monument section, led by James Conaty and Joseph Stynes, won the day in 1949 and notified the anti-monument leaders by letter of their expulsion from the movement.

The anti-monument section led by Tadg Brosnan, Paddy Smith, Paddy Thornbury and James Brislanne, was still relatively powerful but it split in 1952, when Brendan O'Boyle went to New York looking for support for a campaign of his own. The pro-monument group healed its row with the Paddy Mahoney section, which had split over the speakeasy issue in 1930, through the good offices of the Dublin I.R.A. which sent over a man called Monaghan to act as peace maker among all the sundered wings of the Clann. He failed, however, to heal the breach between the pro- and anti-monument sections and in fact the pro-monument section subsequently suffered a split itself in 1956.

Apart from the Clann, which was and is strongest in New York, Chicago and Philadelphia, the many Irish-American groups which exist throughout the States were also likely supporters when bombs began to go off along the border. Some of these societies were little more than a joke. In 1969, I was given a circular seeking support for a group whose letter-heading proclaims that it has branches in New York, Boston, Philadelphia, Cleveland and San Francisco. Accompanying this was a handbill showing a starving, sad-eyed child behind barbed wire. The caption to the drawing reads:

'This child's father is in a concentration camp in occupied Ireland.'

Despite the claims of this circular, there were no concerntration camps in Northern Ireland at this time. By 1979 of course, Long Kesh (see chapter 20) had been opened. The H Block issue had arisen and, in the grim, self-fulfilling prophecy nature of Anglo-Irish relations, what could be pointed to as uninformed Irish-American propaganda at the start of the decade was very near the truth at the close. Then came the hunger strikes. I will leave it to readers to draw their own moral, particularly when they have read Part II of this book describing in more detail what happened over the decade.

One day in the late 1960s I was visited in my office by Roddy Connolly, a life-long Republican socialist. He was accompanied by a young Irish-American priest anxious to make contacts in the North on behalf of a civil rights movement founded in New England to help the Northern Catholics. Because he was in Connolly's company I contented myself with the quickest questioning of his background, and provided him with several introductions. Two days later Eoin MacNamee called in, fresh from Boston, where he told me that he had been told in Clann na Gael circles about a Protestant clergyman, who was seeking support for civil rights—a man of the same name as the young priest. I did not check into the Boston civil rights movement, but if I were in the I.R.A. and a similar confusion arose over a Clann emissary I can understand the tensions and uncertainty which might arise.

Along with the splits and the confusions, the generosity of the average Irish American also exists and is a very real and all-pervasive fact of Irish-American life. Charlie Murphy told me he met with several acts of personal generosity from Americans. Men donated their personal savings to the movement when the border campaign began, or collected money for the movement like the member of the Red Branch Knights' Society of San Francisco who came to Ireland personally to hand over a cheque for $3,000 raised by the Branch. At its peak American aid averaged about $3,000 a month, continuing the tradition of Irish Americans in every decade, whether they were supporting Tom Clarke and his newspaper *Irish Freedom*, or Maurice Twomey and *An Phoblacht*, or Brendan O'Boyle and his ill-fated campaign of 1952–55.

In the hot-house atmosphere of fears and splits after 1945 O'Boyle decided to form his own group. He had joined the I.R.A. while a student at Queen's University, Belfast, in 1940 been captured the following year and was one of the escapees from Derry Jail in the big break-out of March 20, 1943.

His American funds campaign owed its inception to the merest fluke. A Mrs Tom Leonard, formerly of Co. Tyrone where her family and that of her husband were active in the I.R.B. and I.R.A., was holidaying in Dublin with her daughter in 1947 when O'Boyle was pointed out to them in O'Connell Street as 'One of *them*. He's a good lad.' That was the only contact the Leonards had with O'Boyle until two years later when Mrs Leonard, attending a meeting in New York of the United Irish Counties Association, recognised him when he stood up to speak from the floor. He was on a business trip and, seeing the meeting advertised, went to it in the mistaken belief that the association might offer some prospect of revolutionary action. (It is, in fact, a highly constitutional body.) Mrs Leonard spoke to him after the meeting and invited him to her home the following Sunday. Among the guests was Harry Short, a kindly fanatic. Crippled from birth in his native Armagh, he had served with the Fianna in the War of Independence and emigrated to America afterwards. Like Joe McGarrity he devoted his life to the movement.

Short invited O'Boyle to meet some friends, including a member of the pro-monument group of the Clann. Realising that O'Boyle did not have the support of the I.R.A.—otherwise they would have been informed of his visit and he would not have been making himself known in circles like those of the United Irish Counties Association—Short and some other members of the group then took him to the home of Tadg Brosnan from Kerry, a former I.R.A. leader and, since emigrating to New York, a worker for Clann na Gael.

After a time of probing and questioning O'Boyle ventured as a general observation the fact that 'there's a good group at home, if they got support. Do you people think they could get support?' The others thought this quite possible despite problems. The Clann was split; O'Boyle was not 'official'; the Clann men were all in their late fifties or early sixties; and American law does not look kindly on the use of its territory and resources for the fomenting of revolution in other countries (unless of course such activities are confined to the hands of government agencies), so there were likely to be difficulties with the F.B.I. (Indeed it is because of these difficulties that I must omit dates and names of surviving group members who still live in the U.S. lest they find themselves behind bars in the evening of their lives.)

O'Boyle returned to Ireland and tried to get control of the younger element of the I.R.A. and become chief of staff. The group in America was to raise funds, purchase and arrange for the shipping of arms and ammunition to Ireland.

O'Boyle wrote to Short in August saying that he would require about ten thousand dollars, five hundred Thompson sub-machine guns and substantial numbers of rifles, ammunition and hand grenades. He would need these to achieve any sort of success against the Stormont government, plus the men to use them and a back-up of friendly houses, doctors, intelligence service and transport, would be required. However in the conditions obtaining in Ireland at the time both the request and its execution were doomed to end in failure and misery. The I.R.A. mistrusted O'Boyle and thought he was getting money for personal use. Murphy and Magan had him shadowed constantly and the Special Branch also watched him because they suspected him of smuggling across the border.

In America also opinion was divided as to the wisdom of helping O'Boyle. One of the most influential figures on the Irish-American scene, the chief representative of the Irish Hospitals Sweepstake's organisation, himself an executive of the Clann and a man who could smuggle elephants in and out of America if he chose, warned Short on the 'Sweep' grapevine to have nothing to do with the campaign. But Short decided to persevere. He told me that he reasoned, 'O'Boyle is a Northerner. We'll have the fight in Ulster and not in the South. We'll get away from bloody civil war in the South.'

With this in view Short contacted a group of Northern Irish emigrants who, with the addition of one Kerry man, formed the Northern Action Committee. Its members were Felix O'Byrne, Paddy Thornbury, Tom Leonard, Frank Curran, Frank Donnelly, Tommy Guy, like the others a former I.R.A. man but who had taken the Free State side in the Civil War, and Tadg Brosnan, the only non-Ulsterman. They met in August, 1949, in a hotel in Times Square (no minutes were taken for obvious reasons), and Short read O'Boyle's letter to them. The committee was then set up.

Committee organisation was simple. For secrecy the members decided that in correspondence they would always sign their mothers' names. The only hard and fast

organisational rule was that if Short thought the subject warranted it any member of
the group must be prepared to meet him without delay at any time. The committee
asked for contributions of $100 from friends and associates and had impressive receipt
forms printed from a design invented by Joe McGarrity's daughter. In all the group
sent about fifteen thousand dollars to Ireland between 1949 and 1960. (About two-
thirds of this was sent to Brendan O'Boyle and when he was killed the group transferred its support to Liam Kelly.) They tapped all the county associations for money but
the greatest support was from Kerry, Cork, Tipperary, Down, Armagh and Tyrone.

The *modus operandi* for raising funds was to show arms to representatives of
different groups and explain the purpose of both weapons and collection, but the
committee's motives were sometimes questioned. A problem also arose because
part of the Clann was supporting the 'official' I.R.A. and opposed O'Boyle's
schemes. Some prominent Irish-Americans, such as the 'Sweep' executive, also
continually used their influence to scotch support for either organisation on the
grounds that both were equally suicidal and futile. Then, too, the minimal secrecy
which the committee imposed was sometimes sufficient to cause trouble. One
holidaying Tyrone man met Liam Kelly in Ireland and, remembering his
subscription in New York, thought that the money was being sent to Kelly. Kelly
understandably made it known that he had no money and this caused controversy.
Another prominent Irish-American, John MacIvor, wrote to Charles MacGleenan
(one of the staunchest and best informed Republicans in the country) in Armagh
to ask him what he knew about an I.R.A. man called MacAllister who was
planning an uprising in the North. Not knowing that O'Boyle was using the
name MacAllister, MacGleenan replied that he had never heard of him. This kind
of incident was always sorted out, but there was enough gossip, among other
problems, to make O'Boyle's plans for a campaign very difficult to put into action.

The committee did do away with one convention which had been a continuing
source of friction between the I.R.A. and Clann na Gael. Historically the Clann and
the I.R.A. were on an equal footing so far as leadership of the joint movement was
concerned, but the committee agreed to place itself entirely under the command of
O'Boyle, and to ask nothing of him except leadership. Short secretly hoped that
O'Boyle would prove himself the strong man of an all-Ireland Republic.

Great ingenuity and daring were shown in securing arms and transporting them
to Ireland, not only under the noses of the American and Irish authorities, but also
of the hostile wing of the Clann in America and of the equally hostile I.R.A. in
Ireland who were ready at any time to commandeer arms intended for O'Boyle.
One shipment of ten revolvers and five tear-gas pencil-guns consigned to him at a
Dublin hotel was, in fact, hijacked by the I.R.A.

The story of the arms procurement activities of the committee reads at times
like a film scenario. On the Pulaski Skyway outside New York one evening a car
driven by one of O'Boyle's sympathisers developed a flat tyre, which was fixed
with the aid of a helpful policeman who duly received a five-dollar bill for his
services, unaware that in the boot of the car were two 100 lb. tins of napalm
which had just been stolen from the Brooklyn Naval Yard.

One of the most useful suppliers of arms was a gangster whom a member of
the group met accidentally. It was he who supplied the tear-gas guns and he was

making excellent progress with the supply of revolvers when he decided to expand his activities and began turning up machine guns. This ceased following a gangland murder involving the use of a machine-gun taken from Brooklyn Pier. The police circulated the serial numbers of stolen weapons and the committee discovered it had been given weapons in the missing serial range.

O'Boyle too proved himself an expert in customs' evasion. He had an almost incredible network of contacts. He once, thanks to a contact, cleared Idlewild Airport with his papers in order but carrying in his luggage several dozen revolvers and many thousand rounds of ammunition. He had the customs at Cobh, where the trans-atlantic liners from America traditionally call, particularly well organised. A shipment from New York of nine cases of ammunition was once sent to him at Cobh without him being told of the number of cases in the consignment. He only collected eight. One case was left aboard the liner and made a round-the-world cruise before the liner again docked at Cobh and a horrified O'Boyle was telephoned in Dublin by a customs official who told him that there was a case addressed to him awaiting clear-ance at the docks. His customary helper was off duty when he arrived but he man-aged to get his case through the customs without opening it to declare the contents.

But all his daring and ingenuity were not proof against the weight of gossip and intrigue that gradually crushed down O'Boyle's spirit. The dour reality of the Northern political scene caused his organisation to dwindle away. By July, 1952, he was dependent on a neighbour and his wife, who were not members of his group, to go with him on a mission to blow up Stormont telephone exchange. When the neighbour's baby fell sick O'Boyle's wife Carmel offered to take her place. They got to their destination safely and Carmel and the neighbour stepped out of the car leaving Brendan making adjustments to a mine. Suddenly there was an explosion.

The neighbour led Carmel away from the car, urging her, 'Don't look back.' She was taken to hospital and treated for shock. The neighbour made his escape and despite her terrible condition Carmel resisted all police questioning and refused to reveal the dead man's identity. The Unionists would not allow her to attend her husband's funeral but no charges were brought against her. Ultimately Cardinal d'Alton intervened privately to have her released.

The Liam Kelly split forced its way into the public consciousness on November 26, 1955, when a mine tore the side out of the Roslea R.U.C. barracks, Co. Fermanagh.

Kelly, who had led the raid, was the founder of two Republican organisations, Saor Uladh (Free Ulster), the military wing, and Fianna Uladh, its political arm, which ceased to count for very much after the year of its foundation, 1953. Kelly was a figure of some standing in east Tyrone and in Nationalist circles generally, having been imprisoned for nine months in 1953 for sedition shortly after his election to Stormont for mid-Tyrone. On his release his homecoming to the town of Pomeroy was marked by severe clashes between police and Kelly's sympathisers—afterwards referred to in the North as the Pomeroy riots.

The I.R.A. denounced the Roslea raid on the day after it occurred and issued a statement appealing to young men 'not to join sentimental or microscopic organ-isations such as those who attacked the R.U.C. Barracks at Roslea'. (The I.R.A.

also attacked it with equal lack of success on October 11, 1957.) However, Kelly refused to admit to the raid and issued a statement through Fianna Uladh on November 28 which said:

'Fianna Uladh neither admits nor denies responsibility for the raid.

'It is our policy now and always not to felon-set, to inform on political prisoners or to give any information whatsoever to the usurpers of our country that would aid the process of elimination, which in our opinion helps the English army of occupation and its satellites.'

At the time it was not generally realised that there were two militant Republican groups at work. Nor did the public or the I.R.A. know that Connie Green, who had formerly served with the British army and was a member of the Saor Uladh attacking party, had been shot in the raid. His death, or rather the irregularities surrounding the inquest into his death, caused such a storm that Saor Uladh was finally forced to issue a statement, in the Fianna Uladh journal *Gair Uladh* on December 16, accepting responsibility for the raid. The statement also showed the differences between the I.R.A. and Kelly's groups. It said:

'Saor Uladh accepts the Constitution of the Republic enacted on July 1st, 1937, and recognises that Oireachtas Eireann is the sole legitimate authority in Ireland.

'Saor Uladh is organised solely in the Six Counties. Application of the laws enacted under the Constitution is by the Constitution itself restricted to the Twenty-Six County area. It is apparent therefore that these laws are not applicable in the case of Saor Uladh.'

These points are clearly at variance with what was then I.R.A. policy, and there was also the attitude of Magan and the older members of the I.R.A. executive to be considered. Their orthodox Republicanism precluded any official liaison between the I.R.A. and Kelly, although younger members did make unofficial contact with the Kelly organisation. Charlie Murphy told me that Kelly once gave him a large quantity of ammunition for use by the I.R.A. but MacLogan later ordered it to be returned and another young I.R.A. man, Terry O'Toole, told me that when he was on the run he found the Kelly organisation both more helpful and more efficient than that of the I.R.A. network in the North.

This, of course, was because Kelly was a Northerner and despite the fact that many Northerners were acting in the I.R.A. the I.R.A.'s concept of the North was of a place 'up there'. It had to be attacked from the South, according to a plan masterminded from Dublin, which, when the attacks were over, was to be the safe resting place and recruitment area. Militarily, however, Kelly saw the Northern situation as one to be solved by Northerners. His campaign failed for the usual reasons: lack of popular support and scarcity of weapons of a sufficiently high calibre to breach the defences of R.U.C. barracks (although he tried to purchase arms in America). Like the I.R.A. he also attempted to drive out the British by attacking the Irish constabulary.

While the Fianna Uladh admission of responsibility was important in clarifying the internal situation for Republicans, it was almost completely overshadowed in the public's mind by the events of the raid itself. These show the hesitancy and confusion of governmental policy towards the Republican movement at this time.

The raid began at 5.40 a.m. when a mine went off at the end of the barracks.

The debris blocked the doorway from the guardroom which the attackers entered through the breach. As the rubble was being removed Sergeant William Robert Morrow, who was living in the barracks at the time with his wife and two little boys, leaped from bed, grabbed a Sten gun, and beat off the attack, which lasted about fifteen minutes. (He was awarded the George Medal for this.) In the shooting, a Constable Knowles was hit seven times, but recovered later and after the raid it was believed that he was the only casualty.

But rumours, which the *Sunday Independent* published on November 28, persisted that one of the attackers had been shot in the raid and buried secretly in Monaghan after an inquest had been held and a coroner had made the usual order for burial. After enquiries by journalists the Government Information Bureau in Dublin made the following announcement:

'In answer to enquiries it was ascertained through the Government Information Bureau that on Saturday afternoon the Coroner for North Eastern Monaghan was informed that the body of an unknown man who appeared to have died from gunshot wounds was lying in a farmhouse in his district. An inquest was held in the evening when it was found by the jury that the unknown man had died from shock and haemorrhage and that there was no evidence to show how the injuries had been received.'

The G.I.B. refused to make any further comment, but a leading Irish journalist, John Healy, succeeded in getting the coroner, Dr Thomas Leonard (aged 77), to talk to him. The old man revealed that prior to the G.I.B. announcement 'no information was to have been given by anyone who participated in the inquest'.

'That,' he said, 'was the position until today. Then Dublin let us dawn with this announcement . . . it was no longer a secret . . . that is why I am able to talk to you now.

Leonard said that the man had died on the morning following the attack. He had been attended by a local doctor who had sent for a priest to give the man the last rites. That afternoon the doctor and two other men called on Leonard, told him that a man had died (without telling him when or where) and asked him to hold an inquest. Leonard explained that he could not do this without informing the authorities and the men left, apparently to do just this. Leonard then got in touch with the Gardai and was visited by a superintendent who at first said he knew nothing about the affair. He later returned and told Leonard that he would be called for at 8 p.m. to carry out an inquest.

That evening Leonard was taken to a farmhouse where he found the body of a 'fine looking man' already in a coffin, and six men ready to act as jurors. Leonard swore them in. The superintendent presided and the inquest was held in his presence and that of a solicitor, a detective, the owner of the farmhouse and the doctor who had examined the man while he was dying. Uniformed guards and members of the detective force were stationed outside the house. Evidence was taken from the owner of the farmhouse and from the doctor, who said that the dead man had had a bullet wound in his left side. A verdict that death was due to shock and haemorrhage was returned.

Leonard went home and made out the death certificate which he described as a 'most unusual one. There is no name. I could not say if the man was married or single, what occupation he had. In the age column I wrote "about 30". That was all.' (The body was buried the following morning at Carrickroe cemetery, about twelve miles north of Monaghan, with the full rites of the church.)

The background to all this was that Liam Kelly sought to have Connie Green buried without an inquest but the doctor insisted that this would not be possible. Kelly telephoned a Clann na Poblachta member who was highly placed in the coalition government, to obtain the permission. However when the Clann na Poblachta contact sought to co-operation of Michael Keyes, the Minister for Justice, he was informed that an inquest would have to be held but it could be held in secrecy.

The entire episode aroused the strongest feelings both North and South and in England. John J. Horgan of Cork, at the time one of the senior coroners of Ireland, wrote to at the time one of the papers saying that a secret inquest, at which the coroner made no attempt to identify the deceased or ascertain the cause of death, and following which he denied all knowledge of the event, constituted 'a breach of both law and practice'. The *Irish Times* printed an interview with 'a prominent barrister' who was quoted as saying:

'Let us take an extreme case. Suppose I and some friends of mine decided to commit a murder. Apparently all we have to do is to take out the victim, shoot him, and bring him to the nearest coroner for an inquest and then to a graveyard for burial. We don't even need to say who he was.'

These two quotations reveal the principal worries and the criticisms of the public in the South at the time, though there were subsidiary consideration arising out of there being only six jurymen empanelled. But in the North, where tension had been steadily rising from the time of the Ebrington Barracks raid of 1951, the Roslea affair aroused much sharper reactions and criticism.

During a debate at Stormont a day after Healy's story, Lord Brookeborough said:

'It is unbelievable that any civilised country which has outlawed the I.R.A. is yet afraid to take action which any civilised country would take to prevent blackguards and scoundrels coming here to commit murder and create antagonism among the people.'

He added that if and when it became necessary to increase the size of the B-Specials, men would join and do their duty 'as their fathers had done in the past . . . We want to assure these blackguards that we won't be shoved around. Nothing is going to put us out of the United Kingdom.'

In the same debate Minister for Home Affairs George B. Hanna announced the banning of Saor Uladh and referring to the inquest said:

'The wisdom of our fathers in refusing to join with the South is evident when one considers the procedure at that inquest, which could not take place in any properly conducted community . . . I charge the Government in the South as being morally responsible for the raid.'

He gave instances of cases wherein the Stormont authorities had given information to the Southern authorities concerning illegal drilling on the Southern side of their border, 'but they took no steps to stop it'. Hanna also pointed out that the Nationalist members who had walked out of the debate claimed to represent the Roman Catholic Church. 'Had the Church no views on what had happened?' he asked. (The Church did in fact have something to say, but it was said too late to have any bearing on tho immediate controversy.)

A significant point which emerged from the Stormont debate was the fact that Lord Brookeborough had been in touch with the British prime minister with a view to getting Great Britain to seek an extradition treaty with the Republic. In London, *The Times* seized on this point in a leader headed 'Murder and the I.R.A.':

'Whatever the technicalities in bringing the offenders to book, it should be a point of honour with all three governments . . . to co-operate in overcoming them. If further agreements between the three governments are required they should at once be negotiated . . . these men are, like pirates, the common enemies of all civilised states and it behoves all Governments to combine against them.'

In Belfast the *News Letter* capitalised the feelings of Orangemen at the time, saying:

'Events since the Roslea raid make the Dublin Government look extremely foolish . . . If the Government is not pursuing a policy of hushing up the affair, and thereby shielding the men who were engaged in it, then its authority is being defied in its own territory, it is a week-kneed and incompetent Administration, and no credit even to the Irish Republic.

'It is the duty of all to give whatever assistance they can and to prove that Ulstermen in 1955 are just as capable of defending themselves, and as ready to do so, as the men who manned the Border and patrolled the gunmen's roads in 1921 and 1922.'

The following day, November 30, the Northern Ireland Minister of Finance Brian Maginess pressed home the attack on the Dublin government saying:

'Those in the North who look southwards saw a people who were afraid to speak out, and afraid to condemn murderous attacks on police and military establishments. They saw a government that was weak and vacillating. As they saw these things they could thank God that we are part of the United Kingdom.'

On the same day Southern Prime Minister Costello made a major speech in the Dail in the course of which he made three central points:

'We must assert and vindicate the people's right to determine national policy and the right of the Oireachtas and the Government to maintain and to uphold the authority that reposes in them . . .

'We are bound to ensure that unlawful activities of a military character shall cease, and we are resolved to use, if necessary, all the powers and forces at our disposal to bring such activities effectively to an end . . .

'In order to prevent any future controversy or discussion on this point . . . there can be no question of our handing over, either to the British or to the Six-County authorities, persons whom they may accuse of armed political activities in Britain or in the Six Counties.'

Both Fianna Fail and Clann na Poblachta supported Costello in his stand and on December 4 he attempted to deal with the alleged government complicity in the secrecy surrounding the Monaghan inquest. Speaking at Abbeyfeale, Co. Limerick he said:

'No order or direction to hold the inquest in secrecy or to maintain secrecy was given or suggested by the Government or any member of the Government or by any member of any Government Department, or by the Commissioner or any officer or member of the guards.' He went on to add that as soon as he had heard of the affair he had given a personal direction that 'there should be publication forthwith'.

(I would be inclined to assess Costello's statement as entirely honest in the light of the information available to him. He was after all the leader of only one party in a coalition supported by Clann na Poblachta which had made Liam Kelly a senator.)

A courageous motion by Dr Owen Sheehy Skeffington in the Senate on December 15 which welcomed the general tenor of Costello's speech, but regretted that he had not actually taken steps to halt 'this crazy militarism, however high its ideals or self-sacrificing its members', failed to attract a seconder.

Nor did church leaders get much further in their efforts to check 'crazy militarism'. At midnight Mass on Christmas Eve Cardinal d'Alton appealed to young men not to use violence in support of their aim in uniting the country, and on January 19 the standing committee of the Irish hierarchy issued a statement condemning the use of force and pointing out the dangers of civil war. The statement was also read out at Masses but it had no effect on the I.R.A.'s recruiting or planning. As Charlie Murphy put it to me, 'When the bishops called down fire and brimstone not a man stirred but when Joe Christle fecked off half the shagging I.R.A. followed him!'

Before describing the 'fecking off' of Joe Christle it is important to pick up the threads of the 'official' I.R.A.'s activities.

Following the Arborfield raid and the severe sentences on his brother and friends, Charlie Murphy began to feel personally responsible for both these and the Omagh imprisonments. A sense of guilt coupled with the exhaustion engendered by years of sleepless nights and punishing travel, almost drove him out of the I.R.A. This point came one day in November when he found Michael O'Donovan, a life-long Republican, sitting in an office of the *United Irishman*. He had just been dropped from the staff by Magan. O'Donovan, or 'Pasha' as he was generally known, was such a keen Irish-speaker that he even spoke to his dog in Irish and Murphy like everyone else in the movement had a soft spot for the old man. He tried to get Magan to reinstate him and when he failed he resigned from the headquarters staff of the I.R.A. although he remained an ordinary member of the Dublin unit. A few days later, the Roslea raid took place. Realising that it was not an I.R.A. job but fearing that it might mean a round-up of I.R.A. men Murphy set off for the hills around Dublin in a car and warned the groups drilling there to lie low. Magan then asked him to return, which he did and so began an association that led to large-scale hostilities against the North.

Sean Cronin was thirty-three when he came back from America. He had become known in Clann na Gael circles in New York, and was accepted into the I.R.A. by Magan. He had been an officer in the regular army before emigrating to America where he worked as a journalist and on his return he joined the *Evening Press* as a subeditor. (Ironically he had known of the editor, Douglas Gageby, in the army where Gageby had earned a reputation for his wartime work in intelligence, as has been mentioned earlier.) From the start Cronin made headway in both the I.R.A. and on the *Evening Press*. On the newspaper he was meticulous about time and used to appear five minutes early in the office every morning. Cronin's American accent earned him the name 'Sheriff' among his colleagues. The staff all liked him and was sorry when he resigned, ostensibly because he had a commission from a newspaper chain in America. A few days later he was picked up on the border and we realised what the commission was and how apt had been his nickname.

I had nearly stumbled on the truth some months earlier when I happened to notice him coming out of the *United Irishman* offices. We knew that he used to write for the paper, but pretending not to know this I said to him the next day in the office, 'I hear Sean that you're getting very prominent in Sinn Fein circles.' He nearly rose out of the chair with surprise, grabbed my arm and barked at me, 'What? Where did you hear that? What do you mean?'

He was so intense that I thought he was afraid that I might say something which would harm his prospects on the *Evening Press* and I relented and told him that I had seen him the previous day and was only joking. I was not aware that his relief stemmed from the fact that the I.R.A. had just agreed to a full-scale attack on the North along the lines of a plan drawn up by himself.

From the moment that he arrived back in Dublin in October, 1955 Cronin had been keen on action, but as he had to go through a recruits' course like everyone else it was not until January, 1956 that he began to be listened to in the inner councils of the I.R.A. Then Charlie Murphy invited him to join him as a co-training officer, because of his military background. (At the time, apart from an active service unit of perhaps fifty men who had taken part in raids, the vast majority of the rank and file of the I.R.A. had no experience whatsoever of soldiering.) Cronin gave Murphy a plan, 'Operation Harvest', for an attack on the North aimed at destroying communications, military installations and public property on such a scale as to paralyse the six county area. Murphy turned the plan over to Magan. It had, of course, very little practical relevance but Magan liked it, and in April, 1956 appointed Murphy and Cronin as joint operating staff. Murphy and Cronin then began repeated visits to the North to meet local I.R.A. units and to reconnoitre targets.

In July, 1956 Murphy and his colleagues arranged for the biggest single operation the I.R.A. carried out, apart from the campaign itself—a battle school in the Wicklow Mountains. The course was devised by a former British officer, a veteran of the Burmese war who had also fought on the Republican side in the Civil War. The site could only be reached by a rope wall over a stream, but he could cross it like a cat, whereas the I.R.A. lads puffed and floundered and very often had to be pushed over.

The day began at 5 a.m. and training involved the use of live ammunition and simulated attacks over ground along which charges of gelignite had been laid to be detonated by Murphy and Cronin. (A film of this exercise was shot and sent to America.) The school lasted for a fortnight and involved making a considerable amount of noise, but there was no interference from either the Special Branch or the regular army, which during lulls in the firing could be heard at their own practice ranges in the Glen of Imaal just over the mountains. The only complaint received was from traders in a nearby town who objected that the I.R.A. had not bought its supplies locally and to allay such criticism it was decided to invite the locals to a supper which was so lavish★ that one shepherd remarked as he laid into a second helping, 'Be Jasus lads if this be war let there never be peace !'

However no date was set for the start of a campaign, nor for security reasons were the rank and file informed of what was afoot. In view of the security position this was necessary but it helped to bring about the Christle split, when most of the active service unit, unaware of what was being planned by the 'Official Army of the Republic', followed Joe Christle in breaking from the I.R.A. because he stood for action against the North and the I.R.A. apparently did not.

Joe Christle had a quality that I can only describe as 'whoosh'—energy, anarchy, male supremacy and learning all canalised into a brand of patriotism that found its outlet in everything from fomenting strikes and laying up explosives to bicycle racing. Apart from organising the marathon round-Ireland Ras Tailteann he cycled twenty miles before work every day himself. His home in Rathgar, Dublin was continually in turmoil. Phones rang. People rushed in and out. Beethoven boomed from the record player. Large young men in track suits carried bicycles through the hall. (Like most things surrounding Christle there was more purpose to the activity than met the eye.) His three friendly young sons were trained to wash dishes and do housework. They were intelligent lads who instead of toy guns were given books at Christmas. One evening chatting with them while waiting for Joe, I was particularly impressed by their knowledge of Greek mythology.

In 1945, when Christle was still a schoolboy at St James's Christian Brothers School, he founded his first revolutionary circle. He was sixteen. He made efforts to contact the I.R.A. but failed and joined the F.C.A. (An Forsa Cosanta Atiuil) the Irish equivalent of the British territorial army. As membership involves taking an oath of allegiance to the state I asked Christle how he squared this with his conscience.

'Oh,' he said, 'we took the oath like Dev did. To break the oath.'

In the F.C.A. summer camps he would distribute leaflets asking his fellow F.C.A. members what were they defending, twenty-six or thirty-two counties? He found a good deal of support for his views and the authorities removed him and a number of like-minded enthusiasts in the summer of 1949. By then he had also joined the Gaelic League and was a member of its Ard Craobh (literally 'high branch') of which de Valera was chairman. That year also he founded the Gate Cycling Club, joined what was left of the N.C.A. and was taken into the I.R.A. by 'Pasha' O'Donovan. Everyone in the Gate Club was a member of the I.R.A. and on the Armagh raid six of the twenty raiders were club members.

He joined the John Mitchel Club of Sinn Fein in 1952 and became one of its principal speakers along with Myles Shevlin and Seamus Sorahan. He saw that 'action' brought a mushroom growth in recruiting and he felt that the movement was too preoccupied with form and not enough with substance. Because of this

---

★ This generosity was a cause of the I.R.A.'s running out of meat during the exercise, but despite the presence of large numbers of sheep in the vicinity, no effort was made to eat them, not through honesty but because, despite the fact that the course was held to increase expertise in human slaughter, no one liked the idea of killing a sheep!

view and as that suspicious person, a university student, he gradually found himself isolated from the older leaders of the movement, in particular Anthony Magan, Michael Traynor and Patrick MacLogan. They felt he wanted to take over the movement for himself—and certainly Joe was a leader rather than a follower.

Never a man to allow revolution to interfere with his lawful activities he sat for part of his bachelor of law examination on the morning of the Armagh raid. He had just completed a question asking, 'What are the safeguards in the Irish Constitution against armed insurrection and rebellion?' when he was called for and driven off to take part in a little 'armed insurrection and rebellion' against the Northern Ireland constitution.

He emerged from both tests with second-class honours, hearing from the university some weeks later and being censured by the I.R.A. for taking it on himself to give orders for the disposal of an arms lorry after the raid, an action which resulted in the lorry's being captured. In August he organised the first of his annual eight-day cycling events, the round-Ireland Ras Tailteann. In October he took part in the Omagh raid. In November he organised the National Students Council, embracing every student society in University College, Dublin. He was wounded during the Omagh raid and was on sick leave from his job in the state-run Electricity Supply Board, when he and Martin Campbell, who had been an important I.R.A. fund-raiser around Chicago in 1921–23, set off in December around the country in a car with the slogan 'Let Christmas Day be Prisoners Day', and was so successful that on Christmas Day he and Campbell carried literally buckets of money into the Castle Hotel in Denmark Street for the Prisoners' Dependents Fund.

Christle continued on his ebullient way during 1955 in a manner gravely upsetting to the older men. As part of their contribution towards helping the election of Mitchell and Clarke three of the Christle group decided that if they could get the support of the veteran Nationalist priest, Canon Maguire of Newtownbutler, Co. Fermanagh, they would have gone a long way towards persuading the Nationalists not to stand against either Mitchell or Clarke and so avoid splitting the vote. The three were Seamus Sorahan, a law student and at the time the best public speaker in Sinn Fein, and the brothers Willie and Joe Fogarty. They drafted a letter seeking the canon's cooperation and had it signed by hundreds of students as coming from '. . . University College, Dublin, where Philip Clarke studied and so often spoke of you as the leader of Nationalist thought in Occupied Ireland . . .'

As far as anyone knew at the time Clarke had never mentioned the formidable old canon in his life, but Sorahan and Willie Fogarty had Fáinnes (gold circles which proclaimed the wearers fluent Irish speakers and Pioneer Pins which proclaimed them teetotallers, which they are not) to their lapels and set off with letter to the canon. The emissaries and letter so appealed to the old man that he promised to help them.

The I.R.A. leadership, particularly Magan, MacLogan and MacCurtain, eventually decided that Christle would have to go. In June, 1956, Charlie Murphy was ordered to hand him his dismissal notice, ostensibly for addressing a Sinn Fein meeting without permission. This had the easily foreseeable result that those who thought like Christle also left the I.R.A. The bulk of the most active and best trained volunteers, including most of the active service unit and twelve out of fifteen of the officer corps followed him. Like Christle they were unaware that a campaign was being planned by the I.R.A. leadership. But their secession and subsequent activities were so embarrassing to the 'official' leaders that they spent as much time between then and December, 1956 trying to dissuade others from following Christle as on planning the campaign itself.

On his dismissal Christle approached Liam Kelly and those sections of Clann na Gael which would always support 'action'. Kelly, however, was not too happy and at first suspected Christle of being an I.R.A. plant, but the two groups, about seventy men in all, finally came to agreement in August, 1956 at a meeting in Dublin at which the Northerners arrived carrying arms. The first joint Christle-Kelly operation took place on Armistice Day 1956 when they burned down customs huts along a 150-mile stretch—almost the entire length of the border. The group carried out about twelve attacks, blowing up customs huts, telephone exchanges, bridges, B-Special drill halls, and demolishing the lough gates at Newry.

Kelly and Christle accompanied their groups on all the raids and on a number of ambushes which failed when the R.U.C., the B-Specials or British military did not arrive. Another plot which Christle hatched but which failed through lack of co-operation from his own supporters, including Kelly whom it horrified, was a plan to seize the town of Newry, with the help of the Catholic population, thus forcing the British to engage them and, he reasoned, forcing the Irish army to become involved also. This, Christle hoped, would lead to a situation in which the United Nations would intervene and send a peace-keeping force to replace the British in the North!

There was some evidence of sympathy for Christle's scheme in high places. Michael Fitzpatrick, chief whip of Clann na Poblachta, told me that he favoured sending the Irish army to the border on manoeuvres just to see what the Orange-men would do—engage the Southerners, he hoped. I have also been told about Dail deputies parking outside Leinster House with car boots laden with arms and ammu-nition which they were transporting for the I.R.A. On at least one occasion a ministerial car was used to transport ammunition for Thompson guns from Kerry to Dublin and Christle did have many contacts in the army. (So much so that on one occasion a serving officer, still in the army, took part in a border raid and was very nearly captured, but had the good fortune to find a farmhouse whose occupants put him in contact with a priest who spirited him safely back across the border. Whether or not Christle had intended him to be captured and so provoke a crisis within the army is still a subject of debate.)

Kelly differed from Christle on other matters also. Christle wanted to 'ostracise' British servicemen by using the EOKA tactics of bombing cafés, pubs and dance halls patronised by British soldiers. Kelly disagreed because Catholics might be killed and this he felt would be murder —an attitude towards taking life typical of the thinking concerning the use of force and the I.R.A. It is best illustrated by a story from the 1930s. A man wanted to have a farmer shot because of a dispute over land. The chosen I.R.A. man asked him if he had any sons. He had three, all in their early twenties. Could they not handle the problem for him. The man was horrified.

'My sons shoot him is it? Sure that'd be *murder*.'

Kelly and Christle disagreed again on what the outcome of a successful revolution should be. Kelly did not care who ruled Ireland so long as she were free. Christle saw himself as a socialist revolutionary wanting to create a revolutionary situation by violent methods. To the Northerners, the police were only guarding the peace. Christle argued, 'Let's break the peace so!'

Both men had to acknowledge one fact although in different ways: Kelly by suddenly departing to the States without telling Christle and Christle by laying down his gun, though not his belief in the use of force. That fact was that a campaign such as theirs could not change the position of the Northern Irish government.

In the event the Kelly-Christle partnership cost no lives nor did they lose a man on the border. When in January, 1959, a group of Christle's men were caught by the Gardai and interned he ordered them to sign out. He was arrested himself but was later released.

Readers will see for themselves how in the decade 1969–79 scruples of Kelly's sort were laid aside as irrelevant as a newer and more ruthless breed of I.R.A. man decided that there was no such thing as justifiable or murderous force—there was only effective or ineffective force, and effective force was decided on whatever the cost.

14

The Border Campaign: 1956–62

While the border was the prime source of political discontent in Ireland during 1956, it was also the principal source of revenue for anyone in the area wanting to get rich quickly. Politics and smuggling, to a certain extent, are still the main preoccupations in a belt of land reaching about forty miles into the hinterland on both sides of the border, which stretches from Derry in the North to Carlingford Lough at its southernmost extremity. Not only does the border divide North from South, it also divides the North. Donegal, which is in the Republic, is more northerly than any spot in the Six Counties and the bewildering loops and curves of the red line marking the division on the map are even more bewildering to an observer standing on a hill a couple of miles north of any of the border counties.

Politically, to the east of the Bann river 80 per cent of the population is Unionist. This is where the good land lies. Driving through the North once with a knowledgeable commentator pointing out the Protestant and Catholic areas to me, I could soon tell for myself which was which—the Orangemen had all the fertile low-lying land, the Catholics generally lived in the hilly marginal areas west of the Bann in east and mid-Tyrone, south Down, west Armagh, south Armagh, south Fermanagh and in the Derry area. At the time of the border campaign these areas were described politically as 'Nationalist'. Apart from a brief interlude of enthusiasm for a Civil Rights policy of reform within the system, circa 1967–69, they could again be so described, and to a heightened degree today.

Geographically the 'North' can be either left or right of you, turning in behind you, running along before you, or all unknown to you falling further and further behind as you drive along an 'unapproved road', one on which a customs patrol can stop you when you fondly imagine you are still in the Republic. Of course, if you come to a sign post you can tell immediately: if you are in the North the names are printed only in English, in the Republic they are given in both Irish and English. Also, rural electrification is further advanced in the Republic and you can tell by the large number of polls and overhead wires where you are. In 1956 it was usually possible to tell North from South by the way the fields were kept. Those in the South looked the way the countryside looks in childhood or on Christmas cards: overgrown, bounded by enormous hedges and ditches and as likely to be occupied by rabbits, hares, flocks of crows, flights of pigeons, or occasional foxes and badgers as by cattle or sheep. The fields in the North were neat trim agricultural units.

As the South's agriculture improved, it became increasingly hard to tell the two sides apart by looking at the landscape—and even more difficult to find someone who knew from living there. Emigration to England, to America and to the towns on either side of the border, drained away the people at a rate that could be measured better visually than statistically. Standing on a hill in 1969 at an old I.R.A. jumping-off point such as Knockatallon, six miles north of Monaghan town, you could see the remains of perhaps thirty homesteads from which people had gone in the last five or six years.

The man on whose land I stood had memories of a boyhood and adolescence filled with dances and card games, cups of tea in neighbours' houses, rabbit hunting, haymaking, bringing in the harvest with the labour shared between one farmer and another, and the excitement distributed evenly among the hordes of children. His children had no one to play with. It was two miles to the nearest shop and three to the local school. They had no car and by the time his wife had looked after the large family she was lucky if she could manage more than two or three visits a year to Monaghan. This man was in the I.R.A. and 'immediate and violent revolution' was his solution to the problems of life in north Co. Monaghan. It may not be a good solution but you could at least have understood his feelings if you looked over his empty countryside on a wet winter's day. He was a skilful man who could have made good money in Dublin, but his father was a widower in his seventies, and would not leave his farm, his only reassurance in his old age, and my friend could not leave his father alone in the green desert where the pressures of economics had left only the rushes and furze to chase men off the land.

Life was traditionally hard in these counties, which is why the natives made poteen to keep out the cold and the reality. Then came the border and they started to smuggle after the land annuities dispute and the economic warfare made a field across the road a part of England so far as tariffs were concerned. It was a smuggler's paradise.

The pattern of smuggling changed with the times. During the war any food was welcome in the North. Car batteries, tyres, razor blades and nylons fetched good prices in the Republic. Butter was a perennial favourite, because the cheap food policy of British governments had left a gap ranging from sixpence to two shillings in the pound between the price of butter in the Republic and the North. Whatever the fluctuation, there was always an inducement for someone with a lorry to run four or five tons of butter down south. Dramatic confrontations between customs men and smugglers, midnight car chases and rammings were so frequent that they rarely made any sort of headlines unless the Dublin evening papers were stuck for news.

The border runs through farms, and even through houses, as in the village of Pettigoe, divided between Donegal and Fermanagh and the entire area is a mass of small, winding roads without signposts. There is a tradition of secrecy in the area as well as the normal suspicion of the law that exists in the Irish countryside. Children mistrust strangers and are trained to regard even the most innocent questions as being aimed at their family's liberty.

While I was driving around the border, inspecting the jumping-off points for raids and the places that were attacked a school teacher told a story which illustrated the local attitude to the police perfectly. A patrolling squad car had picked up a child wandering along the side of a by-road, at a time in the morning which suggested that the child was either lost or a truant from school. The child, a boy of about seven, appeared not to know his own name or where he lived. Neither did anyone at the farms at which the squad car called. Eventually the police sought the teacher's help and he immediately recognised the child as one of his pupils, the son of an established local family. Everyone the police had called on earlier must have known this also, but they, and the child, mistrusted the police's motive in trying to identify the boy. 'Tell them nothing', is the motto of the border counties.

Such were the traditions of the countryside in which the I.R.A. launched on December 12, 1956, a campaign against the North.

The actual beginning of the campaign was as untidy and as straggling as the countryside itself. One cannot point to a quickly implemented decision to start the campaign, but shortly after 'Operation Harvest' was proposed the I.R.A. leadership decided that some such scheme should be put into effect. The 'three Macs' were not, however, enthusiastic. MacCurtain argued that they had no armaments to justify such a campaign, but the urge for 'action', founded on a lack of appreciation of the real partition problem and fired by the optimism of youth, overcame his and other object-ions (Magan was irresolute for a time and MacLogan and Traynor were not happy either). Murphy, Russell, Cronin, Brady and the younger element in the leadership carried the day, and from April, 1956 on the I.R.A. made plans for the campaign.

In these early days of the campaign and its planning Charlie Murphy was com-paratively little known. He was, however, a key man in organising the campaign, was later involved in a *cause célèbre* and was the central figure in a dispute which split the I.R.A. internally.

On January 13, 1957, a month after the campaign had officially started, Murphy, Magan, MacCurtain and Sean Cronin (not the Cronin of the I.R.A. leadership but a namesake) were arrested at Murphy's home after they had attended Mass. The arrests were made by Detective Inspector Philip MacMahon, later head of the Special Branch and the man who was to prove the nemesis of Murphy and the movement. Along with the men the police seized incriminating lists of money sent from America to the I.R A.

MacMahon turned the captured evidence over to the state solicitor's office and ten days later it was produced in court before Judge Michael Lennon.★ Lennon created something of a sensation by openly siding with the accused men. When the prosecutor produced a copy of the declaration which brought the Offences Against the State Act into force, Lennon remarked ironically, 'This proclamation does not end with the words "God save the King".' The prosecutor asked if he were expected to reply and the judge said, 'Yes. I remember proclamations of the kind made in relation to myself and they always ended with the words, "God save the King".'

Further exchanges followed and at a later hearing Lennon ordered that the

---

★ In 1931 Lennon had attacked James Joyce, in the American *Catholic World*. He revealed that mixture of shame and chauvinism which so many Irish intellectuals show to the 'one who got away', because they feel that such a person is condemning them by force of example to the role of timeservers in a land where, as Joyce put it, 'Christ and Caesar are hand in glove'. The attack so infuriated Joyce that six years later he wrote to his friend Constantine Curran refusing to visit Dublin because to him the map of Ireland was marked 'Hic Sunt Lennones'.

property belonging to the two I.R.A. men before him—Magan and MacCurtain —be returned to them. The 'property' consisted of ammunition and, order or no order, MacMahon refused to hand it back.

Lennon's actions cost him his judgeship. After an inquiry he was retired on a not very impressive pension. But this stern treatment of an eccentric but humane judge should be assessed against the background of a time during which many judges were reluctant to include I.R.A. cases on their lists and sentences on I.R.A. defendants tended to be of the order of three to six months. At the same time the I.R.A. was attempting not to recognise the courts.

Murphy had meanwhile served three months and he was to remain at liberty for almost a year. He married on February 16, 1958, the day of the abortive raid on the Blandford military barracks in Dorset, England. (This was another example of daring and planning going to waste. Before the raid Murphy and Frank Skuse paid several visits to the camp and familiarised themselves with the layout. The raiding party of nine men was led by Sean Cronin and included Skuse but the attack was completely bungled. The only result was that a British soldier was shot in the stomach; no arms or ammunition were seized and the raiders were forced to abandon a new car obtained for the occasion.) Shortly afterwards the I.R.A. learned that the Special Branch was about to arrest a captain in the regular army who had been helping the I.R.A. Someone had to warn him and Murphy volunteered. MacMahon immediately learned of this (the Special Branch by this stage had the I.R.A. riddled with informers) and MacMahon was waiting.

Murphy went back to prison and MacMahon then singled him out as the victim of a ploy designed to split the I.R.A. down the middle—which it did very successfully. Murphy was depressed at his capture, the various disastrous raids and the failure of the campaign in general and was disposed to listen to tales of the hardships which families of imprisoned I.R.A. were suffering. For several days MacMahon tried in vain to talk with Murphy, but eventually MacMahon got him to accept a week's parole during which he was to contact the Army Council and report that if the campaign were called off all the prisoners would be released.

Sean Cronin, the leading man of the hour, was furious at Murphy's action. Cronin believed that if the I.R.A. decided to end the campaign the prisoners would automatically be released, an assumption which was open to question in the light of what had happened during the war. Having encountered great hostility, Murphy returned to jail after two days and refused from then on to have any dealings with MacMahon. But the damage had been done. The I.R.A. was subsequently driven by controversy as to the rights and wrongs of Murphy's action.

The first decision the campaign planners made was to send organisers to a number of centres: north Antrim, south Derry, south-east Derry, south Fermanagh, south Down, south Armagh, Derry city. These were all Nationalist areas and all were easily reached from the border. Belfast did not require a special organiser as Paddy Doyle lived there. Then this was interrupted by the Joe Christle split in June, and the energies of the I.R.A. were devoted to dissuading volunteers from following Christle. (When twelve out of the fifteen officers in the Dublin area did follow him, eighteen-year-olds in some cases succeeded them.) For a time Christle's followers kept their weapons, but tensions subsided when these were handed back. As a result the organisers were not sent in until August, but they managed to remain undetected, despite their Southern accents, until the outbreak of hostilities. There were approximately twenty of these organisers and their job was to train volunteers locally, act as intelligence agents, pick out targets and report back to Dublin in person at regular intervals.

The Army Council had voted to begin the campaign in November, 1956, but the irresolution of some members of the council, and a number of other snags pushed the date into December. During the planning period Paddy Doyle was captured with a Belfast newsletter to local units and the council decided to cut Belfast out of the campaign altogether. It had been feared all along that the I.R.A. might be too weak to defend Belfast Catholics and this setback decided the issue. Then there was a row between the emissary sent from Dublin to Derry concerning the smuggling of arms into the North. Derry had been chosen as the entry point but as a result of the row it was decided to send the arms in by south Fermanagh. This caused a twenty-four-hour delay on the very eve of the campaign, almost getting Charlie Murphy captured on December 10. He had to drive through the border areas postponing everything and between the psychological let-down and the exhaustion caused by travel and lack of sleep he failed to notice that he was driving without his lights on. He was stopped by an R.U.C. man in Pomeroy, Co. Tyrone, but was let off with a caution. (On Armistice Day he had an even narrower escape when Joe Christle and Liam Kelly burned down customs huts. Murphy, Noel Kavanagh and Sean Daly were in the North casing likely targets. Their method of operation was to drop a petrol cap off their car as they passed an R.U.C. barracks and then get out to look for it, inspecting the area as they did so. They were doing this outside an R.U.C. barracks when charges went off under the customs huts, but they escaped.)

Approximately one hundred and fifty men took part in the opening night of the campaign which between then and its end in 1962, was to cost, according to figures supplied to me by a Stormont spokesman, £1 million in outright damage (paid for by the British exchequer) and approximately £10 million in increased police and military patrols. Six young R.U.C. men and eleven Republicans were killed. In the South increased patrols and the opening of the Curragh internment camp cost in the region of £400,000 a year for the campaign's duration. The campaign was certainly a factor in the fall of the government in Dublin in 1957, and had other effects. An official concerned with attracting new industry to Ireland told me that some British and Continental investment was scared off by the disturbances.

But though matters appeared serious to foreigners, and poisoned the relations of Dublin with both Belfast and London, the Irish, both North and South, viewed it with less excitement. In the North the Nationalists refer to the campaign today as 'the incidents', because that is in fact what it was: a series of incidents along the border, impinging very little on Belfast and annoying rather than terrifying the Northern administration. It did, of course, arouse terror in the hearts of Unionist sympathisers living along the border—even on the Southern side. In the early stages of the campaign some Southern Protestants living in border areas made a practice of crossing over to earn pocket money as B-Specials, but after it became known that the I.R.A. was aware of this practice the Gardai warned moonlighting B-men that it would be impossible to guarantee their safety in the South. In the South public interest flared up for the first few days of the campaign or at dramatic moments like the Brookeborough raid with its subsequent emotive funerals; the opening of the internment camps; the trial which led to Judge Lennon's dismissal; Sean Cronin's trial at which 'Operation Harvest' was read out in court, and the trial of two young Co. Tyrone men for the murder of an R.U.C. sergeant blown to pieces in a booby-trapped cottage. But once it became obvious that the campaign could have no effect on the permanency of the Northern regime public interest diminished.

Interest reached its highest point in the Republic's elections in 1957, when Sinn Fein candidates polled 66,000 votes, but by the 1961 election this total had fallen by half and no Sinn Fein candidates were elected. At no time did this interest ever betoken any hostility to England or indeed towards the North. Most people in the Republic were rather puzzled by the whole thing and were inclined to write the whole thing off as 'the I.R.A. at it again', without any clear appreciation of why it should have been at it again. British tourists were as welcome as ever in the South. In fact, except for a time of great emotion such as the 1916 Rising, or the time of the 'Troubles', and isolated episodes which we shall come to later, such as the killing of Lord Mountbatten or the burning of the British Embassy, it is difficult to find a time in this century when anyone in Ireland would attack an Englishman—despite the efforts of some schoolteachers and politicians who, failing any coherent philosophy of their own, often do make efforts to equate being pro-Irish with being anti-British.

One incident which I can authenticate shows the degree of incomprehension that exists in Irish-English affairs. It occurred at the time of the 1955 Ras Tailteann, the day after the Northern authorities had prohibited the carrying of the tricolour in Northern areas by Ras cyclists. The prohibition, and its breach by some cyclists, had led to violence and a number of cyclists were beaten up by Orangemen. An N.C.A. supporter, employed at Killarney Mental Hospital and normally one of the gentlest of men, was so incensed when he read of this that he swore to take retributory action if he could. He was on his rounds as a van driver on a deserted country road when he saw a British car coming towards him. He stopped his van, halted the car, seized the Union Jack fluttering from the bonnet and tore it into pieces and jumped on them while the middle-aged couple in the car, both visitors from the north of England, looked on in astonishment. The destruction accomplished he drove off leaving Mum saying to Dad (as they later reported), 'Eeh lad. The man in Aer Lingus never said owt about anything like that!' But as the van drove over the hill they noticed in large letters on the rear doors 'Killarney Mental Hospital' and the whole incident thereupon (wrongly) lost all political significance.

The campaign began with a satisfactory bang. Ten different areas were attacked on the night of December 12 1956, in a ring from Antrim round to Derry. The targets included the B.B.C. relay transmitter at Rosemount, Derry, which was demolished, and Gough Barracks, Armagh, which survived. A Territorial Army headquarters, being built at Enniskillen, was blown down. The Magherafelt Quarter Sessions Courthouse, Co. Derry, was burned down. Near Magherafelt, Toome Bridge was destroyed. At Newtownbutler, Lady Brooke Bridge was damaged and Carry Bridge at Inishmore Island also suffered. In Newry, a B-Special hut was partly burned.

Most of the explosions took place early in the morning and in Charlie

Murphy's words, 'The place looked like the western front. Bombs going off, flames, Very lights, Sten guns—the lot.' He, together with Magan, Robert Russell and others, directed operations from Monaghan, a campaign centre. A guard on his rounds wanted to know what was going on and finally Russell told him that he was a chicken farmer up early to catch the market—a remark rendered nearly inaudible by a loud explosion a few miles to the north. The guard went off complaining that he would have to make a report about this.

The raids were greeted with predictable denunciations in Dublin, London and Belfast, but not in Moscow. On December 29 *Pravda* denied British claims that the raids were only 'isolated actions without popular support' saying: 'The Irish patriots cannot agree with Britain transforming the Six Counties into one of its main military bases in the Atlantic pact.'

In Dublin the government a day later said it would take every action needed to prevent loss of life. In London the government ordered the British ambassador in Dublin, Sir Alexander Clutterbuck, to express Britain's 'very great concern' at the incidents and the hope that Dublin would live up to its promise.

In Belfast of course reaction was more decisive. Lord Brookeborough referred to the I.R.A. as 'hooligans who raid this country' in a speech on December 13 to a meeting of the Shankill Unionist Association which was also addressed by the chairman of the British Conservative party, Oliver Poole. Poole pledged support for the Unionists and promised that as soon as Sir Anthony Eden, then on a visit to Jamaica, returned to London he would inform him of the raids. At this time Eden was under heavy attack from the 'Suez rebels' and the twelve Unionists at Westminster could not be lightly lost by the Conservative government. The price of their support was seen in a strong statement which Eden made in the House of Commons on December 19.

Before this the North had already looked to its own defences. The Special Powers Act's regulations were reintroduced on December 15 (providing for arrest and internment without warrant or trial) and further orders provided for the imposition of curfew, the immobilisation of cars and a strengthened police force. On December 22 the R.U.C guided British support in the drastic step of blowing up unapproved roads in border areas, destroying bridges and spiking roads at intervals. Deep craters greatly restricted transport along the border and the only usable roads were guarded by police and customs posts. Three thousand R.U.C. men and 12,000 B-specials were caused into action, and the North became an armed camp.

South of the border the number of guards in border areas was doubled and despite the fact that Belfast continually thundered that Dublin was not doing enough to curb the raids it was in fact the Southern Gardai who brought off the first large-scale capture of I.R.A. men and who throughout the campaign posed a greater threat to the I.R.A. than did the R.U.C. It was also the Gardai who eventually seized the 'three Macs', Murphy, Cronin, Laurence Grogan and the rest of the principal leaders. If the Southern authorities had not been so vigilant the campaign would have certainly been more destructive.

On December 16 the Gardai and units of the Irish army surrounded a farmhouse at Knockatallon and seized Murphy, Cronin and eleven other I.R.A. members but this time released them the same day. Their release caused great annoyance in

Stormont where the Minister for Home Affairs, W. B. Topping observed that he hoped that this was not the sort of 'necessary and appropriate' action which the Southern government had referred to in its statement of December 14.

Unionist M.P. Nat Minford, replying to Topping, said that he did not think that the British government was treating the situation seriously enough to 'bring to justice those damned scoundrels nor to bring pressure to bear on the Dublin authorities to stamp out I.R.A. drilling and prevent the raids'.

'We Protestants,' he declaimed, 'are running this country, and are going to run it. We want to live in a country where peace will prevail. If we find that these attacks are going to continue, then we Protestants ourselves will have to determine what the future will be. I'm not content to sit back and see these things continue.'

It was Lord Brookeborough who calmed the atmosphere, saying that Eden had assured him that the North would get the same support in defending itself as any other part of the United Kingdom. He counselled against any efforts to meet force with force, 'no matter how tempted', because such action 'would put the country in a state of chaos, bloodshed and hatred . . . the defence of the country must rest with the Government and no one should take any action on their own.' Eden said the next day that 'The safety of Northern Ireland and of its inhabitants is therefore a direct responsibility on Her Majesty's Government, which they will of course discharge.'

Costello replied to Eden, reiterating his statement of November 30, 1955, saying that the six-country area was a part of the Irish national territory and that any claim that the six counties were 'an integral part of the United Kingdom' could never be accepted by any Irish government. He called on Britain, as being primarily responsible for partition, to take the initiative in doing away with it and wound up by saying again that the government would do everything it could to bring 'unlawful military activities to an end'.

But Costello's government had less influence on the campaign than the campaign had on the government. The campaign helped in bringing down the coalition government, returning Fianna Fail to power and thus ultimately leading to the downfall of the I.R.A. Untroubled by divided councils, as was a coalition having to deal with I.R.A. sympathisers in Clann na Poblachta, Fianna Fail was able to take vigorous and successful action against the movement.

The end of the coalition came on January 28, 1957, when, on behalf of Clann na Poblachta, Sean MacBride moved a vote of no confidence in the government on economic grounds and because of its 'failure to formulate and to pursue any positive policy calculated to bring about the reunification of Ireland'. Deprived of the Clann's support, Costello had no option but to dissolve the Dail which he did on February 12, 1957. A general election was held on March 5 and in the post-Suez economic crisis the coalition took a bad beating, Fianna Fail winning fourteen more seats than it had held in 1954. Clann na Poblachta lost some thirty thousand of the fifty thousand votes it had got in 1954, but Sinn Fein won almost sixty-six thousand. (Their four seats meant nothing because the candidates refused to sit in the Dail and thus lost, if nothing else, the chance of a national platform to state their case.)

One of the most interesting developments of this period was an attempt on the part of the Church to find a solution to the border problem. On March 3, Cardinal d'Alton put forward a plan proposing that each of the six counties be allowed to choose between Dublin and Belfast. If the North agreed to federation with the South, Ireland was then to associate with the Commonwealth as an independent republic on the same basis as India, and offer bases to N.A.T.O. (At the time the cardinal's idea was a non-starter, but so far as Dublin and Westminster were concerned, relations were so harmonious, behind the scenes, on the partition issue that something could well have been worked out. The 'not-an-inch' extremists of the North of course remained a big stumbling block, but even these were considerably weakened by having Harold, rather than Sir Henry Wilson, in London's Corridors of Power. Had Edward Heath found himself dependent on the ten Unionist backbenchers it might have been a different proposition however.)

In the campaign itself the organisation was of course poor as is obvious from the experiences of a typical I.R.A. organiser. Gerry Higginbothom was nineteen when he attended a Sinn Fein meeting in Middle Abbey Street, Dublin, after the Omagh raid in 1954, and he joined first Sinn Fein and then the I.R.A. His feelings about partition were simply a vague notion that Ireland would be better off with thirty-two counties than twenty-six, and he was personally anti-British. He was shaken by the Church's letter of January, 1955, but after a chat with a Jesuit he decided that this need not affect his political activities. An amiable, able lad, the gap left by the Christle defections brought him to the fore rapidly, and in September, 1956 he resigned his job as a clerk and went to Fermanagh under the name of Gerry Cronin. He was joined there by Dave O'Connell from Cork and they began training in Fermanagh and Tyrone.

Young Higginbothom always felt that the predominantly Catholic counties of Derry, Fermanagh and Tyrone, of which he had personal knowledge, were never suitably organised for lengthy guerrilla warfare or even for hit-and-run operations. Training with Thompson and Sten guns and rifles was carried out across the border in Monaghan and was confined to groups of approximately twenty young men at a time. Everyone thought that the movement would snowball when the campaign began, but they were shattered when the Southern police began picking up columns as they recrossed the border and it very soon became clear that no one was going to replace the captured men.

Only luck had kept Higginbothom from being caught before the campaign began. His car had broken down at Derrygonnelly, Co. Fermanagh, and an R.U.C. sergeant asked him his name and what he was doing in the area. Gerry explained that he was interested in exploring caves but he could not answer the policeman's request for the correct name for such activity (he called it archaeology instead of speleology). The sergeant walked off saying resignedly, 'I suppose you'll be coming back some night to put something against the gable end.'

When the campaign began Higginbothom's chosen gable end was Lisanelly Barracks, not far from Omagh. The attack called for the use of gelignite to breach the rear wall, but after obtaining the gelignite from Mountfield quarry, seven miles away, his lorry stuck in a ditch. While the lorry was being extricated sirens went off as other points were attacked and when Higginbothom and his group finally got back to the mustering point the rest of the raiding party had disappeared. Only their possession of two Thompson guns enabled him and his companions to secure a night's lodgings in a mountain farmhouse. (Another young I.R.A. man of the period, Terry O'Toole, told me that in his experience food and lodging had become so hard to find by 1958 as the campaign wore on that he frequently had to brandish a revolver to get in for a night.) There followed eighteen days in a shack with food being supplied at intervals by local sympathisers.

On New Year's Eve 1957 he and his column were ready to attack Carrickmore Barracks about ten miles away from their hideout when they learned of the Brookeborough affair (described below) and Carrickmore had to be abandoned because the area was alive with police and soldiers. They were advised to retreat to Strabane where Saor Uladh members put them up. They crossed the border with the aid of friendly girls who paired off with them as if they were going across to the Republic for a 'court'. In Dublin Higginbothom made contact with the leadership and was asked to return to the North, to Donegal, and to attempt to recross the border and organise a column around Strabane.

By this time, however, the more reliable men in Strabane had been picked up and he could get nothing done. In desperation he took twelve men to Clady one night and let off a mine at an old bridge in the hope that the military would be attracted to the scene and that an ambush could be carried out. However the R.U.C. made it a policy to ignore things that went bang in the night and this ploy failed. He returned to Strabane later dressed as a Franciscan friar and was saluted with due reverence. But he spent the first afternoon in dread because there was a woman dying nearby and for a time it seemed likely that he would be called on to administer the last rites. In the end he gave himself away in a shop by asking for a brand of Southern cigarettes that was not sold in the North. There are no Franciscans in the North anyhow and this slip enabled the R.U.C. to apprehend him. The campaign knew him no more.

A farmhouse at Knockatallon was intended as the operational H.Q. for the border area, the place from which raids could be launched and to which men could return. It was only about a mile and a half to the border from the house but on December 13, a cold, sleety night, to avoid the roads which were alive with police an I.R.A. patrol led by Charlie Murphy followed a route thirty miles over mountain and bog to attack the R.U.C. barracks in the town of Lisnaskea. In the town there were some anxious moments when it was learned that an I.R.A. suspect had been captured and was in a cell at the rear of the barracks. It was feared (wrongly) that he might have given away the raid and while Murphy and the others were going over the final plans in an outhouse not far from the barracks, the woman whose husband owned the farm burst in and exclaimed, 'That fucking bollocks has spilt the beans.' Murphy was thunderstruck, not because of the suspected leakage but because he had never heard a woman swear before. However they decided to go ahead.

Lisnaskea Barracks is a three-storeyed building in the main street of Lisnaskea with houses on either side, one of them the local curate's, who was then a Father Fergusson. Across the road lived the parish priest, Canon Donnelly. The I.R.A. party got word to him that they were shortly going to free 'occupied Ireland' and would he care to vacate his part of it in case something nasty came through his window during the war of liberation?

(Solicitude for the welfare of parish priests is not normally a characteristic of the I.R.A., but all had received confession a short time earlier from a Republican-minded young chaplain who had turned his Volkswagen into a roadside confessional.) The old canon sent back word that at his time of life death might as well come to him in his own house and he stayed put.

As the raid began Murphy was just removing a mine from the back of a truck when the driver put his foot on the accelerator instead of the brake, the truck moved forward and the mine dropped at Charlie's feet. The mine, which was made of gelignite, failed to explode. Half of the group then dashed across the road with it, and placed it in position. It went off perfectly at 1.20 am. and blew in the side of the barracks, and with it the staircase, which meant that the attackers could not get at the fourteen R.U.C men. The aim of the raid had been to destroy the barracks and take whatever arms were available, but without heavy weaponry this was impossible. Neither of the two Bren guns used by the attackers functioned properly. The police replied with Sten guns and revolvers and between them the two parties managed to break almost every window in the town. After twenty minutes the I.R.A. broke off the attack and made off in the truck, sheets of tracer bullets pouring down the street after it. 'It made a very pretty sight' one of the residents of the town told me.

Derrylin Barracks was also attacked that night without any damage. Two bridges outside Lisnaskea were blown up to delay pursuit. Everyone concerned got back safely to Knockatallon, arriving in broad daylight, much to Sean Cronin's horror. Here they heard Costello's statement about 'appropriate action' and decided that weapons not immediately needed should be dumped.

The main column then returned across the border hoping to ambush a patrol. Cronin, Murphy and eleven others stayed on, Murphy intending to go next day to south Fermanagh with a sack of ammunition for Noel Kavanagh. He then fell asleep and was shaken awake a few hours later to find that police and soldiers had surrounded the farm and that the kitchen was full of police. Everyone was very polite. 'Excuse me, sir,' said the soldier who had awakened him. 'Not at all,' he replied and when police and soldiers vanished upon discovering a mine upstairs, Murphy rendered it harmless for them.

There were a number of incriminating documents in the house and when the party was taken to Monaghan police station none of them expected to see home again for some time. But the police officer in charge of the operation telephoned Dublin from the room in which they were detained and to their incredulity they realised from the conversation that they might not be charged.

'No sir, they'd no ammunition,' they heard him say and they were told that they could go—whereupon they immediately refused to move unless they were given transport! The police contended that they had no transport, but Cronin and Murphy persisted and finally two taxis were hired and paid for by the police and the whole party driven to Dublin, Murphy and Cronin in a squad car. The pair walked up Emmet Road, where Murphy lived, in their American army battle dress, but finding that Mrs Murphy had gone to England to visit Donal they called round to a neighbour for breakfast.

A little later Magan came and told them that the campaign had been called off because of their arrest and that Laurence Grogan was in Drogheda contacting those concerned to tell them this. After much argument an Army Council meeting was called and it decided to reactivate the campaign, the men on the border being recalled, however, not only for Christmas but also to regroup and reorganise.

In a sense the Brookeborough ambush explains everything about the I.R.A. and its hold on Irish tradition. It shows all the courage, the self-sacrifice, the blundering and the emotional appeal that have characterised and kept alive the I.R.A. spirit for centuries. The two young men who lost their lives in the Brookeborough affair, Fergal O'Hanlon and Sean South, were given two of the biggest funerals in living memory—but during their lives there was never sufficient public support for their aims for them to receive proper military instruction or even to be correctly briefed on the target that claimed their lives: the R.U.C. barracks in the centre of the little Fermanagh town of Brookeborough.

O'Hanlon was nineteen at the time of his death and South twenty-seven. South was cut from the same cloth as Pearse or Liam Lynch. A clerk in his native Limerick city, he was a prominent member of An Realt, the Irish-speaking branch of the Legion of Mary. The Legion, the physical manifestation of the Mariolatry which characterises so much of Irish Catholicism, is dedicated to social worker and missionary activity in the developing countries for the Roman Catholic Church. South showed himself in his few writings to be a staunch though not uncritical Catholic and possessed of a social conscience. His attraction to the military calling is shown by the fact that the only photograph of him in circulation shows him in his uniform as an officer in the F.C.A., the regular Irish army reserve.

O'Hanlon was also an outstanding young man in his native Monaghan town. A keen footballer interested in Gaelic culture, he leaves several references in his diaries to the need for training and self-discipline in order to do his duty for Ireland. His I.R.A. comrades remember him as a particularly winning and promising boy.

I once called on O'Hanlon's parents and visited the farm where he died. Mrs O'Hanlon looked and acted like the mother of a martyred saint. She had the same passionate dedication to the cause which claimed him as had her son and she spoke about his death as something holy as well as patriotic. It hurt her to hear anyone suggest that the cause should be abandoned or that the Republican movement should forswear force as a means of reuniting Ireland. To her, this was a betrayal of all that Fergal and those who went before him died for.

After a meal his father drove me to the place called Baxter's Cross. Hard by the Cross there stands an old-fashioned, two-storeyed farmhouse and beside it a cowbyre. It was in this byre that the bodies of O'Hanlon and South were found. A few miles away to the north is Brookeborough. (Ironically things had become so peaceful that the barracks which was the scene of the raid had become a private house occupied by a family.) Both the farmhouse and the byre at Baxter's Cross are deserted. There are no windows or doors in the byre and one has to look closely to pick out the bullet holes in the wall and the two tiny crosses which Mrs O'Hanlon set into the cement at the spots where her son and his comrade died.

It was frustration after so many failures that led to the Brookeborough raid, plus the fact that the raiders, who had been out on long, fruitless patrol duty, had been supplied with detailed plans of the barracks by a local. On the night of the raid, January, 1957, the raiding party got its first full meal since Christmas at a friendly house and set off in a truck for the attack.

Brookeborough is an Irish town of the sort best described by the quip, 'It has only one Main street and the further you go, the mainer it gets.' The barracks was located in the middle of the town in a house which looked no different from those adjoining. The plan was for the truck to pull up outside the barracks, five men acting as a cover group staying in the truck to open fire and divert attention while an assault group armed with two mines, two Thompson guns and four rifles, augmented by a half-dozen or so home-made grenades, breached the barracks walls and gained entrance. While this was going on, two other men would keep watch on the roads leading into the town.

There was nothing to distinguish the barracks and in the badly lit street the driver, Vincent Conlon, who had given up a job in America to come home when he read of the raids, almost missed it. However, one member of the party, a local man, shouted out, 'Oh Jasus, there's the barracks,' and the truck stopped immediately outside the building. The cover group opened fire with a Bren gun and four rifles while the assault group attempted to let off a landmine. It failed to explode and the party had to dash back and get a second mine from the truck. This also misfired, even when someone tried to trigger it by shooting at it. Then South's Bren gun ran out of ammunition—they had only three magazines for it, a microscopic amount for such a quick-firing gun. As soon as its noise died away the raiders realised that the occupants of the barracks were returning their fire. South was hit first; like the others in the truck he was a sitting target from the upper windows of the barracks. One of the attackers threw a grenade at the barracks, but it bounced off a window-sill and fell under the truck. Just as this happened a burst of Bren-gun fire wounded Phil O'Donoghue, Sean Garland and Fergal O'Hanlon. Then the grenade went off and O'Donoghue was blown off the truck; as he hit the road he was struck by three bullets one of which ran right around his stomach under his belt without scratching him. All it left was a red weal.

Despite the rain of bullets, the party somehow scrambled back into the truck while the R.U.C. concentrated its fire on the driver. The windscreen was cracked and frosted by the bullets. Conlon could not see where he was going, but one of the men who had been guarding the approach to the town came back directly under the windows of the barracks and broke in the windscreen with his rifle butt. Conlon was unhurt but the truck's tipper gears had been shot to pieces and every time the truck went over a bridge or bump its back went up in the air and everyone in it slipped to the rear. Conlon managed to keep going for a few miles despite this damage and the ruined tyres and then at Baxter's Cross the party halted, realising that the R.U.C. must be close behind and that Roslea which lay ahead would be alerted.

There was no one in the farmhouse and the only shelter for O'Hanlon and South, who were both unconscious, was the open cow-byre. Four other members of the party were wounded and one, Sean Garland, wanted them to leave him behind so that he could make a fight of it and gain time for the rest to escape. He was dissuaded and the survivors retreated up the hill a few hundred yards in the direction of the border. About ten minutes later the R.U.C. drove up, stopped by the abandoned truck and, taking no chances, opened fire on it for what seemed like five minutes. A few minutes later the I.R.A. party heard one long burst of fire coming from the direction of the cowbyre and they believed afterwards that this was the *coup de grâce* being administered to O'Hanlon and South. However, Pat Regan (upon whose personal account I have based this description of the raid) went back to the spot some years later and found that the line of bullet holes was approximately waist to chest high on the wall facing the cow-byre entrance and he concluded that none of these bullets struck either O'Hanlon or South, unless perhaps by ricochet. He attributed the firing on the cowbyre to the normal military tactics, employed when approaching a strongpoint supposedly held by the enemy, of falling on one knee and firing a burst. However, this explanation did not percolate through I.R.A. circles for some years and the deaths of O'Hanlon and South were a source of immense bitterness.

The survivors reached the Monaghan border safely where, after resting in a friendly house, they gave themselves up to obtain medical attention for the wounded. They were treated in the Mater Hospital, Dublin, and although the police were supposedly keeping a keen eye on them, and their names were printed in the papers, they all managed to leave their sick beds at varying intervals and get out of the hospital, which has a long Nationalist tradition, without being detained.

The greatest single disaster of the entire campaign was Edentubber explosion in Co. Louth which claimed five lives in November, 1957. In some parts of the Irish countryside where tragedy has walked across some green corner it is possible to recreate the event from a relic of some sort—a tumbled-down church, a ruin, a cross perhaps but at Edentubber today all that remains is a five-barred gate leading into an empty field. Not a stone stands to mark the spot where four young I.R.A. men and the owner of the forester's cottage were blown to pieces when a home-made landmine went off just before the four set off to cross the Louth border a few yards away. Behind the hill there is a lane which leads to a Mass rock inscribed with a cross, a memento of the religious division of the penal days that began the whole affair. Behind rise the Carlingford Mountains, ahead lies Newry, home of one of the dead boys, Oliver Craven, nineteen. In the distance there is Armagh, the birthplace of a second victim, Paul Smith, also nineteen, and away to the south far beyond the reach of eye is Co. Wexford, which gave a title to one of President Kennedy's favourite songs, 'The Boys of Wexford'.

> We are the Boys of Wexford,
> We fought with heart and hand
> To burst in twain our Captive Chains
> And free our native land.

George Keegan, twenty-nine, and Patrick Parle, twenty-seven, had been singing that song since boyhood, and on the night of November 12, 1957, they had left their native Wexford to play a part, as they saw it, in freeing their native land. The fifty-five-year-old bachelor who went to death with them had lived alone since his mother died. His life and death were symbolic of the Irish: love of his mother denied him a wife; love of his fatherland took his life. Little wonder that the news of this affair shocked Murphy and Cronin. Murphy in particular became prey to a melancholy, suffering for years afterwards, losing weight and frequently waking up sweating in the grip of nightmares.

It is here worth looking briefly at the career of a prominent I.R.A. man of the border campaign period— Terry O'Toole. He saw much active service over a long period, was one of the 'activists' while interned in the Curragh and was very aware of the intrigues and splits that affected the movement.

O'Toole joined the I.R.A. in June, 1954, influenced by the Armagh raid and by the fact that his uncle, Tom Maguire of Mayo, was and is a life-long Republican. He joined the Heath unit (named from the heath near Portlaoise, another traditionally Republican area where MacLogan had his pub). Nothing happened beyond routine drilling and meetings until August, 1957, despite repeated appeals by Terry and the unit to be sent north. MacLogan was the leading figure in the area and was not in favour of such action.

Then in August word came from Dublin that five men were required immediately for active service. Terry could not supply the request and went to Galmoy in neighbouring Kilkenny to get two volunteers. With these he went to Dublin and was directed to Donegal. The first operation was to be an ambush of British soldiers from Omagh Barracks along the Omagh-Derry road. However the ambush party, about fifteen strong, was forestalled and a police raid seized 150 lbs. of gelignite which had been made into mines.

O'Toole and the others withdrew to Mountfield in south Tyrone and began to train about fourteen local youths, there and in Carrickmore.* The local people were friendly but the I.R.A. was very poorly organised and Frank Morris of Convoy, Co. Donegal, who was strictly speaking in Saor Uladh, was their mentor in the area. It was to him that they looked for guidance rather than to Dublin. O'Toole and his group worked with local farmers cutting turf and sharing farmhouse chores. There was no difficulty about freedom of movement by day but night raids by police on suspected houses became so heavy that accommodation was hard to find.

It was decided to build a dug-out in a farmhouse which was used as a piggery by a friendly farmer. Working at night, they removed the floor of one room and dug down eight feet, scattering the yellow clay in a nearby potato field lest it attract attention. The hole was then covered with railway sleepers provided by sympathisers, and the sleepers were covered with concrete. Entry was provided by a shaft which was cut from under a small porch outside the house. Covered by a camouflaged trap-door the shaft and dug-out were completely hidden. After giving the concrete a week to settle straw was sprinkled over it and the pigs were allowed back in. In all it took ten days to build during which the I.R.A. group lived on packets of chicken noodle soup and potatoes from nearby fields. It seemed a small price to pay in return for the safety of the dug-out, but in fact the hiding place nearly killed them all. When they woke up after the first night in the shelter all of them were suffering from excruciating headaches. There was such am acute lack of oxygen that matches would not strike. Worse, they could not force open the trap-door, because the pigs were lying on it. Eventually the tallest man in the group managed to get his shoulder to the door and forced it and a surprised pig into the air. He almost collapsed from the effort. Had his strength not sustained him for the moment all those in the dug-out would have died.

Supplies were now needed for their raids as they had only approximately two hundred rounds of Thompson and three hundred rounds of revolver ammunition.

---

* Carrickmore became a flash-point in Anglo-Irish relations during October-November, 1979, when at a time, following Mountbatten's death, the British were pressing the Irish on security, the I.R.A. again took over the village for several hours, for the B.B.C.'s *Panorama* programme, under the noses of the nearby, and unsuspecting, British army.

Intelligence was another problem for although the locals were friendly their information was usually so outdated as to be useless. Information about troop movements was finally obtained only after several nights were spent in the open watching B-Specials setting up road blocks a few yards away from them. Then, having discovered when and where to carry out ambushes the supplies problem reasserted itself; four separate lots of equipment sent from Dublin were all seized.

In a hopeless position they decided to move to Monaghan where they thought organisation and opportunities would be better. It took them two days on foot, sleeping out at night, and when they got there they learned that two of their number were named in an R.U.C. leaflet as being wanted in connection with the death of a sergeant the previous August. They could all have faced a capital charge had they been caught, and the fact that they were not informed of the leaflet earlier is indicative of the lack of communication between border units and G.H.Q. in Dublin. Then in December O'Toole, Sean Cronin and J. B. O'Hagan, the leading figure in the North, decided that O'Toole's column should be broken up and that he would try to organise the adjoining areas of Lifford, Co. Donegal, and Strabane, Co. Tyrone.

Between Christmas and Easter his group succeeded in blowing up four trans-formers on a line between Lifford and Derry, a customs hut and an R.A.F. hut. The plan in each case was to attract the military to the scene and ambush them. The Northerners refused to be drawn and neither shooting nor loss of life took place.

Another operation that failed to materialise was planned for Easter under the direction of a Dubliner, Jimmy McGilligan. Over sixty men were to have taken over the village of Clady and make a stand there, similar to that envisaged by Tom Barry in the 1930s. The approaches to Clady were to have been ambushed for some con-siderable distance so that Easter Monday 1958 would rival Easter Monday 1916. The scheme fell through when the extra men required from Dublin were not forth-coming. Instead Sean Cronin ordered a 'demonstration' in the village.

Seven men accordingly entered the village on Easter Monday night. The Army Council's Easter message was read out, a number of I.R.A. leaflets were distributed and the proceedings concluded with the hoisting of the tricolour and the firing of a volley over the post office. The group waited outside the town hoping to stage an ambush but nothing happened until the following day when a tank arrived at the village to supervise the removal of the tricolour. The next day O'Toole and his group had planned to blow up a B-Special hut but their hideout was discovered and they were taken in handcuffs to the Curragh.

While the bombs continued to go off during 1958, particularly during July, the most significant I.R.A. activity was hidden from the public and in fact took place within the Curragh internment camp.

After a number of skirmishes on the border and raids on quarries in the Republic for gelignite de Valera had reintroduced the Offences Against the State Act on July 4. Sixty men were picked up in one swoop on July 8 and by the following March a total of 131 were interned in the reopened Curragh. (The camp, however, did not remain open long. The campaign fell into such disarray that the last of the internees were released on March 11, 1959.)

Compared to the rigours of the war years the Curragh now was almost a rest camp. The food was plentiful if unvaried and could be supplemented from outside or by meals cooked in the huts on electric rings. Tea could be obtained from an immersion boiler. There were four huts at the peak of the internment containing about forty detainees in each. Each hut had its own O.C. and there was a camp council of prisoners with Thomas MacCurtain as O.C. The huts were opened at 7 a.m. and breakfast was served in the dining hall at 8. Anyone who was sick got breakfast in his hut, served by a member of the Legion of Mary, until he recovered or was transferred to hospital. Everyone did a spell of orderly duty, cleaning out the lavatory (renamed 'Boland's' in honour of the Minister for Justice), or washing dishes and generally tidying up. Showers were compulsory once a week, and could be had more often. A nearby field was made available for games and the prisoners were also encouraged to read or to make wallets and crosses which were sold outside the camp to raise funds.

The worst feature of internment was the lack of privacy. No one could ever get away from his fellows, or from the sound of chipping and snipping as yet another wallet or cross began its journey to the outside. To a sensitive person the conditions were hell, but several of the internees told me that if you overlooked the defences the place was 'more like a factory than a camp'.

The camp was protected by five sets of fences. Two lay between the camp and a trench six feet deep and eight feet wide, which was booby-trapped with flares and tripwires, and three more fences had to be surmounted when and if this was negotiated. At the four corners of the camp elevated sentry posts were manned by an armed guard. In addition the perimeter was patrolled by guards armed with revolvers and ammonia grenades.

The prisoners were divided among themselves as to escaping. The camp council frowned on escape attempts believing it best to avoid doing anything that might get someone killed. The activists thought this a cowardly attitude and felt that the proper course for Republicans was to make life difficult for their jailers in the time-honoured manner. Two of the activist group, O'Toole and Conlon, the driver at the Brookeborough raid, brought the debate to a head by trying to escape without the sanction of the camp council.

On first being interned O'Toole was almost glad of the rest and food apart from the 'patriotic eggs', which were so called because, he claims, when cooked they assumed the national colours of green, white and orange and were apt to turn into concrete if left on a plate. But the novelty wore off soon and he gladly fell in with Conlon's suggestion that they escape. At the time the two men were receiving treatment for slight illnesses in the camp hospital and Conlon thought they could get out through a window in the shower cubicle which was protected only by two iron bars. This window also opened on to clear ground away from the camp defences.

On Whit Sunday they attacked the bars, taking a shower each on each guard's watch and by the following night, although somewhat chilled from their series of unwanted showers, they had sawn through the bars with saws from the handicraft classes. A third occupant of the ward, a young volunteer named Kelly, was to accompany them and he unwittingly caused the escape to fail. Conlon, as arranged, went into the shower first leaving O'Toole playing draughts. A few moments later O'Toole also went to the shower, on the pretext of washing some shirts and underwear. This was the signal for Kelly to follow, first putting some turf on the fire and thus necessitating his washing his hands.

Conlon, a large man, stuck in the window for a moment and had to be pushed through. O'Toole followed more easily. They waited for five minutes for Kelly, unaware that the guard had begun chatting with him just as he made for the shower, and then decided to head for Kilcullen, a village on the main Dublin road. Incredibly, they had made no plans for hiding places, although Terry was reared less than twenty miles from the Curragh. After about ten minutes the pursuit began but they got away safely to a place called Yellow Bog, about six miles from the camp. They then decided to knock on the first house they came to, and by good fortune it turned out to be the home of a member of Sinn Fein.

They stayed there for the night, but did not dare to sleep. Next day planes circled the area and soldiers appeared nearby. Kelly, who had finally escaped, had been in the vicinity, attempting unsuccessfully to gain admission to three neighbouring houses, so that their presence in the area was known. They left through the back of the house, deciding not to cross the Liffey which flowed nearby. Later in the day a lorry dropped some troops near their hiding place and they made a run for it. It was now Tuesday and as they had had no sleep since the previous Sunday they slept in a ditch, covering themselves with sacks.

O'Toole awoke to find a young soldier prodding him with a bayonet and that was the end of the escape bid—a fact which was not made any the more pleasant by the officer in charge telling than that had they crossed the Liffey they would have got away as the far side was not being searched.

This short-lived burst for freedom renewed the issue of escape especially when militant members, in particular Charlie Murphy, J. B. O'Hagan and Willie Gleeson, were picked up and interned. These grouped under Murphy's leadership, along with O'Toole and Frank Driver, a phenomenal character who never allows his humorous brand of anti-clericalism (based mainly on the position of the bishops on the Act of Union issue in 1800) to interfere with his Christian charity.

Driver was particularly active in planning escapes. One suggestion of his was that the wife of an internee who had ten children should take them all to the house of the Most Rev. Dr John Charles McQuaid, Archbishop of Dublin, and deposit them on his doorstep for safekeeping until her husband was released Another was that the wives, female relatives and sympathisers of the internees should make a mass march on the barbed wire from the outside, cutting their way in with wire cutters. 'Jesus,' said Frank, 'think of the publicity if one of them got shot.' The camp council thought of it and turned the proposal down with horror.

When Murphy arrived in camp there were two escape projects in train. One involved cutting a tunnel under the wire, but it came to nothing as a sergeant spotted some of the clay from the tunnel that had been carelessly dumped on a path. Th second one worked though not the way the activists had intended.

A blanket was taken from the hut where most of the activists lived (it was called 'Little Rock' after the Arkansas trouble spot) and covered with grass in a corner of the playing field. Two detainees slipped under it while another group stood around to mask them from the sentries. When it was dark the two simply slid under the wire while back in the huts two dummy beds were made up so that the customary inspection found nothing wrong. The trouble was that when the camp council, which had been pressed into sponsoring the escape sent word to Sean Cronin about the scheme, he nominated Dave O'Connell and Rory Brady as his candidates for escape whereas those in the camp wanted Murphy and O'Hagan to go out. Cronin's men went.

Cronin himself was interned not long before the camp elections to choose a new O.C. It had been expected that MacCurtain might stand down and that Murphy would stand in his place, but in the event MacCurtain went forward and Murphy preferred not to stand against him. J. B. O'Hagan stood in Murphy's place and was narrowly defeated. Cronin remained neutral until the night of the election when he advised that policy be left as it was, in the hands of the official leadership, the 'three Macs'.

To the militants the election result meant that if they wanted action they would have to bring it about themselves, and that Murphy was the only leader they could look to to support such a policy. The activist group now gained two supporters, Frank Armstrong, and a young Limerick man, Jimmy Devereux, an expert fitter who could make wire-cutting equipment. The hacksaws used in making souvenirs had all been withdrawn and their only wire-cutting tool was a pair of pliers which a detainee had hidden. But using angle-irons and a six-foot-long poker from the laundry Devereux made three wire-cutters, tempering the steel in the hut fire while members of the group lounged around screening the operation not only from the camp authorities but also from the supporters of the 'no escape' policy, who would certainly have attempted to stymie the attempt if they could. The poker was used to make extended arms for the cutters.

The escape was planned for December, 1958. Twenty-six men were to take part and after getting away they intended to go to Meath to regroup and recommence operations on the border. Everyone went to confession before the escape bid, which in the event failed to come off on the chosen date for it was discovered that soldiers were stationed all around the big trench. The minister for justice was visiting the camp and a general stand-to had been ordered.

The next day, Willie Gleeson, Tom Ferris, Terry O'Toole and Devereux cut their way through the first fence before the guards realised what was happening. Then a guard ran up firing two revolver shots which struck no one. O'Toole noticed as he ran that the sentry in the elevated post nearest to him had his rifle in the air and this seemed to confirm the theory that the escapees would not be fired on. He ran on, passing within eight feet of the guard who was firing the revolver, not knowing that behind him Brian Boylan had already been shot. Charlie Murphy, who had stayed at the gap assisting the others through, went to Boylan's assistance. The rest of the group cleared the second and third fences and reached the dyke without further casualties. Then ammonia grenades were thrown at them. Hampered as they were by trip wires that set off flares they floundered among the coils of barbed wire, everyone injured or cut or temporarily blinded. O'Toole was shot in the right thigh, but kept going. By the time the last fence was reached the cutters had been abandoned and the group, by now reduced to ten, attacked the fence with bare hands and clawed it down while the ground was cut up by flying bullets.*

It was approximately a mile to the nearest cover, a field with a thick ditch, where they carried out what first aid they could. One of them, Pat McGirl, was completely blind from the ammonia gas and was later captured as was Liam Fagan who had been shot in the knee and had to crawl on his stomach. First aid had to be abandoned as the soldiers drew near again and the group split up. Some of them then went to Moone, near the camp, and called inadvertently at a house where a man was being waked. The widow was not a Republican herself, but her husband had been one and she paused in her grief to arrange that the escapees be taken to friendly houses.

Equipped with maps O'Toole and his companions (Gleeson, Devereux, Gerry Houghey, and Dan Donaghy) circled Kildare and headed for Portarlington town, following a route that took them thirty-five miles instead of the normal eighteen. They reached a friendly house on the outskirts of Portarlington the next morning, wounded and exhausted, and a doctor was sent for (he turned out to be a state medical officer). He tended their wounds and the others moved on but O'Toole's leg prevented him from travelling. He stayed there for two days until the woman of the house dressed him as a woman and drove him to the west of Ireland where a sympathetic surgeon got him into a hospital, and the bullet was removed from his leg, nearly four days after he was shot.

Back in the camp and in the ranks of the I.R.A. throughout the country the escape deepened at the split in the movement. To the official leadership, that is to say the remnant that remained of an organisation, the escapees had put themselves outside the movement and almost every Army Council meeting between then and June was devoted to discussing what should be done about them. And on top of this issue there was heated argument over the control of Sinn Fein. Should the party be autonomous or should it be controlled by the I.R.A.?

There was one distraction during this arguing. Joseph Christle dumped an unwanted hero into the I.R.A. ranks, James Andrew Mary Murphy whom he had rescued from Wakefield Prison, February 12, 1959. Then the London *Daily Express*, whose Irish correspondent Seamus Brady, was known to be particularly well informed about all levels of Irish politics, constitutional and otherwise, printed a report asking, 'Is Murphy Skuse?' Controversy blew up within and without the I.R.A. as to whether he was Skuse and, if he was, whether he should be extradited to England. Ultimately he was not but for a time this issue drew attention away from what was left of the campaign and from the controversy within the movement, most of it directed against Charlie Murphy for his acceptance of parole at the time of the MacMahon incident and his leadership of the escape.

There were two legal proceedings during the campaign of which mention must be made here. The more important was the case of Gerrard Lawless—the first to be judged by the Court of Human Rights in Strasbourg.

---

* The Republicans were particularly bitter about this shooting, but in fairness it should be underlined that the sentries in the elevated posts could probably have killed many of the escapees had they wished. The number of leg wounds seems to indicate that they deliberately aimed low. The soldier with the revolver who first inflicted casualties was disarmed by an officer as he prepared to fire at some of the escapees from point-blank range.

Lawless, who had an I.R.A. record, was arrested by Detective Inspector MacMahon on July 11, 1957, just as he was about to leave Ireland for England. Lawless said that MacMahon offered him a job and money if he would give information about the I.R.A. but that he had refused, claiming that he was not in the I.R.A. (he had sided with Christle in the split). He was then interned in the Curragh where he was, in fact, ostracised by the I.R.A. detainees.

From the Curragh Lawless contacted a Dublin lawyer, Ciaran Mac An Ali, asking him to take his case. Some of the finest lawyers* in Ireland joined Mac An Ali in doing so and on November 8, 1957, an application on behalf of Lawless was filed before the European Commission on Human Rights asking immediate release from the Curragh, payment of compensation and damages, and payment of all costs before both the Irish courts and the Court of Human Rights. On the advice of his lawyers Lawless then reluctantly availed himself of the machinery for release from the camp by signing an 'undertaking' and he was freed on December 10.

After a lengthy argument, first through the European Commission and then through the Court of Human Rights to which the Commission's judges had referred the case, judgement was given against Lawless on July 1, 1961, but despite this some important principles were set out. Lawless's lawyers established that the 'undertaking' which Curragh internees signed to release themselves had no legal status as it was not provided for by the Offences Against the State Act to which it referred. More significantly the court set the precedent that it did not have to accept a member country's own opinion as to whether a state of emergency existed within that country sufficient to warrant such measures as internment, but that it could exercise its own judgement as to the extent of the internal crisis, and consequently could rule on the measures adopted to deal with that crisis.

This decision had a direct effect upon Irish politics. When the border campaign flared up again temporarily in 1961–62 the government did not resort to internment camps but instead had recourse to military courts. These imposed sentences of several years—which were quickly commuted to months when the I.R.A. called off the campaign. It is, indeed, doubtful that any Irish government will use internment camps again except in the gravest emergency.

The most dramatic court case of the entire period was the 'Mallon and Talbot affair' which, although it received far more publicity than the Lawless case, had far less long-term significance.

The affair began on August 17, 1957, when R.U.C. Sergeant Arthur Ovens kicked open the door of an unused cottage near Coalisland, Co. Tyrone, and was blown to bits by a mine. The R.U.C., understandably enraged by the death of a colleague who was also the father of three children, nearly took Coalisland apart looking for those responsible. After lengthy interrogations the R.U.C. came up with Kevin Mallon and Patrick Talbot, both twenty-one, as the chief suspects.

In Dublin (where to this day it is not known exactly who set the booby-trap) Charlie Murphy and Sean Cronin decided that regardless of the policy of not

---

* Senior counsels Sean MacBride and Tommy Connolly, junior council Seamus Sorahan and one of the country's leading solicitors, P. C. Moore. They continued the tradition of defending the I.R.A. men without payment.

recognising the courts Mallon and Talbot would have to be defended or they would
be hanged. Again Sean MacBride came to the rescue after Murphy and Cronin had
failed to get another Dublin lawyer interested in the case. MacBride advised them
that no Unionist lawyer would take the case, that a Nationalist would be too
timorous and that the best thing to do was to get an Englishman. He then arranged
for Elwys Jones, later a Labour attorney general, to defend the two young men. A
vigorous publicity campaign (in which the *New Statesman* was prominent) highlighted
the tortures to which Mallon and Talbot were allegedly subjected and a special
committee was formed in Dublin to raise funds for the defence. As a result of this,
and of Jones's effort, Mallon and Talbot were sentenced to prison rather than to
execution and they were freed when the campaign ended.

The campaign had manifestly failed, although with Irish doggedness the movement was on one hand looking for a scapegoat to blame for the failure and on the
other trying to prolong the attacks on the border. It eventually did find a formula
whereby the Curragh escapees could be received back into the fold. They signed
readmission forms, which were a sort of admission that they had been thrown out
but now accepted the authority of the official section of the movement. In fact
O'Toole and the others planned to eject the 'pacifist' section of the movement at
the convention elections in June, 1959, but for the moment they co-operated
with the existing leadership.

By June the rift in the I.R.A. had become public knowledge. Reports of a split
appeared in the papers and denials by the I.R.A. publicity bureau certainly failed to
convince the Special Branch at least whose members frequently accosted I.R.A. men
in the streets and asked them, 'Which I.R.A. do you belong to, Charlie Murphy's or
the official I.R.A.?' without even bothering to arrest any of them. Worse the authorities publicly showed their contempt for the movement by gradually releasing the men
in the Curragh. By March, 1959 the movement was no longer a real threat, despite the
British ambassador's formal protest against the releases and de Valera's angry exchange
with British Prime Minister Harold Macmillan. Yet even after de Valera retired on
June 17, 1959 (he became president) I.R.A. activity continued to poison British-Irish
relationships. De Valera's successor, Sean Lemass, worked unavailingly for a revision of
the Anglo-Irish Free Trade Agreement of 1948, which by the terms of the Agreement
should have been revised by 1959. It was not until 1965 under the Labour government
that the Irish secured a new and satisfactory trade agreement.

Within the I.R.A., the campaign against Charlie Murphy reached a poisonous
intensity, and Myles Shevlin tried to heal the rift at a meeting in Monasterevan,
Co. Kildare, on Spy Wednesday, April, 1959. Everyone reacted amicably and
parted friendly but nothing came of the meeting. In fact for a time relations got
worse when, after the June convention the Murphy wing, having failed to secure
his elevation and the overthrow of the 'pacifists', resolved to carry out border raids
on its own and commandeered weapons from the 'official' I.R.A. These were
given back after Cronin informed O'Toole that his section had a series of
operations planned along the border. When Murphy heard this he realised that the
situation was drifting not towards war against the North, but towards war within
the I.R.A. and he ordered that the captured weapons be handed back.

Charge and counter-charge flew with the dum-dum destructiveness of character that the Irish can so well employ. When Murphy tried to clear his name by calling for an inquiry the report praised Murphy with faint damns in such a way as neither to make the past forgettable nor the future attractive. Murphy resigned and entered a black period of self-doubt, financial stringency and readjustment. Throughout this time the kindness of Sean MacBride was one of the things that kept him sane. Murphy's wife Carmel worked as a waitress and he was taken back by the Guinness brewery. He and Carmel became the most law abiding and popular members of their suburban community, devoting their energies to nothing more revolutionary than residents' association and bring-and-buy sales. Myles Shevlin and Thomas MacCurtain also parted with the movement shortly after the Monasterevan meeting and Sean Cronin was made the subject of an inquiry after allegations of Communism were directed against him. The inquiry found no substance in the allegations but Cronin too resigned from the army. He is now a successful journalist in America.

During all this time blood was still being shed. On July 2, 1958, a police patrol fired on an I.R.A. patrol near Clontivern, Co. Fermanagh, and killed the column leader, Aloysius Hand, a twenty-year-old unemployed labourer. He had a loaded Thompson gun, and according to the evidence given at the inquest had fired two bursts before the R.U.C. shot. A verdict of justifiable homicide was returned.

Later on July 15, 16 and 17 the campaign flared up all along the border in the major show of activity since its inception in December, 1956. Explosions took place from Down to Derry, resulting in two deaths, a number of injuries and some destruction to customs huts and to bridges.

The first death was deliberate. Constable H. B. Ross, Forkhill, was cycling through Moircastle on the south Armagh border when an electrically triggered mine was detonated from behind a hedge. Although he was badly injured he managed to walk to a nearby house to wait for an ambulance. He died in hospital the next day leaving a wife and child. The second death was caused by the I.R.A.'s faulty bomb-making. Patrick MacManus, twenty-seven, the principal I.R.A. leader at liberty in the North was removing a gelignite mine, made in a biscuit box, from a cache on the roadside at Drumask, Co. Cavan, when it went off, blowing him to pieces. The physical damage wrought in this short-lived offensive ranged from the destruction of the biggest customs post between North and South, the Killeen post on the main Dundalk-Belfast road, which was wrecked, to craters blown in unapproved roads.

One particularly distasteful killing occurred on August 24, 1958: the shooting of James Crossan by the R.U.C. in ambiguous circumstances at the customs post at Mullan, Co. Fermanagh.

The I.R.A. claimed that Crossan was murdered and this is how his death is described in its roll of honour. The R.U.C. said in a statement that 'the suspicions of a police patrol on duty near the British Customs post at Mullan, Co. Fermanagh, were aroused by persons approaching the post from the direction of Eire. Police called on these persons to halt, whereupon they bolted towards the Border . . . They again called on them to halt. One man stopped but the others continued running. Police opened fire and later . . . the dead body of a young man was found. The other man, who like the dead man is a native of Eire, has been detained.'

However a statement from 'An Enniskillen correspondent', in the *Irish Press* said,

'Crossan and McHugh parted from three Fermanagh friends, two of them Unionists, on the Fermanagh side of the Border at Mullan at about 3.30 a.m. The three Fermanagh friends drove off in a van towards Kinawley and the two Cavan men were walking back again to another van which had brought the five to the Cavan [Southern] side of the Border when Mr Crossan was shot dead by Six County police who had taken up positions near the Customs hut.'

At the inquest a verdict of justifiable homicide was returned and this was met by an indignant press release from the I.R.A. saying that '. . . James Crossan was unarmed. The suggestion that he and Ben McHugh were on a reconnaissance mission at Mullan British Customs post is ridiculous.'

While 1960 was uneventful, 1961 began and ended with deaths, and of all the deaths of the campaign these are the least defensible. Public support for the 'physical force' policy had been falling away and this, combined with new political proccupations and new political figures and philosophies that greatly improved the standard of living in the South pushed the whole border question well into the background. (In the general election of 1961, Sinn Fein lost all four seats and its poll fell by over 50 per cent.)

Nevertheless the militants struck again. On January 27, 1961, a young R.U.C. man, Corporal Norman Anderson, was taken up a lane shortly after he had said goodnight to his sweetheart, and thirty-four bullets were shot into his back. The I.R.A. believed that he had been spying on its movements. In the wake of condemnation, South and North, the I.R.A. pulled in its horns for the summer, but on November 12, a police patrol was ambushed at Jonesborough, Co. Armagh, and another policeman, Constable William Hunter, was shot dead. There were protests from Belfast, from the British government and from Dublin and the Southern government decided to act.

On November 22, it was announced that the government was setting up the Special Criminal Court again. The court was composed of army officers and there was no doubt that the government, and in particular the new minister for justice, Charles Haughey, a young man who had come to the fore after the 1961 election, were determined to take the most drastic measures to scotch not alone the campaign but also the I.R.A. at the next possible opportunity. The I.R.A. decided not to give them that opportunity.

On February 26, 1962, the Irish Republican Publicity Bureau announced that:

'The Leadership of the Resistance Movement has ordered the termination of "The Campaign of Resistance to British Occupation" . . . all arms and other materials have been dumped and all full-time active service volunteers have been withdrawn.'

The statement added that one factor responsible for the decision had been the attitude of the public, 'whose minds have been deliberately distracted from the supreme issue facing the Irish people—the unity and freedom of Ireland'. Another juncture had been reached in Irish history in which it appeared that the I.R.A. were finished once and for all.

15

New Initiatives: 1962–70

After the campaign ended the dissension within the ranks of the Republicans continued. The dispute centred upon who should control the Republican movement henceforth and again the situation resembled that at the end of the Civil War. The 'physical force' men had been beaten; disillusion and depression had set in; scapegoats had to be found, and there was no clear leadership.

Eamonn Boyce is an example of what I.R.A. men were like at the time and of what they encountered. Boyce emerged from prison to find that his mother had suffered through the loss of his income and through helping his colleagues. She had slept for months with several hundredweights of gelignite under her bed, worried by his absence and the presence of the explosives and, as Boyce said, 'wondering where she got the headaches'. Eventually he found a job as a bus conductor, but first he had to master his nerves so that he could cross a road unaided, make a simple purchase in a shop, sign on at a Labour Exchange, or do any of the normal things which prison keeps a man from doing. Many of Boyce's comrades decided they could take no more and dropped out of the movement completely. Patrick MacLogan was found dead in his back garden with a revolver beside him, causing allegations and counter-allegations in the I.R.A. as to how he died.

Gradually, after 1964 the movement began to build itself up again, and a Republican debating society, the Wolfe Tone Society, became popular in circles outside the I.R.A. The most significant single individual was perhaps Roy Johnston, a young Marxist computer scientist who became so trusted by the I.R.A. leaders that he was appointed to the Army Council as a kind of education officer cum political commissar. Under his influence I.R.A. policy moved steadily left. The absence of a strong ideological grounding (apart from the crusading to end partition by force) made this a relatively easy process, at least at leadership level; among the grass-roots members and those of a right-wing cast of mind the new developments were worrying.

In 1965 the political arm of the movement, Sinn Fein, announced that it would continue to sit on local government bodies but would also continue to boycott Stormont, the Dail and Westminster. However the party decided, somewhat paradoxically, that in the event of Sinn Fein winning an over-all majority, which would enable it to take over the Dail, the party would do so: constitutionalism, too, was growing during this period. In the North Sean McCaughey, who had been a vice-president of Sinn Fein, resigned and concentrated on building up an Irish union movement along much the same lines as Denis Ireland's efforts of the 1940s. Helped by the emotionalism of the 1916 anniversary celebrations in 1966 Sinn Fein increased its strength, openly in the South and in the North under the guise of Republican clubs. At the 1966 Ard Fheis Sinn Fein was pledged by its president, Tomas McGoilla, to an effort to win a majority in the Dail within five years. At Bodenstown in 1967 Cathal Goulding made his speech in favour of socialist policies and decried the movement's concentration on the 'physical force' policy found in the writings of Dan Breen.

But the activist tradition inevitably re-emerged and throughout 1966 several incidents and bombings took place, the most celebrated being the destruction of Nelson's Pillar. One young Republican, Richard Behal, in jail in Limerick on charges arising out of a visit to Ireland by Princess Margaret, made a dramatic escape at midnight on New Year's Eve 1966, and for the greater part of the year, on the run from both the left-wing I.R.A. and the Special Branch, was openly associated with some of these incidents. Another group of Republicans which favoured the use of force began to coalesce into what became known as the Saor Eire Action Group and this took a hand at bank raids. Between 1967 and mid-April 1970 either it or the I.R.A. carried out seventeen bank raids. In the last, disavowed by the official I.R.A., a garda was killed.

Throughout this period the *United Irishman* struck up a medley of Fenian and Marxist airs despite the fact that there were rumblings from Clann na Gael in America that the leftward swing was not to its liking. In England the movement made some ground by dropping the title Sinn Fein and trying to amalgamate all the various emigre Irish parties and associations under the banner of a new grouping: Clann na hEireann, 'the family of Gaels'. In Dublin the Republicans' greatest success in terms of publicity was the sponsorship of the Dublin Housing Action Committee, a body which existed independently of the I.R.A. to do something for Dublin's homeless. The I.R.A. put muscle into its demonstrations and sit-ins, and in the country also, wherever disputes arose over small farmers seeking to have large estates broken up, the I.R.A. became active in land leagues. Foreigners who owned land in Ireland or who held Irish ground-rents were singled out for verbal and sometimes physical attack. In May, 1968, the I.R.A. burned out £60,000 worth of buses used to take workers to a factory owned by an American company, the E.I. Company of Shannon, during a dispute over union recognition. In the west, in Rossaveal on the Connemara coast, a £6,000 fishing boat owned by an American-financed company was wrecked in August by an I.R.A. bomb, and in June, 1969, a number of buildings on farms owned by Germans were set alight.

But the I.R.A.'s most significant initiative was its behind-the-scenes involvement in the Northern Civil Rights movement. The broad-based Civil Rights movement, which captured the world's headlines, began appropriately enough in the fiftieth anniversary year of 1916 with a private meeting of interested parties in Derry at the home of a prominent Derry Republican, Kevin Agnew, a solicitor, in August, 1966, and a public meeting the following November in Belfast. Cathal Goulding attended the Derry meeting and while he said frankly that he did not think it would work, he pledged the I.R.A. to give it a trial. When the North of Ireland Civil Rights Association was officially founded in Belfast at a meeting in the International Hotel on January 29, 1967, the broad-based Committee of 13 which was founded to run the movement included, apart from a number of communists, trade unionists and reform-minded individuals such as Dr Con McCluskey, both Agnew and two Wolfe Tone Society Representatives as treasurer and P.R.O., Fred Heatley and Jack Bennett. The association worked brilliantly: Unionist spokesmen continually thundered that C.R.A. (Civil Rights Association) was only another way of saying I.R.A., but never a shot was fired, never an I.R.A. man showed himself as such and the I.R.A. deserves some of the credit for the great success of the Civil Rights movement, although politically it got swallowed by it much as it did in Fianna Fail's success in 1932.

As the Civil Rights movement spread figures such as John Hume, Ivan Cooper, Gerry Fitt and Bernadette Devlin came to national and then international prominence and the radical movement, People's Democracy, received much publicity. Behind the scenes, however, many older Republicans of the generation of 1940 disagreed violently with the passive resistance policy. The idea of going up to a policeman at a barricade and allowing him to baton one into the ground without any attempt at retaliation was common ground with the Southern opponents of the socialist policy generally but all criticism was stifled by the enormous publicity the Civil Rights movement received after October 5, 1968. Then a peaceful march in Derry was batonned by the R.U.C. and there began the decline into anarchy, the erosion of respect for the R.U.C. as an impartial force and the build-up of Protestant feeling which on August 2, 1969, made of the Apprentice Boys' march in Derry a torch that very nearly lit a powder keg in all Ireland.

As Protestant passions mounted, inside Stormont hardline Unionists such as William Craig began to rail against Prime Minister Terence O'Neill and his policy of liberal Unionism and a gradualistic approach to friendship with Dublin. Unconstitutional leaders and movements began to make themselves felt on the Protestant side. The Ulster Volunteer Force was heard of again and in May, 1969, a group of I.R.A. leaders in Belfast became worried enough at the build-up of Protestant strength and emotion that it went to Dublin to ask the Army Council for large supplies of arms without delay.

The request was not granted. In the first place the I.R.A. had become almost de-militarised—most of its weapons had been sold to Welsh nationalists—and was vir-tually without funds. (The *United Irishman* was only saved by an emergency appeal for money.) To have given the few arms at its disposal to Belfast would have left the I.R.A. in the South unarmed. Then too, in the event of weapons being discovered in the North, the work for the Civil Rights movement would have been discredited and a stick given to Stormont to beat the I.R.A. out into the open from behind its facade of Republican clubs. Moreover, Belfast had not distinguished itself during the border campaign and the conversion to militancy did not wholly convince the Dublin leaders. The Northerners went away unhappy and from then on there were suggestions that a separate Northern Command be formed.

On August 12 the Apprentice Boys were allowed to hold their traditional march in Derry despite warnings that this could lead to a bloodbath. In the event, the procession passed off peaceably enough but eventually, maddened by the provocations of some Catholic hooligans who had been pelting them with stones, the R.U.C. instead of being withdrawn from the Bogside area baton-charged its assailants and hurled stones back at them. Batons and bricks failed to dislodge the Bogsiders from behind their barricades and, for several days, there was enacted another siege of Derry. This time history was reversed and the Catholic defenders withstood the Protestant onslaught.

In Dublin the prime minister was Jack Lynch, a quiet, pipe-smoking Corkman who had never shown himself a militant in any sense. He had continued the hands-across-the-border policy initiated by his predecessor, Sean Lemass, visiting Stormont and being entertained by O'Neill, and having O'Neill on a return visit to Dublin. But Lynch now escalated the partition issue to a plane it had not reached since the days of the treaty debates. Speaking mildly, with sincerity in his voice and a haggard look about the eyes, he went on television to announce that he had moved units of the Irish army up to the border and was opening field hospitals so that people injured in the Bogside battles could be treated without fear of being reported to the R.U.C. Refugee centres were set up in military installations in the South.

London was immediately forced to take notice of a situation which raised the spectre of Irish troops being engaged against British forces. In Belfast the news was received with fear and horror by Protestant extremists and rioting broke out in which millions of pounds worth of property and some lives were lost. Whether the rioting would have come anyway as a result of the summer's build-up of tension and the fighting in Derry or whether the Irish government's action precipitated it will always be arguable but, once and for all, it forced the British government to take the most decisive action it had taken on the North of Ireland since the creation of the state itself. British troops poured into the North and British politicians poured in after them; a spate of commissions and tribunals ensued, and the British government guaranteed, publicly, that all the reforms sought by the Civil Rights movement would be conceded and, privately, that if the government of Major Chichester Clarke, who had succeeded O'Neill, fell, there would be no further Northern government. Westminster would take over.

It seemed for a moment that in one year the Civil Rights movement had done more to end injustice than fifty years of anti-partition policies had begun to do. Where was the I.R.A. during all this? Apparently not there at all as an organised body. As far as can be reasonably ascertained, approximately six Republicans took to the streets of Belfast during the rioting which broke out after August 12 to defend the catholic areas. One of these, at least, was a middle-aged man who had not been active since the 1940s. He somewhere got a tommy-gun and for his exploits that night has forever earned himself an honoured place in the hearts of Belfast Catholics. There seems little doubt that had the handful of I.R.A. men not been present, Orange mobs led by B-Specials would have burned the Falls Road to the ground and, with it, every Catholic family which did not flee. But this circumstance, much as it may have redounded to the credit of the individuals concerned, redounded very badly indeed on the I.R.A.'s public image.

The principal public activity of the I.R.A. during this period was to issue a ridiculous statement claiming that units of the I.R.A. were active in the North and ready to take any and every action, short of throwing the British Crown into the Thames, in the defence of Catholics and liberation of the North. It did nothing except bolster the charges by hard-line Unionists that the C.R.A. and the I.R.A. were identical. Relations between Belfast and Dublin reached their nadir.

Republicans congregated in farmhouses along the border waiting for arms from Dublin that never came and once again the Northern I.R.A. decided to act on its own and the plan for a Northern Command began to take shape. Distraught Republicans began scurrying around the country to lay hands on weapons to give to the desperate Catholics—with sometimes bizarre results. A Dublin Capuchin monk, for instance, gave five rounds of revolver bullets and a Dominican dressed five I.R.A. men as priests to enable them to get into Belfast undetected.

Concomitant with the I.R.A. troop movements, the Irish government mounted an ill-advised publicity campaign to draw world attention to the partition issue, a campaign which recalled the anti-partition efforts of 1948. The government also appealed to the United Nations, through Irish Foreign Minister Dr Patrick Hillery, where he made a seemingly strong effort (at the time the Irish army had only enough ammunition for 72 hours' firing) to get a U.N. presence into the North. For a time the Americans were sympathetic but the British mounted what an Arab delegate told me during a subsequent visit to the U.N. was the 'strongest diplomatic offensive of their history since Suez' and swayed the Americans with the argument: 'This is a Civil Rights issue, domestic to the U.K. You have Civil Rights issues too, domestically (Martin Luther King was still alive and marching). If international observers are admitted to the U.K.'s domestic affairs a precedent will have been set and you will have U.N. observers, possibly Russians and Chinese, in Selma . . . do you want that?'

Shudderingly, the U.S. said it did not want that and, debating from a position of having to because of the sudden eruption rather than because of long-felt, planned-for conviction, the Irish were not altogether displeased to let the issue slip having been seen to raise it honourably and loudly—Ireland was after all applying for an E.E.C. membership for which Britain's support would one day be essential, even though a prime reason for joining was to gain more independence of Britain economically and hence politically.

In fact, subsequently, though Ireland did take Britain to the Court of Human Rights it is arguable that her preoccupation with the problems and prosperity of E.E.C. membership, its fat subsidy for farmers, its butter mountains, M.C.A.s and wine lakes, fish quotas and the rest of it, did distract Ireland's relatively small Foreign Affairs Department and her decision makers in the cabinet from concentrating on the North. As the main thrust of government policy swung towards Europe and international investment, away from the old catch cries about 'reintegration of the national territories' arguments about de jure and de facto recognition and so on, one sometimes got the impression that the baby of interest in the North was thrown out along with the bathwater of shibboleth.

But this is to anticipate. Along with the U.N. initiatives some of Lynch's colleagues reportedly began taking more private and unconventional initiatives. Allegedly some of the arms which began to find their way to the North did so as a result of a prominent Fianna Fail politician's action and at one stage there were rumours of £50,000 being paid to the I.R.A. But this referred to the total cost of an arms shipment in the international market and, I am told, only approximately £2,300 was paid to the I.R.A. for arms purchases to assist the Northern Catholics. Catholics could also receive training in the Donegal area and at some of the military centres set up in the South for refugees. Reports that six Irish army officers were sent across the border to co-ordinate Citizens' Defence Committees, again with Republican co-operation, circulated in Dublin.

Certainly the Fianna Fail government appeared to speak at times with two voices on the North. Two ministers in particular, Neil T. Blaney and Kevin Boland, took harder attitudes than did Lynch. Boland laid the continuing blame on Britain and Blaney repeatedly said that the use of force was not ruled out on the part of the Irish government as a means of ending partition. Rumours that some of Lynch's colleagues had not wished him to stop short of the border but to push on to Derry gained currency; but on December 28 Lynch gave a very frank radio interview in which he said that he had had a 'firm chat' with Blaney. 'He understands,' Lynch said, 'that the members of the government must adhere to government policy. In fact, he does.'

Whether this broadcast had anything to do with governmental policy towards the I.R.A. is a matter of conjecture, but it is a fact that six Derry youths who had been training openly under arms near Buncrana, Co. Donegal, were suddenly arrested in early January, 1970, charged under the Firearms Act and lodged in prison in Dublin before being released under the Probation Act. Despite this leniency the arrests were clearly designed to indicate that the blind-eye policy regarding drilling was at an end and Lynch won a thunderous ovation at the Fianna Fail Ard Fheis on January 18 when he again ruled out force, challenged anybody (his audience included Blaney and Boland) to oppose him, refused to allow organising for Fianna Fail in the North and said frankly that the South would have to recognise the fact that the majority of the North's inhabitants wanted to remain linked with Britain.

Exactly one week before Lynch's speech the Republican movement had split down the middle in a crisis that was as public and almost as damaging as that which led to the formation of Fianna Fail itself. The stated issue was the recognition of the 'partition parliaments' of Dublin, Stormont and Westminster. The I.R.A. had held a secret convention in mid-December which had voted 39 to 12 in favour of recognition and the Sinn Fein Ard Fheis meeting (in the incongruous surroundings of the American-financed Intercontinental Hotel) was supported to do likewise and give Sinn Fein a mandate to oppose foreign investment and set about the 'reconquest of Ireland, shop by shop and factory by factory'. There seemed little doubt that the Ard Fheis would give the required two-thirds majority.

A commission set up by the 1968 Ard Fheis to examine the movement and make recommendations as to its future had circulated a report, 'Ireland Today', in March, 1969 saying that there was no need for the leadership of Sinn Fein and the I.R.A. to be amalgamated as 'the present degree of mutual understanding of overall policy and strategy renders any such amalgamation unnecessary'. The usual overlapping of membership had occurred and many of those who had voted to recognise the parliaments at the I.R.A. convention were highly placed on the Sinn Fein executive.

News of the I.R.A. vote was leaked to the press and the *Sunday Press* carried the story two weeks after the convention, on December 28. The report helped to crystallise opposition to the new policies. The March document had recommended that 'all embargoes on political participation in parliament be removed from the Constitution and Rules of both bodies [Sinn Fein and I.R.A.]', but this was accompanied by a directive 'that the undermining of confidence in existing parliaments and eventual abstention from them in order to establish an alternative form of government must be a major objective of the movement'. Now, however, it was out in the public press that Sinn Fein was going to recognise the 'partition parliaments' without any provisos. A new 'provisional' Army Council was set up and various I.R.A. units and Sinn Fein bodies around the country gave the 'provisional' council their allegiance. These groups included important figures such as Tom Maguire, John Joe Sheehy and eighty-nine-year-old Joe Clarke, who fought in 1916. By the time the crucial vote was taken at the Ard Fheis on January 11, the traditionalists had so rallied their forces that the proposal to abandon the abstentionist policy was only carried by 153 votes to 104, less than the required two-thirds majority. There may have been other, deeper motives behind the proposals to enter parliament. The 'Ireland Today' document posed the possibility of a link-up with the Southern Irish Communist Party and, interestingly enough, in mid-March the Southern and Northern Communist Parties completed a merger at a meeting attended by several Russian journalists. The idea of a 'National Liberation Front' had come very close to giving Moscow a voice in an Irish national movement for the first time in history.

Far from agreeing on the 'creation of the National Liberation Front' called for by the March policy document, Sinn Fein was as split as ever it was. The 'Provisional Army Council' had brought out its own newspaper, *An Phoblacht*, and it was hard to prophesy what the future held.

The I.R.A. tradition is one of physical action and separatism. It is not an intellectual one, which is why I have carefully refrained from discussing events or personalities which some historians might feel were influential in the Republican story: the constitution of 1937 or the declaration of a Republic in Ireland in 1948, for examples on the political side, or the writings of Sean O'Faolain or of Brendan Behan on the literary one. These are not important to Republicans of the 'physical force' school. Deaths, commemorations, holding firm with the past—these are and will be the preoccupations that nourish the I.R A.

For those who think of this as a cheerless prospect, let me quote a letter (published in the *Irish Press*, November 6, 1969) to his mother from Conor Lynch, son of a prominent I.R.A. man of the 1930s, who had just received a seven-year sentence in England.

'Cheer up, Mother,' he wrote. 'It could have been worse, I could have got seven years and a month.'

Part II
1969–1979

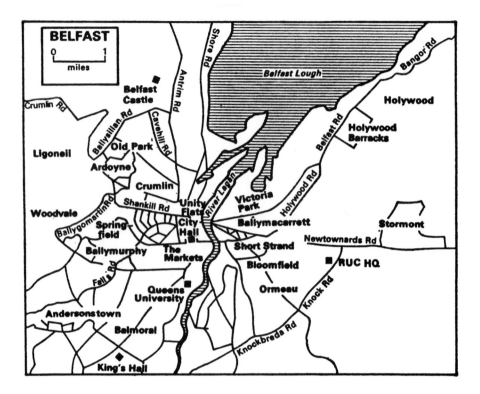

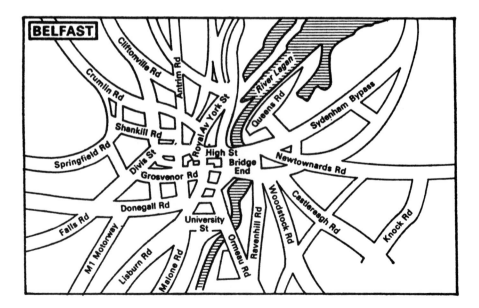

16

The Roots of the Conflict

How did the blackened, almost unarmed and certainly very largely discredited I.R.A. resurrect itself to become a national force moving the North of Ireland issue to the fore throughout all the dismaying events of the 1970s? At the time of the I.R.A.'s initial regrouping following the setting up of the Provisional Caretaker Executive, I met an I.R.A. friend who had been picking up the threads of family and business life but now appeared to be going downhill again through becoming involved in I.R.A. activities. As he told me both of his hardships in the past and of what he was doing at that time, I remember saying to him: 'Eamon, you are mad! You have done your bit for your cause and now you risk wrecking your own happiness and everyone else's to join a splinter of a splinter group.' For that was how most people in Southern Ireland would certainly have described the I.R.A. in the early part of 1970; but as it happened I was both completely right and totally wrong. My friend did undergo terrible traumas but the I.R.A. blossomed into one of the major guerilla organisations to emerge since World War II.

Events moved at two levels—the constitutional and the paramilitary. They also moved in a number of different arenas, in a way that makes understanding very difficult. Let us, nevertheless, make a start by taking the constitutional level as it affected the major actors in the drama in London, Belfast and Dublin.

The catalyst in Northern Ireland was the Civil Rights movement—though the British Education Acts also contributed by ensuring that in the ranks of this movement there would be several young men and women equally, if not better, educated than their Unionist opponents, and well able to hold their own on television and in political techniques. But these factors were compounded by the particularly obdurate type of resistance with which the Unionist hierarchy and those who wished to join it—or control it—like the Rev. Ian Paisley, met the Civil Rights demands.

It is hardly an over-simplification to say that the Catholics were forced off the streets into the arms of the I.R.A. who were subsequently maintained in their recruiting by the activities both of the Protestant paramilitary mirror organisations which grew up to combat the I.R.A. and of the British army.

Yet while all the old wounds of Irish history were re-opened by the contemporary political situation and the bloody conflict began, it became clear that no side had enough strength to deliver the knock-out punch necessary to achieve its aims.

The strongest partner in the dilemma was the British government. Yet though it had an army, large resources and a native 'Ulster security force' at its disposal, it could never hope entirely to exterminate the I.R.A., for the following reasons:

1. *The high birth rate* in the Catholic ghettos of Belfast, Derry and elsewhere.

2. *The supply of money and guns* from America and later, to some degree, training, weapons and money from the Arab States.

3. *The support generated for the I.R.A. by events*: the growth of the Civil Rights movement, the Falls Road curfew of July, 1970, the unilateral introduction of internment in August, 1971, when no Protestants were interned, stimulated the Catholic population to extend a far greater degree of support to the I.R.A. than had existed at any time since the end of the Anglo-Irish War of 1916–21 and arguably even during it. This support, which probably peaked in 1972 when Stormont fell, suffered many rises and falls but never wholly disappeared. It is arguable whether tradition, fear, the need for protection against sectarian assassinations, or the popularity generated by I.R.A. activity itself through daring raids, spectacular exploits, dramatic hunger strikes and so on was the stronger reinforcement of this support.

4. *British policy*: this was certainly hard to overestimate in terms of its benefit to the I.R.A. For although the troops entered Derry and Belfast as 'saviours', it might have been predicted that the troops would inevitably be drawn into conflict with the civilian population—given the nature of armies, and the fact that as soon as it had mustered itself into any semblance of organisation the I.R.A. did its utmost to make pariahs of the soldiers and to turn the population against them. The army, to be an effective impartial peacekeeping force, should have been briefed to counteract this. But the army seems to have been unnecessarily psyched up against the situation—for instance, the Sinn Fein 'oath' in Chapter 17 of this book was reproduced from the first edition as the genuine article in the manual issued to every soldier who came to Northern Ireland. The manual was withdrawn from circulation and the 'oath' deleted after I published the manual's contents in the *Irish Press*.

Not only the troops and police warders, but British personnel generally seemed either to have a natural antipathy for the Irish or to have been indoctrinated against them. I remember a young Protestant ex-warder at Long Kesh telling me why he left the prison service. 'I don't like the "Ra" [I.R.A.],' he said. 'You see that "knuckle",' he said, showing me his hand—'I broke that on a Ra man's head one day. But I'd always use my hands and I'd never hit a man unless I had to. But you should hear the way the fellows over from England talk. "The Paddys", they call us Protestants and Catholics. They treat the prisoners like scum. They'd use boots, batons, anything. They sickened me, and I got out.'

There were and are many individual exceptions; soldiers and police who tried to understand the people and involve themselves in helping the community. But where these were not regarded with outright suspicion and hatred as potential spies, they came up against the inevitable 'them' and 'us' syndrome which a young soldier from Dublin encountered one night when he stopped a Belfast architect of my acquaintance at a roadblock and tried to show his friendliness towards him while going through the motions of searching his car. He was coldly rebuffed. 'But,' he tried, 'I'm one of you. I'm a Catholic—from Dublin.'

'Your bullets are just as hard,' said the architect.

Thus the way in which the police and military assessed the situation was a key element—one which affected not only the decision to opt for internment or to impose the Falls Road curfew but other vital happenings in the province.

For instance, the internment swoop was seen solely as an anti-Republican and Catholic measure to be carried out in the same spirit and against the same type of foe as it had been in the 1950s. Accordingly no Protestants were seized although there was a litany of criminal activity on that side of the fence visible for all to see—if they wanted to see. (The first killings of any sort, the Malvern Street murder, the first explosion and the first constable killed in the North, Constable Arbuckle, were all carried out by Protestants.) Moreover the Catholics who were locked up for the most part had little or nothing to do with the I.R.A., a fact which, magnified by the ill-treatment the internees received, did however considerably boost the I.R.A.'s support.

The Bloody Sunday massacre of January 30, 1972, when British paratroopers fired on one unarmed Civil Rights procession through Derry was another example of the British lack of understanding of the overall situation. Thirteen people were shot dead and, in the countrywide wave of indignation which followed, the British Embassy in Dublin was burned down. The subsequent inquiry by Lord Widgery (published on April 19, 1972) into the shootings exonerated the paratroopers whose basic case was that they thought they were in danger of their lives, shots having been fired at them. However, no one else in Derry that day, including some journalist eyewitnesses of the calibre of Simon Winchester, then of the *Guardian*, heard any shots until the army began firing. Nor was it ever explained why the army viewed that particular march with such anticipation. It was banned in advance, and was therefore technically illegal, but this in itself would not explain the heavy concentration of top military figures present in Derry that day, nor the type of orders the soldiers were evidently acting on. On the evidence it would appear that either the army simply wanted to teach the natives a lesson or that they were given a heightened and misleading impression of what was likely to happen.

Less publicised outside the country but still of invaluable benefit to I.R.A. propaganda was the tactic of road cratering in border areas which the army initiated on October 11, 1971. As a measure aimed at diminishing guerilla activity it was like damming a stream with palings. Moreover British statistics put the total number of border incidents (out of the total number of violent acts since the trouble began) at 3 per cent by September of 1979. What the cratering was meant to achieve in 1971 is beyond belief.

Another circumstance affecting the troops' morale and behaviour was the fact that they were left to find a military solution, in a society divided by hate, to a problem which was essentially political. Their responses to I.R.A. provocations were military ones, invariably involving and alienating anti-I.R.A. members of the Catholic community so that they soon became pro-. It's just not possible to fire C.S. canisters down narrow teeming streets and affect only I.R.A. lungs.

But instead of being reined in while the politicians got down to sorting out the mess, the troops were left to blunder forward. The result was a morass of brutality, and propaganda fodder—kicked-down doors, ripped-up floorboards, beaten-up young men and, worse, occasional bursts of ill-directed rifle fire that claimed civilian life and helped on the one hand eventually to land Britain before the European Court of Human Rights and on the other to build up the I.R.A.'s strength. In the crucial formative period of 1970–1, the man directly responsible for Northern Ireland was Reginald Maudling. He did absolutely nothing to halt the drift into anarchy and is chiefly remembered for a remark he made on leaving Belfast in an aeroplane after inspecting his new field of responsibility: 'Christ,' he said calling for a large Scotch, 'what a bloody awful country.'

The result of the June, 1970, election was the cause of the initial series of disasters which gave the Provisionals strength through placing power in the weak and faltering hands of Maudling. The Labour handling of the province during the later part of the decade does not entitle one to believe that ultimately they would have been any more effective in their handling of the situation, given the way things turned out. But it was the Conservatives whose policy first helped to make events happen as they did.

Under Labour the army was considerably restricted in its operations, the Minister of Defence at Westminster, Roy Hattersley, keeping a day-to-day check on army operations such as their use of the water cannons in crowd control. And the Unionist squirarchy and its bigotry was becoming increasingly distasteful to the Labour Cabinet in which James Callaghan was one of the most powerful advocates of a 'seize them neck and crop' attitude to the Unionists—by suspending Stormont, for instance.

However, the Tories were, apart from Maudling's lack of drive, encumbered by the traditional relationship with the Unionists so that the army was allowed to fall from an impartial role of peacekeeping between Protestant and Catholic to one of implementing Unionist-inspired policy. Heath was eventually to become highly disenchanted with Brian Faulkner, in particular after his advice on internment proved to be disastrous. In fact he said openly (in an interview with Shirley Williams on B.B.C. TV) that it was Faulkner's attitude on security which caused him to suspend Stormont. (Faulkner wanted to retain control over the R.U.C. in Unionist hands.) But this was two years further on. By then the damage was done and the Provisional I.R.A. was a full-fledged fearsome reality. It may well be that no single change in British governmental policy or party can accurately be blamed for what happened. For while the North and all that happened there for fifty years was ultimately Britain's responsibility the sudden quickening of events there with the growth of the Civil Rights movement and the reaction to it simply took all parties to the problem, North and South, and in England by surprise and Britain as the controlling power had no policy either to hand or in prospect with which to meet the erupting situation.

As one of the best pieces of insight* into the whole decade illustrated, Stormont was an 'Ultima Thule' to decision-taking London where practically no one that counted had the faintest idea as to the background or direction of events, and it took an appreciable time for London to discount the theory which was hitherto dogma, that anything which happened in 'Ulster' came under the sole purview of Stormont. It took even longer to acknowledge that Dublin had any

---

* 'Ulster', by the Insight team of the *Sunday Times*, London, 1972.

say in the matter. When the then Foreign Minister, Dr Patrick Hillery, drove up to see the aftermath of the Falls Road curfew there was outrage in the British press at this outsider's presumption!

By Wednesday, September 10, 1969, the most tangible evidence—apart from the presence of soldiers—of the army's activities in Belfast was the 'peace-line', a mile-and-a-half-long line of fencing composed of strips of corrugated iron stretching from Cupar Street (in the Falls) to Coates Street and allegedly partitioning Catholic areas from Protestant so that neither side could slip through to strike at the other. In real terms it was about as effective as the Border road-cratering policy and the 'line' has become rusted and obviously ineffective. A fitting piece of symbolism for the decade of army involvement.

5. *Reform policy*: though reform was introduced, often with a genuine desire on the part of a wide section of British public opinion (if not of some decision-taking mandarins in Whitehall) to do something possible about the problem, these changes were like firing sticking plaster to a broken limb.

This point deserves examination in some detail, especially as in Ireland, in a situation of tremendous political passion, events of profound significance have often been masked by more exciting, but ultimately far less important happenings. For example in 1920 the Government of Ireland Act was passed. Few Nationalists of the time, preoccupied as they were with the course of the Anglo-Irish war, saw this Act for what it was—permanent statutory recognition by the British of the strength of Unionist and Conservative politicians. For the rest of Ireland the notion that a once-universal Protestant domination of Ireland should be ceded from the Crown to Catholic and Nationalist control was now becoming an inevitable part of political philosophy.

Not surprisingly, during the next fifty years Unionist hegemony, deriving from the 1920 Act, offered very little in the way of democracy to the Catholics, and Britain did equally little to ensure that it should.

Now, in August, 1969, as the Catholics protested against their situation in a new Civil Rights fashion to the tune and inspiration of 'We Shall Overcome' rather than 'The Soldier's Song', Britain too seemed to be moving in a new way to redress old grievances. Harold Wilson, the British Prime Minister, met the North of Ireland Prime Minister, James Chichester-Clarke, a cousin of Terence O'Neill, who had fallen in the uproar of Unionist and in particular Paisleyite disapproval of his reformist policies. Following the meeting (on August 20), Wilson drafted and issued the Downing Street Declaration.

This stated that Catholics were to become equal under the law; local government was to be democratised; and housing was to be re-allocated. But, and it was a very big 'but' to the Unionist mind, anything in the way of a fair share for a Catholic meant less of a share for a Unionist—and a possible weakening of his privileged position derived, as he saw it, from and through his cherished link with England.

The Joint Communiqué pledged itself to reform in three major areas thereby, of course, implicitly forcing a Stormont administration to admit publicly that such reform was needed. The three areas were:

(i)   the fair allocation of house by public authorities;
(ii) the avoidance of any discrimination in any form of public employment; and
(iii) the promotion of good community relations by methods including the
      prohibition of incitement to religious hatred

Some of the disabilities Catholics laboured under were physical, i.e. jobs and housing, and some had a legal and psychological effect—though these could have an acutely physical outcome also, as, for instance, in the operation of the Flags and Emblems Act of 1954.

> The Flags and Emblems (Display) Act (Northern Ireland) 1954 'gives special pro-
> tection to the occupier of land or premises who wishes to display a Union Jack. It is
> an offence to prevent or threaten forcibly to interfere with such display. In respect of
> other emblems any police officer may, if he apprehends a breach of the peace,
> require the person displaying the emblem to remove it, and in the event of failure to
> comply may enter the promises to remove and detain it. Failure to remove such
> emblems on police request constitutes an offence.'

The 'other emblems' referred to usually meant the tricolour which if displayed by a Catholic, say around St Patrick's Day or at election time, could be deemed an incitement to riot and supervision whereas the Union Jack had to be treated with respect even while its symbolism was visibly being misused so as to make of it a symbol of supremacy and injustice.

For instance one of the principal stepping stones in Paisley's rise to power was the 'Cromac Square' saga which began during the Westminster election of 1964 with Paisley holding a Union Jack leading a demonstration to the Catholic district of Cromac Square in West Belfast in protest against a tricolour being displayed in the window of a Republican candidate's election HQ. After days of riots and bus burnings the tricolour was eventually removed by the police, though it was acknowledged at the time that had Paisley not seized on the opportunity for self-publicity, very few people in Belfast would have known of the flag's existence and fewer taken offence at it. But once singled out, the law decreed that it was the display of the tricolour and not Paisley's opportunism which caused the disturbances.

Similarly the local government laws allowed the Unionists to pack the local bodies which allocated County Council housing so that there was blatant injustice and discrimination against Catholics in housing. Limited companies and occupiers of premises with a rateable valuation of £10 could appoint nominees—as could companies for each £10 of their valuations—under a system of plural voting, which even allowed such votes to be cast in another constituency (where Catholics might have a majority) so that the poorer Catholic community was in effect electorally disenfranchised.

The electoral laws were finally reformed (by the Electoral Act of 1968–9) and as a result of this and the lowering of the voting age to eighteen the local government electorate rose from 694,483 in 1967 to 1,031,694 in 1972, almost a 50 per cent increase. However, as we shall see, 1972 was one of the worst years in the history of the North and the benefit passed unheeded. Over fifty years of injustice had created a disease for which the cure had come too late.

One has to see the situation on the ground to understand how the Unionists used it to their own advantage. For instance, in Fermanagh and Derry, Civil Rights protesters could point to the fact that the numbers of Catholics exceeded those of Protestants yet the Protestants returned more representatives!

In Fermanagh, where the Catholic electorate for Stormont elections outnumbered Protestants by 29,400 votes to 23,500, the Unionists created three seats (Enniskillen, Lisnaskea, South Fermanagh) so that the first two areas lost much of their Catholic representation and a majority Catholic area returned two Unionists while the Catholics could only elect one Nationalist, in South Fermanagh. In local government elections the result was worse: the minority Unionist element managed to return twenty Unionists to only six Nationalists.

Derry city, which had 36,049 Catholics and 17,695 Protestants, was carved up so that it returned a Unionist.

The plural voting system which, of course, favoured the commercially dominant interests, coupled with the gerrymandering produced results which could be seen in their darkest colours in Derry where the Unionist managed so to arrange matters that their 9,235 electors returned twelve representatives whereas the 14,325 Nationalists could only return eight members.

Dungannon, which I mentioned at the outset as being a particularly black spot for violence during the troubles, was 53 per cent Catholic in 1969, yet returned fourteen Unionists as against only seven Nationalists (the electoral figures may not justify but they help one to understand the bombing statistics).

An article in the *Belfast Telegraph* on January 30, 1969, summed up the position thus: 'Roughly a quarter of the total adult population is denied a local council vote . . .'

This manipulation was not carried out for reasons of abstract political power— to maintain laws of significance to the Protestant conscience, for instance. It was intended to achieve a specific result in jobs and housing too.

For instance, again taking Dungannon, we find that a housing survey carried out by a team led by Austin Currie (January, 1968) discovered that between 1945 and 1968 the allocation of new houses to Protestants and Catholics on a percentage basis was Protestants 71 per cent, Catholics 28.9 per cent. It was no accident that the entire Civil Rights movement should have taken its rise in the Dungannon area, being led first by Dr Con McCluskey and his wife Patricia who compiled statistics on discrimination, and then receiving a tremendous impetus from a sit-in ordered by Austin Currie at Caledon—over the allocation of a house to the eighteen-year-old secretary of a prominent local Special who was jumped over a housing waiting list that included Catholic families with up to a dozen children.

In Derry at the time of the Civil Rights genesis, there were practically no Protestants unhoused whereas the younger, faster growing, majority Catholic population had 2,000 unhoused families.

In fact it was gerrymandering that caused the Unionists' downfall ultimately in Derry because the high-rise flats, which the Unionists had built to pen the Catholics into the Bogside area so that they could not spread out and dilute the Protestant vote, were the stronghold from which Catholic petrol bombers successfully withstood the charges of B-Specials and R.U.C. jointly trying to enter the area during the August, 1969, rioting that first brought the troops to Northern Ireland.

One could go on for pages itemising further instances of discrimination.

Sufficient to say that apart from its existence in private commercial firms or large-scale government-subsidised firms like the Harland and Wolff Shipping Company, which at the time had probably less than 100 Catholics employed out of 10,000 workers, the practice was also part of the public employment system. In Derry, for instance, as the Civil Rights movement began, the heads of all fifteen departments in Derry City Council were Unionists. Catholics held only 33 per cent of the County Council jobs—the lower paid ones, as 79 per cent of all salaries were paid to Unionists and the general Catholic representation in Public Service Boards (transport authority, etc.) was only 11.1 per cent. Out of such percentages are gunmen made.

Though the Downing Street Declaration threw a fair light on specific Catholic grievances, it was drafted in such a way as to shed very little light on Nationalist aspirations—a fact which in the welter of debate about the reforms proposed in the Declaration was not very extensively discussed. So far as the link with England was concerned the Declaration was a direct extension of the 1920 Government of Ireland Act and its lineal descendant the Ireland Act of 1949 which stated that no change would take place in the statutory position of Northern Ireland without the consent of the majority of that state—the Unionists.

The significant portion of the Declaration read as follows:

The United Kingdom Government reaffirm that nothing which has happened in recent years in Northern Ireland derogates from the clear pledges made by successive United Kingdom governments that Northern Ireland should not cease to be a part of the United Kingdom without the consent of the people of Northern Ireland or from the provision in Section I of the Ireland Act 1949 that in no event was Northern Ireland or any part thereof cease to be part of the United Kingdom without the consent of the Parliament of Northern Ireland. The Border is not an issue.

In the same spirit of giving with one hand, but taking with the other, the Declaration both emphasised Britain's responsibility for law and order and stressed at the same time that its military presence was not limitless. To the Protestant or Republican extremist the Declaration might be taken as encouragement to try to push Northern Ireland in the direction either desired.

But in constitutional terms the Declaration meant that Unionism continued to receive the British government's underscoring of its legitimacy.

However, while the British angered the national-minded amongst the Catholics by continuing to affirm the link with England and the sanctity of the Union, they also incurred the disapprobation of the Protestants by dismembering what they considered to be fundamentals of their state. The B-Specials were stood down. The Royal Ulster Constabulary were disarmed. Plural voting was abolished. And, finally, Stormont was suppressed. However, having initiated these developments, the British then backed down when the Loyalists staged their largest and most definitive stand against British policy in the Ulster Workers Council Strike of July, 1974.

After Stormont was suspended in March, 1972, William Whitelaw was appointed to administer Direct Rule from Whitehall as Secretary of State for Northern Ireland—giving rise to the Dublin joke that the tricolour would henceforth be green, orange and Whitelaw. He demonstrably tried to break new political ground from the word go, as we shall see, holding talks with the Provisionals that July, and on

September 25 opening talks at Darlington on the future of Northern Ireland which eventually, through a series of conferences and Green and White Papers, led on to the Sunningdale Agreement.

The Sunningdale Agreement was named after the conference between the British and Irish governments and representatives of some sections of Unionism (but not Paisley or the extremists like the Ulster Defence Association and of course the I.R.A.)—the Alliance Party and the Catholic Social Democratic and Labour Party (S.D.L.P.)—which all met at Sunningdale from December 6 to 9, 1973.

The Agreement reiterated the Downing Street Declaration stipulation that no change would be made in the status of Northern Ireland without the consent of the majority. It envisaged the setting up of an Executive to run Northern Ireland which would share power between the Catholic and Protestant elements. There was to be an all-Ireland court procedure which would combat terrorism and at the same time recognise the existence of the two separate states by trying suspects within the jurisdiction in which they had been apprehended.

But recognising at least the fact that Ireland was one island the Agreement also provided for the setting up of a Council of Ireland which would provide a link between Belfast and Dublin, provide an 'Irish Dimension' to meet with the aspiration of the S.D.L.P. towards eventual peaceful unity, and would carry out tasks of mutual benefit to North and South in the realms of E.E.C. membership, agriculture, trials, terrorism and so on.

Lest this should be seen as a diminution of the North's constitutional status in Unionist eyes, it was proposed to register the Declaration at the U.N.

However, domestic British problems rate higher than those of the 'U.K. Overseas' and the very day after the Agreement was signed, Whitelaw was transferred back to England to deal with the miners. Lesser men succeeded him; power swung back to Labour which showed itself unable to control either the army or mob rule, and the North was allowed to degenerate into the bloody political slum it has since become.

The U.N. proviso did not assuage Loyalist anger at this ultimate 'betrayal' coupled with all that had gone before, and a province-wide strike was embarked on which, as we shall see later, wrecked both the Agreement and Faulkner's political position. The fact that the British security forces subsequently arrested and imprisoned Loyalists, although still to nothing approaching the degree to which they had tried to suppress Catholic organisations, had the effect of increasing the move towards an 'Ulster consciousness' among the Loyalists.

Protestants began to feel that the British were one day going to do them down and depart, 'stopping only to write a large cheque' as a Protestant apologist put it to me once. Loyalists for the first time in a position of conflict with the British began to experience something of an identity crisis. Just where were his roots? What in 1970–80 terms is the percentage in shooting Catholics? Who gains?

At this time there were small but definite signs that some of the Protestant paramilitary leaders had become imbued not only with these feelings but also with the belief that they should have had some of the powers, and trappings, which the Unionist ascendancy traditionally garnered to themselves. These trappings were the rewards of a society whose values were secured by the efforts of the Orange paramilitary overlap with the regular police, and sometimes the army in keeping the 'White Niggers', the Catholics, in their place. Now the paramilitary leaders were thinking seriously of what the position would be *when* the British withdraw, not *if*. They did not welcome such a possibility but they envisaged it as being likely to occur at some stage in the undetermined future. And they wanted some of the political spoils which would be going begging when this happened.

17

The Constitutional Participants

1. *The British*

The question which one often hears and which logically arises at this junction is, why don't the British pull out? Why haven't they gone already? Why go on putting up with their soldiers being shot and with bombs going off in the U.K. mainland when the problem of the Northern Ireland Protestant and Catholic is outside their power to control?

Regrettably the answer is not what British apologists would have us believe, that they are holding the ring out of a sense of duty, because they can see no way of withdrawing from their 'Northern Ireland commitment' without leaving behind a situation where Protestants slaughter Catholics. The fact is that the Tories are by tradition and definition the Conservative and Unionist Party and the traditional Unionist alliances (which generally represent about ten Westminster Unionist pro-Tory seats) and sympathies were clearly and disastrously shown when within a matter of days after the election of June, 1970, which returned them to power, the Tories allowed the British army to be used to ransack the Falls Road during a period of two days' curfew which recalled nothing so much as General Massu's descent on the Casbah during the Algerian War. The anger that this episode aroused gave the Provisional I.R.A. a strength in Belfast which it possesses to at least some degree to this day. There certainly were some scores, probably even a few hundreds, of weapons in the Falls Road—acquired at this stage as much for defence as offence by the Republicans of both Official and Provisional wings. But this should be compared to the revelation in Hansard that at this period the Protestants held 107,000 *licensed* weapons including two machine guns, for which an obliging Justice of the Peace had issued a license to a gentleman who said that he needed them 'to kill otters'. The Shankill, however, was not curfewed.

The Queen is still the Queen of Britain, the United Kingdom and Northern Ireland, and on B.B.C. TV the weather maps still show the weather for England and the top right-hand corner of Ireland. The strong Nationalist movements in Scotland and to a lesser degree Wales were a powerful disincentive to a British government to 'let Northern Ireland go'. Though these waned in strength during the late 1970s they also made clear the possibility that if one part of the U.K. broke off, others could too. The Scots Nationalists' slogan, after all, was: 'It's *our* oil!' Jim Callaghan's coming to power generated a good deal of optimism in Ireland.

Yet neither Labour administrations of the period had the power or the will to do anything substantive. The British Labour Party leadership is a balancing act between contending forces within the party, at the best of times.

Under James Callaghan the party suffered from the additional need to maintain itself in power with the aid of minority groups in parliament.

As readers are by now aware, successive British administrations had concluded that the Unionists were not to be trusted with power. They had progressively dismantled or attempted to reform all the instruments through which that power was administered, local government, the B–Specials, the R.U.C., the housing executive, and finally Stormont, the seat of government itself. There could be no more damning indictment of a regime than this concluding stripping away of all its executive powers. Nevertheless when dependent on the Lib-Lab pact and on the smaller parties, Jim Callaghan in a desperate attempt to prolong his stay in office for another six months actually did a deal with the Westminster Unionists whereby, in return for their support, he would give the Unionists more power by introducing proportional representation into the North—which was estimated as possibly meaning an extra five seats for the Unionists.

Appalled at this opportunism, Gerry Fitt, a life-long supporter of Labour, which meant in Belfast risking his life, abstained in the crucial vote of no-confidence moved by Margaret Thatcher which brought on the 1979 election that returned the Tories to power. Callaghan lost by one vote—the Unionists of course voted with their traditional allies, the Conservatives; had Fitt voted, there would have been a tie—the Speaker would have voted for the status quo and Callaghan would have survived.

Yet, although the Irish issue in a sense brought on the General Election, the 'bi-partisan policy', as the all-party agreement not to rock the boat over Ireland was euphemistically termed, meant that the Irish question was not raised during the election campaign despite the murder of Airey Neave.

The fact that Mrs Thatcher had a comfortable majority (and nothing to the right of her over Northern Ireland) might on the surface have given grounds for optimism concerning her administration, though her stated approach had been a militarise, 'Northern Ireland is British' one. But the only real indications of what her policy was had been the customary diffusing emphasis in British and Irish ministry pronouncement following the first official visit to Dublin of the new Northern Ireland Secretary, Humphrey Atkins, in July, 1979, and, more importantly, following the murder of Mountbatten; although it should perhaps also be noted that the first Head of State received by Mrs Thatcher after her election was Jack Lynch. The Irish spoke of the need for a political initiative, the British of the need for increased security.

2. The Northern Irish

Looking at the period 1969–79, one got a false impression of movement. Northern Irish political life appeared to be changing radically. The once monolithic Unionist Party burst apart under the strain of the times. Terence O'Neill and his cousin Chichester-Clarke who succeeded him, a captain and a major respectively, were of the old ascendancy Church of Ireland type, landowners with British army records. Brian Faulkner, who took over from Chichester-Clarke on March 20, 1971, represented the triumph of the Presbyterian business tradition of the North over the landowners. He was not to enjoy his premiership for long. A decision he

29. Massed Loyalists jeer in the background as British troops charge Nationalists, firing rubber bullets. Belfast, May, 1971. (*Colman Doyle*)

30. The chaos of January 30, 1972—Bloody Sunday—as British troops fired on the peaceful demonstration, killing thirteen unarmed civilians and injuring many more. (*Colman Doyle*)

31. Civil rights marchers in Newry in the shadow of heavily armed British forces in 1972. (*Colman Doyle*)

32. British Army soldiers on patrol in Northern Ireland. (*Colman Doyle*)

33. Uniformed U.D.A. paramilitaries with British Army protection. Belfast, 1972.
(*Colman Doyle*)

34. Provisional I.R.A. leaders (left tto right) Martin McGuinness, Daithi O Connell, Sean MacStiofain, and Seamus Twomey, on June 23, 1972. (*Pacemaker*)

35. Michael Gaughan's funeral as it passed through Dublin, June 8, 1974. Gaughan, of Ballina, County Mayo, died on hungerstrike in Parkhurst prison, Isle of Wight, England. (*Colman Doyle*)

36. Michael Gaughan, who died on hungerstrike in an English prison in June, 1974.

37. Bobby Sands became an icon of the Republican movement in 1981 when he died on hungerstrike while in Long Kesh Prison.

38. Prisoners inside Long Kesh Prison during internment in the 1970s. This snapshot was taken by one of the prisoners and smuggled out.

39/40/41. I.R.A. volunteers, mid-1970s. (*Colman Doyle*)

42. Members of the R.U.C. search Republican suspects before making an arrest in 1970s Belfast. (*Colman Doyle*)

43. The presence of the British Army is an aspect of everyday life in Belfast (as shown here in the 1970s) throughout the Troubles, and right up to the present day. (*Colman Doyle*)

44. Arms from the United States bound for the I.R.A. captured aboard the trawler *Marita Ann* off the Kerry Coast on September 29, 1984. (*Irish Times*)

45. Inside the Grand Hotel, Brighton, England, after the I.R.A. bomb exploded on October 12, 1984. British Prime Minister Margaret Thatcher narrowly escaped death in the explosion which killed five people and injured many more. (*Press Association Photos*)

strongly advocated—the introduction of internment on August 9, 1971—helped to create such turmoil throughout the province that Stormont was suspended on March 24 the following year. Effectively speaking, with the exception of the Power-Sharing Executive set up as a result of the Sunningdale Agreement of December 9, 1973, which collapsed in May, 1974, the North has been governed by direct rule from London since Stormont fell on March 24, 1972.

Bereft of a British initiative, constitutional North of Ireland politics did not develop, they simply polarised. Brian Faulkner was killed in a riding accident and succeeded by an innocuous Fermanagh farmer, Harry West, who, after his poor showing in the June, 1979, election, was succeeded by James Molyneaux. But already by June, 1978, the Unionist Party was in a situation analogous to that of the I.R.A. There was an 'Official' Unionist party and a number of rival groupings, the more vigorous of these being the Rev. Ian Paisley's Democratic Unionist Party. How democratic the organisation is, is open to question, but it is beyond question that Ian Kyle Paisley, the fundamentalist Free Presbyterian with a doctorate from Bob Jones's Bible Belt University, lungs like the Bull of Basham and a theology from the Apocalypse, has established himself as the leading political figure in Northern Ireland. Certainly in the early days of the Northern conflagration it was he above all others, including even William Craig, who was at the time Minister for Home Affairs, who incited opposition to the Civil Rights marchers. He would have appeared to have been a prime target for the Provisionals but they let him live for two reasons: 1. his onslaughts on the Unionist Party leadership had the effect of bursting the party asunder; 2. 'he only says publicly what the rest of them say privately; he shows them all up,' explained a Provisional spokesman.

Paisley, whose church grew richer by the week, continually attracted new recruits from the Church of Ireland. He still sits in both the Westminster and European Parliaments, being returned by unassailable majorities.

In fact it was to be a noteworthy feature of the period that the murder of politicians was about the one form of killing generally, if not totally, eschewed by all groups. The Official I.R.A. did kill two Senators, one Northern (Senator Barnhill), one Southern (Senator Billy Fox), but neither was premeditated. John Taylor, the Unionist M.P., was their most considered target and he survived his wounds. And, for their condemnation of the I.R.A. violence, Austin Currie of the S.D.L.P. and Gerry Fitt, its leader, both had their homes raked with gunfire by Provisional supporters, a mob of whom on one occasion broke into Fitt's home in West Belfast, but were held off by him with a revolver until the police came. Fitt showed me the revolver once after a meeting in Queen's University. 'It won't save me from an assassin,' he said, 'but they won't be able to kidnap me—they won't get me into that car.'

Apart from the fact of having to contend with hostility from the differing wings of Republican extremism, who detested the S.D.L.P. almost as much as the Unionists, the S.D.L.P. also had cause to fear Orange extremists. A third member of the party was his election agent, Senator Paddy Wilson, who did not carry a gun. Not long afterwards in Belfast on June 26, 1973, Senator Wilson and Miss Irene Andrews, a Protestant, were found beside his car, ritually murdered. Senator Wilson's body had literally been stabbed dozens of times; the Ulster Freedom Fighters, a Protestant

paramilitary group, claimed responsibility for the murders. And Protestant paramilitaries were also responsible for the other major killing on the Catholic side, that
of Maire Drumm, vice-president of Sinn Fein, on October 28, 1976, while she
was staying in the Mater Hospital, Belfast, for cataract treatment.

The foregoing is a grisly list of horrors but mercifully short in relation to the
high visibility and vulnerability of politicians in Northern Ireland.

The middle of the road and middle-class Unionist Party, the Alliance grouping
led by Oliver Napier, a solicitor, at one stage seemed to offer the possibility of a
new departure for Unionism. A leading member of the party, driving to London
with me after a meeting at Cambridge, confided that he could see himself 'coming
out in favour of a United Ireland one of these days'. That interesting political
phenomenon—a Unionist supporting a United Ireland—disappeared in the years
which have elapsed since, and it seems unlikely that it will be seen in the years
which lie ahead. In contemporary Northern Ireland members of political parties
are better thought of as media spokesmen for the differing Northern viewpoints
than as men who can 'deliver'.

The most interesting examples of this unfortunate truth are the members of the
Catholic Social Democratic and Labour Party. The party contained some of the
brightest political talent to appear on the Irish scene for years, including the
outstanding figures of Gerry Fitt, John Hume, Seamus Mallon and Austin Currie.
Growing out of the Civil Rights movement, the S.D.L.P. built on the foundations
of the old 'Green' Nationalist Party but appeared to offer a chance of progress to
the old Northern problems, being reformist rather than preoccupied with the border.
This could have had profound reprisals on Southern opinion and in America. Until
mid-1971 it appeared to many people in Ireland that the fluent, articulate S.D.L.P.
men who ran rings around their Boer-like Unionist adversaries on TV were
inevitably destined to move world and domestic opinion (particularly in Ireland) to
a degree that was certain to bring change and reform in all the traditional areas of
Northern bitterness.

However, the conflicting currents of the Provisional campaign, Loyalist reaction
to the Provisionals and army response to the general situation, produced a tidal
wave of disorder that washed the S.D.L.P. out of effective political life in July of
1971 when, following the shooting of two innocent Derry men, Seamus Cusack
and Desmond Beattie, by the army on July 8, the party's deputy leader, John
Hume, came under such pressure from his electorate that he persuaded his
colleagues to withdraw from Stormont a week later, to the annoyance of Fitt who
constantly withstood similar pressure in Belfast. The TV screen can mislead those
who appear on it as to their effectiveness just as much as those who view it. From
being forced into adopting the Abstentionist tactics of the Nationalist Party, the
S.D.L.P. was ultimately driven, as the decade ended, to adopting the central policy
of Eddie MacAteer's party, what was known as The Full National Demand of
Irish Nationalists down though the years—a British withdrawal from Ireland,
however long-term this aspiration might appear.

The S.D.LP. did make some important contributions to developments during
the decade—particularly in influencing Dublin's policy towards the North and,
largely through John Hume, in interesting American politicians of Irish descent into

taking an interest in the Irish issue. Edward Kennedy in particular took a keen and continuing interest in the North, getting a regular weekly briefing on the day-to-day situation; and Tip O'Neill, then Speaker of the House of Representatives in Washington actively embroiled himself in controversy through his criticism of British policy. He appeared to have been quite genuinely shocked at Callaghan's opportunistic deal with the Unionists. Other distinguished figures such as Governor Carey of New York, Patrick Moynihan and Hugh Byrne, along with life-long campaigners for Irish interests such as Paul O'Dwyer, the Civil Rights lawyer, or Judge James Comeford, former Chairman of the New York St Patrick's Day Parade, that annual assertion of Irish strength in the U.S., were increasingly making their voices heard on specific issues such as the behaviour of the security forces. President Carter, too, had interested himself in the Northern issue. American politicians' statements had almost inevitably condemned violence and then gone on to task Britain to do something about her responsibilities in the area.

The American dimension has not been regarded as an unalloyed plus by the Dublin governments. First, the Irish in America have long supported force as a tactic for achieving reunification—a tactic to which Dublin is straightforwardly opposed. Opposed in fact to a degree which may have proved counter-productive because a succession of Irish Prime Ministers and Ministers going out to America since the troubles began, warning Americans against subscribing to the Provisionals, have certainly created something of a backlash against the idea of foreigners coming to the U.S. to tell Uncle Sam how he should spend the dollars in his pocket; and the Provisionals have in fact thus been given some subscriptions which they would not otherwise have received.

Secondly, some American politicians who interested themselves in the Irish issue were too close to the physical force aspect in Dublin's view—most notably Congressman Mario Biaggi whose ad hoc committee on Northern Ireland claimed the support of over 130 senators and congressmen. This sizeable lobby of pro-Irish sentiment was outweighed in value in Dublin's view by virtue of Biaggi's close links with the Northern Aid Committee (the Provisionals' major support group in the state led by the old-time Tipperary Republican Michael Flannery), and later with the Irish Caucus (an umbrella committee of Irish-American organisations, led by Fred Burns O'Brien, an Irish-American civil servant, and by Father Sean MacManus, the Redemptorist priest who helped to get Sean MacStiofain off his hunger strike [see Chapter 21] and whose brother Jackie was killed in the 1956 campaign). Although in true Irish style all these organisations related to each other in a manner which proved they were Republican—they almost immediately split— nevertheless, as a result of these cross currents in Irish-American sentiment, as much of the Irish Embassy in Washington's time was spent on anti-Provisional activities as was devoted to positive lobbying on the Northern issue. It was the old dilemma of trying to be pro-Irish or sometimes anti an aspect of British policy without *inter alia* helping the I.R.A.

Britain's response to the American influence was low-key, subtle and so far quite effective. The style of the State Department tends to be English in the sense that the style of diplomacy generally tended once to be French. Tea, tweeds and a posting to the Court of St James tend to be highly favoured. This natural sympathy to the British position—combined with the fact that most media coverage of the North of Ireland tends to come through agencies, correspondents and TV crews based in London—makes for an understanding approach to Britain's difficulties in 'Ulster'.

In this period the calibre of America's ambassadors to Dublin had risen sharply; men like John Moore, Walter Curley and William Shannon, a former policy maker at the *New York Times* and author of a standard work on the Irish in America, had performed that rare feat of furthering both their own country's interests and those of the country to which they had been accredited. But the view from Dublin was not as readily accepted in Foggy Bottom as that from St James and the dispatches of William Shannon had sometimes to contend with those of Kingman Brewster, his counterpart in London. However, as a U.S. Presidential election neared, one in which the importance of men like Edward Kennedy and Tip O'Neill did not need to be stressed, the odds appeared to favour a view more sympathetic to Dublin. 1979 saw more interest in, and speechifying about, Ireland than America had seen in any other time in that troubled decade.

3. *The Southern Irish*

Finally to the last principal set of actors on the constitutional stage—the Dublin administrators and in particular Jack Lynch and Fianna Fail. For although by one of the ironies of history it was the Coalition—which by tradition might be expected to be less than enthusiastic concerning the fulfilment of Republican goals—just as it was John A. Costello's Coalition of 1948 which declared a Republic so it was the Coalition of 1973 between Fine Gael and Labour (the latter containing such an avowedly anti-Republican figure as Dr Conor Cruise O'Brien) that came nearest in the period under review to furthering Republican ambitions with the Sunningdale Agreement.

Nevertheless Fianna Fail were in power for nearly twice as long as the 1973-7 Coalition since the troubles began and were—and are—the major Irish constitutional force to be reckoned with during the era. As it is also the constitutional embodiment of Republicanism, the party whose leader drafted the constitution, Article 3 of which lays claim to Northern Ireland, it is the party on which the moral responsibility for finding a solution to the problem lies heaviest. But although a Fianna Fail study group was working to produce a full policy on the implications of unity, there was as yet in existence no detailed blueprint as to what exactly the party intended to do to create a peaceful, post-British-withdrawal Ireland in which Protestant fears would be assuaged and liberties protected. In a general atmosphere of 'Oh Lord make me good but not yet', one was aware that the party was generally in favour of unity, this to be achieved at an unspecified future date, at some sort of conference at which the Protestants' reservations about the South's constitution and laws would be resolved.

The main line pushed abroad—in Washington, for instance—was that Dublin would like to see Britain withdraw her 1949 guarantee to the Unionists so as to make them more amenable to negotiation. Of course, as we have seen, the Downing Street Declaration reinforced rather than dismantled this barrier. The keystone of the Lynch policy was that, while distancing itself from the I.R.A. demand that Britain should make a declaration of intent to withdraw from Northern Ireland, she should nevertheless exercise herself towards working for unity, rather than checkmating it. There is no doubt that a sizeable segment of the rank-and-file of Fianna Fail favoured a more activist policy than that of Lynch.

In July, 1979, before the parliament recessed for the summer, there were angry parliamentary party Caucus meetings protesting at aspects of the party's performance including its policy on the North; and finally Lynch had to devote a full day to a parliamentary meeting at which the various grievances were aired. While these were as much related to the handling of the economy as to the North and to a damaging strike in the postal service, the North was the issue which was viewed almost in theological terms. And for a very good reason: apart from their undoubted ancestral feelings on the issue, the party was aware that the substantial portion of their huge majority, gained because of the Northern situation two years earlier, was in imminent danger of being lost to them. For the West of Ireland had returned Neil Blaney, one of the men sacked over the Arms Trial affair, as its member for Europe—against Fianna Fail's nominee. Blaney has always maintained that he hadn't left Fianna Fail; Fianna Fail had left him! Blaney was not to be heard referring to the Provisionals as terrorists—he called them Freedom Fighters. From all this, Charles Haughey, that other major figure of the Arms Crisis, emerged to become Lynch's main rival for the leadership.

On top of these symptoms of Northern-occasioned disquiet, Lynch had to endure another particularly unwelcome challenge just four days after he had returned from seeing Margaret Thatcher in London to discuss the North in the wake of the Mountbatten murder.

He unsuccessfully sought to prevent Síle De Valera, the youngest deputy in the Dail, and a granddaughter of Eamon De Valera, from delivering a speech at the Commemoration of Liam Lynch on September 9 in Fermoy, Co. Cork. He had seen an advance copy of her script, which she had circulated early to gain publicity. It was couched in old-fashioned, *An Phoblacht*-style rhetoric, and seemed both by its timing and content to be an effort to undermine Lynch. He had to issue a statement publicly rebuking her and to call a special parliamentary party meeting to discuss the issue on the eve of the Pope's visit so that the details would be lost in the coverage of the Pope's visit. Lynch weathered that storm, occasioned not so much by the speech or the age of the girl concerned as by her surname, but it served to highlight the weakness of his regime in other areas, economic as well as political, so that ultimately the death of Lord Mountbatten brought other unlooked-for results for the I.R.A.

One other circumstance which aided the I.R.A. tremendously should be noted here. Despite all the apparently genuine efforts that had been made at reform, all the expenditure of life, money and effort, a report published by the Fair Employment Agency in January, 1978, showed that though adult Catholics number only one-third of the population of Northern Ireland, they contributed twice as many unemployed than the numerically superior Protestants. In fact, due to the higher birth rate, Catholic children were generally reckoned to be in a majority of 52 to

48 per cent to Protestant children at school-going age. But the employment situation was like the ring the Chinese fishermen place around trained cormorants' necks to prevent them swallowing the fish they catch—Catholic children could catch an education but this could not necessarily enable them to earn their daily bread—hence they had to emigrate.

Discrimination and political inertia have ensured both a continuity and a steady recruitment to the I.RA. The obvious analogies between the situation of Irish Catholics and of the Palestinians (whose poverty and lack of opportunity provide a continuing stream of recruits to the P.L.O.) have meant inevitable contact between the I.R.A., the P.L.O. and other such organisations.

So much for the story of the progress of the constitutional actors in the drama of Ireland over the ten years from August 1969 to 1979. To turn now to the activities of the unconstitutional actors who in a sense both brought up the curtain and refused to let it drop—the Provisional I.R.A.

18

The Provisional I.R.A.—The Rebirth of a Movement

As the I.R.A. themselves put it, their strategy in the years which saw the rebirth of the 'movement' between 1969 and 1971, fell under three headings:

1. Defence
2. Retaliation
3. Offence (in 1971 and continuing apart from various truces to the present day)

A Provisional apologist given the history and theology of the movement could make a case under all three headings, defence being the most obvious. Around 1969/1970, Belfast was the cockpit of activity in Northern Ireland. Later, as we shall see, other areas such as Crossmaglen in Co. Armagh were to become scenes of bloody and momentous deeds, and some towns, apart from the obvious centres of Belfast and Derry, were particularly badly hit during the troubles. Three of these were Dungannon, Strabane and Coleraine which were devastated several times by bombings.★

However, Belfast remained the key area for a number of reasons. The Protestants struck there most continuously, and there was both a plentiful source of recruitment and a nucleus of older leaders so that the Provisionals regrouped there as a result. There was, for instance, William McKee, later to become O.C. of the Belfast Brigade of the Provisional I.R.A., who was badly wounded as he conducted a successful defence of St Matthew's Church off the Newtownards Road, in the face of determined Protestant efforts to burn it down in July, 1969. The Protestant mobs who also attempted with some success to burn out areas in the Falls Road in August, 1969, were in the minds both of the Catholics and, in some cases, of themselves, always ready to return to finish off the work so begun. So the need for defence was a powerful motive force in the strengthening of the Provisional I.RA. in the early 1970s.

The Provisionals, or Provos† as they became generally known, began to group in the Falls area generally. For instance, the Andersonstown branch of Sinn Fein, the Rodger McCorley Cumann, split from the Official I.R.A. of Cathal Goulding

---

★ One of the worst of these occurred on June 12, 1973, when a bomb killed six people in Coleraine and injured thirty-three more, some, in hospital parlance, 'very seriously', i.e. crippled for life.

† The Provisionals came to be known as Provos or Provies or Pinheads. This last is not a term of abuse but to differentiate them from the 'Stickies' the Officials, who use gum to affix their Easter Lilies to their lapels as opposed to the Provisionals' pins.

when the section led by Albert Price—father of the Price sisters, Dolores and Marion, who went on hunger strike in Brixton prison after being sentenced for their part in the London bombings (see Chapter 21)—differed from the socialist policy of the rest of the Cumann and reverted to the traditional Republican aim of getting the British out of occupied Ireland. This sort of re-alignment of forces went on everywhere there was a Sinn Fein branch. But most notably in districts like the Clonard area, in which the Bombay Street burning had occurred, and in which other deeds of Republican significance had also taken place. For instance, it was in the 'little India' area of the Clonard district in Cawnpore Street that Tommy Williams and his companions were arrested after the fatal shooting of an R.U.C. man, for which Williams was subsequently executed. Amongst his companions who escaped the noose was Joe Cahill, who now became something of a household name through his appearance at press conferences as he and other figures from the past—'forties men'—who had seen active service in that area began to come together and re-organise.

Within the ranks of the I.R.A. as a whole Sean MacStiofain (in English, John Stephenson) was emerging as the principal leader. He became Chief of Staff of the Provisionals after the Intercontinental walk-out. Born in England of an Irish mother, service in the Royal Air Force as John Stephenson had accentuated rather than dulled his ancestral nationalism, and a capacity for mastering the internecine politicking of the I.R.A. carried him upwards through the ranks of the movement, which he had joined along with various Irish Language movements during the 1950s. He served a jail term with Cathal Goulding, who now faced him across the ideological divide, for his part in the Arborfield raid. Apart from the fact that his was the hand on the throttle that moved the I.R.A. from 'neutral' to 'go' in the organisational build-up period of 1969–71, his principal contribution to Republican strategy as the introduction of the snipers' technique of only firing one shot before disappearing, which claimed several soldiers' lives.

Daithi O'Connell, who is credited with being the architect of the car bomb, and later became one of the movement's principal political thinkers, had taken part in the famous Brookeborough ambush and escaped from the Curragh internment camp in the 'Three Macs' era, as we saw with another young I.R.A. man who was also to become a household name during the post-1969 hostilities—Ruairi O'Bradaigh, President of the Provisional wing of Sinn Fein.

Little India, full of Victorian red-bricked, dry-closet houses born to huddle and hate under the shadow of long-silent mills, now began to echo to the murmur of old aspirations and old leadership. The Kashmir Road, Cupar Street, Bombay Street, Cawnpore Street, and many other names from England's colonial past, began to come alive in contemporary Ireland in a manner that was to provide John Bull with one of his last and worst heartaches of the Empire.

As the Shankill Road loops around the Clonard district, there was, in its early days, little need for the I.R.A. leaders to stress the need for 'no-go areas'. Later, barricades manned by vigilantes met both the Catholics' requirements for security and the Republicans' instinct to deny Britain's security forces a right of access.

The I.R.A. had an odd sort of life of its own, as much based on the fears and aspirations of the Catholic population as on separatist theology. It is literally true, for instance, that in August, 1969 the only weapons known to be available to the I.R.A. were ten guns. Subsequent to the Bombay Street burnings, Jack McCabe, with another Republican sympathiser, Myles Shevlin, a solicitor, smuggled in some guns to the North which had been cached since the 1950s campaign—one of them a Schmeisser machine-gun. McCabe, a veteran of the forties who subsequently blew himself up when a spark from a shovel with which he was mixing explosives on the floor of a garage in his home on the Swords Road, Dublin, sent the explosives off, injuring him terribly and fatally, was probably the main I.R.A. bomb supplier of the period. His eyes and his testicles were blown away but on his deathbed he used his last strength to give Shevlin details of what had gone wrong so that someone else would not make the same mistake. 'An iron man,' Shevlin told me, 'an iron man.' After his death, on December 30, 1971, the Northern hydra was to ensure that many others with expertise gained in armies both at home and abroad would be found to follow in his footsteps.

Immediately after the burning and appearance of troops on the streets, anyone in the Falls Road area who could lay their hands on a weapon did so, for defence. This was not done under I.R.A. auspices, although the I.R.A. of course did begin sending emissaries far and near to search for armaments.

The famous 'Arms Crisis' which exploded in Southern Ireland and resulted in two cabinet ministers being unsuccessfully prosecuted for arms importation—Neil Blaney and Charles Haughey, whose brother Jock was also charged and acquitted— was the result of a chain of events which included the allocation by the Southern government of public monies for the relief of distress in the wake of the burnings (there was a very wide-ranging set of appeals from the North to help the Catholic population). There was also a general feeling in the South that somehow all the momentous happenings in the North were in some way going to help the South 'to get back the six'.

It became known that an Irish army officer, Captain James Kelly, had been moving in different circles north of the border, and in the subsequent court proceedings it was revealed that he and Jock Haughey had indeed gone to Germany on an arms mission. Kelly believed sincerely that he was acting with official government knowledge during this time. But in fact he seems to have acted as a result of ad hoc personal initiatives on the part of senior politicians. The result was that Kelly departed from the army and abandoned his military career in the wake of the dismissals and resignations of other political figures. The most ironic resignation was that of Kevin Boland, a son of the wartime Fianna Fail Minister of Justice who had had the task of carrying out De Valera's stern policy towards the I.R.A. of the war years. The contemporary Minister for Justice, Micheal O'Morain, also resigned.

John Kelly, a Belfast I.R.A. man whose sincerity when on trial in October, 1969, in the company of Blaney, Haughey, Captain James Kelly and Albert Luyks, a Belgian resident in Ireland, impressed even opponents of Republicanism, said bitterly in the course of an oration that ranks in the best tradition of Irish speeches from the dock: 'We did not ask for blankets or feeding bottles. We asked for guns— and no one from Lynch down denied our request or told us this was contrary to government policy.'

What seems to have happened, to put the most charitable interpretation on events, is that neither Kelly at one end of the scale, nor Lynch at the other end knew exactly what the Northern sub-committee of the cabinet, which the government set up as a result of the crisis, was doing.

I remember one enthusiastic Dublin public relations practitioner whose services had been engaged at this juncture breezing into the office of the *Irish Press* to give me a preview of what one minister, whose name he liberally quoted, had planned to 'get the word out to the rest of the world when the banging started'. The P.R.O. envisaged that in order to bring the matter to U.N. attention, the Irish army was going to be used to cross the border to seize 'even a football field'; and the Irish government had, he assured us, a communication network set up through Paris in case the British seized the lines through London.

The only tangible evidence of communications which emerged from all this was a newspaper, the *Voice of the North*, produced by another former *Irish Press* (and *Daily Express!*) journalist, Seamus Brady, a confidant of Neil Blaney, and a brief appearance on the Irish scene of Markpress, the publicity organisation which had acquired some experience of wartime propaganda during the Biafran conflict.

A postscript was added to the affair many years later in 1979 by James Gibbons, the Minister for Defence at the time of the Arms Trial and Captain Kelly's supposed ultimate boss. As Charles Haughey's bill to legalise contraceptive sales was sneaking embarrassedly through the Dail, it became known that Gibbons, who from the time of the bitterness engendered by the Arms Trial could never be reckoned amongst the ranks of Haughey's admirers, alone of all the Fianna Fail parliamentary party was being allowed to abstain from voting on 'grounds of conscience', an unheard-of happening in Fianna Fail.

As many political observers in Dublin felt that the contraception bill had only been brought forward at that time both to obscure the controversy over the government's handling of the E.M.S. issue—entry to the European Monetary System for a time greatly depreciated the value of the Irish punt against sterling when Ireland went in and Britain stayed out, thus breaking the 150-year-old link with sterling—and to try to check the ascent of Haughey's star by forcing him to pick up some political dynamite, the consensus was that Gibbons's memory (of the events of 1969–70) as much as his conscience played a part in his exemption.

Boland subsequently founded a Republican Party, Aontacht Eireann (Irish Unity Republican Party), intended to topple Fianna Fail.★ But by the General Election of 1977 his party had gone the way of earlier splinter parties—into oblivion.

Whether the I.R.A. benefited substantially from all this is a hotly debated point in Ireland. Fianna Fail's political opponents say that the intervention of some of the party's leading figures at this stage did give the I.R.A. the springboard it needed to leap into yet another round in the cycle of English and Irish blood and destruction.

In fact the evidence, such as it is, that I have been able to uncover from the people who might be presumed to know best, the I.R.A., tends to suggest otherwise. Some Irish government funds were paid over to a German arms dealer in

---

★ He put his money where his principles were following the signing of the Sunningdale Agreement when he took an unsuccessful and costly action to prove the Agreement contrary to the Irish Constitution.

Hamburg but the arms never left for Ireland and the Irish government subsequently sued unsuccessfully to have the money refunded. The public money that did come to Belfast seems to have gone on paying vigilantes to patrol the streets at night, watching for Protestant assassination squads. There was at this stage a strong Catholic grouping known as the Central Citizens Defence Committee (C.C.D.C.) which was composed of Catholics of every political hue including that of the I.R.A.—its chairman was Jim Sullivan of the Official I.R.A.—but was exactly what its name implied, a defence committee which assisted the victims of rioting with funds provided from the South, but took no role other than that. (The C.C.D.C. eventually split over the issue of giving support to the families of I.R.A. men on the run which some senior Catholic clergy opposed because it helped the I.R.A. activities.)

I.R.A. leaders from the past negotiated under the guise of community leadership with the British military authorities, particularly General Farar-Hockley, on issues such as whether or not the barricades should come down and on law and order problems. These talks were held to have broken down when Farar-Hockley named on television four of the principals with whom he had negotiated. They were Liam Hannaway, Billy McKee, Leo Smith and Frank Card—or Proinsias MacAirt as he prefers to be known.

The principal military activity in the I.R.A. at this time (1969–71) was stone-throwing and sometimes petrol-bombing, which could just as easily have been attributed to high spirits on the part of local youths who had inherited, along with the attitude of the urban, unemployed proletariat anywhere towards uniforms, the particularly Irish ancestral antipathy for 'their law' and 'their order', as manifested by 'their' troops and 'their' R.U.C.

To the outside eye, nothing very significant in terms of I.R.A. development seemed to be happening, apart from acts of hooliganism and destruction, and the fact that the Protestant apologists and Ian Paisley were working themselves into paroxysms of rage at the spectacle of members of Her Majesty's security forces being denied access to part of the United Kingdom by Republicans in parts of Belfast and Derry. These finally came to an end when on July 31, 1971, 'Operation Motorman', a major, motorised, British army thrust into Derry's I.R.A. controlled areas, brought an end to the no-go areas—but not to the I.R.A. who simply were not there when the troops arrived and re-emerged to fight another day.

Within the movement, as new faces and new ideas emerged, an old debate also re-surfaced the idea of 'going political'. The debate was not on the customary lines of force versus constitutional action (the Provisionals were clearly in favour of force), but of having a political programme to put forward to show that the Provisionals were not merely mindless gunmen. O'Bradaigh and Daithi O'Connell were strongly in favour of a political programme, but MacStiofain and his supporters, chiefly the Northerners, were mistrustful of anything that might dilute the military effort. However, the politicals ultimately won out to the extent that a socialist-sounding policy for a new order in Ireland, the 'Eire Nua' (New Ireland Policy), was adopted.

A part of the new policy revealed to the public on August 21, 1971, in Monaghan Town (the venue was chosen because it was in the South but near the border) contained one fundamental new idea, namely that there should be four regional

parliaments for Ireland, catering for regions drawn up on the old provinces of
Leinster, Munster, Connacht and Ulster. Ulster was to be restored to its original nine
counties with its own parliament, Dail Uladh, the idea being that the Protestants
would gain three more counties, albeit with a much reduced overall majority,
which would on the one hand reduce their fears of being swamped by Catholics
and at the same time give the Catholics a larger share in the running of the new
Dail Uladh. The idea was keenly discussed at least in Republican circles, though I
for one could never see that the Unionists, having sown the dragon's teeth they
did with six counties, could be expected to do any better with nine.

The Provisionals also drew up a five-point programme which was issued on the
eve of the Lynch-Heath meetings at Chequers on September 6, 1971, and which
subsequently formed the basis of discussions on a cease-fire with Whitelaw. The five
points, though dismissed by everyone concerned, are a useful thumbnail description
of the Provisionals' aims and still stand, though the provision regarding Stormont
clearly no longer applies. They asked that the British government should:

1. End its campaign of violence against the Irish people.
2. Abolish Stormont.
3. Hold free elections to establish a regional parliament for the Province of Ulster as a first
   step towards a new government for the thirty-two counties.
4. Release all Irish political prisoners, tried or untried, in England and Ireland.
5. Compensate all those who had suffered as a result of British violence.

Still the only overt signs of I.R.A. activity on the streets of Belfast were riots,
stone-throwing youths and 'up the I.R.A.' graffiti. But behind the walls of the red-
bricked terraced houses a stranger, had he penetrated, might have observed here
and there groups of men sitting around walky-talkies imported from America and
heard exchanges like these:

'Foot patrol coming up Kashmir Road . . .'

'Roger, will open up a second front in Dunville Street.'

The 'second front' might have consisted of five or six youths armed with stones or
an occasional petrol bomb. But their activities would have diverted the patrol
from the Kashmir Road and from possibly finding an arms cache or radio transmitter,
and in any event another group of soldiers was pinned dawn. Also at this time
(roughly late summer of 1970/early spring 1971) one began to read of the soldiers
being taken to hospital after 'accidentally discharging their own weapons'. I
remember a hospital orderly in Musgrave Military Hospital in Lisburn telling me
that his ward at that stage was already filled with gunshot victims—'shotgun
pellets, twenty-twos, everything'—but the army were not issued with those types
of guns and yet 'they were making out that it was accidental discharges that did it',
said the orderly. Yet despite the obviously deadly nature of the steadily fermenting
yeast, the first British soldier to die in the troubles, Gunner Curtis, was not shot
until February, 1971.

The ultimate object of the campaign that began to get off the ground was not to
pin an outright victory over the British army, which was clearly impossible, but to
render the existing state inoperable so that the army would have to withdraw. The
army is still there but the I.R.A. have certainly succeeded in making the state a heavy
liability to Britain. The British government estimated at the end of August, 1979

that the operational cost since the army first moved in, on August 15, 1969, at around £404.3 million; the daily cost of terrorism was said to be running at about £500,000, or £5.50 a second.* The overall bill for holding on to the North was £1 billion annually—the same as Britain contributed to the E.E.C.

After a period in 1971/2 following the introduction of internment, which was characterised by riots, bus burnings and prolonged gun battles with troops, costly in terms of ammunition, the pattern changed; rioting gradually died away and the campaign developed along a three-fold path.

1. The shooting of personnel—security forces, police, members of the Ulster Defence Regiment and so on.

2. The use of bombs, placed both in premises—some large, but some ludicrously small, 'soft' targets such as insignificant shops and pubs—and in parked cars. One of the biggest single 'economic targets' was destroyed on July 17, 1971, when the Provos blew up the £2m *Daily Mirror* plant at Dunmurry outside Belfast (one of the most advanced in Europe), partially because it was regarded as the 'Soldiers'' paper. Despite, or perhaps in part because of this, the *Daily Mirror* in London published an editorial in August, 1978, calling for a British troop withdrawal.

3. The use of propaganda, at which the Provisionals soon proved themselves to be enormously adept. Another related field at which the Provisionals were to show considerable prowess was intelligence.

All through the decade they proved themselves able to get hold of top secret information which had both a military and a propaganda value. For instance, in 1969 they learned of internment in advance so that instead of being a crushing blow, it proved a launching pad—so few of their key personnel being picked up that the blow fell mainly on the innocent, with consequent enormously damaging repercussions for the authorities. They learned that British intelligence was operating behind the cover of at least one seemingly ordinary business and brutally crippled this endeavour by eliminating the team, including a woman, that operated in Belfast behind the cover of the Four Square Laundry. In early 1979 they brought off a coup which really displayed arcane knowledge, taking from the English mails a top-secret British military assessment (published in *An Phoblacht* in May) of their own strength in which the British concluded, among a number of other judgments, that the I.R.A. could not be defeated—an incredible morale booster to receive from an enemy.

Recruitment was very largely from the young of working-class Catholic strongholds in Belfast, Derry, Armagh, Down and Tyrone, though later, as the campaign began stretching on and on, Southerners started to be drawn into the ranks also. The widespread nature of I.R.A. support in ghetto areas, though it contained inherent weakness in terms both of its potential for infiltration and for ghastly errors of timing and inefficiency which led some British security forces to sneer at the 'Paddy factor', did offer great advantages to a guerilla movement.

---

* *Sunday Independent*, August 26, 1979.

The 'Paddy factor' arose because much of the movement was young, working class, limited in vision and experience, very often cut off from central direction by the duress of the circumstance, and had to rely therefore on 'targets of opportunity' or personal initiative. These last two circumstances in particular were sometimes responsible for awful tragedies of bungled warnings as to bomb explosions, or for the unforeseen tragedies such as the kidnapping of Dr Niedemayer.

A bomb could be made in one place, transported to a second and picked up by a third party who might not have known either of the others, for delivery to the target—be it a restaurant, hotel, public building, shop or pub. In all cases the basic motivation was the same, the waging of economic warfare. This particular aim was pursued to its extreme limits with the policy, later on in the decade, of actually shooting industrialists and businessmen. This began in January, 1976, causing widespread criticism even amongst I.R.A. supporters, particularly after the very able managing director of Dupont in Derry, a man who had done a great deal to attract investment to the province, Mr Jeffrey Agate, was shot. The I.R.A. did try to justify the businessmen's killing, issuing a statement on March 22, 1977:

> In all cases, those executed by the I.R.A. played a prominent role in the effort to stabilise the British-orientated Six County economy.
> This economy has never served the interests of the people. It is geared completely to their exploitation and is to the benefit of those in control. The war is not merely a conflict between Republican and British forces. It is a conflict between the interests which these forces represent. Those involved in the management of the economy serve British interests— they represent and maintain economic interests which make war necessary.

But, despite the foregoing, the campaign was recognised for what it was, an ugly and unpopular affair, and was quietly dropped without public declaration. But as we shall see in our examination of the events of 'Bloody Monday' on August 27, 1979, in which Earl Mountbatten was blown up at Mullaghmore, Co. Sligo, the idea of striking at the prestigious continued intermittently to be reactivated by the movement to a point where it became major policy.

The I.R.A. benefited from the traditional passive support given to the movement. The bed for the night, the blind eye, the co-operation in money or services. For instance, the I.R.A. are not invulnerable, bullets do wound them, but one very rarely hears* of a doctor or a hospital reporting the fact that a wounded man is receiving treatment—'traffic accidents' are widespread! But political support, in the form of the vote, continued to be withheld—or rather the type of person who might have drawn the vote continued to stand aloof from the movement.

All through the decade both the cause of constitutionalism (as represented by the S.D.L.P.) and of physical force have suffered because the two wings of Catholic assertion were divided. This in a sense makes the I.R.A.'s struggle all the more remarkable. It was far more lengthy and costly in life and destruction than the Anglo-Irish war of the 1916–21 era but, unlike that era, it was carried out without a significant political movement and, hence, without the sanction of being able to point to a voting support for its activities.

The changing times forced new techniques on the Provisionals as the campaign

---

* In fact in the South, never.

wore on and British surveillance and technology improved. For instance, during March, 1973, because searches and heavily increased surveillance were making bombing more difficult, the I.R.A. introduced the tactic of proxy car-bombing, i.e. forcing the driver of a hijacked lorry to drive his own vehicle to the target under the threat of his own or his family's death and leaving the driver to raise the alarm. On March 28 of that year, one of the most spectacular of such bombs caused three-quarters of a million pounds-worth of damage in the centre of Belfast.★ At different times, as we shall see, judges, businessmen and prison warders were added to the death lists. On April 8, 1976, the first prison warder claimed as a 'legitimate target' was shot dead. (The hitting of one such legitimate target on April 17, 1979, well exemplified the increasing inhumanity of the campaign; he was at a wedding holding the hand of a three-year-old child at the time.)

Up to the summer of 1978, when a re-organisation of the movement into a cell system, not unlike the old I.R.B. model, was carried out, the I.R.A. was modelled on the old army-style lines and engaged out in activities under familiar banners: the I.R.A. itself; Sinn Fein, its political wing; Cumann na mBan, the women's wing; Na Fianna Eireann, the youth organisation; and one new departure, the I.R.A. auxiliary, which did not show itself in overt operation but existed as low-profile support groups of considerable value to the movement as a whole. As the campaign wore on, the movement issued a wide variety of pamphlets and newspapers, the principal being the *Republican News* in Belfast and *An Phoblacht* in Dublin, which were subsequently merged into *An Phoblacht*.

Apart from the premeditated direct attacks carried out by the I.R.A. on security forces, warders, informers, loyalists and the organisation's own disciplinary activities, which could and did include shaving off women's hair, tarring and feathering, kneecapping and even death, there was the loss of life as a by-product of the I.R.A.'s activities. For instance—not including the enraged response against innocent Catholics by Protestant killer squads such as the U.V.F., the Tara Organisation or the Shankill Butchers Gang, all of which tortured and killed Catholics as a direct consequence of the I.R.A. campaign—there were the members of the public and of the I.R.A. itself, accidentally killed as a result of premature explosion or a faulty warning system.

When thinking of the I.R.A. operatives one should not visualise hardened neo-psychopaths of ice-cold nerve. There are a few, but they are a minority. This may sometimes, particularly in the wake of a miscalculation which has cost civilian casualties, seem very hard to accept, but the I.R.A. make a firm and fixed distinction between attacks on U.D.R. and R.U.C. personnel and sectarian assassination. It is official I.R.A. policy (broken only very rarely and in exceptional circumstances—see Chapter 24) that a Protestant is not a target for his religion. It is the status of the target as an upholder of the Northern status quo which determines the choice of target.

★ The principal destructive agent used in the North has been gelignite, although more modern substances including napalm bombs which destroyed La Mon, for instance, have been used. The gelignite has been obtained under the traditional guise of 'Staff exports' from quarries all over Ireland and England and from America where in New York it took five years and a suspiciously large amount of explosives to blast out the New York City Water tunnel.

The only time civilian casualties have been deliberately caused was during the British campaign.

The majority of volunteers are young working-class men and women of varying degrees of education, intelligence, nerve and experience. Some grow tougher under the duress of circumstances, jail, interrogation, placing bombs and so on. Some do it as a matter of reluctant necessity. Some, a few, may even enjoy killing—the near sexual satisfaction of a gun. Many, many caught up in all sides of the conflict drink far more than is good for them or the people on whom their decisions have impact. Drink must be more of a factor in this campaign than in any other.

The bulk of Northern volunteers also come from a background in which the system is regarded as so evil that any evil may legitimately be used to destroy it. This and the sense of historical continuity of keeping faith with the patriots who have died in this and earlier struggles makes up the 'justification factor'.

I remember one I.R.A.-supporting housewife on the Falls Road saying dismissively of a Protestant housewife (like herself a good mother to a young family) who had lost a brother and a husband to I.R.A. action, 'Ah sure, what is she but an auld orangie?' The more havoc the I.R.A. wreaked, the more the Loyalists lashed out at Catholics—any Catholics—and the more action and reaction intertwined, the more callous everyone got.

The I.R.A. women who lured three British sergeants to a party on the Antrim Road in Belfast one evening so that they could be lined up and machine-gunned to death, or the I.R.A. squad who caught two off-duty R.U.C. sergeants, who were buying wine to take home to their evening meal with their families, and forced them to lie on the floor for 'execution', had one thing in common: they weren't killing flesh-and-blood people, they were destroying cyphers. 'We've nothing against them personally. It's the uniform we are after. It's just business,' said one I.R.A. apologist to me in a comment that might have come straight out of *The Godfather*.

Yet that spokesman and the bulk of his movement would have been highly insulted at being compared to the Mafia. The 'justification factor' is compounded of a combination of 'the cause' and dialectic. Basically the I.R.A. man feels that he is fighting for freedom, for an end to injustice, while his opponents seek supremacy, so the end justifies the means.

It was, after all, though at another place and in another time, another Republican upheaval which caused Madame Roland to exclaim as they took her to the guillotine, 'Oh Liberty, what crimes are committed in thy name.' The other component of the 'justification factor', the dialectic one, means that all action can be rationalised in de-personalised language.

An opponent is not murdered. He is 'hit', 'done', 'knocked off' or 'executed'. A bungled bombing which cost civilian life is defended by pointing out that 'civilians die in war. It's a regrettable inevitability.' So much for the 'them'. If one of 'us' gets killed it is a matter for empathising with the families, and a ritualistic black berets, military-style funeral perhaps, but certainly an occasion for human emotion.

The ranks of the 'them', the security forces and in particular the Loyalists, see the Catholics in a similarly de-personalised, demonised guise, of course.

A partial breakdown of the statistics involved in the death toll, 1971–79

	1971	1972	1973	1974	1975	1976	1977	1978	Jan.–March 1979
Shooting incidents	1,756	10,628	5,018	3,206	1,803	1,908	1,081	755	189
Explosions	1,022	1,382	978	685	399	766	366	455	90
Bombs neutralised	493	471	542	428	236	426	169	178	35
Weight of explosives (in lbs)[1]									
In explosions	10,972	47,462	47,472	46,435	13,753	17,596	2,839	5,443	2,015.5
Neutralised	3,001	19,978	32,450	27,094	11,159	16,252	2,188	5,860.5	559.5
Armed robberies	437	1,931	1,215	1,231	1,201	813	591	439	132
Amount stolen (in £s)	303,787	790,687	612,015	572,951	572,105	545,497	446,98	231,250	64,354
Malicious fires[2]			587	636	248	453	432	269	58
Deaths: civilians[2] (sectarian, interfactional & intra-factional assassinations shown in brackets)	115	322 (122)	171 (87)	166 (95)	216 (144)	245 (121)	69 (42)	50 (14)	7 (1)
Deaths: army/U.D.R.	48	129	66	35	20	29	29	21	3
Deaths: R.U.C./R.U.C.'R'	11	17	13	15	11	23	14	10	–
Injuries: civilians	1,838	3,813	1,812	1,680	2,044	2,162	1,027	548	113
Injuries: Army/U.D.R.	390	578	548	483	167	264	188	117	22
Injuries: R.U.C./R.U.C.'R'	315	485	291	235	263	303	183	274	51
Houses searched[3]	17,262	36,617	74,556	71,914	30,092	34,939	20,724	15,462	1,285
Finds: firearms	717	1,264	1,595	1,260	825	837	590	400	95
Finds: ammunition (in rounds)	157,944	183,410	187,399	147,202	73,604	70,306	52,091	43,511	8,419
Finds: explosives (in lbs)	2,748	41,488	38,418	26,120	11,565	21,714	3,809	2,108	744.25

Apart from the figures for deaths and explosives, a breakdown of violence over the period gives an idea of the scale of the upheaval, of the enormous outpouring in energy and resources involved. Either the shooting incidents for 1972 (over 10,000) or the house searches for 1973 (over 7,000) tell a story of disruption and danger that was all the more acute by virtue of so much of it being compressed into a small area that made up many of the Catholic districts of West Belfast and the working-class ghetto areas of the Catholic towns throughout the North. Then if one thinks of all the security and legal personnel involved in the apprehension, prosecution and ultimate detention of those involved in the figures below, the scale of the war really emerges. And those figures are of course not financial. One has also to think of the figures for compensation, for injury, death or destruction.

Persons charged with serious security-type offences[a]

	31 July–31 Dec. 1972	1973	1974	1975	1976	1977	1978	Jan.–March 1979
Murder	13	71	75	138	120	131	60	11
Attempted murder	16	85	75	88	121	135	79	13
Firearms offences	242	631	544	460	353	301	225	49
Explosives offences	86	236	161	100	215	146	79	9
Theft act	111	186	232	314	188	203	151	42
Other	63	205	275	97	279	392	249	63
Total	531	1,414	1,362	1,197	1,276	1,308	843	187

[a] Estimated weight only.
[b] Consolidated figures not available for earlier years.
[c] Includes occupied and unoccupied houses searched.

Out of this medley of emotion one gets a cold statistic of nearly 2,000 dead in the troubles to mid-1979 (see table).

But then if one analyses how and why some of them died, names and events swim through the haze of incident—The Abercorn, McGurk's, Donegall Street, Bloody Friday, La Mon—in a confusing yet ultimately all too explicable montage.

McGurk's bar was blown up by Loyalists in reprisal for I.R.A. activity because it was owned and frequented by Catholics. Fifteen people died including Mrs McGurk and most of her family. This was one of the first of innumerable other premises destroyed for sectarian reasons. The Abercorn could have been the work of Loyalists also, or it could have been caused by a Provisional bomb in transit to another target. Anyway, one nondescript March day in 1972, a bomb exploded amongst a restaurant full of women and children, killing two people and leaving some of the hundred injured without arms, legs, eyes, and with psychological trauma probably never to be eradicated.

That year also, bungled communications were responsible for two awful incidents, the Donegall Street explosion (March 20) which killed six people, and the Bloody Friday explosions (July 21) which killed nine.

In the case of the Donegall Street blast, a car bomb went off in a street crowded with children who had been cleared from a street nearby by troops who had received a bomb warning. The Provisionals claimed that the security forces deliberately misunderstood their warning so as to maximise the casualties. But it is more likely, in the tension and confusion of Belfast, that the Provisionals overestimated the capacity of their opponents to deal with a profusion of bomb scares, phoned in moreover by excited, possibly very youthful, callers.

The Bloody Friday bombs, for instance, involved twenty-two separate explosions in a one-mile radius of the Belfast city centre over a period of forty-five minutes. Between them the explosions injured about three hundred people, crippling some of them for life. It's one thing to phone a warning, it's another to estimate how soon it will take effect. In the La Mon disaster nearly eight years later, warnings were phoned but not sufficient time elapsed between the time they were received and the bombs going off to avoid carnage: the bungled napalm bombing of the La Mon Restaurant in the Protestant district of Comber in February, 1978, in which twelve people died was one of the worst episodes of the entire period.

But to hark back to the 'justification factor', an I.R.A. spokesman whom I met after the La Mon bombing, though he showed himself mindful of the loss of life and of the possible Orange retaliation, was at least equally disgusted at the fact that the news had blanketed the reports of the I.R.A.'s achievement in shooting down an army helicopter. *An Phoblacht*, for instance, led the issue following La Mon with the helicopter story and recorded La Mon on a back page under a list of the week's happenings.

To look back through the pub bombings, tortures and assassinations for one year, that of 1972, we see that the total killed in that one twelve-month period was 468 persons. Most of these were civilians—323. Some 103 were army, the rest R.U.C. and U.D.R. The happenings deserve to be reckoned alongside the Munich Olympics massacre, or the kidnappings of Signor Aldo Moro or Herr

Schleyer, but they become lost in the welter of Northern Ireland horror—hence but one of the reasons why the Provisionals decided to try for a British campaign and later for 'prestige targets'.

19

The British Campaign

As in Sean Russell's day, there was always a body of opinion within the movement which favoured 'having the war on England's sod'. Theoreticians like Daithi O'Connell reasoned, regrettably correctly, that the Irish could kill each other off until Tibbs Eve, and even throw a bunch of working-class British soldiers into the deadly stew for good measure, without anyone in England becoming unduly worried—but should a few of the bombs which went up so frequently in Belfast go off in Britain, then the public consciousness would be galvanised—hopefully into action on a British withdrawal.

The difference between Sean Russell's day and the contemporary campaign was that the contemporary one was better organised. Those opposed to the I.R.A. could point to the ease with which the police captured some of the bombers—after the Birmingham and Scotland Yard explosions, arrests were made within hours of the blasts as groups of young men and women were apprehended trying to buy air and rail tickets back to Ireland—but it was more protracted and destructive than the earlier campaign and had, as the bombings in December, 1978, and January, 1979, showed, more potential for being re-started should the I.R.A. so decide.

Although many of the bombers and gunmen were new to the British scene and inexperienced in getaway techniques, others were trained according to the lessons of the I.R.A.'s past and of post-World War II guerilla experience generally. Men took names and used them to acquire passports—inspired by those appearing on tombstones over graves whose occupants, had they lived, would have been the same age as their impersonators. 'Sleepers' (people who had lived for years in England without mixing with other Irish) came to life and went into action. The means used embraced everything from petrol bombs, fire bombs, explosive bombs to direct assassination.

The list of incidents which began on March 8, 1972, with explosions at the Old Bailey and Whitehall (the Aldershot bombing of February that year was an Official I.R.A. reprisal for Bloody Sunday) was to include episodes as diverse and bloody as the Birmingham bombings which killed 21 people and injured 168, and shootings and bombings in the West End of London which for a period in 1974-5 severely affected the commercial and social life in the area.

The campaign often looked meaningless and cruel—a bomb in the Tower of London, frequented almost exclusively by tourists, in July, 1974, for instance, injured forty-one innocent children and killed a woman; but apart from the general theory of spreading the war to England there was also often a specific reason for individual actions.

The coach bombing on the M62 motorway in which nine soldiers, a woman and her two children were killed in February, 1974, the pub bombings at Guildford and Woolwich in October of that year, which between them claimed seven lives, all occurred during election periods and were designed to underline the fact that Britain had not yet found an answer to the Irish question. Ross McWhirter, the compiler of the *Guinness Book of Records*, was shot because he was sponsoring a reward scheme for the apprehension of those responsible for the campaign.

The most striking example of how the I.R.A. could tie their British campaign to specific demands of the moment probably occurred during a set of truce talks in 1975 between the Provisionals and British civil servants (James Allan and Michael Oatley under the direction of Sir Frank Cooper, Permanent Secretary to the Secretary of State for Northern Ireland, then Merlyn Rees). The British told the I.R.A. negotiators, James Drumm and Pronsias MacAirt, that they could not control the British bombers whom they alleged were simply I.R.A. mavericks. The I.R.A. men replied to the civil servants (after consultation with their principals) that there would be a spate of bombings until midnight on January 27 and that then an undeclared truce would occur. Sure enough, the 27th was punctuated by a series of explosions. The truce was formally agreed to at a meeting on February 10, but it, like the others, was to peter out.★

The I.R.A. intended to resume operations in England very shortly after Balcombe Street (described below), and would have done so had not the Gardai in Dublin succeeded in breaking a captured I.RA. man, an epileptic, and seized a load of explosives en route to England. The man who talked was subsequently executed by the I.RA. in a Dublin pub. A little later in the year, two I.RA. men were arrested in England. Both went to jail, in England and in Belfast, although on somewhat lesser charges than they might have incurred had they been captured after some of their planned operations.

Operations did resume, as mentioned earlier, in the late winter of 1978 and, though peaks and valleys in the campaign have occurred, the will to wage such a campaign remains constant.

While it would be impossible within the present compass to deal fully with the entire bombing campaign, the career of the 'Balcombe Street four', as the I.R.A. unit became known after they were sentenced at the Old Bailey on February 10, 1977, to a total of over thirty years apiece by Mr Justice Cantley, is worth examining in some detail.

Readers will readily see the similarities in the attitude and background of the young men concerned to those involved in the pre-World War II campaign, but the difference in the degree of sophistication, training and ruthlessness will also be readily apparent.

★ Although it was subsequently denied from the British side, one of the more interesting side-effects of the talks seems to have been the channelling of British public monies to the Provisionals via Provisional-minded builders under the auspices of the Northern housing executive. No sane author would attempt to describe the labyrinthine world of the Belfast housing executive with complete authority. But it does appear that a substantial amount of what seemed like legitimate building activity was in fact only a Provo fundraising front which the authorities are now trying to crack down on.

The four were Martin O'Connell, a native of Co. Clare, who came to London in August, 1974; two months later Eddie Butler and Harry Duggan arrived, and Hugh O'Doherty did not arrive until March, 1975. They were convicted of six murders; one manslaughter; a series of bomb attacks; possessing firearms with intent to endanger life (at Scott's Restaurant, Mayfair); using guns to resist arrest; kidnapping John Matthews and his wife Sheila, who were held hostage during the six-day Balcombe Street siege; plotting to cause explosions; and plotting to discharge firearms with intent to endanger life. In all they caused fourteen explosions in London and one in Surrey.

Another member of the unit, Brendan Dowd, is also serving life imprisonment for other I.R.A. offences. The five were operating together until the murder of a policeman, Constable Tibble, after which Dowd left London for Manchester.

In just over a year of guerilla activity the four averaged more than one attack a week. Their slide into capture began on the night of December 6, 1975, when, from a stolen car with all four aboard—the first and last time they had all gone on a mission together—they raked Scott's with gunfire; the second time they had hit the building, but they were pursued by police and then sought refuge in Balcombe Street where they commandeered a flat and eventually surrendered after a six-day siege, leaving the owners of the flat (Mr and Mrs Matthews) unharmed.

Until January, 1975, the unit was under orders to attack military targets, including pubs frequented by soldiers. The principal aim was *not* to kill, but in the bitterness after the end of the six-month ceasefire in 1975, the orders from Dublin switched to killing.

The four were then living in two flats in different parts of North London: O'Connell and Duggan in Milton Grove, Stoke Newington; the others in Crouch Hill. Both areas were filled with coloured immigrants, but contained very few Irish; they avoided pubs and districts frequented by the Irish. They got their money and supplies via couriers who visited them monthly from Ireland—their identities (they were mostly women) still remain secret. They kept social life to a minimum—a film, perhaps, or a football match, but rarely drinking or going out with girls.

On a mission the normal *modus operandi* was for only two to take part, usually one employed in planting the bomb and one keeping an armed watch. The night Ross McWhirter was shot, for instance, Duggan did the actual shooting (with an Astral Magnum) and Doherty drove the getaway car belonging to Mrs McWhirter.

Duggan planted the bomb under Edward Heath's car in November, 1975, but O'Connell made it. As well as making most of the bombs, O'Connell organised the intelligence and drew the maps of target areas. Duggan came next in seniority. Doherty mostly did reconnaissance, and Butler generally acted as back-up man.

Normally the unit chose its own targets, though occasionally Dublin might recommend something or someone in particular, and they concentrated their attacks on the wealthier areas and strata of society.

Harry Duggan was born in Kilburn. His parents were told in 1973 that he was dead, 'killed in action in the North'. He was supposed to have been buried in Feakle, Co. Clare, at that time. Eddie Butler, from Castleconnell, went missing soon after Duggan's 'death', in December, 1973. Hitherto he had had a background of minor I.R.A. activity, selling Republican papers on a Sunday and so on. Hugh

Doherty met the others in London. He had spent most of his life in Scotland, his parents having emigrated, like many Donegal folk before them, to the transported orange and green rancours of Glasgow. During the period of the campaign all four were in their middle twenties.

Ironically Duggan might not have been involved at all had the Canadian authorities not turned down his application for a visa to Canada where he had an opportunity of working as a carpenter during the early 1970s. He then rejoined the I.RA. and took part in a number of operations including the £8 million robbery of paintings from Sir Alfred Beit's collection in Co. Wicklow (see Chapter 20).

Duggan's 'death' and resurrection formed part of a Provisional plan to utilise key men in specialised operations under a cloak of anonymity gained by announcing their deaths after explosions in which victims could not be identified. (Incidentally a variant of this idea is used by the British army to cloak their casualties, some of whose Northern losses have been attributed to accidents suffered by B.A.O.R. personnel while in Germany so as to delude the Provisionals and possibly the British public. The Protestant paramilitaries also buried their dead secretly for a time to avoid giving the I.RA. the satisfaction of learning their casualties.)

It was only during the siege at Balcombe Street that Irish fingerprints experts discovered that Scotland Yard had fingerprints which matched those found at an abandoned house near Charleston, Co. Mayo, after Duggan and another I.R.A. man had shot their way out of a Garda force which had surrounded the house after the art robbery.

Scotland Yard had no inkling of the four's whereabouts until the Scott's episode when by chance they ran into one of the police patrols saturating the West End as a result of the bombings. The Yard had hitherto been concentrating its surveillance on known Irish haunts and on known Sinn Fein sympathisers, all of whom the group of course sedulously avoided. Until they were captured they terrorised the West End to such a degree that I once crossed Oxford Street at rush hour without having to watch for traffic!

The explosions and killings caused by the Balcombe Street group, which, of course, had their effect heightened by other occurrences such as the Birmingham, Woolwich and Guildford death tolls, left an ancillary trail of maimings and shock. This explains, though it does not forgive, a phenomena closely related to the bombing campaign, the treatment meted out to the captured I.RA. men while in custody.

The *Irish Press* and the *Guardian* newspapers were instrumental in revealing the ill-treatment of the six Northern Irishmen arrested for the Birmingham killings. To say that the 'confessions' on which their successful prosecutions were based were not yielded voluntarily is to understate very considerably what happened. It is a tradition of the bombing campaigns against England undertaken by Irish extremists, stretching back through the days of the Coventry explosions to the Fenian times, that Irish captured as a result of the activities invariably receive rough justice when apprehended. Brendan Behan, who gave a glimpse of this facet of the age-old struggle between the Irish and English, carried an indentation in his forehead to the grave; a memento from the Liverpool police who arrested him for his part in Sean Russell's campaign.

Warders at Hull prison were brought before the courts on charges arising out of the treatment of Irish prisoners, and in Parkhurst prison on the Isle of Wight, Irish prisoners voluntarily sought solitary confinement to escape their fellow prisoners who, led at one stage by both the infamous Kray brothers, offered them violence and threats of death without interference from the warders. (The moving of one Kray brother to a criminal lunatic institution didn't improve the situation.)

Hatred between political prisoners and their captors is not a phenomenon confined to the I.R.A. in England. As noted elsewhere, there were riots and incidents involving a high degree of brutality in Mountjoy and Portlaoise jails in Ireland also, to say nothing, of course, of what transpired in jails in Northern Ireland, such as Long Kesh or Crumlin Road or, above all, in interrogation at centres like Hollywood and Palace Barracks.

Such bitterness is probably inevitable in a situation where not only are people losing life, liberty, limbs and happiness, but the freedoms of democratic society are being utilised by their assailants to carry on their campaign. What is really surprising is not the bitterness but the degree of apathy in Britain about the whole Northern Ireland position, despite all the catalogue of horrors listed above.

Nor are things much different in the South of Ireland. For instance, the worst single set of happenings of the entire course of events was the simultaneous bombings in Dublin and Monaghan in which over thirty people were killed outright and scores more were maimed. Yet within a matter of days after Dublin had seen gutters run with blood, bodies fused together with the force of the explosion, arms and legs blown across pavements and through shop windows, it was as though there was a social determination to forget the horrors, and the subject dropped completely out of conversation except for the families of those directly involved. In fact in the case of Dublin there was a determination to forget or more particularly to forgive, lest the episode spark off an unimaginable escalation of revenge. But the absence of response from London has the effect of goading the I.R.A. to see just what action is required to provoke the response which they seek. And so more young Irishmen go to their destiny.

Although nothing can restore life (or limb), in some ways the most pathetic victims of the bombing campaigns are the perpetrators themselves. The Birmingham-Woolwich-Guildford bombers were all too young to have come any nearer to bombs than a television screen had they not been born Catholics in Northern Ireland. They were given life sentences in the hostile atmosphere of English prisons for deeds none of them can recall with comfort.

The names of those imprisoned for life for the Birmingham-Woolwich-Guildford bombs are Gerry Hunter, Richard McIlkenny, William Power, Hugh Callaghan, Patrick Hill. All are from Belfast. The sixth, John Walker, is from Derry. All have consistently asserted their innocence. Leave to appeal was refused in 1977. The Woolwich-Guildford four also sentenced to life imprisonment are Paul Hill, Patrick Armstrong, Gerald Conlon and Carole Richardson. The three men are all from Belfast; the woman is from London. Hill, who was twenty-one at the time of sentence, was also given a life sentence for the murder of a soldier. His girl-friend Eugenie Clarke gave birth to his child seven weeks before the sentence was passed. A disturbing circumstance that surrounded the whole affair was that after their arrest the Balcombe Street four, who refused to take any other part in the proceedings against them, claimed that it was they who were responsible for the Woolwich and Guildford attacks and not any of the foregoing. Given the climate that surrounded the arrest and detention of all concerned, it was not an easy issue to offer judgment on.

Guiseppe Conlon, Gerald Conlon's father who died in prison in England in February, 1980 was entirely innocent of any crime. He was a very sick man entirely unconnected with the I.R.A. when he learned of his son's arrest. He set off from Belfast for London to do what he could for his son; but he was arrested, accused of having had explosives in his possession and, on the basis of a 'scientific' test, jailed, and he died in prison.

20

Response to Violence

One of the unpleasant truths concerning the attitudes of the various constitutional parties to the Northern turmoil was (and is) the degree of hypocrisy that permeated everyone's dealings with the situation. Once the Civil Rights movement stalled in the face of Protestant extremism, it became evident that what kept the situation moving was the activities of the hard men on the extremes of Republicanism and Protestantism—particularly the Republicans and specifically the Provisional I.R.A.

Yet the common cry on all sides was 'no talking to gunmen'. The only acceptable political activity concerning the gunmen was to denounce them, legislate against them, imprison them, torture them and generally to devote most of one's political waking hours to them, but never, never to negotiate with them. Not surprisingly, after a decade of this the problem had neither gone away nor been solved, but neither had there been any formal acknowledgement that they, or more importantly their cause, existed.

While maintaining this public posture, however, the British did in fact 'talk' to the I.R.A. on a number of separate occasions. The first came during a visit by Harold Wilson to Dublin (on March 13, 1972) when he took a break from his official duties to talk with top Provisionals including Sean MacStiofain and Daithi O'Connell. Nothing came of these discussions. The most substantial contact occurred in July, 1972, when there was a dramatic meeting in London between William Whitelaw and a top-level I.R.A. delegation comprising Sean MacStiofain, Daithi O'Connell, Seamus Twomey (then O.C. of the Belfast battalion), Martin McGuinness (then O.C. of the Derry battalion), and Ivor Bell and Gerry Adams, the senior officers in the Belfast command structure. A Dublin lawyer, Myles Shevlin, acted as secretary to the I.R.A. delegation.

The I.R.A. men were first flown to Belfast in a British army helicopter for transshipment to Oxfordshire in an R.A.F. turbo-prop Andover; and the worst moment of the entire talks (for them) occurred then because the helicopter circled for a time, and they feared, though they couldn't show it, that at any moment they could be shot down by an I.R.A. rocket. Although the talks were in a sense historic—in Anglo-Irish terms the first in which Irish guerillas had fought their way to a conference with the British Government since Michael Collins had debated with Lloyd George—they were also abortive. The British army refused to honour the Agreement made at the talks to counter Protestant militarism. At that stage, despite the history of the movement, the I.R.A. seemed to be merely one competent, and a rather uncertain and gangsterish one at that, of the Irish problem. One can only conjecture as to whether or not there would have been a Protestant backlash had the British kept to the Agreement. A backlash certainly seemed more possible then than it does now. But if one looks at the loss of life subsequently, one sighs over what the Agreement could have led to had the meeting justified its hopes.

It was held at 96, Cheyne Walk, Chelsea, the home of Paul Channon, a Guinness heir and a member of William Whitelaw's team of junior ministers. Quite apart from the complexities of the situation outside the room, the cultural gap within it was such that meaningful understanding would have been difficult to arrive at anyhow. The Scottish landowner Whitelaw, the millionaire Channon, the suave career civil servants, David Steel and Phillip Woodfield, and the I.R.A. delegation came from yawningly different backgrounds. Seamus Twomey had been a bookmakers' 'runner' in Belfast, invaluable training for street warfare but not for Cheyne Walk; Martin McGuinness had been a butcher's assistant, Gerry Adams a barman, Ivor Bell a mechanic. Only O'Connell, who had been a teacher, and Myles Shevlin, had a degree of academic training.

O'Connell impressed the British most, but the others, conscious of the historic dangers encountered by Irish insurgents in dealing with British statesmen, displayed a kind of rough sincerity that came across unimpressively. As so often happens in Republican affairs, a man's natural intelligence and, very often, qualities of character and judgment, are belied by the theology of the movement, its symbolism and anti-Britishness. A British informant on the talks wonderingly described one of the Irish participants to me afterwards as being 'like a dog'.

For their part the British gave an imprison of condescension and heartlessness that repelled the I.R.A.—'Whitelaw is a ruthless bastard. "We can accept the casualties," he said, "we probably lose as many soldiers in accidents in Germany." ' That sort of philosophy, which was not confined to Whitelaw, was a major factor in the I.R.A.'s decision to have a bombing campaign in England —where the casualties would not be 'acceptable'.

The meeting had been foreshadowed by an I.R.A. ceasefire which had followed the granting of political status to I.R.A. and Loyalist prisoners on hunger strike in Crumlin Road jail and a diminution of British army activities in Catholic ghetto areas. There was a general mood in favour of conciliation on the part of the Catholic community which Whitelaw, who by now realised what an enormous blunder internment had been and understood better the historical position of the Catholic minority, was anxious to build on. But he was thinking in small-scale terms—not of acceding to Irish wishes for a United Ireland.

He had opened by saying that the Provisionals had observed their ceasefire undertakings honourably, and went on:

I hope that the trust set between us is reinforced by this meeting. I record that the histories of our two countries give the Irish grounds for suspicion. I hope that in me you will see a British Minister you can trust.

Look on me as a man who will not make a promise that he will not keep.

He told the I.R.A. team to make any point they wished; he had come there to listen to them. MacStiofain called for a general amnesty for all political prisoners, in Irish and British prisons, all internees and detainees and all persons on the wanted list. A suspension of offensive operations by the British army and an immediate end to internment.

Whitelaw said he noted the Republican attitude in relation to internment and said, 'without agreeing entirely' with Mr MacStiofain, that he understood the feelings of the Republican movement on the matter. 'I hope you understand our difficulties at this time of year with the 12th of July coming upon us. Any moves on my part might bring about a worse situation,' he said. 'Give me the time and the opportunities and I will surprise you gentlemen with the rapidity with which I will act.'

Whitelaw said that recognition of this principle (the principle of the right of the people of Ireland as a unit to decide the future of Ireland—the central I.R.A. demand) would have to be 'very carefully discussed' with his cabinet colleagues. Both the Tory and Labour parties had given repeated assurances to the majority in the North on this point and this very point had been given 'statutory fact' in the Government of Ireland Act.

At this stage the Irish delegation intervened, saying that if Mr Whitelaw was going to quote the Government of Ireland Act, then any negotiations would become sterile. They told Whitelaw that this was 'the very root of the trouble' and discussion on this line would serve no useful purpose.

'Neither of us is a plenipotentiary. I am an Englishman in an Irish situation. The minority in the North have been deprived of their rights. I set myself the task of conquering this. You can give me some help in the matter,' said Whitelaw.

MacStiofain said that the best contribution England could make would be to rescind the principle involved in the Government of Ireland Act. 'We have had talks with many shades of Unionism and are satisfied that there is a growing realisation that such a declaration [rescinding of the Government of Ireland Act] by the British government would bring home to many Unionists the realities of the situation.'

The Irish side made a number of proposals of which the following were crucial:

1. Britain should make a public declaration that it is for the whole people of Ireland, acting and voting as a unit, to decide the future of Ireland.
2. The British government should give an immediate declaration of its intent to withdraw from Irish soil, such withdrawal to be completed on or before the first of January, 1975.

From the foregoing it is obvious how wide apart were the objectives which the Irish and the British were seeking.

One side wanted full-scale independence; the other a peaceful return to the status quo albeit to a reformed and more just one.

Daithi O'Connell said there had been too much talk about a 'Protestant backlash' and this and previous British governments had been intimidated by such talk. 'These are our people,' he said, 'and we do not desire nor would we welcome a clash with them. But the fact must be faced that they cannot be allowed to intimidate and hold out on the whole people of Ireland.'

During the meeting the I.R.A. delegation told Whitelaw and his officials that it was desirable to use the term 'Unionist' rather than 'Protestant'. They stressed that a confrontation with the U.D.A. was not being sought, but that the possibility of it could not be ignored.

Despite the divergence in the two points of view, a fourpoint agreement was hammered out:

1. A bilateral suspension of offensive operations would continue until July 14.
2. In the event of a resumption of hostilities, twenty-four hours' notice would be given.
3. On July 14, a further meeting would take place at which the British government's submissions and documents in reply to points one and two would be made known.
4. In the event of the documents being unacceptable to the Irish, they would be at liberty to resume offensive operations without notice.

Two days later it all came to nothing—ostensibly over a nondescript housing estate called Lenadoon on the western fringe of Andersonstown. Some time earlier, Protestant extremist leaders had visited the Protestant residents of this area and 'advised' them to leave their homes because, it was stated, they were in danger from their Catholic neighbours. Catholics in the area said the real reason was because the U.D.A. wanted a clear field of fire at the Catholics when *Der Tag* dawned. Whatever the reason, the houses lay empty and it was decided that Catholic families who had been intimidated out of their homes from elsewhere in Belfast should be rehoused there. However, when the Catholics sought to take up their allotment the U.D.A. said they would burn them out

The army decided not to accept this challenge and barricaded the area. Outraged Catholic crowds gathered as, after a period of negotiation, Seamus Twomey sought to get an army barricade removed to allow through a Catholic owner with a lorry piled high with the furniture belonging to one of the homeless families. At this stage Protestants were carrying arms openly behind the troops who were using C.S. gas, a water cannon and rubber bullets to keep back the Catholic crowds. At Twomey's insistence the troops disarmed a revolver-carrying U.D.A. man, but then they used a Saracen armoured car to ram the furniture lorry. As Whitelaw had not proved responsive to the barrage of frenzied Provisional phone calls which preceded this incident, Twomey took the ramming as the signal that the ceasefire was over—and very speedily shots rang out and battle recommenced.

Whether the I.R.A. were wise to attempt to force the housing issue during the July period or whether the truce would have ever come to anything is arguable—what is certain is the ensuing death toll.

While it was largely conducted on Irish soil and had none of the drama involved in flying Irish terrorists under safe-conduct in British aircraft to meet with British statesmen in London, what became known as the 'Feakle' peace initiative both led to the most important truce of the decade and was certainly the most effective peace movement of the decade.

Prior to the foundation of the Peace Movement two years later, there had been other peace groupings in the North aimed at improving community relations and the cessation of violence. PACE—Protestants and Catholic Encounter; Peace Point, an off-shoot of the New Ulster Movement; and the would-be ecumenical 'Women Together'. All of these seemed in working-class eyes (whether Protestant or Catholic) a little too middle class and where the I.R.A. were concerned they were all viewed as actual or potential British front organisations working to sap their war effort.

The Rev. William Arlow and a group of Protestant fellow clergymen did not do what the other peace movements did—largely confine themselves to attacking the I.R.A.—but instead tried to understand them. The Rev. Arlow and the group, all active in the Irish Council of Churches, had had their interest in trying to promote ecumenical contact in Ireland whetted by their experience in meeting Catholics in Holland and when it was suggested—according to a popular Belfast story, by a Republican on the plane home—that they should try this ecumenism a little nearer to home, Arlow agreed and began making contacts with Sinn Fein.

It had been a very bad year both in Ireland, which had seen, apart from the collapse of Sunningdale and the hopes placed in a power-sharing executive, a ferocious outburst of murder of all sorts, including the Dublin bombings, and in England which had suffered a spate of bombing both in London and in centres such as Aldershot, Birmingham, Bath and Bristol. Accordingly, Arlow's seeds fell on fertile soil. First the Provisionals showed meaningful intent by turning up at the little Clare town of Feakle on December 20, 1974, in an inconspicuous hotel, with a heavy-weight delegation. Three of these, Seamus Twomey, Kevin Mallon and J. B. O'Hagan, later went to prison. The others were Ruairi O'Bradaigh, Seamus Loughran, Billy McKee and Daithi O'Connell. The only woman present, the best known in the leadership of the Republican movement, Maire Drumm, was subsequently murdered in her hospital bed.

Apart from Arlow, the Protestants present at the meeting were: Dr Arthur Butler, Church of Ireland, Archbishop of Armagh; Rev. A. J. Weir, Clerk of the Assembly of the Presbyterian Church in Ireland; the Rev. Eric Gallagher, former President of the Methodist Church in Ireland; the Rev. Ralph Baxter, Secretary of the Irish Council of Churches; the Rev. Harry Morton, General Secretary British Council of Churches; the Rev. Arthur McArthur, Moderator of the General Assembly of the United Reformed Church of England and Wales; Stanley Worrall, former Headmaster of the Methodist College, Belfast.

Arlow had also contacted Sir Frank Cooper, Permanent Secretary to the Northern Office, Stormont, so everyone present knew they were not talking in a vacuum. However, before anything definite could be decided, they were informed that the Special Branch were on their way—the Provisionals had eyes and ears in all sorts of unexpected places—and the immediate aftermath of the meeting appeared to be nothing more than an inquiry initiated by an angry Irish Prime Minister (Liam Cosgrave) to find out where the leak was in the Special Branch. It was never discovered but meanwhile, though interrupted, underground Feakle continued to bear fruit! The Provisionals decided to declare a ceasefire from December 22 to the following January 2—a hopeful way to begin the New Year. Merlyn Rees said three days before the ceasefire ended that in the event of a 'genuine and sustained cessation of violence' the British government 'would not be found wanting in its response'. The next day, New Year's Day, 1975, the Provisionals announced a fortnight's extension of the ceasefire. It seemed like a breakthrough but on January 16, 1975, came the depressing announcement that for a variety of reasons, including a British failure to reply to a demand that the army withdraw to barracks and an escalation of British military activity, the ceasefire would end.

This was not the first time over the period that the various British parties appeared to go in different directions. Not only did the army frequently appear to chafe at the restraints imposed by politicians and civil servants, but there was also a considerable and continuing rivalry between the army and the R.U.C.* During the talks one of the civil servants surprised the Provisional side by remarking when in a discussion of army attitudes which the I.R.A. called for, following which the Provisionals had lashed out, killing a number of soldiers, 'Oh well, we will play at soldiering won't we . . .' However, Arlow, the Provisionals and the Foreign Office persisted, and on January 19 Arlow introduced Proinsias MacAirt and James Drumm, husband of Maire and holder of the hardwon distinction of being the most imprisoned Republican in Northern Ireland, to the Foreign Office officials, James Allan and Michael Oatley.

After a frigid opening session, the meeting led to more talks which resulted in a number of important, tangible developments. On February 12, for instance, Rees publicly announced the opening of a number of 'incident centres', which were ostensibly to monitor a hoped-for ceasefire but were also to provide, in Provisional eyes and in the eyes of their foes, a base for local political and community involvement. The Provisionals gave point to the discussion by displaying an ability to turn the off-stage bombing on and off like a tap until finally, on February 9, there was an I.R.A. announcement of a ceasefire to take effect from the following day. This was matched by a British commitment to maintaining the army at a 'low profile' from February 10. The 'incident centres', each with a 'hot-line' to Stormont Castle, followed.

This was a hopeful and important breakthrough but it ultimately petered out the following October in the closure of the incident centres, a spate of bombings and a number of other episodes, such as I.R.A. feuding, unrelated to but affecting the ceasefire. The principal factor ending the ceasefire was that each side wanted different things from it. The I.R.A. wanted a formal British declaration of intent to withdraw from Ireland. This, it seems, they were certainly led to believe they were getting, but the smooth Foreign Office diplomats, skilled in the art of the misleading nuance, had not actually committed their masters (who were of course bound to the Downing Street Declaration) to this Holy Grail of Republicans.

What the British sought, and got, was a respite from Provisional harassment of the security forces, and a somewhat improved climate in which an effort could be made to bring the various factions together in a convention and perhaps to rescue something from the midst of Sunningdale, just as in the wake of 1916 the British had tried to quell awakened Nationalist sentiment by staging a convention to be attended by all political factions. However, elections were held on May 1, 1975. The anti-Sunningdale Loyalists won forty-seven seats to thirty-one. The summer bled on, and it became clear that there was no hope of a new power-sharing

---

* On January 11, 1977, the R.U.C. were appointed the principal security force in the province, but this primacy was damaged by the I.R.A. blows struck against Lord Mountbatten and the British army on August 27, 1979. Subsequently Sir Maurice Oldfield, the intelligence supremo, was appointed from London to try to co-ordinate security.

formula emerging from the 'politicals'. In their innermost hearts the British could not really have expected a 'convention' held in the wake of Sunningdale's collapse to do what Sunningdale could not, but it provided at least a political figleaf to cover the real lack of will and hopelessness, where Ireland was concerned, in the Labour government.

Meanwhile, throughout 1975, although the I.R.A. and the army left each other more or less alone, some of the cruellest and most dramatic events of the decade occurred. Maddened by the suspicions engendered by the talks and the establishment of the 'incident centres', the Loyalist paramilitaries lashed out at innocent Catholics both by means of pub bombings and individual killings, in a wave of murder that reached a crescendo with a slaughter at Bessbrook the following January (see Chapter 24). All three major paramilitary groups had their splits and feuds. The Provisionals with the Officials. The Officials with the Irish Republican Socialist Party. And the U.D.A. within itself—Charles Harding Smith, shot on February 6, being the most notable victim of this feud.

While this was going on, Southern Ireland had its share of incident with episodes like the effort by the Provisionals to break into Portlaoise with an armoured bulldozer, the Larry White shooting in Cork, the Herrema siege at Monasterevin and a U.D.A. bombing of Dublin airport. England had its share of bombing throughout the autumn until the Balcombe Street siege rang down the curtain on that particular chapter of events. The incident centres were closed down in October after a month in which one of their O.C.s, Seamus MacOsguir of New Lodge, was shot in the Officials-Provisional split.

As with the Boal/MacBride talks (described later in Chapter 24), the situation, still *sub regnum* Downing Street Declaration, had not matured to the point where unilateral talks involving just one section of the combatants could end the violence. Also ended that year was detention which in effect meant nothing as the prisoners were still held; only the methods of seizing and prosecuting changed, and an end was signalled for political status for prisoners from March 1 of the following year.

The last was a decision that was to provide much adverse publicity for the British and to provide a rallying point for Provisionals during the low point of their campaign from the end of 1977 to the summer of 1979.

Finally to the most publicised response to violence, the Peace Movement which began on August 10, 1976, when British troops in hot pursuit of a car driven by Danny Lennon, a member of the Provisional I.R.A., fired on him, fatally wounding him and causing the car to go out of control on Finaghy Road North, mounting the pavement and killing the three young Maguire children, Joanna (aged eight), John (two-and-a-half) and baby Andrew (six weeks), before the eyes of their traumatised mother, Mrs Anne Maguire, and their aunt, Mrs Pat O'Connor, whose children mercifully escaped unhurt.

Watching another aunt, Mairead Corrigan, weeping on TV that evening, Mrs Betty Williams, no relation, decided that the afternoon's slaughter of the innocents was just too much and she contacted Mairead Corrigan and the pair began circulating a peace petition.

Spontaneously the Peace Movement mushroomed into the biggest mass movement of the decade. It was aided by Ciaran McKeown, then an *Irish Press* journalist, who wrote them a prayer for the movement. Some of its rallies were spectacular, particularly an early march down the Shankill Road which was genuinely inspirational. In full view of the cameras Protestant women embraced marching Catholic nuns. Very large sums of money were collected, particularly in Norway, and Corrigan and Williams were awarded the 1977 Nobel Peace Prize.

However, the movement allowed itself to give the appearance of being more anti-I.R.A. than anti *all* forms of violence, understandably, perhaps, in view of its genesis, and was used by the Northern Ireland Office as a smokescreen for political inertia and ultimately left no lasting imprint on the campaign.

21

Prison: Riots, Escapes, Unlucky Freedoms, Personalities and a Place Called Crossmaglen

The decision in 1975 to end political status for prisoners after March 1, 1976, led to the H Block blanket protest where the I.R.A. prisoners sought to win back political status by not wearing prison clothes. There was a consequent withdrawal of privileges and the situation escalated until the prisoners ended up in cells befouled with their own excrement, wearing nothing but blankets, sometimes for periods of over three years.

The Provisionals managed to smuggle out a film showing the conditions inside the block and this had a considerable impact when it was shown on television. The impact was heightened and spread by the *Washington Post* columnist Jack Anderson who gave American readers a bombshell insight into the H Block affair in his widely syndicated column. The situation escalated to one of far greater anguish and danger an any other prison drama of the period, with warders shot dead outside the jails situated in the Long Kesh compound area—and beatings, bad diet and conditions of indescribable filth inside the jail provoking many humanitarian people including Cardinal O Fiaich to call for an end to the horror.

As in other eras, prison occupied a real place in the I.R.A.'s mind and in publicity. How to avoid it, how to beat the system either by riot or hunger strike and, above all, how to get out.

'The Crumlin Kangaroos' was the name of a popular ballad written about a group of nine men who escaped from the Crumlin Road Jail, Belfast, on November 16 1971. Two were recaptured but the other seven reached the Republic safety having had the benefit of the traditional right of sanctuary in a Cistercian Monastery in Tyrone. This was the first major escape of the period and it also provided marvellous propaganda opportunities for the Provisionals to provide living refutation of the Compton Report's attempt to whitewash reports of army brutality.

Less than two weeks after the 'Kangaroos' episode, on December 2, 1971, two of the Provisionals' toughest volunteers, Martin Meehan and Dutch Doherty, were amongst a trio (the other was Hugh McCann) who again escaped from over the Crumlin Road wall. The prison at the time was bursting at the seams with over 900 inmates, and supervision was not what it normally was, allowing the three, with the aid of a friendly warder, to get away using knotted blankets and sheets.

They, too, gave evidence of being tortured. The army tried to refute this, using a doctored picture of Doherty allegedly pleading for mercy which was published in the *Daily Mirror*, in an attempt to show that the pair had 'squealed'. However, the army boot in his ribs was airbrushed out.

Meehan's escape, in particular, jolted the army who were anxious to interview him. It jolted the South, too, where there was always the danger that war could spread from the North. On January 27, 1972, Meehan and his henchmen both compounded this risk and added to the South's difficulties in trying to refute Unionist claims that it was not a haven for terrorists, by engaging the British army in a four-hour cross-border gun battle. Later that day, Meehan nonchalantly told reporters, 'We pasted them. You could have heard them squealing for miles.' No one suffered in the incident, the only casualty being London-Dublin understanding.*

On January 17, 1972, another seven-man escape team made headlines by following the example of a seal. They were being detained on the *Maidstone* prison ship in Belfast Lough when a member of the group spotted a seal slip through a gap in the barbed wire draped around the ship, and it was decided that if the seal could come in, they could go out. This they did, camouflaged in black boot-polish and smeared in butter to keep out the cold. Though badly cut by the wire, they managed to get safely through the icy water to shore although some of them could scarcely swim. They hijacked a bus and drove to the Catholic markets area of Belfast where they disappeared only to reappear at another propaganda-bonanza press conference.

The foregoing were all, as it were, the 'acceptable face' of the I.R.A. legend. Such episodes fitted into the movement's daring, romantic side and involved no loss of life; but they came early on in the decade before the dull, horrific campaign was well under way. Later a grimmer note was to enter the prison saga. The hunger strikers and the bitterness of Portlaoise jail are described elsewhere.

Mountjoy jail in Dublin had its riots and damage but the principal flair up of the period occurred in the North. On October 13, 1974, Long Kesh went up in smoke with the Republican prisoners attacking warders (over the food) and being subdued by soldiers. To complete the subjugation process helicopters dropped C.S. gas into the wire-enclosed compounds.

As the burned-out Long Kesh huts were still smouldering, women I.R.A. prisoners in Armagh prison seized the governor and three prison officers and imprisoned them! There was a sympathetic riot in Crumlin Road for which troops and police were called out; and at Magilligan prison camp in Derry the I.R.A. also burned their huts. Subsequently there were conflicting claims as to how many were injured in the riots, the Provisionals claiming one hundred and the North of Ireland Office a third of this number.

The Armagh governor was surrendered uninjured after two days but the Provisional prisoners were left for some days afterwards to weigh the effects of the publicity they had gained against their bruises and their discomfort in trying to sleep amidst ashes and muck.

Probably the most dramatic escape of all occurred in Dublin, giving rise to yet another ballad, 'The Provie Bird'. The Provie Bird was the name given to the

---

* Again that year (July 9) Provisional sympathisers demonstrated at the Curragh, hurling abuse, physical as well as verbal filth, at the soldiers who did not respond even while stones were hurled. Ultimately C.S. gas was fired and the crowd was dispersed harmlessly.

helicopter which, with a suborned pilot at the controls, dropped into the exercise yard of Mountjoy jail on the afternoon of October 31, 1973, and took off again with three of the most important I.R.A. men in the country while the others prisoners stood around and cheered and the warders made a futile attempt to get through the cheering throngs.

This escape really created a sensation not only because of the dramatic means but because the three prisoners were Seamus Twomey, Chief of Staff; J. B. O'Hagan, a pillar of the movement from Lurgan; and Kevin Mallon who, toughened and hardened from the days of his beatings as one of the two prime suspects in the Sergeant Ovens case, had become one of the most formidable and daring I.R.A. figures of the century. He is yet another example of how I.R.A. men get hammered out in the anvil of circumstances: sometimes the beatings and jailings break them but when they don't, a Joe Cahill or a Kevin Mallon emerges.

Many of these escapees would have been better off had they stayed in jail, because here and there, without headlines, as the campaign wore on, several who had reported back to duty were either killed or re-arrested and charged with more serious crimes committed after their escapes.

One of the more ironic cases was that of John Francis Green whose escape from Long Kesh on September 9, 1973, dressed as a priest caused a great deal of knowing head-shaking; his brother, Fr Gerrard Green, who had been visiting him prior to the escape, was found after it, tied up in a compound. Green went back on active service and was found shot dead in a farmhouse south of the border twenty-two months later. The Provisionals blamed the S.A.S. and cited his death as one of the reasons for ending their ceasefire on January 16, 1975.

Because of the nature of the campaign and sometimes of the theatre in which it was waged, splits, or at least cases of 'separate identity', within the Provisional movement also occurred, in and out of prison. Apart from the ideological reasons recorded elsewhere, two of the most celebrated centred around personalities on the one hand and a place (see Chapter 20) on the other. We will look at the personality difference first, that of one of those who was to find freedom unfortunate.

Some of the loudest headlines generated by the I.R.A. were detonated from within the Provisionals by an active service unit (A.S.U.) which the I.R.A. heartily detested by the time it was run to ground. It was led by Eddie Gallagher, the son of a small farmer in Co. Donegal, who while working in London met the woman who was to bear his child and eventually to marry him in Limerick Jail, Rose Dugdale, the English heiress. She was active in a sit-in at the London School of economics (which, incidentally, attracted a number of young Irish revolutionaries whose Republicanism thus became impacted on to socialism) that had caught his attention.

The A.S.U. began 1974 by seizing a helicopter and forcing the pilot to fly them to Strabane where they dropped two milk churns filled with explosives on an R.U.C. barracks. Neither exploded. On February 23 Manchester Magistrates Court issued a warrant for Dr Dugdale on the charge of conspiracy to smuggle arms and explosives to Northern Ireland and it became known also that the British army were anxious to discuss milkchurn delivery, as practised in Strabane, with the lady in question.

But the Garda Siochana in Southern Ireland became even more eager to make contact with her when in an uncharacteristic display of appreciation for the finer things of life, an I.R.A. squad raided Russborough House, near Blessington, Co. Wicklow, and departed with the cream of Sir Albert Beit's collection of art valued at eight million pounds sterling.

Rose Dugdale was arrested, and the paintings recovered on May 4 in a house rented by her in Glandore, Co. Cork. On June 25 she was sentenced to nine years for the theft of the paintings.

Eddie Gallagher was also picked up later that year and consigned to Portlaoise jail on August 15. Four days later he was free again, one of the group that blasted its way out of the jail with smuggled explosives. Gallagher, who was also suspected of the Lord and Lady Donoughmore kidnapping, was one of those who would have been better off staying in jail. For he really hit the headlines the following autumn before police ran him and Marion Coyle to ground on October 21, 1975, in a house in Monasterevin, Co. Kildare, some forty miles south-west of Dublin, with Dr Tiede Herrema, the managing director of Ferenka Limited, a subsidiary of the giant Dutch multi-national Akzo, whom they had kidnapped in Limerick earlier in the month.

After a seventeen-day siege, all were released unharmed. But there were some consequences apart from the fact that Marion Coyle joined Rose Dugdale in Limerick instead of securing her release which was one of the objects of the kidnapping (along with freeing Kevin Mallon, who had been recaptured, and James Hyland); and Eddie Gallagher returned to Portlaoise, this time with a thirty-year sentence.

One side-effect was that many Republican sympathisers visited by the police during the search for Herrema were so disgusted by the kidnapping that they volunteered valuable information about other Provisional activities.

Another was that because of this and the generally unfavourable and unwelcome publicity surrounding Gallagher and company's activities, the Provisionals placed him at or near the top of their black-list.

A third was that Ferenka closed down with the loss of 1,500 jobs. This was largely due to labour relations and the fact that the tyre manufacturing process carried on at the factory had been rendered near obsolete by newer technology, but the kidnapping will always linger on in some people's minds as the main causative factor.

However, though Dr Herrema was subjected to a ghastly ordeal through no fault of his own, he was at least able to live to tell the tale. Not so another kidnap victim of the I.R.A. prison saga, Thomas Niedemayer, the German Consul in Belfast and head of the North of Ireland branch of Grundig. Like Herrema a highly popular figure in the community, he was kidnapped without authorisation by an I.R.A. party on December 27, 1973, acting on impulse in a confused gesture of retaliation for the ordeal of the Price sisters and the other hunger strikers in jail in England. He suffered a heart attack as a result and died. His body was subsequently disposed of and his wife and family were left to mourn his loss in an agony of uncertainty.

The final and most improbable footnote of the Gallagher saga (to date, that is) is that a sizeable strike of uranium has been made on land in Co. Donegal owned by— Eddie Gallagher.

The place which gave rise to a state of 'separateness' within the Provisionals, amounting almost to a sort of 'independent Republic' within the physical force spectrum as a whole, is of course the Provisional-oriented area of Crossmaglen. Ironically, Crossmaglen—or more specifically the district of South Armagh in which it is situated—gave both the British army and the Provisionals two of their most authentic heroes of the period. Captain Nairac, whom the Provisionals captured, beat severely and shot while he was on undercover work in South Armagh, certainly would be accounted a hero on the British side. On the Provisional side was Michael McVerry, whose short life was shaped through being born not alone to a parish but to a history.

The market town of Crossmaglen in South Armagh boasts the largest square in Ireland but this is not why Crossmaglen is a name that strikes a disturbing chord in the mind of any British soldier who has served in Northern Ireland since 1971. Set in a little 'U' of land enclosed in Northern Ireland by the border, Crossmaglen is the prime example of the Unionists' chickens coming home to roost.

By tradition and religion it is a Gaelic-minded Catholic enclave with a minuscule Protestant population. Lying in the shadow of the Sliabh Gullion mountains in a cobweb of narrow twisting roads, bordered by high overgrown hedges, its inaccessibility from the rest of the North meant that in centuries gone by rebels flourished there long after the rest of the country was conquered. Naturally the people of Crossmaglen turn towards the South for all the things that make up a cultural pattern—shopping, holidays, careers.

Only the most mindless gerrymandering could have included Crossmaglen, or nearby Cullyhanna for that matter, into a state proclaiming itself Protestant and British. But included it was, and today the lists of British soldiers 'killed in action' bears witness to that folly. Unionists claim, as they have done throughout the fifty years of the state's existence, that it is the proximity of the border which makes South Armagh such an I.R.A. hot-bed. The I.R.A. are able, they say, to take advantage of the terrain and retreat to Dundalk.

The I.R.A. of the Crossmaglen district don't retreat anywhere. After they have set off their tripwire bombs—or nowadays radio-controlled bombs—fired their lethal snipers' bullets or even, on one celebrated occasion, downed a helicopter (the day of the La Mon débâcle in Belfast), they simply go home, protected by the unseeing eyes of their families, friends and neighbours.

There is also a flourishing G.A.A. club at Crossmaglen which the soldiers have frequently disrupted. Deplorable though this conduct was, I felt I had an insight into it, one day, when on a visit to the town I saw part of a group of young soldiers watching a rugby international on a television set in a shop window. The other part faced outward, guns at the ready. The British Garrison there has to be serviced by helicopter because the roads are too easily and too frequently ambushed.

The archetypal Crossmaglen I.R.A. figure, one of the folk heroes of the decade, was Michael McVerry who was killed on November 15, 1973, during an attack on Keady R.U.C. barracks in Co. Armagh. Aged twenty-three, McVerry was the officer commanding the First South Armagh Battalion. He was a native of the townland of Skerriff near Cullyhanna.

McVerry exploited the countryside he knew so well to the full, sometimes opening fire on troop-carrying vehicles from a car and being chased by them blazing away like something out of a film until he lost his pursuers. Apart from using bombs and timing devices, he used bluff and sheer cheek as well—as for instance when having caused an explosion in a shop in Crossmaglen he made no effort to get away but, picking up a child, stood with the child on his shoulders talking to the soldiers while the debris was shifted.

A young man of McVerry's dedication could not understand or accept that the I.R.A. leadership could descend to internecine politicking and position-seeking. Even for an outsider it is sometimes very unpleasant to go to a public occasion, a funeral say, or to Bodenstown and to watch the preening and publicity-seeking of some of the movement's top figures. It's hard to accept that men who have risked, and taken, life for 'the cause' could behave like any ordinary small-time self-seeking politician, seeking public notoriety. At times like that one may be forgiven for speculating that in some cases intense dedication to the cause may be a cover for some deep-rooted lack in character rather than a sincere, thought-out resolve.

Towards the end of his brief career McVerry also seems to have become somewhat disillusioned by the type of recruit coming into the movement. There was a good deal of drinking—there still is—a general laxity and a falling away from the high standards he set himself. He felt that the war was not being pushed with sufficient vigour and was attempting to heighten the tempo of activities with a barracks raid carried out in the unfamiliar district of Keady, Co. Armagh, where he was killed.

Today his memory is recalled by an imposing memorial—a set of inscribed gold-leafed tablets reached up a flight of steps in Cullyhanna. The effect of this memorial is to provide both a source of inspiration to like-minded young men of the district and, as such, a source of affront to the security forces and the Loyalists who each sometimes daub the memorial with insults and obscenities, a regrettable but apposite example of what a 'them' name on a monument means to an 'us' in Northern Ireland.

22

Hunger Striking: the I.R.A. Reach Beyond the Bars

Of all the facets of the decade-long campaign, the most typically Irish was hunger-striking, that powerfully weak form of protest in which, as we have seen in other eras, the case of the participant seems to the public to get morally stronger as the victim gets physically weaker.

There were six major incidents of hunger striking in the course of the post-1969 campaign. Five of these ended in failure—although one, a mass strike at Portlaoise, was to have far-reaching effects as we shall see. Two of the strikes ended in death and only one resulted in the prisoners demands being met.

The first involved Joe Cahill and the O'Bradaigh brothers, Ruairi and Sean. Just a week after the Republic voted by a majority of approximately five to one in favour of the government's proposal to join the Common Market, Lynch felt strong enough to move against the I.R.A. after the Mountjoy jail riots of May 18, 1972. He brought in an Emergency Bill to enable civilian prisoners to be transferred to military custody and followed this up a few days later on May 31 with the setting up of Special Courts under the 1939 Offences Against the State Act.

The Special Courts consist of three judges who sit without a jury. The I.R.A. decided to respond to this tactic by hunger striking and for eight, thirteen and nineteen days respectively Sean O'Bradaigh who was director of Sinn Fein publicity, Ruairi O'Bradaigh who was its president, and Joe Cahill who was on the I.R.A. army council went on hunger strike after being picked up as part of a new drive. All were released for lack of evidence and though the strike aroused some publicity—O'Bradaigh's sister also joined in—it caused nothing like the controversy which was to develop over subsequent strikes.

The successful strike was the strike which included the Price sisters, Dolores and Marian, who were arrested with five others after car bombings in London in March, 1973, and who went on strike in order to be sent back to Ireland to serve their sentences. Two of the men arrested with them, Hugh Feeney and Gerard Kelly, also went on hunger strike with the same demand and were also force fed for a period which lasted over 200 days, and were also ultimately successful. But somehow the men's struggle never captured the public's imagination in the same way that the girls did. Apart from the fact of being women, Dolores wrote poetry and Marian had a descriptive touch about her writings which made her letters on forced feeding particularly arresting. For instance a letter which another Price sister, Claire, was prevented from reading on Radio Eireann contained the following:

Well this morning we had our force-feeds. Dolores was a bit sick and I was the sickest I have ever been. As soon as the tube went down I started to retch and then when the liquid was poured in, it all came up again, so half way through the doctor pulled up the tube and started all over again.

I don't think that helps much because I still puked the remainder up. Very unpleasant, but this is the first day of the New Year and if I have to go through the same for the next 364 days I will.

However she concluded:

We read in the paper about Dolores being at 'Death's door'; she did not think that she looked that bad on the visit, but I don't suppose we are very good judges. Anyway, don't be worrying about us because I assure you we are both still alive and kicking and living in Brixton.

During their captivity the girls were transferred from Brixton prison to Durham and Dolores wrote a poem which read in part as follows:

> The light has gone out of my existence
> No reason left but the great one
> The one that overrides all others.
> That takes my whole being
> Reserves and demands it.
> Still there is a longing for the little ones.
> The wave of your hand
> That stirs my heart and makes me smile
> To think that for me it is there
> The sound of your voice,
> That I know from among many
> That too is one of the little.
> Perhaps it is the little that is great,
> The great just is.
> And I could say such things to you
> Could tell you of my dreams,
> How once there was a little girl
> Who danced in summer streams,
> and sat upon a mountain,
> And thought that she was God,
> Knowing in her innocence,
> All wrongs that she must solve
> Then I could show the woman
> Still so much the child
> Who knows to hold your hand in hers,
> If only for a while
> And would you gladly give yourself
> To one who soon may die . . .

A very sizeable publicity campaign built up in support of the girls' demands and respected public figures as disparate as Bishop Daly of Derry, the S.D.L.P. Assembly man, Paddy Devlin, Lord Longford, Fenner Brockway, the Labour M.P., joined in the campaign to have their requests granted. The girls finally ended the strike on June 7, 1974 but they were not transferred to Armagh jail until March 18, 1975, because the bombing campaign in England in the interim made their transfer politically inadvisable. Ironically it was the deteriorating position of the Provisional ceasefire which helped Roy Jenkins, the then Home Secretary, to make up his mind in March, 1975, that the transfer of the Price sisters might have a beneficial effect on the situation. Ultimately it had no bearing on it, but for a time the conciliatory attitude gave hope of better things to come. Kelly and Feeney were transferred the following month as was a member of the U.V.F., William Campbell, who had been in jail in Glasgow on explosive charges.

At one stage the Price sisters' affair looked like being compounded by deaths other than their own, when the popular Tipperary peer, Lord Donoughmore and his wife were kidnapped by I.R.A. elements in support of the Price sisters' case. This was one of those sidebar dramas, as was the kidnapping of Dr Herrema, that were thrown up by a mixture of impulsiveness, daring, and a lack of foresight by groups within the I.R.A. which in themselves did the I.R.A. considerable damage and could have done even more had they not ended without bloodshed.

The Donoughmores are a particularly popular family in Ireland. Their son, Mark Hely-Hutchinson, a leading amateur jockey in his time, is the managing director of the Guinness Brewing Company and the family were known to be sympathetic to Sinn Fein during the Anglo-Irish war of the 1920s. The Donoughmores' ordeal came to an end when the news of the Price sisters' transfer broke and though they came to have a high regard for their captors there was an ominous note of what might have been, in the words used by one of them when he broke the news of the Price girls' victory to Lord Donoughmore: 'You're lucky,' he said.

The hunger strike of Sean MacStiofain actually occurred before that of the Price girls and could have had more damaging long-term effects because he was at the time chief of staff of the I.R.A. But again, by some benign turn of fate, confronta-tion and bloodshed were avoided. His arrest came as the result of an interview on Telefis Eireann, the Irish television station. As a consequence the government later tracked down on Telefis Eireann and fired the nine-member Authority which the government appoints as watchdogs of what is transmitted.

Despite the presence of this board of governors and with the war in the North hotting up, the government had earlier in the year introduced an additional safe-guard in the shape of a loosely worded and to the Broadcasting Act, Section 3 (now referred to in Ireland in much the same way as the phrase Catch 22 is used in America). Aimed at debarring I.R.A. spokesmen or propaganda from the station, Section 31 is very difficult to interpret u government lawyers have advised the government what it can be taken to mean in a particular circumstance.

The particular circumstance that brought down the government's wrath on R.T.E. was an interview with Sean MacStiofain by Kevin O'Kelly, at the time news features editor of R.T.E.

The government killed two birds with the one stone by arresting MacStiofain in the early hours of Sunday morning, November 19, 1972, as he drove away from O'Kelly's home where he had given the interview, and then by sacking the R.T.E. Authority for allowing the interview to be transmitted later that day.

MacStiofain heightened the atmosphere of drama by going on a hunger and thirst strike and he was sentenced to six months' imprisonment on November 25 for I.R.A. membership. That evening bombs went off in Dublin causing injuries to some forty people. Kevin O'Kelly was sentenced to three months' imprisonment for contempt of court, for refusing to answer a question about the interview, and the R.T.E. Radio and TV service closed down for a forty-eight-hour strike. Large meetings were held in Dublin, addressed by Provisional spokesmen, demanding that MacStiofain be released; and armed men dressed as priests burst into the Mater Hospital to which MacStiofain had been transferred in an unsuccessful attempt to rescue him. Shots were fired in the hospital itself but mercifully no one was injured. MacStiofain's would-be rescuers were all captured and sentenced to seven years' imprisonment. MacStiofain himself was transferred by army helicopter to the Military Hospital at the Curragh to prevent any further rescue attempts. He continued his hunger strike but accepted water and glucose.

The backdrop to his incarceration turned particularly rancorous because of the visits to MacStiofain in hospital by both the present Catholic Archbishop of Dublin, Most Rev. Dr Dermot Ryan, and his predecessor, Dr John Charles McQuaid.

Critics of the I.R.A. and of clerical influence in the Republic had a field day with both visits, which were particularly Irish crises of conscience for both prelates. Once they were asked to visit a man who through hunger and thirst strike could be termed in *articulo mortis* (and whose death moreover, if he did die, could be the cause of widespread bloodshed with the Northern conflict once and for all engulfing the South), both had a moral and a spiritual obligation to visit him.

But politically, of course, the visits exposed both men to attacks from critics in the Republic and in the North. In the Dail, Dr Noel Browne, T.D., an old political opponent of Dr McQuaid, was particularly scathing on the visit to a gunman by his old 'Mother and Child' scheme adversary.

The Dail was convulsed at the time with far more weighty matters, because at a juncture in the passage of the second stage of the Offences Against the State Amendment Bill when it looked as though the proposal might founder, two bombs suddenly went off in Dublin on Friday night, December 1, 1972, in Sackville Place and at Liberty Hall (blowing in the windows of my office). To this day many people in Dublin swear that the bombs were planted by British intelligence. Two people were killed and scores were injured. The Bill passed by seventy six to twenty-three at four a.m. the following Saturday morning. Ironically, one man blown into the division lobbies on the amendment side had hitherto been one of the Bill's sternest critics, Patrick Cooney, of Fine Gael who, when power changed hands in the election on February 28, 1973, became Minister for Justice and was to become one of the most controversial law and order figures to hold that office in the history of the state.

MacStiofain stayed on strike for fifty-seven days and finally came off it the following January when the I.R.A. army council asked him to. A statement issued by the council said that 'after fifty-seven days of hunger strike no useful purpose will be served by Mr MacStiofain continuing his protest against unjust imprisonment.'

MacStiofain never again regained the position of power he had held in the Provisionals. It was alleged that he had sought the statement from the Provisional leader which enabled him to come off the strike to save his face. The Dublin wags of the time had it that his telephone number was Curragh 888 but from his biography it is clear that he suffered considerably during the strike and certainly for a time it appeared that if he were to die the result would be civil war in the South of Ireland.

The two saddest occurrences of the hunger-striking episodes were the deaths of Michael Guaghan and Frank Stagg, the former in Parkhurst on the Isle of Wight on June 3, 1974, and the latter on February 12, 1976, at Wakefield prison. Stagg had initially gone on hunger strike with Gaughan on his death-fast and though he decided not to make the supreme sacrifice on the first strike, he followed the route of Terence McSwiney, Terence McCaughey, D'Arcy and MacNeela on the second occasion.

The basic demands of both men were for political status, the right to wear their own clothes and not to be forced to do prison work. Gaughan, the eldest of six children, was twenty-one when he was sentenced for his part in a bank robbery in Hornsey in North London which netted only £530 for the Republican movement. He was in fact a member of the Official I.R.A. through its English wing, Clann na hEireann. Stagg, who was two years older than Gaughan, also came from Mayo and unlike Gaughan was married. He was sentenced to ten years in October, 1973 on charges of conspiracy after being arrested with Father Patrick Fell and five others—the Coventry seven, as they were known.

Gaughan's death was made all the more poignant by virtue of the fact that it came a week after the successful Loyalist strike to which the government capitulated. But there was to be no capitulation to the demands of a lone I.R.A. hunger striker in a British jail. He went on hunger strike on March 31, was artificially fed from April 22, but refused medical treatment and died of pneumonia eventually. The two men could only be seen by their relations through a glass screen during visits supervised by police and prison warders. In these circumstances Gaughan received a single visit from his mother three weeks before he died and in describing the visit afterwards, Gaughan's brother John said: 'They both cried.'

His death raised a controversy in English medical circles as to whether doctors should render medical assistance in a case like his even though some forms of treatment, if given without a patient's consent, could have led to charges at law of technical assault. In fact the use of hunger striking as a political weapon posed the same dilemma for doctors as voluntary euthanasia—'does the patient have the right to end his own life?'

However, a discussion of the issues by the British Medical Association's ethical committee later in the month in which Gaughan died, failed either to yield an answer to the problem or to avert Stagg's death two years later.

A far greater controversy obscured this issue when Gaughan was buried with the full I.R.A. honours in Ballina in his native Mayo after a funeral, which took place following a procession from the east to the west of Ireland, virtually closed down the town of Ballina with I.R.A. supporters. This created vast publicity for the Provisionals and an even greater headache for the government, which did not want to allow itself to be drawn into confrontation with the Provisionals during the funeral and so generate worldwide publicity. The Provisionals got their publicity anyhow.

The government was annoyed on a number of fronts: the domestic flouting of its authority; the criticisms which the television and newspaper accounts of the proceedings gave rise to in England; the consequent pressure this brought on from London; and, no small consideration this, the very evident proof of its strength which the Provisional I.R.A. had openly given in moving in very large numbers from Dublin airport in the east (where Gaughan's body was landed) right across the country to Ballina in the west.

Consequently when Stagg died on February 12, 1976, having been on hunger strike for sixty-two days, the government took a decision expressly to deny Stagg what according to his lawyer, Michael Connolly, was his principal last request, namely that he be given a military funeral along a route from Dublin to Ballina which he specified. The Provisionals were equally determined that a major propaganda funeral should be held and the stage was set for a confrontation.

This situation was made all the more distressing by virtue of the fact that a split developed between members of the Stagg family over the affair. His widow Bridie, who with Stagg's seventy-year-old mother was present at his bedside when he died in the hospital wing of Wakefield prison—having shrunk to approximately four stone in weight and gone blind in the process—blamed the Provisionals as much as the British Home Office for his death. His brother Emmet also held the Provisionals responsible and objected to a military-style funeral, but other members of the family, in particular another brother, Joseph Stagg, supported the idea. Apart from the family bitterness which this split engendered there was so much pressure and intimidation from Provisional sources on Emmet Stagg and the widow that for months afterwards Emmet Stagg had to have police protection.

Against this unseemly backdrop an almost tangible state of national tension built up as the media of the world waited at Dublin airport for the plane bringing Stagg's body back from Yorkshire and for the expected clash between the authorities and the Provisionals.

However, while the plane was en route to Ireland the government diverted it to Shannon and despite some scuffling with Provisional sympathisers, successfully whisked the coffin away to Ballina where it was buried on February 20 in Leigue Cemetery near Gaughan, but not in the same Republican plot as Stagg had wished.

The next day, Joe Cahill who, with a party of other prominent Republicans including the President of Sinn Fein, Ruairi O'Bradaigh, had had a fruitless wait at Dublin airport for the fought-over, wasted corpse, delivered a funeral oration over the grave promising that one day Stagg would lie in the Republican plot.

Stagg was buried in a grave dug by police which was concreted in to a depth of eighteen inches and watched over round the clock by police; but the guard was withdrawn some six months later and shortly after midnight on November 6, 1976, a group of Provisionals accompanied by a priest dug through the night to tunnel under the concrete, recover the coffin, bless and re-inter it in the Republican plot a hundred yards away.

Today there are three tombstones bearing Frank Stagg's name in Leigue Cemetery: one over the concreted grave erected by his wife and some other members of the family; another over an empty plot bought by his brother George; and the third includes his name amongst those buried in the Republican plot.

But the most potent inscription of all is the invisible one, in the pantheon of Republican martyrs which, if the Northern Irish situation is not resolved, will one day surely inspire some other young Irishman to follow Stagg's example—with possibly more deadly consequences.

The largest outbreak of hunger striking of the period, a mass strike by Republican prisoners at Portlaoise led by Daithi O'Connell, Leo Martin and Dan Hoban, lasted for forty-seven days and ended deceptively on April 22, 1977, in apparent failure. However, it proved subsequently to have very far-reaching effects, and contributed to the downfall of the Irish government.

The strike itself was called off to the sound of a national sigh of relief after a Catholic bishop, Bishop James Kavanagh of the Dublin diocese, interceded. He had been collected by the nationalist-minded Senator Michael Mullen, General Secretary of the largest Irish union, the Irish Transport and General Workers Union, at the behest of I.R.A. sympathisers to see if intercession might get the prisoners, the authorities and the country off the hook. The prospects of mass death appalled everyone.

The prisoners failed to get any concessions as a result of their strike in the short term but the circumstances and personalities involved are worth examining in one detail, as they do illustrate how the Northern issue and the I.R.A. can suddenly erupt from being a peripheral issue to become once again *the* Irish political concern.

The economic situation had contributed to the downfall of Fianna Fail in the General Election of February 28, 1973, and the return to power of a coalition between Fine Gael and Labour led by Liam Cosgrave, son of William T. Cosgrave, the first Prime Minister of the Irish Free State after independence.

But Fianna Fail had been in power for sixteen years and the accretions of office had done their work. There was a general wish for improvement throughout the country when the Coalition took office and an expectation that new faces, particularly in the Labour Party which included intellectuals like Dr Conor Cruise O'Brien and Justin Keating, would provide a leavening of brilliance rare to the normal atmosphere of Irish parliamentary debate.

In fact Irish political debate is not noticeably below the level of, for example, the standards of West European parliamentary debate, but Fianna Fail has the tradition of machine politics in which the leader is habitually the central figure and spokesman for the government, and ministers are expected to be competent rather than compelling in their public persona which very readily leads to the charge that Fianna Fail are the duds and the Opposition, the intellectuals.

The presence of figures such as I have mentioned and of Dr Garret FitzGerald, then leader of the Fine Gael party, certainly added substance to the charge in the abstract, but, tested in the reality of politics, the result was a great disappointment for people who felt that Fianna Fail had gone stale and needed a rest to regroup and rethink, and that a change would be good for the country.

Part of the problem stemmed from the interaction of the personalities of two very different men, Liam Cosgrave and Dr Cruise O'Brien. Both in different ways anathematised the I.R.A.: Cosgrave because his father had led the Treaty side into victory in the civil war by taking stern action against the Republicans whom he saw as attempting to wreck the country, and the son shared the father's feelings towards the I.R.A.; O'Brien, because he objected to the nationalist movement on principle, feeling that the 1916 revolution had delivered the country into the hands of bogmen, priests and Fenians.

He had a belief that to have credibility and integrity in Irish politics one had to confront both these forces and though he never became noticeably embroiled in controversy over the Church he was not alone in assailing the I.R.A. with great vigour at the time of his election. He subsequently espoused a course of confrontation of all the Irish nationalistic beliefs—or myths, as he and his at one time large body of supporters, would have seen them.

He publicly stated on more than one occasion that he did not think it helpful to work for Irish unity and he continually said that if the British left Northern Ireland the result would be a holocaust.

He was appointed Minister of Posts and Telegraphs and as such the operations of Radio Telefis Eireann fell within his purview. He believed that the Provisional I.R.A., if not in actual occupation of the building, at least greatly influenced programme-making and found himself the centre of a controversy on censorship which gradually had the effect of alienating a considerable body of Irish public opinion from the new government.

Meanwhile Cosgrave through his Minister for Justice, Patrick Cooney, who as mentioned earlier had been a liberal during the course of the passage of the Offences Against the State Act Amendment Bill, pursued a particularly tough law and order line. A few major developments may be mentioned here to exemplify the attitude of those years.

One was the introduction of an Emergency Powers Bill which gave the police the right to hold suspects in detention for seven days without charges; in other words subjecting them to duress and stress during that period in order to extract damning evidence. The other was more difficult to identify: the formation of what became known as the 'Heavy Gang', a flying squad of policemen who conducted interrogations with suspected I.R.A. men in different parts of the country and whose activities again gave rise to the very considerable disquiet and widespread allegations of police brutality.

Since it has been fashionable in England, particularly in the popular press, to say that if the Irish government stepped up its security measures then the I.R.A. would be defeated, it will, I think, be instructive to look at what happened when an Irish government did take an unusually harsh line on the I.R.A. (After years of conflict it should not be necessary to point this out—since the components of the problem should be known to everyone in a senior position in Fleet Street and the British media generally.)

As Mary Holland pointed out writing in the *New Statesman* (September 7, 1979):

The nadir of recent British experience in Northern Ireland was reached precisely when the army, spurred on by a Unionist government at Stormont, had control of the fight against the terrorists in the province. Those were the years that produced internment, no-go areas, Bloody Sunday, the complete alienation of the Catholic community and a situation of such volatility in the South that the Irish government was unable to prevent the burning down of the British embassy.

It was the closest Ireland has come this time around to the much prophesied civil war, and what averted it was the suspension of Stormont in 1972 and the arrival of William Whitelaw, who immediately saw that his first priority must be to tie the army's hands back where they belonged.

Fate decreed that I and the *Irish Press* played a role in inflicting the first defeat on the Coalition and then bringing about the resignation of an Irish President, Cearbhall O'Dalaigh. These events, particularly as can be imagined the resignation of the President, led to vast public controversies and ultimately, as the subsequent election results were to show, built up into one of the few occasions in Irish history when under native government the public refused to go along with a government in measures aimed at the I.R.A.

The affair began when in August, 1976, after five men had blasted their way out of the basement of the Special Criminal Court at Green Street in Dublin, the government decided it was time to really put the boot into the I.R.A. Using the Offences Against the State Act, a State of Emergency was declared and some draconian legislation was drawn up under an Emergency Powers Bill. It was proposed to increase the length of time wherein I.R.A. men could be held in detention for questioning from two to seven days and no one was under any misapprehension that the extra five days were intended to provide the suspects with a more thorough knowledge of prison cooking. In addition the penalty for I.R.A. membership was increased from two to seven years. Additional powers of search and arrest were conferred on the army, and in another bill, the Criminal Law Bill, there was a provision aimed specifically at the media, and, as it turned out, even more specifically at myself and the *Irish Press*, section 3 of which read as follows:

Any person who expressly or by implication directly or through another person or persons or by advertisement, propaganda, or any other means, incites or invites another person (or persons) generally to join an unlawful organisation or to take part in, support or assist in its activities shall be guilty of an offence and shall be liable on conviction on indictment for a term not exceeding ten years.

The distinguished *Washington Post* journalist, Bernard Nossiter, then the paper's correspondent in London, came to Dublin to interview Dr Conor Cruise O'Brien about the package which at the time, though it was not liked, was expected to go through the Dail, with the veiled assistance of Fianna Fail—accepted as just another distasteful procedure necessitated by the situation in Northern Ireland. Nossiter's interview changed that.

He discovered that O'Brien had intentions beyond the stated scope of the bill. He wished also to 'cleanse the culture' of such malignities as revolutionary ballads and if necessary he agreed that the bill could be used against teachers of history who glorified Irish revolutionary heroes (readers will remember that earlier in the book I referred to the link between the teaching of history and I.R.A. recruitment).

These targets intrigued Nossiter but what shook him was O'Brien's pulling open of a desk drawer to produce a collection of cuttings of 'Letters to the Editor' from the *Irish Press* as further examples of the sort of thing the bill would put a stop to. He did not propose, he said, to use the bill against the authors of such letters, but against the editor of the paper. He left Nossiter in no doubt that an editor 'offending' in such a fashion would find himself in trouble.

Immediately on leaving O'Brien, Nossiter contacted me and warned me to look out for myself. I declared editorial war on O'Brien, reprinting the *Washington Post* interview which appeared on September 3, 1976, and printing a series of strong editorial attacks on the bill.

Politically the climate altered sharply. It was one thing to swallow distasteful security measures against the I.R.A., it was another to use the I.R.A. to cloak the launching of a vendetta against the press. (Though no one should really have been surprised at this for as far back as August 3, 1973, Eamon MacThomas, editor of *An Phoblacht*, had already been given fifteen months for I.R.A. membership for his activities which were strictly confined to the paper.) Accordingly, after a period of uproar in the media and in the Dail, the government backed down—the first time it had suffered a defeat of any sort, since taking office.

The Minister for Justice, Patrick Cooney, announced that the bill was not intended for the prosecution of editors, and the wording was watered down to give effect to their promise; and there the matter should have ended.

However, while the foregoing had been taking place, President O'Dalaigh, whose office had certain powers in relation to the legislation, had been becoming increasingly disturbed about the drift of events. O'Dalaigh had made Irish legal history in 1946 when at the age of thirty-five he became the youngest-ever Attorney General. He then went on to become Chief Justice and a Judge of the Court of the European Communities. But above all, for the purposes of this narrative, he was also a former Irish editor of the *Irish Press* (from 1931 to 1942). His late brother Aengus was, in addition to being one of the few Saints in contemporary Irish history, the *Irish Press* librarian.

Over the years I had known O'Dalaigh to take a keen interest in matters affecting the welfare of the press generally, sending me documentation on E.E.C. Legislation concerning press freedom, newspaper taxation, or newspaper cuttings on related topics which he thought I should read.

Although he had been an all-party-agreed presidential nominee in 1974 on the death of his predecessor Erskine Childers—he had been, prior to his Chief Justiceship, firmly in the Fianna Fail camp and now, two years after his accession to the presidency, he was, in addition to his disquiet over the danger of a curtailment of press and other freedoms, feeling the draught of Coalition antipathy to this background. His very office derived, of course, from a constitution which scrapped the one drawn up by Liam Cosgrave's father; and he found that he was being offered petty slights to his own and the presidential dignity. For instance, he told me that an invitation to the Head of State to attend the canonisation of Blessed Oliver Plunkett ceremonies in Rome was taken up instantly by Cosgrave without reference to him.

Perturbed at the authoritarian drift of events and by the legislation, he decided (as he was entitled to under the constitution) after a four-hour consultation with the Council of State not automatically to sign the bill into law as expected but to refer the Emergency Powers Bill to the Supreme Court to be tested for repugnancy to the constitution. This bill was found not to be repugnant and was duly signed by him and passed into law. (Both bills, including the Criminal Law Bill containing the now famous, but sanitised Section 3, had been drawn to the attention of the Council of State.) There the matter apparently ended.

However, on October 18, 1976, at an army ceremony at St Columb's Barracks, Mullingar, the then Minister for Defence, the convivial Patrick Donnegan, a County Louth politician, spoke of the President's referring of the legislation to the Supreme Court and referred to him as a 'thundering disgrace' saying in the same breath that 'the army must stand behind the state'. O'Dalaigh took this as a clear implication that the minister who was probably only voicing the cabinet's opinion felt that the President did not stand behind the state. He felt that in addition to anything personal which might be derived from Donnegan's statement-there was an open affront to the dignity of the office of President in whom the constitution vests the supreme control of the defence forces, all commissioned officers, on the government's nomination, holding their commissions from the President.

Accordingly, following the utterance of Donnegan's statement in the presence of an army audience, O'Dalaigh felt that he had no way of preserving the dignity of the presidency save to resign which he did on October 22.

The combination of Section 3, the O'Dalaigh affair and the Portlaoise hunger strike affair so moved public opinion that the security issue exploded in the faces of the government the following February, and the old Clann na Poblachta vote resurfaced to help give Jack Lynch his overwhelming total of eighty-four seats.

Neither he nor the I.R.A. welcomed the support. The I.R.A. Leadership in particular, knowing that Fianna Fail would be more subtle adversaries than the Coalition in power, but equally opposed to subversion, vainly tried to prevent a stampede of their sympathisers to vote and campaign for Fianna Fail. In fact, though Fianna Fail's popularity had waned, chiefly on economic grounds, by the time of the European Elections two years later in June, 1979, but also because of lack of progress on the Northern issue, this Republican component was still strong enough to work the other way, against Fianna Fail, some of whose supporters turned against their own party to assist Neil T. Blaney, who had been sacked by Jack Lynch over the Arms Crisis in 1970, but who always averred that he had not left Fianna Fail (Fianna Fail had left him), to a resounding victory over a Fianna Fail candidate.

The other legacy from the Coalition's over-zealous pursuit of 'security' has been the fact that because of the increase in the penalty for I.R.A. membership to seven years, many senior I.R.A. men now recognise the courts, plead their cases and get off to fight another day, much to the chagrin of the security forces on both sides of the border.

It was an era of considerable significance for anyone who had believed that there was no difference intrinsically between Fianna Fail and Fine Gael. Arguably there isn't on matters of social and economic policy to any very marked degree; but when it came to dealing with the I.R.A. the essential division certainly showed up.

Fianna Fail have taken stern action against the I.R.A. on occasion. But they manage to convey whilst doing this that it is a question merely of a government being only concerned with the putting down of unlawful acts and meeting the challenge posed by the I.R.A. and of a second authority raising its head in the state.

Fine Gael, however, gave the impression of pursuing the second course in a mood of theological righteousness. 'We did it during the civil war and we'll do it again,' was an attitude one encountered in government circles at the time. There was a prevailing zeal—a desire to hunt, to root out the devil and his works and props rather than an objective governmental attitude towards dealing with a problem which has bedevilled Irish administrations since the foundation of the state.

In fairness to the Cosgrave administration, one would not have required any theological aversion to the I.R.A. to have found government in 1973 a particularly difficult task in Ireland. Specifically where prison conditions were concerned, the I.R.A. had already distinguished themselves under Fianna Fail by burning down a new prison during a riot in Mountjoy jail, Dublin, and so leading to the transfer of some of them to the Curragh under military custody. Accordingly the question of internment continually flickered around the edges of Irish political debate, though public opinion was generally against it in the wake of the fiasco of the Northern experience in August, 1971. However, it always remained an option in the wings and the Curragh transfer had overtones of internment policy. The transfer was not in effect a backdoor effort to bring in internment but a recognition of the fact that prison conditions in Ireland were woefully inadequate to cope with the rise of urban crime, let alone the I.R.A. The principal prisons with which the I.R.A. are connected were Portlaoise and, to a degree, the women's prison in Limerick. The prison service was so inadequate that the women warders had to be augmented by policewomen—Ban Gardai—in Limerick, and after the transfer these for the Alfred Beit robberies and the Herrema kidnapping respectively, of Rose Dugdale and Marion Coyle, the pair drew attention to these shortcomings by throwing boiling water in the face of a Ban Garda which led to some more prison staff being employed. In Portlaoise there was pretty rough fighting between prisoners and warders which left both sides battered in the extreme.

But the worst single episode of this phase of the Portlaoise saga occurred outside the jail in the early hours of October 16, 1976, when a booby-trap bomb in a deserted cottage near the town claimed the life of one policeman, Garda Clerkin, and blinded a second for life. Not only was this a deliberate, planned murder—the Gardai were lured to the cottage by a phone call—but it was a calculated breach of the Standing Order No. 8 policy which the Provisionals had hitherto (and subsequently) observed and which could have had very far-reaching consequences indeed, including the implementation of the death penalty,[*] against whoever was found guilty of the crime.

It was against this backdrop that the Provisionals launched their mass hunger strike seeking political status.

Portlaoise was still the vile place in which Sean McCaughey died in the 1940s. Governments had been reluctant to expend money on 'coddling' prisoners and the influx of politically motivated Provisionals into the Irish prisons was totally unforeseen.

But the contemporary Provisional prisoner was quite different to anybody who had gone before: he was highly motivated, highly organised, and his only contact with the prison authorities came through his spokesman. On the other hand the government had an absolutely rigid attitude, as outlined earlier, and when I visited

---

[*]   The death penalty was very nearly carried out against the Murrays—a husband and wife team who were responsible for the death of the off-duty Garda Reynolds who pursued the pair after an attempt at bank robbery (on September 11, 1975) at the Dublin suburb of Clontarf. The Murrays, who belonged to a revolutionary socialist group unconnected with the Provisionals, had their sentence commuted at the last moment by the Supreme Court. By then the death cell at Mountjoy had been readied and the cabinet, I am told, were determined, had the appeal failed, to carry out the execution, even though there was a woman involved, Mrs Murray, who actually fired the fatal shot.

the prison myself in November, 1977, after the turbulence had subsided, some of the prison staff and justice officers confided to me that 'we were pushed all the time' to ensure that the Provisionals were confronted at every hand's turn, when the familiar Republican defiance of prison regulations began. Between them, the two sides made of Portlaoise a pressure cooker within which temperatures steadily rose and common humanity boiled away. (Outside also, since the Gardai were ordered to baton protestors away from the gates when a demonstration began).

My visit came as a result of the national disquiet which became widespread as reports of prison conditions spread and the incoming Fianna Fail administration invited the editors of the three national daily papers to tour the prisons to see that all was well under their benign tenure.

Of course by the time the journalists were invited, all was comparatively well, given the archaic nature of the buildings and the fact that the existing prison regulations were written in the last century. But evidence of tension still remained, besides the fact that there were armed soldiers on the roof and gun emplacements on the walls. There were sixteen members of the uniformed Gardai patrolling one door of the jail alone, in addition to the normal staff. Since sixteen visible Gardai in this forty-hour-week era means that when holidays are included a total of forty-two men are involved in all, one can see what the concentration of police power in the prison must have meant to the crime statistics outside.

Under the Coalition, its obsession with 'security' and the checkmating of 'subversives' as the political prisoners are known in department of justice circles, this payment in manpower was willingly made against a backdrop which included episodes like a bombing which nearly cost the life of a prison governor's wife—part of an iron railing was blown into her kitchen. Another abortive effort if it had gone off would have claimed the life of Governor O'Reilly or the lives of his family, but before it had a chance to detonate, a bomb under his car was defused. Provisional prisoners made a daring escape by blowing their way out of the jail in August, 1974, using explosives smuggled in a box of Lucky Number sweets. Another attempt to smuggle explosives into the prison was foiled when a lady visitor to the jail was discovered in the act of passing over a string to a prisoner she was visiting in the jail, the cord being attached to a contraceptive, crammed with explosives, inserted in her person. On yet another occasion the following year a prisoner was shot dead by soldiers on duty at the jail during an unsuccessful raid on the jail in which an armoured bulldozer was used in an attempt to batter down a side door.

The prisoners' protest resulted in all forms of concessions being withdrawn—handicrafts, study and reading facilities, television viewing. The strictest surveillance was made of visitors whose conversations were conducted through a thick wire mesh in the presence of prison warders.

Surveillance was so tight that one woman who had travelled from Donegal almost 200 miles away, getting up at 4 a.m. in order to catch the bus to see her son, had her visit terminated within seconds because she addressed him in the Irish that the family normally used in their Gaeltacht district. There were reports of prisoners' relations being left standing in the rain outside the jail; of people being denied visits after making long journeys to see relatives; parcels of all kinds were forbidden after the Lucky Numbers episode and another involving the smuggling in of explosives to prisoners in a hollowed-out shoe heel (this resulted in a dramatic escape by prisoners appearing on remand in Green Street Court before appearing in the Special Criminal Court).

But the most degrading and most detested form of retaliation was the incessant strip searching whereby prisoners, sometimes several times a day, were stripped and searched in a procedure which involved manual parting of the buttocks and inspection of the testicles (prisoners had been known to hide explosives by taping them behind their testicles). The strike lasted for forty-seven days without any apparent gain for the strikers but it did have the more far-reaching effects already outlined. The situation in Portlaoise was, under Fianna Fail, at least contained as a result of those days' experiences.

23

Arms

One of the side effects of the violence was that groups of young men, uprooted by the troubles, roamed around the country pulling off robberies, either on behalf of some paramilitary organisation or for themselves—it was, and is, often very difficult to tell which—the skills and the guns required for such activities becoming all too easily available in the disorder of the times. But on top of this one can never be sure whether a bank robbery or a payroll snatch, both of which now happen, North and South of the border, so often that no one raises an eyebrow any more (the police reckon in the Republic some £2 million was taken between January, 1978, and August, 1979), even if they do not appear to be politically motivated, could in fact be the work of a front organisation working for the I.R.A., like the Saor Eire activists; or a joint venture between two Republican organisations—for example, the Provisionals and the Irish National Liberation Army or even an outside criminal hired by one or other organisation for the job. For instance, a train robbery at Sallins, Co. Kildare, appropriately enough not far from Wolfe Tone's birthplace, netted the Provisionals some £¼ million.

But a group of young men from the Irish Republican Socialist Party were found guilty of the crime after confessions were extracted from them by methods which had aroused widespread controversy and unrest. I was approached by a Provisional source to explain to the government that they had done the robbery but obviously couldn't claim it publicly. My informant said that they found this circumstance particularly embarrassing because Deisun Breannacht, the father of one of those sentenced over the Sallins robbery, Osgur Breannacht, was at the time editor of the Provisional newspaper, *An Phoblacht*. But in the welter of confusion surrounding the robberies, which of course the government finds outrageous, officialdom did not show itself to be impressed by the Provisionals' submission which, in view of the calibre of the source who approached me, I feel could be true; Breannacht and the others have since been released.

Another Kildare fundraising venture which the I.R.A. found highly embarrassing concerned a haul of cannabis worth approximately £1 million which the Gardai seized on August 25, 1979, near Naas, also in Kildare, and by coincidence near to Sallins.

One of the three men seized by the Gardai in this swoop was James 'the Fox' McCann, known to the popular press as the 'Green Pimpernel' of Republicans because he succeeded in escaping from Crumlin Road jail by cutting his way through his cell bars. But Fox's escape seems to have been doubly unlucky for him. Apart from being captured by the police in very serious circumstances, he was badly kicked and beaten by Provisional prisoners when transferred to Portlaoise jail, and into the bargain the Provisionals issued a statement denying any connection with him on the drugs.

Drugs, or rather drug traffickers, have at times been the subject of very severe I.R.A. punishments. Even women have not been exempt, and the fact of being implicated through the capture of a man once prominently associated with the I.R.A. in drug-running was both infuriating and, particularly where their conservative supporters both in Ireland and America were concerned, was potentially highly damaging to the Provisionals.

The captured British army document referred to earlier put the Provisionals' annual income at around £1½ million. I would be inclined to assess it higher. Apart from the foregoing, there is the American connection, the various drinking clubs controlled by the Provisionals such as the Prisoners' Defence Fund Club in Andersonstown or in what is known as the Pound Loney area off the Falls Road, the very large Pound Loney Club.

The Provisionals also control pubs, hold collections, levy 'protection' and in fact so control West Belfast that no builder could operate there without Provisional consent. In fact it is highly doubtful if any builder can survive there anyhow, because ripping off the system has become such a way of life in Belfast that between materials 'falling off lorries', never getting put on lorries in the first place, and being removed from sites when and if they ever get there, building in Belfast—including East Belfast where the U.D.A. holds similar sway to the I.R.A.—has become one of the world's most bankruptcy-prone professions, as a talk with any Northern accountant will speedily verify. What all this has done to the character of people is of course a matter of conjecture, worth a study in itself.

Yet despite the manner in which it is acquired (there was much talk about racketeering and 'Godfathers of Crime' in the media during and since Merlyn Rees's tenure in office when a determined effort to 'criminalise' the I.R.A. was set in train as part of the British propaganda effort), the money generally speaking—there is of course some incidence of outright pilfering—is administered for 'legitimate purposes'. These include the welfare of prisoners' relatives and supporting men on the run and their families, and above all the purchase of arms and explosives.

In the earlier stages of the campaign the I.RA. mainly relied on couriers to transport relatively crudely made, highly volatile bombs to the point of detonation. But the army's techniques of cordoning off shopping areas and searching everyone who entered, forced a change of method on the Provisionals. Firstly the car bomb was favoured—hijacking a car, putting a bomb in it and parking it outside the chosen target. As noted already, this technique, though devastating, had the drawback that synchronising the warning often posed problems. Then came radio bombs and other more sophisticated methods. The I.R.A. began to use radio-controlled devices, trip wires and 'sleeper bombs' that could be planted weeks in advance of the arrival of a V.I.P. and then detonated.

The 'sleeper bomb's' most illustrious target was Her Majesty, Queen Elizabeth II of England. One of these devices went off some hours after she had visited Coleraine University during her visit to the North in August, 1977. The then Secretary of State, Roy Mason, claimed at the time that the bomb was thrown over the university perimeter before it exploded. Mason had been most zealous in lobbying for the visit even though it occurred during the worst possible week as far as Catholic sensibilities were concerned—one which combined both the anniversaries of internment and the Apprentice Boys' Parade in Derry. It was this parade which had first put a torch to the situation in 1969. The week after the visit, on August 19, the army's chief bomb disposal officer, Lt.-Col. Derrick Patrick, stated that the Provisionals did have a sleeping bomb.

For the rest of Mason's reign, Ulster Television's nightly broadcasts faded out with a clip of film showing Her Majesty arriving from a helicopter with the ineffable Mr Mason smirking in the background (good taste finally prevailed and the clip was removed).

Despite some spectacular captures both while arms were en route to Ireland and when they were found in dumps, the I.R.A. managed to build up a sizeable armoury over the years. Russian RPG-7 rockets have been used and Russian Kalashnikov and Chinese Simarol rifles have been found in arms raids, but the principal Provisional weapon became the Armalite, whether it be the M16 or the AR180 version. These are very high velocity weapons which weigh only seven pounds and have a collapsible butt which enables them to be used both lethally and inconspicuously.* Apart from these, the Provisionals laid hands on a small quantity of a variety of weapons from all over the world: a few German Landmann .22 hunting weapons, some Magnum French hunting rifles, also .22 calibre, some Garand semi-automatic rifles, Springfields, Lee Enfields, a few Thompson sub-machine guns, the lawyer's German Schmeisser sub-machine gun made its appearance as did a wide variety of revolvers, hunting guns, petrol bombs, nail bombs, hand grenades—in fact practically every device of the smaller sort which man developed to kill man in recent years showed up in Belfast.

And not all of the smaller sort either. It was confirmed that the Provisionals had acquired M60 machine guns which fire Nato issue 7.62 bullets, and I had from time to time been given indications that the Provisionals possessed even more deadly heavyweight equipment which for various reasons—the risk of civilian losses being one—had not been used yet. This consideration would not apply in the type of situation which might arise should wholesale warfare break out between Protestant and Catholic, and in conversation with U.D.A. leaders one day, I found that they too believed that the Provisionals had more heavy armaments in stock and had a healthy regard for it.

British intelligence was particularly effective in halting any major flow of arms from the Middle East, although at different times organisations such as Al Fatah and the P.L.O. have declared themselves sympathetic to the Provisionals (although Yasser Arafat distanced himself from the Provisionals at the time of the Mountbatten murder).

The skill of British intelligence in priming the relevant authorities was shown in the seizure of a number of major consignments of armaments destined for the I.R.A. at Holland, Canada and off the Irish Coast (one could include the shipments which

---

* The guns are manufactured under license by the Stirling Armament Company Ltd of Great Britain which means in fact that the British manufactured the guns the Provisionals use to kill British soldiers.

precipitated the famous Arms Trial but it was a smaller consignment involving only some hundreds of pistols intended primarily for the defence of Catholics in the North against Loyalist mobs—not as part of an aggressive war on the British army). The major seizures occurred:

1. October 17, 1971, when Dutch police swooped at Schipol Airport, Amsterdam.

2. On Wednesday, March 28, 1973, when the Irish government seized a shipment of arms aboard a 298-ton motor vessel registered in Cyprus as the *Claudia* which was intercepted off the coast of Waterford: 250 rifles, 240 small arms, anti-tank mines and explosives.

3. On July 4, 1975, in Canada when the Mounties swooped on a number of centres: Toronto, St Catherines, Tavistock and at Windsor, Ontario. The Mounties captured a variety of weapons including machine guns, sten guns, semi-automatic weapons, hand grenades and ammunition, but the raids did not have the impact of the other two seizures which, of course, occurred much nearer home.

4. On December 21, 1977 when a triphammer blow fell on further arms importation on a large scale from countries other than the U.S.A. as the Dublin police pulled off a two-for-the-price-of-one' coup (as they had done with the arrest of Sean MacStiofain) by picking up both Seamus Twomey, who had been at large since the Mountjoy helicopter escape, and another important I.RA. figure, Seamus McCullum.

The Schipol haul of Czech-made armaments including Bazookas, rocket-launchers, hand grenades, machine guns and rifles was so large that it filled 166 crates and it created a sensation partly because the I.R.A. had sent a pretty young woman along with Daithi O'Connell to Amsterdam to finalise the deal. She was Maria Maguire whom the Provisionals took into the movement because she seemed the type of university-educated, politically minded type which the movement was then trying to attract. However, the following year Miss Maguire left the movement and wrote a series of articles for the *Observer* which were highly critical of the Provisionals and of Sean MacStiofain in particular. She followed this up with a book, *To Take Arms*, which gave a penetrating but to the Provisionals a highly unwelcome★ portrait of the movement and of MacStiofain who was then temporarily in obscurity.

The Amsterdam affair was a non-starter from the word go because as O'Connell and Maguire arrived in the city, the *Daily Telegraph*, generally regarded in Ireland as the mouthpiece of Whitehall and of British intelligence, came out

---

★ Apart from Miss Maguire, the second most celebrated departure from the ranks of the Provisionals during the decade was Peter McMullen who wrote his Life in the Provisionals' story for the *Boston Globe* in September, 1979. He was a former British paratrooper who deserted, after bombing his own barracks. Before deserting the Provisional he bombed other targets including Claro Barracks in Ripport Yorkshire, and is wanted by both Britain and the Provisionals. At the time of writing he is fighting extradition from America on the grounds that his offences were political'.

with a report that O'Connell was on the Continent, involved in an arms deal. The nearest the pair actually got to the arms was watching them on Dutch television being inspected by a Scotland Yard detective, although in the end the publicity gained may have made up for the arms lost.

The *Claudia* affair too caused great discussion in Ireland. This arms shipment, which occurred following a visit by Daithi O'Connell to Tripoli, was apparently monitored by British intelligence until it was practically in the arms of the Irish security services—the *Claudia* crew reported seeing a British submarine shortly before they were picked up. As a result the irrepressible Minister for Defence, Patrick Donnegan, commented: 'We gave her [the *Claudia*] a good kick up the transom.' In fact the ship was allowed to go free eventually.

McCullum had been using a false name, Robin Kingsley, owner of the Progress Electro Company, Middle Abbey Street, Dublin, to cloak his real name and purpose—the importation of a large shipment of arms from Cyprus. McCullum, who also had a prison record in England for possession of explosives, had been interned during the 'Three Macs' era and used the name of a dead Dubliner, John O'Neill, to secure a valid passport for travelling purposes.

He managed to get two huge transformers, weighing over three tons each, shipped aboard the *Tower Stream* filled with a wide variety of arms supplied by Al Fatah. However, the scratch-my-back-and-I'll-scratch-yours world of intelligence services soon buzzed with the information that the Israelis had news of an Arab shipment headed for Dublin. The British saw to it that the Belgians prevented the shipment getting any farther than Antwerp, and McCullum getting any farther than Martello Terrace, Sandycove, Co. Dublin, in the shadow of James Joyce's tower, where his Ulyssian Odyssey began. McCullum's ended in the arms of the Irish Special Branch. Twomey was picked up a little later in the afternoon having been shadowed from a visit to McCullum.

The seized shipment included two Bren guns, twenty-nine Kalashnikov rifles, twenty-nine sub-machine guns, over a hundred hand grenades, thousands of rounds of ammunition of different kinds, large amounts of T.N.T., rocket-launchers and rockets to go with them, and substantial amounts of plastic explosives.

An obvious source of armaments on the face of it was the Soviet Union. But the conditions described at the time of the Russell-Boland-Cooney visit hadn't changed all that much. Ireland still hadn't shot any bishops; although in his book *The Secret Work of Society Secret Agents*, John Barron, the former American intelligence orative, says:

The K.G.B. has worked secretly through Czech, Cuban and Arab terrorist intermediaries to arm and train both wings of the I.R.A. The Cuban operational plan for 1972 drafted under K.G.B. supervision stipulated that the Cubans would train Irish Republican army personnel in the tactics of terrorism and guerilla war.

Barron's views, considering his sources, have to be treated with some respect, but while the Russians were obviously keen on infiltration in Ireland, the conservatism of the Moscow régime and the manner in which they went about implementing their policies had to be taken into consideration. One Provisional Leader, with disgust in his voice, said to me at the time: 'The Russians don't recognise revolutionary movements, they only recognise revolutionary governments.'

At Russian Embassy parties in Dublin one noticed the respect accorded to figures on the revolutionary left, not the revolutionary illegal who were not invited. Tomas MacGiolla, President of Sinn Fein, the Workers' Party (the old official wing), for instance, was usually to be seen encircled by Russian 'diplomats'. The 'Workers' Party' tag was adopted to differentiate further the Official I.R.A.'s political wing from Provisional Sinn Fein and to give the party more distinction of identity and purpose in the minds of potential young recruits, who might not be attracted to banners inscribed merely Sinn Fein (Gardner Street) Officials or Sinn Fein (Kevin Street) Provisionals.

One also learned that the Russians, who were supposed to account for their movements when going outside Dublin, did not always do so, and Russian Embassy personal were observed crossing the border at unguarded points.

The main thrust of Russian influence would appear to have been educational and propagandist. It was directed at the Official I.R A., the Irish Republican Socialist Party and its military offshoot the Irish National Liberation Army (I.N.L.A.) which is described below. There was certainly some form of Russian-P.L.O. co-operation in supplying the I.N.L.A. with weapons, and some P.L.O. involvement in providing training for both Provisionals and the I.N.L.A. at Middle Eastern centres.

This was confirmed by both the Irish police and the Israeli Embassy in London which issued a booklet (on February 15, 1978) on I.RA.-P.L.O. Links.

The Provisionals also have links with other separatist guerilla movements. For instance, with the Basque E.T.A. These were acknowledged as far back as March, 1974, when a spokesman for E.T.A. was quoted in *Der Spiegel* as saying that E.T.A. had 'good, very good relations with the I.R.A.'. Perhaps the 'goodness' of these relations may be assessed in the light of the continuing reports one hears that I.R.A. training and experience contributed to such E.T.A. activities as the blowing up of Señor Blanqui, or the spate of bombings at Spanish holiday resorts in the summer of 1978.

But the principal source of weapons and money for the Provisionals was, is and will be, the United States. Anyone who has an Irish-American entrée in the States will very speedily learn this for themselves. I encountered I.R.A. collections on the east and west coasts, and, of all places, in Peoria, Illinois. The American connection also limited the I.R.A.'s freedom of movement in making communist bloc contact because the ultra-conservative Irish American trade unionists, on whom the I.RA. relied to get the hardware through the docks, would have turned in horror upon any sort of red involvement

Congressman Aspin said (on September 2, 1975) that the I.RA. had stolen weapons from U.S. bases. Quoting from a U.S. army report, he said that the I.R.A.. were amongst the extremist groups who between 1971 and 1974 had stolen enough arms and ammunition from U.S. depots to arm ten battalions or 8,000 men. Apart from the fact that there has been an evident penetration of the American network which resulted in the capture of a consignment of Armalites and two M60 machine guns at Dublin docks from an American ship on November 1, 1979, this ideological balancing act continued until the demise of the Communist bloc.

A Provisional leader told me on leaving prison that they found it nearly impossible in jails and camps to interest the young volunteers in traditionalist Republican indoctrination. A diet of socialism and Marxism was required. And the Provisional assessment of the temper of its Belfast Brigade was that it was unlikely, following the attitude of the church over the decade, that the Provisionals would have gone to the aid of a church as Billy McKee did over St Matthews in 1969. Ireland today has the youngest electorate—over 50 per cent under the age of twenty-five—of any country in Western Europe. It also has one of the highest rates of youth unemployment, a potentially highly important consideration for the I.R.A. of the future—and for whoever controls it.

The educated unemployed who have had the benefit of the revolution in Irish education which has occurred since universal free secondary education (and a consequent increase in university numbers) was introduced in the 1960s, are not likely to be as passive as the traditional dole queues in the acceptance of their lot.

24

The Use of Torture

The question of the use of torture has been, as can be imagined, highly emotive. Although constantly alleged by the I.R.A., it was not until the *Sunday Times* published the fact that the army were using such techniques that 'respectable' opinion in Ireland accepted its existence and the Irish Department of Foreign Affairs began opening a file on torture with a view to governmental action.

The law case of Ireland against the United Kingdom and Northern Ireland began before 1971 ended (the Irish application was introduced before the Commission of Human Rights on December 16) and did not end until 1978 began, when, on January 18, the European Court of Human Rights delivered its verdict.

The court found that the following five techniques were used:

1. hooding the detainees except during interrogation;
2. making them stand continuously against a wall in a spreadeagled and painful posture for prolonged periods of some hours;
3. submitting them to continuous and monotonous noise;
4. depriving them of sleep; and
5. restricting them to a diet of one round of bread and one pint of water at six-hourly intervals.

It found therefore: 'By sixteen votes to one that the use of the five techniques in August and October 1971 constituted a practice of inhuman and degrading treatment, which practice was in breach of Article 3.' (Article 3 of the Convention on Human Rights states that 'No one shall be subjected to torture or to inhuman or degrading treatment or punishment.')

However, the court found 'that the said use of the five techniques did not constitute a practice of torture within the meaning of the Article'. The court did not visit the barracks mentioned—Palace, Girdwood, Hollywood—nor did they go to Northern Ireland at all. Judges did visit Greece during the Greek torture hearings to interview witnesses but not during the Irish ones because the British had claimed that the lives of witnesses would be imperilled, though this consideration was not advanced during the Widgery and other tribunals.

The one vote against the other sixteen judges in the finding of the breach of Article 3 was Judge Sir Gerald Fitzmaurice. He had this to say: 'According to my idea of the correct handling of languages and concepts, to call the treatment involved by the use of the five techniques "inhuman" is excessive and distorting, unless the term is being employed loosely and merely figuratively.' The Judge went on to give examples of figurative use within most people's experience:

'One hears it said, "I call that inhuman", the reference being to the fact that there is no dining-car on the train. "It's degrading for the poor man," one hears with reference to an employee who is being given all the unpleasant jobs. "It's absolute torture to me," and what the speaker means is having to sit through a boring lecture or sermon. There is a lesson to be learnt here on the potential dangers of hyperbole.'

Sir Gerald's semantics are one of the classic examples of how a lawyer can use words so as totally to dehydrate a case of all humanity or reality, and recalled to me an occasion some years earlier when I discussed without 'hyperbole' with Kevin Hannaway, one of the hooded men and like his father Liam a life-long Republican, the experience which had led to the Belfast courts awarding him damages for his experiences. 'After they arrested me, I was thrown into a lorry where I got a kicking. Then I was taken to another barracks where I got another kicking and they took me up in a helicopter and told me they were going to throw me out. I thought we were hundreds of feet up but we were only a few feet up. They set Alsatians on me, my thigh was all torn, and they made me run in my bare feet over broken glass.' Following these happenings, Hannaway underwent the 'five techniques'. When it was all over, he told me, lowering his voice because his wife was in the room, 'My privates were the size of a football from the kicking.'

How did you manage to get through it all, I asked him? 'I kept thinking of *The Last Words*, and I thought of what those men went through and I said to myself, sure what am I getting—nothing! So I stuck it out.'

(*The Last Words* is a book about the last words and writings of the executed 1916 leaders. It is doubtful if any political science course includes it on its reading list but such works have more relevance to the making of a revolutionary than the learned tomes that are written about them afterwards.)

The case caused a good deal of rancour between successive governments in both Britain and Ireland while it proceeded—the British continually sought to have it dropped—but not amongst lawyers who made large sums of money from it. Some of the victims were also compensated.

However, despite Strasbourg, torture as described (however the word is interpreted) continued to be used by the security forces.

On December 20, 1972, the British government published and accepted the report of Lord Diplock's commission into the administration of law in Northern Ireland. Stemming from Diplock, an Emergency Provisions Bill was introduced at Westminster the following April tightening up the conditions on which bail was granted, shifting the burden of proof of innocence to the accused in the 'terrorist' type cases and enabling such cases to be heard without a jury because of fear of intimidation. The I.R.A., Cumann na mBan, Fianna Eireann, Saor Eire, Sinn Fein and the U.V.F. were produced under the bill. Under Roy Mason pressure mounted on police to obtain convictions and the statistics show that from 75 per cent to 80 per cent of convictions in these 'Diplock' courts were obtained on the basis of 'confessions'.

Concern over reports of torture led to the Amnesty report which was sent to Mason on May 2, 1978. The revelations in the document destroyed Sir Kenneth Newman's allegation that prisoners 'were injuring themselves as part of an I.R.A. propaganda campaign against the police', and in June, 1978, a committee of inquiry was set up under Judge Harry Bennett, Q.C., to instigate police interrogation procedures in Northern Ireland. On March 16 the Bennett report confirmed that there had been mistreatment. A number of police doctors had already protested about the statement and one of them, Dr Robert Irwin, had gone on television just before the Bennett report was published to describe what was going on at Castlereagh where he was police surgeon. The North of Ireland Office's response was to orchestrate a campaign against him, using the fact that his wife had been raped, to try to belittle his witness. In the welter of disclosures surrounding the Irwin affair it also became known that the police authority had three separate meetings with Sir Kenneth Newman to discuss the doctors' complaints during which they told him that having appointed him they could fire him. He quoted the Northern Ireland Police Act to prove that they could only hire him—not fire him!

There did not seem to be any great grounds for optimism either that the matter was simply one of replacing Sir Kenneth. His deputy, who succeeded him, Deputy Chief Constable Jack Hermon, was as involved as Newman in what happened.

The problem lay at the very heart of the British connection. On the one hand, the North of Ireland was officially regarded as being as much a part of England as Bradford or Leeds. On the other hand, to continue her presence in 'the U.K. overseas', Britain was forced to adopt methods which would drive those responsible out of public life for ever, were they to be employed in the 'U.K. mainland'. Even if one were to adopt the *Realpolitik* morality that the Provisionals' record leaves them open to any sort of treatment, the problem was that a great deal of the time the treatment was meted out to people who were not Provisionals. I had a graphic illustration of the nature of the problem one evening in Belfast while doing research for this book.

I was driven to a pleasant middle-class suburb, as remote from the slums where the I.R.A. flourish as one could imagine, to meet the I.R.A. leadership. The people who owned the house were apparently returning from a continental holiday and all was bustle and suntan and reminiscence; a world removed from the preoccupation of the people drinking tea and eating cake in their living-room. One of the group was a businessman who, it transpired, used his various bank accounts to cover the movement of I.R.A. funds.

Apart from discussing I.R.A. policy, our conversation switched for a time to the R.U.C. There was bitter condemnation of the force for their unfair treatment of a group of students whom those present apparently knew in a non-I.R.A. capacity. Seemingly the students were picked up one evening, taken to a barracks, questioned all night and then charged with loitering, drunkenness and other misdemeanours of a like nature. The charges necessitated appearing in court on the eve of their exams. All the students were represented by lawyers when the cases came to Court and they were found not guilty and acquitted. The point the I.R.A. men made was there was never any question of the lads behaving as charged because of the proximity of their examinations. They had simply been harassed because they were Catholics, and in the hope of interrupting their studies. I could not of course evaluate the allegation but I found it fascinating to hear these men, law-abiding in one compartment of their minds, sworn to bloody revolution in another, complaining about the police force not because on one level they were at war with them—the R.U.C. are 'legitimate targets' to the I.RA.—but because they regarded them as 'bent coppers'.

For their part, the R.U.C. are formed by the traditional view of the Catholics as either potentially or actually disloyal, killed and maimed by the I.R.A. and baffled by the I.R.A.'s code of secrecy—a code most terribly enforced on those who would break it—and by the knowledge that houses like the one I was driven to actually do exist. The R.U.C. attempt to overcome their difficulties by using tactics which Europeans associate with pre-war Germany, rather than E.E.C. England and the reforms proposed by the Bennett report won't change that situation in a hurry.

The level of feeling towards the R.U.C. Special Branch investigators on the part of the I.R.A. may be gauged from the fact that the I.R.A. say that if they ultimately win, as some day they confidently expect to, the one category of their opponents for whom there will be no amnesty are the 'police torturers'. 'They'll have to get out or be shot' I was told bluntly by an I.R.A. spokesman.

25

Sectarian Murder

Sectarian assassination is such a feature of the struggle that it deserves a special examination, as do the Protestant paramilitary forces and their endeavours. The sectarian assassin can be either a bigoted racialist or a genuine patriot. He can strike to punish, as he sees it, treacherous and rebellious members of a sub-species which is threatening life, love, liberty and the pursuit of happiness. This is how many Protestant assassins, particularly in the U.V.F., see their actions. Or he can coldbloodedly retaliate for an earlier killing as the I.R.A. did at Bessbrook in South Armagh on January 5, 1976, when ten Protestant workmen were machine-gunned to death after they had been ordered out of their mini-bus and forced to line up for death, one of the few occasions when the I.R.A. went in for outright sectarian murder.

Why? I asked an I.R.A. spokesman. Looking me straight in the eye he replied: 'Why not? It stopped the sectarian killings in the area, didn't it?' Unfortunately he was right. Five Catholics had been killed in two attacks in that area on the previous day. The attacks stopped immediately.

However, a very hopeful rapprochement between the U.D.A. and the I.R.A. was aborted by the killings. The U.D.A. had actually prepared documents on what they saw, as the way forward for exchange with the I.R.A. when the news of the massacre broke; but when the U.D.A. leadership turned up to discuss the exchange the morning after the shootings, the projected discussion instead tools the form of one man picking a copy of the *Daily Mirror*, with a massacre headline on page one, from the table and saying, 'How could you exchange papers with the people who would do *that*?' It was one of the many episodes throughout the curse of the ten-year tragedy in which overall development was stunted by individual action at ground level—though, as we shall see, there were many attempts at I.R.A.-U.D.A. contact then and before. Still, the massacre must rank, apart from its intrinsic horror, as being one of the most unfortunate turning points of the decade no matter what claims can be made for its effect on sectarian assassination.

Assassination reached the peak during 1972 when of the total of 322 civilian deaths, 122 were classified by the R.U.C. as assassination; of these 82 were Catholic and 40 Protestant.

Things have improved since then. It is possible that I may have contributed to the improvement, since at a certain juncture early in 1978 I was able to use the contacts I had built up over the years to help arrange an unofficial agreement whereby in return for the I.R.A. abandoning the use of car bombs the U.D.A. forswore sectarian assassinations. Although an occasional car bomb went off, more as a result of a local I.R.A. unit's initiative than because of official policy, the pact more or less held up until the time of Mountbatten's murder.

In fact there were signs of strain showing before Mountbatten. The reorganisation, and the revelations about R.U.C. interrogation methods had visibly strengthened the Provisionals and cut the number of security 'successes' when at a Provisional rally in Belfast's Casement Park, G.A.A. Ground, during August, Provisional volunteers displayed modern automatic weapons—enraging Loyalists.

The U.D.A. deemed it advisable to respond with a statement promising 'a shift of emphasis towards a more positive paramilitary role'. That this did not go far enough was demonstrated later in the month—on the very morning of Mountbatten and Warrenpoint—on August 27, when it was announced that some members of the U.D.A., the U.V.F. and the Red Hand Commandos were going to assassinate known members of the I.R.A. and of the I.N.L.A. In fact prior to this announcement a number of assassinations and assassination attempts had been made on known I.R.A. men and on innocents mistaken for I.R.A. men.

In one of these, the previous April, the assassins called at the home of Billy Carson, who was a member of the Provisionals, and waited for him to return, chatting to his children and watching television, till he walked into the house and they shot him dead. Then after Mountbatten, the U.F.F. (generally regarded as a U.D.A. hit group which can be disowned if necessary) called a press conference to announce that they would retaliate for the deaths of August 27; a number of shootings resulted. However, all this killing was remarkably small-scale in the light of what happened and, though they sometimes made ghastly mistakes, U.D.A. or Protestant paramilitary attacks were carried out at least on the initial presumption that the victim was an I.R.A. man—not merely a Catholic.

This was a considerable advance on the type of selection made earlier in the decade when Protestant 'hit men' would sit on a bus until it passed a Catholic church, watch who blessed themselves, shoot them and then get off.

Of course, long before it was possible for any outside initiative to be undertaken the Protestant paramilitary organisation had matured and altered almost beyond recognition. There were two reasons for this; one external, the other internal. The U.D.A.'s fastest growth was principally in the year 1972—a year of particular Unionist ferment; it was the year which saw the growth of William Craig's Ulster Vanguard movement with its Grand Old Duke of York militarism (his speeches marched his hearers up the hill of apparently strong action but then contrived to march them down again without actually committing anyone to violence). The Loyalist Association of Workers (L.A.W.) led by Billy Hull, a prominent shop-steward at the Harland and Wolff shipyards, also preached traditionally Protestant politics. It was of course also the year in which Stormont fell.

The Vanguard movement (the Ulster was speedily dropped) soon found itself uncertain how to advance. But the U.D.A. and the U.V.F. had no such inhibitions. There was only one way that its members wanted to or could reply to what the I.R.A. were doing, which was to meet force with force. Interestingly enough, a principal force in the U.D.A.'s rise in late 1971 and in the early months of 1972 was the influence of militant Protestant women. These said to their husbands and boyfriends (in some cases even to their sons) in effect, 'What are you doing about it all? You are not men at all. You are letting the I.R.A. get away with it.'

The traditional response of the Protestant establishment when the natives became restive had always been to crack down hard. The appearance of the U.D.A. in military formation and paramilitary battledress was in some senses the gut reaction of Ulster Protestantism to the feeling that somehow, somewhere, its traditional leaders had sold them out.

The U.D.A.'s birthing stages were almost an exact mirror image of those of the I.R.A. Men scurried around looking for weapons; a few Smith and Wessons, some Webleys and some automatic pistols from Czechoslovakia. Some weapons were bought by sympathisers in Scotland, others from armament factories in Britain which did not seem unduly curious as to why all the gentlemen with North of Ireland accents should want so many of the trade-in police guns and the old rifles. These did not cost much—about £15 to £35—because they were in bad condition, but the traditional engineering skills of the Ulster Protestant soon had them in good working order again.

While this was going on community relations in Belfast were worsening. As always in times of communal tension, mixed districts were the first to feel threatened; Ballymurphy and New Barnsley rapidly lost their Protestant admixture and the Catholics in districts like Finaghy, Woodvale and the Newtownards Road became even thinner on the ground.

I remember feeling at the time as I went about the various districts, shepherded by either a Protestant or a Catholic interlocutor, that fear wasn't just a feeling, it was as easy to see and as ugly as facial cancer.

Here one met a shaken Catholic family after an intimidatory visit by U.D.A. men in masks who warned that a home must be abandoned or the visitors 'could not be responsible for the actions of people in the neighbourhood'. There one met a Protestant lady whose furniture had just been thrown out on the street by her Catholic neighbours.

And so the fears and the confusion, the inculcated bigotry, the hates were fed into the mindless computer of Belfast history and the answer came out in bullets.

Scores of young Catholics were found with hoods over their heads and bullets through their brains. Others were found in a condition better imagined than described, with mutilations, throat cuttings and every form of atrocity.

Modelling itself on the I.R.A., the U.D.A. held its first military-style funeral (for a U.D.A. man, J. L. Brown, found shot to death a few days earlier) on June 28, 1972—the same day that the Provisional I.R.A. issued its policy document, Eire Nua ('a New Ireland'), in Dublin. A murder trial in October the following year, in which Albert 'Ginger' Baker got life for the murders of four Catholics and for some eleven robberies totalling £15,000, revealed the activities of the 'romper room'—a torture chamber in the Shankill Road. Hoisting torture victims ceiling-high by means of a pulley and then letting them crash to the floor was only one of the techniques used there.

Men were done to death in every conceivable and inconceivable way. There was a feeling among the Protestants that the I.R.A. were no better than animals and should be treated as such. They adapted and improved on such I.R.A. tactics as kneecapping by using a Black and Decker drill.

But eventually this wave passed, though not before the U.D.A. had detonated a number of bombs in Dublin and Monaghan on May 17, 1974. The Dublin bombs killed twenty-five people, and those in Monaghan killed six.

It was as if in Mafia terms the organisation had 'made its bones', killing to prove its manhood to show that it could do in Dublin what the I.R.A. did in Belfast. Within the movement there was a dawning realisation that this sort of brutality alienated not only the Catholic population but also a very large section of the Protestant community on which the U.D.A. would have to rely if it ever intended to be taken seriously as a political movement or even for funds to continue as a paramilitary movement. (Interestingly enough, at the time of writing these are not as readily forthcoming as formerly, and there is a marked difference in attitude between now and the time of the successful Loyalist strike of May, 1974.)

On May 25, 1974 Harold Wilson went on British television to castigate the Loyalist strikers and call them spongers on the British public. But the effects of the Dublin bombings and the Loyalist strike proved stronger than his rhetoric. Three days later on May 28, Merlyn Rees issued a statement saying that 'there is now no statutory basis for the Northern Ireland Executive'. In other words, Faulkner had lost support in the Assembly.

There was more than a whiff of the Curragh Mutiny about the army's attitude during the Loyalist strike. British soldiers were photographed talking amiably to U.D.A. members at barricades and the G.O.C., Lieutenant-General Sir Frank King refused to take his 17,500-strong force into action against the strikers on the grounds that he hadn't enough men. The army saw its role as fighting the I.R.A. only. The R.U.C. did absolutely nothing to restrain the strikers either, and several of them told journalists that their orders in fact precluded them from doing anything.* This was at a time when per contra the Secretary of State for Northern Ireland Merlyn Rees and his civil servants were vainly attempting to prod the force into action.

The elasticity with which Protestant groupings could stretch to cover the constitutional and un-constitutional wings of the Loyalist spectrum was well exemplified by the formation of the Ulster Army Council on December 10, 1973. This was founded to oppose the Council of Ireland idea contained in the Sunningdale pact. The Ulster Army Council was influenced, as is so much Protestant paramilitary thinking, by the I.R.A., whose supreme governing body is of course the 'Army Council'.

Its membership included the U.D.A., the U.V.F., the Ulster Special Constabulary Association (the former B-Specials) and the Red Hand Commandos who had played such a distinctive role in the August, 1969 burnings in Belfast. It is worth noting that Glenn Barr,† who was an Assembly man representing Vanguard at Stormont, was also a U.D.A. Commander. The Down Orange Welfare organisation which with the Vanguard took part in the Ulster Workers' Council, the body which organised the strike, had at its head a former British Army Colonel, Peter Brush. Catholics did not enjoy witnessing such a grouping taking place but the only difference for them was that on this occasion the paramilitaries were offering their services and encouragement to the politicians, rather than the other way around.

---

* The best account of this crisis is Robert Fisk's *Point of No Return*, an excellent guide to the Northern problem generally.

† Barr said after the strike that the army could have broken it, had it wished, by moving early in its development.

It is worth digressing here to note that this trend continued following the Mountbatten murder. John Taylor, a particularly venomous Unionist apologist, made a 'hold-me-back, let-me-at-them' speech saying that if there was going to be retaliation by Loyalist paramilitaries then he hoped that it would be directed against the South. The Official Unionist Party Secretary, Norman Hutton, concurred in this statement saying that the remarks by Taylor, a member of the European Parliament, were official Unionist policy. However, Sam Duddy, speaking for the U.D.A., said that the organisation would not be retaliating on behalf of Mr Taylor or anyone else in the Unionist Party, and disassociated itself from Taylor's remarks.

In the case of the Loyalist strike, the politicians who were being helped by the paramilitaries were the Loyalists opposing Faulkner over Sunningdale (Ian Paisley, William Craig, and Harry West). The more perceptive of its leaders came to accept that the role of the organisation was not simply to exist to do the dirty work for Unionist politicians who could and would disown them when the going got rough. A newer, more reactive breed of leadership began to emerge particularly after the Loyalist strike when it became evident that men like Glenn Barr, Andy Tyrie, Harry Chicken, Sam Lyttle and others were thinking on political lines, although they continued to make extremist Protestant noises. Privately, however, men like these would admit in conversation with people like myself that some form of Irish Ireland appeared inevitable; that the British would go one day and that their dilemma was to try to win public support for some form of acceptance for these ideas while at the same time keeping their more extremist followers in check by making the usually threatening noises.

As one leader said to me with grim humour, 'There's no redundancy in my job!' After the second Loyalist strike, called in 1977, flopped because the electricity workers would not join in this time, the U.D.A. became increasingly bitter against the British who began increasingly to mete out to them the same type of treatment which the I.R.A. and the Catholic community had long experienced.

This process was accelerated on the British side by a growing realisation that the policy of 'the enemy of my enemy is my friend' had severe limitations, in particular when it gave rise to wholesale protection rackets and to internecine bloodshed. Several leading members of the U.D.A. including Tommy Heron, Ernie Elliott and Sammy Smith were murdered by their own people, and some like Charles Harding-Smith and Vogel had to flee the country for their lives.

These pressures combined to produce a situation where, at the time of writing, the U.D.A., now short of funds (since it has nothing even remotely approaching the I.R.A.'s overseas sources of money) and driven to a realisation that protection rackets, knifings and sectarian assassination were counter-productive in terms of political advancement, actually launched a political campaign in March, 1979, to gain support for the U.D.A. goal of an Independent Ulster. Independent of both Dublin and London, that is. This idea, though still mistrusted by old-time Belfast Republicans like Billy McKee and Proinsias MacAirt who felt that it in some way was a policy that would result in a continuing British presence, was nevertheless the subject of continuing secret contact which had begun some years earlier between the U.D.A. and I.R.A.

The principal figures involved in the earlier talks were two lawyers outside the ranks of the paramilitaries. On the I.R.A. side one of the most distinguished living Irishmen, Sean MacBride, a top U.N. administrator, Nobel Peace-Prize winner, Clann na Poblachta founder, and former Chief-of-Staff of the I.R.A.; and, for the U.D.A.,* Desmond Boal, a politician and a confidant of Paisley. He is a noted traveller and a Protestant apologist who had been flickering around the edges of religious controversy in Ireland since the mid-1950s.†

From the end of 1976 to around April the following year these talks proceeded more or less fruitfully. The framework of an agreement between the two factions appeared feasible—at least to the negotiators! It was intended that the European Convention on Human Rights would be used to safeguard both Protestant and Catholic, North and South of the border. The North was, under this safeguard, to have a kind of independence with, however, some links to the South which would both reassure the Northern Catholics that in some way the South's numbers could if needed be used to weigh in their favour, and loose enough to prevent the Protestants fearing that they would be engulfed in an All-Ireland Catholic state. There was to be a ceasefire during which, most surprising of all, the document was to be presented to London—accompanied by a U.L.C.C.C.— Provisional I.R.A. demand for a British withdrawal from Ireland.

However, the situation simply had not matured sufficiently to bear the weight of all this. During April on the Provisional side attention was distracted by a renewed outburst of warfare between the 'stickies' and the 'pin-heads', and on the Loyalist side Paisley diverted action by calling for a second Loyalist strike. He wanted more action against the Provisionals at a time when because of their internal re organisation overt activity was at a low ebb and Roy Mason mistakenly thought that the security forces were winning. Mason had since mid-January sanctioned an agreement whereby the prime responsibility for security shifted to the R.U.C. Paisley also wanted, or said he wanted, a restoration of Stormont More likely he simply wanted to show that he was still a power in the land.

In any event the strike began on Monday, May 2, 1977, and petered out a few days later. Mason did not bow to the intimidation this time; London and Belfast had learned the lessons of 1974 when it was realised too late that a firm attitude at the start could have prevented the situation escalating. The Protestant paramilitaries were discredited by the failure of the strike and on both sides the paramilitaries' powers appeared to be on the wane.

Against this background it proved possible to salvage something from the carnage and chaos—civilian casualties went down from 145 (in 1976) to 69 (in 1977), principally due to a decline in sectarian assassination which thus provided a basis for the 'no car bombing' pact which survived even the La Mon carnage

---

* Strictly speaking, Boal was speaking on behalf of the Ulster Loyalist Central Co-ordination Committee. But without the U.D.A. there would have been very little need for 'coordination'!

† He then figured as a negotiator in a national controversy which erupted over mixed marriage in which a Protestant lady left her husband, a Catholic, in Fethard-on-Sea in Co. Wexford and returned with her children to the North and to Protestantism rather than submit any longer to the dictates of the Ne Temere decree. There was for a time a boycott by Catholics of Protestants in the area as a result.

described below. In fact with the exception of the occasional inevitable breach on either side the pact could have been said to have lasted until after the Mountbatten murder. Following this the Ulster Freedom Fighters called a press conference while Andy Tyrie, either for reasons of strategy or relaxation, was on holiday, to announce a resumption of retaliatory killing, but even this subsequently proved to be considerably less than was feared.

Against the scale of deaths in the decade the agreement over car bombing and the MacBride-Boal talks do not bulk large. But without them these things might have been incalculably worse. To the question, 'What did you do in the war, Daddy?' it is at least possible to reply: 'We tried.'

One of the main architects of the U.D.A.'s shift in emphasis from the bullet and the knife to political activity is Andy Tyrie, a skilled mechanical worker who has worked in England. He has reached a place of leadership within the movement. At moments of crisis, such as in the aftermath of the La Mon bombing when he was besieged by heated calls for an exemption of the assassination campaign, he has been known to throw a list of top I.R.A. men's names on to a table and with them a gun, saying, 'Those are the men you want, pick up the gun and I will give you as many more as you want to do the job—but there's no use shooting Catholics just for revenge.'

Neither the list nor the gun was picked up. On another occasion Tyrie, who had successfully negotiated for a U.D.A. man, Freddy Parkinson, who was at the time serving a sentence for attempted arson in Mountjoy jail, Dublin, to be released for his mother's funeral in Belfast, completed his side of the bargain by personally picking up the reluctant Parkinson on the Shankill Road and driving him to Dublin to complete his sentence.

On the U.V.F. front (the U.V.F. is largely subsumed into the U.D.A., particularly in Belfast, but it does have an identity of its own), a similar metamorphosis took place. This was attributable to the twin pressures of attrition, jail and internment and the dawning realisation that their idealism or hatred had been misdirected. Jail is a great leveller. Many an ardent Orange supremacist who went into Long Kesh for his U.V.F. activities became so unsettled in his traditional beliefs by observing Republican fellow prisoners and by his own treatment at the hands of the warders and soldiers that he changed to the extent of actually learning Irish. To be sure some kept up the brave pretence that they are only doing so for the same reasons that the Americans used Indian dialects during World War II because it was a language that the Germans could not understand. Similarly, the Protestants wanted to find out what the Catholics were saying.

Many of the younger U.V.F. men in particular had been imbued with patriotism, myth and prejudice to the extent that the only way they could see of 'defending the Protestant heritage, the liberty of religion and the British connection', was to take a gun and shoot some seventeen-year-old Catholic of their own class.

However, as the time in jail passed, remorse began to set in—and conscience has proved a powerful causative factor in bringing about a change of heart in many a youthful killer. Remorse apparently ended one of the biggest murder hunts of the decade, that for the killers of U.D.A. leader, Hugh McVeigh, and a lesser U.D.A. figure, volunteer David Douglas, who were done to death by the U.V.F. on April 7,

1975. The idea behind the murders seemingly was to try to provoke the U.D.A. into taking action (and so to shatter the ceasefire between the I.R.A. and the army) against the Provisionals who were widely assumed to have done the killings. Eventually, almost two years later, however, in a four-hour reserved judgment, Mr Justice McDermott handed out a total of 700 years in sentences to twenty-six U.V.F. men whom he held to be guilty not alone of the murders but of a series of other crimes as well.

It was the evidence of one man, 'Witness A', as he was referred to all during the trial, which formed the basis of the breakthrough which led to the finding of the murdered men's bodies and the ultimate sentencing of the killers. Witness A had taken to going at regular intervals and praying beside their grave and these pangs of conscience were causing people in the district to wonder at his actions and leading his colleagues apparently to think of silencing him and thus led him to go to the police. Witness A was spirited out of the country following the trial after threats were made to him from the dock.

However after a spell in jail, young men like these begin to ponder on the nature of their heritage and on the fact that it was the British uniform which they were trained to revere which was now keeping them behind lock and key. It was the British handing out beatings, whenever tension arose in the camp, over prisoners' demands or infringement of rules. It's a hard thing for a young man barely out of adolescence to find that he has gone into prison believing himself to be a patriot and to find himself christened a murderer instead. It's even harder when unlike his young I.R.A. counterpart, who has a far greater historical continuity to look to, he finds that his cause and his culture crumble under examination into a crisis of identity (rather like the disappearance of the Blueshirt movement of the 1930s while many of its members were in jail). Hence there has come on the Protestant side a general consciousness of being Irish—an Ulsterisation process, as some commentators put it. They know at least that they belong to Ulster; that much is safe and sure, as Dublin looms closer and London apparently prepares to betray them.

In the Protestant dilemma there is a hope for the future. A voyage of self-discovery has begun and it is a giant step forward. Until the murder of Mountbatten one could have said with reasonable confidence—nothing is of course certain in the Northern Ireland morass—that a backlash from the Protestant side would not necessarily occur if the British left. And though events since the murder have weakened that confidence, they have not wrecked it.

One of the more distressing aspects of the I.R.A. campaign was (and is) the tactic of shooting off-duty Ulster Defence Regiment personal, sometimes in circumstances of particular horror, such as when they are taking their children to school, or in their homes watching television. In some of the talks between the U.D.A. and the I.R.A. which have flickered on and off through the years, these shootings have been used as a bargaining counter for a cessation by the U.D.A. of its sectarian assassination campaign.

Partly this was because many U.D.A. men are in the U.D.R. but the reason for the U.D.R. killings goes deeper than anger at this or the need to have a bargaining position in the grisly subterranean horse-trading. I have written earlier about the role of the B-Specials and their formation by Lord Brookeborough.

Readers will therefore be aware of the key position the corps occupied in the maintenance of Protestant hegemony and then consequent detestation by the Catholic population whose leaders frequently called for the force's disbandment

Catholic detestation came to a head with the events of August, 1969, in which B-Specials took part in the acts of burning and violence not as a legitimate aid to the forces patrolling the border but as a Protestant militia seeking to extirpate the Catholics in the centre of cities exactly as their forefathers had done.

Some of the episodes in which the B-Specials were involved were shown on British television (during the Falls Road burnings of August, 1969) and enlightened English public opinion was enraged. Harold Wilson, the then British Prime Minister, expressed himself strongly on the corps in the House of Commons during a debate on Northern Ireland, and a committee of inquiry into the activities of the police and the B-Specials was set up under Sir John Hunt, the Everest conqueror. His report was published in October, 1969, and accepted by the government that day—an alacrity that was as pleasing to the Catholics as it was dismaying to the Protestants.

Sir John recommended that the B-Specials be disbanded and replaced by another body, the Ulster Defence Regiment. Protestant sentiment was so outraged by the disbandment of the 'Specials' that some replacement had to be found. But it was hoped that the new corps, which was finally set up during April, 1970, being ultimately responsible to the G.O.C. Northern Ireland, would therefore be more susceptible to orthodox discipline since security was henceforth to be a matter not for militias but for Whitehall.

Sir John Hunt had proposed that the U.D.R. be 2,000 strong but by 1979 it had just under 8,000 members and a women's auxiliary unit, the Greenfinches, which had 600, with about 1,000 members on duty every evening and 2,000 at weekends. A strong advertising campaign on television and in newspapers sought to keep those numbers up despite the I.R.A.'s attrition. Initially the force was not a 'legitimate target' for the I.R.A. but it was not long in operation before there were Catholic complaints that the new U.D.R. was just the old B-Specials in a new guise. Initially the force had a 16 per cent Catholic enrolment. This had fallen to 8 per cent by the end of a year (Hansard, November 25) and must be virtually non-existent now.

I noticed when driving in the North with Catholic friends that they appeared to be more fearful of being stopped by the U.D.R at road blocks than by the army. As I have never encountered anything but courtesy myself whenever I have been stopped in the North by either the U.D.R. or the army I cannot add anything by way of firsthand experience to this observation. In the abrasion of Northern Irish life both the Catholic population and the I.R.A. very obviously could, and after reports of U.D.R. involvement in the various killings of Catholics and, of course, in the arrests and weakening of I.R.A.—the I.R.A. declared open season on the U.D.R in 1971 when five members of the force were shot in the course of the year. By the end of 1979, some eighty members of the force, including two women, had been assassinated. At first sight that figure would seem to indicate that the U.D.R. had been most foully set upon—and in some cases its members were— but there is another figure which should be considered in this context.

In March of 1979 the R.U.C. admitted that U.D.R. members had been involved in thirty known cases of murder, the two most spectacular or horrific examples of which were the massacre of the Miami Showband, a Southern group whose members were ambushed, three being murdered and two wounded on August 1, 1975, near the border,* and by the activities of the Shankill murder gang known as the 'Butchers'.

The 'Butchers' day of reckoning came on February 20, 1979, in Belfast when Mr Justice O'Donnell sentenced a group of eight 'Butchers' to a total of forty-two life sentences for nineteen deaths. One of the most prominent members of the group, Robert 'Basher' Bates, was an ex-U.D.R. man. To anyone familiar with the North it was inconceivable that a group not actively connected with either of the major sources of paramilitary activity could have put away with the spate of torture, throat cuttings and shootings which the 'Butchers' practised over a period of several years. Yet this apparently was the case, even though the 'Butchers' met regularly and openly in such Belfast haunts as the Lawnbrook drinking club and in other Protestant pubs.

Many Catholics believed that authorities connived at or at least turned a blind eye to such activities, because, acting on the theory that 'the enemy of my enemy is my friend', it was felt that such pressures would 'soften up the Papes' and make them more willing to yield up the guerillas in their midst, the I.R.A.

The official version of the 'Butchers' downfall is that they had left one victim, Gerard McLaverty, a Catholic, for dead, but through a change in their *modus operandi*, he recovered and with the aid of excellent police work on the part of two police officers, Detective Chief Inspector James Nesbitt and Detective Sergeant Chambers, was able to identify his assailants standing outside a pub.

Instead of using a meat cleaver or an axe on McLaverty, after the customary bout of torture, they tied a bootlace around his throat to silence him and then slashed his wrists with knives and threw him in an alleyway where his blood congealed in the cold so that the bleeding stopped and saved his life.

Sentencing the killers, Mr Justice O'Donnell made it clear that in the case of two of them, William Moore and the ex-U.D.R. man, Bates, life was to mean life and that no reason was to be accepted for terminating this sentence save terminal illness.

The most substantial journalistic effort to prove the links between the security forces and the paramilitaries came in October, 1973, when *Political Murder in Northern Ireland* was published by Martin Dillon and Dennis Lehane. But Loyalist paramilitaries' spokesmen, post the Sunningdale strike, been to make public claims about their U.D.R links (I was flatly told during one visit to the U.D.A. H.Q. that 'you can take it we more or less control the U.D.R.') and there was a notorious case in the Bawnmore district of Belfast in September of 1979 in which a Catholic who had spent three years in jail on an arms charge was murdered within minutes of a U.D.R. patrol passing by.

Wherever the truth lies, the development of the U.D.R., the subsequent onslaught on it and its involvement with episodes like the 'Miami' affair and the 'Butchers'' activities help to illustrate yet again why to Catholics in the ghetto the term 'law and order' has to be defined as to whose law and whose order. To the people of Andersonstown, Ballymurphy, the Clonard and so on, the R.U.C. and

---

* In a botched effort to blow up the Miami van two U.V.F. men died on the same occasion.

the U.D.R. and any similar grouping are either instruments of oppression in themselves or source of information for their associates in the ranks of sectarian assassins.

As readers will be aware by now, a characteristic of 'The Movement' is its tendency to split whether over ideology or personality. This trait also asserted itself strongly in the 1969–79 decade.

While the Provisionals are of course the principle physical force unit within the Republican movement, it is just conceivable that they will not always remain so. For just as when the Provisionals split from the Officials they seemed to be but a splinter group, and then established themselves as the strongest guerilla movement in Europe, so too might the Irish National Liberation Army movement prove in the long run to be even stronger than the Provisionals. Apart from the speculation, and the fact that the organisation was responsible for assassinating Airey Neave, the birth and survival of the I.N.L.A. is significant inasmuch as it shows yet again the strength of the revolutionary current which constitutes extreme Republicanism in Ireland and the impossibility of that current ever being completely short-circuited so long as the border issue remains—British uniform in Ireland is an irritant in the political oyster around which no pearl will ever form.

Like the Provisionals, the I.N.L.A. was born out of a feud within the Official I.R.A. This came to a head in a bloody feud which began with the shooting of Hugh Ferguson (I.R.S.P.) on February 20, 1975, and lasted until May as the Officials tried unsuccessfully to put down the mutiny. Apart from Ferguson, the shootings and counter shootings included Sean Garland, badly wounded in Dublin a few days later on March 1. Within the Official movement he was regarded as one of the heroes of the I.R.A. having been wounded in the Brooksborough ambush. The following month Billy McMillen, the Officials' leader in Belfast, also a respected figure inside and outside the movement, was murdered on April 28 and an unsuccessful attempt was made to machine gun Seamus Costello as he was overtaken by a motor-cycle while driving from a meeting in Waterford on May 7.

The I.N.L.A. support centred for a time on Divis Flats in the Falls Road and there was for a time a joke about the nickname given to the flats based on the initials of the I.N.L.A.'s political wing—the Irish Republican Socialist Party. The flats were called 'Planet of the I.R.P.S.', but no one is laughing now after episodes like the assassination of Airey Neave, and bank robberies of the scale of the one carried out in June, 1979, at Barnagh Gap, Co. Limerick, which netted £500,000. The Irish Republican Socialist Party has its own newspaper and disclaims any connection, save a shared aim, with the I.N.L.A. This aim is a united socialist (thirty-two county) Irish Republic achieved through physical force. The I.R.S.P. was set up by and under the leadership of Bernadette McAliskey (née Devlin) and Seamus Costello in 1974 but she split from the party a year later because of its 'militarism' and Seamus Costello was assassinated in 1977. Interestingly enough the I.R.S.P. is currently also run by a woman, the articulate Belfast political activist Miriam Daly.

The I.N.L.A. is largely financed through raiding banks in Ireland and by Middle Eastern subventions. It has carried out a number of attacks against the army, U.D.R.

and R.U.C. which were for a long time ascribed to the Provisionals because it was not until after the Neave killing that the very tightly knit, secretive, Republican unit publicly claimed an operation. It is now known that the I.N.L.A. also attacked U.D.A. and U.V.F. members because, it says, of their known sectarian activities. The I.N.L.A. is known to be close to the Provisionals, possibly to the extent of engaging in what in business circles are known as 'joint ventures', while remaining bitterly opposed to the Officials and other left-wing groupings, Trotskyites, socialists, and so on. They had, before the Provisionals themselves tightened up, a tighter recruitment policy than the Provisionals, screening applicants for membership rigorously and keeping numbers small and anonymous—though the organisation claims at the same time to be organised in all the important Irish towns and certainly has strong support in the Falls Road district of Belfast and in Derry.

The sophistication of its weaponry—which include Kalashnikov (AK47) rifles, Russian hand grenades, taken together with the bomb-making ills, so potently demonstrated in the mercury-triggered device which killed Airey Neave as he drove his car from the House of Commons car park make the I.N.L.A. a formidable foe indeed. The organisation decided to kill Neave because he had been calling for a strengthening of the S.A.S. and the U.D.R. and for the introduction of hanging and the re-introduction of internment. As he was expected to succeed Roy Mason, those views could well have become policy for Northern Ireland where his intelligence background would have been of further assistance to him and a drawback to the revolutionary groups opposing him.

As for the Officials themselves during the period, the story is no more cheerful than for any of the other parties concerned. After the split the Officials continued in being, attracting numbers of young people by their blend of Marxism and revolutionary Republicanism which after May 29, 1972, did not even carry the risk of the Provisionals' brand—death—because on that day, the Officials declared a ceasefire. This ceasefire has held more or less intact to the time of writing, barring some feuding with the Provisionals, and more especially with the Irish National Liberation Army which split from them. Had the Provisionals not been preoccupied with their anti-British activities, the original Provisionals' split might have had a different and a bloodier end—one of the Provisionals shot and permanently injured by the Officials, for instance, was Thomas Cahill, Joe Cahill's brother. As it was, a short vicious spate of fighting between the two wings in October, 1975, claimed eleven deaths and fifty wounded before two priests, Father Alex Reid and Father Desmond Wilson, managed to negotiate a settlement.

The stated aim of the Officials—to unite Protestant and Catholic workers in an All-Ireland Socialist Republic— does not have a snowball's chance in hell of succeeding and it would be easy to dismiss them as pretentious and unreal rhetoricians. There is a joke told in Belfast concerning an army haul from the Provisionals, the U.V.F. and the Officials. The Provisionals yielded some bombs, Armalites and machine guns, the U.V.F. some rifles and revolvers, and the Officials 'five thousand copies of *The Thoughts of Chairman Mao*, five thousand copies of *Das Kapital* and a library of books on world revolution'.

In addition to this, their record of military operations is a litany of brutal bungling. A bombing at an army billet in Aldershot, in retaliation for Bloody Sunday, killed a Catholic chaplain and some cleaning women—'workers of the world unite'! And their other activities included the assassination of Senator Barnhill;* an attempted assassination of John Taylor (which failed, according to Belfast gallows humour, because they shot him in the head!); the dragging of a U.D.R. man, who was also a bus driver, off a school bus and shooting him dead in front of the screaming children; and finally the murder of a popular young Derry lad, Ranger William Best, who was home on holidays from the British army and who had been known to join his friends in the Provisionals in throwing stones at the British army. This last murder precipitated a wave of condemnation for the Officials and the ceasefire.

However, despite this record of literally murderous folly, the 'Stickies' appeal— or perhaps more correctly that of left-wing Republicanism—is not to be underestimated. For instance, when after the ceasefire the Officials' Belfast leader, Joe McCann, was shot by British troops, Gusty Spence, the U.V.F. leader, wrote to his widow in sympathy and appreciation of McCann's views; and in the 1974 Westminster General Election the Republican Clubs, as the Officials' political wing is known in the North (in the South, it is Sinn Fein, the Workers' Party), received 21,633 votes, a thousand more than Brian Faulkner's wing of the Unionist Party. It may not be the Official I.R.A. wing which ultimately benefits from this residual support, but the hard men in the I.N.L.A., some of whom were mixed up in the Best affair and in other murders of a similar nature both since and before the split.

But certainly in a country with high unemployment and the youthful electorate already referred to, this smouldering socialist torch is one that the authorities are very keenly aware could put sparks to the political fabric of the country, if circumstances were right.

To wind up the litany of fractiousness, it might be noted that Saor Eire† too had a split which yielded an offshoot 'Saoirse Eire'. Larry White, one of its members, was shot dead in Cork on June 10, 1975. I was to acquire a particular interest in this last death because as a result of publishing allegations concerning police brutality towards the men accused of his murder, made by their solicitor, I found myself in the High Court, successfully defending, I am happy to say, a contempt of court charge.

One of the tactics used by the Coalition was to try to muzzle the papers on the subject of the I.R.A. by using the contempt of court laws. The four major newspaper groups in the Republic and even the weekly opinion journal *Hibernia* were all prosecuted by the state between 1974 and 1977. In this unprecedented outburst of state legal assault, the *Irish Press* was the only paper successfully to defend itself.

Apart from the difficulty of trying to determine who shot who and why in Northern Ireland (generally over guns or money), which one side or the other probably felt belonged to it—there is also the fact that sometimes 'contract' killers are used by both sides—Republican and Protestant—on top of this, the activities of the S.A.S. and the 'dirty tricks' brigade have never been satisfactorily explained.

---

* The Stickies only intended to destroy his home in Co. Tyrone as part of their 'class warfare', but the Senator put up a struggle and was killed more or less accidentally. His home was then destroyed.

† Saor Eire officially went out of business on June 27 when a statement was issued on behalf of the organisation saying that it was suspending operations 'in the interests of the working class'.

One of the issues which continually caused trouble between London and Dublin was the vexed question of extradition. For the Dublin governments, bound by history and the Irish constitution, the position remained exactly that enunciated by John A. Costello on November 30, 1955, when he said (Chapter 13) '. . . there can be no question of handing over either to the British or to the Six County authorities, persons whom they may accuse of armed political activities in Britain or in the Six Counties.'

After Sunningdale a 'law enforcement commission' was set up which reported on the advisability of an all-Ireland court which would try offenders within the jurisdiction within which they were apprehended, for instance Dublin could try an I.R.A. bomber wanted by the British without having to hand him over for trial; but the British never availed of this facility and continued to seek extradition.

This pressure was accompanied by a publicity campaign which, apart from irritation it caused in Dublin, sometimes backfired—at least once with tragic results, in the case of Margaret McKearney. In September, 1975, Miss McKearney was twenty-one, a native of Moy, Co. Tyrone, a member of a fiercely Republican family in which two of her brothers had been jailed and one, Sean, killed with a comrade* in a premature bomb explosion. She was also, according to Scotland Yard, 'possibly the most dangerous woman terrorist in Britain'.

She was wanted in connection with a number of the British bombings, London, Liverpool, Southampton, Glasgow and Manchester, police believing that she was one of the team of women who brought over supplies, money and instructions to the I.R.A. units in Britain. However, Scotland Yard issued the Press Association with a picture of her, allegedly taken at a dance in Dublin. This was later said, however, to have been found during a raid in Manchester and it also became known that at the time that Scotland Yard was allegedly seeking help in apprehending 'the most wanted girl in Britain' she was known to be back in Ireland. Moreover the Irish Special Branch were able to substantiate the fact that Miss McKearney was also in Ireland on dates when the Yard claimed she was active in Britain.

The discrepancy in the dates gave rise to a belief that the British authorities were using the McKearney affair to bring pressure to bear on the Irish government over extradition and there was a resultant flurry of diplomatic activity between the two governments.

However, while the matter was still being discussed privately and diplomatically, publicly and bloodily a group of Loyalist assassins took a hand in the affair by shooting an innocent couple (on October 23) in their garden—Peter McKearney and his wife Jane, who were mistaken for Margaret's parents. They were in fact unrelated.

British intelligence was of course far from quiescent over the period. An obvious centre of activity was and is the embassy. Sir John Peck, the popular British diplomat who had the doubtful privilege of having his embassy burned down† after Bloody Sunday, had an intelligence background in the Middle East—though

---

*   Eugene Martin of Charlemont.
†   Perhaps the Foreign Office made a point of sending to Dublin men versed in incendiarism; Peck's predecessor, Sir Andrew Gilchrist, was also present at the burning of the British Embassy in Djakarta.

neither he nor the Irish saw any reason why this should prevent him settling down subsequently to an enjoyable retirement in Dublin. A successor of his, Christopher Ewart-Biggs, was of course apparently struck down because of intelligence considerations. One I.R.A. version of the reasons for his deathwish I was given was that it was the military attaché, not the ambassador, who was the real target.

This would at least be a more convincing explanation than the fact that Brian Cubbon, Permanent Ulster Secretary of the Northern Ireland Office, who was in the car at the time of the explosions, was the reason for the attack. For while it would not be difficult to monitor the ambassador's movements with a view to ambushing him, it would be very difficult indeed with up-to-date information from the embassy itself or the security forces guarding it to say just when Cubbon would be in the car. Cubbon, incidentally, survived the blast and has lived unattacked since, as has Merlyn Rees, another supposed passenger in the car.

Obviously over the decade I, like other journalists, had heard stories of an espionage connection with some leading Fleet Street journalists who had come to Ireland because of the troubles (and sometimes similar stories concerning people residing in the Republic). But it is better not to dwell on these and to give only concrete proved examples. I will content myself with two; one involving Britons, the other an Irishman. The Britons, of course, were the celebrated Littlejohn brothers, Kenneth and Keith, whose British army background was apparently put to other uses by the British authorities. On February 19, 1973, this pair lost their appeal in the London High Court against being sent back to Ireland to face charges arising out of the armed robbery of £67,000 from the Allied Irish Bank in Grafton Street, Dublin, the previous October. For the offence Kenneth received twenty years and Keith fifteen from the Special Criminal Court. Stiff sentences for mere bank robbery nowadays. The London case was heard in camera because the Attorney General said that 'matters of national interest' might be involved.

What these matters might be became somewhat clearer in the Dublin proceedings during which it was revealed that the money was thought to have gone to the Official I.R.A. whom the Littlejohns had infiltrated, quoting as their authority for this action the British Ministry of Defence. They named a number of leading figures in public life as being party to their actions, saying that in particular, Geoffrey Johnson Smith, Minister of State and Minister of Defence, knew about them.

It never became clear at what point the Littlejohns came to be regarded not as agents but as bank-robbers by the British, thus allowing them to be returned to Dublin. Nor did the full extent of their activities—some of them known to be carried out in border areas—ever become public. But the Irish government sent its ambassador to the Court of St James, Donal O'Sullivan, to lodge a protest over the affair on August 9. And it also took the unusual step of issuing a statement through the government information office expressing 'dissatisfaction' with the British government's assurances concerning espionage in the Republic, saying that spying was 'unacceptable' and 'counter productive'. (The British government took some of the sting out of the exchange by pointing out that it had officially informed Lynch of the Littlejohns' activities. He acknowledged this but pleaded a 'lapse of memory').

The file on the case involving the Irish citizen, which presumably formed part of the 'unacceptable' background to the O'Sullivan protest, was closed at the

Special Criminal Court on February 27 of that year, 1973, when Patrick Crinnion of Dublin was found guilty of a number of charges under the Official Secrets Act and sentenced to three months' imprisonment which he did not have to serve as he had been in custody since the previous December. John Wyman, the Englishman to whom he had been supplying the information, received a similar sentence and discharge from the court. One can only hazard a guess as to what Wyman's real job was—but before he was found out, Crinnion had been a member of the Irish Special Branch, a fact which caused very great annoyance in government circles. To this day, no one can say with certainty whether or not there are Crinnions engaged on the Provisionals' interest in the Special Branch but no decision-takers in the Department of Justice will, or can, rule out the possibility entirely.

26

Return to Secrecy and Discipline

After eight years of the foregoing, and much, much else, some of which will probably never be known even after cabinet, police and army records are laid bare, the I.R.A. found itself under heavy pressure. British technology, war weariness, attrition North and South of the border and a number of other factors were taking their toll. Losses mounted and Roy Mason was talking about squeezing the I.R.A. like 'toothpaste'.

Talks about the I.R.A. as being 'finished', 'degenerating into Chicago-type gangsters' and so on became common.

However, where the I.R.A. is concerned such talk can be highly misleading.

It was not that much of what the I.R.A. was seen to be doing—kneecapping, bank-robbery, increasing civilian casualties, shootings of off-duty U.D.R. men and so on—did not come well within the 'Chicago' description. What was important was what they were not seen to be doing—planning and reorganisation.

But over and above the reorganisation there are paramount considerations about the current I.R.A. campaign which differentiates it from all earlier Fenian or I.R.A. activity and that is the way in which it departs from the normal pattern of cyclical violence. In this case it is not a matter of generations coming to maturity and striking a blow to maintain the Fenian tradition of a Rising in every generation. This time the pattern is continuous—the I.R.A.'s fresh 'generation' is next year's school leaver, or his younger brother or sister. Consequently when the I.R.A. started to reorganise it had something to reorganise (unlike the fifties' campaign when the tactic of attacking barracks, as in Tom Barry's day, was found to fail in the face of modern communications). This time the issue was not targets or how to attack them. As has been demonstrated, the I.R.A. could choose and hit these all too effectively. The problem was largely structural. The 'Army' was modelled on an outmoded pattern which was proving susceptible to penetration. Belfast, for instance, had a 'Brigade' structure in which Andersonstown, Ballymurphy and most of the Upper Falls Road area were organised into the 'First Battalion'. The Lower Falls and Clonard were the Second Battalion, and northern and eastern Belfast (also with large Protestant populations), the Third Battalion.

One only had to stroll into an I.R.A. haunt like the Prisoners Defence Fund Club in Andersonstown and listen to the audience join in a rousing rebel chorus to the music of the Wolfehounds or some other group, popular in Republican areas, to tell where the spectators came from—they used to raise their arms in the air, swaying in time to the music, holding up on, two or three fingers on each hand to show which battalion they belonged to, supported, or lived under the aegis of. In either case a useful starting point for any police agent present.

It was decided to change the battalion system to a cell structure and to move younger, unknown figures into positions of responsibility leaving well-known, established, older men in a high-profile position as front men. (The social conditions ensue that the supply of young men is never in doubt.)

A blueprint was drawn up incorporating these and other sweeping changes that envisaged transforming the shape of the I.R.A. into a more deadly, more secretive organisation. By a double irony, the blueprint became public—being seized at the time of Twomey's recapture on December 2, 1977. However the reorganisation did become more secretive and more effective.

The document was entitled simply 'Staff Report' and included the following:

The three-day and seven-day detention* orders are breaking volunteers and it is the Republican Army's fault for not indoctrinating volunteers with the psychological strength to resist interrogation.

Coupled with this factor which is contributing to our defeat we are burdened with an inefficient infra-structure of commands brigades, battalions and companies. This old system with which the Brits and Branch are familiar has to be changed. We recommend reorganisation and remotivation, the building of a new Irish Republican Army.

We emphasise a return to secrecy and strict discipline. Army men must be in total control of all sections of the movement.

1) A new rank of Education Officer must be created.

G.H.Q. must have a department of education officers available for lectures and discussions at weapons training camps. Anti-interrogation lectures must be given in conjunction with indoctrination lectures. The ideal outcome should be that no Volunteer should be charged unless caught red-handed.

It should be pointed out to new recruits the failure of our past structures—the number of men who have been arrested and who signed their freedom away. The commonsense methods of personal security should be thrashed out. Any new recruit mixing with known volunteers should be suspended pending discipline.

We must gear ourselves towards Long Term Armed Struggle based on putting unknown men and new recruits into a new structure. This new structure shall be a cell system.

2) Ideally a cell should consist of four people. Rural areas, we decided, should be treated as separate cases to that of city and town Brigade/Command areas.

For this reason our proposals will affect mainly city and town areas, where the majority of our operations are carried out, and where the biggest proportion of our support lies anyway.

CELLS: As we have already said, as from now, all new recruits are to be passed into a cell structure.

Existing Battalion and Company Staffs must be dissolved over a period of months with present Brigades then deciding who passes into the (reorganised) cell structure and who goes into the Brigade controlled and departmentalised Civil Administration (explained later).

The cells of four volunteers will be controlled militarily by the Brigade's/ Command's Operations Officers, and will be advised by Brigade's/Command's Intelligence Officer.

Cells will be financed through their cell leader, who will be funded through the O.C. co-ordinator. That is, for wages, for running costs, financing of operations (expenses, etc., will be dealt with through the O.C.).

Cells must be specialised into I.O. cells, sniping cells, executions, bombings, robberies, etc.

The cell will have no control of weapons or explosives, but should be capable of dumping weapons overnight (in the case of a postponed operation).

---

*   The North's Special Powers Act, like the South's Offences Against the State Act, can be altered as the moment dictates to bring in any security remedies caused for.

The weapons and explosives should be under the complete control of the Brigade's/ Command's Q.C. and E.C. respectively.

Cells should operate as often as possible outside of their own areas; both to confuse Brit Intelligence (which would thus increase our security) and to expand our operational areas.

Disguises should be made use of in all operations. The breaking up of present structure into administration sections and operational cells will make for maximum military effectiveness, greater security, a more efficient back-up structure to increase support and cater for our people's problems

Thus our Operations Officer can go straight into an area and deal exclusively with Military Operations and problems.

All present volunteers under old structure must be re-educated and given up-dated lectures in combating new interrogation techniques.

Women and girls have greater roles to play as military activists and as leaders in sections of civil administration in propaganda and publicity.

Cumann na mBan, we propose, should be dissolved with the best being incorporated in I.R.A. cells structure and the rest going into Civil and Military administration.

Na Fianna Eireann should return to being an underground organisation with little or no public image. They should be educated and organised decisively to pass into I.R.A. cell structure when of age.

I.R.A. Auxiliaries: To be trained for defence, but with an increasing emphasis on a policing role under Brigade civil administration.

Aux. Batt. Structures (in Belfast) should be maintained. The present I.R.A. should use them less and less, with Brig. Q.M.'s having discretion to pick out potential workers. These Aux. structures should be transferred under co-ordination department.

CLUBS: Clubs are bases of support, places of cultural activity and fund-raising venues. Clubs should now be expanded into Community services (e.g. for the youth, mothers, pensioners, etc.).

Sinn Fein: Sinn Fein should come under Army organisers at all levels. Sinn Fein should employ full-time organisers in big Republican areas.

Sinn Fein should be radicalised (under Army direction) and should agitate around social and economic issues which attack the welfare of the people. S.F. should be directed to infiltrate other organisations to win support for, and sympathy to, the Movement. S.F. should be re-educated and have a big role to play in publicity and propaganda departments.

How effective was the 'building of a new Irish Republican Army'? The answer to that question is best explained in a British army document seized in the mails by the Provisionals and reproduced triumphantly (after being vetted for some months by I.R.A. intelligence) in *An Phoblacht* on May 10, 1979, a few months before the Mountbatten killing underlined the accuracy of the army's appraisal.

It said that the Provisionals were acquiring weapons at a faster rate than the army could recover them and it predicted that the Provisionals may acquire more sophisticated Soviet-designed anti-aircraft missiles, the SA7, similar to those used by Nkomo's guerillas to shoot down two Rhodesian Viscounts near Lake Kariba in 1978.

The document said:

The Provisional I.R.A. (P.I.R.A.) has the dedication and the sinews of war to raise violence intermittently to at least the level of early 1978, certainly for the foreseeable future.

Even if 'peace' is restored, the motivation for political inspired violence will remain. Arms will be readily available and there will be many who are able and willing to use them. Any peace will be superficial and brittle. A new campaign may well erupt in the years ahead.

Commenting on the calibre of Provisional I.R.A. volunteers the report said:

LEADERSHIP—P.I.R.A. is essentially a working-class organisation based in the ghetto areas of the cities and in the poorer rural areas. Thus if members of the middle class and graduates become more deeply involved, they have to forfeit their lifestyle . . . Nevertheless, there is a stratum of intelligent, astute and experienced terrorists who provide the backbone of the organisation . . .

TECHNICAL EXPERTISE—P.I.R.A. has an adequate supply of members who are skilled in the production of explosive devices.

RANK AND FILE—Our evidence of the calibre of rank and file terrorists does not support the view that they are mindless hooligans drawn from the unemployed and unemployable.

TREND IN CALIBRE—The mature terrorists, including, for instance, the leading bomb makers, are sufficiently cunning to avoid arrest. They are continually learning from mistakes and developing their expertise.

The report contained the first official admission of the risk faced by Queen Elizabeth during her visit to the North during her Silver Jubilee in August, 1977. At Coleraine University, which was visited by the Queen, an I.R.A. bomb exploded several hours after she left.

The report concluded:

The Provisionals' campaign of violence is likely to continue while the British remain in Northern Ireland. We see little prospect of political development of a kind which would seriously undermine the Provisionals' position. (Nor can anyone else see such a 'political development' on the horizon.)

The murder of Lord Mountbatten on August 27, 1979, in a Sligo bay was the most shocking single political assassination in Irish history, ranking in importance if not exceeding it, with the Burke and Cavendish slayings in the Phoenix Park in Parnell's time, making a high-water mark in ferocity for the Provisionals' campaign and a correspondingly low one in Anglo-Irish relations. The I.R.A.'s hammer blow smashed into the world's consciousness with a force that was underlined when as the wavelets were still lapping up wreckage from the Earl's bombed launch at Mullaghmore in the West of Ireland, eighteen members of the Second Battalion Parachute Regiment including a Lieutenant Colonel were blown up on the north-east coast at Narrow Water Castle near Warrenpoint in County Down.

This last was in fact the better planned of the two, and in numbers alone the more horrific; the families of working-class soldiers also feel grief, after all, and there were more of these affected than in the Mountbatten party. There were two explosions, the first designed not only to kill the soldiers in a vehicle in a passing army convoy but to lure more troops to the scene. The Provisionals reckoned (correctly) that these would be helicopter borne and that they would take refuge in a nearby castle gate. They did and a Provisional Unit which had remained at the scene then detonated a second bomb, inflicting the greater part of the day's casualties.

But neither blow was unprecedented. Soldiers had been bombed before and more significantly. Although no one realised it fully after Mullaghmore, the I.R.A. had declared it was going after 'prestige targets' as early as November, 1974. Daithi O'Connell, when speaking on an I.T.N. programme during an interview with Mary Holland, the English journalist who has most consistently and most informatively reported* on the Irish scene, said unequivocally that not only would

---

★   A small coterie of English journalists have reported on Ireland with accuracy and insight all through the Troubles. John Whale, and the Insight team of the *Sunday Times*, Keith Kyle, the Dimblebys and the *Tonight* programme-makers on B.B.C. being prominent among them.

there be more bombing in England, but that the I.R.A. would strike at targets of an 'economic, judicial, military and political nature'. On November 21 the sound of the Birmingham explosions gave a grisly resonance to his words.

Even before Birmingham the interview created a furore, more because of O'Connell's demeanour, and the mere fact that he was allowed on the air at all, than for what he threatened. But even before the interview the Official I.R.A. had tried to shift their war out of the ranks of the working class and the unemployed and move death up the social scale. Within the Provisionals there had been condemnation of the Officials when they, prior to their ceasefire, began making attacks on targets other than installations or military figures. 'Look at that,' said a Provisional leader to me one day, showing me a clipping from the *Irish News* in which the Officials claimed responsibility for an attack on a director of the no-Catholics-need-apply firm of Mackies, the engineers. 'Just look at that. Sheer class warfare, that's what it is.'

However, prior to Mullaghmore, the Provisionals themselves were already deeply involved in 'class warfare' on 'prestige targets', as they choose to call them. Apart from the businessmen campaign already described and dropped, judges had been shot*—Rory Conaghan, Martin MacBirney and Liam Staunton; there was the murder of the British Ambassador to Dublin, Ewart-Biggs, followed in the year of Mullaghmore by that of Sir Richard Sykes, British Ambassador to the Netherlands, on March 22, 1979, whom the British had placed in charge of the investigation. And of course there had been a spate of upper-class targets in England during the various bombing splurges of the decade. The Adjutant-General of the British Army, General Sir Cecil Blacker, had had a narrow escape as far back as January 4, 1974, when a thirty-pound bomb was found outside his home in London. As that year ended, a bomb was thrown into Edward Heath's Belgravia home causing material damage only. Apart from Ross McWhirter, the Balcombe Street group were wanted for an unintended death in the upper-social register, that of Professor Gordon Hamilton-Fairley whose accidental and very regrettable loss to medicine occurred as he passed a booby-trapped car owned by Hugh Fraser, Conservative M.P. Above all, the Provisionals made a much more deadly and much more serious attempt than was generally realised at the time on the person of Her Majesty, Queen Elizabeth II herself when she visited Northern Ireland.

Nevertheless, despite the foregoing, the death of Lord Mountbatten and three members of his party, the Dowager Baroness of Brabourne, his fourteen-year-old grandson, and another fourteen-year-old, Paul Maxwell, a local lad, who was aboard acting as a pilot but was no relation of the Mountbattens, produced a reaction of shock, anger and incredulity which elevated the Mountbatten episode to a new place in all the outrage that had gone before. Ireland, and in particular Jack Lynch,

---

* Prior to these killings, a study of court cases for the previous two years, published on October 18, 1973, in Belfast by two university lecturers, Tom Hayden and Paddy Hilliard, found that there was marked discrimination against Catholics in the judicial system. However, two of the murdered judges mentioned above, Conaghan and Staunton, were Catholics, and Conaghan, a well-loved figure on all sides of the community, had actually once sent Paisley to prison! MacBirney was well known through his appearance on a BBC Radio Quiz programme.

was placed in the dock of British public opinion, and security emerged as the key issue for the British.

Lynch found himself the target for attack particularly in the *Irish Times*, because he did not immediately cut short his holiday in Portugal on hearing of the Mountbatten murder (a decision which contrasted with Mrs Thatcher's descent on Northern Ireland to comfort the troops after Warrenpoint). The two sets of killings did not produce comparable results, of course. In the case of Mountbatten the public reaction in Ireland, no less than in England, was caused by the felling of a Titan in world affairs and a well-loved gentleman in private life. But in the British army, Warrenpoint set up a crisis of morale in a corps that was already unenthusiastic about service in Northern Ireland, whose recruitment was falling off and whose general commanding officer, General Creasey, and presumably other officers were already highly resentful at not being able to take the gloves off *à la* Oman (where Creasey had served) and where water supplies could be blown up or poisoned, villages destroyed and a welter of parallel activities engaged in without any fear of meddling press publicity.

If Mrs Thatcher had not gone to Northern Ireland there might have been no army to go to a little later. (A 'troops out' march held at the time attracted, instead of the usual few hundred marchers, a following of over 10,000.)

Papers like the *Star* and the *Express* had banner headlines calling the I.R.A. 'bastards', and editorials, particularly in the Beaverbrook group, referring to Ireland in terms in which the description a 'stinking country' passed almost unnoticed. Against this background it was decided to set up a top-level meeting between the Irish and English governments to discuss the situation on the afternoon of the service in Westminster Abbey for Lord Mountbatten.

After a morning feeling the effects of the full weight of British ceremonial at its best and taking part in a sad and moving ceremony (witnessed amongst others by six kings and three queens) necessitated by the activities of Irish assassins, the Irish Prime Minister met the fourth English Prime Minister he had dealt with since the troubles began years earlier.

To say the least of it, it was not the best psychological backdrop for such a meeting, in which the Irish pressed for a political solution and the British stressed only the need for improved security. Moreover in an effort to prove the genuineness of his desire for reconciliation and to promote a political settlement, Lynch had said in a radio broadcast (Radio Eireann, September 2, 1979) prior to the talks that he would seek simply a power-sharing form of devolved government in the North without insisting on an Irish dimension, e.g. a Council of Ireland. Lynch left himself open to the charge of being intimidated and falling far short of the Full National Demand. However, insofar as the I.R.A. were concerned this would have been an irrelevancy anyhow, as five years after Sunningdale something considerably less than that package could only be expected to be ignored by them. Where the general Irish public was concerned, anything that was not too obviously a climb-down in the face of British pressure would have been acceptable after years of the Northern horror—at least temporarily after Mullaghmore. But four days after the Thatcher meeting, the first of a promised series of talks, the explosive nature of the Republican issue for Fianna Fail was dramatically illustrated yet again by the speech delivered by Sile de Valera at the annual commemoration of Liam Lynch. By holding the party meeting which the speech necessitated on the eve of the Pope's visit to Ireland (September 28) Lynch effectively dodged press scrutiny of the meeting which in the end supported him. However, coupled with the bad showing of the party in the Euro elections of June, 1979, Lynch was irretrievably on a slide; and the Northern issue, combined with rising inflation, resulted in his losing the two by-elections in his own native county of Cork in November, 1979. The particular *causus belli* was an agreement which is still not fully understood by the public at large, or anybody else in the Republic for that matter, whereby apparently an 'air corridor' was created along the border so that Irish and British helicopters could fly into each other's territories for a distance of some kilometres.

Lynch apparently agreed to something of this nature at a meeting with Mrs Thatcher and her cabinet after the Mountbatten funeral. Militarily speaking the arrangement was totally ineffective as a means of suppressing the I.R.A. but evidently it was a project dear to the heart of the British military authorities who favoured 'hot pursuit of the I.R.A.' across the border.

The notion of British troops or aircraft infringing Irish sovereignty awoke every sleeping fibre of Nationalism there was in the Fianna Fail party—as well as widespread fears that Irish helicopters might be shot down by the I.R.A. in mistake for British ones; and after some pretty severe internal in-fighting within Fianna Fail, Lynch resigned on December 11, 1979, and was succeeded by Charles Haughey after some even more intense in-fighting with Deputy Prime Minister George Colley. Haughey elevated the Northern issue, at least in terms of verbal republicanism, in Fianna Fail's priorities at the annual party conference on February 15, 1980. He said Northern Ireland was *the* political challenge facing the government and said flatly that the Northern state had failed.

The S.D.L.P. also acquired a change of leader when Gerry Fitt found himself in a minority of one within the party because of his enthusiastic endorsement of Britain's proposals for a constitutional conference which the incoming Thatcher administration offered as a means of solving the imbroglio—specifically excluding the Irish dimension contained in the Sunningdale pact. John Hume succeeded him.

Where the I.R.A. itself was concerned, *An Phoblacht* in the issue after Mullaghmore/Warrenpoint (September 1) served to reveal how far the I.R.A. had come in targets, language and sentiment from the time Billy McKee got himself shot to pieces in a gun-fight that killed four Protestants defending St Matthew's Church. Above a photograph of Mountbatten with 'Executed' emblazoned across it, a sneering half-page article signed by 'the Brigadier' described how the Queen took the news without a blink, merely informing the butler that 'there would be one fewer for dinner' but 'groaned in anguish' when 'the Brigadier' accidentally smashed the Meissen tea set. 'Personally,' said the Brigadier, 'I never had much time for the old fool, but *noblesse oblige* and *de mortuis nihil nisi* slobber . . .' *An Phoblacht* also marked the occasion by printing a cartoon, headed, in a play on the pop song title, 'I hate Mondays'.

The official *An Phoblacht* statement was headed 'Execution of Soldier Mountbatten' and it went on:

In claiming responsibility for the execution of Lord Mountbatten (former Chief of the United Kingdom Defence Staff, cousin of the Queen of England and symbol of all that is imperial Britain) the Irish Republican Army stated that the bombing was a 'discriminate operation to bring to the attention of the English people the continuing occupation of our country',

The statement went on:

The British army acknowledge that after ten years of war it cannot defeat us but yet the British government continue with the oppression of our people and the torture of our comrades in the H-Blocks. Well, for this we will tear out their sentimental imperialist heart. The death of Mountbatten and the tributes paid to him will be seen in sharp contrast to the apathy of the British government and the English people to the deaths of over three hundred British soldiers, and the deaths of Irish men, women and children at the hands of their forces.

On the same day in the *Irish Times*, talking with Niall Kiely, a Provisional spokesman gave one of the most chilling—and important—interviews of the entire decade. To underline its importance *An Phoblacht* reprinted it in its next issue.

In one sentence it laid down I.R.A. policy for the future:

We will do exactly the same thing again—against prestige targets.

That was the language of the brutal and the brutalised. It was the authentic note of Belfast 1979—ten years on from the Falls Road burnings and the Downing Street Declaration and still nowhere near a solution.

Part III

1979–1986

27

The Ignition of the Crisis

'Pat' was an important figure in the I.R.A.'s Command structure. Middle thirties, five foot nine, black haired, moustached, an unremarkable, windcheatered figure, he might just as easily be blond and wearing pin-stripes when, and if, I see him again. We met in Belfast and 'Pat' devoted an afternoon to the interview. He was friendly, knowlegeable, and completely frank in his replies to my questions; he answered precisely what was asked, volunteering nothing. A shortened version of the upshot is reproduced here in his own words; it gives some impression of the effect of the war on the thinking of the I.R.A. of the mid-1980s and the changes that had taken place over the past decade.

In the early seventies the I.R.A. was hugely popular. We had big companies. Everyone was volunteering. Lads would be well known in this area. They'd be known to the Brits too. So they began to be picked up. There was internment, Sunningdale, all that, and a bit of war weariness set in. Young people began dropping off. So the numbers in units got smaller. Remember there was the truce with the Brits. After the Miami the numbers went up. But in the Truce the Brits got wind of us. Touts, then Mason and the stuff about 'squeezing the I.R.A. like toothpaste'—numbers started going down again.

We had the Brigade Structure, at least formally and they were on to us. The Peace People. Everything was coming down on us. Seventy-six was a very significant year. We began going over to the Cells generally, with A.S.U.s [Active Service Units] operating independently. We had to contend with the war weariness. We had the problem of people looking for protection. We were trying to organise local policing. Paisley's strike was terrifying our people. There was talk of Civil War. Numbers were definitely down. I think an average volunteer only lasted about three months then. Anti-interrogation became the big thing. We started going over to the *Green Book* philosophy. Mason was one of the best things to happen to us.

Also La Mon made us realise the need to politicise the struggle. Implementation of the Cell structure really took over and by 1979 I'd say we were on the way to defeating Castlereagh and the Conveyor-Belt System. Everyone knew what happened if you got caught. We started operating only on the 'need to know'.

The prisoners understood what the Brits were about. Volunteers were politicised: the *Green Book* philosophy took over. There was analysis of history. Lectures on how to deal with isolation. The rhetoric definitely changed from 1916 and Pearse, Connolly and so on. We began looking at other struggles. Vietnam especially. The hunger strike cemented the position about education. Don't mind that talk about Libya. The Libyans were trained in conventional warfare. They couldn't teach us anything. There's no international conspiracy. The I.R.A. makes its own news. We have waiting lists waiting to join up.

There's always a debate of course about soldiers against politicians. But the war's about people, not kills. Destroying the economic infrastructure* wouldn't help the people. A

---

* Pubs were favourite targets for I.R.A. bombings in the early '70s, as well as factories and shops. However local opposition and changes in compensation awards systems altered this.

THE I.R.A.

thing like the Agate thing was different. Mason was in the States trying to encourage American investment. In theory American businessmen support the MacBride principles*, in practice no.

G.H.Q. men went through the Brigade areas talking to the A.S.U.s explaining electoral strategy, explaining how military decisions could affect people's attitudes. A lot of the Army were apathetic to Sinn Fein. They weren't interested in politics. We had to argue Standing Order No. 8 through with them. They see the Gardai as Brits in different uniforms. But Standing Order No. 8 is a realistic policy even though the Gardai and the R.U.C. are collaborating. They talk to each other across the Border on radio. The Free State's Security policy, in essence, is a pro-Brit policy. The danger is the Brits will manage to get some permanent foothold on the island through the Free State Security co-operation. They've got a strategic N.A.T.O. interest. They don't want the Republic neutral.

If Section 31† were removed it would help Sinn Fein but it wouldn't affect the I.R.A. The arms seized on the *Marita Ann* are standard issue to the I.R.A. We already had that type of armament. We'd have preferred of course that the particular shipment got through but you can draw your own conclusions about the weapons position from the fact that the *Marita Ann* stuff was already standard issue, before the capture.

Getting arms, or explosives or planning anything is the same for us as for anyone, the B.A. or the R.U.C., except we don't have recourse to back-room 'boffins' with resources, science and so on to bear down on any problem. Our back rooms can be raided or under surveillance at any time, but still we do analyse any situation we come to, though it takes us longer than our enemies. The analysis and adaption goes on all the time. Sometimes people think the I.R.A. is on the run. The truth is the I.R.A. is *always* on the run, and always learning‡, reading about other struggles, the history of colonialism; it videos films like *The End of Empire* or Julian Pettifer on Vietnam. Analysing things that happen to us like the supergrass thing. We realise the need for volunteers to have a stable, committed background. We try to pick people who'll last the distance, we recruit the over-twenties for preference—an eighteen-year-old might be inclined to marry and give up, maybe joining up out of a sense of identity and local status, but he mightn't have the commitment. We do have some Protestants in the I.R.A., mostly in rural areas, but they're mostly Catholic. We have some university types—mostly in Sinn Fein. Yes, of course a volunteer can leave when he wants to. He's expected not to talk, of course.

Our aim is to create such psychological damage to the Brits that they'll withdraw. Sick of the expense, the hassle, the coffins coming back to England. But we know we can't defeat them in a military sense, no more than they can beat us. So there's a kind of stalemate. But we always retain the ability to bring the situation to a crisis. Bomb a county target to switch the troops from the cities. Then hit city targets. Or do a Brighton, a Mountbatten. We analyse each result and act accordingly. If it doesn't work *then* we'll worry, but remember, we live here; Maggie Thatcher doesn't. Yes, we have plans for a Doomsday situation.

We're organised into cells, as you know, five to ten people, independent of the organisation except for the O.C. who knows the Brigade Adjutant. He (and his own men of course) gets his orders from him. The Cell has its own pool of weapons, and explosives, intelligence. It arranges houses and transport outside the organisation. There are five to six Cells active in greater Belfast. Single men get £10 a week. Married men £20. You're so busy you

---

* Named after Sean MacBride, the Nobel and Lenin Peace Prize winner, these are analogous to the Sullivan Principles, and relate to the participation of American companies in South Africa under apartheid. They attempt to lay down ground rules for fair employment, between not black and white but Protestant and Catholic.

† Section 31 of the Broadcasting Act prevents Sinn Fein spokesmen being interviewed on R.T.E.

‡ The 'Republican University' Jail, North and South of the Border produces its quota of university graduates and third level qualifications. One can see the lights blazing in the cells of Portlaoighise in the small hours of any morning as the prisoners avidly make use of study opportunity.

don't need money. But there's the dole and people help out, food and so on. You learn to live with the risk, the threat of prison—I've been in prison myself. Yes, I've taken life, or at least I must have done judging by the casualties after operations I've been in. But I was never conscious of hitting anyone at the time. You're so keyed up during the operation. You lead two lives. One for the family. You're always at risk. There's a Shoot to Kill policy in Armagh just now. But that's nothing new. Remember Ronnie Bunting, Miriam Daly, Bernadette, a lot of innocent people get . . . caught up. No I'm not talking about the likes of the Stronges. If you encourage sectarianism, you pay for it. Look at the people in for the Birmingham and Guildford bombings. They're completely innocent.

There's a lot of talk about Marxism and left-right splits about, but that's nonsense. Everyone knows they have to hang together. You get political discussion in any organisation. The main thought is to get the Brits out. Everyone can follow his own political theory then. Danger makes for pragmatism not grand theory. The I.R.A. is not riddled with racketeers and Godfathers. There's strict control of weapons.★

If some 'loose horse' I.R.A. men did decide to go in for bank robberies, with their training they'd be inclined to go for a million. No, most of the crime in Belfast is either I.N.L.A. or 'sticky' off-shoots, hoods, or petty criminals.

We're stripped down for a long war.

The awful authenticity of the Provisional I.R.A. was tested and proven in the crucible of the H Blocks of Long Kesh in 1980 and 1981. In those years the I.R.A.'s capacity for endurance—the obverse side of the coin of infliction—was brought under the microscope of the international media and was seen to triumph in death in a manner which captured the attention of the world. The 'armed struggle' was elevated from being almost exclusively a matter of guerrilla warfare to a political plane on which Sinn Fein succeeded in winning nearly half the votes of the Nationalist population of the Six Counties and gained a degree of purchase in the affections of sympathisers throughout the island which it still retains. For the contemporary Provisional I.R.A., where Northern Ireland is concerned, the outcome of the hunger strike led by Bobby Sands was the equivalent of the 1916 Rebellion aftermath to the Nationalists of that era.

Like bankruptcy the crisis came in two ways, gradually and suddenly. The public at large were unaware of what was building up in the H Blocks; to them the I.R.A. meant deeds like La Mon and the Mountbatten killing. These were what got the headlines. But the situation inside the H Blocks increasingly became the I.R.A.'s own focal point.

These H Blocks are named from their construction: cells down each arm are linked in the middle by the administration offices, like an H. They were built on the site of the Second World War airstrip of Long Kesh, ten miles west of Belfast, as the result of a conscious political decision to criminalise the I.R.A. Since internment in August, 1971, I.R.A. prisoners (and subsequently Loyalist ones also, though separately) had been housed in wire compounds in a corner of the site. Here, they behaved like prisoners of war, responsible only to their officers, acting in a military manner, but—central to what happened subsequently—wearing their own clothes. They also received a plentiful supply of parcels, news and mail from outside. As we have

---

★ How strict I can vouch for. One day a friend brought a pleasant young fellow into my office for me to autograph a copy of the book. Well dressed, good looking, he seemed like an accountant or a lawyer. I asked after him a year later and found that he had been an active service volunteer. He had sold some guns from a dump—and was executed.

seen, their virtual prisoner of war status, certainly a *de facto* version of it known as 'Special Category Status', came about as a result of an effort made by the British to neutralise the I.R.A. after the fall of Stormont in 1972, when a top level conference took place in London between Cabinet Ministers and an I.R.A. delegation. From the I.R.A. side the price of this conference was the calling off of Billy McKee's hunger strike in Crumlin Road jail in return for conceding in substance to his demands for political status.

For roughly four years the I.R.A. prisoners enjoyed Special Category Status, but increasingly Unionist and Tory anger became focused on the 'Sandhurst of terror', on which was conferred a near Libyan bogeyman status. Concurrent with this burgeoning distaste, the British themselves were evolving a new counter-insurgency strategy. Like the Americans in Vietnam they decided to 'Vietnamese' the conflict, that is, let the natives do the fighting, chiefly the R.U.C. and the U.D.R. This policy became known as 'Ulsterisation'. A second wing of the strategy, 'Normalisation', meant what it said: an attempt to restore the Province to an appearance of normality so as to counteract the I.R.A.'s economic campaign and its efforts at sabotaging normal political and economic activity. 'Criminalisation' aimed at taking away whatever dignity the Special Category Status conferred and making the I.R.A. not an organisation with a political ambition and its roots in history, but a mafia-like conspiracy differing only in its methods from what the North of Ireland Secretary of the time, the hapless Merlyn Rees, termed 'ODCs'—Ordinary Decent Criminals.

The crucial step towards the ignition of the H Blocks crisis was taken on January 30, 1975, with the publication of a report from Lord Gardiner, a former Lord Chancellor, who had been asked by the Government post-Sunningdale to consider 'in the context of Civil Liberties and Human Rights, measures to deal with terrorism in Northern Ireland'. Lord Gardiner reported as follows:

The introduction of Special Category Status was a serious mistake . . . It should be made absolutely clear that Special Category prisoners can expect no amnesty and will have to serve their sentences . . . We recommend that the earliest practicable opportunity should be taken to end the Special Category.

This did not altogether escape the attention of the I.R.A. negotiators, who told the British that any tampering with Special Category would mean a drastic I.R.A. response, including the shooting of warders—a threat which was duly carried out. However, at the time of its publication, debate centered on another recommendation in the report.

In the best British tradition of calling a spade an agricultural implement—which caused Long Kesh to be rechristened 'The Maze'—the unpopular term of 'internment' disappeared but 'detention' remained. In effect this was internment by another name; once picked up or 'detained', prisoners were remanded in custody almost indefinitely—thus adding to, rather than lessening the problem, as by the time Lord Gardiner made his report, prison numbers had risen from a total of 727 in the early days of the Civil Rights Movement to 2,848. As almost 1,200 of these were Special Category prisoners Britain had an embarrassing number of political prisoners on her hands to account for internationally. Lord Gardiner decided to get rid of them and their type of accommodation at one fell swoop, recommending the building of the H Blocks:

71% of male prisoners, 1,881 out of a total of 2,648, are now in temporary prisons of the compound type rather than in conventional cellular accommodation.

Prisons of the compound type, each compound holding up to 90 prisoners, are thoroughly unsatisfactory from every point of view; their major disadvantage is that there is virtually a total loss of disciplinary control by the prison authorities inside the compounds. The layout and construction of the compounds make close and continued supervision impossible.

From the British point of view the phrase 'thoroughly unsatisfactory' accurately sums up what happened following the adoption of Lord Gardiner's report. Prison totals continued to rise, to over 3,500, largely because of an essential component of the 'Conveyor-Belt System': the extra-judicial 'Diplock' courts. These were set up as a result of Lord Diplock's Commission, which reported to Parliament on:

What arrangements for the administration of justice in Northern Ireland could be made in order to deal more effectively with terrorist organisations by bringing to book, otherwise than by internment by the Executive, individuals involved in terrorist activities, particularly those who plan and direct, but do not necessarily take part in, terrorist acts, and to make recommendations.

Lord Diplock's recommendations, which Parliament accepted immediately, (December 20, 1972), were far-reaching indeed. After analysing the problem he said:

We are thus driven inescapably to the conclusion that until the current terrorism by the extremist organisations of both factions in Northen Ireland can be eradicated, there will continue to be some dangerous terrorists against whom it will not be possible to obtain convictions by any form of criminal trial which we regard as appropriate to a court of law; and these will include many of those who plan and organise terrorist acts by other members of the organisation in which they take no first-hand part themselves.

We are also driven inescapably to the conclusion that so long as these remain at liberty to operate in Northern Ireland, it will not be possible to find witnesses prepared to testify against them in the criminal courts, except those serving in the Army or the police . . . The only hope of restoring the efficiency of criminal courts of law in Northern Ireland to deal with terrorist crimes is by using an extra-judicial process to deprive of their ability to operate in Northern Ireland those terrorists whose activities result in the intimidation of witnesses. With an easily penetrable border to the South and West the only way of doing this is to put them in detention by an executive act and to keep them confined, until they can be released without danger to the public safety and to the administration of criminal justice.

Deprivation of liberty as a result of an extra-judicial process we call 'detention', following the nomenclature of The Detention of Terrorists (Northern Ireland Order, 1972). It does not mean imprisonment at the arbitrary diktat of the Executive Government, which to many people is a common connotation of the term 'internment'. We use it to describe depriving a man of his liberty as a result of an investigation of the facts which inculpate the detainee by an impartial person or tribunal by making use of a procedure which, however for to him, is inappropriate to a court of law because it does not comply with Article 6 of the European Convention.

For so long as 'the troubles' lasted, Lord Diplock prescribed that certain types of offences, murder, possession of arms or explosives, grievous bodily harm—in short the type of offence commonly associated with terrorism— should now be termed 'scheduled offences' and dealt with as follows:

1. Trials of scheduled offences should be by a Judge of the High Court, or a County Court Judge, sitting alone with no jury, with the usual rights of appeal.
2. The armed services should be given power to arrest people suspected of having been involved in, or having information about, offences and detain them for up to four hours in order to establish their identity.
3. Bail in cases involving a scheduled offence should not be granted except by the High Court and then only if stringent requirements are met.

4. The onus of proof as to the possession of firearms and explosives should be altered so as to require a person found in certain circumstances to prove on the balance of probabilities that he did not know and had no reason to suspect that arms or explosives were where they were found.

5. A confession made by the accused should be admissible as evidence in cases involving the scheduled offences unless it was obtained by torture or inhuman or degrading treatment.

6. A signed written statement made to anyone charged with investigating a scheduled offence should be admissible if the person who made it cannot be produced in court for specific reasons, and the statement contains material which would have been admissible if that person had been present in court to give oral evidence.

The paragraph concerning confessions was destined to create lasting bitterness throughout Northern Ireland. In effect it contains the third element of the 'Conveyor-Belt System', for despite Lord Diplock's stipulation as to the use of torture, it became an accepted fact of life that the way to get confessions out of suspects was to brutalise them.

In November, 1977, thirty solicitors who did most of the work in the 'Diplock' courts wrote to the Secretary of State for Northern Ireland, Roy Mason, stating:

Ill treatment of suspects by police officers, with the object of obtaining confessions, is now common practice, and . . . most often, but not always takes place at Castlereagh R.U.C. station and other police stations, throughout Northern Ireland.

As I have indicated earlier (see Chapter 24) this complaint was only the tip of the iceberg. Throughout the 1970s there was a whole series of official investigations arising out of the methods used to obtain confessions These generally concurred in substance if not in form with the findings of Lord Parker of Waddington's Report (adopted January 31, 1982), which found that the methods then in use were illegal under U.K. law, though not 'immoral' given the circumstances of the time. Interestingly enough in view of his H Block report, a minority report from Lord Gardiner held that even where terrorists were concerned such methods were immoral.

Britain would probably not have been prepared to go even as far as commissioning Lord Parker's Report had not another brutality investigation a few months earlier aroused such derision when it appeared in November, 1977, that the Government felt it had to be seen to give the issue serious attention.

Lord Compton had been charged with finding out the truth behind the widespread belief that the treatment of suspects during the internment swoops of August, 1981, had been very brutal. He investigated the techniques used and reported that 'our investigations have not led us to conclude that any of the grouped or individual complainants suffered physical brutality as we understand the term'.

As the reader has in earlier chapters studied these techniques, I will leave the matter there, with the obvious comment that prisoners treated by the above listed 'Special' methods of interrogation, courts, and imprisonment felt with a burning conviction that they belonged to a 'Special Category' in both name and deed, as did their families and friends when the time came to support them in public protest.

28

Five Demands and Hunger Strikes

Knowing that the I.R.A. would resist the abolition of Special Category Status, the British attempted to negotiate away the prisoners' opposition, dealing through their leader of the period, David Morley. They offered special treatment and concessions, the most notable of which was a sort of Head Office of terrorism which the authorities intended to provide in downtown Belfast, in Rosemary Street. There, not only the I.R.A., but also the U.V.F., U.D.A. and sectarian killers of all persuasions were apparently supposed to meet in paramilitary ecumenical bliss under the one roof so that the British could safely keep tabs on them all. However, as the prisoners in the Long Kesh compound saw before their eyes the H Blocks growing daily, other offers, such as increased recreational and educational facilities, fell on increasingly hostile and deaf ears.

Realising this, the British took quite extraordinary steps during the negotiating period, allowing Morley to go not only out of jail to negotiate with Northern I.R.A. leaders, but down to the Republic, which was outside the State's jurisdiction. Ostensibly this was to confer with I.R.A. leaders there, though in reality, as Morley himself told me, for no other purpose than to see how far the I.R.A. could stretch British credulity. Morley even sought for and obtained the right to carry a gun on these jaunts. The only stipulation was that, having signed for it, he had to give it back to the authorities on his return.

Something of a division in medium-term objectives developed at this time between the I.R.A. members inside and those outside the jails.

Outside, they were preoccupied with such phenomena as the adverse effect of the Peace People Campaign and the fallout from catastrophes like the La Mon bombing. Action took the form of intensive debate on how the structure of the I.R.A. might be reorganised (the outcome of which chapter and verse will be detailed later) and, most importantly, how to resist the new British counter-insurgency techniques of the 'Conveyor-Belt System', which were not only adversely affecting the campaign, but also swelling the prison totals quite dramatically. The Army Council was also preoccupied with drawing up a philosophy for dealing with interrogation and for articulating Republicanism in the contemporary era. These various strands were drawn together to become one of the I.R.A.'s most secret and highly prized documents, the *Green Book*. Like Colonel Gadhafi's *Green Book*, it sets down all one needs to know about the philosophy of the Revolution, its history, and the means whereby the struggle is to be prosecuted, and after much internal debate, it came to be the I.R.A.'s bible.

As I have explained elsewhere, I.R.A. prisoners lose their rank, revert to the position of volunteer, and endeavour to carry on the war from within, practically speaking responding to the command structure in the prison rather than to that outside. As they had traditionally done, prisoners now defied the British efforts at criminalisation. The first man to lose Special Category status, Ciaran Nugent, refused to wear prison clothes, saying after his sentence in 1976, 'They'll have to nail them to my back.' He served out three and a half years with nothing but a blanket to wrap around himself in a cell from which all furniture had been removed as a punishment for his refusal to wear the official garb. He was denied outdoor exercise, visits, parcels and educational facilities.

Nugent's example was followed by hundreds of others as the 'Conveyor-Belt System' went into overdrive. The Republic at large was unaware of what was happening, although Castlereagh, the barracks in which many of the interrogations were conducted, became notorious, partly because of the effect of its name alone. The original Lord Castlereagh, prime architect of the Union of 1800 which the I.R.A. of the 1970s were trying to break, is best known to most Irish people today from Don Byrne's couplet:

> *I met murder on the way*
> *and he had a face like Castlereagh.*

But inside the jails the pressure cooker boiled up dangerously. The situation became both more horrific and more farcical. Certain Loyalist warders had developed the practice of kicking over the prisoners' slop bowls in the mornings so that the contents spilled over the cell. This resulted in the prisoners refusing to 'slop out' and spreading excrement on the wall instead. (An earlier attempt to throw it out of the windows was foiled by warders who threw it back in again.) The 'battle of the bowels' resulted in the prison cells, the most modern in Europe, becoming filthy, maggot-infested caves, in which young men stood naked save for their hate and a prison blanket. This phrase 'on the blanket' was to acquire a new dimension in Irish prison history, though initially not one welcomed by the I.R.A. outside.

The H Block prisoners were also engaged in debate. They were going back into history, to the memory of Terence McSwiney, the events of the 1940s, and the example of I.R.A. prisoners from time immemorial who, when all else was taken from them, fought the battle with the only weapon left, their wills, crystallising into a stark and skeletal resolution: to fast to the death. Preoccupied with its own external reorganisation, and mindful of the potential disaster should a strike break out and be defeated—'break the lads in jail and you break the movement' is a fundamental I.R.A. tenet—the I.R.A. failed until 1980 to realise the potential which the H Block issue held, and sought instead to avert a strike.

By an accident of fate, in January, 1980 I came to be involved in these events, and I am convinced that the principal I.R.A. thrust of the period was aimed at keeping the hunger strike at bay, not encouraging it. Prison chaplains, prisoners' families and others with whom I was friendly at this period, all feared that the situation would escalate out of control and that the prisoners would put into operation their declared intention of having a hunger strike, with or without I.R.A. sanction and with potentially devastating effects on themselves, their families and the community as a whole. In an effort to head off the potentially explosive situation, I highlighted the problem of the dirty protest in my book *On the Blanket.*★ As a result of my research, I was quite clear at the time that a magnanimous gesture on the part of the British Government, coming down, as such things often do, to simple pieces of symbolism—such as in this case the right of prisoners to wear their own clothes—could have brought about a complete change in the position. It was not to be. Ironically, my book appeared on the very same day that the European court passed an adverse judgement on a case brought by a Belfast solicitor on behalf of a number of prisoners in Northern Ireland seeking to have themselves declared 'political'.

Their 'five demands' were:

1. The right to wear their own clothes.
2. The right not to do prison work.
3. Free association with fellow prisoners.
4. Full 50% remission of their sentences.
5. Normal visits, parcels, education and recreational facilities.

The situation worsened and eventually the prisoners, under the leadership of Brendan Hughes, decided that unless the 'five demands' were met, they would go on hunger strike.

These demands were not conceded despite warnings as to the possible consequences of a hunger strike and high level negotiations with the British, involving figures such as Cardinal O'Fiaich and Charles Haughey. A hunger strike duly broke out on October 27 and lasted until December 18 when an eleventh hour settlement, reached after frenzied negotiations between Dublin, London, Belfast and various meditators, including myself, seemingly produced a formula which got everyone off the hook, while allowing prisoners the crucial right to wear their own clothes. It turned out to be a false dawn and both the strike and its aftermath produced a lasting bitterness which was ultimately to lead to another, fatal hunger strike. To understand how this came about it is necessary to examine the situation which developed both before and during the first strike (December, 1980).

As the pressure on the prisoners built up (prior to the commencement of the October, 1980, strike) they, in turn, began to look for ways to put pressure on the authorities to alleviate the situation. Off-duty warders were shot. Prisoners' relatives formed H Block defence committees, and the spectacle of women in blankets walking barefoot on Belfast (and eventually on Dublin) streets began to be seen. Influential people in the Nationalist community began to be perturbed about what was happening. In February, 1980, Cardinal O'Fiaich held a series of meetings with Humphrey Atkins, the Northern Ireland Secretary of State, and he and Bishop Edward Daly of Derry urged Atkins to find a formula which would get both parties off the hook before a full-blown hunger strike broke out. They pinned their hopes on the definition of prison work being broadened and permission being granted to allow the prisoners to wear their own clothes.

The relationship between prisoners and warders is an abrasive affair at any time. But in the summer and autumn of 1980, after years of defiance on the part of the prisoners, retaliation by the mostly Loyalist warders, and the I.R.A. campaign of

---

★   Ward River Press, Dublin, June 1980.

shooting them when they were off-duty, relationships in the prison were at such an appalling level that informed people began to worry that something unique and dangerous was brewing in Northern Ireland. Messages to this effect went to the British Government from a variety of sources including the Government in Dublin, to no avail, but as the storm clouds built up to the point where a hunger strike appeared inevitable, a breakthrough apparently occurred on October 23. The Northern Ireland Office announced that instead of prison uniform the men would be permitted to wear civilian clothes. This gave rise to great hopes, which were dashed and turned to even greater anger when it was discovered that what the Northern Ireland Office meant was 'prison issue civilian clothes'. The difference between these and the prisoners' 'own clothes', the first of the 'five demands', may not appear much at first sight but in the cauldron of Long Kesh symbolism was all. The prisoners were determined that having, as they saw it, come from an unjust society, through an unjust legal system, fighting for a just cause, they were not going to admit that they were wrong, or that their enemies were right, by allowing themselves to be 'criminalised' in any particular. A hunger strike duly broke out four days later on October 27. It was led by Brendan Hughes and his six companions were Tom McFeeley (with Hughes Joint O.C. of the Provisional prisoners), Sean McKenna, Leo Greene, Tommy McKearney and Raymond McCartney. John Nixon, O.C. of the I.N.L.A. prisoners, a much smaller group than the Provisionals, was accepted as a member of the hunger striking party.

As the hunger strike wore on the seven men in Long Kesh were joined by three women in Armagh jail, Mairead Farrell, O.C. of the Armagh Provisional prisoners, Mairead Nugent and Mary Doyle. Like the men in Long Kesh they had been on a dirty protest from February 7 of that year. This protest began when male warders attempted to seize the berets and black skirts from which the women had fashioned a type of uniform. During the raids for this clothing, several women were injured, and as a protest, having been locked in their cells and refused the use of toilet facilities, used the same method as the men to make their objections known.

I visited Long Kesh and Armagh during the strike and found the Armagh conditions the worst, a combination of the prison building itself being older and the fact that in addition to faeces, the women's menstrual blood was smeared on the walls of the cells, which I found particularly nauseating. The women had neither washed, brushed their teeth nor received a change of clothes or underwear for ninety days. Prior to the strike, prisoners had only been allowed one hour's outdoor exercise per day; those on dirty protest now lost this hour as punishment.

Understandably, responsible people in many walks of life throughout the country were deeply perturbed by the possible consequences of all this. As the publicity generated by the strike built up, it appeared that the British were prepared to go along the same face-saving lines as had the Republic in order to defuse the Portlaoise situation, and come to some agreement over the 'Five Demands' which would concede substance without name. There was continual communication between Charles Haughey's office and Downing Street throughout the period and, amongst others, Cardinal O'Fiaich maintained his efforts. All this seemed to bear fruit when on December 10, 1980, an official of the North of Ireland Office spoke to the hunger strikers. After this visit a very lengthy document, some thirty-four pages, and a statement which Humphrey Atkins was about to make in the House of Commons, were given to the prisoners.

The part which influenced the I.R.A. read:

> I want to spell out for you and your families what will happen when the protest ends. First of all, any such prisoner will be put into a clean cell as, I hope, all prisoners end their protest. We shall have the task of cleaning out all the cells right away and this should take a week or 10 days.
>
> Within a few days clothing provided by the families will be given to any prisoners giving up their protest so that they can wear it during recreation, association and visits . . .

It was hoped that a formula based on the fact that the prisoners would get 'clothes provided by their families' would do the trick. The prison issue civilian clothing would be distributed, or so the prisoners believed, after their families' garments arrived, and the prisoners for their part would come off the dirty protest and consequently off the 'blanket' as well. This was the message with which Bobby Sands, who had succeeded Hughes as the prisoners' O.C., accompanied by two prison chaplains (Fathers John Murphy and Tom Toner), went through the wings of the prison on December 18. The hunger strike was ended.

There was one very important element in Sands's acceptance of the settlement terms: the condition of one of the hunger strikers, Sean McKenna. He was a particularly tragic product of the troubles. His father was one of those who, after the 1971 internment swoops, received the type of treatment which led to the Dublin Government bringing Britain before the European Commission of Human Rights. The treatment meted out to McKenna senior was some of the worst to have been suffered by anyone and when he died in 1975, at the age of forty-two, it was generally accepted by his friends, family and neighbours that it was the 'inhuman and degrading treatment' that had brought him to an early grave.

Young McKenna was an embittered I.R.A. activist during 1976 and living in the Republic at Edentubber (near where the four I.R.A. men were blown up in the 1956–62 campaign) when he was kidnapped, it is believed by the S.A.S., and taken across the Border to Bessborough Barracks, Co. Armagh. There he underwent the customary brutalising treatment before being placed on the 'Conveyor Belt' that eventually landed him in Long Kesh. By the forty-eighth day of the strike he had gone blind and his mental condition was giving rise to concern amongst his comrades. He had begun the strike with an indifference to the prospect of death, described to me by a priest who visited him as 'tantamount to a death-wish'; and then, as the strike progressed, he apparently moved in the other direction, recalling his father and expressing a wish not to die—though not seeking to come off the strike.

I was close to people in Dublin taking part in negotiations with the British at the time, and thus in a position to know that one of the arguments used against Dublin's wish that concessions be made was the fact that the British felt that the strike was going to end shortly in collapse anyhow because of McKenna's failing health. Apparently, also, Sands and his friends decided not to tease out the documents or to have more extensive discussions with the prisoners before calling off the strike because they feared that by the time this process was completed, McKenna would be dead. Accordingly, when over Christmas and in early January it became apparent that the Atkins proposal contained a chicken and egg element, Sands felt particularly embittered and betrayed.

As rumblings that all was not well reached me in Dublin from sources as different as Father Brendan Meagher, who had been in the jail bringing messages from Dublin, and from Father Faul, who was the most active of the prison chaplains and at that time the one most respected by the prisoners, I made some inquiries myself. During these I remember Padraic O'Hannrachain, Charles Haughey's political assistant, saying worriedly: 'Maybe it's just a case that all these fellows in Whitehall have gone home for the Christmas and they're watching television and everything will be all right when the holidays end . . .'

Things were far from all right after Christmas. What none of us had realised at the time was, as Mr Michael Alison, the Minister in charge of prisons, was to put it later: 'There was a lady in the case.' Mrs Thatcher remembered Airey Neave. 'Crime was crime', as she was to repeat subsequently, and the combination of her inflexible nature and the Loyalist prison administration's reluctance to concede anything to Republicans completed the lighting of the powder fuse.

As early as January 2, the I.R.A. obviously realised that there was trouble ahead and released the following statement (from the Republican Press Centre in Belfast): The statement deserves to be read in full as its significance was not at the time appreciated, nor was it as widely publicised as hindsight suggests it might have been:

Belfast Republican Press Centre Tel. 46841
2nd January, 1981

We have been asked to issue the following supplied statement to our office from the PRO of the protesting prisoners in H Blocks 3,4,5, and 6, Long Kesh:

On Thursday, 18th. December 1980, the British Government presented the Republican hunger-strikers and our O/C with documents which contained in our estimate 'the requirements of our five demands'.

In response to this development, and against a background of apparent flexibility and co-operation within the prison, the blanket men, were hopeful that the ending of the blanket and no wash protest would follow quickly.

This depended obviously upon 'a responsible and sensible attitude from the British Government in implementing their proposals'. Given the above we declared that we would make a positive response.

Immediately before Christmas, with a noticeable absence of movement from the British, we issued a further statement drawing public attention to the manner in which the British Government, contrary to earlier indications and assurances, was handling the situation.

We feel we must again draw the public's attention to the continuing deadlock. The British are intent on deliberately creating as much confusion as possible and upon protracting the deadlock in order to sow suspicion and dissension among our supporters and families.

The blanket/no wash protest can be resolved quite simply. The British Government and their prison administration are fully aware of this, but it appears to us that they lack the will to resolve this issue and that they are committed to going back on their original assurances, including Humphrey Atkins' statement about what would happen as the protest was deescalated.

So, we call upon all those in authority, in Church and State, who urged the British to act in a sensible manner, to immediately and publicly bring pressure to bear upon the British to ensure the speedy resolution of the blanket/no wash protest and the defusing of the H Block/Armagh prison crises.

We ask our relatives and supporters to remain alert and vigilant. We assure them that we will not continue indefinitely to accept the present unsatisfactory situation. The British Government are past masters of deceit and double-dealing. We were aware of this when we accepted, with some qualifications, their document. We were dubious about the sincerity of their intentions, but were convinced that even they would not be stupid enough to waste yet another opportunity to settle this issue.

Should they remain intransigent we will be forced to fall back upon our own resources. In that event our only guarantors, the masses who supported us during the recent hunger-strike, will once again be called upon by us to take to the streets.

If the British Government cling to the forlorn hope that they can yet break the men and women of the H Blocks and Armagh, they have but to look at their failures during the last 4½ years of our protests.

We will not be found lacking in illustrating our ability and will to, if necessary, once again escalate our protest.

Signed PRO, H Blocks 3,4,5 and 6, Long Kesh

However, the statement had no effect on the situation in the prison and Bobby Sands obviously began to feel that a hunger strike was inevitable. It has been suggested that this strike was orchestrated from without by the I.R.A., but, as I think the following hitherto unpublished letter from Sands himself makes clear, this was not the case.

The letter was written on a sheet of toilet tissue paper, in tiny lettering and smuggled out. Readers will need a little explanation as to some of its contents. For instance, 'Brownie' was Gerry Adams. 'Comm' is a communication. 'Rat' was the prison governor, Mr Stanley Hillditch'. 'Sid' was Sidney Breathnach, Sands's adjutant: 'Angel' was Father Brendan Meagher. 'The Germans' was probably a reference to a German Jesuit who was visiting the prison at the time and attempting to mediate. 'Marcella' was the name of Sands's sister, with which he often signed letters and statements. 'A move' was generally accompanied by violence as it involved forcibly washing the prisoners, often with wire brushes and carbolic soap, in water that was either too hot or too cold. The purpose was to move the prisoners to clean cells to allow the dirty ones to be cleaned up. Finally the reference to the I.R.S.P., 'accept one on H.S.', illustrates the respect given to the hunger striking tactic. It was felt that the I.R.S.P. prisoners deserved the honour of joining the hunger strike and Patsy O'Hara was the prisoner selected as a result of initiative.

14. 1. 81. 5 p.m. Brownie.
Comrade: Got your comm (date 9 p.m. 13. 1. 81) read to me at pipe today at dinner. Then I asked for Rat directly after dinner lock-up, (2.30 p.m.) saw him almost immediately with No. 2 Rat, A Chief and P/O. Now I went at him very delicately on clothes. I said relatives were confused and that we had considered statement telling only those in moved wings to bring up our clothes on Friday. I said perhaps we could avoid that by informing them personally etc. I went on to subtly suggest that simultaneous gesture of clothing would be handy to everyone and that we'd immediately wash upon receiving them. I read into his statement given to us to-day using the 'request of clothes' and 'encouragement to come off protest'. Now I didn't get to how could relatives best do this, i.e. deliver clothes, what amount etc. when I came under attack from the old attitude again. Firstly, the Rat called the simultaneous delivery farcical, but I beat that back and he said okay, I will forget the principle involved in that, and then said, but we must be clear, what will happen on Monday morning, will prisoners be standing at their doors in prison issue clothing? I said we're talking about a step by step procedure bla, bla, and tried to get off the point. He kept hitting me up the face with it. I said I don't know, it depends on what happens. He said your own clothing is a privilege, your asking for a privilege before you declare that you are a conforming prisoner who is so available for industry work etc., etc. He asked me then, 'if you were to get clothes together would you be a conforming prisoner?' I said if we got clothes, and we washed and put clothes on we'd be nonprotesting prisoners. He questioned this. I elaborated, i.e. we'd not

be on blanket/non-wash. He quoted document, prisoners to come off protest altogether and emphasised 'altogether' and repeated work etc. He mentioned education once and said that it was only for sub-normal people, i.e., remedial education. Any way comrade, I was throwing him every sort of chance and had to make my stand on having achieved clothes that is only a step and there must be further steps and suggestions, etc. I kept getting Secretary of State's statement on the prison regime shoved down my throat etc. At the end up, I said well what of the simultaneous clothes delivery and so on. He said he'd have to consider all this and that I should read Atkins' rubbish. He said he'd get back to me. I didn't try to get visit with Sid, the climate wasn't favourable. I was militant enough, but only when I had no choice. Rat said that as it stands now that anyone who leaves clothes in for prisoners will be leaving it in for to be held in reception until prisoners ends his protest.

So, there you have it, comrade. Now I'll comm Sid on this as soon as I can. My impressions were, they could have been seeking a major compromise on our behalf or weakness, but am more convinced that they are just downright intransigent, and want us at the very least off non-wash protest. We can't hold back for very long. Other 8 wings will be moved soon. So, I'll wait and see if Rat changes tune, (I doubt it). I was expecting Angel never saw him. I doubt if he has anything helpful. Screws in this block believe we're winning. Screws in H 5 the opposite. It's all my running around here does that. Still think Germans are trying to defuse issue. Got comm from I.R.S.P. accepting one on H/S. So 'if' we go (which I think we'll have to do) we'll go with 3 Provos and one I.R.S.P. We thought that this morning's document, i.e. Rat's statement, left some manoeuvreability, shows you how wrong you can be. Yahoo!! Well, that's about it. Think you may hold statement on clothes now cause if they don't come across they'll just hold them in reception and people will think we have them. Okay, comrade, I'll get back to you.

Marcella XXXXX

The fatal sparks were struck by the events of the weekend of Friday, January 23, 1981.

The prisoners were given to understand that a selected group of twenty men would wash, shave and have their hair cut, after which they would collect their own clothes for that weekend. The clothes were delivered at eleven o'clock on Friday morning by the prisoners' relatives. Sands contacted the Governor and formally told him that the prisoners wished to end the protest and wanted washing facilities and their own clothes. The Governor, Mr Stanley Hillditch, said he would reply later. After consultation Hillditch returned at two-thirty that afternoon with word that the men could wash and shave, though he added that they would not get their own clothes until there was 'strict conformity'. The washing and shaving went ahead and at four o'clock all should have been well. (According to prison rules the week ends on Friday and there is no prison work to be done after four o'clock.) The custom was that prisoners who conformed to regulations normally were allowed to wear their own clothes throughout the weekend. However, despite repeated requests, the prisoners were refused the clothes which their relatives had brought in. On January 23 Sands circulated a statement within the prison, which contained a clear warning of his intentions:

For our part we must realise that another hunger strike, should it collapse, would present the Movement with disastrous consequences. Therefore a second hunger strike cannot and will not end in defeat because as I have said before, when the balance of conformity outweighs that of resistance, then criminalisation is indeed winning . . . So, comrades, once again under the duress of the British barbarity and in the ugly face of further British intransigence, we are forced to embark upon a hunger strike in the coming weeks. The announcement of this should be made public, along with the date, on Friday, 30 January. The number of hunger strikers shall be small, myself and three others, amongst them of course a representative of the I.R.S.P. . . .

I accept now that men will sacrifice their lives on this hunger strike. But you must all cast aside everything for total unity within these blocks—unity and steadfastness. You should, when a comrade dies, remain steadfast. Because, comrades, at the end of the day, men will die and the responsibility of ending this protest for once and for all will not lie with dead comrades, but with you. Because only your unflinching resistance and steadfastness will force an end to this protest.

Therefore, stand together and give your fullest support to the O.C. of these blocks. And in one way or another, comrades, victory will be ours, because we have the will to win. And we will win.

Just over a month later on March 1, 1981, Bobby Sands began his passage into Republican immortality. He was to be joined by nine others: Francis Hughes, Raymond McCreish, Patsy O'Hara (I.N.L.A.), Joe McDonnell, Martin Hurson, Kevin Lynch, Kieran Doherty, Tom McElrea and Mickie Devine. They were all carefully screened before beginning the protest; there could be no oscillation between determination and despair, as in the McKenna case. The strikers came from each of the North's Six Counties and, in addition, they were outstanding figures within the Republican Movement.

Everything that was known or could be ascertained about hunger striking was studied. The I.R.A. even contacted a Palestinian who had survived a hunger and thirst strike for a lengthy period, so that his experiences could be put to use. The H Block committees were revived, though with some misgivings, because as always the I.R.A. outside the prison was fearful that a collapse of the strike would have harmful effects on the Movement as a whole. However the temper of those outside proved to be almost as determined as that within, and despite its reservations Sinn Fein, having as I know from my own sources attempted and failed to dissuade the strikers from going ahead, gave its full support.

This time the strike was a staged affair, with prisoners joining at intervals; in all it lasted 217 days until officially being called off on October 3, 1981. By the time it ended Anglo-Irish relationships had been badly soured and Sinn Fein itself had come from behind to threaten to obliterate the S.D.L.P. Its new leaders, Gerry Adams, Martin McGuinness, Danny Morrison, Joe Austin, Richard McAuley, Jim Gibney, Tom Hartley and Owen Carron persuasively talked their way into the public consciousness via television, newspapers and radio in a myriad of interviews. The character of Sands himself made a powerful impression on the country as a whole. The circumstances of his life and his treatment in Castlereagh could have served as the stereotype for the thousands of Catholic lads whom Sands came to symbolise in Northern Ireland.

Born in 1954, he lived with his Catholic, but not Republican, family in the predominantly Protestant district of Rathcoole, from where the family were driven by Loyalist gangs after the troubles escalated in the 1960s. Bobby Sands thus lost not only his home but his apprenticeship as a coach builder. They moved to Twinbrook where apparently after the Burntullet March intimidation of the family, combined with the attacks on the People's Democracy marches, induced him to join the I.R.A. at the age of eighteen. Shortly afterwards a number of guns were found in a house and Sands was charged with possession. He received three years in the cages of Long Kesh, where at that time Special Category Status was in full swing, and devoted his time to a programme of reading and learning Irish. After being released in 1976 he again became active in the I.R.A., married and had a son. The marriage did not last under the duress of the times but the affiliation with the I.R.A. did. Sands became prominent in his district in the address of local grievances, edited a newspaper, *Liberty*, and developed the talent, which he later showed in Long Kesh, for producing articles and letters in great quantities. A good singer, much in demand at parties, and subsequently in jail for prison concerts, he appears to have become fascinated with the story of the skylark who, when placed in a cage, refused to sing. Its owner then covered the cage with a black cloth, so that eventually the bird died. Sands would later write a book which had a powerful effect on the younger members of the I.R.A. in particular, *The Skylark Singing Her Lonely Song*, a compendium of his thoughts on prison experiences.

He went to jail again in October, 1976, for his part in the fire bombing of the Balmoral Furniture Company. One of those involved with him in that operation was Joe McDonnell who, like Sands, would die on hunger strike in Long Kesh. Sands received the customary treatment in Castlereagh, a six-day programme of kicks and blows, sleep deprivation and lack of food aimed at producing a confession. He refused to sign this, and resolved that the important thing was not to give up. His companions of the time say that he found consolation in the Prophet Sirach: 'Blessed is he whose heart does not condemn him, and who does not give up hope.' He coined an Irish phrase which was to resound around the country, 'tiocfaidh ár lá' ('our day will come'), and constantly preached that the treatment of I.R.A. prisoners was part of the British effort to criminalise the Nationalists outside the jail. No matter how bad the beatings or the pangs of hunger, the important thing was to withstand them as Terence McSwiney had done, and some day '*tiocfaidh ár lá*'. To Sands, as to thousands of young men of his type, life in a Nationalist ghetto was merely a sojourn in a larger prison while awaiting one's time to be picked up and sent via the 'Conveyor Belt' to the smaller prison of Long Kesh. Both systems had to be destroyed.

What was known about Sands's personality and record, and the fact of his being on hunger strike, made him an attractive candidate, and when the Sinn Feiners out-manoeuvered the S.D.L.P. into not contesting the vacant Fermanagh—South Tyrone seat after the death of Frank Maguire in March, 1981, Sands was the sole candidate for the Nationalist vote. On April 9, he won the seat. It was a media event of the first magnitude—the campaign had been closely followed by the world's press and TV cameras, Civil Rights-minded young people had come from as far away as America to campaign for him—and the publicity, his personality and the hunger strike combined to overcome reluctance that a vote for Sands was a vote for the I.R.A.

However, although he won political status at the polls, and died a member of the British parliament, he did not manage to move Margaret Thatcher. He continued his fast despite visits to his cell from members of the European parliament, the European Commission of Human Rights, and the Pope's private secretary, and the publicity attendant on refusals to grant permission to visit him to such notables as Ramsey Clarke, the former United States Attorney General, or the American anti-Vietnam campaigner, Father Daniel Berrigan, SJ. He died on Tuesday, May 5, and it is estimated that close to a hundred thousand people attended his funeral in West Belfast. All over the world his death was marked by signs of respect—in New Delhi, for example, the Indian parliament observed a minute's silence—but apart from Northern Ireland, it was in America that the hunger strike had the most lasting effect. The heightening of the consciousness of being Irish resulted in people of all classes rediscovering their ancestry, with tangible results. For instance, in 1985–86, opposition by Democratic Senators in the debate on the Anglo-Irish aid package significantly watered down the extradition clause so prized by Margaret Thatcher, so that the Republican Senators failed to link extradition to the Aid Bill in any meaningful way. It is worth noting here that apart from the constitutional clout shown by the Irish-American, the underground physical force factor is being increased almost daily by illegal immigration. Young people are going into America from both sides of the Border on tourist visas and then disappearing into the Irish network to work in bars and on building sites. Some ultimately get 'green cards', most live just one jump ahead of the F.B.I. and the social welfare system, unable to return home for a family wedding or funeral lest they are not allowed back again. These young people, many of whom are understandably bitter towards the society which educated them and then failed to provide them with employment, support revolutionary groups far more uncritically than they would, say, the S.D.L.P. or Fianna Fail.

The month after Sands died, hunger striking candidates were proposed as candidates in the General Election called by Charles Haughey in the Republic. One of these, Kieran Doherty, was actually elected in County Cavan, and in a number of other constituencies, Fianna Fail's loss of the H Block vote was enough to turn the balance of power in favour of the Coalition. Margaret Thatcher still held firm. One after another Sands's nine skeletal companions followed him to their graves. Eventually the strike was called off in circumstances of considerable controversy and bitterness, with Republicans contending that Father Faul had induced the families of hunger strikers to pressurise their men into ending it.

One of the ironies of the whole affair was that in so far as actual prison conditions were concerned, by December the prisoners had (*de facto* if not *de jure*) won most of the concessions for which the hunger strike was held. They were wearing their own clothes; they had 50% of the full remission they had sought (despite the fact that Lord Gardiner whose recommendation it was that the H Blocks should be built in the first place, had stipulated that it was essential that there should not be an 'amnesty' and the prisoners should serve their full sentences); prison work was confined to around ten things which they could agree to do or not, but only under orders from their own O.C. They were allowed a form of 'association', so that some forty prisoners in a wing were able to gather at one time, in the presence of only five warders, which meant that prisoners could not be intimidated. They had the facility of leaving their cells every night for some two hours after dinner time, and also an hour's exercise in the fresh air during the day. Their command structure was recognised implicitly, though not officially, by the prison staff; a prisoner making a request did so through his O.C., not directly to the Governor. And some of the more degrading customs of the jail which had had a bearing on the strike—the hated mirror search, for instance, in which prisoners were spreadeagled naked over a mirror so that an anal inspection could take place—were also abolished. In a word, much the same situation as had been reached in Portlaoise in 1977, and has continued with only intermittent hiccups of confrontation ever since, was also arrived at in Long Kesh, but only after ten deaths and far-reaching political changes.

29

The Test of the Ballot Box

The younger street-wise, Northern activists whom I mentioned as coming to the fore in Sinn Fein, had been pressing for the adoption of the *Green Book* philosophy by the Republican Movement as a whole. After the hunger strike, the largely abstentionist-minded Sinn Fein became not a mere appendage of the I.R.A., but a serious constitutional threat to the S.D.L.P. in Northern Ireland and, for a short time apparently, also to the constitutional parties in the Republic. The votes won by the nine H Block candidates who stood in the Republic during the June, 1981 election totalled some 10.2% of the vote, though candidates stood under the banner of 'H Block'. In February, 1982, Sinn Fein stood as a party in its own right, but its vote fell by over 50% in the June election; the party won no seats and did not contest the November, 1982, election.

However, in the North the momentum of the hunger strike continued. The Northerners were, in fact, more keen on political action than the Southerners, and it was for this reason that at the 1981 Ard Fheis, Danny Morrison asked the celebrated rhetorical question: whether the delegates would object if Sinn Fein took power 'with a ballot box paper in one hand and an armalite in the other.' Many constitutionalists outside the Movement recoiled in horror at such a prospect but in Northern Ireland the argument served to reassure those who thought along the traditional lines, that seeking political power meant going soft on physical force. The next year's Ard Fheis again showed the influence of the Northerners' 'no sops to Loyalists' policy, and the Eire Nua Federal policy was dropped. A single unitary state was the preferred goal and the Ard Fheis passed unanimously a resolution which sought: 'that all candidates in national and local elections and all campaign material be unambivalent in support of the armed struggle'. The armalite was clutched in the hand as firmly as any ballot paper. The young tigers were cock-a-hoop at that Ard Fheis.

A week earlier Sinn Fein had taken just over 10% of all votes cast at the Northern Ireland Assembly Elections and the party went on to win 13.4% of all the votes—approximately 40% of the Nationalist vote—in the Westminster Election in June, 1983.

These external changes were reflected in the internal balance of power the following November when the Sinn Fein Ard Fheis saw Ruairi O'Bradaigh and Daithi O'Connell stand down as President and Vice President. Their stated reason was that as they were the main architects of the Eire Nua Federal policy opposed to Dail Elections and taking seats in the European parliament, there was no point in continuing in their posts. The real reason was that the hunger strike had made out of Sinn Fein a Northern Movement led by Northerners; and Gerry Adams and his cohorts were now firmly in the saddle. Adams, who personally defeated Gerry Fitt in the West Belfast Westminster Election in June of that year, was a particularly potent figure, the equal of anyone who had come to the fore in constitutional politics, North or South of the Border. Highly politicised, with a background of the 'Republican University' and street politics, and an unusually well-developed gift for political analysis, Adams believed that the time was ripe for a Sinn Fein electoral onslaught on the Republic, given the widespread alienation, particularly of the young, from established parties as a result of unemployment. His analysis might well have been proved correct. Up to the time of the hunger strike the penetration of the Northern conflict throughout the island as a whole had been remarkably slight, given the size of the country and the scale of what had happened over the previous sixteen years. It seemed inevitable that at some stage the Northern knell would begin to toll in Southern constitutional policies.

However, shortly before Christmas, 1983, the unacceptable face of Sinn Fein showed itself in the fatal events at Ballinamore, Co. Leitrim. Gardai and Army seeking to free the captured English industrialist Don Tidey were fired upon by I.R.A. men and a Garda and a soldier were killed. Subsequently there was controversy as to whether at least one of these deaths was caused by blind shooting from their own side—there was considerable confusion amongst the security forces at the time—but the fact of the deaths themselves, combined with the revulsion felt throughout the island at the kidnapping, had the effect of creating a serious setback for Sinn Fein. Indeed, from that date it is true to say that Sinn Fein went backwards, winning only 4.9% of the vote in the June, 1984, European parliament election, thus bringing home to Sinn Fein the difficulty of operating a national movement from North of the Border. Accordingly, the Adams faction persuaded the November 1986 Sinn Fein Ard Fheis to drop the Abstention Policy, causing traditionalists led by Ruairi O'Bradaigh and Daithi O'Connell to set up a new movement: Republican Sinn Fein. Whatever chance this movement might have had of achieving any sort of success faded with the sudden death, from natural causes, of Daithi O'Connell, on New Year's Eve, 1990.

Writing in the prestigious American foreign policy journal *Foreign Affairs* in April, 1986, the former American Ambassador to Ireland, William B. Shannon, an authorative commentator on Irish and Irish-American affairs said:

Prime Minister Thatcher, by refusing any of the graceful compromises that were offered to her by the Irish Catholic Bishops and other intermediaries early in the strike, may be seen by history to have made a major strategic error. The hunger strike was the greatest political propaganda coup for the I.R.A. in the last decade.

Watching the rise of Sinn Fein in the early post hunger strike period, the British Government certainly did not make any public statement of agreement with Shannon's sentiment, or those of like-minded people, but it certainly acted as though it agreed. In particular James Prior, a leading 'wet' in Mrs Thatcher's Cabinet, who was appointed Secretary of State for Northern Ireland in 1981 and lasted there until 1984, decided that something new was called for.

Starting in the spring of 1982, Prior attempted to breathe life into at least that part of the Sunningdale Agreement which provided for a Power Sharing

Executive. He worked to resurrect a Northern Ireland Assembly but did not seek as a prerequisite from those taking part that they would share power. The assembly was to start from small beginnings, to have legislative not executive powers, and to elect Committees which would hold inquiries or examine Civil Servants. If this experiment were to succeed, the Committee Chairmen could, it was thought, evolve into full-blown Cabinet Ministers with Government Departments at their disposal. This experiment in 'Rolling Devolution'* as it was known, was in fact the brainchild of a Unionist-minded Tory back-bencher Dr Brian Mawhinney, who in fact became a Minister in the Assembly. Unionists of all stripes eventually agreed to co-operate, while Sinn Fein said it would contest the elections but boycott the Assembly. The influence of Sinn Fein at the time was such that the S.D.L.P. followed suit and also declared a boycott.

The S.D.L.P.'s position requires some explanation as it illustrates how the hunger strike impacted on the larger political scene outside Sinn Fein's own particular following. As I indicated earlier, the intervention of H Block candidates cost Fianna Fail the 1981 General Election. It also cost Dublin, or London, depending how one looks at it, the friendship of the other administration. Early in his Premiership, on May 21, 1980, Haughey had gone to Downing Street and presented Mrs Thatcher with a Georgian silver teapot. After their meeting, which according to him had gone swimmingly, particularly their *tête-à-tête* session, glowing accounts of progress between the two leaders were put out by Haughey.

Those who, like myself, thought they were too glowing and overly optimistic had their doubts somewhat reassured when the most tangible evidence of Haughey's claims emerged in the shape of a top-level delegation visiting Dublin in December, 1980, after which one of the most far-reaching communiqués in the history of Anglo-Irish relations was issued. Prime Minister Thatcher was accompanied by Lord Carrington, Sir Geoffrey Howe, and Humphrey Atkins; Haughey, by his Deputy Taoiseach, Brian Lenihan, the Minister of Foreign Affairs, and by Michael O'Kennedy, the Minister for Finance. The communique noted that the meeting had been the first agreed in the May Summit and spelt out a wide range of national and international issues on which the two Governments agreed to cooperate, but the key was the sixth paragraph.

They accordingly decided to devote their next meeting in London during the coming year to special consideration of the *totality of relationships* [my italics] within these islands. For this purpose they have commissioned joint studies, covering a range of issues including possible institutional structures, citizens rights, security matters, economic co-operation and measures to encourage mutual understanding.

That paragraph contained the seed of subsequent major Anglo-Irish developments but, for the time being at least, it was blown out of the water by the issue referred to in paragraph seven—H Blocks, concerning which the two leaders merely reiterated the hope that 'the issues could be resolved'.

In the event they were not. After the December meeting Haughey said in a speech typical of his rhetoric of the period that what had happened had been an

---

* The idea was that the committee deal would 'roll on' to a stage where the province would achieve full devolution with the exception of London's control over security.

'historic breakthrough which did not rule out *any* possibility including a new type of federal or confederal arrangement involving Ireland, Britain and Northern Ireland'. Mrs Thatcher said at her press conference, however, that there was 'absolutely no possibility of a confederation flowing from the agreements reached'. Despite this, in Anglo-Irish relationships, fairly predictable disagreement on what words meant, all sides agreed that a very significant step had been taken and pointed unofficially, in the off-the-record briefings to journalists, to the fact that it was hoped that by the time the next Summit was held the following June, substantive proposals would have been worked out for signature. By next June however, Anglo-Irish relationships were at their worst since the de Valera-Churchill animosities of the Second World War.

The H Block issue had cost Haughey his Premiership and so embittered him that when he regained it the following February (1982), he stood aside from the E.E.C. support for Britain in the Falklands War, directing the Irish delegation at the U.N. to abstain also, which meant in effect that Ireland was opposing sanctions against Argentina. He also criticised the Prior Assembly, saying that Northern Ireland was a 'failed political entity' requiring direct Dublin and London talks leading to reunification to resolve the problem. With Sinn Fein (also favouring unity) riding high in the opinion polls and popularity stakes of the time, the S.D.L.P. Leader, John Hume, tacitly concurred with this view, and turned his attention from the Assembly and Prior's efforts to a campaign aimed at getting a new consensus from the South and from constitutional politicians in Northern Ireland and Britain. A tall order, but one he went very far with.

Hume got on better with Jack Lynch and Garret FitzGerald than he did with Haughey. Therefore he was probably aided in his efforts by the fact that Haughey again fell from power in November, 1982, and FitzGerald returned once more as Prime Minister. At all events, Hume succeeded in getting all-party agreement to his ideas so that on April 14,1983, Fianna Fail, Fine Gael, Labour and the S.D.L.P. met to announce that they were setting up a Forum to examine the realities of a United Ireland. The Unionist parties boycotted the proceedings and Sinn Fein, whose success had occasioned the whole thing, was deliberately not invited. The-deliberations, held in Dublin Castle, were to be for constitutionalists only: the armalite had to be laid aside while the test of the ballot box was being applied.

The initiative was probably somewhat oversold as it could not of itself produce anything—substantive progress, of course, depended on London—but there was something high-minded about the whole affair which caught the Irish public's imagination. The reports on economic policy, the legal systems North and South, the cost of violence, the cost of the division of Ireland since 1920, and all the other matters which the Forum went into in its eleven months of painstaking analysis earned respect. In particular, the fact that all the Nationalist parties took part in the discussion had a comparable effect on public opinion as would have occurred in England had the Conservatives, Labour, and Alliance parties, participated in a single political task.

Accordingly, when the Forum reported its major findings on May 2, 1984, there was considerable expectation in Ireland that something was going to happen as a result. It defined three possible models for a New Ireland, the most favoured being a unitary state governed from Dublin. Alternatives were a federation or confederation of the two parts of Ireland, something along the lines of the Haughey-Thatcher communique of 1981, or joint authority in which Britain and Ireland would share the governance of the North. But the Forum also pledged itself to 'remain open to discuss other views which may contribute to political development', in the unrealised expectation that the Unionists might want to come forward even at that late stage.

The Unionists, of course, never did. There was some initial skirmishing after the Forum report was published, Haughey contending that the only resolution acceptable to Fianna Fail was the unitary option. On July 2, 1984, just two months after the report had been published, Prior, who had announced that he was leaving the North of Ireland Secretaryship and the Government to go into business, opened the North of Ireland debate in the House of Commons. Mrs Thatcher sat beside him as if to underline the importance of what he had to say. In a few paragraphs he indicated that none of the three major options defined by the Forum was likely to receive British Governmental support, though he angled for Dublin co-operation on security and there were indications that the joint sovereignty option might be a runner. This was the most dangerous course from Dublin's point of view because it involved the South in the responsibility of security without giving it the authority to control organisations such as the U.D.R. and the R.U.C.

Senior Civil Servants continued the discussions in Dublin and London throughout the summer and autumn, and finally at yet another Anglo-Irish Summit on November 18 and 19 in London, FitzGerald and Thatcher met again. Mrs Thatcher, as always, was determined that Britain retain its sovereignty in Northern Ireland, and her major concern at the time was that the Ulsterisation policy should continue. However, while the communiqué issued by the two leaders did not build anything substantial on the Forum workings, neither did it diminish the status of the exercise.

At their subsequent press conference, however, a chasm opened. While FitzGerald was clearly concerned to keep the talks alive at all costs, Mrs Thatcher displayed all the intransigence which she had shown over the hunger strike issue itself—with this difference: she did it before Irish television cameras. Speaking of the three models put forward by the New Ireland Forum she said: 'I have made it quite clear, and so did Mr Prior, when he was Secretary of State, that a unified Ireland was one thing that was *out*. A second solution was a confederation system: that was *out*. A third solution was joint authority: that is *out*.'

I can speak with some authority when I say that for once the vast majority of the Irish people agreed with the editorial I wrote in the *Irish Press* for the next day, in which I said that Mrs Thatcher managed to make 'out' sound like a four-letter word.

Not only was constitutional Irish public opinion outraged; Mrs Thatcher was criticised internationally, particularly in America. Gradually the realisation sank in in Whitehall that she had made a mistake and that as a result Garret FitzGerald was damaged. They met again in Milan in June, 1985, at a European Community Conference and FitzGerald took the opportunity to impress on her how damaging to the S.D.L.P. and beneficial to Sinn Fein her attitude had been.

She got the same message from Washington. It was pointed out to her, by a friendly administration into the bargain, that if she failed to find an accommodation with the moderate Hume or FitzGerald she was unlikely to find it with any Irish politician. Accordingly she went back to the drawing board. Negotiations recommenced between top-level British and Irish Civil Servants. On the British side the team was led by Sir Robert Armstrong, the head of the British Civil Service, a man of considerable ability and one whose observation of the Unionists' behaviour over the years at close quarters had not endeared him to their cause. On the Irish side the team was led by the able Sean Donlon, Secretary of the Department of Foreign Affairs, who was close to both FitzGerald and Hume—so much so that Haughey, when in office, once tried unsuccessfully to shift him from his post as Irish Ambassador to Washington.

What the two teams worked out between them, and eventually unveiled at Hillsborough Castle outside Belfast (symbolically the former seat of the Governors of Northern Ireland) on November 15, 1985, was another version of the Forum's joint sovereignty option based on the 'totality of relationships' clause in the December, 1980, Dublin Communiqué. Haughey rejected the agreement immediately, saying it was a 'sell-out', thus bringing to a head a party split, and Mr Desmond O'Malley left, taking three other deputies with him to found a new party, the Progressive Democrats. Nationalist opinion North and South of the Border, however, was more welcoming and Haughey eventually modified his position.

The Hillsborough Agreement provided for an Irish Minister being designated as the permanent Irish Ministerial Representative, with the British Secretary of State for Northern Ireland as co-Chairman of an inter-governmental conference which was to meet at Maryfield not far from the sacred precincts of Stormont itself. The conference was to discuss all matters of interest to both North and South, to meet at 'regular and frequent' intervals, and the Agreement stipulated that 'the United Kingdom Government accept that the Irish Government will put forward views and proposals on matters relating to Northern Ireland'.

So far as Unionists were concerned the plain meaning of the Agreement was that an Irish Minister and Dublin Civil Servants were North of the Border as of right, Dublin accents could be heard in Stormont as of right, and after all the years of murder and mayhem on the part of the I.R.A., the Fenians and their Dublin allies had at long last triumphed. In fact the Agreement stipulated that there was to be no change in the constitutional position of Northern Ireland for so long as the majority wished to remain in the United Kingdom and Dublin. Apart from thus consenting to legitimise partition in an Agreement which was moreover to be lodged at the United Nations, the Irish Government also had to swallow the bitter pill of being seen in the Nationalist community to take responsibility for the U.D.R., the 'Diplock' courts, strip-searching in Armagh and such like, without having the power to address these grievances—in effect this was the joint sovereignty option by another name. However, the Nationalist community perceived that whatever was making the Unionists mad must have something in it to make *them* joyful, and at this time it was difficult to say what the long-term outcome of the accord would be.

As a respected U.D.A. confidant of mine said: 'Look, you surely don't think any of our people *read* the Agreement, do you? We don't have to. We *know* what's in it.' Obviously it represented, for the Protestant community, a high-water mark of Nationalist influence, at least on the symbolic front.

The Unionist response was to withdraw from Westminster immediately on learning the Agreement's contents and to organise a series of protests at every level throughout the Province. Broadly speaking these may be defined as falling in stages into three categories, all equally ineffectual:

1. Withdrawal from Westminster and from participation in County Councils, Corporations and so forth
2. A campaign of Civil disobedience.
3. A campaign of violence, including violence directed against Southern targets.

The earlier stages were not long lasting and the last stage was not reached, although it was abundantly telegraphed by statements from Loyalist spokesmen and by deeds such as the continual intimidation of R.U.C. men who sought to uphold the Agreement and the burning out of policemen's families in Protestant areas.

Where Sinn Fein was concerned, the effect was not long lasting either. British determination overcame R.U.C. recalcitrance—the three R.U.C. men who appeared on British television on April 21, 1986, wearing masks and saying that they would not uphold the Hillsborough Accord, were not reflective of a general resolve within the force. As briefers on the Accord put it in Dublin and London, the aim was to give the 'alienated' Nationalist supporters something to look forward to (code for 'win support back from Sinn Fein').

I am aware from contacts in the Gardai and in the Army that U.V.F. cars were seen, presumably on scouting missions, in the vicinity of police and military installations on the Republic side of the Border. It is very difficult to work out which strand of Loyalism actually means what. I have given above the three main Loyalist responses to the Agreement. The people making these responses may be sub-divided as follows.

On January 23, 1986, the election necessitated by the withdrawal of the Unionists from Westminster gave them 418,000 votes, a seeming rebuff as both Paisleyites and the official Unionists had called for a poll of 500,000 votes. In the election they actually lost a seat to Seamus Mallon, Deputy Leader of the S.D.L.P. Constitutional Nationalists now had two forceful and articulate spokesmen at Westminster, John Hume being the other. (One question posed here, of course, is what would happen to the remaining fourteen Unionist seats should a hung parliament loom. Would these return to whichever party promised to scuttle the hated Agreement?) On the actual ground level, however, the 418,000 votes were less significant in themselves than which strand of Unionism would win out. Currently the hard men of the U.D.A. and of bodies such as the Ulster Clubs, which have sprung up just as did the Ulster Loyalist Council in the wake of the Sunningdale Agreement, are the actual motor force of militant 'Loyalism'. It is they, not the Democratic Unionist Party led by Ian Paisley and his increasingly thrustful Deputy Peter Robinson, nor the Official Unionist Party led by Jim Molyneaux, which count. However, it should be noted that Robinson distinguished, or disgraced himself, depending on how one looks at it, by being arrested by Gardai in the company of a group of marked, cudgel-carrying men who took over the border town of Clontibret on the Republic side of the Border at 2 a.m. one night, thereby, of course, terrifying the inhabitants of that County Monaghan town. The invasion was ostensibly staged to highlight security lacunae, but at the time, in August, 1986, Ian Paisley was abroad. Paisley returned to the subsequent court hearing so promptly that it was widely commented that he was concerned about Robinson's stunt—a highly dangerous one in the tense border area—not because of its physical dangers but because of its political one to his leadership. The initial court hearing sparked off riots in Dundalk. The affair ultimately ended in farce. Robinson, who had been reported as intending to refuse to pay his fine, ultimately escaped any consequences of his action. Someone paid the fine anonymously. Robinson added to his unsavoury reputation after the American raids on Baghdad in June 1993. He proposed that the R.A.F. should emulate the American example and bomb what he termed the 'I.R.A. strongholds' in Dublin and elsewhere in the Republic. It was a highly irresponsible piece of incitement at anytime, but doubly so coming during the North's traditionally perfervid 'marching season'. But certainly Clontibret was the first occasion on which any Westminster MP led a paramilitary invasion into the Republic's territory. Meanwhile, in the underworld of Loyalism a debate is raging as to whether the correct course to follow is U.D.I.; a repartition; closer integration with Britain—or outright sectarian warfare. The outcome of Northern Ireland's present turmoil will be dependent to a large extent on which of these schools of thought wins. Ominously, the years 1991–3 showed a decided tilt towards the sectarian option.

The I.R.A. always maintains the capacity to create a crisis unexpectedly. It cannot strike a decisive blow at the British to achieve its objective, nor can the British crush the organisation, a familiar pattern, as readers of these pages will by now have grasped. Personally, I doubt that the I.R.A. or Sinn Fein can be defeated. They must be part of any settlement which brings a final resolution to the Northern agony. As readers have seen already in the interview with the I.R.A. leader 'Pat' and will see later in the extracts from the *Green Book*, the 'army' is stripped down for a long hard war. And the statistics show that six months after the Accord was signed, one of its main effects was thwarted already: the hope that Unionist opposition could be overcome through increased Garda-R.U.C. co-operation, resulting in a defeat for the I.R.A. The I.R.A. killed more than two dozen members of the security forces in that time and the tempo of attacks, both shootings and bombings, was stepped up after an initial three months' lull, during which the strategists digested the effects of the Agreement. The Army Council had obviously deduced correctly that these could be withstood.

Things would have been different had Mrs Thatcher allowed Bobby Sands the right to wear his own clothes while he was a prisoner in Long Kesh Jail.

It is not the skylark singing its lonely song that one hears now high over Belfast's Cave Hill, where Wolfe Tone and the others back in the eighteenth century lit the fires of Republicanism from where emerged the I.R.A. tradition, but the croaking of the raven of war.

30

Bombs in Britain and Counter-Insurgency

Let us turn our attention to some of the other principal developments caused or influenced by the Republicans in the period 1980–86.

Unquestionably the major event was the hunger strike and its chain reaction effect of bringing about the Anglo-Irish Accord of November, 1985. But other incidents also had a bearing in bringing about that Accord, occurrences in England, the Brighton bombing in particular, the Harrods bombing and the attack on Chelsea Barracks. In Ireland the 'highlights' of those years, if that is the correct term, included a spate of kidnappings, sometimes with fatal results, the massive jail break from Long Kesh, attacks on security forces, such as the mortar bombing of Newry Barracks, the seizure of the *Marita Ann*'s cargo of arms off the Kerry Coast; and one must also take note of the depredations of the I.N.L.A., the bombing at the Droppin' Well in Ballycastle, Co. Down, the Darkley Massacre and the great controversy surrounding the extradition of the I.N.L.A. leader Dominic McGlinchey. All of these will be examined in the following pages, but let us begin with the British bombing campaign.

Curiously, it was the bomb which claimed the lives of animals as well as people that created the greatest controversy of the period. On July 20th, 1982, two bombs detonated in London killed a total of eleven soldiers, four of them members of the Household Cavalry and seven members of a band of the Royal Greenjackets.

The Cavalry were ambushed by a bomb set off by a radio signal in Hyde Park, which contained 25lbs of gelignite and about 30lbs of nails. This killed and maimed a number of horses, which seemed to create as great an outrage both in England and Ireland as the deaths of the soldiers. In Dublin the Royal Dublin Society replaced the horses which had been destroyed, and some £50,000 were raised, apart from the R.D.S. gesture, for the families of the soldiers.

I happened to be in London the week after the explosions. People were still laying wreaths on the spot in Hyde Park where the horses were killed, but I saw no signs of activity in Regent's Park where the bandsmen were blown up. My strongest impression at the time was the remarkable lack of anti-Irish feeling that my Irish accent elicited, even though the TV pictures, nightly it seemed, carried pictures and reports of the surviving horses' condition, giving these greater prominence than the medical bulletins for the surviving soldiers.

Eight days before Christmas, 1983, a car bomb exploded outside Harrods, one of the world's best-known stores, claiming the lives of six people and injuring ninety others, some of them very drastically—PC John Gordon, for instance, lost a leg in the blast. Apart from horrifying the public all over the world, this cruelly underlined the deep-rooted nature of the I.R.A. problem. Hans Crescent, where the bomb was planted is just around the corner from Hans Place, where the Irish delegation stayed in 1921 during the Treaty negotiations which were supposed to have solved the Irish problem once and for all. Exactly why that target was chosen during that week has never satisfactorily been explained. Did the planners of the raid deliberately set out to take life in a shocking context and at a particularly shocking time? A quite high-ranking Republican figure did flatly say to me that it was 'deliberate'. However, while there is a continuing desire to export as much of the terror and destruction of the Northern conflict as is possible to the British mainland, it must be said that this theory, like much else about the I.R.A., remains to be proven.

Other I.R.A. apologists told me that the bombing was just 'a job that went wrong', one of the inevitabilities of war. They pointed to the fact that Natalino Vella, a Dublin fish and chip merchant who was sentenced at the Old Bailey on March 7, 1985, to fifteen years on a variety of arms charges, was apparently an I.R.A. 'quartermaster' who had been sent over to London especially to find out what had gone wrong with the Harrods bombing and to order the unit responsible back to Ireland. Mr Justice McCowan, who sentenced Vella, also condemned Paul Kavanagh and Thomas Quigley, both of Belfast, to thirty-five years in prison on the same occasion. They were found guilty of the Ebury Bridge nail-bomb blast near Chelsea Barracks on October 10, 1981, which killed a widow—Mrs Nora Field and a teenager, John Patrick Breslin—instead of the intended victims, Irish Guardsmen returning to their barracks in a bus. Mr Ken Howorth, a bomb disposal expert, was killed on October 26, when a bomb which Kavanagh and Quigley were accused of setting went off in an Oxford Street Wimpy Bar. The Judge also found them guilty of the attempted bombing of Debenhams in Oxford Street, also in October, and of the explosion at the Attorney General's Wimbledon home on November 13.

The police believed that it was an I.R.A. unit run by Kavanagh which planted the Harrods bomb. Apparently they stumbled on the unit more or less by accident when estate workers at Pangbourne, Berkshire, discovered an arms cache in which Kavanagh's and Quigley's fingerprints were found, along with the car keys used in the Chelsea Barracks bombing. When Vella came over to London after the Harrods bombing he walked into a police trap. He had ordered Quigley and Kavanagh to show him where their arms and explosives were hidden; police tailed them to two dumps, one at Salcey Forest in Northants. and another at Annesley Forest in Nottinghamshire, where they found what the prosecuting Counsel described at the Old Bailey as 'a comprehensive collection of terrorist hardware'. In his statement, Vella, whom the prosecution alleged had supplied 'the terrorist hardware' for the 1983 campaign, said that he had not known that Harrods was to be a target. 'I would rather hit the economy of England than see people killed,' he said. 'Things went badly wrong. The unit stepped outside its instructions. There was a lot of trouble about Harrods. We didn't want all those people killed. We didn't know if they had given the general forty-five-minute warning. Anyhow it shouldn't have been the target.'

This pretty comprehensive disavowal would, I know, be in line with a good deal of I.R.A. thinking on the outrage, but where such statements are concerned in an era of Castlereagh-type interrogations and supergrasses, one has to be somewhat wary of accepting statements at their face value. However, there is no doubt that there was no division whatever within the I.R.A. over the target chosen for the attack on October 12, 1984: the Grand Hotel in Brighton, at which Mrs Thatcher and members of her cabinet were staying during the British Tory Conference. There were five people killed in the blast: Sir Anthony Berry, Tory MP; Mrs Roberta Wakeham, wife of the Conservative Chief Whip; Mrs Jeanne Shattock, wife of the Chairman of the Party's western area; Mr Eric Taylor; and Mrs Muriel MacLean.

Apart from the deaths and the television footage showing the victims being recovered, notably Mr Norman Tebbit whose wife was very badly injured in the blast, the idea that the entire British Cabinet had nearly been wiped out by the I.R.A. traumatised people both in England and Ireland and caused considerable alarm as to the possible repercussions. Mrs Thatcher herself only escaped by a hair's breadth: she had used the bathroom which took the full brunt of the explosion only minutes before the bomb went off. The I.R.A. could have planted the bomb at the previous year's Tory Conference but decided that their chances of a major coup were better if they waited until Mrs Thatcher herself would be reasonably certain to be in the line of the blast. One of the brutal simplicities of terrorism is that despite intelligence, counter-insurgency and sophisticated equipment of all sorts, it is virtually impossible to guard against the obvious. In this case the world and his wife knew with certainty that the one place during the year that anyone could be sure of finding Mrs Thatcher was at the hub of her own Party Conference. The idea of hitting the British Government is not new in Republican circles. During the Anglo-Irish War, for instance, Cathal Brugha devised a scheme which involved taking a suicide squad into the House of Commons and mowing down the front bench. Individual members of any British Administration who deal with Ireland can incur an outstanding amount of opprobrium—for instance, Mr Roy Mason is still very badly thought of by Republicans and others. The Brighton blast was the result of more than simply a desire to 'get the people responsible'. It was a direct and calculated response to Mrs Thatcher's handling of the hunger strike and was intended to avenge the deaths of the ten strikers. It was also an underlining of a cardinal feature of I.R.A. strategy.

Speaking to me in 1986, an Army Council spokesman said: 'We can't be beaten; there is no question of us winning in the sense of driving the British Army into the sea. But we always maintain the capacity to bring the situation to a crisis at some stage'.

In the wake of such a deep-rooted problem it is inevitable that the innocent of all sides suffer along with the guilty. I referred earlier (see Chapter 19) to the treatment of Irish prisoners in England and to the fact that claims of innocence had been made by those convicted for serious crimes. In my interview with the Army Council spokesman I raised this issue and was categorically assured, as I had been on earlier occasions, that the prisoners in jail for the Birmingham and Guildford bombings were totally innocent. This claim was not new—this had been the contention of Civil Rights campaigners like Father Faul for several years and there had been sporadic media interest in the subject—but, from what the I.R.A. spokesman said to me I now believed even more strongly than I had five years before that a gross miscarriage of justice had occurred.

While those serving long sentences, as in the Birmingham and Guildford cases, are the worst examples, it is also true that the inevitable prejudice excited by the I.R.A. has resulted in some very small-minded and unjust actions being carried out against Irish prisoners. Strip-searching in Armagh jail for instance, has apparently been employed as a tool to break the prisoners' morale and is seen by the Northern Ireland Office in much the same light as the issue of prison uniforms was during the hunger strike.

The official reason for the introduction of strip-searching in Armagh jail in November, 1982, was given in Hansard on March 15, 1983: 'On 22 October in the course of a detailed search of cells two keys were found in the possession of two remand prisoners.' Since then, however, prisoners have been searched, not merely on admission to the prison, or before, or after, a court appearance when there might be a possibility of something being smuggled to them, but on random occasions when they have not left the prison for weeks or had any visitors. According to statistics provided by the Irish Information Partnership in November, 1985, the prisoners were searched thirty times per capita of the average number of inmates between 1982 and 1985. According to the prisoners themselves the number of searches was much higher and the women in particular regarded it as a direct tool of humiliation. They described being asked to remove sanitary towels or tampons and place them in a bag while the search was in progress; being searched while five and six months pregnant; and there were also ancillary complaints such as the searching of members of their families, including children, during prison visits. Independent witnesses such as the Tribunal on Strip-Searching, set up by the Irish Trade Union Movement in Dublin and comprising not only trade unionists but academics, politicians, clergy and journalists (including myself), established that the allegations were broadly true.

One can imagine the impact of this practice on two girls in Brixton Prison, Martina Anderson and Ella O'Dwyer, who were remanded on charges of conspiracy to cause explosions in Britain and found guilty on June 11, 1986. It was accepted in Ireland that these girls were strip-searched hundred of times during their period on remand. The authorities may have stated otherwise but this belief was strongly reinforced by the continuing impact of the Maguire family saga. I referred earlier to the Guildford affair. The controversy surrounding this heated up in Ireland in April, 1985, when the prestigious R.T.E. current affairs programme *Today Tonight* screened a two-hour investigation of the trial which had linked the Maguire family to the bombing. Subsequently the programme led to the case being examined on Channel 4 and on Yorkshire Television.

In the programme, the *Today Tonight* team, led by editor Joe Mulholland, proved through the interviewing of expert witnesses that the evidence which convicted the Maguire family was extremely shaky. The prosecution case centred exclusively on scientific tests which 'proved' that there were traces of explosives on the defendants. However, the tests were carried out by a seventeen-year-old apprentice and the results could never be challenged as the samples were destroyed in the process. Even Dr Yallop, the scientist who invented the test, said that it was not reliable evidence as cigarettes or household cleaning agents could have given similar readings. Nevertheless the Maguires were sentenced in a trial in which the prosecution admitted that no explosives were ever found. Despite this anomaly Annie Maguire served nine years of a fourteen-year sentence imposed in 1976 when she was forty years of age. Her husband Patrick, her sons Vincent and Patrick, her brother William Joseph Smith, her brother-in-law Patrick Giuseppe Conlon, who died serving his sentence, and a family friend Patrick O'Neill, were all found guilty at the Old Bailey of possessing nitroglycerine. The Maguires were devastated by the trial and lived for several months in great penury after Annie was released in February, 1985. Their flat in Kilburn had no furniture and they encountered bureaucratic difficulties in getting council grants.

Understandably all this had considerable impact on Irish public opinion and even Lord Gerry Fitt, no friend of the I.R.A., was amongst those who raised the case with the British Government. Out of such dragon's teeth have I.R.A. men traditionally sprung.

The efforts to curb the I.R.A. have resulted in some tactics being employed which would not be countenanced elsewhere in Western Europe, and can only be justified in counter-insurgency terms, not legal ones. One of the best known and most odious of these is the use of so-called 'supergrasses'.

The supergrass phenomenon was first seen in action in the trial of four I.R.A. men who in March, 1980 were sent away on the word of an informer, Stephen McWilliams. Later that year, in September, another one, James Kennedy, put twelve more men behind bars.

Supergrasses who retracted their evidence have mentioned astronomical sums of money being offered to them if they implicate Republicans. One such, David Lean, told reporters that he was offered £300,000 to implicate Gerry Adams, Danny Morrison and Martin McGuinness. 'The sky was the limit' was how he termed his offers. But this is only the start. After the supergrass has done his work he has to be protected for the rest of his life. The R.U.C. say that the police can only offer an informer a top payment of £5,000 and that the rest comes from British intelligence, from the so-called 'reptiles fund' which pays for the informer's new life abroad, including a new name, new home and a new face with plastic surgery.

Giving details of such figures in March, 1985, the Northern Ireland Secretary, Mr Douglas Hurd, said that in the previous seven years the British Government had spent almost £1½ million in protecting and resettling informers who gave evidence in court. He said this figure represented total 'direct expenditure' for such items as paid information, hotels, living allowances, pocket money, assistance in finding accommodation and jobs abroad, but the total cost must be far higher. By March 1985 there had been twenty-seven supergrasses who were given total immunity for their own crimes in order to implicate others but Hurd's figures only referred to eight of the twenty-seven, who by that time had *disappeared* to start new lives abroad under new names, but very much under the same old dread. His figures did not include such 'indirect spending' as wages and overtime for the R.U.C. men assigned to rehearse the supergrasses in their evidence pre-trial—

often in luxury hotels out of the country—and the amount spent afterwards in guarding not only the informers themselves, but their relatives. It was known by March, 1985, that the taxpayer had spent more than £5 million on court costs alone for these trials. One case, that of Christopher Black, whose evidence convicted thirty-five people on I.R.A.-linked charges, cost £600,000.

The supergrasses' evidence, which the 'Diplock' courts naturally accept *without corroboration*, became less valuable as community and other pressures built up.

In a fourteen-month period during the years 1980–81 the I.R.A. executed six men they found guilty of informing and in their own words 'took less drastic action against others' (anything from kneecapping to exile). Of the first twenty-seven supergrasses, from the years 1980–85, fifteen retracted their evidence, and Lord Gifford, himself a former judge, said in a report on the system published in 1984 that the supergrass system was 'not justice', that it led to 'telling of lies' and to the conviction of the innocent. He accepted the fact that the R.U.C. regularly programmed supergrasses to 'concoct and rehearse statements'.

Lord Gifford's view was echoed by Mr Justice Higgins, who described one 'supergrass', William 'Budgie' Allan, as a 'liar' and threw out charges, based on his 'evidence', against forty-four Loyalists who were brought to trial in 1983. The waste of money and time involved in this trial can only be guessed at. Nevertheless, Allan, a former U.V.F. activist who at the time of the trial was serving a fourteen-year sentence on a total of fifty-two charges, including attempted murder, was granted the Royal Prerogative of Mercy by the Secretary of State for Northern Ireland, Mr Tom King, on May 11, 1986, following a deal done between Allan and the Chief Constable, Sir John Hermon.

The supergrass system thus differs from the ordinary use of informers, who are, of course, also used in the Province, though merely as spies to collect information. The R.U.C. adopted the system after they began to find it increasingly difficult to obtain confessions in the absence of full internment (a variant of which still exists: internment by remand) and institutionalised torture, which was ruled out in the wake of reports by Amnesty International, the European courts and the Bennett Report. It comes in for heavy criticism for reasons other than the use of uncorroborated evidence. Many of those used either to manufacture or to give evidence were themselves convicted killers who thus got immunity from their crimes. However, in the early stages of the system the R.U.C. and the Unionists were able to weather the storm by pointing to the number of suspects rounded up; by March, 1983, there were three hundred behind bars of whom eighty-two were actually convicted. Privately Unionists were cock-a-hoop at such results. One prominent Unionist politician said to me in London at a convivial occasion one evening: 'The Republican Army has always been vulnerable to informers. We have them now—that is if the Rescue Brigade, the do-gooders like yourself, don't manage to bugger up things!'

The Chief Constable, Sir John Hermon (Annual Report 1985) was more restrained. He said that the 'converted terrorist process', as he termed it, 'undoubtedly dealt a severe blow to the morale of both Republican and Loyalist terrorist organisations and to their ability to murder and destroy'. He claimed that in one area of Belfast alone, 'terrorist murders dropped by 73% and all terrorist crimes by 61% following information supplied by this process'.

But it was neither the activities of the 'Rescue Brigade', nor of Lord Gifford, who recommended that trial by jury should be restored, albeit with safeguards for the security and identities of jury members—that dealt the supergrass process a telling blow. This came when supergrasses themselves began to retract their evidence. The R.U.C. attempted to counteract this failure of nerve by invoking an archaic legal measure, the Bill of Indictment, which had the effect of bypassing the customary preliminary hearing of evidence so that defendants were automatically returned for trial, thereby giving the police a fresh chance to apply psychological tactics on the waverer.

At present, the supergrass tactic, while much diminished in effectiveness, is still in operation. It was revealed by a Northern Ireland spokesman during August, 1986, that since the previous month 'the four remaining supergrasses who were serving jail terms are now held at Maghaberry'. Behind this bland statement lies an astonishing tale of expense, deceit, and muddle. Maghaberry took ten years to build, and cost £40 million, but, at the time of the statement, the prison, situated some twenty miles from Belfast, housed nobody but the four supergrasses as the Government still felt it was insufficiently secure. However the supergrasses probably didn't complain. They had been housed in a specially designed cell block containing private bathrooms, gym, library, and other comforts such as arm-chairs, videos and television. Although these four must have been the most at risk, both from Loyalists and the I.R.A. enemies, of any prisoners in the world, they were probably better off than their twenty or so counterparts who lived in Britain because other countries of their choice had refused to take them.

Both inside and outside prison the wretched supergrasses were both a symptom and a cause of the disease they were intended to cure: the poisonous political scene in Northern Ireland.

31

Action in Ireland

If the hunger strikes displayed the 'acceptable' face of the I.R.A., on the other side of the coin were the detestable features of kidnapping. The need to provide the sinews of war and the attrition of the security forces campaign drove kidnapping further up the Movement's scale of priorities, especially at times when certain personalities, people less susceptible to the nuances of Irish public opinion than other, more experienced members of the Army Council might have been, held particular influence. Alongside this unwelcome development was the fact that criminal gangs sometimes got in on the act so that a spate of actual or threatened kidnappings accompanied the I.R.A. campaign, particularly from 1979 onwards, when the exigencies of the time seemed to have overcome the revulsion caused by the Herrema affair four years earlier. In that year there was a series of raids in Dublin and Wicklow directed at the families of bank managers, and money was paid over before the Gardai became involved. This type of extortion had been common in the North for a long time, though it was officially denied by the banks. It attracted widespread publicity when in December, 1979, the Gardai succeeded in rescuing Mrs Margaret Fennelly, the wife of a Cobh bank manager, before a ransom of £60,000 could be paid. Two years later they captured a gang with extremely dubious political connections which had sought to extort £100,000 from Mrs Anne Hudson of Enniscorthy, Co. Wexford, who had been kidnapped in Courtown. Mrs Hudson was eventually discovered in a flat in my own area of Glenageary, Co. Dublin. Later that year the Gardai were paid a back-handed tribute when the Provisionals kidnapped the Dublin businessman Ben Dunne and held him for five days—North of the Border, releasing him on October 23 in South Armagh. There was considerable controversy over whether or not a ransom was paid for Mr Dunne. I have heard the sum of £750,000 being discussed in Republican circles. Crossborder kidnappings continued with the snatching of two bank managers' daughters, one from Dundalk and the other from Ardee, who were released in Newry after £50,000 had been handed over in each case.

It is thought that kidnappings in June and August 1983 may have been connected with the I.N.L.A., not the Provisionals. Certainly, Mr Richard Hill and his daughter Dianna, who were seized in a holiday home in Co. Mayo, are thought to have been taken by the I.N.L.A. The Hills, like Mrs Heloise Jones seized earlier in the year in Co. Dublin, were released safely. In August, after a wild shootout, the Gardai arrested five Provos who were subsequently sentenced for the attempted kidnapping of Mr Galen Weston, the Canadian multimillionaire. The Special Branch had been lying in wait at Mr Weston's home in Roundwood, Co. Wicklow, obviously acting on a tip-off, when the Provisionals drove up. Later that year, kidnapping mania led to the seizure of Mrs Alma Manina, who was released by the Gardai after being kidnapped in Greystones, Co. Wicklow on October 21. A number of local men were arrested but it is not clear what happened to the £60,000 ransom.

The two most celebrated kidnappings to occur in 1983 were, of course, the stealing of the thoroughbred horse Shergar, the Derby Winner from Ballymoney Stud at the Curragh on February 8, and the Don Tidey drama in December. Shergar was apparently put down by his kidnappers when the syndicate led by the Aga Khan which owned the horse failed to pay the ransom. The horse's body was never recovered. This kidnapping is associated with one particular maverick I.R.A. man whose daring exploits have often been in the news.

The Don Tidey kidnapping made appalling headlines. A policeman and a soldier were killed in the fusillade which broke out as the security forces closed in on the dugout where the Provisionals had hidden him, in Ballinamore, Co. Leitrim. Mr Tidey, who was employed by the international combine Associated British Foods, apparently cost the insurers some £2 million. Garret FitzGerald had intervened personally with Mrs Thatcher to ensure that no ransom would be paid and received assurances in this regard. However, I understand that the Gardai believe that the money was handed over by the insurance company in Switzerland. Subsequently the Gardai began an action against a prominent Irish-American businessman, having arranged the seizure of some millions of his money from Irish bank accounts.

One bizarre side-effect of the affair was the leaking by R.U.C. sources to Loyalist paramilitaries of the fact that the ransom had been paid to the I.R.A.

The Loyalist paramilitaries promptly counter-attacked by demanding a like amount of money from the stores owned by Associated British Foods in Ireland. There were some reports of vegetables being poisoned, causing the Quinnsworth chain to install videos carrying warnings to shoppers and requests to report anything suspicious. This episode petered out without it being ascertained whether or not the Loyalists had received any money.

After the Ballinamore débâcle the I.R.A. went cold on kidnapping and there was a merciful respite of the practice in Ireland until an English criminal gang seized Mrs Jennifer Guinness, the wife of a prominent Dublin merchant banker, in April, 1986. She was released by the Gardai on April 16 unhurt and without a ransom being paid. The only good thing to be said about kidnappings in the period under review is that the Gardai showed a consistent and successful record against them.

The power of the Irish American link was amply demonstrated on September 29, 1984, when some seven tons of arms were seized by the Irish authorities aboard the *Marita Ann* off the Kerry Coast. The five men arrested aboard the trawler were Gavin Mortimer, Martin Ferris, John McCarthy, John Patrick Crowley, and Michael Browne, the skipper and a member of one of Ireland's best-known fishing families.

The *Marita Ann* was captured by the Irish naval vessels the *Emer* and the *Aisling* after being fired at by tracer bullets. The trawler had transhipped the arms from a bigger American trawler, the *Valhalla*, which had crossed the Atlantic from Boston (and was seized there by U.S. Customs on October 16). The arrangements for the purchase and shipping of the arms were well known to some members of the

46. Mortar launchers used in I.R.A. attack on Newry R.U.C. Barracks on February 28, 1985. Nine members of the R.U.C. were killed and thirty-two injured. (*Pacemaker*)

47. Plain clothed policemen and Army at the scene of the shooting of Sinn Fein President Gerry Adams in 1984. (*Pacemaker*)

48. Signing of the Anglo-Irish Agreement on November 15, 1985, at Hillsborough, County Down by Irish Prime Minister Garrett FitzGerald and British Prime Minister Margaret Thatcher. The three men standing in the centre are, from left to right, Irish Deputy Prime Minister Dick Spring, Northern Ireland Secretary Tom King, and British Foreign Secretary, Sir Geoffrey Howe. (*Pacemaker*)

49. Rev. Ian Paisley salutes the crowd gathered at City Hall, Belfast, during the massive Loyalist demonstration against the Anglo-Irish Agreement on November 23, 1985. (*Pacemaker*)

50. Sinn Fein President Gerry Adams carries the coffin of James Lynagh, an I.R.A. unit commander killed by the S.A.S. in a shoot-to-kill ambush at Loughall, County, Armagh, on May 8, 1987. (*Colman Doyle*)

51. The scene at Enniskillen on November 8, 1987, where an I.R.A. bomb exploded during the annual Remembrance Day commemoration. Eleven civilians were killed and sixty-three were injured in what is one of the worst I.R.A. atrocities of the Troubles. (*Pacemaker*)

52/53. Two scenes of the violence that broke out in the streets of Belfast in March, 1988, in the wake of the killing of three I.R.A. members in Gibraltar by the S.A.S. in a shoot-to-kill operation. (*Pacemaker*)

54/55. Recent pictures of members of the Ulster Volunteer Force (U.V.F.) in training. There are many alleged links between the U.V.F. and other Loyalist paramilitary organisations and British Intelligence, including the provision of equipment and training for Loyalist hit squads. (*Pacemaker*)

56. Gerald Conlon, one of the Guildford Four, outside the Old Bailey court in London after his release on October 19, 1989. He served fifteen years for a crime that he was totally innocent of. (*Press Association*)

57. Hugh Callaghan, one of the Birmingham Six, in Dublin after his release in March, 1991. (*Colman Doyle*)

58. Smoke billows from the burning van in Whitehall, London after the mortar bomb attack on Prime Minister John Major and his Cabinet in Number Ten Downing Street on February 2, 1991. (*Press Association*)

59. A Scotland Yard security picture showing the devastation to the City of London by the massive I.R.A. bomb on April 24, 1993. The final bill for the damages could well exceed two billion pounds. (*Press Association*)

Boston police force, whose help in providing bodyguards, and advice in guiding the purchases through the underworld of American arms dealers, greatly assisted the *Marita Ann* project—initially, that is. Although the capture was hailed as a triumph of F.B.I. detection coupled with satellite surveillance, which was supposed to have monitored the *Valhalla*'s progress across the Atlantic, it was the age-old Irish role of the informer which played the most important part. At the time of the seizure, in an effort to protect the identity of their 'moles', a story was issued by 'Washington sources' and printed by the papers, stating that the capture 'was connected with a top-secret U.S. Customs operation code-named Leprechaun which has been underway in New York for two years (*Sunday Press*, September 30, 1984). However, the I.R.A., my sources tell me, were not thrown off the scent by this theory. The I.R.A. shot one man in connection with the event and other deaths may have followed. The power of the I.R.A.'s 'doctrine of continuity' was ironically underlined by the occasion: some of those arrested were caught waiting at Banna Strand, a place made famous by its association with the capture of Sir Roger Casement, who was hanged for his part in the attempt to smuggle arms from Germany in the *Aud* prior to 1916. The ballad about Sir Roger and 'the lonely Banna Strand' is one of the most popular in Ireland and, though the authorities were naturally delighted by the arms seizure, the song—and its symbolism—received a renewed burst of popularity.

Garret FitzGerald also was delighted by the *Marita Ann* episode, for two reasons. Firstly, he hoped that this demonstration of Anglo-Irish security co-operation, in the most spectacular arms seizure since that of the *Claudia* off the coast of Waterford eleven years earlier, would help incline Margaret Thatcher favourably towards the Forum proposals; and secondly—as his statement of congratulation to the Security Forces indicated—because the arms had been prevented 'from coming into the country to murder people both North and South of the Border'.

It was the I.R.A. statement* on the affair, however, which eventually proved to contain the correct long-term pointer to the outcome of the seizure. After criticising the Dublin Government for continually postponing Ireland's freedom by acting as Britain's agent, the statement promised that the I.R.A.'s campaign 'would not be curtailed'. Decoded, this meant that though deprived of a highly important arms shipment, they could and would improvise. The degree of efficiency with which they could do this was demonstrated a few months after the *Marita Ann*'s seizure. An attack was launched on Newry R.U.C. Barracks at 6.30 p.m. on February 28, 1985, using home-made mortars fired at a range of two hundred metres from steel tubes four and a half feet long and bolted to the floor of a hijacked lorry. The mortars wiped out a canteen made from two portacabins that had been filled with a teatime crowd. The attack was obviously launched with a great deal of local knowledge; nine members of the R.U.C. were killed (including two women) and thirty-two others were injured. It was the highest single death toll suffered by the R.U.C. since the troubles began. The dead† included a chief inspector and a sergeant.

---

*   *Sunday Press*, September 30, 1984.
†   The names of those killed were: Chief Inspector Alexander Donaldson; Sergeant John Dowd; Constables David Topping, Ivy Kelly, Rosemary McGookin; Reserve Constables Geoffrey Campbell, Sean McHenry, Paul McFerran and Denis Price.

But shattering as the blow was to the morale of the force, it was only the bloody tip of an iceberg continuously grinding away at it. Apart from outright attacks and threats of attacks, there was a constant campaign afoot to isolate the police by various methods, including shooting contractors who repair R.U.C. barracks or provide them with supplies. I have even known of a band which played at an R.U.C. Social Club to be warned to desist.★

The I.R.A. broadened the 'legitimate' target list with their announcement on August 7, 1986, that they would attack civilians who work not only on military contracts, such as barracks and so on, but for government installations such as British Telecom.

Apart from provoking fear and resentment amongst Catholics, for whom such employment is the only possible work opportunity, this provoked a backlash from the U.V.F. Hooded spokesmen appeared on television reading out what amounted to a tit-for-tat death threat against Catholic workers in Protestant firms, and this particular threat was further underlined on August 18, when a group, thought to be from within the U.D.A., having first stolen the clocking-in cards of the few Catholics allowed to work at Shorts Brothers, announced that it would take action against them.

This firm had just won an important American defence contract with the assistance of John Hume, in the teeth of opposition mounted by Irish-American spokesmen such as Father MacManus of the Irish-American Caucus, on the grounds that there was discrimination against Catholics in the factory, in flagrant contravention of the McBride principles, among others. However the real point about Shorts is that the number of Catholics was so small, approximately 3% of a workforce of 7,000, even though the management had the full backing of all the firm's trade unions in its threat to dismiss anyone found guilty of stealing the clocking-in cards, or engaging in sectarian intimidation.

The Shorts situation merely serves to underline the continuing facts of life of Northern Ireland employment, whereas the I.R.A. threat added a new dimension of terror to both Protestants and Catholics in the Province, a further step in their aim of isolating British installations.

The strain on the R.U.C. in dealing with attacks mounted by Loyalists after the signing of the Anglo-Irish Agreement, can well be imagined. But although the Agreement is widely and deeply resented within the R.U.C. as it is within the wider Loyalist community, the force has not shown any great difficulty in controlling Loyalist mobs if ordered to do so (and sometimes the 'if' is highly relevant, as was apparent during the Loyalists' Province-wide work stoppage of March 3, 1986, when intimidation was widespread and unchecked) despite the spate of attacks on individual policemen's homes. The R.U.C. is a highly trained force, particularly in counter-insurgency, to a degree that gave rise to a belief within the I.R.A. that fear of Loyalist backlash from paramilitaries should more properly be directed at the R.U.C., who had training, equipment and local knowledge. It remains to be seen how the R.U.C.'s reaction to the growing threat posed by loyalist paramilitaries affects that calculation.

★ Members of the group were Catholics. The threat was a boon to their careers, as they emigrated to Ibiza where they became highly successful.

Despite the fact that, post Hillsborough, the R.U.C. obviously did enough impartial policing to enrage the Loyalists, the Stalker affair confirmed Nationalist suspicions that the force was not to be trusted. One of the most controversial aspects of the R.U.C.'s activities was highlighted by this affair. Following complaints from Nationalist leaders, in particular Seamus Mallon, Deputy Leader of the S.D.L.P., and repeated representations by clerical leaders, most notably Cardinal O'Fiaich, on May 24, 1984, Mr John Stalker, Deputy Chief Constable of Greater Manchester, was appointed to head an eight man team of detectives investigating reports of an R.U.C. 'Shoot to Kill' policy in Armagh, which had claimed the lives of at least six people in the preceding months. His report was handed over to Sir John Hermon on September 18, 1985, and little was heard of it officially until it was sent to the Director of Public Prosecutions on February 13, 1986. On March 4 it became known that the D.P.P. had asked for further information. Unofficially, however, there was widespread discussion about a series of leaks which held that Mr Stalker had recommended prosecuting a number of high-ranking officers and had severely criticised some of the R.U.C.'s operations in South Armagh. Then, on June 6, 1986, it was officially announced that Mr Stalker was being replaced as leader of the inquiry by the Chief Constable of West Yorkshire, Mr Colin Sampson. He was suspended from duty pending the outcome of an internal police investigation in England concerning an alleged serious breach of the disciplinary code. Apparently this stemmed from a trip he had made to Miami with a local businessman, Mr Kevin Taylor. The same day, he gave a press conference accompanied by his solicitor, at which he stated that he was completely innocent of any wrongdoing and did not know what the suspension related to. British newspapers, however, speculated freely that he had uncovered highly embarrassing information about the R.U.C. and that efforts were being made to silence him. Mr Stalker himself refused to be drawn on reports that the R.U.C. had shown a lack of co-operation.

In Northern Ireland experienced observers shook their heads and recalled the Irwin case. Doctor Irwin's report was eventually confirmed, but not before the North of Ireland Office and the R.U.C. had orchestrated a smear campaign against him, using the fact that his wife had been raped in an effort to discredit him.

The B.B.C.'s *Panorama* programme of June 16, 1986, did a great deal to substantiate fears that Mr Stalker had in fact been 'set up'. The official inquiry found so little to criticise in Stalker's conduct that he was restored to duty—making people wonder all the more why it had been found necessary to suspend such an apparently conscientious officer in the first place. The wonderment was shared by the S.D.P. which held a full-scale debate on the affair at its Harrogate conference on September 16, 1986. Not surprisingly, Stalker subsequently found the atmosphere in the police force uncongenial and retired. He has since done well for himself through activities as diverse as writing a book, *Stalker*, TV appearances, and acting as a security consultant to a football team. Nevertheless, as he has said himself publicly many times on both sides of the Atlantic, he would have preferred to continue working as a police officer because: 'It's what I do best.'

Apart from the immediate publicity attracted by the hunger strikes, a series of escape attempts ensured that the prisoners remained the focus both of tension and media attention. In the 1980s prisons in both the Republic and the North flickered into the headlines briefly, as escape attempts were discovered and foiled, not unusual for a movement which during the first five years after internment dug so many tunnels under Long Kesh—more than two hundred of them—that it was afterwards revealed (*Irish Press*, September 26, 1983) that had the tunnelling continued, there was a real danger of the place collapsing. The tunnel diggers were apparently defeated by underground sound detectors and infra-red cameras mounted on helicopters, but in a manner typical of the I.R.A.'s method of coping with its enemies' technological advances—shown also in the armament field, for example in the case of the Newry home-made mortar attack—they went back to the drawing board and succeeded in 'springing' thirty-eight prisoners on September 22, 1983. This break-out had, and still has, a significant effect on the I.R.A. because of its scale and the calibre of the men who were thus released back into the Movement.

The escape took some four months to plan. The prisoners made a virtue out of necessity, using the work which had been enjoined on them by the hunger strike and visiting the workshops to gather intelligence on the prison layout, becoming so diligent in cleaning duties that often they were found polishing and scrubbing areas normally out of bounds. H Block 7 was chosen as the wing for the escape because the adjoining block was being renovated and its gates were deserted. Six handguns fitted with silencers were smuggled into the prisoners. Armed with these, and led by Brendan McFarlane, who had succeeded Bobby Sands as the prisoners' leader, at 2.15 p.m. on a quiet Sunday afternoon prisoners moved into the central accom- modation block of H Block 7, on the pretext of cleaning out the store and the Medical Officer's office. Within half an hour they had the block under control and were scanning files both to gain information and to destroy anything which might lead to their identification and capture. They climbed into a lorry which had brought supplies to the prison, one keeping a gun on the driver. They cruised effortlessly through the first two security gates and stopped at the van pool near a lodge at a prison exit, where they encountered about a score of warders coming on duty, stopped and attempted to hold them up. Fierce fighting broke out. Some of the prisoners had knives as well as guns and the warders were armed with truncheons. One warder was stabbed to death, five others received stab wounds and a man on each side was shot. The prisoners had intended to drive out of jail but the exit was blocked by warders' cars, so they made off on foot across the fields.

Some hijacked cars, others hid in barns or took over houses. Several were captured or, like Seamus McElwaine (shot on April 24, 1985), killed in subsequent encounters with the security forces. One of the saddest cases was that of Kieran Flemming, aged 24. He had spent more than a quarter of his life in jail after being imprisoned for an indefinite period in 1976 for his part in an ambush which resulted in the death of policewoman Linda Baggley. His colleagues told me that he was badly hurt in the swirling bludgeoning that broke out in the van pool, and had to be urged on by his comrades to face the second bout of fighting that broke out at the blocked prison gate, where he again suffered injury. He escaped and recovered from his wounds, but while on active service on a cold sleety day on December 2, he and a colleague, Anthony MacBride, ran into an S.A.S. patrol near Beleek, Co. Cavan, close to the Border. MacBride and a soldier were killed and Flemming escaped, only to find his route barred by the River Bannagh on the Fermanagh side of the Border. He suffered from a fear of the water, and often had nightmares about drowning, a colleague told me. With the S.A.S. behind and the river ahead he made an attempt to cross, but drowned, probably out of shock and horror.

The escape was both a body-blow to the Northern authorities and a corresponding lift to the I.R.A.'s morale. Following an enquiry conducted on behalf of the Government by Sir James Hennessy, the prison Governor, Mr Ernest Whittingham, resigned. He was replaced by the formidable figure of Mr Stanley Hillditch who had governed the prison during the grim days of the hunger strike. It was felt in many quarters that others should have followed Mr Whittingham at the political level but neither Mr Prior nor Mr Nicholas Scott, the North's prison Minister, acceded to the resignation calls from enraged Unionists and prison officers.

Apart from morale, the I.R.A. gained from the expertise of the men released. Brendan MacFarlane in prison in Holland, fighting attempts to extradite him back to Ireland, speedily acquired folk hero status within the Republican Movement. He has been credited—whether correctly or not is a matter for conjecture—with being the brains behind almost every noteworthy I.R.A. activity to occur subsequent to his escape, and something of the calibre of the others may be judged from the following potted history of their careers to the date of their escape.

Kevin Barry Artt (24) of Madden Gardens, Belfast. Life for murdering assistant governor, Maze prison, Mr Albert Miles, 1978, convicted in Christopher Black 'Supergrass' trial.

Brendan McFarlane (31) of Ardoyne, Belfast. Life for murdering five people in a bomb attack on Shankill Road bar, in 1976. Succeeded Bobby Sands as prison leader during the hunger strike.

Hugh Joseph Corey (27) of Moneymore, Co. Derry. Life for murdering part-time U.D.R. man in 1976.

Terence Damien Kirby (27) of Andersonstown, Belfast. Life for murdering 77-year-old garage owner, William Creighton, in 1976.

Seamus Joseph Clarke (27) of Holmdene Gardens, Belfast. Life for murdering five people in Shankill Road bar explosion.

Kieran Gerard Flemming (23) of Nelson Drive, Derry. Indefinite sentence for murdering, when he was a minor, policewoman Linda Baggley in an ambush in 1976.

Anthony McAllister (25) of New Barnsley, Belfast. Life for murdering a soldier in 1979.

Seamus Turlough McElwaine (22) of Knockna Cullion, Co. Monaghan. Life for murdering a U.D.R. man and R.U.C. Reserve Constable in 1980.

Anthony Edward Kelly (22) of Garvan Place, Derry. Indefinite sentence for murdering as a minor—an R.U.C. Reserve Constable in 1976.

Brendan James Mead (25), of Rockdale Street, Belfast. Life in 1980 for his part in the murder of a U.D.A. man.

James Joseph Smyth (38) of Ladbrooke Drive, Belfast. Jailed for 20 years in 1978 for the attempted murder of a prison officer, possession of illegal documents.

Gerard Patrick McDonnell (32) of Rockmount Street, Belfast. Jailed for 16 years in 1978 for having bomb-making material and illegal documents.

Robert Peter Russell (25) of Springhill Crescent, Belfast. Jailed for 20 years for the attempted murder of an R.U.C. superintendent in Belfast in 1978.

Dermot Joseph McNally (26) of Lurgan. Life in 1977 for causing explosions and other serious crimes.

Gerard Kelly (30) of Moyard Crescent, Belfast. Life in 1973 for his part in the Old Bailey bomb blast. He and the Price sisters, Dolores and Marian, were transferred from English prisons to Long Kesh in 1975.

Dermot Finnucan (22) of Buncrana Gardens, Belfast. Jailed for 18 years for possessing arms used in a murder bid on an Army patrol in 1981.

Paul Brennan (30) of Flenalina Park, Belfast. Jailed for 16 years in 1977, for having a bomb.

Paul Anthony Kane (28) of Nortwick Drive, Belfast. Jailed for 18 years on evidence given by Christopher Black of attempted murder and having firearms.

Patrick Oliver McKearney of Moy. Jailed for 14 years in 1981 for having a loaded gun.

Patrick John McIntyre (25) of Letterkenny. Jailed for 15 years for murdering a U.D.R. man.

James Pius Clarke (27) of Letterkenny. Jailed for 18 years for attempted murder in June 1979.

Gerard John Friers (24) of Ardmonagh Gardens, Belfast. Jailed for 14 years in 1981 for having a lorry bomb near Dungannon.

Sean McGlinchy (27) of Balaghy. Life for murdering six people in car bomb explosions in Coleraine in 1973.

William Gerard Gorman (24) of Carlisle Road, Belfast. Indefinite sentence, as a minor in 1980, for murdering a policeman in 1974.

James Joseph Burns (34) of Lenadoon, Belfast. Jailed for a minimum of 30 years for murdering a man at Suffolk.

Henry Harrison Murray (35) of Lenadoon, Belfast. Life in December 1979, minimum 30 years, for murdering an R.U.C. man.

Peter Christopher Hamilton (29) of Butler Street, Ardoyne. Life for murdering five people in a Shankill Road bar in 1975.

Robert Kerr (27) of Pim Street, Belfast. Life in 1979 for killing a woman civilian searcher, and a soldier at city centre security gates.

James Gary Roberts (24) of Riverdale Park Drive, Belfast. Indefinite sentence, as a minor, for murdering a 64-year-old grandfather in a Dunmurray pub.

Dennis Martin Cummings (31) of Stewardstown. Life for murder.

Edward Joseph O'Connor (24) of no address. Life for murder.

James Patrick McCann (27) of Andersonstown. Jailed for 25 years in 1977 for the attempted murder of soldiers and policeman.

James Gerard Donnelly (21) of Ardoyne. Jailed for 15 years for conspiracy to murder, and other offences on evidence of informer Black.

Marcus Laurence Murray (22) of Lisnaskea. Jailed for 20 years for conspiracy to murder, and possession of firearms.

Martin Gerard McManus (27) of Moyard Crescent, Belfast. Jailed for 15 years in 1979 for possessing guns and ammunition.

Robert Storey (27) of Riverdale, Belfast. Jailed for 18 years, for the attempted murder of soldiers.

Joseph Simpson (30) of Gweedore Park, Belfast. Jailed for 20 years in 1981 for the attempted murder of policeman and possessing incendiaries.

32

THE I.N.L.A.: 1980–93

The history of the I.N.L.A. in the five years from 1980–85 was largely that of one man, the extraordinary Dominic McGlinchey, who acquired a latterday Ned Kelly reputation largely through his habit of stripping Gardai of their uniforms after hold-ups.

McGlinchey had a strong Republican background. He was the third eldest of a family of eleven, of whom one brother, Sean, is currently serving a life sentence for a bombing in Coleraine; another, Paul, got a fourteen-year sentence for attempted murder; and at the time of his capture on St Patrick's Day (March 17) in 1984, his brother Michael had been sentenced for I.R.A. membership. McGlinchey, labelled by the media as 'Ireland's Most Wanted Man' or 'Mad Dog', was leader of the I.N.L.A. and, on his own admission, a killer thirty times over with some two hundred 'active service' operations behind him before his arrest by Gardai in Co. Clare. His road to notoriety began, as did that of so many other young I.R.A. activists of the time, with internment. He was picked up at the age of seventeen in Bellaghy, Co. Derry, during the fatal August of 1971, and for five days sustained the sort of treatment which, as I have indicated, led to Britain's being arraigned before the Bar of Europe. During the next ten months he was held in Ballykelly Camp, Magilligan, and finally Long Kesh, the 'Republican University'.

Prior to his incarceration McGlinchey had taken no interest in politics beyond attending any Civil Rights marches which occurred in his area, but when he was released in the summer of 1972, by order of the then Secretary of State for Northern Ireland, William Whitelaw, he embarked on the course of conduct which gained him notoriety.

The year after his release he was back inside again, this time for eighteen months, having been one of the first to be tried by the 'Diplock' courts, for possession of arms. The sentence served, he joined up with another another young man, Francis Hughes, who had become active in the I.R.A. after getting a bad beating from soldiers one evening at a road block. Hughes was destined to be the second man to die in the Long Kesh hunger strike, after Bobby Sands. With a third South Derry Provo, Ian Milne, (subsequently imprisoned in Long Kesh) they became a legend, so much so that the R.U.C. took the unprecedented step of issuing 'wanted' posters for them, categorising a long list of murders, shootings, bombings and hijackings, which they had perpetrated by 1976. However, it was not the R.U.C. but the Gardai who captured McGlinchey in November, 1977, on charges of hijacking a Garda car, resisting arrest and threatening a Garda with a gun, and he was not released until February 1982.

Given the temper of the Southern courts at the time, the question of extraditing him back to the North did not arise. Nor did the question of his going back to the I.R.A., as in jail he had clashed with the leadership. Prior to going to Portlaoise he had been Operations Officer for South Derry; now he assumed the same position for the I.N.L.A. and in less than six months became its Chief-of-Staff. At the time the organisation was riven by feuding, which in some cases had resulted in deaths (I have been told of at least four such killings), and was based mainly in Dublin and Belfast. McGlinchey stopped the feuding, ruthlessly it is said, and built up the organisation throughout the country, so that cells started operating from South Armagh, South Down, Tyrone, Louth, Donegal and many other places. There were several robberies in the North and South during his time as Chief-of-Staff, two of which in Cork netted over £300,000, and by the end of 1982, his first year in office, the I.N.L.A. had claimed responsibility for the deaths of twenty members of the British security forces.

McGlinchey did not plant the bomb in the Droppin' Well Inn at Ballykelly, Co. Down, which killed eleven soldiers and six civilians in December, 1982, but he admitted to being 'involved' in the attack and argued that prior to the incident there had been six warnings about soldiers using the pub.

In 1983 a number of Catholics in the Portadown area were shot by members of the U.D.R., who afterwards boasted openly not only that they had committed the murders, but that they would continue to kill other members of the dead men's families. One family warned the police that unless action was taken something drastic would occur. Nothing happened, so the brother of the dead man contacted the I.N.L.A. leader, McGlinchey, and requested a weapon with which to kill a known U.V.F. man. He was given a Ruger semi-automatic rifle but, clearly deranged by the death of his brother, used it instead to attack the Darkley Gospel Hall, where he shot three church elders and wounded people later described by McGlinchey as 'entirely innocent hill-billy folk'. After the massacre, the man again warned the police that unless they took action, 'what happened at Darkley Hall will look like a picnic'. This time, arrests followed.

Other 'innocent folk' were killed as a result of McGlinchey's campaign. For instance, in June, 1982, a sixteen-year-old boy's head was blown off when an I.N.L.A. bomb went off on the back of a parked motor-bike, and in September of that year, a nail bomb claimed the life of a British soldier in the Divis Flats complex and also killed two children. But McGlinchey, who felt the need to explain himself to the media after the Darkley shooting, said that 'never at any time have I killed or been responsible for killing civilians'. He said of his victims, be they U.D.R., Army or R.U.C. 'they are agents of an oppressive and violent state'. Where the Gardai were concerned, apart from repeatedly holding them up and taking their uniforms, he operated a Standing Order No. 8 policy.

'I genuinely wish,' he said, 'that there were other ways of dealing with repression, but I believe it is the only way. Therefore I do what has to be done and don't think about it thereafter. I take no pleasure whatever in it as some people would like to suggest.'

McGlinchey has admitted to planting several bombs personally, at Magherafelt, Toomebridge, Bellaghy, Portglenone, Castledawson, Ballymena, and many other places. He said of his *modus operandi* when shooting someone: 'I like to get close to minimise the risk for myself. It's usually just a matter of getting in first and by getting in close you put your man down first . . .'

In the midst of this lurid career he managed to get married (on July 5, 1975, at Toomebridge) to Mary O'Neill, with whom he had two sons, Declan and Dominic. His career ended, temporarily at least, when Gardai surrounded a cottage near Newmarket-on-Fergus, Co. Clare. McGlinchey was captured after a fierce shootout, but the controversy he generated continued.

There were of course extradition warrants against him, and immediately after his capture it was proposed that he be sent back to face charges in Northern Ireland. His lawyers objected to this, and in the High Court Mr Justice Barrington granted a temporary injunction against his extradition. However, although there were a variety of serious charges which could have been laid against him in the Republic, that same day the State made a decisive and successful effort to extradite him. A special sitting of the Supreme Court was held, with Justices Griffin and Henchy sitting in company with the Chief Justice Mr Tom O'Higgins, a former Fine Gael presidential candidate and a nephew of Kevin O'Higgins, whom three I.R.A. men had shot in 1927, thus creating a political climate which forced Fianna Fail into the Dail. Now, in 1984, the political climate was one in which a Fine Gael Taoiseach, whose father (Desmond FitzGerald) had succeeded the murdered O'Higgins in the 1927 Cabinet, wanted to create circumstances favourable to impressing both the Unionists and the British as the Forum deliberations continued. Extradition had long been something stoutly argued for by the Unionists and rejected by the Republic.

After a two-hour hearing Chief Justice O'Higgins ordered that McGlinchey be extradited. He said:

To prove that an offence was political, an appellant must demonstrate that he or she was engaged in what reasonable, civilised people would regard as political activity.

This court is invited to assume that because of the existence of widespread violence organised by paramilitary groups in Northern Ireland, any charge associated with terrorist activity should be regarded as a charge in respect of a political offence or an offence connected with a political offence. I am not prepared to make any such assumption.

McGlinchey, the 'Mad Dog', the 'most wanted man in Ireland', was driven North to face what everyone assumed would be an immediate court appearance on a variety of charges. Back in Dublin the decision was criticised on the grounds that the haste with which he had been passed across the Border indicated a supine attitude on the part of the Irish authorities, who should at least have had the national self-respect to try him for crimes committed against the Irish State before caving in on the important principle of extradition. This controversy worsened as the months dragged by and, despite the speed with which the 'most wanted' man had been extradited, it became evident that the Northern authorities had little or no evidence on which to justify McGlinchey's presence in their custody. It took over six months to bring him to trial, for the murder of a sixty-seven-year-old post-mistress in her home at Toomebridge, Co. Antrim, eight years earlier. The death of Mrs Hester McMullen was what the Pentagon would term a 'collateral casualty' of one of McGlinchey's many raids, and he received life imprisonment for it on Christmas Eve, 1984.

However, the following October Belfast Appeal Court quashed this conviction. Mr Justice Gibson said that the evidence against McGlinchey consisted solely of two fingerprints found on the getaway car and two affidavits which he made in Dublin to resist his extradition. He held that the fingerprints could have been made at any time before the murder and were therefore insufficient evidence on which to base a conviction, and he ruled that the affidavits were inadmissible. Two days after the trial, on October 12, McGlinchey was handed back to the Gardai, just a few days short of two full years after they had first apprehended him. He was sentenced on March 12 in the Dublin Special Criminal Court to ten years in Portlaoise for firearms charges in connection with the Co. Clare shootout. By then the pendulum of public opinion had swung back towards him considerably. The pictures in the papers and on TV made him seem less terrible than his reputation; there was considerable sympathy for his attractive wife and children and, as the Presiding Judge Mr Justice McMahon said while sentencing him, it was to his credit that on a number of previous occasions he had not fired on Gardai while in a position to do so. It was widely felt that had he wished it, a marksman of McGlinchey's calibre could have accounted for some of the Gardai in the Co. Clare gunbattle; he had previously stated that he would never be taken alive. Many people sympathised with, if they did not condone his Counsel's version of events. Mr Paul Callan S.C. said that on the day of his arrest, McGlinchey had arranged to meet his children and had reacted instinctively when surrounded. (One Garda was hit in the shoulder by a bullet when McGlinchey aimed a burst of submachine-gun fire at a Garda car). He continued: 'He is an intelligent man of ability and great energy and, but for the fact that he was born in the Community of South Derry, it is highly unlikely that he would ever be before any court . . .' With the names and the places changed, one could probably say the same about thousands of young men in Northern Ireland, both Republican and Loyalist.

The Chief Justice who originally tried McGlinchey's case, Mr Justice Tom O'Higgins, a neighbour of mine, was immediately placed under twenty-four-hour armed guard; his house was floodlit with detectives stationed in huts at the front and rear. He had once been his country's most prestigious judge, the sort of man one met walking his dog, driving in the district, or occasionally sipping a pint of Guinness; he now became an incessantly guarded hate-object. Eventually he resigned and took up a post in Europe, saying frankly that the strain was too much for him and his family.

During his time in Portlaoise, McGlinchey had asked me to visit him. I found a low-sized, slight, balding man of whom prison and other happenings had taken their toll. Shortly before I visited him his wife Mary had been shot dead as she bathed their two children. I knew that there was considerable tension within the prison, because a man popularly suspected of the murder, Dessie O'Hare, had recently been captured and sent to Portlaoise also. I asked McGlinchey how he felt about O'Hare's coming to the jail. To my surprise McGlinchey answered: 'I don't think that Dessie O'Hare had anything to do with my wife's death.' McGlinchey seemed to harbour no animosity towards anyone, except, to a degree, the R.U.C., who had made such a song and dance about extraditing him and then, having subjected him to the stress of this process, tamely sent him back to the Republic. All he wanted to do was serve his sentence and be re-united with his sons. At the time, though well-cared for by relatives, the children were being subjected to considerable harassment and bullying by loyalist kids.

I was subsequently informed that McGlinchey was correct in exonerating O'Hare of complicity in his wife's death. According to my informant, Mrs. McGlinchey, who had run McGlinchey's operation for a time in his absence, had been shot in reprisal for a killing for which, rightly, or wrongly, she had been held responsible. The dead man's brothers had returned from the U.S., shot Mary McGlinchey, with borrowed weapons, and were back on the plane to America next day. McGlinchey was released in March, 1993, and immediately set about making good his promise to spend time with his children.

Amongst other treats he took them on a holiday to the Aran Islands, the Irish-speaking islands off the coast of Galway. On a Saturday evening, shortly after his return, (on June 12, 1993) he went to a party arranged for them at Darver, near Ardee, Co. Louth. A car drew up which McGlinchey mistakenly assumed to contain Garda Special Branch. He left the children, aged 9 and 12 in the car and went to talk to the occupants. A man got out carrying a machine gun. He moved to cock the weapon and McGlinchey grabbed it. A burst of fire caught him in the head and side, but he succeeded in jamming the gun. The attacker then produced a handgun, but miraculously, though wounded in the head, arms and side, McGlinchy succeeded in grabbing this also. As he struggled, his would-be killer emptied the pistol at him. McGlinchey was shot twice more, but managed to escape into some shrubbery. A second man in his assailant's car called to McGlinchey's attacker, who got into the car and drove off. At this, McGlinchey's twelve-year-old ran out into the road to take the number. The car stopped and the gunman got out and made towards the children, who ran into the house where the party was to have been held.

McGlinchey recovered from his attack and said that it had been carried out by British agents. 'They had English accents and the man who attacked me was a trained man. He was wearing a flak jacket under his coat. They meant to shoot me and the children in the car. Only I made the mistake of thinking they were Gardai, and got out and surprised them or they would have killed us all.' He denied that he was still a member of the I.N.L.A. or its splinter organisation the Irish People's Liberation Army. He said that Republican or Nationalist movements would not have had any interest in attacking him. The only people who would gain from his going 'home to Bellaghy in a box were the British', McGlinchey said.

I simply cannot evaluate McGlinchy's claims. In the murky underworld of the splinters of splinters of the paramilitary organisations it would be a brave man who would say where the truth lies. But a brief look at the fearsome history of the I.N.L.A. after McGlinchey's capture gives a chilling indication of the violence which the Northern conflict has spawned. In 1986, Dessie O'Hare, who already had a long history of murder, and prison sentences behind him, joined a wing of the I.N.L.A. led by John 'Big man' O'Reilly, a man of the gun. The other wing was led by Gerald Steenson, who called himself 'Dr. Death'. O'Hare is thought to have commited several crimes, including the murder of a 70-year-old woman who had been friendly with his family. However, she had a son in the U.D.R., which was enough for O'Hare.

An effort to bring the two wings of the I.N.L.A. together erupted in blood. 'Dr Death' took advantage of a 'peace-meeting' at a Drogheda hotel in January, 1987, to murder both O'Reilly and a friend who had arranged the meeting. Several other killings followed over the next few months, including that of 'Dr. Death', until a truce was agreed in March. It was in the course of the feud that Mrs. McGlinchey was shot (on January 31, 1987). O'Hare took an active part in a number of the killings including that of one Tony McCluskey. Before shooting McCluskey, whom he blamed for 'setting-up' O'Reilly, O'Hare chopped off his fingers with bolt-cutters. He was quoted as saying that he wanted to give him a 'hard death'.

O'Hare, who for a time was the most wanted man in Ireland, was finally captured by Gardai in a shoot out at Minister's Cross near Urlingford in Co. Kilkenney, in which one man was killed. But before being caught he had kidnapped a wealthy Dublin dentist, John O'Grady, and cut off his finger tips in chagrin at not being paid a ransom. O'Hare, 'The Border Fox', is still in Portlaoise, but another splinter group of the I.N.L.A., (from the 'Dr Death' wing') the Irish People's Liberation Organisation is still extant and has continued to contribute to the North's death toll. This brief chronicle of the I.N.L.A. feuding would in itself be sufficient to warrant an end to the Northern slaughter—O'Hare boasted to journalists of being responsible for 26 murders—but alas, it is only a bloody exclamation mark in a much longer chapter of violence.

33

The Green Book: I

As we have seen, the I.R.A. prepared a structural plan based on the cell system which became public when Seamus Twomey was captured in 1977. The report found on him isolated the I.R.A.'s central problem as follows.

The three-day and seven-day detention orders are breaking volunteers and it is the Republican Army's fault for not indoctrinating volunteers with the psychological strength to resist interrogation.

What did not become public was the *Green Book*, an important blueprint drawn up to give recruits the ability both to withstand outside pressures and to constantly keep political goals in mind. While it dealt with all aspects of training and the movement's aims, it clearly regarded the most important thing for a volunteer as being not so much what he carried in his hands, or what shape his organisation took—though such considerations are crucial—but what he carried around in his head and heart.

One of the first documents drawn to every recruit's attention, equal on a plane of importance with the 1916 Proclamation, is the Democratic Programme of the First Dail which met after the Sinn Fein landslide victory in the 'khaki election' of 1918 with a mandate for the whole of Ireland. In the first lecture of the *Green Book* the recruit is told:

Commitment to the Republican Movement is the firm belief that its struggle both military and political is morally justified, that war is morally justified and that the Army is the direct representative of the 1918 Dail Eireann Parliament, and that as such they are the legal and lawful government of the Irish Republic, which has the moral right to pass laws for, and to claim jurisdiction over the territory, air space, mineral resources, means of production, distribution and exchange and all of its people regardless of creed or loyalty.

In the same lecture he is warned:

The most important thing is security, that means you:
DON'T TALK IN PUBLIC PLACES:
YOU DON'T TELL YOUR FAMILY, FRIENDS, GIRL-FRIENDS OR WORK-MATES THAT YOU ARE A MEMBER OF THE I.R.A. DON'T EXPRESS VIEWS ABOUT MILITARY MATTERS, IN OTHER WORDS YOU SAY NOTHING to any person. Don't be seen in public marches, demonstrations or protests. Don't be seen in the company of known Republicans, don't frequent known Republican houses. Your prime duty is to remain unknown to the enemy forces and the public at large.

Being an Irish Revolution, drink of course has to be taken careful note of.

Another important thing volunteers must realise and understand is the danger involved in drinking alcohol and the very real danger of over-drinking. Quite a large body of information has been gathered in the past by enemy forces and their touts from volunteers who drank.

Volunteers are warned that drink-induced loose talk is the MOST POTENTIAL DANGER facing any organisation, and in a military organisation it is SUICIDE.

The recruit learns from Day One that:

The Irish Republican Army, as the legal representatives of the Irish people, are morally justified in carrying out a campaign of resistance against foreign occupation forces and domestic collaborators. All volunteers are and must feel morally justified in carrying out the dictates of the legal government, they as the Army are the legal and lawful Army of the Irish Republic which has been forced underground by overwhelming forces.

The recruit is told that 'the British Army is an occupying force', and the R.U.C., Gardai, U.D.R. and Free State Army are 'illegal armies and illegal forces whose main tasks are treasonable and as such morally wrong, politically unacceptable and ethically inexcusable'. The volunteer is, as we have seen, told under 'Standing Order No. 8' that 'the Southern forces are not to be regarded as targets'. This, as we saw, was an acknowledgement of the fact that times had changed in the Republic and that any other attitude would be unacceptable to the public. The recruit is also made aware of the importance of another tenet forced on the I.R.A. by harsh experience: motivation. Mindful of the splits and informers which grew out of both internment and more particularly the I.R.A.'s own blanket style of recruiting, he is warned:

The Army as an organisation claims and expects your total allegiance without reservation. It enters into every aspect of your life. It invades the privacy of your home life, it fragments your family and friends, in other words claims your total allegiance.

All potential volunteers must realise that the threat of capture and of long jail sentences are a very real danger and a shadow which hangs over every volunteer. Many in the past joined the Army out of romantic notions, or sheer adventure, but when captured and jailed they had after-thoughts about their allegiance to the Army. They realised at too late a stage that they had no real interest in being volunteers. This causes splits and dissension inside prisons and divided families and neighbours outside. Another important aspect all potential volunteers should think about is their ability to obey orders from a superior officer. All volunteers must obey orders issued to them by a superior officer regardless of whether they like the particular officer or not.

This motivation is not merely expected to carry the volunteer through vicissitudes such as capture, interrogation and prison; it is expected to sustain him to the Movement's ultimate political goal—a socialist Republic. It is dinned into him that military action is an extension of political action, therefore the military campaign of the I.R.A. is in effect a political campaign. The recruit is told bluntly: 'people with no political concepts have no place in the Army.' Furthermore, those concepts must be of a particular type: 'All potential volunteers must be socialist in outlook.' The recruit is given a very clear eyed vision of the facts.

Before any potential volunteer decides to join the Irish Republican Army he should understand fully and clearly the issues involved. He should not join the Army because of emotionalism, sensationalism, or adventurism. He should examine fully his own motives, knowing the dangers involved and knowing that he will find no romance within the Movement. Again he should examine his political motives bearing in mind that the Army are intent on creating a Socialist Republic.

Nowhere are the facts spelt out more specifically than in the briefing given on how political goals are to be arrived at by military action.

Volunteers are expected to wage a military war of liberation against a numerically superior force. This involves the use of arms and explosives. Firstly the use of arms. When volunteers are trained in the use of arms they must fully understand that guns are dangerous, and their main purpose is to take human life, in other words to kill people, and volunteers are trained to kill people. It is not an easy thing to take up a gun and go out to kill some person without strong convictions or justification. The Army, its motivating force, is based upon strong convictions which bonds the Army into one force and before any potential volunteer decides to join the Army he must have these strong convictions. Convictions which are strong enough to give him confidence to kill someone without hesitation and without regret. The same can be said about a bombing campaign. Again all people wishing to join the Army must fully realise that when life is being taken, that very well could mean their own. If you go out to shoot soldiers or police you must fully realise that they too can shoot you.

Life in an underground army is extremely harsh and hard, cruel and disillusioning at times. So before any person decides to join the Army he should think seriously about the whole thing.

He should indeed.

'Analysis' is a word which a recruit soon becomes aware of; it figures prominently in all I.R.A. teaching. For, having warned the would-be guerrilla of what he is up against and told him what he is striving for, it is then of course essential to explain how both the 'for' and 'against' arose.

The nationhood of all Ireland has been an accepted fact for more than 1,500 years and has been recognised internationally as a fact. Professor Edmund Curtis, writing of Ireland in 800 AD says that 'she was the first nation North of the Alps to produce a whole body of literature in her own speech', and he is told how the Danes were driven out or assimilated by a people 'whose civilisation was a shining light throughout Europe', prior to the Norman invasion of 1169 with which there 'commenced more than 8 centuries of RELENTLESS AND UNREMITTING WARFARE that has lasted down to this very day'.

The objective of the 800 years of oppression 'is economic exploitation with the unjustly partitioned 6 counties remaining Britain's directly controlled old-style colony' and the South under the 'continuing social, cultural and economic domination of London'. This last led to Irish savings being invested in England 'for a higher interest rate' and many hundreds of thousands of boys and girls from this country had to emigrate to England to seek the employment which those exported savings created.

Another aspect of economic imperialism at work is the export of raw, unprocessed materials: live cattle on the hoof, mineral wealth, fish caught by foreign trawlers, etc. Further, from 1958 on, the Free State abandoned all attempts to secure an independent economy, and brought in foreign multi-national companies to create jobs instead of buying their skills and then sending them home gradually.

'Africanisation' is the word for this process elsewhere. Control of our affairs in all of Ireland lies more than ever since 1921 outside the hands of the Irish people.

The logical outcome of all this was full immersion in the E.E.C. in the 1970s. The Republican Movement opposed this North and South in 1972 and 1975 and continues to do so. It is against such political economic power blocks East and West and military alliances such as NATO and the Warsaw Pact.

It stands with our Celtic brothers and the other subject nations of Europe, and with the neutral and non-aligned peoples of the Third World; it seeks a third, socialist alternative which transcends both Western individualistic capitalism and Eastern state capitalism, which is in accordance with our best revolutionary traditions as a people.

It can be imagined how potent this teaching was (and is) to an unemployed young man in Andersonstown, Ballymurphy or the Bogside with British soldiers patrolling the streets. But as the hunger strikers lay dying, moved by their ordeal and by his own circumstances, such a young man would even more readily accept the fact that:

The position of the Irish Republican Army since its foundation in 1916 has been one of sustained resistance and implacable hostility to the forces of imperialism, always keeping in the forefront of the most advanced revolutionary thinking and the latest guerrilla warfare techniques in the world.

He would accept the legitimacy of linking 'the 1916 Rising, the Black-and-Tan War, the War against the Free State and the new Six-County State, the Bombing Campaign in England 1939–40, the Resistance Campaign 1956–62 and finally the present most heroic campaign of all dedicated to final victory . . .' He would also be moved and recognise grace notes struck in his own day by the description of those dates, albeit with hyperbole as:

The milestones, the battle honours won, the blood-stained trail of sacrifice, imprisonment, hunger strikes, executions, yet with telling blows delivered to the enemy, often in the heart of British imperialism itself, commanding the open admiration of freedom-loving peoples around the world.

And finally, with hammer-blows of moralistic continuity, any remaining doubts he might have of himself setting out to follow those 'milestones' would be broken down with the following:

NOTE: The moral position of the Irish Republican Army, its right to engage in warfare, is based on: (a) the right to resist foreign aggression; (b) the right to revolt against tyranny and oppression; and (c) the direct lineal succession with the Provisional Government of 1916, the first Dail of 1919 and the second Dail of 1921.

Regarding point (c), the first Dail declared itself the successor to the signatories of the 1916 Proclamation when it met in January 1919. Later, in March 1921, it declared that if enemy action reduced its ranks to a minimum, the remaining Deputies should hand over executive powers of government to the Army of the Republic, which would constitute itself as a Provisional Government. In 1922, when the majority of the Dail approved the Treaty of Surrender, and were thus guilty of treachery, the I.R.A. withdrew its allegiance from the Dail. Later that year it recognised the minority of the 1921 Deputies as the 'final custodians to the Republic'.

In 1938 the seven surviving faithful Republican Deputies delegated executive powers to the Army Council of the I.R.A. as per the 1921 resolution. In 1969 the sole surviving Deputy, Joseph Clarke, reaffirmed publicly that the then Provisional Army Council and its successors were the inheritors of the first and second Dail as a Provisional Government.

From that point on the recruit would accept the I.R.A. premise that it was fighting 'a long war of liberation' on the three grounds outlined above. It is then explained that the type of society the recruit sees around him is a product of economic and cultural imperialism manifested in the 'living conditions, life style and political power of the minority in comparison with those of the majority'.

Economic imperialism is evident on every main road and city street of Ireland: in Banking, Insurance, Merchant Marine, the Motor Industry, Mining, Fisheries, Industry in General, I.C.I., Courtaulds, Pye, Phillips, Grundig, Shell-BP, Wimpey etc.; and cultural imperialism, epitomised in the Conor Cruise O'Briens of this Island, has been reinforced since the Treaty sell-out by successive Free State Governments via mass media, R.T.E., and the press and through education.

He is taught that a Republican must fight these and all other forms of imperialism and Neo-Colonialism so as to overthrow the unjust systems prevailing in both Free State and Six Counties.

The injustice of being as an individual politically impotent, the injustice of unemployment, poverty, poor housing, inadequate social security, the injustice of the exploitation of our labour, our intelligence and our natural resources, the injustice of the bloody-minded destruction of our culture, our language, music, art, drama, customs, the inherent injustice of the state repression which is necessary to maintain the present system as a whole.

So long as partition lasts, a unified national concentration on correcting these injustices is not possible. 'We must therefore first of all break the British connection.' The I.R.A. promises a democratic and socialist state:

A Government system which will give every individual the opportunity to partake in the decisions which affect him or her: by decentralising political power to the smallest social unit practicable where we would all have the opportunity to wield political power both individually and collectively in the interests of ourselves and the nation as a whole. Socially and Economically we will enact a policy aimed at eradicating the Social Imperialism of today, by returning the ownership of the wealth of Ireland to the people of Ireland through a system of co-operativism, worker ownership, and control of industry, Agriculture and the Fisheries.

Culturally we would hope to restore Gaelic, not from the motivation of national chauvinism but from the viewpoint of achieving with the aid of a cultural revival the distinctive new Irish Socialist State: as a Bulwark against imperialist encroachments from whatever quarter. Internationally our alignment would hopefully be with the progressive Governments or former colonies like ourselves with the dual purpose of mutual advantage and of curbing the endeavours of imperialistic military and economic power blocs throughout the world.

In order to achieve the long-term goal of the Democratic Socialist State every member of the Movement is urged to concentrate on short-term objectives which might be accomplished en route to the long-term goal.

A new recruit's immediate obstacle is the removal of his (her) ignorance about how to handle weapons, military tactics, security, interrogations etc. An O.C.'s might be how to put a unit on a military footing; an I.O.'s how to create an effective intelligence network; a Cumann Chairman's how best to mount a campaign on a given issue, e.g. H Blocks etc., and for all members of the movement regardless of which branch we belong to, to enhance our commitment to and participation in the struggle through gaining as comprehensive an understanding as possible of our present society and the proposed Republican alternative through self and group education.

The approach of the *Green Book* is a cunningly thought out mixture of philosophy and guide to action. Each lesson or lecture is in part repetitious, in part a thinking forward to the next stage, a constant preoccupation with the problem of how to win friends and influence people while at the same time killing others and setting off explosions. The basic formula chosen to deal with this lethal paradox is 'get your defensive before your offensive'. This is explained to the recruit thus:

Before we go on the offensive politically or militarily we take the greatest defensive precautions possible to ensure success, e.g. we do not advocate a United Ireland without being able to justify our right to such a state as opposed to partition; we do not employ revolutionary violence as our means without being able to illustrate that we have no recourse to any other means. Or in more everyday simple terms: we do not claim that we are going to escalate the war if we cannot do just that; we do not mount an operation without first having ensured that we have taken the necessary defensive precautions of accurate intelligence, security, that weapons are in proper working order with proper ammunition and that the volunteers involved know how to handle interrogations in the event of their capture etc., and of course that the operation itself enhances rather than alienates our supporters.

The book does not hesitate to point out the I.R.A.'s own mistakes in order to highlight this point. It warns about how the enemy can exploit for publicity reasons bomb situations, there having been some horrific cases of bombs going off before buildings could be cleared:

Even the given situations of adequate bomb warnings are exploited which is again our mistake in not having sufficiently considered our defensive before going on the offensive: the so-called Bloody Friday being the prime example. Either we did not stop to consider that the enemy would 'Dirty Joe' us on the warnings or we overestimated the Brits' ability to handle so many operations. But regardless of which is the case we made the mistake and the enemy exploited it.

Other more everyday examples: [the enemy] exploits the mistake of a volunteer who stays in his own home by arresting him; he exploits the careless dumping of war materials by lifting them or, as is the more recent tactic, by assassinating volunteers who return to pick the materials up; he exploits I.R.A.-sticky* confrontations by staying out of the way to allow the subsequent detrimental publicity and effect on support to run its course; he exploits I.R.A.-Loyalist confrontations by moving in behind the I.R.A. unit and attacking it, plus again the detrimental international publicity.

But the recruit is also taught how to exploit the enemy's mistakes.

We exploit these mistakes by propagating the facts. So it was with their murderous mistakes of the Falls Road curfew, Bloody Sunday and internment, which were exploited to our advantage support-wise as was the murder of John Boyle in Dunloy.

The grim flexibility of the I.R.A., which can 'legitimise' a target at the drop of an ideological hat, is contained in the directive on tactics.

Tactics are dictated by the existing conditions. Here again the logic is quite simple. Without support Volunteers, Dumps, Weapons, Finance, etc., we cannot mount an operation, much less a campaign. In September 1969 the existing conditions dictated that Brits were not to be shot, but after the Falls curfew all Brits were to the people acceptable targets. The existing conditions had been changed.

Likewise at present, for example, although the leadership of the S.D.L.P. has proved itself to be collaborationist and thus an enemy of the people. At various stages since 1974 we could have employed the tactic of making them subjects of ridicule by tarring and feathering them when for instance they were members of an Executive which tortured and interned Irishmen, which penalised rent and rates strikers, etc., or when they recently declared at Westminster in a debate on H Block that 'Life should mean Life and there should be no Political Status'. The defensive precaution in the latter example being of course that the people be made aware beforehand that they actually did make such an utterance.

The rule of thumb for all our actions can therefore be clearly seen to be that we must explain by whatever means we have at our disposal why we bomb, why we punish criminals, why we execute informers etc.

In that concluding phase, the 'etc.' can be the most important—and deadly—word. The 'existing conditions' can indicate a chilling range of 'etceteras'. For instance, the businessman Jeffrey Agate was shot because at the time the Secretary of State for Northern Ireland Roy Mason was touring the U.S. trying to attract investment

---

*   Official I.R.A.

to the Province. Sir Norman Stronge and his son were shot and their home burned because sectarian assassinations were claiming the lives of Catholics. The death of Sir Norman, a former Speaker of the parliament of Stormont and one of the Province's leading Orangemen, made the sectarian assassins give up their campaign—at least temporarily. Edgar Graham, the Unionist Assemblyman, was shot because it was discovered that he had been aiding the prisons administration with advice which was felt to be outside a politician's normal term of reference. The Carrolls, a husband and wife who had been 'turned' by the R.U.C., were executed both as informers and to respond to the tactic of 'turning'. Whole categories of people can be declared 'legitimate targets' for a period. During the H Block crisis, for instance, over a score of warders were shot; throughout 1985 and 1986 contractors who either did building work on R.U.C. barracks or even performed catering duties were targets.

So far as the I.R.A. were concerned, these people were helping to 'service the war-machine' of their enemies. And the *Green Book* itself says:

> We do not exclude taking an action which does not completely fill the criteria of this analysis on how to conduct the struggle. Many instances have arisen and will arise again when we have had to step outside these general terms of reference to our immediate detriment propaganda-wise and support-wise. However even in such an eventuality, if we rationalise our action, get our defensive before our offensive, try to ensure that we have an alternative, relatively unaffected area of support from which to operate if the support in the area in which the detrimental but unavoidable action takes place, we are adhering as best as possible under the circumstances to a proper conduct of the war.

The young recruit is left under no illusion as to the power and extent of the enemies ranged against the I.R.A. both from outside and within.

THE ENEMY: CATEGORISE—CURE: The enemy, generally speaking, are all those opposed to our short-term or long-term objectives. But having said that, we must realise that all our enemies are not the same and therefore there is no common cure for their enmity. The conclusion then is that we must categorise and then suggest cures for each category.

Some examples: We have enemies through ignorance, through our own fault or default and of course the main enemy is the establishment.

The enemy through ignorance we attempt to cure through education though such an attempt is obviously futile if we do not firstly educate ourselves. Our means are marches, demonstrations, wall slogans, press statements, Republican press and publications and of course person to person communication. But as already has been stated, we must first educate ourselves, we must organise the protests and demonstrations efficiently, we must be prepared to paint the wall slogans and to sell and contribute to Republican press, Publications and Press statements.

The enemy through our own fault or default is the one we create ourselves through our personal conduct and through our collective conduct of the struggle: the wee woman whose gate or back door gets pulled off its hinges by a volunteer evading arrest and who doesn't get an apology as soon as possible afterwards or more preferably has the damage repaired by one of our supporters; the family friends and neighbours of a criminal or informer who has been punished without their being informed why. In brief our personal conduct as well as our conduct of our Republican activities must be aimed at if not enhancing support, at least at not creating enemies unnecessarily.

The establishment is all those who have a vested interest in maintaining the present status quo in politicians, media, judiciary, certain business elements and the Brit war machine comprising, the Brit Army, the U.D.R., R.U.C. (r) [reserve], Screws, Civilian Searchers. The cure for these armed branches of the establishment is well known and documented. But with the possible exceptions of the Brit Ministers in the 'Northern Ireland Office' and certain members of the judiciary, the overtly unarmed branches of the establishment are not so clearly identifiable to the people as our enemies as say armed Brits or R.U.C.

It is our task therefore to clearly identify them to the people as such and again depending on the existing conditions and our ability to get our defensive before our offensive, effect a cure. Execution, as earlier stated is not the only way of making this category of establishment enemy ineffective: we can variously expose them as liars, hypocrites, collaborators, make them subjects of ridicule etc., e.g. The 'Mason—Superthug' poster image, the 'Captain Nervewreck' cartoon strip, the Conor 'Booze' O'Brien pun etc.

If Dr O'Brien did in fact 'booze' to the extent the I.R.A. pun attempts to suggest, he would not have created the body of writing which makes him the object of their propaganda. But as has been said before it is an Irish Revolution, and no opportunity for humour, however slight, can be lost sight of even when summing up something as important as the Movement's strategy (as opposed to tactics).

GUERRILLA STRATEGY: Many figures of speech have been used to describe Guerrilla Warfare, one of the most apt being 'The War of the Flea' which conjured up the image of a flea harrying a creature of by comparison elephantine size into fleeing (forgive the pun). Thus it is with a Guerrilla Army such as the I.R.A. which employs hit and run tactics against the Brits while at the same time striking at the soft economic underbelly of the enemy, not with the hope of physically driving them into the sea but nevertheless expecting to effect their withdrawal by an effective campaign of continuing harrassment contained in a fivefold guerrilla strategy.

The Strategy is:

1. A war of attrition against enemy personnel which is aimed at causing as many casualties and deaths as possible so as to create a demand from their people at home for their withdrawal.
2. A bombing campaign aimed at making the enemy's financial interest in our country unprofitable while at the same time curbing long term financial investment in our country.
3. To make the Six Counties as at present and for the past several years ungovernable except by colonial military rule.
4. To sustain the war and gain support for its ends by National and International propaganda and publicity campaigns.
5. By defending the war of liberation by punishing criminals, collaborators and informers.

The greatest threat posed to the I.R.A. is that of penetration either by enemy agents and informers or by the supergrass system. To guard against this threat, volunteers learn tactics such as anti-interrogation techniques, which the *Green Book* concentrates on in particular—an indication of how importantly this is viewed by the I.R.A., and which we will examine shortly. But even more important than the counter-interrogation techniques is the creation of a good self-image on the part of the volunteer, by dinning into him the justice of his cause and his personal superiority to the 'Brit' enemy, who has 'not only the sympathy of, but a degree of control over the elements which largely formulate people's opinions—TV, Radio, the large circulation press'.

While one of our chief considerations in deciding tactics is the concern for our friends, relatives, neighbours, our people in the midst of whom we operate, the enemy is simply dealing with an impersonal, inferior foreigner, a 'Paddy', 'Muck-Savage' or 'Bog-Wog', and with the great added advantage of all the resources and back up of a conventional army, paramilitary police, etc., e.g. M.R.F., S.A.S., plain clothes units, covert surveillance teams etc.

At this juncture the most obvious differences between the Brit and the I.R.A. volunteer, apart from the fact that the Brit is an uninvited armed foreigner who has no moral or historical justification for being here in the first place, are those of support, motivation and freedom of personal initiative.

The Brits support, his billets, dumps, weapons, wages etc., are all as stated earlier provided for by involuntary taxation. His people who pay the taxes have never indicated nor indeed have they been asked to indicate by any democratic means their assent to his being here at their expense.

The I.R.A. volunteer receives all his support voluntarily from his people.

It is pointed out to the volunteer that 'the Brit, apart from the adventurist elements, has no motivation for being here'.

A member of the I.R.A. is such by his own choice, his convictions being the only factor which compels him to volunteer, his objectives the political freedom and social and economic justice for his people. Apart from the few minutes in the career of the average Brit that he comes under attack, the Brit has no freedom or personal initiative. He is told when to sleep, where to sleep, when to get up, where to spend his free time etc.

The I.R.A. volunteer, except when carrying out a specific army task, acts most of the time on his own initiative and must therefore shoulder that responsibility in such a way that he enhances our necessary stated task of ensuring that his conduct is not a contributory factor to the Brit attempt to isolate us from our people.

The threat of capture looms over all I.R.A. activity, even more omnipresent than death. It is a situation from which the I.R.A. can draw either defeat as in earlier confrontations in the Curragh for instance, or victory in death as in the H Block struggle. But capture and interrogation are circumstances for which all volunteers have to be prepared en route to the Movement's long-term objective of a Democratic Socialist Republic, before the actual prison, or rather interrogation programming commences. Immediately before the subject of interrogation is dealt with all that a volunteer has learned to date is summarised in chart form as shown on the following page.

The summary continues:

By now it is clear that our task is not only to kill as many enemy personnel as possible but of equal importance to create support which will carry us not only through a war of liberation which could last another decade but which will support us past the 'Brits Out' stage to the ultimate aim of a Democratic Socialist Republic.

Resistance must be channelled into active and passive support with an on-going process through our actions, our education programmes, our policies, of attempting to turn the passive supporter into a dump holder, a member of the movement, a paper-seller etc., with the purpose of building protective support barriers between the enemy and ourselves, thus curbing the enemy's attempted isolation policy. And of course the more barriers there are, the harder it is for the enemy to get at us while at the same time we increase the potential for active support in its various forms.

The immediate protective barriers are of course, our own security, the other branches of the movement, our billets etc. But we must build up other barriers by championing the various causes in our support areas through involvement in the various enemy structures which have been brought down as a result of the war: Policing, Transport, Bin-Collection, Advice-Centres, etc.

The alternative to our plotting such a course is obvious. IF, for example, we have an area with a unit of I.R.A. volunteers and nothing else: no Sinn Fein Cumann, no Green

Cross committee, no local involvement etc., after a period, regardless of how successfully they have been against the Brits, they end up in jail leaving no structures behind: no potential for resistance, recruits, education or general enhancing of support.

It will be seen from the foregoing that despite all the political and military training and advice, the recruit must be warned that jail is something he will almost inevitably experience. Interrogations are frequently simulated in training to increase the volunteers' awareness of what confronts them.

LONG TERM OBJECTIVE: Democratic Socialist Republic
SHORT TERM OBJECTIVE: Brits out

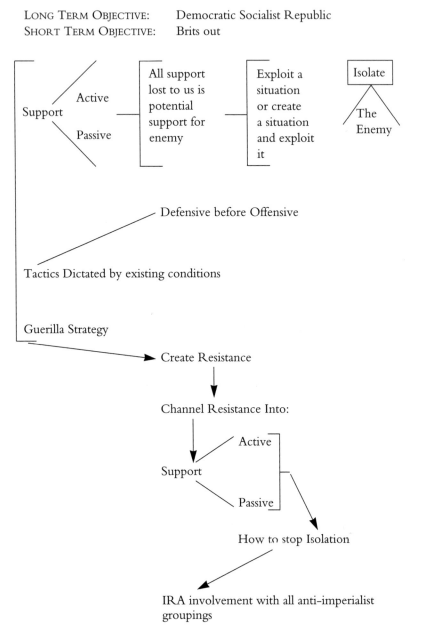

34

The Green Book: II

It is when studying what the volunteer is told will happen to him in the eventuality of capture that one fully realises the commitment of the rank-and-file I.R.A. man to the 'Cause'. The use of interrogation techniques has been documented in a variety of ways: reports by Amnesty, Lord Compton, Judge Bennett; the case brought by the Government of the Republic before the Court of Human Rights at Strasbourg over the treatment of men caught in the internment swoop of August, 1971; and the accounts given by individuals seeking damages for experiences which befell them while in custody. From my own research into prisoners' experiences, particularly for my book *On The Blanket*, I have found that, if anything, the *Green Book* lectures *understate* the horror of what lies in store for a captured I.R.A. man. Certainly whatever makes them face such risks, it is not the £10 a week (£20 for a married man) which was the standard pay in the mid 1980s.

In view of the important light it sheds on a volunteer's conditioning, I am reprinting this section of the *Green Book* at some length:

ANTI-INTERROGATION

I ARREST

Most volunteers are arrested on or as the result of a military operation. This causes an initial shock resulting in tension and anxiety. All volunteers feel that they have failed, resulting in a deep sense of disappointment. The police are aware of this feeling of disappointment and act upon this weakness by insults such as 'you did not do very well: you are only an amateur: you are only second class or worse'. While being arrested the police use heavy handed 'shock' tactics in order to frighten the prisoner and break down his resistance. The prisoner is usually dragged along the road to the waiting police wagon, flung into it, followed by the arresting personnel, e.g., police or Army. On the journey to the detention centre the prisoner is kicked, punched and the insults start. On arrival he is dragged from the police wagon through a gauntlet of kicks, punches and insults and flung into a cell.

What A Volunteer Should Do When Arrested

1. The most important thing to bear in mind when arrested is that you are a volunteer of a revolutionary Army, that you have been captured by an enemy force, that your cause is a just one, that you are right and that the enemy is wrong and that as a soldier you have taken the chance expected of a soldier and that there is nothing to be ashamed of in being captured.

2. You must bear in mind that the treatment meted out to you is designed to break you and so bleed you of all the information you may have with regard to the organisation to which you belong.

3. They will attempt to intimidate you by sheer numbers and by brutality. Volunteers who may feel disappointed are entering the first dangerous threshold because the police will act upon this disappointment to the detriment of the volunteer and to the furtherment of their own ends. Volunteers must condition themselves to the obvious fact that they can be arrested and if and when arrested they should expect the worst and be prepared for it.

II INTERROGATION

After the prisoner has been placed in a cell, he may be left for some time alone. During this lull, police officers, 'The Interrogators', will crowd around the outside of the cell door from time to time, shouting threats and insults, telling the prisoner what they will do to him when they go into the cell.

After some time the interrogators will enter the cell and ask the prisoner to make a confession. During this period he may be subjected to assaults and abusive language, depending on the circumstances surrounding the charge. At this stage he will be fingerprinted and other questions will be put to him, related to the specific charge or other charges. Usually his name and address will be taken, place of employment, occupation, educational standard and so forth. After this he will be again isolated in his cell while his 'interrogators' check his identity, usually with local police, his home and place of employment. In this period of time the police will try to establish his political beliefs, if any, his associates, his police record, if any, and in this way build up a file on him. Most probably 'his associates' and general pattern of movement will give a pretty good idea to the police, if the person is involved in or is sympathetic to a political organisation. Armed with this body of information the police will re-enter the cell and accuse the prisoner of all sorts of activity. If the evidence does not indicate a degree of guilt on the specific charge, he will be accused of all kinds of vague activity.

The purpose of these vague accusations is to implant a feeling of guilt in the prisoner. If, however, the police have some evidence or strong beliefs, linking him with a specific charge, pressure will be applied immediately. This pressure will take the form of physical and psychological torture, most probably he will be punched and kicked around the cell while they scream at him to make a confession, indicating to him that they know all. One or more of the interrogating officers will act in a particular and brutal manner, if they fail to get a confession or an admission of guilt they will leave the cell, telling the prisoner they will be back and threatening him with the most barbaric forms of torture, implying that they extracted confessions from better men than he.

Another set of interrogators will enter the cell, possibly carrying a file with the prisoner's name written on it. They will act quite friendly and sympathetic towards him, telling him that they do not condone the activity of the previous interrogators, that they were mad, crazy and possibly they may kill him when they come in later, they will go to extremes to impress the prisoner of their own sympathy towards him, and ask him to make a confession to them indicating that they do not want the previous interrogators 'to get at him again'.

They will probably guarantee him that if he makes the confession they will not allow the former interrogators to re-enter the cell, this will be coupled with a warning that otherwise they can not guarantee him safety. When the prisoner refuses to confess they will pretend to become very annoyed and disappointed at his lack of co-operation. They may strike him across the face or in the stomach while telling him that he ought to be thankful to them, that they saved him from the previous interrogators and indicating that his behaviour and attitude is a thankless way to repay their kindness.

The interrogators will then open up the file and pretend to read extracts from it, related to the prisoner's past life and activities, even the most intimate and private aspects of his life will be read to him, and possibly a general account of his movements and associates. Most of this information may have been supplied by his friends, employer, school, family, or girl-friend, it may also be 'Pub Talk', local gossip, information supplied by touts or information extracted from other prisoners. This detailed information is designed to frighten the prisoner and to shatter his confidence in his associates and his organisation. If, however, they get no confession, they will leave the cell, but before doing so they will give the prisoner their names and tell him to ask for them at any time he wishes to, again indicating that the next set of interrogators are crazy, drunk, and will do him severe damage, they then leave the cell.

After a period of time another set of interrogators will enter the cell, again these interrogators will be particularly brutal and nasty towards him. They will attack him immediately in a most hostile and vicious manner, suggesting to him that if he did not confess to the former interrogators he will confess to them, they will let him know that they have a reputation of getting confessions from people like him, implying that everyone they met confessed before they were finished with them. The torture used will now take on a three-fold purpose:

1 Physical Torture.
2 Subtle Psychological Torture.
3 Humiliation.

1 Physical Torture

The physical torture will be in the form of beatings, kicking, punching and twisting of limbs, it may even be burning from cigarette ends.

2 Psychological Torture

This will be in the form of threats to his family, his friends and himself, e.g. threats of assassination and threats to castrate him.

3 Humiliation

This takes the form of stripping the prisoner of his clothes and remarks passed about his sexual organs. This period of interrogation may last for as long as two hours or more and at the end of that period they may produce a factual or faked confession from an associate. Failing to get their confession they leave the cell, telling him they will be back and when they do come back they will break every bone in his body.

This process can continue for seven days without a break, the minimum of sleep is allowed and if they deem it necessary, no sleep will be allowed. Lack of sleep causes the prisoner to become confused.

Because of the existing laws which authorise the police to detain a person for seven days, it means in effect that the process of interrogation can continue to disorientate their victim, due in the main to lack of sleep.

Interrogation can have many different phases, depending on the evidence or information which the police have gathered. It is obvious that a volunteer captured carrying out an operation is already seen to be guilty, especially if captured with a weapon bomb, etc., in this case the police have all the evidence needed to obtain a conviction and interrogation becomes unnecessary. Most likely the volunteer will be beaten up in the police stations for what he has done, not for what he knows, if interrogated under these circumstances it will be to get information on the organisation to which he belongs and on his comrades. Another shady aspect directly related to interrogation is blackmail and bribe. When the police cannot obtain a confession they may attempt to blackmail the volunteer, this may be in the form of threats to spread scandalous stories about the volunteer, stories or threats may be designed to hit at the character of the volunteer such as a threat to tell his comrades or his organisation that he told everything or that he had been working for them for years. The other phase of this shady interrogation is bribe. A volunteer may be promised money, a passport and a safe passage to any country he so desires if he co-operates.

THE INTERROGATION—ANALYSIS

The best defence in anti-interrogation techniques is to understand the techniques as practised by police forces. The purpose of interrogation is to get a confession. If the interrogators knew what they were searching for then there would be no need for interrogation, therefore interrogation is necessary only when the police are unaware of information, which would lead to a conviction. The best anti-interrogation is to SAY NOTHING . . . All police forces work from a story suspicion or a clue, therefore when a volunteer is arrested they strive to build that clue on that suspicion and the only way that can be done is to obtain information from their victim. They usually start by questioning their victim, writing down a recording of what he says, comparing this information with information already in their possession, looking for differences which contradict the information previously gained, going back to their victim, pointing out these differences, resulting in the victim changing his alibi in order to suit this difference. The police will again check this new story with other information and again look for a difference or mistake narrowing the prisoner's alibi down until finally it breaks. All of these changes in his statements will be recorded and used as evidence against him, evidence which will without doubt be accepted by the court and so lead to his conviction. This cannot be over stressed: when arrested SAY NOTHING . . . Ask to see your solicitor and doctor immediately and keep on doing so.

DO NOT INDULGE IN CONVERSATION WITH THE POLICE.

After the prisoner had been placed in his cell, we have seen earlier in the lecture how the police had crowded outside the cell door shouting insults and banging on the door. The purpose of this exercise is to frighten the prisoner and so arouse anxiety in their victim. When anxiety has been aroused all natural, rational defence barriers break down or weaken. When this happens the prisoner becomes irrational and becomes more prone to interrogation, in other words an anxious or frightened man is easier to intimidate by interrogation than a cool, calculating person. During the time the prisoner is left alone in the cell, he should: in as far as is possible ignore the police, the threats and the insults and he should marshall all facts surrounding his arrest. He should bear in mind that he can be detained for no more than seven days and he should understand clearly the issue involved, detention for seven days if he remains silent or possibly years in prison if he speaks. Most volunteers speak from a sense of fear thinking mistakenly that if they speak, torture or ill treatment will not be used. It is a recorded fact that interrogators are guided by a simple rule of thumb: 'If a prisoner won't speak he may be innocent and interrogation may be a waste of time, if he speaks a little there is always more and so interrogation is necessary', therefore the prisoner who speaks a little in order to avoid abuse is in effect inviting more abuse from his interrogators who will always assume there is something more. Therefore the best defence is to remain COOL, COLLECTED, CALM, and SAY NOTHING.

We have seen earlier in the lecture how the first batch of interrogators will enter the cell usually insulting, shouting and beating the prisoner. Volunteers should understand that this first batch of interrogators usually fingerprint, ask name, address etc. At this stage a little is known about the prisoner and therefore the task of the interrogator is to identify him positively. Again the prisoner must bear in mind that everything he says will be recorded and compared with existing information in the possession of the police. The purpose of abusing the prisoner at this stage is called the 'softening up period', usually one or more will act in a particularly nasty manner. This interrogation period may last not more than one hour and is only a preliminary investigation. The purpose of using heavy handed techniques and sheer hostility is an-opening for the following batch of interrogators, whom we have seen act in a particularly sympathetic manner.

This set of interrogators, we have seen, acted in a friendly and sympathetic manner towards the prisoner, offering him cigarettes and friendship. Volunteers should be well aware and on guard against this feigned friendship. These interrogators pretend to be sympathetic towards the aims and objects of the movement, going to lengths to impress the volunteer, pretending that they too believe in a united Ireland. They will, no doubt, tell the volunteer that their father or grandfather was in the same organisation and that they were forced by economic circumstances to join the police force and that they are now merely passing the time until they are pensioned off. They will try to convince the volunteer that it is in his interest to make a confession, that they advise him to make a confession to them in order to escape from the previous interrogators who, they claim, are anti-Republican and are not interested in getting a confession but are only interested in beating the prisoner up. The volunteer should understand that these seemingly kind police officers may be acting the tough cop with his comrades who had been or are arrested. Finally we have seen how these interrogators, pretending to become upset, have stretched forward and beat the volunteer about the face and body, declaring that their advice and friendship was being returned or repayed with a stubborn attitude and a refusal to make EVEN PART OF A CONFESSION. This technique is as old as police forces, they attempt to win over the friendship and trust of the prisoner, hoping that if their prisoner falls into that trap he will become upset, not so much at the punching about the face which he received from them but at his own refusal to co-operate: this perhaps is the most dangerous type of interrogation and one which leaves the prisoner in a psychological vulnerable position.

Another technique is called TOP SECRET FILE TECHNIQUE, this involves the interrogators bringing into the cell a file with the prisoner's name printed on it. The police will open this file in the presence of the prisoner as we have seen earlier in the lecture. They proceed to read from this file parts of the prisoner's past life, even to the most intimate details and a general account of his movements and friends, especially those associated with or known to have contacts or sympathies with a political organisation, e.g., Sinn Fein. They also have information gathered from various sources such as employer, neighbours, PUB TALK OR LOCAL GOSSIP. Very often the PUB TALK and gossip is factual, this arises from the volunteer or volunteers in general speaking in pubs under the influence of alcohol, telling close friends and girl friends and boasting in a bravado manner about their exploits and the exploits of others. This type of bravado is POSITIVELY DANGEROUS, not only to the volunteer and his associates but to the Movement in general. Another dangerous aspect of interrogation is 'an associate's confession', this involves an interrogator approaching the volunteer with a signed or unsigned, factual or unfactual confession of an associate. Volunteers must understand, (in the first place) this confession may be a hoax and in the second, even if it is a factual confession of his associate, this confession is not an indication of guilt and will not be accepted in court unless his associate who made the confession is prepared to turn State or Crown witness and is prepared to swear its truth in the witness box. Very often a volunteer may break under severe physical and psychological torture and make a confession, but rarely is prepared to turn Crown or State witness and swear against his comrades. If this technique is employed by the police DON'T FALL FOR IT, it is a trick to weaken the volunteer and so get him to make and sign a statement.

Another dangerous technique employed, is bringing the prisoner who made a statement into the same room as the volunteer who refuses to co-operate, usually they are left on their own and the prisoner who made a statement may try to entice his comrade to do likewise. If this happens to you always bear in mind that you are not alone because the room is always bugged and any talk is recorded. Another important point to bear in mind is when the prisoner who confessed and perhaps implicated you approaches, don't launch a verbal attack on him because this verbal attack on him would be an implication of your guilt, always speak friendly to him and suggest he must be mistaken, that he is ill and advise him to seek medical attention.

Another important point to be remembered and one which is extremely important, DON'T GET INVOLVED IN A POLITICAL CONVERSATION, this technique is a universal tactic and one which recurs repeatedly. When volunteers refuse to make a confession and when all other tactics of interrogation have failed, the police usually, if not always, attempt to get the volunteer to speak on political matters. This is a technique which many volunteers fail to recognise, its purpose is to fling the volunteer off balance, to sound out his political thinking, to break his silence and so make it easier for him to speak freely. This tactic has been used against volunteers and very often to their own detriment. When a volunteer has been arrested and the usual terror tactics used against him, this display of friendship has a weakening effect upon him and can be explained in psychological terms.

As we have seen earlier in this lecture, these seemingly friendly interrogators will give their names to the prisoner before they leave the cell, telling him that the next set of interrogators are crazy, anti-Republicans who are out to do him harm, they will tell him to call upon them at any time he so wishes and they will do their best to save him from brutal treatment. All volunteers must understand and understand in the clearest possible way that no interrogator is his friend, that they are the enemy, the instruments of coercion, the tools of suppression and a more dangerous enemy than the interrogators who will beat him up. These people act a part in a well-rehearsed play, and are using subtle psychological techniques in order to undermine the morale of the volunteer. All volunteers are well versed in brutal treatment as practised by the police and Army. They understand what physical torture means, but now you will have to understand the meaning and application of psychological torture, perhaps the term is an uncommon one, but its effects are far reaching.

We have seen earlier in this lecture how the 'heavy squad' now enters the scene and proceeds to attack the volunteer in a most vicious and brutal manner.

This shock treatment is well rehearsed and is meant to push the volunteer into a physical and mental corner, in other words they hope that their shock treatment will knock the volunteer off balance, and off guard in the hope that he will confess. They will shout statements to the effect that they have a reputation for extracting confessions, that they have never yet failed and that he will not fool them. Now we must analyse this approach, the first thing we note of importance is, the shouting in conjunction with the physical torture, the shouting as we shall see is a more important interrogation technique than the physical torture. Again, why shout? Why boast? Why tell the volunteer that they are experts at extracting information? This shouting and boasting is merely an assurance to the police that they can get a confession, it is the first obvious sign of their own weakness, a compensation for their own shortcomings and all volunteers should and ought to look upon this display as a modern war dance. Just as primitive peoples held war dances, and built totem poles in order to compensate themselves for their own known weakness, so too frustrated interrogators will shout and boast in front of the prisoner to compensate themselves for their own weakness. The best anti-interrogation technique when a volunteer finds himself in this situation, is to look upon the police interrogators as he would look upon primitive people, wearing the head of a dead animal, hoping that by doing this they gain the strength or cunning of the animal whose head they wear. All volunteers should look upon shouting, boasting policemen as they would look upon primitive people doing a war dance.

While the sole object of this frightening lecture is to defeat the British and all British influences, reading the following passage one could be forgiven for thinking that the I.R.A., for all their Irishness, had acquired the peculiarly British characteristic of understatement.

PSYCHOLOGICAL TORTURE

We have seen that this type of torture is widespread and usually in the form of threats to the volunteer in question, to his friends and family, threats to assassinate him, to blacken his character, to castrate him; loss of sleep, poor quality food and continuous noise. This in conjunction with physical torture and the fear of physical torture builds up anxiety and borders on hysteria. All of this is designed to smash down the volunteer's natural defence mechanism, usually a person held for a period of time, perhaps seven days, living in an environment of fear and indecision, constantly being threatened, cut off from all natural contacts, deprived of his usual social surroundings, lack of sleep etc. This can and does, form disorientation and disillusionment: during this period the volunteer will get no sleep or very little sleep, living this type of vague existence for a number of days can leave its mark and deserves an independent lecture.

The sexual overtones of some interrogation techniques are graphically described in a section devoted to humiliation.

HUMILIATION

We have seen that this type of interrogation technique invariably is stripping the prisoner of all his clothes and remarks passed about his sexual organs. Volunteers should be aware of the proven fact that clothes are an important aspect of the individual's character or make up. By removing his clothes the interrogators hope to remove the volunteer's character and make up, psychologically this is symbolic and by doing this the police like to humiliate the volunteer and so lift away the barriers, just as they find barriers preventing them from getting a confession. A person's clothes become symbolic of this barrier and by removing them they hope to remove the natural defence mechanism of the volunteer.

The second part of humiliation is to pass derogatory remarks about the volunteer's sexual organs. This is quite common in all police stations, North, South and in England. Volunteers should attempt to understand the mentality which underlies this act and so be better prepared to meet this angle if and when it happens to them. Just as they removed the volunteer's clothes which symbolised a defence mechanism or natural barrier so too by passing derogatory remarks about the volunteer's sexual organs they attempt to humiliate the volunteer and by so doing to weaken his will to resist. The mere act of doing this has deeper undertones than one would guess. Volunteers should understand that from a psychological point of view this act is called a penis complex. This complex is inherent in the homosexual and although the interrogators themselves may be married men with a family it indicates suppressed homo-sexual tendencies. When the volunteer realises and understands this proven fact he should not have great difficulty in triumphing over his interrogators. He should look upon them as homosexuals with the immunity of the establishment, as people who become sadistic from the homosexual tendencies which underlie them.

BRIBERY and BLACKMAIL are also discussed with a grim warning for those who succumb to such techniques.

The police sometimes attempt to use blackmail and bribe in the last vain attempt to obtain a confession. All volunteers should ignore this type of carrot-dangling. Blackmail rarely works effectively and can backfire against the police in libellous action and so bad publicity. Bribery never works, despite the fact that a volunteer may be offered money and protection in exchange for information. He should bear in mind that when he is of no further use to the police they drop him and the protection means nothing, for example, Kenneth Lennon.*

To avoid ending up like the unfortunate Lennon, volunteers are finally given some advice on how to make MIND triumph over MATTER.

While being tortured in a brutal, physical manner it is important that the volunteer should consolidate his position, he should realise that it's seven days if he keeps silent, perhaps seventeen years if he speaks. It's no easy thing to dismiss physical torture as a small meaningless thing. It is by no means small and by no means meaningless to the receiver. From time immemorial, from histories recorded as far back as the Babylonian Empire up through the days of Imperial Rome, from the Spanish Inquisition to Nazi Concentration Camps, Free State and British police stations, come stories of how people coped and defeated the attempts of police to beat information from prisoners.

One notable technique was the prisoners' ability to form images in their minds or on the surrounding walls. People who were brutalised found that by directing their powers of concentration away from their interrogators and diverting it to images formed in their own mind they could in effect overcome the physical pain. Some people pictured images in their own mind or in the mind's eye, this picture may have been a flickering candlelight, a leaf or a flower, but by concentrating upon it, by building it and by stabilising it, it seemed to attract their concentration so strongly in fact, that physical abuse became meaningless. This mental exercise is called by some psychologists mind over matter and is said to be a highly successful and invincible anti-interrogation technique.

---

* Lennon was found shot dead in a ditch after the I.R.A. tracked him down—in England.

Little is known of the laws surrounding this technique but all authorities associated with its research maintain that people under severe physical and mental pressure seem to adapt themselves to this state. People without previous experience or knowledge of the subject, but who under interrogation stumble across this technique maintained that it worked but they did not know why.

Again, some people found that by staring at a certain spot on a cell wall they experienced a similar sensation. It may be that the ancient Indian practise of Yoga has close or similar sensations, but one thing is certain that when a person's concentration is directed away from his interrogators he seems to triumph and perhaps torture is a method employed by the police to hold the prisoner's attention on them. This advice should be at least considered by volunteers.

In conclusion, if and when arrested:

SAY NOTHING, SIGN NOTHING, SEE NOTHING, HEAR NOTHING.

But to illustrate just what one has to train the mind to deal with, the most shocking warning on psychological torture is kept until the end.

A technique at present being practiced by the Brits and Police is one of shock aimed psychologically. This involves exposing blown up photographs, usually of dead bomb victims, dead soldiers and policemen and more often than not the corpses of the suspect's comrades. The technique behind this tactic is to arouse emotions of hysteria in the suspect and by so doing to disorientate him temporarily. All volunteers must understand and be fully aware of the anxiety, the shock and the hysteria it can arouse in the unprotected suspect.

By understanding this technique and by looking at it logically and the tactic behind it, volunteers should be ready to meet the situation of that nature, with confidence in the knowledge that its purpose is to shock the volunteer into confession. Another tactic of this nature is throwing the limb or limbs of a corpse into the cell of the suspect. To the best of our knowledge this tactic has been used only once, but successfully, again in the Miami Showband case.★

The best protection while being interrogated is LOYALTY to the Movement. This implies LOYALTY to all YOUR COMRADES and PROTECTION of all members of the Movement. Again commitment to the aims and objectives of the Movement, a deep and unmoving POLITICAL COMMITMENT to the ideas of the Socialist Republic, CONSTANT AWARENESS that you are a REVOLUTIONARY with a sound POLITICAL base, NOBLE and JUSTIFIABLE CAUSE, and a deep and firm belief that those holding you and interrogating you are MORALLY WRONG, that you are SUPERIOR in all respects, because your cause is RIGHT and JUSTIFIED.

★ Members of the Miami Showband, a popular group from the Republic, were ambushed and murdered during the wave of sectarian assassinations (see Chapter 25) in Armagh. An attempt was made to destroy their bus and bodies with bombs.

Part IV
1986–1993

35

The Enemy of My Enemy is my Friend

Legitimate Targets and Shoot-to-Kill

The years that have elapsed since 1986 were filled with incident. An attempt to chronicle all that happened within the present compass would result in just that, a chronicle, a litany of horror, salami of the mind. Instead, I propose to concentrate on a selected number of the major developments of the period; episodes which made world news, or which I know from some involvement of my own to be especially significant.

In their battle against the I.R.A. the British have relied more and more on the talents of the Special Air Services (S.A.S.). Based in Hereford, the S.A.S. are the British Army's elite hit-unit. They are particularly effective when deployed on behalf of friendly sultans in Brunei or Oman—away from the media. S.A.S. commandos are highly paid and trained to an unusual pitch of fitness. S.A.S. men commonly perform operations such as waiting for days in a hole in the ground for a suspect to show up. In this time they will remain immobile, sleeping in wet clothes, and defecating into plastic bags. The suspect, if he arrives, ceases to be regarded as a suspect and becomes a target. S.A.S. men are trained to shoot to kill.

The S.A.S. played a leading role in one of the worst blows suffered by the I.R.A. since 1986 in the village of Loughall, County Armagh, on May 8, 1987. Nine men were killed, one of them an innocent passerby, Anthony Hughes, a Protestant, whose car was fired on by the S.A.S.. The eight I.R.A. men who were killed included at least four senior I.R.A. figures, James Lynagh, James Lynch, Patrick Kelly and Patrick McKearney. Lynch, from Tully, County Monaghan, had done several jail terms, but though released, was on the R.U.C.'s 'most wanted' list. Kelly was the principal leader of the I.R.A. in County Tyrone. Lynagh, the commander of a particularly active unit which, amongst many other operations, is thought to have carried out the 1981 attack on the home of Sir Norman Stronge and his son James, two of the north's leading Unionists, in which both men were killed. McKearney was one of the men who led the Great Escape from Long Kesh in 1983.

The conventional wisdom is that the security forces had an informer close to Kelly and Lynagh—a woman called Colette O'Neill was later kidnapped by the I.R.A. for this reason, but was rescued by the R.U.C.—and that both men were kept under close surveillance as they planned an attack on Loughall R.U.C.

station. The resulting intelligence enabled the S.A.S. to be in waiting as the raiding party drove up to the barracks, shortly after seven p.m. In the resulting shoot-out all the I.R.A. men were killed. Like the curate's egg the story is good in parts. The I.R.A. attack was expected and a shoot-to-kill policy was applied with ruthless efficiency. Indeed it is said that an I.R.A. killing was allowed to go ahead less than two weeks earlier, on April 25, so that the stake-out would be successful.

In this fatal incident a member of the U.D.R., William Graham, was shot dead in front of his wife at Pomeroy, County Tyrone. The link with Loughall was established in two ways. Weapons captured at Loughall were proved to have been used to shoot Graham. Moreover, a footprint left by one of his killers matched that of one of the Loughall dead. It is said that the R.U.C. informer had warned of Graham's intended murder but I do not have any first hand knowledge on this point. What I can say with certainty is that, apart from encapsulating in a single incident all the brutality of the Northern conflict, Loughall was highly significant in a number of other ways.

There was the importance of the I.R.A. unit which was taken out; the demonstration of the existence of the oft denied 'shoot-to-kill' policy on the part of the British; and the manner in which both psychological warfare and straightforward happenstance play a part in the war. History has ingrained into the I.R.A. a deep-rooted fear and detestation of informers. The R.U.C. seek to increase the fears and uncertainties by allowing it to be believed that their informants are more effective than they are in fact. As a result, acting on the principle that just because you are paranoid does not mean they are not out to get you, the I.R.A. are sometimes driven to act in a manner damaging to their own side. Misplaced suspicions are thought to have cost the lives of some I.R.A. victims wrongly executed as 'touts'.

It happened that at the time of the Loughall incident I was acting as an intermediary in discussions between a Republican contact and a high-ranking Dublin Government figure. The contact had been originated by Roman Catholic clergy who were trying to further dialogue between the various parties to the conflict. The process eventually led, amongst other conversations, to the talks between the Sinn Fein President, Gerry Adams and the leader of the S.D.L.P., John Hume. Loughall occurred shortly after I had introduced my Northern contact to the Dublin cabinet member, who asked if I could find out what had really happened. I did so and my contact came to Dublin to deliver his report in person, in my presence. Significantly his account contradicted the official S.A.S. version. As I have known this man for over twenty years and can vouch for both his character and his standing I give its substance here:

The attack on the barracks formed part of the I.R.A.'s overall objective of driving the R.U.C. out of the countryside. A number of other Tyrone barracks had already been attacked, at Ballygawley, Carrickmore, Castlederg and elsewhere. Once destroyed, the I.R.A. targeted, and sometimes killed, building contractors who attempted to rebuild them, regarding anyone who assisted the R.U.C. or the British Army as collaborators. The object of the Loughall attack was to destroy the barracks, not to take life. That is why the operation commenced after the barrack's normal closure time, 7 p.m. Two vehicles were used, a mechanical digger and a van. The digger, holding two of the party, was intended to smash through the barracks' protective fence, after which it was planned to use a bomb, carried by the digger, to blow up the building.

Prior to the attack, the barracks, situated in a predominantly Loyalist town, had been extensively reconnoitred. However, the party—based across the border—which carried out the reconnoitring, used a car belonging to one of the raiding party's leaders. On one occasion it broke down, attracting Loyalist attention. The number was noted and the R.U.C. computer did the rest. It was obvious that the only thing which would cause an I.R.A. man of the calibre of the car's owner to come to Loughall was the barracks.

Heavy surveillance was instituted and by May 8, the authorities were in possession of sufficient intelligence to enable them to ring the Loughall area with hundreds of hidden, armed police and soldiers. The actual killing was left to the S.A.S. who were deployed in and around the barracks a few hours before the attack was scheduled to begin. Five of the I.R.A. party from the van were killed in the opening fusillades. The two in the digger managed to detonate the bomb, destroying the barracks. Then they and the single survivor from the van were captured. All three were ordered to lie on the road and shot dead.

The I.R.A.'s view, said my contact, was that this was 'fair enough', the wiping out of an enemy unit. 'It was war. They'd have done the same.'

Loughall was a short term gain for the authorities. Each of the dead eight's funerals probably drew more than fifty replacements for the I.R.A. and greatly increased support for Sinn Fein. It is difficult to overstress the potency of funerals in generating this kind of support for Republicanism. A month before Loughall, the television screens were filled with images from the delayed Lawrence Marley funeral in Belfast. Marley was a prominent I.R.A. man who had been murdered by the U.V.F. In order to guard against military displays at his funeral, the R.U.C. surrounded the Marley home. But the family refused to take the coffin through the cordons, and after three days the police compromised sufficiently for the funeral to go ahead—followed to the grave by thousands of sympathisers. Once again, the 'funeral factor' was back at work for the I.R.A., reversing another S.A.S. inflicted defeat.

The phrase 'Death on the Rock' covers a triple series of killings, which like a three stage rocket, blasted the I.R.A. on and on into the consciousness of the world's media during March 1988. The phrase had its origins in an I.R.A. decision to extend its European campaign to Gibraltar in the spring of 1988 by car-bombing a changing of the guard ceremony. The intended bombers were three well-known I.R.A. figures, Mairead Farrell, Daniel McCann and Sean Savage. McCann had served two years on explosive charges and though Savage had not been in jail, he was on R.U.C. records as being an active I.R.A. man. Farrell was the most prominent of the three. When I interviewed her in 1980, she was the leader of the Republican women prisoners on a Dirty Protest in Armagh Jail as part of the campaign for political status which eventually led to the Bobby Sands led hunger-strikes of 1981. She was caked in filth and the walls of her cell were smeared with excrement and menstrual blood. Farrell had been destined for a medical career but her studies were interrupted by a ten year sentence for attempting to blow up a Belfast hotel. She never resumed them.

The I.R.A. unit's presence in Spain became known as early as November, 1987, after the trio checked in their false passports at their hotel. The checking requirement had not been foreseen apparently. I am told that one of the documents did not contain a proper passport number, but the subject's social security number or some such. In any event, the Spanish authorities, thinking they might be involved in drug-running, notified Interpol, who informed the British. Farrell's presence in particular led the British to react initially by getting the Spanish to ensure that the trio were closely monitored. Subsequently, at Cabinet level in Mrs Thatcher's Government, a judicial murder was decided upon. On March 2, 1988, an S.A.S. 'hit squad' was flown to Gibraltar with instructions to kill the I.R.A. party.

On March 6, the unarmed I.R.A. unit carried out yet another reconnaissance mission into Gibraltar. They were shadowed to the border by Spanish security who were in radio contact with their British opposite numbers. As in Loughall they drove not into an arrest, but an ambush. They were shot dead on the streets of Gibraltar. This was the first stage of the fatal rocket. The second ignited at their funerals at Milltown Cemetery Belfast, on March 16. A Protestant gunman, Michael Stone, made a grenade and pistol attack on the huge attendance in revenge for an I.R.A. atrocity (the Enniskillen bombing described below). Three people were killed and fifty injured. The third stage exploded three days later, on March 19, at the funeral of one of Stone's victims, Kevin Brady. Two off-duty British corporals, Robert Howes and Derek Wood, were set upon by the crowd who mistakenly took them to be on another S.A.S./Stone mission. The men, who may have simply taken a wrong turning, were dragged out of their car by members of the crowd, stripped, beaten, and then shot dead.

The continuing controversy over the rocket's first stage, the Gibraltar killings, was heightened by the Thames TV documentary, *Death on the Rock*. The programme, for which Roger Bolton was responsible, was screened despite strenuous efforts by Mrs. Thatcher's Government to have it stopped. It highlighted not alone the circumstances of the shootings, but the British tabloid campaign, notably in Rupert Murdoch's *Sun*, against witnesses who had helped to discredit official attempts at a cover-up. Bolton later worked with me on the making of another, lengthier, drama-documentary on the Anglo-Irish Treaty of 1921, which explained how the entire Anglo-Irish problem had come about in the first place. He was at the editing stage of the programme in November, 1991, when the final stage of the Gibraltar rocket crash-landed. The Conservatives announced that, in the review of broadcasting franchises which had been in progress for some months, Thames Television was to lose its licence.

Currently, Roger Bolton is an independent TV producer, Michael Stone is serving life imprisonment, as are some of the people who dragged the two corporals from their car, but the identity of those who shot them has not been established. Nor has it been made known who was responsible for the I.R.A.'s worst single atrocity of the period, the Enniskillen bombing on Remembrance Day, November 8, 1987, which ushered in the a period during which the I.R.A. campaign reached its nadir.

Enniskillen, and its aftermath, illustrates how, even for supporters of the I.R.A., the terrorist line of acceptable targets can be crossed into unacceptability. But it also demonstrates how the Northern Ireland situation generates circumstances that inevitably win back that support for the I.R.A. It serves too to encapsulate all the problems posed for a volunteer, underground army, depending largely on targets of opportunity, stemming from a recruitment of individuals whose emotions can outrun their educational or political attainments. The 'funeral factor' or, perhaps, hatred of the system, prejudice, whatever, may provide the courage and motivation for an attack, but not the foresight to gauge its political outcome.

At Enniskillen there was, as usual, a respectable turn out of Protestants for the annual commemoration of locals who had died in Britain's wars. To the attendance the fallen had given their lives to maintain a way of life, and a set of values symbolised by the Union. Suddenly, without warning, a bomb went off at the speakers' platform killing eleven civilian men and women, and injuring sixty-three others. The inexcusable slaughter caused the unit responsible to be disbanded, the I.R.A. to apologise publicly, and Gerry Adams to declare at the subsequent Sinn Fein Ard Fheis (in January, 1988) that the accidental killing of civilians would have to stop. Gordon Wilson, a Protestant shopkeeper whose daughter died in the blast, forgave her killers and aroused such widespread admiration that he was subsequently appointed a member of the Seanad, the Dail's Upper House.

But the toll of innocent civilians continued to grow. The following December an I.R.A. bomb accidentally claimed the lives of two pensioners and over the ensuing months there was a series of equally ghastly events. The sister of a man wrongly thought to be in the U.D.R. was shot in mistake for her brother. Two Catholics were killed by an I.R.A. bomb set on the Falls Road, where it could hardly have failed to kill 'some of their own'. In July, 1988, the entire Hannah family, apolitical Protestants, was wiped out by a bomb placed not for their car but that of a judge. In all, from Enniskillen to the Hannahs, there were seventeen grisly I.R.A. mistakes, one of them a Dublin nun, Sister Catherine, accidentally caught in a blast that killed four R.U.C. men. It was a time during which the I.R.A. sustained an unprecedented barrage of criticism from London, Dublin and Belfast. A recurring theme both during and after this period was that the I.R.A. were nothing more than an Irish version of the Mafia, Green Godfathers involved in racketeering.

If this were the simple truth about the I.R.A., the movement would have come to an end years ago through lack of popular support. But racketeers do not produce hunger strikers to the death from their ranks, nor volunteers willing to inflict and endure for stipends of often less than twenty pounds a week. The more complex truth about the I.R.A.'s finance is that both in the present era, and in the glory days which led to the setting up of an Irish Republic in twenty-six Irish counties, the I.R.A. has always financed itself by a system of levies. Its theory of banking is based largely upon withdrawals. In the vast majority of cases these levies or subscriptions were and are given willingly. In a very small percentage of cases straightforward extortion has been known to occur, both in the previous and present I.R.A. campaigns. Generally, however, when the I.R.A. leadership has become aware of extortion or theft for individual gain, it has put an end to the practice; sometimes by the horrible punishment of kneecapping (crippling the victim with a bullet in the kneecap).

This is not to say that the I.R.A. has not, and will not, continue to derive funds from highly illegal and reprehensible activities such as bankrobberies, kidnapping and building site scams, but it does so to fund a war effort, not to enrich Godfathers. Of my own knowledge I can state that over the past quarter of a century I have carried out interviews in the homes and families of many of the top I.R.A. leaders. Certainly these very often cramped 'kitchen houses' of back street Belfast showed no sign of affluence, nor did the lifestyle of their occupants. In dealing with the vexed question of the I.R.A.'s finance, one should perhaps keep in mind the axiom of a medical friend of mine who ran a hospital for the treatment of alcoholism. His rule of thumb about patients' consumption levels was to believe: 'half what the wife says he drinks and twice what he says.'

The period of the I.R.A.'s 'mistakes' was horrific, but instructive; for despite the outrage generated by the I.R.A.'s blunders, that generated by the authorities' S.A.S.-type response and the continuing bending of the rules of the judicial system enabled the I.R.A. to survive. Indeed, not alone to survive their mistakes, but to deliberately perpetrate fresh horrors: the introduction of the repulsive proxy bomber tactic. This, mercifully short-lived, initiative consisted of forcing people to drive bombs to targets by threatening their families. It reached its peak on October 24, 1990, when the I.R.A. tied three alleged informers to the seats of trucks and compelled them to drive the lethal vehicles to British Army installations. One terrified, screaming, but inarticulate, driver failed to communicate his mission to puzzled soldiers and the resultant explosion claimed seven lives including his own.

However, coming against the background of all that had gone before, the continuing impact of Loughall and Gibraltar helped to level up the sympathy scales on the one hand, while on the other, episodes such as shooting down a helicopter at Crossmaglen, in June, 1988, or blowing up a bus killing eight soldiers at Ballygawley, County Tyrone in August, showed the I.R.A. to be engaged in a military campaign, not indiscriminate murder. One incident I know of may be cited as attesting to the depth of support for the I.R.A. that exists in some areas of Northern Ireland.

Kevin Barry O'Donnell, aged 21, was one of four I.R.A. men ambushed and killed by the S.A.S. in a shoot-to-kill operation at St. Patrick's Church near Coalisland, County Tyrone. (The others were Sean O'Farrell, 23, Peter Clancy, 19, and Daniel Patrick Vincent, 20.) They had driven to the Church, as part of their pre-arranged getaway plan, after shooting up Cookstown R.U.C. barracks. A year earlier, O'Donnell had been cleared of arms charges at the Old Bailey in London. Somehow he convinced a jury that the rifles found in the boot of a car he was driving had been put there without his knowledge. During the period following his arrest, a source of mine in Tyrone, who has I.R.A. contacts, was approached several times on O'Donnell's behalf by lads who knew him, either as a neighbour, or who had played football with him. None of them were in the I.R.A. themselves, but they wanted my source to find out from the I.R.A. what O'Donnell was doing with the rifles and to let it be known that they would complete the mission for him.

Of course on the Unionist side of the war, that admiration is paralleled by an equally intense detestation. The importance of Unionist outrage had been demonstrated the month before O'Donnell and the others were shot when the I.R.A. blew up a van at Teebane, County Tyrone, on January 17, 1992. It had been taking Protestant workers from an Army base. Seven were killed, seven more terribly injured.

The Northern Ireland Secretary, Peter Brooke, who had impressed most people, in the Republic at least, as a decent man, had earlier agreed to appear on Dublin's *Late Late Show*, the State's most popular TV programme. Once on he yielded to the urging of Gay Byrne, the show's star, to sing his party piece, 'My Darling Clementine'. Unionist politicians chose to regard the singing, a few hours after the blast, as a calculated insult and called for his sacking. Along with Clementine, another British political reputation had fallen into the foaming brine of Anglo-Irish relationships. For although initially backed by John Major, the British Prime Minister, who refused to accept his resignation, Brooke went in a Cabinet reshuffle which followed the Tory general election victory on April 9, 1992. He was replaced by Sir Patrick Mayhew, a plummy traditional Tory with a quiff and a pinstripe. As Attorney General he had alienated Nationalists by his refusal to prosecute R.U.C. personnel alleged to have been involved in shoot-to-kill incidents. The man John Major wanted to send to Belfast, and who wanted the job, was the likeable, and intelligent, Chris Patten, who had experience of working in the Tories' Six County team. However, he lost his seat in Parliament in the general election. Appropriately enough, a place was found for him as Governor of Hong Kong, smoothing the path for eventual British withdrawal.

Mayhew's equally plummy and pin-striped colleague, who was awarded the Northern Ireland Defence portfolio, aroused Nationalists' sense of humour, but not their enthusiasm. Michael Mates, a former Colonel, had served with the Army in Northern Ireland. It was also noted that he shared a surname with that of the largest selling brand of condoms in the Six Counties, a new definition of a security posting! Mates' career was short and characterised by a series of bloopers. He was ultimately forced to resign in June, 1993, not over matters Irish, but because of his involvement with Asil Nadir, a businessman who jumped bail in England while awaiting trial on fraud charges.

The comings and goings of British politicians made no impact on the I.R.A. A new type of bombing campaign was introduced in Northern Ireland and activities were not alone stepped up on the U.K. mainland, but extended to take in British targets in Continental Europe. As stocks of semtex were used up, the Provos reverted to making bombs out of fertiliser and sugar, and launched an economic war, not against personnel, but against commercial targets. A Press Association report, dated July 6, 1993, stated that it was estimated that the bill for 1990–93 would be £200 million. A Unionist M.P., David Trimble, complained to the newspapers (*Irish Independent*, January 20, 1992) that there were fertiliser plants in the Republic manufacturing fertiliser with a higher potential explosive content than those in the North. He wanted the authorities to confirm that it was Republican fertiliser, not the Unionist variety which was causing the damage!

Wherever it came from, huge fertiliser bombs, sometimes weighing over a ton, were systematically employed to destroy whole commercial districts right across the province. The bombs caused havoc in Belfast, where targets included the Opera House and the much targeted Europa Hotel, both of which were regarded by the authorities as showpieces of the 'Normalisation Policy'. But the bombers also caused devastation outside the city in a range of towns chosen to indicate that the I.R.A. could strike at will across the Six Counties: Lurgan, Coleraine, Bangor, Portadown, Magherfelt and Newtownards. Sometimes the fertiliser bombs were alternated with firebombing devices which were used to destroy individual shops. Miraculously no lives were lost in the commercial blitz.

The same could not be claimed for the I.R.A. campaign in England. An I.R.A. man deliberately shot a prowler who broke into his car in London in 1988. The man, Patrick Sheehy, returned to Ireland, took to drink, became depressed and committed suicide three years later. Meanwhile, in 1989, ten Marine bandsmen were intentionally killed in a bomb attack on a Barracks in Deale, Kent. Twenty-one were injured, one of them so badly that he died later. Although they could be considered soft targets, the view of I.R.A. apologists was that they were Marines first and bandsmen second. Ian Gow, the notably pro-Unionist Conservative M.P., was also deliberately blown up by a bomb placed under his car in July of the following year (1990). There were echoes of Gibraltar that September when Sir Peter Terry and his wife were attacked. Sir Peter, who was the more seriously wounded of the two, was a former Governor of Gibraltar. The following month the I.R.A. were foiled in an attempt to give a practical demonstration of the subject at a conference on terrorism held in London at the Royal Overseas Club. A semtex bomb was discovered under the speaker's lectern less than two hours before the Conference was due to open. The speakers included the Metropolitan Police Commissioner, Peter Imbert.

A more spectacular I.R.A. attack was also foiled on February 7, 1991, by the branch of the tree in the garden of Downing Street which deflected the rocket intended for the War Cabinet (see below). But the bombing campaign continued against a variety of other targets: railway stations; that Tory citadel, the Carlton Club; the Stock Exchange. The railway campaign was especially widely felt. Beginning in the same month as the Downing Street onslaught with bombs at Paddington and Victoria stations in London, one (at Victoria) killed a man when police disregarded a phoned warning. This particular facet of the campaign played havoc with commuters' schedules when, after the Victoria fiasco, the authorities reacted promptly to every subsequent warning with the result that hoax calls frequently halted London's underground.

The 'prestige target' of the 1992 phase of the bombing campaign was the Baltic Exchange in the heart of London's financial nerve centre, the City of London. It seemed that the I.R.A.'s Irish strike-at-will commercial campaign had been successfully transported to England. But on a Saturday afternoon in March of the following year, 1993, it went terribly wrong. I.R.A. bombs planted in a far from prestigious target, a shopping centre in Warrington, Chesire, claimed the lives of two little boys. Again it was an occasion which created a situation in which one could measure accurately the depth of anti-I.R.A. feeling in Ireland and England and the corresponding power of the I.R.A. to ride out the storm.

I visited nearby Birmingham shortly after the Warrington bomb to take part in a TV programme involving a representative studio audience. Both the programme and the opportunity which the visit afforded of sampling opinion in the area were instructive. The audience were in a justifiable state of outrage at the atrocity. But they also showed how British public opinion viewed Northern Ireland. The audience erupted into spontaneous applause on three occasions. Once when a speaker suggested that Sinn Fein should be declared illegal. Again when someone else proposed re-introducing internment and the death penalty; and finally when someone, disagreeing with my proposal that the U.N. and the E.E.C. be invited to play a role, raised the cry: 'Ulster is British.' There was a stony, disapproving silence when I pointed out that, inexcusable as the outrage was, nevertheless; four Catholics in Northern Ireland had been murdered—allegedly by Loyalist death squads—by way of reprisal in the immediate aftermath of the bombing. Were not each set of deaths worthy of sympathy and analysis as to why they had occurred? There was booing and disagreement when I suggested that a political solution as opposed to a security one, was the desired objective. And yet, when I met the audience after the show, they thawed, grew friendly, and were disposed to discuss the problem rationally. But the bottom line was that Mr and Ms British Average do not think about Northern Ireland, or help to form any part of a political consensus on the subject, rather than apathy and distaste, except in the wake of 'the atrocity nearby', when the reaction is likely to be of the knee-jerk variety: no giving in to terrorism. This was, of course, no surprise.

A more telling example of this attitude had come after Ian Gow's death. The Conservatives used his murder to the utmost in the subsequent by-election to elect his replacement. He had been a popular M.P. and the campaign invoked his fate and memory by every means imaginable. Yet, the Liberal Democratic Party obliterated his huge majority to take the seat. British politics are more concerned with bread and butter issues than with the side effects of the Irish involvement. But, for a time after the Warrington explosion, Irish nurses, taxi drivers, waiters, and barmen, told me they were keeping their heads down in Birmingham. The anonymous phone call in the small hours of the morning, and insulting comments about Ireland and the Irish gained a nasty, but fortunately short-lived currency. Shorter at any rate than the more deep-rooted anti-Irish prejudice that exists in some official circles.

In the Republic of Ireland the reaction to Warrington was one of guilt mingled with outrage. Again there was no empathy with the Catholics killed in the Six Counties, but there was an immediate, genuine outpouring of feeling for the stricken of Warrington. Though selective, it was the same sort of decent national response to what one got, or gets, at moments like Bob Geldof's marathon rock concert for famine relief in Ethiopia, President Mary Robinson's visit to Somalia, or even the achievements of the Irish soccer team managed by an Englishman, Jack Charlton. The Irish have a keen perception of national pride. Warrington was not done in their name.

Two remarkable women spearheaded the response. One was a Dublin housewife, Susan McHugh, from the middle class suburb of Clontarf. One day in the wake of the bombing, after dropping her children at school, McHugh decided that she had to do something. Without discussing it with anyone, she phoned Trinity College and secured a room. Then she got on to a live radio chat show, announced she wanted the killing stopped, invited people to meet at Trinity, and launched what turned out to be an enormous, but short-lived, peace movement, Peace Initiative '93. McHugh's generous impulse was corralled by a group called New Consensus, which grew out of the old Official I.R.A. It is suspected by Republicans as being manipulated as part of the British counter-insurgency effort. For a short time New Consensus added an amount of organisational muscle to McHugh's effort and for a moment there was a re-run of the Peace Women Initiative. There were monster rallies in the centre of Dublin, cross-border meetings and much media attention. The mood of reparation and sympathy was heightened by President Mary Robinson, who supported McHugh's initiative and went to Warrington herself to attend a commemoration service for the dead children.

But the moment faded. The I.R.A.'s ability to maintain both its campaign and its support proved stronger than the public's capacity for sustained outrage. While the Peace Movement was at its height, the I.R.A. detonated the most successful and devastating explosion of the entire British campaign. Just over a year after the Baltic Exchange bomb had caused damage to the tune of £350 million, another explosion, at Bishopsgate, on April 24, 1993, ripped the heart out of the financial district for a second time. This time the bomb, consisting of over a ton of fertiliser contained in a parked truck, claimed the life of a newspaper photographer who had been sent by the *News of the World* to cover the alert. It also caused an astronomical damage bill.

Initially there were efforts to minimise this. Insurance experts said that talk of £1.5 billion was exaggerated. Prime Minister John Major, the Chancellor of the Exchequer, Norman Lamont, and the Lord Mayor of London all made public statements saying that the bombers had failed to achieve a lasting effect, and that it would be business as usual for the City. But, as the days passed, and the full nature of the damage became known, it became evident that the final bill could well exceed the £2 billion mark. I visited the scene myself some weeks later and found that the TV and newspaper pictures had not conveyed a sense of the full extent of the devastation.

The confined nature of the city had ensured that the blast had burst along several narrow streets, ricochetting from one building to another. Over a million and a half square feet of office space was affected. Structures hundreds of yards apart had their windows blown out and their interiors damaged. The tallest building in the City, the 52-story Nat West Tower, was badly damaged, and a number of other landmarks had suffered such irreparable harm that I was told they would have to be demolished. These included St. Ethelburg's, a medieval church which had survived the German blitz of World War II.

And the toll could have been far worse that Saturday morning, for two other I.R.A. attacks did not come off when hijacked taxis exploded at Finsbury Park and King's Cross. The drivers had been ordered to make for Scotland Yard and Downing Street, but instead, they abandoned their vehicles and phoned the police. Not surprisingly, after visiting the City, I found webs of scaffolding in and around Downing Street; vast new, and expensive, bomb and bullet-proofing works were in progress. Clearly the British were not pinning all their hopes on Peace Initiative '93.

The I.R.A. campaign in Britain has not been cost free to the movement. Several supporters have vanished into prison for terms of twenty years and more, for either aiding and abetting the campaign, or being found in possession of weapons or explosive. Nevertheless, it has been characterised by a high degree of success. Apart from individual actions such as the City of London bombings, the British campaign carries a special value to the I.R.A. inasmuch as a bombing or shooting on the 'U.K. mainland' draws many times the attention of similar activities in the 'U.K. overseas', as one often hears Northern Ireland referred to in England.

The same is true of I.R.A. activity on the Continental European mainland, where language and logistics barriers have not assisted the I.R.A. in its long running attempts to extend the theatre of war to attack British bases and personnel in Europe. The British Ambassador to Holland, Sir Eric Sykes, was killed as far back as 1979. There was also a bomb attack that year on a British Army Band in Brussels, injuring seven bandsmen and nearly twice that many civilians. But, in I.R.A. terms, the campaign was more costly than the results warranted. An effort to kill Christopher Tugendhat, a British E.E.C. Commissioner, failed. Then the Dutch police put an end to the European operation for a time with the arrests, in 1982, of two prominent I.R.A. men, Brendan McFarlane and Gerry Kelly, both of whom had escaped from Long Kesh.

Five years later, in 1987, thirty people were injured by an I.R.A. car bomb outside the British Army Headquarters at Rheindahlen, West Germany. This bombing ushered in a wave of approximately twenty gun and bomb attacks on British servicemen which petered out in 1990. Three members of the R.A.F. were killed on the same day (May 1, 1988) in separate incidents in Holland (at Roermond and at Nieuw Bergen), in which a machine gun and a car bomb were used. The campaign was characterised by a spate of I.R.A. mistakes. In one case the wife of a British serviceman was shot in her car when gunmen mistook her for her husband. In another, two Australian tourists were gunned down in the belief that they were off duty British servicemen.

Apart from bad publicity, the campaign cost the I.R.A. about a dozen experienced personnel, who were captured by police, and a good deal of money and equipment. It probably also helped to heighten European reactions against terrorism generally and the I.R.A. in particular. Yet, if the campaign did more to underline for the I.R.A. the difficulty of operating away from Ireland, than to further its cause, it did mark a significant step in the movement's development. Also it increased British security costs and, of course, it underlined the fact the I.R.A. had come a long and bloody way from the five hand guns on the Falls Road at the outbreak of the troubles over twenty years earlier.

Though proven unsuccessful by 1990, there is no guarantee that the European campaign will not be resumed.

Even further away were America and Libya, both of which were important to the I.R.A. in recent years. Two incidents, which serve to highlight that importance, also demonstrate how the I.R.A. can expect to be treated differently by a legal system not susceptible to pressure from the British compared to one which is. By the mid-eighties Libya had come to represent the I.R.A.'s best source of arms. Earlier assistance from the P.L.O. had dried up as that organisation came to forge stronger constitutional links with the Irish Government. I visited Libya in 1987, to interview Colonel Ghadafi and was struck by the interest shown in the I.R.A. by many people I met. One Army officer openly said: 'Tell them [the I.R.A.] to come over here and we'll train them.' Ghadafi himself quizzed me about the level of support for the movement in Ireland and made me promise to send him an edition of this book. I later discovered the reason for Tripoli's preoccupation with the I.R.A.: the enemy of my enemy is my friend. As part of his general campaign against the West, and Britain in particular, Ghadafi had turned again, as he had done in the *Claudia* affair, to supplying the I.R.A. with weapons.

The story broke after what would have been the biggest consignment ever, one hundred and fifty tons, was seized off the coast of France aboard the *Eksund* at the beginning of November, 1987. At the end of the month, as information flowed from the seizure, the Gardai began what was probably the largest ever house-to-house and farm-to-farm search that had ever been mounted in Ireland. Tens of thousands of homes were visited. A small number of arms were found, and some amazingly large and well constructed bunkers, but that was all.

The most important seizure was that of two more participants in the Long Kesh escape, Joseph Clarke and Anthony Kelly. However in the wake of the searches, and the subsequent trial of the *Eksund* crew in Paris, it emerged that at least four separate shipments had been landed on the Wicklow coast before the *Eksund* voyage. They constituted a remarkable breach in the invisible and, hitherto, supposedly impregnable screen against such arms shipments to Ireland from the Middle East. (Britain has reciprocal arrangements with various military alliances and intelligence networks, including the Israeli secret service, Mosad.)

The shipments would appear to have amounted to some one hundred tons of rockets, rifles, short arms, hand-grenades and ammunition. Above all they included large amounts of semtex. This light, easy to handle, and immensely powerful plastic explosive added enormously to the I.R.A.'s bomb and rocket making capability in subsequent years. The British were so angered by Ghadafi's lethal largesse to the I.R.A. that he felt it necessary to attempt to assuage their wrath in the wake of the Lockerbie bombing of Pan Am Flight 103 on December 21, 1988, by turning informer on the I.R.A. During British/Libyan negotiations in Geneva in 1992, on the British demands that Libya hand over two Libyans suspected of the bombing, the Libyans instead handed over details of what they knew about the I.R.A. For once the British and the I.R.A. agreed about something. 'Not a lot', was, I am told, the joint verdict on the worth of the information.

When the *Eksund* crew were eventually put on trial in Paris in January, 1991, I was afforded an opportunity of witnessing a factor that adds even more capability to the I.R.A. than semtex—family support. After appearing before the court as an expert witness, I was introduced to the daughter of one of the defendants. Following the arrests she had given up her job in Ireland, learned French, and got herself work in Paris, so that she could visit her father in Fresnes prison three times a week. In company with the families of some of the other accused she attended every day of the hearing.

In the case of the defendants whose case I was called in, the judges decided that the I.R.A. were a politically as opposed to a criminally motivated organisation and the men were freed a year later. Even allowing for the time they had already spent in prison, it was a slap-on-the-wrist sentence which would have been infinitely more severe had they been caught in Irish, English, or, it appears, American waters.

The most controversial American case involving the I.R.A., was that of Crumlin Road jailbreaker, Joe Doherty, who had been an active I.R.A. man since being interned in 1971. After the break-out, Doherty, who was accused of the murder of an S.A.S. Captain*, fled to the U.S. where, under an assumed name, he worked in a New York bar. Eventually the F.B.I. caught up with him and a protracted trial began in 1984. Sean MacBride and I made lengthy appearances during the trial to explain the background to the Irish troubles. The prosecutor, who was instructed by officials from the British embassy, had the appropriate name of Ira H. Block! Judge Sprizzo apparently accepted our descriptions of the origins of the I.R.A. and of the Northern state as indicating that the I.R.A. was a historically based organisation with a political goal, as opposed to a purely criminally motivated one, like the Mafia. The verdict, delivered in 1986, was that the British application for extradition should not be allowed on the grounds that he had been engaged in a legitimate conflict.

However, this did not prevent his continuing to be detained in prison while the battleground changed to a move by the U.S. authorities to have him deported back to Belfast on charges of having entered America illegally. They were ultimately successful, and Doherty was extradited back to Belfast on February 19, 1992, to begin serving the life sentence imposed in his absence. His American incarceration was not taken into account. By contrast, the Irish Supreme Court had decided in the case of two of his fellow escapers that, as they had served ten year sentences in the Republic, they should not be extradited.

The Doherty case provided a focus for Irish-American concentration both because of the nature of the issues raised and because during his term in prison he manifestly matured and became a very different personality to the young revolutionary of the 1970s. The 'Republican University' had produced a well-read, reflective, analytical character who had developed into an independent-minded writer prepared to criticise I.R.A. excesses such as the bombing of Musgrave hospital. A number of distinguished personages visited him in prison, including Cardinal O'Connor of New York and the Irish Cardinal, the late Cardinal O'Fiach. O'Connor publicly took issue with the prosecution's stated belief that Doherty's deportation was desired by the State Department as a matter of foreign policy. What business of the State Department's was it, the Cardinal asked, what went on in the courts? The interest taken in the case by Irish-American politicians—many of whom, as part of their campaign on his behalf also made a point of visiting Doherty—was reflected in the naming of a New York street corner in his honour.

---

* Captain Richard Westmacott, during a shootout in Belfast in May, 1980.

Ironically, what cost Doherty his freedom in the end was an outburst of Republican independence of spirit on the part of Charles Haughey and the Dublin Government. Working behind the scenes, influential Irish-American lawyers like Paul O'Dwyer had succeeded in doing a deal with the authorities whereby Doherty would be sent out of America to a country which did not have an extradition treaty with any of the parties involved. Argentina agreed to take Doherty, but because Haughey had tilted towards Argentina and against Thatcher during the Argentinean-British conflict over the Falklands, which had resulted in an extradition treaty between Buenos Aires and Dublin, this proved unacceptable and Doherty stayed in jail. Accordingly, there was considerable resonance for Gerry Adams' comment to the *Irish Times* (February 20, 1992) on Doherty's being sent back: 'The decision to extradite . . . showed that the legal system in the United States had become a victim of British rule in Ireland.'

The British had earlier scored another notable legal victory in securing the extradition of a native born American, Michael Quinn. Quinn was born in San Francisco and was wanted for his part in the British mainland campaign. He had been in captivity in the U.S. from 1981 to 1986, fighting charges which included the murder of a policeman, Constable Stephen Tibble. Unlike the Doherty affair, the courts held that the British campaign was not legitimate.

Quinn is currently serving a life sentence after an Old Bailey trial whose conduct has also been criticised because the jury were not allowed to hear evidence which would have undermined the prosecution's case.

A friend of Quinn's, Dr Frank Foster, of Santa Barbara, also figured in a case which became a cause célèbre in Irish-American circles. Foster was head of the local chapter of the Northern Irish Aid committee (NORAID) which is often accused of supporting the Provisionals. He refused to allow any demonstrations by NORAID against Queen Elizabeth's visit to Santa Barbara in 1983 on grounds of propriety. However, Foster, who was also a noted civil rights activist in the area, wrote to the Queen prior to the visit to suggest she meet him and some other Irish-Americans for a cup of tea. Dr Foster proposed a chat in which he said Her Majesty would hear views on Northern Ireland which would differ from those she might otherwise hear on her tour! Niall O'Dowd's *Irish America*, a glossy, prestigous magazine, described what happened next (in its March, 1986 issue):

Dr Foster was first arrested in January, 1983, on the eve of Queen Elizabeth's visit to Southern California. The technical charge was for improperly prescribing medication and Dr Foster was to go through a Kafkaesque two years and four weeks in the courts system before being finally cleared.

However, though he won his case, Foster, an Assistant Clinical Professer of Medicine at the University of Southern California, lost both his house and his extensive private practice. Because of the publicity, he was forced to take a job 125 miles away from his home.

In another unusual case Gerry McGeough, a native of Tyrone, became the first Irishman to be extradited to the U.S., from Germany, where he had been held for four years on arms charges. McGeough was sentenced to three years on June 17, 1993, in New York on charges of trying to buy 'Red Eye' surface-to-air missiles for the I.R.A. The judge in the case, Federal Judge Sifton, after sentencing McGeough, then proceeded to grant him bail. He said that in twelve years of dealing with cases involving Irish Nationalists he had always been impressed with their honesty.

Irish-Americans are keen to point to several other examples of collusion between the F.B.I. and the British. All are said to stem from the Reagan/Thatcher relationship which President Bush continued with. One of the most notable examples involved an admitted F.B.I. 'sting' which put three supporters of the I.R.A. behind bars in Florida in 1990. They are Kevin McKinley, Seamus Moley and Joe McColgan. The F.B.I. approached them with an offer to sell a Stinger missile, 'the war winner', constantly dreamt of in some I.R.A. circles, because it would make possible the shooting down of British helicopters. The men raised the money, handed it over, received the missile and were then arrested. The F.B.I. then followed the money trail through several locations, including Arizona, Toronto, Palm Beach and New York, and, after widespread raids in New York and Arizona, more arrests followed on November 11, 1992. Those arrested were Patrick Moley, Tony Brannigan, Denis Leyne and Tommy Maguire, the owner of a popular pub in the Bronx, the Phoenix Bar. The indictment, read before a Grand Jury in Tucson, related to both the Stinger affair and the purchase of detonators.

An attorney prominent in Irish-American legal and political activities, Frank Durkan, told the New York *Irish Voice* (on November 24, 1992) that the arrests were part of 'a witch hunt against Irish-American businessmen.' He pointed out that it was common for members of the Irish-American community to regularly contribute money to defence funds and to various Irish political organisations. However he said that : '. . . now decent and respectable business people are being subjected to harassment and are under threat at the direction of a pro-British State Department in Washington.' This sort of complaint would appear to have borne fruit under President Clinton's regime.

Good contact has been established between the Irish-Americans and the Clinton administration. To my knowledge the President has assured leaders of the Irish-American community that there would be 'no more Joe Doherty cases,' and there is tangible evidence of the F.B.I. being reigned in. In the same month (November, 1992) in which the four were indicted in Tucson, I had been asked to appear as an expert witness in a ludicrous case in Chicago which has evaporated since the Republicans exited the White House. It originated in a discussion between five men in the back bar of a run down bar on North Milwaukee Avenue, Chicago, The Irish Wolfhound. The group had a record of contributing to the relief of distress in Northern Ireland. The issue was whether or not it would now be politically correct to give money to a Republican fund-raiser who was expected in the city. During the discussion one member of the group, John Tuttle, was observed to be behaving oddly. He was a recent addition to the circle and the others thought that he was trying to pull a gun on them. They seized him—and found he was fiddling with a concealed microphone.

Within seconds the F.B.I. had burst in and removed Tuttle, who later turned out to be a rather unstable young man. (He had also served a jail term after being dishonourably discharged from the army for selling LSD to his buddies.) A month before the Irish Wolfhound incident, the F.B.I. had induced a state prosecutor to drop charges against him (for punching a woman), because he was a 'protected witness'. Following the Irish Wolfhound incident, the other four were all arrested. They were Chris Fogarty, his wife, Mary Sullivan, Tony McCormick and Frank O'Neill. They were charged with assault, of Tuttle, and damaging F.B.I. property, a Nagra tape-recorder. If convicted they would have faced five years in jail.

The leading F.B.I. man in the case, Ed Buckley, had already become an object of criticism in Irish circles in Chicago. Someone in law enforcement had floated a bizarre theory concerning the particularly savage murder, in the wealthy Chicago suburb of Winnetka, of husband and wife Richard and Nancy Langert. It was said that the murders were linked to the I.R.A., who were annoyed at Nancy's sister, Jeanne Bishop, a Chicago lawyer who had done *pro bono* work for a Protestant group interested in Northern Ireland called The Truth About Northern Ireland. In fact, the group tends to be sympathetic to the Republicans and Jeanne Bishop blames Buckley for planting the story. She says he had harassed her, even before the murders, to obtain the names of Irish contacts. After the murder story surfaced she suffered increased pressure, both from the authorities and the media. But then a local teenager, who was said to have been on drugs, was arrested and convicted of the Langert murders. It also emerged that the F.B.I. had paid more money to Tuttle ($20,000) in the nine months prior to the Irish Wolfhound raid than the Fogarty group, The Friends of Irish Freedom, had been able to raise.

However, after Clinton entered the White House the F.B.I. dropped the charges. Obviously the Chicago Four case is not typical of Irish-American collection activity on behalf of the I.R.A. The Four, in fact, had a history of donation to Irish relief funds, not the purchase of arms. But so long as there is trouble in Northern Ireland some Irish-Americans will support the Provisionals. The Libyan connection may have dried up but the Irish-American one will not be dammed. And to the ranks of first, second and third generation Irish-Americans one must add the constant stream of energetic, intelligent, pro-I.R.A. activists who are constantly emigrating to the U.S. With or without a Green Card their sympathies are green. The guns, the money, the expertise and the political pressure will continue to be exerted.

Miscarriages of Justice

George Bernard Shaw once said that a Royal Commission reminded him of a man going to the lavatory. It sat for a long time, during which nothing was heard. Then there was a loud report—and the matter was dropped. He would have found nothing to make him revise his opinion in the Report of the Royal Commission on Criminal Justice. It had been set up in 1991 because of the publicity aroused by some appalling injustices perpetrated on Irish prisoners. One of the most respected journals in England said this of the Report's findings:

When the Royal Commission on Criminal Justice was convened around two years ago, the phrase 'English justice' had become something of an oxymoron. A string of names and numbers—the Maguire Seven, the Guildford Four and, most poisonously—the Birmingham Six was humiliating shorthand for the manifest failure of what was once one of the world's most envied criminal systems.

The foregoing appeared in the staid economic journal, *The Economist* (on July 10,

1993). Writing in the better tradition of English journalism the magazine was acknowledging that The Birmingham Six, Guildford Four, Maguire Seven, Winchester Three and the unfortunate Judith Ward, were in the words of Michael Mansfield, the English barrister who defended many of them, subjected to 'unthinkable suffering handed down in the name of justice.'*

The outcome of the Maguire Seven case has been described earlier (Chapter 30). The innocence of the Birmingham Six, to which I have previously alluded also, was not admitted until they were freed in March, 1991. Judith Ward was held until May, 1992, before being let go. Hers was the worst case of injustice. A woman with psychiatric disorders, she had spent eighteen years in prison, two years longer than the Birmingham Six, for a crime of which she was totally innocent. The Guildford bombings took place in October, 1974. It was October, 1989, before the wrongfully accused men were released. The sort of evidence which moved the appeal judge to free them may be judged from a file on the supposed ringleader of the group, Gerald Conlon, who was in London when the bombs went off in Surrey. The file contained a police interview with a witness who corroborated Conlon's statement that he was in a London hostel on the day of the explosions. Yet, the witness was never produced at the trial, and the state prosecution marked the file, which would have acquitted Conlon fourteen years earlier: 'Not to be disclosed to the Defence.'†

The Winchester Three were also set free during this period. They were the luckiest of all. They had been found guilty of conspiring to murder the then Northern Secretary of State, Tom King. Had they received sentences of five years or so no one would have complained unduly. The trio had been captured while apparently observing King's movements at his Wiltshire estate. In fact, after a trial which at times appeared to be conducted by the tabloids, they got twenty-five years each. They had claimed the right to silence. But in the middle of the trial King gave a press conference and using language which many felt was in contempt of court, he announced that the Government was withdrawing the right to silence in Northern Ireland. On appeal it was accepted that the timing of the announcement must have prejudiced the jury and the three were set free.

One could argue that these cases and many others grew out of a combination of circumstances: the latent anti-Irish feeling I encountered in Birmingham; the need for the police to be seen to get someone, anyone, for a series of horrifying bombings; the challenge posed to a democratic society by a ruthless, undemocratic enemy. In fact the cases, and their parallel activities in Northern Ireland, Diplock Courts, the use of the S.A.S. in undercover, shoot-to-kill operations, and a whole panoply of other bendings of the law, illustrate that it is not possible for Britain to remain in Northern Ireland without doing severe damage to its democratic traditions.

The Executive and the law are being drawn into the counter-insurgency process. Even the Royal Commission referred to earlier, while it has recommended some reforms—an independent authority to review potentially unjust sentences

---

* The quotation and the others used to describe the Birmingham Six, and similar cases, is taken from Mansfield's book, *Presumed Guilty*, Heinemann, London, 1983, (p. viiii).

† Mansfield, pg. 234.

and improvements in forensic testing, which, for instance, would have acquitted the Birmingham Six if in force—has reported with one eye on Northern Ireland. It proposed the ending of the right to trial by jury, and forcing defendants to disclose their defence in advance. As *The Economist* said: 'A royal commission designed to restore public faith in the courts has produced proposals that are more likely to erode it.'

In a nutshell, Britain is back where it was during the Anglo-Irish war of the 1916–21 period. Once more, because of public opinion, it can not be seen to use its army in an all-out war of conquest. Therefore, once again, she has had to resort to the concept of a 'police war'. This time instead of Auxiliary Police Cadets and The Black and Tans, she makes use of the Special Air Services Unit, the S.A.S., and allows Protestant paramilitary death squads to operate on the principle of 'the enemy of my enemy is my friend'. Just as in the early Anglo-Irish war, the existence of such undercover dirty tricks was at first strenuously denied. But, inexorably, as in the first phase of warfare, revelations in the media (now augmented by the power of TV) have begun first to cast doubt upon and, increasingly, to seriously discredit official disclaimers. More and more, by 1993, the 'police' war was becoming revealed as being no more attractive, or effective, than its predecessor.

The Amnesty International Report for 1992 said flatly that the United Kingdom's behaviour in Northern Ireland had made it into one of the worst human rights violators in Europe. The report cited very disturbing court cases where bending of the rules occured to secure convictions. Most notably, in the conduct of the trial of the seven men accused of charges arising out of the murder of the two British corporals seized at Milltown cemetery in 1988, the report stated 'Courts drew adverse inferences against defendants for having remained silent during police questioning or at trial'. Another Birmingham Six or Guildford saga appears to be under way. But, most damningly of all, the respected international organisaton said that there was evidence of collusion between the security forces in Northern Ireland and Loyalist paramilitary groups.

In his fine book *Big Boys' Rules*★, Mark Urban, a B.B.C. correspondent and an ex-*London Independent* Defence Correspondent, was able to give chapter and verse of S.A.S. shoot-to-kill ambushes which had claimed the lives of more than three dozen I.R.A. men. However, he was less successful in establishing official collusion with outlawed Protestant paramilitaries. He states:

. . . in many interviews with people involved with undercover warfare, none has endorsed these allegations of widespread collaboration between intelligence officers and loyalist paramilitaries; on the contrary, they deny them with vigour.

Urban was commenting on separate claims made by two former British Army officers, Fred Holroyd and Colin Wallace, and by a convicted Loyalist terrorist, Albert Baker. My experience is that getting corroboration depends on who the person 'involved with undercover warfare' is and how much he or she is in awe of the Official Secrets Act. I know at least one such figure who will not deny with 'vigour' the existence of 'widespread collaboration'. He has talked openly to me

---

★ *Big Boys' Rules: The SAS and the Secret Struggle against the IRA*, by Mark Urban, Faber, London, 1992, pps., 54–55.

about what he knows, and, as a result, has written a book which will be published in 1994.

This man, whom I will call 'Maxwell', is a former U.D.R. officer and member of the U.D.A. In the U.D.A., Maxwell, who had been commissioned into the U.D.R. at Sandhurst, worked with John McMichael, the number two man in the U.D.A. leadership who was blown up as a result of collusion between a U.D.A. racketeer called James Craig and elements in the Provisional I.R.A. McMichael had 'made his bones' by killing a number of Catholics and by arranging the killing of many others, including most of the leadership of the anti H-Block campaign in 1980. He was responsible for the deaths of Miriam Daly, a Queen's University lecturer, John Turnley, a Protestant turned Republican, and Ronald Bunting whose father had once been one of Paisley's closest associates. However, in the flux of Six County revolutionary change, Bunting had become an I.N.L.A. leader and was responsible for the ass.a.s.sination of Airey Neave, M.P., Margaret Thatcher's close advisor who was blown up in a House of Commons car park. The one H-Block leader McMichael failed with was Bernadette McAliskey, formerly Bernadette Devlin.

A respected writer, Martin Dillon, who worked in Belfast as a B.B.C. correspondent, and is the author of a number of authorative books on Loyalist terrorism, described what happened.*

She lived with her husband in County Tyrone, near the town of Coalisand. On January 16, an S.A.S. team was in place in the grounds surrounding her house. She was unaware of their presence or the fact that they had cut the telephone wires to her home. A U.D.A. active-service team arrived, entered the house and shot her several times; they were arrested as they left the scene. An Army officer rushed to Bernadette McAliskey's side and kept her alive until a medical team arrived. The presence of the S.A.S. has never been explained. Some observers have concluded that their behaviour proved a connection between the UFF and Military Intelligence and ten years later, this belief hardened the suspicion that McMichael was an agent of British Intelligence.

McMichael always considered himself to be actually at war with the Provisional I.R.A., with justice as his fate indicates, and potentially, engaged in hostilities with the Republic. The fear that some day the Republic's army will cross the border is a deep-rooted one in Northern Ireland's Protestants. After the signing of the Anglo-Irish Agreement, McMichael began taking precautions against this 'Doomsday Day' situation as he termed it. A hit list of targets in the Republic was drawn up that included people, locations and national treasures. Teams of U.D.A. men were sent southwards to scout the targets and their findings were collated on McMichael's computer.

Maxwell's targets included the Book of Kells, the Cuchulain statue in the Dublin G.P.O., and Peter Barry, then the Republic's Minister for Foreign Affairs, who had been one of the signatories to the Anglo-Irish Agreement. The first two had a symbolic value in U.D.A. eyes. Cuchalain was a legendary hero who had defended Ulster against invaders from other parts of Ireland. The monastery in which the Book of Kells is thought to have been created was also in the North.

---

* *Stone Cold*, p. 65, Arrow, London, 1992. Dillon's other books include *Rogue Warrior of the SAS, Political Murder in Northern Ireland* and *The Shankill Butchers*.

Barry, owner of a flourishing tea business, lived in faraway County Cork. This did
not deter Maxwell and his companion. They drove to Cork to monitor Barry's
movements. Once, when they became afraid that their Northern car and accents
might be attracting attention, they brazenly went up to a security man employed
by Barry's company to say that they were becoming distracted by the Cork one
way system. Would he mind if they used the company car park to compose themselves with the aid of their flasks and sandwiches? The obliging security man let
them use the car park, where undisturbed, they observed departures and arrivals,
videoing the proceedings to their hearts' content.

Readers have seen the sentence meted out to the Winchester Three when found
guilty of taking part in a similar mission involving another signatory to the Anglo-
Irish Agreement, Tom King. No such fate befell Maxwell. Instead he was
employed by the R.U.C. Special Branch to keep them informed on what was
going on in the U.D.A. No meeting of the Anglo-Irish Conference, perennially
preoccupied as they were by repeated British demands for closer Dublin co-
operation with the R.U.C. and U.D.R., was ever troubled with the information
that both these organisations had *cezanne* of a plot to murder one of the Irish
principals taking part in the discussions and much more besides. This, of course,
need not surprise us in the light of what has since been revealed about British
Army involvement in paramilitary atrocities. I am merely citing Maxwell's case to
indicate that such collusion was a widely used tactic in the counter-insurgency
effort. He was a trusted officer in the U.D.R., being one of those chosen to give
Douglas Hurd, now the British Foreign Secretary, an unpublicised tour of his area.
He also worked with Captain Robert Nairac, the British Intelligence officer whom
the I.R.A. captured and shot, after torture, in 1977.

McMichael himself once told me that the U.D.A. effectively controlled the
U.D.R. Maxwell confirmed this. In his experience, the sharing of information and
the overlapping of membership were two of the givens of the situation. A third
generation Orangeman—he once walked in a parade with his father and grandfather—he eventually became disillusioned with the entire paraphernalia of the
Loyalist world: the Orange Order, R.U.C., U.D.A., U.D.R., and all the rest. For
a while, he says, he fed the R.U.C. 'duff' information about the U.D.A., then
finally quit all four organisations. Along the way he suffered the almost inevitable
Six County tension-induced crack-up, hitting the bottle and undergoing a short
prison sentence for petty crime. He subsequently pulled himself together and is
now happily re-married, building up a business and a staunch member of the
Church of Ireland. His local vicar is one of those who supports his decision to
write his memoirs, feeling that the ultimate message is that a man can go through
such experiences and emerge a good Christian.

Maxwell says he thinks that the public should be made aware of how the
British, through the security forces, are manipulating people and of the sort of
incident to which this manipulation can lead. He cited the intelligence gathering
units of the Army and the R.U.C. Special Branch. He told me: 'If by writing the
book I can help one other poor sod not to get involved it will be worth it.'

One of the people who worked in the U.D.A. at the same time as Maxwell
was its intelligence director, Brian Nelson, who was also a top British agent. On

February 3, 1992, Nelson was sentenced to ten years imprisonment by a Belfast court. He had pleaded guilty to five charges of conspiracy to murder and fifteen other offences. A British officer, identified only as Colonel 'J' of Military Intelligence, stated at the trial that he was Nelson's boss. The judge who sentenced him described him as a man who had 'shown the greatest courage,' and the former Northern Ireland Secretary, Tom King, wrote a letter on his behalf. By way of illuminating the origin of this high level solicitude, it might be noted that Colonel 'J' told the court that he conducted regular briefings for the North's senior military figures at which Nelson's evidence was passed over. Furthermore he said: 'The Secretary of State for Northern Ireland might also be interested in such information.'

Nelson's arrest had followed an inquiry into allegations of collusion between the security forces and Loyalist death squads which had grown more persistent following the Stalker affair. The inquiry was conducted by John Stevens, a British police officer who, like Stalker, encountered sustained resistance by British Intelligence to the uncovering of evidence, including the fact that Nelson was supplied with over 1,000 photographs taken by the security forces.

Just before his trial the Crown prosecutors withdrew two charges of murder. This deal, which was sanctioned by the then Attorney General, Sir Patrick Mayhew, effectively closed off avenues of cross-examination which might have revealed highly explosive information about Nelson's links with British Military Intelligence. Nelson is a native of Belfast, but he was sent to England to serve his sentence. Nationalist lawyers say that he is likely to serve only some three to four years. Even if this does not prove to be the case, the leniency of his sentence in relation to the seriousness of the offences with which he was charged, compares very oddly with that handed down to the Winchester Three.

The fallout from the Nelson trial included leaks from those in the security forces who feel as Maxwell does about 'dirty tricks' operations, and some sustained investigative reporting by highly reputable sections of the media. These included *The Irish Times*, *The Irish News* and the B.B.C.'s *Panorama* programme. It became known that the British intelligence handlers who 'ran' Nelson knew that he had travelled to South Africa to purchase weapons in 1985. They allowed a South African shipment of arms to be landed on the County Down coast in January, 1988, to protect his position within the U.D.A. In the three years prior to the shipment's landing the U.D.A. and its hit squad, the U.F.F. (Ulster Freedom Fighters), are reckoned to have killed three people. Between the landing and January, 1993, the Loyalist death squads accounted for the murder of 160 people.

The dead, all of whom were killed with weapons from the South African consignment, included Michael Stone's victims at Milltown Cemetery, Patrick Finnucane, a Catholic solicitor famous in the Six Counties for defending Republican prisoners, and random targets such as taxi drivers, or punters who had the bad luck to wander into bookies' shops in Catholic areas. Throughout this spate of killing the British had Nelson and several other agents in the U.D.A. 'There would have been dozens of them in the U.D.R. and the U.D.A.' Maxwell reckons. The information from these sources should have been sufficient to not alone prevent the sectarian killings, but also the protection rackets which the U.D.A. indulges in. But on top of this there is the British intelligence effort itself.

One intelligence officer quoted by Dillon said:* 'Files are kept on the whole population. In Northern Ireland which is not much larger than Yorkshire that is feasible. No one would believe the extent of phone tapping for other phone surveillance. It is very sophisticated'

Why were the crimes allowed to continue? Mark Urban writes†:

> Despite evidence of Nelson's success as an agent, the case raised uncomfortable questions about the difference between the security forces' response to foreknowledge of republican and loyalist attacks. Clearly Nelson's intelligence and that of other loyalist informers has been used to thwart attacks, in the same way as information from republican groups. But it is clear that attempts to exploit this intelligence to ambush loyalists have rarely if ever been made.

That's one way of putting it. 'The enemy of my enemy is my friend,' is another. When a regular R.U.C. report turns up information such as the present whereabouts of a targeted I.R.A. man, or the name of the café where a Sinn Fein Councillor is having lunch, an intelligence handler in the information chain has only to lift the phone to his agent. One more Loyalist killing will not only leave the security forces with one less opponent, but with clean hands into the bargain.

McMichael himself gave me an account of how one of the nastiest episodes of the entire period came to light. This was the Kincora Boys Home affair. The boys in this Belfast refuge were systematically preyed upon by the man responsible for running the hostel, William McGrath, who also ran a Loyalist murder gang called Tara. He abused the boys both for his own—and for his friends'—sexual gratification and hired them out to stag clubs and, as we shall see, other more highly placed customers. According to McMichael, two of the children who found they could no longer tolerate the abuse, made a suicide pact. On the ferry back to Belfast, after performing the duties for which McGrath had hired them to a stag club in Scotland, they would jump overboard. One child did jump, but the other's nerve failed and the affair came to light when the R.U.C. questioned him about his companion's death. However McGrath was protected as Martin Dillon has noted.‡

> McGrath was shielded; he had been working for British intelligence . . . Tara to cloak his secret activities. He also monitored the life of his fellow Loyalists, but his other life included the provision of boys for homosexual colleagues within the British intelligence community in Northern Ireland and for several leading members of the British Establishment who visited Belfast regularly . . . In 1979 a Military Intelligence liason officer sabotaged R.U.C. attempts to trace the history of McGrath and his British intelligence connection.

Dillon says the cover-up was to prevent a scandal which would 'damage the reputation of well-known homosexuals within the British Military Intelligence community, and would also compromise others well-known in British public life.' McGrath received only a *two year* sentence for his Kincora crimes. His Tara activities were overlooked and journalists who attempted to follow up his story were intimidated into silence. A U.D.A. leader who interrogated McGrath in jail was murdered not long after his release. His U.D.A. colleagues say his death was connected with the McGrath investigation.

---

*   *Stone Cold*, p. 136.
†   Urban, *Big Boys' Rules*, p. 217.
‡   *Stone Cold*, p. 57.

By 1993, the weight of evidence concerning British involvement in an underground dirty war was mounting. There were several books attesting to the fact. Apart from those I have mentioned by Dillon, Holroyd, Urban and Wallace, there was also Fr. Raymond Murray's, *The S.A.S. in Ireland* and Peter Wright's *Spycatcher.* Television programmes were also being made, most notably the one in Channel Four's *Dispatches* series, which so enraged the R.U.C. with its descriptions of Loyalist/R.U.C. complicity in killings, that legal proceedings were instituted. Then came the most spectacular illustration of undercover British involvement in the dirtiest trick of all. Yorkshire TV's *First Tuesday* programme on July 6, 1993, reconstructed the events of the worst single day of the entire troubles, the Dublin and Monaghan bombings of May 17, 1974, which claimed thirty-four lives.

Shortly after the bombings, I had been informed by contacts in the Gardai that the Irish police suspected that the car bombs which exploded in rush-hour Dublin that day originated with Loyalist paramilitaries in Portadown operating under the tutelage of British Intelligence. Apparently the object of the slaughter was twofold. Firstly, Loyalist determination to bring home to the south, which they held partly culpable, the realities of the car-bombing they lived with. Secondly, British Intelligence wanted to lay a marker on the Dublin Government as to what might happen if they did not co-operate, as Britain desired, in the fight against the I.R.A. Later, as the jigsaw was pieced together by the police and Irish Military Intelligence, the names of those thought to have been involved became known.

However, two factors militated against any action being taken. Firstly, the R.U.C. refused to assist the Gardai in making enquiries in the Six Counties. Therefore, hard evidence against the men suspected could not be obtained. Secondly, as we have seen, the Fine Gael/Labour Coalition Government of the time, which was particularly anti-I.R.A., believed in a policy of wooing the Unionists, and set a high premium on good relations with London. So much so that a 'Heavy Gang' within the Gardai was allowed off the leash in its treatment of I.R.A. suspects to such an extent that it later became a factor in the Government's subsequent downfall.

In the circumstances, the Coalition decided that pursuing the matter might result only in the generation of publicity which would bring aid and comfort to the I.R.A. Accordingly, the Government tamely allowed the matter to drop. There is no evidence of any attempt being made by Dublin to bring pressure to bear on London to enjoin co-operation on the R.U.C. Over the years, as time took its toll, the bombers died or were killed, either in feuds amongst Loyalist factions, or by the I.R.A. Their names were well known to the security forces on both sides of the border. About a year before the showing of the programme I had a conversation with a friend of mine in the Special Branch who mentioned names quite casually, and for good measure threw in details of their identification. In one case, a farmer in County Monaghan had backed his tractor out of a field into the path of a green Avenger car being driven at such speed that a collision was barely averted. In the resultant altercation he got a good look at the occupants' faces and later identified them from photographs shown to him by the Gardai. The four men were the chief suspects in the Monaghan bombing. (They escaped across the border moments before the bomb went off.)

I also had had a meeting with Maxwell a week before the showing of the Yorkshire TV programme. There had been advance publicity which led us to a discussion about both the programme and the bombings. Of his knowledge, and quite unprompted by me, he mentioned the same names as had my Special Branch friend in Dublin. The only difference was that, in addition, he mentioned two British officers, Capt. Tony Ball and his second-in-command, the then Lt. Robert Nairac. In the subsequent programme, their names were amongst those cited as being involved in the preparation of the bombs. The operation was run by an S.A.S.-trained unit known as the 'Fourth Field Survey Troop', which was then based at Castledillon, County Armagh. All the other suspects I had been told of by both the Special Branch man and the ex-Loyalist paramilitary, were squarely implicated. Most were members of the U.D.R. as well as being in the U.V.F. Ex-British Intelligence officers appeared on the programme to state that at that time in Northern Ireland, British Intelligence controlled the U.V.F. and that the U.V.F. did not have the capability to manufacture the sophisticated timing devices needed to trigger the bombs. It was implied that these devices, and training in their use, were provided by the S.A.S..

The Gardai gave the programme makers access to material and granted interviews with former senior officers, as did the Irish Military Intelligence authorities, in a manner which could only have been sanctioned by the Government. Again it was a Coalition involving Labour, the difference was that this time it was with Fianna Fail. But it was a much different Labour party from that of the seventies. Gone, for example, was a figure whom many regard as a Unionist with a Southern accent, Dr Conor Cruise O'Brien. And its new leader, Dick Spring, who was both Deputy Prime Minister, and Minister for Foreign Affairs, was known to be increasingly frustrated by the lack of political initiative from London. The question of political progress, or lack of it, during the last few years will shortly be discussed, but two points concerning British/Loyalist paramilitary involvement should be made.

One, it has added to the possibilities for a Loyalist backlash in the event of London and Dublin concluding a political agreement away from the murky underworld of 'special ops'. I know from R.U.C. sources that nowadays they sometimes find it hard to distinguish Loyalist suspects from Provisional I.R.A. ones when they are brought in for questioning. 'They're just like Provos,' said one police officer. 'You get nothing out of them. They just sit there for days and say nothing. You have to let them go.' But along with anti-interrogation techniques, the new generation of Loyalists have also acquired more lethal skills, which constitute a problem for the future.

Part of this improved expertise, of course, came about simply because the conflict has gone on for so long. A new generation of Loyalist paramilitaries has grown up; younger, harder men, sons and nephews of the men who first founded the U.D.A. But part of it is also a result of undercover British training. Many a Loyalist paramilitary, like Brian Nelson, having served in the British Army or the U.D.R., came to the notice of agencies like the Field Research Unit and was then recruited for undercover work. Nelson, for example was working in Germany when British intelligence contacted him to return to Belfast and join the U.D.A.

The Field Research Unit is one of the British Army's most important agent recruiting operations. Colonel J, who gave evidence at Nelson's trial, was once the Commanding Officer of this unit. Its operations will assuredly leave Ireland with problems to solve in the future.

The final point I wish to make on this subject is that all the foregoing fully accepts the fact that the I.R.A. has proved itself an implacable, ruthless foe. Apart from the list of its operations I have detailed, including proxy bombing, I could mention countless others, ranging from the killing of judges, to the placing of a bomb in Musgrave military hospital, a 'legitimate target' which claimed the lives of two army medical officers on November 4, 1991. When D Squadron of the S.A.S. were sent into South Armagh in 1976, it was because the I.R.A. had previously shot, or blown up, forty-nine soldiers.

Nevertheless, the basic instructions the S.A.S. received would be illegal in England, the U.K. mainland. At the time the S.A.S. were first dispatched to Ireland, a British Army spokesman writing anonymously in *The Times*, said their mission would be: 'what the Army has failed to do, kill terrorists.'* With no qualifications about a restrained use of force, the instructions, known as 'the yellow card', which govern an ordinary soldier's tour of duty, gave to the S.A.S. a straightforward shoot-to-kill policy.

There are other factors which I have not gone into, which complicate the control of military operations; inter-security forces rivalry, for example. The 'police war' concept has resulted in the police and the army often being at loggerheads. This has led to confusion and ambushes where simple arrests would have been possible had the Army really being acting 'in aid of the civil power'. None of this comes about through any inherent British brutality. It stems, like the My Lai massacre in Vietnam, from the fact of a normally disciplined army getting involved in a dirty, unwinnable war. A war which should be addressed by negotiation and political methods, not the force of arms and undercover murders. But at present, British soldiers are as cruelly and as hopelessly entrapped by the ditches of South Armagh as were the Americans in the jungles of Vietnam.

Neither is the R.U.C. to be thought of as an Irish *Stasi*, the notorious East German secret service. In fact, the force includes some of the best and certainly some of the bravest policemen in Europe. But the way the force was founded and operated for years meant that Protestants regarded it as being an instrument of 'their' law and 'their' order; the means of imposing a Unionist policy which, in plain language, came down to an Irish version of apartheid. The evils of that system generated the troubles and turned the Force into a counter-insurgency weapon, with the result that to the I.R.A., the police became 'legitimate targets'. The absence of a political resolution of the conflict has kept them in the firing line.

Political Developments

During most of the period 1986–93, there was a great deal of political activity on both sides of the Irish Sea, but little movement. Naturally the resignation of the 'iron lady', Margaret Thatcher, as Prime Minister on November 28, 1990, gave

---

* Quoted by Urban, p. 8.

rise to lively hopes in some circles that a change in British policy might follow. But an episode which occurred less than three months later aptly symbolised the reality of the Irish situation for top British decision makers. It was deadly, but peripheral— an I.R.A. rocket exploded in the garden of Number Ten Downing Street.

The man who succeeded Thatcher, John Major, was sitting in the Cabinet Room at the time of the explosion, February 7, 1991. With him were a group which included, amongst others, the Chancellor of the Exchequer, Norman Lamont, the Foreign Secretary, Douglas Hurd, and the Defence Secretary, Tom King. Both Hurd and King had been Secretaries of State for Northern Ireland. But it was not Northern Ireland which had brought them to the Cabinet Room. They formed part of the war cabinet assembled for Britain's priority war, the Gulf War. They were temporarily distracted by the rocket but that was all. The attack itself was a particularly daring piece of outrage. The rocket was one of three fired from a homemade rocket launcher based in a van with holes cuts in its roof. The I.R.A. had parked the vehicle a couple of hundred yards from the back of Number Ten. Those with a knowledge of history afterwards commented on the appropriateness of the parking site in Whitehall—alongside a statue commemorating the Duke of Devonshire who had led the opposition to Gladstone's Home Rule Bill in 1886.

Those around the table, however, were content to get on with bombing the Iraqis and leave the Northern Ireland Minister, Peter Brooke, to attempt to deal with the I.R.A. bombers by holding a series of talks about talks with the Northern Ireland political parties. These were frustrated by a combination of Unionist stalling tactics and a fiercesome spate of sectarian killings which marred the spring of 1991. There was some internal dialogue within the Six Counties, but nothing meaningful occurred in the larger Dublin-London-Belfast context. The Unionists wanted the Anglo-Irish Agreement suspended before they would agree to talks with Dublin. Sinn Fein were to be excluded whether or not the Agreement went because of the party's backing for the I.R.A. campaign. As neither condition offered a foundation for success, the talks, predictably, died without achieving anything tangible beyond preventing Irish-Americans from raising the profile of the Irish problem during the 1992 American Presidential election campaign. Nobody wanted to say anything that might get in the way of the mystical 'talks' that were said to contain a prospect of peace. In fact, after over a year of preliminary skirmishing, the 'Brooke initiative', as it was generally known, boiled down to a short-lived set of conversations. These began on June 17, 1991, after a seven week suspension of the Anglo-Irish Agreement, and petered out on July 3, so as not to inflame the temperatures of those involved in the Six Counties' 'marching season'.

Charles Haughey ceased to be the Irish Prime Minister on January 30, 1992. He was succeeded by Albert Reynolds, about whom little was known beyond the fact that he was a wealthy dogfood manufacturer and former dancehall operator. Reynolds did not carry any of Haughey's ideological baggage stemming either from the arms trial era or the many political controversies which Haughey had been involved in subsequently. One of these had led to the creation of an Adam's rib party from the Fianna Fail body politic, the Progressive Democrats, led by Desmond O'Malley, a long standing critic of Haughey's. By one of the ironies of political life, the two men had been thrown together into a coalition Government. But in

January, 1992, yet another scandal, over phone tapping, caused O'Malley to state that he would withdraw from the coalition if Haughey did not resign. Haughey duly went but before doing so he had been helpful in the process that had led to the talks between John Hume and Gerry Adams which may yet yield more solid dividends than the more visible meetings between Reynolds and Major.

The two Prime Ministers discussed Northern Ireland on April 27, 1992. They got on well together socially, but politically were frustrated in their attempts to find common ground by the Unionists' continued 'not an inch' posture, and by Major's inability to manoeuvre while relying both on the Northern Ireland Unionist M.P.s, and the thirty or so 'Euro-sceptics' sitting in the Conservatives back benches. (The term 'Euro-sceptic' in Tory circles being interchangeable with that of 'Thatcher supporter'.)

There was a further bout of 'talks about talks' that culminated in the opening of a set of formal, but inconclusive, meetings in London on June 12, 1992, between all the Northern Irish political parties, except Sinn Fein, under the Chairmanship of Sir Ninian Stephen, an Australian who was found to be acceptable to all concerned after much argument. One of the Unionist ploys used to abort the talks was a pre-condition set by Ian Paisley. Before agreeing to substantive discussion with Dublin he wanted the Republic to drop Articles 2 and 3 of its Constitution which can be interpreted as laying claim to the Six Counties. However, the notion that there was a 'talks process' still extant survived and was used to good effect in America by the British. Irish-American support for Clinton did yield a return in a pre-election proposal to appoint a Peace Envoy to Northern Ireland. But adverse reaction from London helped to stall fulfilment of this promise. More importantly, Albert Reynolds, during a St. Patrick's Day visit to Washington in March, 1993, asked President Clinton to put the proposal on hold until the possibilities of talks resuming was more thoroughly teased out. However, both on the ground and in Westminster, the British guarantee to the Unionists, that they need not face change so long as they did not wish to, effectively froze the situation in a poisoned political aspic.

It soon became clear that Reynolds had no intention of allowing this situation to continue indefinitely. He had had some initial difficulties as leader of Fianna Fail. One of Haughey's legacies had been a long running judicial inquiry into alleged scandals in the meat industry. A clash of evidence between O'Malley and Reynolds at this Tribunal resulted in O'Malley departing the coalition, a general election being held at the end of the year, and Reynolds returning as Taoiseach in the New Year (on January 12, 1993). However he did so with a greatly reduced number of Fianna Fail deputies and in Coalition with Labour, which had gained substantially under the leadership of Dick Spring. It took him some time to work out an agreed programme with Spring and he was still proceeding cautiously in March when he saw Clinton. Nevertheless, when the dust settled, the political arithmetic in the Dail meant that Fianna Fail's sixty-eight seats, combined with Labour's thirty-three, gave the two parties an enormous advantage over the (fractured) opposition parties' combined total of sixty-five seats. If decided upon, new policies could be pursued from a position of strength.

Seemingly they were decided upon, for a new sound began to be heard in the political chorus emanating from Nationalist Ireland. Sinn Fein's Gerry Adams and the S.D.L.P.'s John Hume had held inconclusive talks in 1988. The underground peace process involving the Roman Catholic clergy, which I mentioned earlier, resulted in talks between the pair resuming in April, 1993. This elicited a chorus of disapproval from all shades of Unionist opinion and from the Dublin opposition parties, but not from Spring and Reynolds. Both of them made muted comments to the effect, summed up by Reynolds, that: 'Mr Hume is a very experienced politician. It is for Mr Hume to judge whether something useful can come out of those talks.' In Irish terms this lack of condemnation amounted to endorsement. That comment by Reynolds was carried in the Irish papers (April 26, 1993) on the same day that Spring weighed in alongside Reynolds with a defence of Articles 2 and 3 of the Constitution. Spring said:' I don't think any party should prejudice the talks by making pre-conditions and that is what we have been trying to explain over the last number of months.'

Reynolds, who was in America when he gave the interview, also said that he would be bringing up the matter of Northern Ireland when he met John Major in June. Pointedly he said that by then the Local Government elections (May) would be held in England, and consequently also in Northern Ireland, and 'the U.K. overseas' would be out of the way. This was code for stating that by June he would know whether the shared hope amongst Unionists, the Irish opposition parties, and most importantly the British Conservative party would be realised. In a nutshell, that Sinn Fein would suffer a reverse. If they did, the British were hoping for results from yet another round of talks, based on an internal settlement within the existing structures. Sir Patrick Mayhew had signalled as much in a speech in Liverpool a few days earlier in which he had stated that he would be bringing forward British proposals for the future of Northern Ireland. Proposals it appeared, concerning which Dublin would have little input.

However, on that April weekend two other things occurred which underlined the impossibility of an internal settlement. One was very visibly external, the Bishopsgate bomb in the City of London. The other was a joint communique from Hume and Adams which expressly ruled out an internal settlement. It said*:

. . . we accept that the most pressing issue facing the people of Ireland and Britain today is the question of lasting peace and how it can best be achieved. Everyone has a solemn duty to change the political climate away from conflict and towards a process of national reconciliation which sees the peaceful accommodation of the differences between the people of Britain and Ireland and the Irish people themselves.

In striving for that end we accept that an internal settlement is not a solution because it obviously does not deal with all the relationships at the heart of the problem. We accept that the Irish people as a whole have a right to national self-determination. This is a view shared by a majority of the people of this island though not by all its people.

The exercise of self-determination is a matter of agreement between the people of Ireland. It is the search for that agreement and the means of achieving it on which we will be concentrating . . . a new agreement is only achievable and viable if it can earn and enjoy the allegiance of the different traditions on this island, by accommodating diversity and providing for national reconciliation.

---

*   *Irish Times*, April 26, 1993.

That statement represented a high water mark for Sinn Fein. The espousal of the right to self-determination marked a shift away from the largely middle-class supported viewpoint of the S.D.L.P. that reform was possible within the system, i.e., while retaining the British presence albeit with an 'Irish dimension'. The accommodation of diversity is also standard Republican dogma going back to the days of Wolfe Tone. The statement was a realistic acceptance of the position in Northern Ireland as it is in 1993 by the two shrewdest political brains in the area. Ironically, its importance was both underlined and overshadowed by the coverage of the Bishopsgate bombing. But the May by-elections duly came and went with no erosion of Sinn Fein's support.

Reynolds saw Major in June and found him impotent politically. The two men like each other, but Major was in fife to the forces of the ineluctable dialectic of history. Even though in the previous March a Gallup Poll had found that only 27 per cent of Britons wanted Northern Ireland to remain part of the United Kingdom; Britain, in irreversible decline, was facing the chill blasts of late 20th Century reality by clinging to the last rags of empire in Northern Ireland. If she divested herself of these, Scotland would be the next to depart the Union, and Scotland might take the North Sea oil revenues with her. In Dublin the Coalition was also concerned with revenues; the honouring by the E.E.C. of a promise, made at the Edinburgh summit, that, as the price of supporting the Maastricht Treaty, Ireland would get some £8 billion from the 'Convergence Fund' set up to help the poorer regions. Britain's bureaucrats were known to be amongst those in Brussels who wanted a cut in the Irish allocation.

But now the strength of the huge Coalition majority came into play. Throughout the latter part of June and the first week of July the Irish Government took a series of strong stands on various issues, including Northern Ireland. It was announced that the national airline was to be streamlined. This involved massive job losses, and the abandonment of the controversial Shannon stopover which prevented foreign airlines from flying into Dublin. If the E.E.C.'s promise to Ireland were not honoured in full, Dublin said that she would veto the E.E.C.'s budget. On Northern Ireland the Government took no action to prevent President Mary Robinson attending a function in West Belfast at which the Sinn Fein President, Gerry Adams, was to be present, despite strong British pressure to do so. The President duly shook hands with Adams. It was a small but highly significant stepping stone on the way to the respectabilisation of Sinn Fein. An opinion poll carried out for the Irish Independent Group showed a 77 per cent approval rating (*Sunday Independent*, June 27, 1993) for the gesture by Robinson, who was well recognised as a critic of violence. In the North, Unionist hackles were raised, but the Nationalist reaction was overwhelmingly favourable.

Then a curious incident occurred. In the House of Commons John Major visibly lost control of himself with Kevin McNamara, the Labour Party Opposition Spokesman on Northern Ireland, in a discussion over a leaked Labour Party policy document.

The document suggested that if the Unionists continued to withhold their consent to an agreed solution, then London and Dublin would have to go it alone without them. The Labour Party's 'preferred option' was that of Joint Sovereignty, one of the three Irish Forum options ruled 'out' by Thatcher. Major denounced McNamara, a supporter of ultimate Irish unity. Uncharacteristically, he lost his temper, branding the Labour Party proposals as 'shameful'. Despite the fact that in earlier speeches Major had given assurances that all constitutional options were open to debate, he now said: 'The Union is vital for all parts of the United Kingdom . . . and we in the Conservative and Unionist Party stand four-square behind it.'

Was the beleaguered Major acting to abort a process stemming from the Hume-Adams talks which had led McNamara, or someone close to him, to leak the document? Did he attack McNamara in order to gain the support of the Unionist M.P.s in what was expected to be a very tight vote over the crunch issue of the Maastricht Treaty? Very likely so must be the answer. For Hume, who was sitting in the chamber, vainly tried to get into the discussion to call Major a 'liar', an unheard of performance for the normally controlled S.D.L.P. leader. He later told journalists that he regarded Major's performance as a 'cheap, destructive and ill-timed bit of partisanship, aimed mainly at winning a few parliamentary votes on issues quite separate from Ireland.'*

The reason for John Major's near hysteria became apparent when on July 22, 1993, the nine Official Unionist M.P.s supported the Conservatives on a crucial vote on ratification of a portion of Maastricht Treaty. It was widely said, although strenuously denied, that the price of their support was a deal whereby a Select Committee on Northern Ireland was to be created, and the Unionists were somehow to be given more power in Northern Ireland.

Concurrent with this development, a leading member of the anti-Maastricht lobby, Norman Tebbit (now Lord Tebbit), said on his London-based television show, broadcast on Sky Television, that bombs in Dublin would be required to make the Irish Government abandon Articles 2 and 3 of the Constitution. Allowances could be made for the fact that both Tebbit and his wife were badly injured in the Brighton hotel bombing. Nevertheless, he is a former Tory Minister and member of Margaret Thatcher's Cabinet, a senior figure in the Conservative Party, and a member of the House of Lords. Inescapably, his words would have been taken as plain incitement to bomb Dublin by some factions of Loyalism.

Many people in Ireland began to uneasily remember the infamous remarks of another Conservative which had fatal results. Douglas Hogg, Under Secretary of State at the Home Office said, under privilege of the House of Commons (on January 17, 1989) that 'there are in Northern Ireland a number of solictors who are unduly sympathetic to the I.R.A. I state this on the basis of advice . . . I have been given by people who are dealing with these matters.' Less than a month later the Belfast solicitor, Patrick Finnucane was murdered. The comment of Gregory Campbell, Paisley's party spokesman on security, on Tebbit's remarks however was: 'we would agree with this.'

Coming after Major's performance and the Yorkshire Television programme about British involvement in the 1974 bombings of Dublin and Monaghan, Tebbit's utterances helped to further worsen the already rapidly deteriorating

---

* *Economist*, July 10, 1993.

Dublin/London relationship. Privately the Dublin Government was known to be furious also about the role played by the British E.E.C. Commissioner, Bruce Millan, in attempting to cut the Irish E.E.C. funds in the same week of the Maastrict vote and the Tebbit affair. Too many coincidences seemed to be occuring all at once.

The components of the deal alleged to have been struck between the Conservatives and Unionists would, if true, have the effect of breaching both the spirit and the form of the Anglo-Irish Agreement. It was apparent to all thoughtful observers that the football of Northern Ireland was once more bouncing around the division lobbies of Westminster.

Dublin clearly thought little of Major's performance either. The Department of Foreign Affairs has always been strongly responsive to S.D.L.P. policies on the North. So much so that critics have often charged that the Department has no policy other than that of Hume. It may be taken for granted that the Department and its Minister, Dick Spring, were fully briefed on the Adams-Hume talks and their long-term possibilities. Following Major's statement, Spring gave a highly significant interview to John Palmer of the *Guardian* newspaper (on July 7, 1993). In it he said flatly that the Unionists could no longer have a veto on progress. If they would not agree to talks, then London and Dublin must agree over their heads. The problem had gone on for too long and would have to be addressed. This was a very different Labour Party attitude from that which had obtained at the time of the Dublin bombings. It was an attitude, moreover, with which Reynolds agreed.

The Irish Government had deliberately chosen to throw down the gauntlet to the British and the Unionists five days before the 'twelfth', the annual July 12 celebration of the Orange high mass. But not alone was the interview timed with an eye on the North, it was given on the eve of a scheduled meeting of the Anglo-Irish Conference. The media briefings from both sides which followed this meeting made no effort to disguise the fact that the encounter between Mayhew and Spring was stormy. Spring was also condemned from the Orange platforms a few days later, but unabashed, returned to his theme the day after the 'twelfth' in the Irish Seanad. He was speaking on the findings of the Opsahl Report*. This was a wide ranging inquiry, to which 3,000 people contributed, into every aspect of the Northern problem. It was financed by the Rowntree Trust, under the Chairmanship of the Norwegian academic, Torkel Opsahl. Significantly, amongst a range of other conclusions, it said:

There was widespread agreement that any settlement that had entirely excluded Sinn Fein from the negotiating process would be neither lasting nor stable, and that some way had to be found to involve the party in future talks.

The Commission also recommended that the broadcasting ban on Sinn Fein should be dropped by the Irish Republic.

Clearly, therefore, there are perceptible shifts of opinion occurring in Ireland. But old tendencies persist. Derry-born John Mathews was held in a maximum security prison for ten weeks on suspicion of being involved in the British bombing campaign. His case provides a good illustration of an attitude towards the Irish in Britain which is too frequently met with. At the end of the ten week interlude a

---

★   *A Ctitzen's Inquiry: The Opsahl Report*, Liliput Press, Dublin, 1993.

magistrate directed that Mathews be discharged 'without a stain on his character', as he was clearly innocent. However, he was taken from the court after the hearing and brought to a police station where he was served with an exclusion order. The next day (July 7, 1993) he was flown to Belfast accompanied by Home Office officials.

Unless the order is lifted he cannot pursue his higher education in England, or hope to succeed in getting a visa for the United States. Commenting on his treatment and that of other Irish suspects also released after being held for several weeks, he told R.T.E. on the day he arrived home that: 'Being Irish meant you were treated like scum. We were innocent and had not even been brought to court, yet the warders, the police, everyone we came in contact with, treated us as if we were convicted terrorists. Every single thing was a hassle, whether you were trying to arrange a routine family visit, or looking for a pair of socks. It was all hassle.'

That British attitude, part ancestral prejudice, part a consequence of the I.R.A. campaign, played its part in the spectacularly unjust miscarriage of justice cases I have already alluded to, those involving the Birmingham Six, the Guildford Four and Judith Ward. The Royal Commission has not altered attitudes. Three factors remain to be dealt with in England. One is the continuing tendency of the Tories—and when it suits them the Labour Party—to play for the Unionist M.P.s support. On July 17, 1993, after all the furore caused by McNamara and Spring, Sir Patrick Mayhew gave a radio interview in which he publicly appealed to the Unionists to support the Tories over Maastricht. Decoded, his message was a blatant appeal to the Unionists to support the Conservatives, who would in turn support them, whereas Labour would sell them out to Dublin. Hume and Sinn Fein reacted to his comments with outrage, pointing out that they made a mockery of Tory protestations that the British had no strategic or political interest in remaining in Ireland. Contemporary British political exigencies had clearly tempted the Tories, yet again, to make a political football out of the Irish issue. However, the second factor, inertia, prevents any constituency arising in British politics to do anything about such opportunism. Only four Tory and two Labour back-benchers took part in the debate on Northern Ireland in the House of Commons, before the House rose for the summer. A third consideration is the *déjà vu* factor.

The situation, as the House yawned its way through the Irish issue in the summer of 1993, was in some ways strikingly similar to that which existed prior to the British declaration of a truce with the I.R.A. in the summer of 1921. Then there was far more interest of course. But then too there was a hawks and doves split amongst British decision makers. On the one hand Lloyd George had unacknowledged civil servants in contact with Michael Collins. On the other the military men pressed for one more big push. Today there are certainly secret contacts between civil servants and Sinn Fein. But by and large the British remain hostile to coming to terms with the party. Even though the conflict is estimated to be costing £3 billion pounds sterling per annum and the death toll has passed the 3,000 mark and is still rising, the hawks in the administration are in the ascendent. They still believe they may yet win in the next few years. However, Sinn Fein and the I.R.A. are equally confident of victory, i.e., forcing the British to the negotiating table and ultimately to withdrawal. In other words, the violence will continue for at least some time yet.

This, of course, immediately raises the spectre of the Loyalist backlash. What is the position regarding the Loyalist paramilitaries?

Obviously they, like the I.R.A., would prefer to step up their campaign, including the Republic in it as well, if possible. But they are limited to what they can do out of their own resources. The inclination might be strong, but the capability, without British support, is far less than that of the I.R.A. However, it may not come to a scorched earth situation or anything like it. The Orange element sense that time is against them.

Despite Dick Spring's remarks to the *Guardian*, the 1993 parades passed off peacefully. Criticism of him was widespread but not unremarkable, whereas, some years ago there would have been riots. Within that spectrum the Loyalist paramilitaries have also been facing up to the future. While details may not be given, I have reason to believe that, accompanying the Hume/Adams process, Loyalist and Republican paramilitaries have also begun a dialogue concerning the position should the British withdraw. The Loyalists do not like the prospect, but they fear they may have to confront it. Meanwhile, it is unfortunately more than likely they will take every opportunity offered to indulge in an Irish version of 'ethnic cleansing'— with unacknowledged, undercover British support.

However, I think it appropriate to conclude this review of political developments with a paragraph from the Adams/Hume statement: 'New agreement is only achievable and viable if it can earn and enjoy the allegiance of the different traditions on this island, by accommodating diversity and providing for national reconciliation.'

That is both the challenge and the formula for the future.

36

Gerry Adams

Gerry Adams carried his weapons with him as he left his job in the famous Belfast pub, the Duke of York, on a fine August day in 1969. The regulars, many of them British TV and print journalists, were sorry to learn of his departure. He had been the most popular barman in the pub. They had not taken much note of his Republicanism. Nor would they have seen much to indicate it from what he was holding as he headed towards the rioting and petrol bombing which had erupted between the Catholic Falls Road area and the Protestant Shankill Road. Gerry Adams was going to war with a dozen large empty stout bottles.

His political evolution between August, 1969, and June 24, 1993, the date of our last interview, in Belfast (much of my knowledge of him is derived from other interviews and contacts over the years★), is a mirror image of the growth in the power and sophistication of the I.R.A. and Sinn Fein in the intervening years. In that time Adams became President of Sinn Fein and the best known figure in the Republican movement. Shortly before we talked, President Clinton, on the basis of material supplied by the British, had decided that Adams should be denied a visa to enter the United States for the launching of a book of his short stories. This caused a great furore in Irish-American circles as Clinton had told Irish American leaders (on April 5, 1993):

I would support a visa for Gerry Adams or any other elected official from a government recognised by the United States. I understand the United States' historical policy towards Sinn fein and on the advocacy of non-violence, but I honestly think that it would be totally harmless to let him [Adams] in†.

The Irish-Americans' anger was heightened by the fact that at around the same time that the British sent the Adams file to Clinton, Sir Patrick Mayhew had refused to accede to a request made by Judge Barbara Caulfield of the U.S. District Court in San Francisco (on June 11, 1993), that she be sent a sensitive file to enable her to make a decision in the extradition case involving James Smith. She had wanted information concerning the Stalker-Samson inquiry into the R.U.C. shoot-to-kill policy and the Kelly report which gave details of the disciplinary measures proposed against R.U.C. officers in the case.

The British argued that the documents might prejudice British security operations in Northern Ireland. Judge Caulfield, who had guaranteed the documents' secrecy, replied: 'It is not whether there is terrorism in Northern Ireland, it's a

---

★ See also *Disillusioned Decades*, Tim Pat Coogan, Gill and Macmillan, Dublin, 1987.
† *Irish Voice*, New York, May 25, 1993.

matter of obeying American law.' But she did not get the documents. According to Clinton, the British file on Adams, which was not made public, had implicated him in terrorism. Whatever the file contains, it is clearly not sufficient to bring charges against Adams because he is one of the most visible public figures in the Six Counties at liberty to come and go as he wishes—within the limits of his own security precautions. But to the British, he would clearly be a dangerous apologist for his cause on American TV. Bearded, good-looking, and disarmingly low-key in manner and speech, he has a sense of humour combined with formidable powers of analysis and logic in debate. He is also a first class writer and pamphleteer. Rightly or wrongly it is alleged that he has had a hand in the composition of every important policy change, and every significant document, ranging from writings attributed to Bobby Sands to the *Green Book*, which has emanated from Sinn Fein or the I.R.A. in the past fifteen years.

He looks more like a tweedy, bespectacled academic than a revolutionary. But one can't help be aware that violence fringes his world. While we talked he casually mentioned the most recent attempt on his life. A few weeks before we met there had been a grenade attack on his home in which his wife and son had narrowly escaped—just as he had himself missed being killed, when fired upon, on a number of occasions. On May 9, 1991, his close associate, Danny Morrison, also a talented writer and more importantly, Sinn Fein's Publicity Director, began an eight year prison sentence for false imprisonment of an R.U.C. informer. Soon after we talked, Adams's brother was arrested for I.R.A. activities, and was then released due to lack of evidence. A cousin, Kevin Hannaway, was one of the 'hooded' men awarded compensation by the British Government because of his mistreatment during internment. Kevin Hannaway, an active Republican, survived an assassination attempt when a U.V.F. gunman who had entered his home, panicked at his own reflection and emptied his gun into a wardrobe mirror which Hannaway flung open in front of him, before departing (rapidly) out the back door.

The Adams boys grew up in the Falls Road in a world of kitchen houses from which one was expected to progress upwards via 'the books'. Study, religion, 'having the crack', a Belfast expression for enjoying life, were the priorities of a lively family of ten brothers and sisters. Adams was the eldest. The Adams are one of the spinal Republican families of Northern Ireland, though for years Gerry was not aware of the extent of the Republican backdrop. There was little or no discussion of things nationalistic that Adams can recall. He had not realised that his uncle, Dominic Adams, was in the I.R.A. (he acted as Chief of Staff, during World War II) until he read the first U.K. edition of this book. The portcullis of years had come down and there was only a dim awareness amongst the children that two other uncles, Paddy Adams and Alfie Hannaway, had done time in the Curragh and in Belfast jail respectively.

The political figure in the family of whom he was most aware was his grand-father, William Hannaway, a remote, patriarchal figure who wore black laced boots. Along with the boots, Adams was impressed with the fact that Hannaway, a full-time labour official in Belfast, had been a friend of James Connolly, and was an agent for de Valera during the 1918 election. But political awareness bore in upon him sharply in 1964, during the Westminster election campaign. At that time it was illegal to display the Irish tricolour in the Six Counties under the Flags and Emblems Act. Ian Paisley, then a scarcely known preacher, discovered that the Republican candidate had a tricolour in his election headquarters window. The H.Q. was in Divis Street, an inconspicuous back street. Paisley, however, made himself conspicuous. Overnight, almost, he became a national figure, leading parades and demonstrations by Protestant Loyalists through the predominantly Catholic area. The resultant riots and petrol bombings saw the first car burnings to occur in Belfast. Television had not long come to Ireland and the public were shocked. After days of rioting the R.U.C. forcibly removed the flag. The Divis Street incident had made Paisley a force to be reckoned with.

Divis Street also had the effect of making the young Gerry Adams join the Republican movement. It was then largely a ceremonial, symbolic organisation. Although some 20,000 self-styled Republicans marched in the Easter commemorations to honour the Anniversary of 1916, only about twenty would have been geared for actual fighting. The I.R.A. was then dominated by the Marxist wing led by Roy Johnston. The thrust of the movement was towards working class solidarity with the Loyalists and the infiltration of trade unions. The folly of this approach in the sectarian climate of the Six Counties immediately became apparent to Adams. Catholics could not infiltrate anything that counted, except the ranks of the unskilled. For example, on the docks the casual workers were generally Catholic, the Protestants were the permanent workers. The craft unions in places like the shipyards, or the power plants, were overwhelmingly Protestant. (A fact which came home to roost during the workers strike of 1974, when the Loyalists successfully defied the British Government, and wrecked the Sunningdale Agreement through their control of the electricity supply.)

Adams took less account of the I.R.A.'s Marxism than of the activities of the Dublin Housing Action Committee. He founded a similar organisation in the New Barnsley and the Ballymurphy areas of the Falls Road. This was successful for a time, agitating over issues like the provision of railings for a pedestrian crossing after a Protestant child was knocked down. He saw how this homely initiative briefly united Protestant and Catholic. However, he also saw how the continuous Paisleyite agitation drove everyone back into their ancestral ghettos so that in the end, Protestant families had to be evacuated from New Barnsley after sectarian riots.

As the sixties progressed, he and the younger men in the I.R.A. who thought like him came to believe that a campaign for civil rights alone would not bring democracy to Ulster. The then leadership of the I.R.A. in Belfast, principally Jim Sullivan and Liam MacMillan, saw the growth of a civil rights movement, paralleling that in America, as leading to reform within the system. Adams argued that Unionism was not capable of democratisation. He and his cohorts wanted to bring about a destabilisation, out of which would grow a new and democratic state. He felt that the colonial relic of Unionist political culture was a decadent creation for which the British were responsible, manipulating the Unionists as they wished. He felt that the backlash factor could be orchestrated to suit British policies. The real backlash threat lay not with the Loyalist mobs, but with the well-armed R.U.C. who had the motivation, equipment and local knowledge to run a successful pogrom against Catholics. Basically this is still his position.

The mid-1960s saw him leave school, and devote himself more and more to local agitation. To his parents' chagrin he did not proceed to university, but took a job in a bar and spearheaded a campaign against the building of Divis Flats on the Falls Road. However, the flats went ahead and duly became prey to all the problems associated with high rise complexes in ghettos everywhere, as Adams and his friends had forecast. The problems were compounded by the growth of paramilitarism. The Irish Republican Socialist Party (I.R.S.P.), the political wing of the Irish National Liberation Army (I.N.L.A.) hung out there. But at the time of their building, they were welcomed by Catholic political and religious leaders as they prevented the Catholic vote being dispersed to other parts of the city. Because of sit-ins and other protests, Adams at one stage faced a grand total of fifty-four summonses for breach of the peace and for illegal entry. His first TV interview came about as a result of these activities.

His education progressed through street confrontations, the study of James Connolly, Irish history and literature. He became a member of the Wolfe Tone Society, the Republican-oriented literary and debating society. Curiously, neither he nor his friends read Marx; they were instinctive, working-class socialists. Ireland overall was experiencing the invigorating shock of the new which the sixties had brought everywhere in the West. There was an explosion in ballad singing and traditional music, always a particularly potent force in Ireland with its tradition of oral culture. Historically a nation on the run did not sculpt or paint portraits, but it could, and did, sing and recite poetry. Now all over the country there was a growth in Fleadhanna Ceol (Irish music festivals).

The Fleadhanna helped to spread the popularity of a Dublin group, the Dubliners, led by Ronnie Drew, who at the time were reviving a medley of Irish airs, old Ulster ballads like 'My Lagan Love', and political ballads like 'James Connolly' which told of his death by British firing squad. Even more potent, because closer to hand, was 'Sean South of Garryowen', who had lost his life only yesterday, in the 1956 I.R.A. campaign. One would have to have witnessed a ballad session in a Republican pub or club to understand the sense of empathy these and similar songs brought, and bring, to young men and women of Adams' type. The drinking, the camaraderie, the shared sense of being 'us' against the hostile 'them' outside is a potent mixture. (The same formula works in Loyalist circles also of course).

Adams' growing consciousness of being Irish was heightened by three factors: the 50th Anniversary Commemoration of the Easter Rising which took place in 1966, his move to a job in the Duke of York bar around this time, and his becoming involved, through the Wolfe Tone society, in the broad based Civil Rights Association which was founded in the International Hotel, Belfast, on January 29, 1967. The effect of the widespread commemoration events (lectures, concerts, Gaelic sporting events and so forth) for the anniversary of the Rising on an ardent young Nationalist can readily be imagined. The Duke of York had another effect, says Adams: 'The atmosphere was heady with ideas. There was a sort of effervescence in the air.' The clientele included actors, journalists, writers, politicians and the B.B.C. and other international television crews being drawn to

Northern Ireland by the clash between the Unionists and the increasingly assertive
civil rights groups.

A London correspondent who remembers Adams from the Duke of York
interlude described him to me as: 'Your classic "favourite barman" type: efficient,
friendly, intelligent. A great loss to the licensed trade!' The amalgamation of like-
minded bodies into the Civil Rights Association broadened Adams's Duke of York
contacts. 'You met all sorts of hues and views,' he recalled. There were British
civil libertarians, communists, members of the Northern Ireland Labour Party,
journalists, professionals like Dr Con McCluskey who first injected the concept of
civil rights into the Six Counties, even some liberal Unionists. But as his contacts
widened, so did two sets of conflict intensify. One, the internal, hidden, struggle
between Adams and the other young tigers of the Republican movement with the
older leadership over the wisdom of pursuing a purely civil rights campaign.
Secondly, the increasingly visible tensions between the civil rights campaigners
and the Unionists, amongst whom Paisley was becoming increasingly active.

Four sets of attacks in particular pushed the Six Counties into 'the troubles'.
An R.U.C. ban on a civil rights march in Derry on October 5, 1968, led to fierce
rioting in which, under the eyes of the cameras, scores of people were injured.
On November 30, Paisley and a henchman, Major Ronald Bunting, intervened in
a civil rights march at Armagh. The Paisleyites arrived in the city in the early
hours of the morning in a cavalcade of cars containing stones, sharpened piping
and cudgels with nails driven through them. They erected barricades and prevented
the marchers traversing a route previously agreed with the R.U.C. The police
made no effort to intervene. Nor did they interfere when at Burntollet, County
Derry, similar mobs ambushed a Peoples' Democracy march. The P.D.s, a student
organisation led by Bernadette Devlin and Michael Farrell, were driven into a
river and beaten while scores of uniformed R.U.C. stood idly by. Again the
scenes were recorded on television.

The pot finally boiled over with the rioting in Derry and Belfast in August of
1969 during which Protestant mobs in both cities attempted to invade Catholic
areas. In Belfast members of the R.U.C. were observed looking at their watches
and departing from their beats, shortly before the mobs arrived, led by their
colleagues in the B-Specials. Since then the people of the Falls Road have fought
to keep the police from re-entering their areas. Today they can only do so under
British Army protection.

The Army arrived to protect the Catholics in Derry, on August 14, and in
Belfast, on August 15. Gerry Adams had his own ideas as to how Nationalists
should be protected. But on August 13, after all the debate about force as opposed
to constitutional action, the I.R.A.'s armament on the Falls Road had consisted
of five handguns. There were no full-time guerillas and no active service units.
Outraged Nationalists altered the letters I.R.A. on gable walls to read: 'Irish Ran
Away'. Gerry Adams left his job in the Duke of York and walked not away, but
towards the fighting.

Fighting in those early years involved home-grown expertise that was often
more harmful to the Republicans than the authorities. Suitcases full of gelignite
sometimes exploded prematurely taking with them the bombers, not the target.

Nail-bombs claimed as many I.R.A. fingers as British limbs. The 'Tipperary rifle', a hurling stick, was frequently employed, as was the 'kidney paver', that stock-in-trade of the Belfast rioter, a cobble-stone. Externally, the reaction to a Loyalist bombing of the Silent Valley reservoir caused the resignation of Captain Terence O'Neill, the Six County Prime Minister. Within the I.R.A. the arrest of the Comanding Officer of the Belfast Brigade, Billy McKee, led to a shake-up wherein new, and unknown (to the R.U.C.) figures moved into positions of authority.

Ironically, McKee was a traditionalist who saw the I.R.A.'s role as defending the Catholics, not attacking the British. Adams, however, increasingly came to be identified with a belief formerly articulated by Michael Collins when he was urging the Sinn Fein of his day to go to war★:

. . . the sooner fighting was forced and a general state of disorder created throughout the country the better it would be throughout the country. Ireland was likely to get more out of the state of general disorder than from a continuance of the situation as it then was.

Adams's own immediate surroundings in the Ballymurphy district of the Falls Road were a scene of 'general disorder'. The inhabitants fought the British Army for a year without firing a shot. There was a plentiful supply of manpower available for the hostilities as male unemployment in the area commonly stands at 60 per cent. Homes were searched incessantly. Five or six searches a night was not uncommon. Gardens were more frequently occupied by Saracen armoured cars than by lawnmowers. But the citizens of Ballymurphy fought back fiercely, the women as much as the men. 'Bin Brigades', sounded the tocsin at the approach of troops by banging bin lids on the pavements. Then the 'hurley brigades' attacked the intruders. Wet sacks were used to gather up the C.S. gas cylinders and hurl them back at the soldiers. Every home had basins filled with vinegar to counter the C.S. gas.

The vocabularies of the unfortunate troops was considerably added to, if not enriched, by the epithets hurled at them by amazonian women who perfected a technique of luring them into cul-de-sacs, where, amongst other things, the soldiers heard many original, and cacophonous, suggestions concerning their ancestry. The psychological injury inflicted must have been greater than anything done with a 'kidney-paver' or 'Tipperary rifle'.

The Adams family was not unscathed. One brother, Dominic, developed a stammer after a C.S. gas attack on their home. Gerry Adams himself was becoming a marked man as the situation escalated. Bloody turning points came and went: Falls Road curfew, July, 1970; first British soldier killed, February, 1971; Internment, August, 1971. Adams was married by Fr. Des Murphy in a room behind the altar in St. John's Chapel on the Falls Road during the height of the internment crisis. Adams's father was in Long Kesh. There was no wedding reception and the honeymoon was a few days in Dublin. On its last evening they heard Southern politicians address an anti-internment meeting in the fiery tones of verbal Republicanism outside the G.P.O. After the meeting ended, Gerry and Colette headed back to Belfast and the Republicanism of Reality.

★   *The Man Who Made Ireland*, by Tim Pat Coogan, Roberts Rinehart, Colorado, 1992, pg. 103.

In 1972 Adams himself was interned. He was interrogated and systematically beaten up. Other methods were also employed:

'You faced the wall for hours at a time, supporting yourself only with your finger tips. You'd be waiting all day for something to happen. Sometimes they came up behind you and dropped a tray with a crash. It would scare the living daylights out of you. Once they showed me a blood stained hatchet . . .'

In Castlereagh Barracks he remained silent for a week, using what he had taught himself of counter-interrogation techniques to defeat his captors. By way of example he indicated the room we were talking in. I had thought it rather spartan but he judged it a good place to be interrogated in: 'You see that curtain for example. It's made of tweed. You could think about how the tweed was made, where the materials came from, how they dyed it, what sort of people worked at making tweed, what their lives were like and so on.' One can certainly find echoes of that technique in the *Green Book*. After his interrogation, following which he lodged a formal complaint about his treatment, he was taken first to the Maidstone prison ship and then interned in Long Kesh prison.

He had no idea as to when he might be released and had gone on a thirteen day hunger strike with a group which included his uncle, Liam Hannaway, a prominent Belfast I.R.A. man. The issue was the usual I.R.A. demand for political status. Unexpectedly, it was conceded in extraordinary circumstances. Out of the blue Adams was freed. One day he heard his name being called for release. When, puzzled, he asked his uncle why his name was being called, all he received in return was a terse: 'Get out.' Outside the jail he discovered that a truce was to be negotiated with the British and that he and Daithi O'Connell were to do the negotiating. A truce was agreed on terms which eventually led to the great hunger strikes of the 1980s. On June 20, 1972, William Whitelaw, the Northern Ireland Secretary of State, announced the introduction of the new prison classification of Special Category Prisoner. This in effect conceded political status by another name to the I.R.A.

Another result of the Adams/O'Connell negotiation was that a group of I.R.A. men, including Adams, were given a safe conduct to be flown to London aboard an R.A.F. plane to meet Whitelaw to discuss a British withdrawal. The Irish and the British delegations met at the luxury home of Whitelaw's ministerial colleague, Paul Channon, in Chelsea, a far cry from Ballymurphy and Long Kesh. Too far, in more respects than one. Historically, it was a significant meeting; the first time representatives of the Irish 'physical force' tradition had met British statesmen since the time of Michael Collins and the Treaty negotiations. But the middle-class Catholics of the Six Counties were not with the Irish delegation because they supported the S.D.L.P. Dublin had not been consulted and the Unionists were completely absent. Politically, therefore, there was no pressure on the British to seriously entertain the I.R.A. demand for a withdrawal. Culturally, too, there was a yawning gulf between the Irish and the British. One of the Irish delegation, curiously the only man with a professional training on the Irish side, was so suspicious of the proceedings that his attitude towards the British was described to me, by an English civil servant, as being 'like a dog'. Not surprisingly all that emerged from the talks in concrete terms were agreements on an extension of the truce.

Adams actually took no formal part in the discussions. His role was that of 'listener'. Listening for the nuances of what the other side meant as opposed to what they said. During a break in the talks he had had a conversation with Whitelaw, whom he found surprisingly nervous, sweating profusely and obviously ill at ease. By contrast, the only time the Irishmen had felt any fear was when they were collected in an R.A.F. helicopter, which circled for a time near the Glenshane Pass in the Sperrin Mountains, preparatory to setting course for their plane to London. They were uneasily conscious of the opportunities for marksmanship being afforded to their colleagues on the ground who had not been made aware of who was in the helicopter!

During his exchange with Whitelaw concerning their pact, Adams agreed that in the event of certain eventualities, 'all bets were off'. The truce only held for a matter of days and the next time Adams heard that phrase he was lying naked on the floor of a cell in the Springfield Road Barracks being kicked by a Special Branch interrogator who punctuated his kicks with the words: 'All bets are off now, Gerry.' He still has kidney problems stemming from that episode. He learned of the birth of his son, Gearoid, from a warder in Long Kesh one September night in 1971. He and Colette were not reunited for another four years and even then their relationship had to adapt to the fact of his being generally on the run.

We have seen how, throughout the seventies, the I.R.A. became reorganised. More time will have to elapse before it can be said with certainty what part, if any, Adams played in that reorganisation. What is undoubtedly true is that increasingly he emerged as the leading political figure in the Republican movement. He deliberately sought to distance himself, in the public mind, from the militant wing of Republicanism, as I discovered accidentally one day when I got a phone call at the *Irish Press* from my solicitor, Con Lehane. It turned out that he wanted to talk, not about my business, but about another client of his, the well-known politician, Mr Gerry Adams, whom the *Irish Press* had recently grossly maligned by referring to him in a report as being a member of the I.R.A. A lively, if not altogether courteous conversation ensued!

However, Adams went on to prove that he was indeed a politician of rare skill and courage. He and the young tigers of Sinn Fein emerged into national, and sometimes international, prominence in the crucible of emotion generated by the hunger strikes which broke out in 1981 over the British proposal to take away the Special Category status which he had negotiated in 1972. As I had some peripheral dealing with the situation myself, on behalf of Irish Government figures, I was able to evaluate the performance of the new generation of Northern Irish Sinn Fein leadership. It was unquestionably of high calibre. Danny Morrison, Martin McGuinness, Tom Hartley, Jim Gibney, Joe Austin and Richard McAuley all conducted themselves with restraint and dignity. Moreover they showed themselves able to rise to the challenge of the moment, whether it involved coping with political negotiation, dealing with the media, or the distraught relatives of hunger strikers.

The hunger strikes lasted for 217 days, from March 1, to October 3, 1981. During that time ten men died: Bobby Sands, Francis Hughes, Raymond McCreesh, Patsy O'Hara, Joe McDonnell, Martin Hurson, Kevin Lynch, Kieran Doherty,

Tom McElera and Michael Devine. They have left an ineradicable imprint on Northern Irish politics. Bobby Sands was elected to the British Parliament as M.P. for Fermanagh/Tyrone as he lay dying. Over 100,000 people joined in his funeral cortège. Adams regards that election as a crucial learning experience for Sinn Fein. The young tigers learned how to conduct a campaign both in nitty gritty detail, like finding out what a personation officer's function is, to the more flamboyant aspects of electioneering.

He told me that it was: 'Exhilarating. Sometimes we'd come into a little town with Catholics corralled away up at the top as usual, the Loyalists living along the main street, with the businesses. We would come in with the tricolour flying and the bands playing and the Catholics would come down from the hills as if we were the relieving cavalry.' That cavalry charge took the young tigers to control of Sinn Fein and to a historic victory in the 1983 Westminster election when Adams defeated the S.D.L.P. leader, Gerry Fitt, for the West Belfast seat. Within Sinn Fein, Daithi O'Connell and Ruairi O'Bradaigh stood down as President and Vice President in recognition of the fact that Sinn Fein was now a Northern movement led by Northerners. Adams has been President of Sinn Fein since, and the movement has followed a hard Northern Republican line. No sops to Loyalism in the form of a federal arrangement as proposed in the Eire Nua document; a unitary state is Sinn Fein's preferred option for the future of Ireland.

However, Adams has not been M.P. for West Belfast since April, 1992. His vote went up slightly but he was defeated by the S.D.L.P. candidate, Dr. Joe Hendron. Hendron, a colourless, unimpressive figure won not on his own merits but because some 3,000 Unionists voted tactically for him rather than support their own candidate, Fred Cobain, in order to defeat Sinn Fein. However, Hendron's popularity is not high, even with his own supporters. He won by less than six hundred votes (17,415 to 16,826) and a thousand new young voters have come on the register since the election. These are almost by definition sure to be Sinn Fein. The Local Government elections in May, 1993, showed the Sinn Fein share of the vote, approximately 40 per cent of the total Nationalist poll, remains constant. Accordingly, Adams is generally expected to regain the seat at the next general election, whenever it may be.

During our interview, Adams and I talked—as inevitably we do when we have a serious discussion—about the possibility of a Loyalist backlash and the linked question of the existence of an R.U.C./Loyalist tie-up. 'I'll put it to you this way,' he replied, 'A few years ago the R.U.C. were shooting Catholics in Tyrone. Catholics are still being shot in Tyrone, but the R.U.C.'s not doing it.' To illustrate his point Adams took as his theme the case of Declan 'Beano' Casey. Casey is yet another example of a paramilitary who worked for the security forces and then became a prey to homesickness and disgust both of himself and the set-up. He went public—at very great personal risk. Casey, though a Republican, has the same motive for speaking out as the Loyalist 'Maxwell'. This former I.R.A. quartermaster from Strabane, County Tyrone, genuinely wants other people to avoid the trap he fell into.

At the time Adams and I were conducting our interview, Casey had told a Belfast Court (on June 22, 1993) that he was :'at all stages under the orders of the

R.U.C. Special Branch and everything I did had the prior and full knowledge of the Special Branch.' He had decided the week beforehand to blow his cover and tell the *Daily Mirror* that he had been allowed to go on killing for the I.R.A. while working for the British Government. The British had set him up in a safe house in England, but Casey decided to come in from the cold. Even though he was under a death threat from the Provisional I.R.A., something I would rank ahead of that placed upon Salman Rushdie, he decided to confront his destiny. He came home and was arrested at the home of his father-in-law. Speaking in a calm voice he told the court that he regretted the traumas he had brought upon his wife, family, and the Republican movement then went on to say, echoing Maxwell:

'I appeal to anyone caught up in the same bizarre position as myself to come forward and make their position known to some public figure and not end up like me—soul-destroyed by the R.U.C. Special Branch.' Casey was charged with possessing two rifles and with withholding information about the death of a U.D.R. man. He said he found it a bit bizarre to be facing 'trumped up charges', having spent five years spying for the unit which had set him up in a safe house in England.

Adams made the point that any mother who had lost a son in the R.U.C. to the I.R.A., or any widow, would feel 'sickened' on reading 'Beano's' evidence. 'Was this what they died for? They'll want to know was their son or husband set-up? Even if he wasn't, what about the wee woman down the road?' It is a fair point that, along with the dawning sense of identity amongst Protestants, very obvious in Maxwell for example, who increasingly sees himself as Irish and wishes that the British would just go away. Such cases do pose a threat to Loyalism.

What else in the province do the authorities know about, say, concerning racketeering of both green and orange hue, and deliberately take no action on for their own purposes? More importantly, in the face of the manifest inability of the authorities to crush the I.R.A., the implications of the fact that only a half dozen Westminster M.P.s bother to turn up for a debate on Northern Ireland takes on an added significance in an era of governmental cutbacks and falling employment. There is a growing sense of betrayal amongst Unionists. In one part of their minds, for reasons of their own self-esteem, Maxwell, and many like him would welcome a backlash. They can possibly stage one, albeit of a short-lived nature, but what then? The Loyalists still control a major proportion of the jobs and better class farms and homes in the Six Counties—precisely the sort of targets that would normally be attacked in a 'scorched earth' situation. But it would be the 'haves' earth which would be scorched, not the 'have-nots'. Where would the former 'haves' go after the scorching?

An essential component of Loyalism was supremacy. Quite obviously the Loyalists are no longer supreme over either the Provisional I.R.A. in military terms or the Dublin Government in political ones. And on top of this, demographic changes are forcing the Protestants out of their traditional areas and out to the northern tips of the Six Counties: East Antrim and North Down. A bastion of Protestant supremacy, Mackie's Engineering Works, has left the Falls area. In the Queen's University, sixty-five per cent of the student body is now Catholic. Many well-off Protestant families, and their Catholic counterparts, are sending their children to

English universities. The enrolment which does attend Queen's thus contains a high percentage of working class Catholics from the hardcore Republican areas. How many science and engineering graduates from this element are advising on the ever increasingly skillful use of technology by the Provos? The answer to that question is: 'No one knows but there is such a thing as the ineluctable dialectic of history.'

I asked Adams what was his guesstimate of the Provos' ability to continue. He declined to reply directly but recalled Mrs Thatcher's comment at the time of the hunger strikes, thirteen years earlier. She had said that the strikes represented the playing of 'the last card' by the I.R.A. Earlier we had talked about the devastation caused by the April, 1993, bomb in the City of London. 'Draw your own conclusions,' he said.

For some years past, before Adams and I spoke, the I.R.A.'s Bodenstown statements had indicated a willingness to talk. The right of the Irish people to 'self-determination' has been a continuing theme. So too has that of asking those who would condemn the armed struggle to suggest another way. It was out of those evidences of willingness to listen to reason that the process which led to the Adams-Hume talks was born. Although Hume endured the public criticism, Adams was taking the greater risk. There are some personalities in the I.R.A. for whom his life would not be worth a cent should it be thought that he was selling out the 'armed struggle'. The feeling stems not from blood-lust, but the same sense of the integrity of the fight which Sean, whom I mentioned in the prologue, displayed when I tried to talk him out of joining the I.R.A. Adams himself visibly has that same sense of the rightness of the struggle. His own experiences and his family background, make calls for truces, and the emergence and disappearance of sunburst peace movements appear, facile at best and, at worse, part of the counter-insurgency effort.

Too many have died to countenance a ceasefire without the possibility of a British withdrawal in sight. On one level 'self-determination' is a deceptively emollient phrase. It means, of course, excluding the British. But it also means including the Irish, all the Irish, and not just the Catholics of Northern Ireland. I found on this occasion, after the series of talks with Hume (who had also, no doubt, learned what the bottom line was for the Republicans), that Adams was prepared to enlarge the horizons insofar as Dublin was concerned. A combination of an elucidation of Dublin's position, which formed part of the discussions, plus Adams's own first hand experience of the lack of support for Sinn Fein in Twenty-Six County elections, had injected a note of realism into the Republican position.

There was nothing of a once familiar refrain: 'To us a Garda is a British soldier in another uniform.' This time he spoke of the necessity to arrive at a solution based on agreement between Dublin and London. 'We would have to be included of course, but London and Dublin must get together in the first instance. 'When his talks with Hume ended, Adams had said (on B.B.C. Radio Ulster, June 12, 1993) that their discussions were the only initiative on the horizon and should be given the same encouragement as the talks Mayhew had been involved in. He said:

'It needs more than John Hume and me. Obviously it needs the Republicans, it needs Dublin, it needs the British, it needs the Unionists. Let us give, if not approval, the same sort of general encouragement to this process as was given to the nonsense that the British were involved in.'

He repeated this sentiment to me, laying great stress on the Dublin–London relationship. 'That's where the settlement has to take place. As Republicans we would of course like to see the solution which eventuates being within a Republican framework. What we seek is a broad democratisation of society: the right of the Irish people to national self-determination. In a post-British withdrawal Ireland we would see the rule of the ballot box as paramount. Contrary to propaganda, we see no role for the armed struggle in the Twenty-Six Counties. The end of Partition and the departure of the British should mean an end to the use of force. And look at the potential for investment, industry, tourism, and so on, that would follow.'

Adams used to be dismissive of a U.N. presence. Now, ironically at a time when the U.N. has rarely shown itself to be less effective, he would welcome an international peacekeeping force. 'But not too many troops. We want less troops, not more in the province.' He is appreciative of such American initiatives as the MacBride Principles, the Clinton proposal for a Peace Envoy, and the support given by American lawyers to human rights cases. 'Basically the problem here is a human rights issue. The British are afraid of Irish-American influence. They are afraid of seeing me in the U.S. But since the hunger strikes, Sinn Fein is a valid and a vital force in Irish and Irish-American affairs. We are entitled to be listened to. We will not give up until we are heard. Thirteen members of Sinn Fein have been killed. To step into their shoes, another candidate has to publish his or her name and address and put their neck on the block. On top of that they have to get eight sponsors. They have to risk their lives too. Yet, every time one of our people is shot, another candidate comes forward. So do his sponsors. That's not Godfatherism.'

'The British are going to go some day. We don't know when. At the moment they're still operating on the belief that they can beat Sinn Fein and the I.R.A. Any more constructive approach is stalled by inertia, lack of vision, the past, everything. But they have nothing to offer. We've had Hillsborough and we're no further down the road. There's a vacuum. What we do know is that until they go we'll keep bothering them and poking at them until they leave.'

And how does young Sean feel about that prospect? At present he is still on remand, and still does not know what his sentence will be. He sent me a 'comm' which gives a fair indication of the state of his morale. It was five cigarette papers long. At the time he wrote it he was in the Punishment Unit 'on the boards' for thirty days for striking a Loyalist prisoner. As a result he was deprived of bedding and confined to his cell twenty-four hours a day. Some forty-six of his companions were in a similar situation because they had worn Easter lillies and conducted an illegal parade to commemorate 1916. He described conditions as follows:

The fun continues. I don't think this place has changed from poor Tom Williams' time, [Williams, as readers will recall, was hanged in the jail in 1942] a real dungeon . . . conditions here are very poor, lads haven't been getting out at all. Not even to empty piss pots, to wash, association etc. The results have been to empty the piss out of the cracks in the cell doors and shit into bags leaving them out the windows . . . I'm not used to this auld crack, the wing I came from was nice and peaceful . . .

The present England campaign indicates that it's definitely winning the war at the moment. Hopefully it'll continue. The previous operations set us back greatly. [Warrington] I was shattered when I heard about it. It's sickening at times. But nothing's changed, I mean from '69 about young children dying. We've lost young ones too. That doesn't make any difference. But when I saw that shower of shit in Dublin I was boiling with anger [The peace demonstrations]. Where have they been for the last twenty years?

He went on to talk about his case and his hopes for the future. One of his fellow accused had 'broke bad'. As a result he expected to get a longer sentence. He told me not to worry about him. He said of Adams:

Big Gerry is a Saint. May God protect him. He is one our best.

When Sean's punishment term had ended, I visited him in the gloomy old Victorian jail. It is set in the Loyalist Crumlin Road amidst houses whose gable ends are decorated with murals showing battle-dressed, balaclaved U.V.F. men firing rifles at an unseen foe—Sean and his comrades. Despite the lowering surroundings, it was like visiting an eager young cadet in a Military Academy. Spotlessly clean, hair cut tightly, he wore jeans and an open necked shirt. He seemed to be taller, certainly leaner, but fit and full of cheer and energy. 'Ah sure they wouldn't let you get down in here. If they [The I.R.A. jail structure] see you gettin' depressed they say 'what are you on about and put two men on you until you just have to get cheerful again.' He showed the same confidence in victory that he had expressed in his comm.

'Ah sure of course we'll win. And we'll get back that seat in West Belfast for Big Gerry. That's a certainty.' His only concern about his trial and sentence was that he wanted it to come quickly so that he could get started on a course of study. In the meantime he was reading everything he could and taking part in prison debates. In the short time which had elapsed since we had last shaken hands he had visibly matured and seemed to have a deeper grasp of affairs. He again mentioned Warrington saying: 'Ah sure that was shocking. You'd have to be against that.' When I suggested that fighting with Loyalist fellow prisoners was perhaps not the best way to secure a United Ireland he replied:

'Sure I know that . . . It was just one of those things, the screws won't allow segregation, and it leads to tensions. I was sorry I belted your man afterwards. We're all going to have to live together one day. You'd be sorry for them in here. They've no organisation, and they feel the pressure. You see them cryin' for their mammies sometimes.' His mother, who had accompanied me on the visit, chided him for making fun of mothers and wagged her finger at him saying: 'Just because you're in here doesn't mean you don't have to show respect like the rest of the family, or I'll chastise you.'

He laughed at her and observed to me: 'Chastised! But isn't she lookin' well?' And indeed she was. The mini-skirted wonder who had opened the door to me so long ago was gone of course. But these days Sean's mother has eschewed the bottle, lost weight, got her hair done and wears smart clothes. Her natural good looks are re-asserting themselves. Like her daughters, she is putting the best possible face on things for Sean. And not merely a face as his arrest has galvanised his sisters in their studies and helped to politicise the family. All are now active on behalf of Sinn Fein. They see their study and work as part of building a new society in which not alone will Sean be free but the goals for which he went to prison will be realised. It's a common phenomenon in Northern Ireland; the same support syndrome I mentioned in the case of Kevin Barry O'Rourke.

When the visit was up, Sean shook hands and waved goodbye like an athletic young freshman bidding friends adieu before returning to his studies. The idea that behind a locked door in the corner of the visiting room he was returning to a world which contained practices like 'shitting in bags' and 'pouring piss through door cracks' seemed incredible. His mother kept the tears at bay until he disappeared. We had planned to have a cup of tea. But when we emerged from the prison we discovered the Belfast traffic had been snarled by a rash of bomb scares. She had to leave immediately. The bomb scares meant that she would be delayed on her way across the city to pick up a granddaughter as she always did in the afternoon, so as to enable the child's mother to work to earn money to pay for her studies. We had met because I had once wanted to encounter a typical Belfast Republican family. Now I was witnessing a typical day in the life of the same family in June, 1993, twenty-five years later. Progress, Northern Ireland style.

Epilogue

How can this mess be resolved?

My formula would be, in shorthand, similar to that evolved by the British in Hong Kong. They set a timetable for withdrawal and started making the requisite plans well in advance of the date set. In the case of the Six Counties, the plans should allow for the active involvement of the U.N. and the E.E.C., with the participation and encouragement of the U.S., whom I would see as the principal motor force in the situation.

All sorts of objections could be raised on the basis of the differences between Hong Kong and Dublin. Only one really counts: instead of a few million pacifically inclined Southern Irish across the border, the British faced the reality of nearly a billion militantly-led Chinese. That fact, not any hypocritically crafted set-piece answer about 'respecting the wishes of the majority' in the artificially contrived Six County area, influenced the decision to withdraw.

If a referendum were held in Ireland as a whole, the result would be in favour of a British withdrawal. Similarly, if the British taxpayers got a chance to register their opinions on withdrawal, they too would opt for encouraging a united Ireland solution. Sir Patrick Mayhew is on record as saying that the cost of the Six Counties is over three billion pounds sterling annually. Much of this money is spent on security. It costs some seven hundred pounds a week to keep one prisoner like Sean in jail, never mind other expenditures such as bomb damage, or the maintenance of a large presence of troops on a war footing. The most important statistic, of course, is the fact that the war has claimed more than three thousand lives and the death toll is rising steadily.

The decaying political culture known as Unionism has no place in European life. Even its nearest exemplar, South African apartheid, has changed, under a combination of external and internal pressures. The Six Counties has more than its share of internal pressures, but there is not sufficient sustained international interest to force improvement.

Nor is it a matter of waiting for a Six County version of South Africa's President de Klerk to surface. Unionism is based on a combination of two things; supremacy and a desire to preserve the British link. Orange power is the basis of this supremacy, as white power is in South Africa. But unlike the Afrikaners, the Unionists have a guarantee from the British Government that they need not heed the winds of changes if they do not want to. Their politics are designed to exclude anyone like de Klerk.

They have a term to describe such figures: a 'Lundy', meaning someone who would come to an accommodation. Even though Unionist desire for linkage with Westminster is only reciprocated these days with waning enthusiasm, and then purely for reasons of expedience, on occasions such as the vote on Maastricht which saved (temporarily) the Conservative Government in July of 1993, reciprocated it is.

Time will tell whether the much disputed deal with the Unionists over their Maastricht support will result in increased Unionist power at the expense of the Nationalists' and Dublin's friendship with London. Certainly, as I write, it is feared in Dublin that this will prove to be the case. What cannot be disputed is the fact that, like a British uniform in Belfast, the Unionists' presence at Westminster is an irritant in the political oyster, around which no pearl will form.

The fraying Westminster link is preventing the acceleration of the natural organic development of a sense of Protestant Irishness which is, nevertheless, increasingly discernible. As the feeling grows that the British will someday be gone, the need to develop a sense of identity becomes more intense. It could and should be encouraged. I believe that decision in principle has to be taken by the British that they intend to withdraw physically from Ireland, as they have clearly done emotionally and intellectually.

Once the principle is confronted, the rest is a matter of mechanics, but potentially highly dangerous mechanics. There are two quite clear-cut recipes for civil war. One is a sudden British pull-out (as the Belgians did from the Congo). The other is any question of an Irish Army involvement. One Irish Army boot six inches north of the border would be the signal for ancestral Loyalist fears, Maxwell's doomsday scenario, to burst forth.

The question of policing is all important. Having Catholic police in Catholic flash-point areas, Protestant police in the corresponding Loyalist areas will be necessary. There is the question of de-fanging the various armed forces in the province. The British have already made a significant step in this direction by subsuming the former B-Special force, the Ulster Defence Regiment, into the regular Army (in 1992).

But far more remains to be done. Ironically, the most powerful grouping, the I.R.A., would be the easiest to deal with, in the event of withdrawal becoming a real possibility. Once Sinn Fein is admitted to talks, as inevitably the party must be, the I.R.A. will be a part of that process. And the I.R.A., it must be recognised, would instantly become far stronger. Some of its best operatives would be freed from prison and the movement would not be under pressure from the security forces, a factor which certainly would give some would-be hit men on the Loyalist side pause for thought. I would not fear that the I.R.A. would attempt any sort of Republican backlash or pogrom. The Provisionals can control their membership. It is on the Loyalist paramilitary front that one has to express doubt.

In one sense these groupings become nobody's children historically, in the event of a united Ireland prospect opening up. Who then controls the U.D.A. and a shadowy grouping like the Ulster Resistance Movement founded by Ian Paisley and Peter Robinson of the Democratic Unionist Party? Amongst other clear links to paramilitary activity, Ulster Resistance members have been arrested in Paris on charges of trying to exchange missile parts—made in Belfast for the British Government—for arms in a covert operation involving South African diplomats.

One must approach the Loyalists in a spirit of putting one's trust in God, but also, very definitely, keeping one's powder dry. There are factors such as the recognition of the inevitability of change, and the basic good sense and law-abiding nature of the vast majority of Northern Ireland's Protestants which will make a positive contribution to any solution. But there is also the visceral anti-Catholic prejudice component of Loyalism that has produced sectarian murder gangs such as the Shankill Butchers, or one-man human death-machines like Michael Stone. Their allies, the British, to whom they are loyal may depart, but their hates will not go with them. Certainly they would wish to stage a backlash.

The question comes down to an appraisal of their ability to stage a backlash without the British connection; without for example, that huge electronic umbrella of surveillance and phone tapping from which so much of their, literally, deadly accurate information comes. One could certainly envisage some sort of outburst of Loyalist hatred and anger, born out of a confused medley of feeling betrayed; being revengeful, needing to demonstrate their pride, to get in some ethnic cleansing while the moment was propitious. But how long would that moment last? How virulent would it be? Would that be the end of it: one last spate of violence which would at least have the merit of being terminal violence? How great or small would the toil be in relation to what has already happened and will happen if the present situation is allowed to continue?

The truth is no one can answer these questions with absolute certainty. What we do know is that the bill in terms of life, property and human happiness, mounts almost daily. I do not believe it is good enough to let it go on mounting out of a vague fear that the backlash cost could be higher. The vexed question of policing is absolutely crucial in any serious discussion of a British withdrawal. The Royal Ulster Constabulary's role is central to the entire process.

The force contains the potential for a backlash, but it also contains the prospect for salvation. If the R.U.C. is told plainly that it can have a backlash, but not its salaries, pension schemes and welfare, then those among its ranks who would opt for the death squads would be in an insignificant minority. The force, more than any other single factor, made the Anglo-Irish Agreement come into operation. It stood up to its fellow Protestants, sometimes at a cost to its members of being attacked and intimidated in their homes. It could do so again.

The international community is also vital to the peace process. While these slow, difficult, dangerous, but necessary, steps are being taken, Ireland needs the assistance, and presence, of a U.N. force, backed by the United States, the E.E.C.— and Britain. Once the British allow it to be recognised that the problem is not merely domestic to Britain, they can allow their friends to help them out of their Irish entanglement.

Last, but not least, is the question of finance. Obviously there is no question of the Republic being in the position to pick up Britain's tab. That will have to remain Britain's responsibility for some years into the future. But the bill will be minus the security costs and there is enough international funding around. The E.E.C. Convergence fund experiment and other sources of finance such as the American backed International Fund could be deepened and enlarged beneficially for less than the cost of producing one obsolete rocket.

Of course, the Irish Government also has a responsibility to assist in the process. Just a few years ago even I would have been harsh on Dublin for sins of omission, rather than commission. Its general attitude of 'oh Lord make me good, but not yet' contributed to the vacuum which the death squads are filling. However, change is coming at such a pace that the old charge of 'Home rule is Rome rule' increasingly has less and less validity.

But Dublin can still do more than it is doing. Holding on to its position on Articles 2 and 3 of the Irish Constitution is a legitimate negotiating tactic—apart from anything else, relinquishing the Articles would involve a most divisive, probably unsuccessful and certainly potentially violent, referendum in the South. This would benefit no one, with the possible exception of the I.R.A., whose traditional claim to be the Nationalists' only real defence would be enhanced. But more needs to be done.

London should be approached with considerably more vigour to address the situation in constitutional terms rather than the narrow ground of security. The foot dragging over the Clinton Peace Envoy proposal should be abandoned. A Southern blueprint for ultimate unity should be published, indicating to the Northern Protestants what safeguards the South guarantees for their liberties of conscience, with reassurances against invasion.

The Irish situation is not an impossibile one. It can be resolved. But the British are part of the problem, not the solution. The grouping which, above all, I look to as being part of the solution are the Irish-Americans. No other component of the equation has the power to make the benign political contribution that they have. This contribution can be made while still conceding that America has a special relationship with Great Britain. I am certainly not advocating an end to this long standing friendly relationship.

But, a true friend will sometimes prove their worth by pointing out where one is going wrong. Relying on a policy of containing the situation to 'an acceptable level of violence' is going very wrong indeed. Connivance in the creation of undercover Loyalist death squads can never be 'acceptable'.

I hope that this book will do something to illuminate the problems, and help towards a better, finer relationship between Ireland and England, and the Irish North and South. I look to all Americans, whether of Irish origins or not, to assist in the realisation of that hope.

I would like to see Sean's family's life alter for the better. I would like to see no more Seans or Maxwells, be they Republican or Loyalist, either in jail or at liberty trying to kill each other. I wish to see no more young working class British soldiers shot on the streets of Northern Ireland, and no more undercover S.A.S. hit squads shooting to kill from an ambush. I want to see my country peacefully united.

APPENDIX I

1980–93: Violence in Northern Ireland

Statistics showing partial breakdown of violence

	1980	1981	1982	1983	1984	1985	1986	1987	1988	1989	1990	1991	1992	1993
Shooting incidents	642	1142	547	424	334	237	392	674	537	566	559	499	506	211
Explosions	400	529	332	367	248	215	254	384	458	420	287	367	371	106
Armed robberies	467	689	693	718	710	542	839	955	742	604	492	608	738	251
Persons charged with terrorist offences	550	918	686	613	528	522	655	468	439	433	380	397	410	152
Deaths: civilians	50	57	57	44	36	25	37	66	54	39	49	75	76	24
Deaths: army	8	10	21	5	9	2	4	3	21	12	7	5	3	2
Deaths: U.D.R.	9	13	7	10	10	4	8	8	12	2	8	8	3	2
Deaths: R.U.C./R.U.C.(R)	9	21	12	18	9	23	12	16	6	9	12	6	3	3

*1993 statistics to May 31.

Figures supplied by the Royal Ulster Constabulary

APPENDIX II

The I.R.A. Court Martial Procedure

1. A Court-marital is set up by the O/C of any Unit or by the C/S to try any Volunteer on a specific charge or charges.
2. The Court shall consist of three members of equal rank or higher than the accused.
3. The Convening Officer will appoint one member of the Court as President.
4. When a Court-marital is set up by a Unit O/C, the Adjutant of the Unit, or some member of the Unit delegated by the Adjutant to do so, will act as Prosecuting Counsel. When the Convening Authority is the C/S, he may appoint any officer other than the Adjutant General to act as Prosecution Counsel.
5. The accused may call on any Volunteer to act as his defence Counsel, or, if he so desires, may defend the case himself.
6. A copy of the charges shall be supplied to the accused in reasonable time before the case is heard to enable him to prepare his defence. The Convening Authority may either supply the accused with a summary of the evidence it is proposed to place before the Court, or arrange for a preliminary hearing at which witnesses for the prosecution will give oath, a summary of their testimony. At such preliminary hearing, neither defence nor prosecution counsel will be present, but the accused may cross-examine the witnesses. The evidence shall be taken down in writing from each witness, shall be read over to him and shall be signed by him. If the accused wishes to make a statement or give evidence on oath he must be cautioned that anything he says may be taken down and used in evidence, at any subsequent hearing of the case.
7. If the accused objects to any of the three officers comprising the Court, his objection will be examined by the remaining two members and, if upheld, the member objected to will be replaced.
8. The Convening Authority will ensure that the Prosecuting Counsel is in possession of all the facts relevant to the case and that all prosecution witnesses are present at the Court.
9. The Convening Authority will supply the Court, with a copy of the charges and with copies of General Army Orders.
10. During the hearing of the case, all witnesses will be kept in a separate room as in the case of a Court of Inquiry. The only persons present in the Court shall be members of the Court, the accused, the defence Counsel (if any) and the witness under examination.
11. The oath will be administered as in the case of a Court of Inquiry.
12. At the start of the case, the President will read each case to the accused and ask him if he pleads guilty to the charge.
13. Witnesses when called to testify will be cross-examined first by the Prosecuting Counsel and then by the Defence Counsel, or by the accused if conducting his own defence. Witnesses may be questioned by any member of the Court. Should either Counsel wish to recall a witness who has already testified, permission of the Court must first be obtained. The Court may recall any witness. Witnesses may not leave the precincts of the Court without permission from the Court.
14. At any time it so desires, the Court may go into private session to decide on points which may arise, such as the admissibility of evidence.
15. When all witnesses have testified, Defence Counsel will sum up and make closing address to the Court. This will be followed by summing up and closing address of the Prosecuting Counsel. The Court then goes into private session to consider its verdict and sentence.
16. For a breach of any General Army Order, the Court shall not have power to impose a lesser penalty than that laid down in such order.
17. The verdict and sentence of the Court shall be set down in writing and signed by the three members. This, together with a summary of the evidence, must be forwarded by the President to the Convening Authority. Sentence is subject to the ratification of the Convening Authority.

Note: In the case of the death penalty, sentence must be ratified by the A/C.

18. The accused may forward an appeal against the verdict or sentence or both to the Adjutant-General who will place it before the Competent Authority. The appeal should be forwarded by accused through his O/C. who in turn will forward it to the Adjutant-General with a signed copy of verdict and sentence and a summary of the evidence. The Competent Authority may order a new trial or reduce the penalty but may not increase the penalty imposed by the Court.

Selected References

The principal source material for Part I of this book was, of course, the more than five hundred interviews I conducted with persons either in or connected with the I.R.A. I also made use of a wealth of Republican publications: I.R.A. directives, regulations, proclamations, pamphlets, newspapers, records of courts-martial and of county brigade activities, letters and personal statements of various kinds. These, and other material not normally available to the public, such as the ritual (adopted 1931) and constitution (adopted 1946) of the Clann na Gael, were given to me through the kindness of individuals.

The principal Republican newspapers, such as *An Phoblacht*, the *Republican Congress*, *Republican File* and the contemporary *United Irishman* provided useful information, as did the national press, in particular the *Irish Press*, *Irish Times*, *Irish Independent*, *Irish News* and *Belfast Telegraph*. A series of articles in *The People* by Joseph Gallagher (commencing December 10, 1961) shed a good deal of light on Nazi-I.R.A. activities.

These activities and other indications of German policy towards Ireland may be studied more formally in the captured documents on German foreign policy published by the Allies after the Second World War. (Some are in German.) Telegram 101410 dated November 24, 1941, is a lengthy assessment of the Irish position, the worth of Goertz's mission, the I.R.A.'s strength and an interpretation of the Hayes affair. It is particularly interesting and well worth translation. But the most comprehensive and easily available study of this aspect of Irish history is Enno Stephan's very fine work, *Spies in Ireland*.

Parts II through IV of this book are based largely on my own experiences, personal files and interviews, many of which must remain unattributable. However the list of Commission reports published below indicates some of the other sources made use of, and I am appending a short bibliography for the reader whose interest in Northern Irish affairs may have been whetted by *The I.R.A.* Concerning these books I would make the following points. A. T. Q. Stewart's book and that of Robert Fisk should ideally be read together, Stewart's work (also mentioned in the references of Part I) coming first. The two books deal with turning-point events in Northern Ireland in which the British army and government failed to confront Loyalists. David Boulton's *The U.V.F.* should ideally be preceded by Bowen's, for the insight they give into Protestant thinking in the last century and in this. My own books I include for those stoic readers who may feel inclined to even more of my own writing, and Bowyer Bell's *The Secret Army* because it is a rival work to my own study of the I.R.A. and, being written by an American, will afford readers an opportunity of seeing how a foreign academic sees the I.R.A. The depth and scope of Dr Bowyer Bell's earlier work is not matched by the chronology of events to which he has virtually reduced the most recent years of I.R.A. activity. The Chronologies on *Northern Ireland Events* published by Blackstaff Press, Belfast, and edited by Richard Deutsch and Vivien Magowan, are among the best things to appear over the whole period of the troubles and are an absolute must for any serious student of the period.

Agreed Communiqué of Conference on Northern Ireland between parties involved in setting up Northern Ireland Executive (Dublin, 1974).

Bennett Commission Report into charges of brutality against the R.U.C. (London, 1978). (The Amnesty International Report which gave rise to the charges was published earlier in 1978.)

Cameron Commission on disturbances in Northern Ireland and Commentary on same by Northern Ireland Government (Belfast, 1969),

Compton Report into security forces behaviour arising from internment August 9, 1971 (London, 1971).

Diplock Report on terrorist activities in Northern Ireland (London, 1972).

Gardiner Report on workings of Emergency Powers (London, 1976).

Green Paper on Northern Ireland (London, 1972)

Scarman Report, 2 vols. (London, 1972)

Hunt Report (Belfast, 1969).

MacRory Report on local government in Northern Ireland (Belfast, 1970).

Widgery Report into Bloody Sunday (London, 1972)

Boulton, David, *The U.V.F., 1966–1973* (Gill and Macmillan, Dublin, 1974).

Bell, Bowyer, *The Secret Army: The I.R.A., 1916–1979* (Academy Press, Dublin, 1979).

Bogdanor, Vernon, *Devolution* (Oxford University Press, Oxford, 1979).

Bowen, Desmond, *The Protestant Crusade in Ireland (McGill-Queen's University Press,* Belfast, 1978).

Coogan, Tim Pat, *Disillusioned Decades* (Gill and Macmillan, Dublin, 1987).

Coogan, Tim Pat, *Ireland Since the Rising* (Pall Mall, London, 1966)

Coogan, Tim Pat, *The Irish: A Personal View* (Phaidon, London, 1975).

Coogan, Tim Pat, *The Man Who Made Ireland: The Life and Death of Michael Collins* (Roberts Rinehart, Niwot, Colorado, 1992).

Coogan, Tim Pat, *On the Blanket* (Ward River Press, Dublin, 1980).

Dillon, Martin, *Stone Cold* (Arrow, London, 1992).

Fisk, Robert, *The Point of No Return* (Andre Deutsch, London, 1975).

Feuchtwanger, E.J., *Gladstone* (Allen Lane, London, 1975).

Jones, Thomas, *Whitehall Diary*, vol. III (Oxford University Press, Oxford, 1971).

Mansfield, Michael, *Presumed Guilty* (Heinemann, London, 1983).

Miller, David, *Queen's Rebels* (Gill and Macmillan, Dublin, 1978).

McDonagh, Oliver, *Ireland: The Union and Aftermath* (Allen and Unwin, London, 1977).

Nairn, Tom, *The Break Up of Britain* (New Left Books, London, 1977).

O'Farrell, Patrick, *Ireland's English Question* (Batsford, London, 1971).

Opsahl, Torkel, ed., *A Citizen's Inquiry: The Opsahl Report* (Liliput Press, Dublin, 1993).

Stewart, A.T.Q., *The Ulster Crisis* (Faber, London, 1967).

Urban, Mark, *Big Boys' Rules: The S.A.S. and the Secret Struggle Against the I.R.A.* (Faber, London, 1992).

Glossary

Ard Fheis Irish language term meaning 'high council' usually used in association with official conventions or conferences of Irish political parties.

Anglo-Irish Agreement A document agreed to by the Fine Gael/Labour Coalition Government of Ireland and Mrs Thatcher's Conservative Government in the United Kingdom in 1985. It stipulates that there shall be no change in the constitutional position of Northern Ireland for so long as the majority wishes to remain as part of the United Kingdom. However, there are provisions for some Dublin influence in Northern Irish affairs which makes in principle for a type of joint sovereignty. Rejected by the Unionists in the North and Fianna Fail in the South, mostly ignored by Sinn Fein and the I.R.A., it seems to have had very little effect on the current situation.

Articles Two and Three of the Irish Constitution These two provisions of the Irish Constitution lay claim to all thirty-two counties of Ireland, and are often cited by Unionists of the Six Counties as the major hurdle to their cooperation with the Dublin Government in any talks concerning the future of the Six Counties.

B.B.C. British Broadcasting Corporation, the state owned media giant (T.V., radio, and publication divisions) of Great Britain.

Black and Tans So nicknamed because of their khaki uniform and black and green belts and caps. These were mainly ex-servicemen sent over by the British as reinforcements for the Royal Irish Constabulary during the guerilla War of Independence. Another related corps set up to assist the police at that time were the Auxiliary Cadets, the 'Auxies', consisting of ex-British officers. Like the I.R.A., they elected their own officers. Both corps are remembered in Nationalist folklore as having committed many atrocities.

B-Specials A Protestant state militia first formed in 1920 by Lord Brookeborough from former U.V.F. and British Army members in the Six Counties as a back-up force for the police in helping maintain Protestant ascendancy. After the troubles broke out in late 1969, their activities so outraged British Prime Minister Harold Wilson, that they were disbanded and reconstituted as the Ulster Defence Regiment (U.D.R.) in 1970.

Clann na Gael An Irish-American Nationalist organisation founded in 1867 in the wake of the failed Fenian rising and later linked with the I.R.B. Its activities included fund-raising, the heightening of awareness and the raising of support for Irish independence. It was the Clann under John Devoy that funded the 1916 Rising.

Conservative Party One of Britain's two main political parties, the Conservatives are associated with right-of-center politics. Also known as the Tory Party, they are allied with the Unionist parties in Northern Ireland.

Dail Eireann Irish Parliament.

D.U.P. Democratic Unionist Party led by Rev. Ian Paisley.

E.E.C. European Economic Community. Founded in 1957, this economic union now has twelve member states. Ireland joined in 1973.

Fianna Fail 'Warriors of Fail' (a poetic symbol for Ireland). Founded in 1923 by Eamon de Valera when he split with Sinn Fein, this is the largest and most powerful of the Irish political parties.

Fine Gael The second largest political party in the Irish Republic, formed in 1933 from the centre Party, the Blueshirts and Cumann na Gaedheal.

Gardai Irish police force.

I.N.L.A. Irish National Liberation Army. A splinter group from the I.R.A.

I.R.A. Irish Republican Army

I.R.B.   Irish Republican Brotherhood, the Fenians, set up in 1858 as a revolutionary movement. It recognised itself as the provisional governing body of a free and independent Ireland. Re-organised by Michael Collins after the failed Easter Rising, it in effect became the leadership cadre of the Volunteers (I.R.A.).

I.R.S.P.   Irish Republican Socialist Party. The political wing of the I.N.L.A.

Labour Party   (Irish Republic) The third largest political party in the Republic of Ireland.

Labour Party   (U.K.) One of Britain's two main political parties. It is usually associated with the labour unions and left-of-center politics.

Loyalists   Loyal to the Union, these are Ulster Protestants opposed to a thirty-two county Ireland. (Same as Unionists.)

Maastricht Treaty   An agreement reached by the members of the E.E.C. in Maastricht, Netherlands in 1992, which lays out several important further steps in the transformation of the Community into a closer federation, and gives new powers to the European Parliament and government organisations.

NORAID   North American Aid. An American organisation that raises money for Irish Republican causes.

Official Irish Republican Army   In 1970 the I.R.A. split into the Official I.R.A. and the Provisional I.R.A., which became the dominant grouping. The O.I.R.A. maintained the old line of the I.R.A., the wish for a socialist thirty-two county Ireland.

Orange Order   (Orangemen) Name taken from the victory of Protestant William of Orange over Catholic King James II. A powerful sectarian order of Protestants characterised by ritualistic pageantry and supremacist celebrations.

Provisionals   (Provos) Now the major I.R.A. force.

Republicans   Supporting a thirty-two county Republic of Ireland.

R.T.E.   Radio Telefis Eireann. Irish radio and television network.

R.U.C.   Royal Ulster Constabulary. Police force in the Six Counties.

S.A.S.   Special Air Services. The special operations force of the British Army against whom most allegations of carrying out a shoot-to-kill policy are directed by Nationalists.

S.D.L.P.   (Catholic) Social Democratic and Labour Party. Constitutional nationalist party of the Six Counties, founded in 1970 and believing in the necessity of majority consent for a united Ireland. It is largely supported by the middle class.

Seanad   Translates as 'Senate'. Upper house of Parliament (the Dail) in Ireland.

Sinn Fein   'Ourselves Alone'. Political party and wing of the Provisional I.R.A. Mainly supported by working class Catholics.

Six Counties   Six of the nine counties which make up the province of Ulster. The Six Counties are part of the United Kingdom.

Taoiseach.   Prime Minister of the Republic of Ireland.

Thirty-Two Counties   The Republic of Ireland and the Six Counties—a united Ireland.

Twenty-Six Counties   The Republic of Ireland.

U.D.A.   Ulster Defence Association. The major Protestant paramilitary group. U.D.A. spokesmen have advocated that Ulster be independent of both Britain and Ireland. Now outlawed, it is alleged to have links with the D.U.P. and U.D.R.

U.D.R.   Ulster Defence Regiment. Formed in 1970 to replace the old B-Special Corps. It too was heavily criticised and was placed under British Army control in 1992.

U.F.F.   Ulster Freedom Fighters. A U.D.A. group which has claimed responsibility for several sectarian murders.

Ulster   This should correspond to the the ancient nine-county Irish province of Ulster. However, when the State was being set up the Unionists rejected the nine county unit because it contained too many Catholics, and settled for the six counties which they could control. The term is now commonly, but erroneously used by Unionists to refer to the Six Counties.

Unionists   Those supporting the 1800 Act of Union when Ireland became part of the United Kingdom and totally opposed to any breaking of ties of the Six Counties with Britain. (Same as Loyalists.)

U.V.F.   Ulster Volunteer Force. Originally formed in 1912 with powerful British and Unionist support to oppose Home Rule. It is now a Protestant paramilitary group who have claimed responsibility for several sectarian killings.

Index of Names

General Index